Women's Voices

This anthology brings together the writings of some Indian women who made pioneering social and literary contributions during the nineteenth and early-twentieth centuries. Traversing a wide canvas, the excerpts taken from letters, tracts, diaries, magazines, articles, autobiographies, short stories, and even speeches discuss theatre, dance, travel, and personal experiences, while others dwell on social issues, doctrinal problems, orthodox practices, and the position of women in society. The book will interest anyone interested in women's literature of modern India.

EUNICE DE SOUZA retired as head of the department of English, St Xavier's College, Bombay. She is an established poet and writer. LINDSAY PEREIRA is currently pursuing a PhD from the department of English, University of Bombay.

Women's Voices

Selections from Nineteenth and Early-Twentieth
Century Indian Writing in English

Introduction by
Eunice de Souza

Biographical Notes by
Lindsay Peréira

OXFORD
UNIVERSITY PRESS

Published in India by
Oxford University Press
22 Workspace, 2nd Floor, 1/22 Asaf Ali Road, New Delhi 110002, India

First Edition published in 2002
Oxford India Paperbacks 2004
21st impression 2022

ISBN-13: 978-0-19-566785-1
ISBN-10: 0-19-566785-9

Typeset in Goudy
by Eleven Arts, Keshavpuram, Delhi 110 035
Printed in India by Replika Press Pvt. Ltd

Contents

Introduction

In one of her letters to her friend Mary Martin, Toru Dutt writes: 'The census of Calcutta was taken a few days ago; I asked Papa to put in my column "Authoress" as a profession, with which request he did not comply!'[1] Despite the exclamation mark at the end of her comment to underscore its playful nature, the comment is still extraordinary for Toru Dutt's confidence (never uncritical) in her abilities.

The writers in this anthology were all, in one way or another, remarkable, sometimes formidable people. They were pioneers in various fields, literary and social, and the word 'first' occurs several times in a list of their achievements. They were political activists, diplomats, legislators, doctors, writers. They travelled extensively, were published and feted abroad. At home in India they often took risks in their personal lives, marrying men their parents did not approve of, or going to jail for their political convictions.

They wrote about their lives and experiences in a wide variety of forms—letters, tracts, diaries, magazine articles, speeches, autobiographies, short stories, novels, biographies. And they wrote about a wide variety of subjects—the position of women for the most part, but also about their travels, Paris in the 1920s, meeting Langston Hughes or Queen Victoria, looking for Dostoyevsky's room in Leningrad, dacoits, doctrinal problems, prison conditions, theatre, dance, travel. For the most part these were writers writing for a cause. There is little of the 'art for art's sake' present in their writing. Nevertheless, they attempted fictional forms with a greater or lesser degree of success. Others were occasional writers, writing for a specific purpose—an essay for an anthology, or an account of a movement. The western region has tended to be neglected in favour of Bengal, but the number of women writing in the western region included here hopefully redresses the balance.

The basic attempt in this collection of Indian women writing prose

[1]Letters to Mary Martin (1876) in Harihar Das, *Life and Letters of Toru Dutt*, London: Oxford University Press, 1921, p. 146.

in English in the nineteenth and early twentieth century has been to draw attention to the range and quality of this writing. Some of it has been almost entirely forgotten. Even standard histories of Indian writing in English club a number of women together in one chapter, often mentioning some of them only in passing. A few—very few—wrote poetry, but it seemed so skimpy beside the sheer volume and originality of the prose that it has been omitted from this collection. For reasons of space, a great deal of the material collected had to be laid aside. In a few cases no material could be found. But hopefully, enough has been included to give the reader an idea of how passionately involved these women were in whatever they were doing.

What this anthology hopes to demonstrate is that in almost every case, these women writers took more than documentary interest in the subject of their writing. The writing is alive. It is observant, sharp. It has an urgency that speaks to the reader very directly. And while most of the women wrote economical, readable prose, some were stylistically brilliant.

Other reasons for such an anthology presented themselves as the material was collected, the foremost being a re-assessment of some of the better-known writers. Toru Dutt, for instance is celebrated as a poet. While this is fair enough as she was the first woman poet in India writing in English, it is really in her letters that she is most marvellously alive. The letters are affectionate, observant, satirical, touching. The prose is completely modern. One has only to compare the prose of her unfinished novel *Bianca* (published posthumously) to see that the novel is almost parodic though it is not meant to be.

Let us examine Bianca's reaction to a kiss from Lord Moore who is in love with her:

> Mr Garcia was in his study when Bianca entered the room. He looked up smiling, 'Well, what is it that you want, child—why, you have been crying—what for?' She came and kneeling beside him, with bent head, took his hand. 'Father,' said she, 'Lord Moore kissed me today.' 'The devil he did,' He exclaimed ...[2]

This treatment is distinct from the direct but heartfelt description in her letters of a horse that was beaten till it collapsed:

> It had been left lying on the damp mud ... After some twelve hours it was lifted up by bamboo props (and a free use of the lash and administration of buckets of cold water into its nostrils and eyes)![3]

[2]Quoted in 'The Women Novelists' in K.S. Ramamurti, *Rise of the Indian Novel in English*, Bangalore: Sterling Publishers, 1987, p. 69.

[3]Letters to Mary Martin, p. 169.

While Sarojini Naidu has been endlessly called The Nightingale of India, it is her somewhat more discordant notes that make her interesting—her famous irreverence, even when she was with Gandhiji, her sense of humour, her ability to make fun of everything and everybody, including herself. Nayantara Sahgal tells us in a piece on Sarojini Naidu, 'She had once told us that she had been introduced to an audience as "India's Number One Public Woman", while another enthusiastic presiding deity had informed a crowded meeting that Sarojini Naidu was an extraordinary lady, "easy of access, quick of conception and prompt of delivery". Only Sarojini on the dais had trouble controlling her mirth. The others present had solemnly awaited her speech ...'[4]

Re-assessments of reputations would also have to include the virtually forgotten novel *Purdah and Polygamy* published by Iqbalunnisa Hussain in 1944. Not only is her novel one of the finest novels of the period under consideration, but of the post-1947 period as well. She has a sustained ironic vision, and a sharp eye for realistic detail. When the head of the household dies, the wife is of course grief-stricken but still remembers that 'A death affords a good chance to the poor to get away with portable articles which can be hidden under the full-size veil.'[5] All big and small things were locked up in the lumber room.

The other reason for this anthology was the wide range of attitudes on issues concerning women. From Vedic times to Buddhist nuns, bhakti saints and so on, there were women who spoke with astonishing freedom. But since the nineteenth century, ideas about women's emancipation started to trickle in from the West. In 1819 the Calcutta Female Juvenile Society established by the Baptist Mission was set up to encourage education for women. In 1848 Jyotiba Phule opened the first girls' school in Poona, and in 1849 Ram Gopal Ghosh and John Elliot Drinkwater established the Hindu Female School (later called Bethune School) in Calcutta.

People held different views on the kind of education to be imparted to the Indian woman. The reformer Keshub Chandra Sen felt that education was intended to make the woman more adept at running the household. His daughter Sunity Devee in her autobiography (1921) tells us that her father 'did not believe in the importance of university degrees. He maintained that for a woman to be a good wife and a good mother was

---

[4]'Sarojini Naidu: A Most Unusual Satyagrahi' by Nayantara Sahgal in *Sarojini Naidu* (Great Women of Modern India Series), eds. Verinder Grover and Ranjana Arora, New Delhi: Deep and Deep Publishers, 1993, p. 479.

[5]p. 8.

far more important than to be able to write MA or BA after her name. Therefore only those things that were likely to be useful in running a household better were taught to the girls who attended Victoria College'[6] founded by Keshub Chandra Sen.

Pandita Ramabai founded the Sharda Sadan in Bombay, then Poona (one of her assistants was Shevantibai Nikambe) for Brahmin widows. Unfortunately, Shevantibai's novel *Ratanbai* (1895) which is about the importance of education even for married Hindu high-caste girls gives us no information about the actual education that was imparted. From other sources however, one learns that Pandita Ramabai stressed literature that would inculcate morals (hence perhaps the reason for asking Ratanbai to recite Casabianca, a poem about a boy who would not desert a sinking ship). Classes were also held in Physiology and Botany, and training was provided in farming, wood-cutting, needlework, tailoring, masonry. However, having converted to Christianity, Ramabai's stress on the religion antagonized a number of people and eclipsed the good work she was doing.[7] On the other hand, Maharani Tapaswani's school in Calcutta, founded in 1893 stressed Hindu religious and moral principles because she believed that Hindu society should be regenerated from within. Cooking lessons were included so that the girls would not become alienated from such chores because of their education.[8]

But in 1911 we find Rani Chimnabai of Baroda providing detailed suggestions for professions that women could aspire to, in her book *The Position of Women in Indian Life* (1911). A progressive and practical woman, she said she had based her suggestions on what she had observed on visits to Europe, England and the US. 'I leave it to my country women,' she wrote, 'to decide which of them—modified to suit local circumstances—are worthy of a trial.'[9] Chimnabai did not neglect the importance of home while talking about professions, but she acknowledged the difficulty of constructing a scheme by which a woman may, 'if called upon to do so, earn her livelihood or contribute actively to the betterment of her fellow-creatures, without unfitting her for the all-important duties of wifehood and motherhood.'[10] She lamented the fact that 'Public matters in India are almost entirely in the hands of men,'[11] while she reminded her readers that 'the good of woman is the good of man.'

---

[6]*The Autobiography of an Indian Princess*, London: John Murray, 1921, p. 21.
[7]Geraldine Forbes *Women in Modern India*, Cambridge University Press, First Indian Edition: Delhi Foundation Books, 1996, p. 48.
[8]Ibid., p. 50.
[9]Longman's Green, p. xiii.
[10]p. 22.
[11]p. 15.

According to statistics, in 1935, there were seven arts colleges for women (only one such college existed in 1886), three medical colleges where earlier there were none. Teacher training colleges had multiplied, and vocational education also included Law, Commerce, Technical and Industrial courses. Child Welfare and Health had, since World War I, become organized departments in every province. And at the basic level of education, 'the schoolable age of girls was longer: in Madras and the Punjab, the enrolment of girls even exceeding that of boys ...'[12]

The difficulties faced by child-brides, wives, widows are central to much of the writing—in both fiction and non-fiction in this anthology. It seems that in 1891, in Bengal, one in three Hindu women was a widow. By 1931 the proportion was down to one in four women.[13] In 1856 the Widow Remarriage Act was passed, followed by the Civil Marriage Act in 1873, the Married Women's Property Act in 1874, and the Age of Consent Act in 1881. In 1893 D.K. Karve established the Widow Remarriage Association.

Despite these achievements in legislation, Cornelia Sorabji felt there was a difference between the old reformers and the new, more politically-oriented ones. Writing in 1938 about the previous fifty years, she said:

> The Pioneers of 1885 were impelled to service by their hearts: they talked little of 'Women's Rights': they were stirred to the core by women's needs. Feeling filtered through the heart. In 1935 feeling would seem to filter through the mind. Service is inspired and directed to a great extent by politics (and it cannot be denied that politics certainly has been the chief factor in loosening the bondage of custom during the last fifty years). Women's rights have become a slogan—rights visualized out of focus because of the belief that Western methods were to be closely imitated, and that the final achievement of English Feminists was to be our starting point ... So that whereas the Pioneers relied on study of local conditions or house-to-house contact with individuals, and on personal conviction as the only stable basis of Reform, the Leaders of today would seem to rely solely on Legislation and Public agitation for the removal of social ills. And many of our too few workers are being diverted from practical personal service to public oratory.[14]

While this scepticism about and even isolation from politics was not a very widely accepted stand when Cornelia Sorabji wrote, her feeling

---

[12]'Position of Hindu Women Fifty Years Ago' by Cornelia Sorabji in *Our Cause: A Symposium by Indian Women*, ed. Shyam Kumari Nehru, Allahabad Kitabistan, 1938, p. 19.

[13]Dagmar Engels, *Beyond Purdah?*, Delhi: Oxford University Press.

[14]*Our Cause*, pp. 20–21.

that women activists should 'even the pace' was shared by women with very different ideologies. Cornelia Sorabji felt that while 'The forward-moving battalion ... is miles ahead, there is still a great gap between this body and the few who are struggling to catch up with them. The majority remain far in the rear, scarcely moving at all.'[15] In one of her later essays Aruna Asaf Ali attacked the 'embourgeoisment of the women's movement'. Among the examples she gave was the 'protest against the male chauvinist requirement by some banks that a woman wishing to open an account should give the name of her husband or father. The protest is legitimate, but the majority of Indian women have no bank accounts.'[16]

In *The Awakening of Indian Women* (1939), Kamaladevi Chattopadhyay voiced these feelings, but said that, 'nevertheless ... there is a base for a women's movement though this base is wider than mere sex. It is largely conditioned by and influenced by the present political and economic condition of the country, a fact which feminists are sometimes apt to ignore.'[17] Paradoxically, she says, working class women, both rural and industrial are 'comparatively freer than the upper class women in India. Amongst the former, a woman being an earning member and an economic factor, enjoys a greater degree of freedom. Economic stress compels this class to be less tramelled by severe social codes.'[18]

Franchise for women was a difficult issue for many reasons. The struggle for franchise for women began in 1917 when Sarojini Naidu led a team of prominent women on a delegation to meet the Montagu-Chelmsford team. Women's organizations in different parts of India held discussions on the subject of franchise. Eventually, Mrs Herabai Tata and her daughter Mithan (later Mithan Lam) went to England with Sir Sankaran Nair, the only Indian on the Viceroy's Council. But there was opposition from Indian men, particularly nationalists, who 'did not relish hearing women speak about the evils of patriarchy',[19] from Gandhiji who felt that the time was wrong,[20] from Cornelia Sorabji who argued that the majority of women were not ready for such a move,[21] and from British men who agreed with these views.[22]

But the demands for franchise were initially limited, and the participants

[15]Ibid., p. 21.
[16]'Bourgeois Feminism is Not Enough' in *Aruna Asaf Ali*, eds. Verinder Grover and Ranjana Arora, New Delhi: Deep and Deep Publishers, 1993, p. 99.
[17]Madras: Everyman Press, 1939, p. 7.
[18]Ibid.
[19]Geraldine Forbes, p. 93.
[20]Ibid., p. 100.
[21]Ibid., p. 99.
[22]Ibid., p. 98.

in the agitation were aware of this. Herabai Tata tells us in *A Short Sketch of Indian Women's Franchise Work* (n.d.), published as a pamphlet, 'for some time to come universal franchise may not be practicable in India, but we do claim that women who possess the same qualifications as are laid out for men ... should not be debarred from the enjoyment of the right to vote on account of their sex.'[23] In 1921 women in Bombay and Madras were granted franchise, and soon after in other provinces as well. The demand was then extended to women's participation in legislative activity, and in 1927, Muthulakshmi Reddy became the first woman legislator in the Madras Legislative Council.

The attempt to reconcile the women's movement with nationalism created many paradoxical situations, the most obvious one being the reaffirmation of patriarchy in the name of nationalism. Political activists fighting for the independence of the country were not necessarily in favour of social reform for women, or even their participation in politics, and tended to make contradictory demands on women. Geraldine Forbes tells us that the husband of a woman who was arrested sent word to the jail that she was not to return home after being released. It was an honour to have a wife arrested, he told the person who tried to intervene, but she had not sought permission to leave the house.[24] According to Partha Chatterjee, the strategy employed was to stress on the spiritual superiority of Indians by putting the onus on women to preserve 'tradition'.[25] Women had to talk, dress, eat and generally behave in a way that clearly distinguished them from Western women, certainly, but especially from the alleged obnoxiousness of Westernized Indian women.

Even Kamaladevi Chattopadhyay, a radical in many ways, abandoned gender terminology for spiritual terms in her account of the women's response to the nationalist struggle, particularly after Gandhiji encouraged women to participate (non-violently). 'Men and women acted as souls, not as sexes, and soul-force was their weapon.'[26] Unfortunately, her idea that women could never be free under colonialism, because the history of British Imperialism was 'one unbroken chain of betrayals'[27] has been belied by the long chain of betrayals in independent India, as even a cursory look at the news will show. And 'tradition', defined in essentialist and narrow terms, has, unsurprisingly, turned demagogic, reactionary and violent.

[23]p. 7.
[24]Geraldine Forbes, p. 121.
[25]*The Nation and Its Fragments*, Delhi: Oxford University Press, p. 126–7.
[26]'Towards Progress and Freedom' in *The Awakening of Indian Women*, Madras: Everyman Press, 1939, p. 56.
[27]'Education and Child Marriage' in *The Awakening of Indian Women*, p. 13.

Arun P. Mukherjee who teaches in Canada has, in an essay entitled 'Some Uneasy Conjectures', put the matter succinctly in her discussion of questions that have come up in her academic work. 'I believe,' she writes, 'that even though post-colonial theory positions itself as the discourse of liberation, it is of no use to those whose battle is against home-grown oppressors. In fact, it works against them because in the post-colonial parlance, these home-grown oppressors become 'the oppressed' who get all the post-colonialist's sympathy for their suffering at the hand of the colonizer ...'[28] Further, she comments on the uncomfortable resemblance between the rhetoric of post-colonialism and that of cultural fundamentalism. 'If I were to use the language of post-colonial theory, I would describe the efforts of BJP/VHP intelligentsia as "resisting" the discourses of the so-called Muslim colonizers of India.'[29]

During the years before Independence various associations for women were set up—the Women's India Association in 1917, the National Council of Women in India in 1925, and Indian Federation of University Women in 1920, the All India Women's Conference in 1926. The *Who's Who of Women in India* gives us hundreds of names of women, Indian and Western, well-known and now not so well-known, who contributed to committees, discussions, anthologies of essays on women's education and other such issues. In 1928 Dhanvanthi Rama Rau set up the All India Family Planning Association. In 1929 the All India Women's Education Fund was established, the Dowry Act was passed, as was the Prevention of Child Marriage Act. One can hardly decry all these achievements. But the implementation of good ideas has remained sporadic and haphazard. And to say that we worship female goddesses and have had a woman Prime Minister is no answer. The caricature of the Westernized woman in Venu Chitale's *In Transit* (1950) indicates the kind of exclusiveness at the heart of the 'essential Indian woman' of the nationalist paradigm.

Purdah is another subject that has elicited a wide range of reactions. Sarojini Naidu, on the basis of her experience of Hyderabad felt, in 1908, that 'incalculably tragic results would follow a premature and total abolition of the system'.[30] She pleaded for a 'deft and wise and almost imperceptible relaxing of its rigorous laws day by day as education increases'.[31] But most of the writers on purdah included here are unambiguous about the

---

[28]*Interrogating Postcolonialism*, eds. Harish Trivedi and Meenakshi Mukherjee, Shimla Institute of Advanced Studies, 1996, p. 17.

[29]Ibid., p. 19.

[30]'A Tardy Renaissance' in *The Stree Bodhe and Social Progress in India*, Bombay: The Stree Bodhe Office, 1908, p. 204.

[31]Ibid., p. 205.

health and psychological damage done by purdah. An unexpected insight is offered by Begum Shaista S. Ikramullah in her autobiography *From Purdah to Parliament* (1963). (This has not been included in the present anthology). Talking of her emergence from the purdah in Delhi, where she lived before leaving India, she writes, 'I had imagined that a mixed society would be composed of intelligent people, who would talk of more interesting things than were talked of in the women's world to which I had so far been confined, but to my disappointment I found that this was not so.'[32]

Perhaps most of the women represented here were so caught up in women's movements and the nationalist struggle, that their autobiographical writing tended to focus more on the public life than the inner person. As Kamaladevi Chattopadhyay said in her memoirs *Inner Recesses Outer Spaces* (1986), a work not included in this anthology, 'Mine has been perhaps an eventful life ... whatever the modern trend may be, I do not think that in a life story one is required to lower the barriers of the discreet reticence which govern our everyday life and affairs'.[33]

In fact, she tells us nothing about key episodes in her personal life, her marriage when she was fourteen to the son of a rich but progressive family of landed gentry. Her husband died a year later, but 'what her memories of this brief interlude in her early life and of the label widow that followed, no one knows'.[34] Later she married the poet Harindranath Chattopadhyay, Sarojini Naidu's brother, but again she tells us nothing of the breakdown of this marriage. She refers to Harindranath only four times in her memoirs, and never refers to him as her husband.[35] S. Muthulakshmi Reddy in *How I Became a Legislator* ruthlessly confined herself to legislative proceedings and quotes in full, proposals she made or legislation she helped to enact. So little is known about the personal lives of many of these women, that it is difficult to assess the differences, if any, between what the women wrote and the experiences that motivated their writings.

Even so, little can equal the zest of Dosebai Cowasjee Jessawalla's *The Story of My Life* (1911) in the pleasure it takes in recording every detail of travel, especially the pleasure of being perceived as revolutionary for travelling in an open carriage at the Delhi Darbar, or going up in a balloon in France. Cornelia Sorabji's books, which concern her many years of work among purdah women whom she helped with legal problems, are full of

[32]London: The Cresset Press, 1963, p. 74.

[33]New Delhi: Navrang Prakashan, 1986, pp. 1–2.

[34]Shakuntala Narasimhan, *Kamaladevi Chattopadhyay The Romantic Rebel*, New Delhi: Sterling Publishers, 1999, p. 149.

[35]Ibid., 153.

sensitivity, humour, and real empathy for the women she was dealing with.

Among the women whose work I could not find are the novelist H. Kaveribai, and Kamala Satthianadhan, notable for children's books. Kaveribai was born in 1897 in Rajamundry and later became Headmistress of her school. She is said to have published novels with a social message which were well received, and articles in English.[36] Kamala Satthianadhan edited *The Indian Ladies' Magazine*, wrote essays, and, among others a novel called *Detective Janaki*. Padmini Sen Gupta however, has written a biography of Kamala Satthianadhan, *The Portrait of an Indian Woman* (1956) which uses quotations from her work.

The novels from which pieces have been selected for the present anthology are a pleasurable read for a host of reasons. Krupabai's novels *Saguna: A story of Native Christian Life* (1895) and *Kamala: The Story of Hindu Life* (1894) contain a lyrical love for nature hardly seen even in the poetry of the time. Zeenuth Futehally's *Zohra* is about the delicate handling of 'forbidden love' while Nalini Turkhud's *The Jagirdar of Palna* (1936) is a pacey narrative.

Short fiction is represented by Cornelia Sorabji's tragic *The Fire is Quenched* (1901). While feminist fantasy provides the bedrock for Rokeya Sakhawat Hossain's *Sultana's Dream* (1905), distress in the time of the Bengal famine is chronicled in Ela Sen's *The Queue* (1944). Ramabai C.T. and Shovona Devi's works comprise children's fiction.

Other pieces are essays which are tributes—Susie Sorabji writes on Ramabai Ranade, Sucheta Kripalani on Langston Hughes, Ela Sen on 'A Woman of Spain'.

The cut-off date for the selections in this anthology is, with a few exceptions, 1947. I have included two novels that have been virtually forgotten—Venu Chitale's *In Transit* published in 1950 and Zeenuth Futehally's *Zohra* published in 1951. Brinda Maharani of Kapurthala's account of her involvement with a jazz café in Paris in *The Story of An Indian Princess* seemed worth including partly for variety, partly because it makes interesting reading. And while Santha Rama Rau's *Home to India* was published in 1945, I have preferred to represent her with an extract from *Gifts of Passage* (1959), easily the most impressive of her works.

While putting this anthology together, dates were a recurrent problem. Sometimes even autobiographies don't mention the date of birth. Prefaces and forewords, while showering praise on the author and the work, have given biographical information a miss.

I was fortunate in a couple of cases. Trying to track down information

[36]NCWI, *Who's Who of Women in India*, Bombay, 1935, pp. 38–9.

about Zeenuth Futehally, I looked at my outdated telephone directory and was amazed to find her name in it. But she had already sold the flat, and as I discovered later, had died a few years earlier. So I decided to try the other Futehallys in the directory on the off-chance that they would be able to provide a clue. As it turned out, Rumanna Denby, Zeenuth Futehally's daughter who lives in York happened to be in Bombay for a few days. I met her and she later sent me press-cuttings and articles about her mother.

Similarly, I wondered if Padma Lokur, a Marathi poet and mother-in-law of a friend of mine knew anything about Venu Chitale. It turned out that she had been a good friend. She put me through to the daughter-in-law's sister who lived in the same building, who put me in touch with the daughter-in-law, and who in turn put me in touch with the daughter Ms Jyotsna Damle who lived in Pune. Ms Damle very kindly gave me copies of both In Transit (1950) and a later book Incognito (1993) that I didn't know existed.

One of the problems in locating books was the varying spellings of the authors' names. In the end it seemed easier to sit on the floor near the relevant stacks and simply take down whatever looked promising. The method worked, and each evening I went home dusty but triumphant.

Reading the books gave me a sense of belonging—to an extended family. So many of the writers refer to each other in their books. Sarojini Naidu turns up in a number of books: in Zeenuth Futehally's Zohra, for instance, where she takes part in a poetry-reading session in Hyderabad; in Venu Chitale's In Transit, and S. Muthulakshmi Reddy's Autobiography, to name only a few. Sarojini Naidu was herself a regular subscriber to the Indian Ladies' Magazine, where Cornelia Sorabji's articles also appeared. The magazine was edited by Kamala Satthianadhan, herself a writer (and mother of Padmini Sen Gupta, another writer who also wrote about Toru Dutt, Sarojini Naidu, and Pandita Ramabai).

Kamala Satthianadhan was Samuel Satthianadhan's second wife. She married him after the death of Krupabai, his first wife. (Samuel, who is said to have encouraged Krupabai to write, wrote Sketches of Indian Christians in which he wrote about Ramabai and Krupabai.) Samuel and Kamala wrote a book together entitled Stories of Indian Christian Life in 1898. The Maharani of Baroda's daughter married the son of Maharani Sunity Devee of Cooch Behar, and their daughter was Gayatri Devi. Of course they too turn up in each other's books. Kamaladevi Chattopadhyay married Sarojini Naidu's brother.

Just when I thought I was coming to the end of what could be realistically achieved, Mr Aroon Tikekar, Editor-in-Chief of Loksatta mentioned some of the books and articles in his collection of rare books. He very kindly lent me all the Cornelia Sorabji titles, Nalini Turkhud's novel *The Jagirdar of Palna*, *Our Cause: A Symposium by Indian Women*, and *Who's Who of Women in India*, the only place in which I could locate information about Shevantibai Nikambe, Ela Sen, Iqbalunnisa Hussain and others. He also lent me vol. I of *Vishrabdha Sharda* (1972) a collection of letters published in Bombay Presidency in the ninetenth century. Anapurna Turkhad's letter to the *Spectator* and the *Times of India* was one of the very few pieces in English. The rest of the letters were all translated into Marathi, or were originally in Marathi. I would also like to thank Adil Jussawalla who gave me the reference to Dosebai Jessawalla.

Eunice de Souza

Dosebai Cowasjee Jessawalla
(b.1832)

The Story of My Life (Bombay: The Times Press, 1911) by Dosebai Cowasjee Jessawalla is dedicated to her mother, Meheribai, for giving the author the privilege of being the 'first Indian girl to receive the benefits of an English education'.

Little is known about the life of Dosebai Jessawalla apart from what her autobiography tells us, though it documents events of her time meticulously. Peopled with pictures and vivid in its descriptions, the book has tremendous importance from a sociological and historical perspective. It also describes the lives of Dosebai, her mother, and her husband.

Opening with a chapter on British rule in India, the book goes on to explore the author's contact with English society, describes innovations in Parsee society, and records her many visits to places like Lucknow, Calcutta, America, and England.

In her Foreword, we are told by Dosebai that it was her mother who prepared her for an active part in the history of Indian women, making her the 'instrument of pioneering the noble cause of higher education among millions and millions of the gentler sex in India'. This desire to break free of convention and live her own life is evident in her at a very early age.

In the chapter, The First Empress of India, for example, Dosebai talks about how something as innocuous as her travelling to Delhi to be present at the Durbar was met with great hostility and surprise. 'I set all necessary preparations in train and kept our intention scrupulously secret to ward off the storm of ridicule and scandal which a rumour of this new departure from old custom would have called down on my devoted head. I fancied I could hear the jeering queries. Is it a Parsee female's business to mix in such demonstrations? How can she be so unwomanly as to venture on such a journey? Parsee men were notoriously selfish and had monopolized to themselves every pleasure and indulgence, fancying that women were only created for household drudgery.'

From then on, however, the author moves from place to place, country to country, discussing people, traditions, and places—a feat that, for a vast majority of her sex in India, must have been unimaginable.

Another chapter reproduced here describes her ascent in a balloon, while the closing pages reproduce an extract from an Indian journal, *The Bombay Courier*. This last excerpt provides insight into the kind of pressure mother and daughter may have had to deal with in order to have Dosebai enter Mrs Ward's seminary as the first young lady. The book remains a testimony to the life of a remarkable woman even now, almost a century after it was written.

The First Empress of India

In April 1876, Lord Lytton was appointed Governor-General, and shortly after it became generally known that our gracious Queen was about to assume the grand title of Empress of India. The entire Indian population received this news with acclamation. An official announcement was issued stating that the public declaration of this event would take place at a grand Durbar to be held at Delhi, the ancient capital of the Mogul Empire. Immediately, the feudatory Princes, Rajahs and nobles began making arrangements to be present and in due time set out on their way to the northern city with their large retinues and numerous followers. Preparations on a grand scale went on throughout the land and the well-to-do of every caste and creed were eager to be present on the occasion, as indeed they were encouraged to show their loyalty by appearing at the Durbar. It was said that something like half the population of India would be drawn towards Delhi and that the demand for edibles of all sorts would be likely to produce a dearth. To attract the attention of the public and to leave nothing undone that could conduce to the splendour of the ceremony, the subject was daily brought prominently forward in the leading native and English journals. As I had long wished to travel through the various districts of my native land, I determined to avail myself of this favourable opportunity for visiting the historical cities of the north. Two months before the time appointed for the Durbar, I introduced the subject to our social coterie and requested my daughter and her husband to bear me company, but they did not enter into the project being apprehensive of the great difficulties of the journey as well as of the expenses at Delhi and *en route*. Mr Pherozshah also declined to join me, so on hearing this I kept my own counsel and said no more on the subject. In the face of these discouragements, my kind husband readily consented to the plan, saying, we could dispense with other company, and go by ourselves. Accordingly, I set all necessary preparations in train and kept our intention scrupulously secret to ward off the storm of ridicule and scandal which a rumour of this new departure from old custom would have called down on my devoted head. I fancied I could hear the jeering queries. Is it a Parsee female's business to mix in such demonstrations? How can she be so unwomanly as to venture on such a journey? Parsee men were notoriously selfish and had monopolized to themselves every pleasure and indulgence, fancying that women were only created for household drudgery. I kept a lookout to see if any of the noteworthy Parsee gentlemen who were honoured by an invitation to the Durbar would take their families with them, but none apparently dreamt of such a thing and thus I was the more bent on going. I have ever taken the lead in matters of female reform and have tried to stimulate the dormant energies of my sisters and to open up to them paths hitherto debarred, leading to innocent pleasures or enlarged interests. It is quite unaccountable to me why native ladies in affluent circumstances should be backward in taking their legitimate place in grand state ceremonials, but they seem devoid of interest and curiosity as regards such things. Every new act of female emancipation at first meets with disapprobation and sarcasm and that frightens many a one from gratifying her inclinations, and on this occasion no other Parsee lady, incited by a keen desire to witness so grand a spectacle, had the courage either to face the ridicule of her people or to undertake the long journey. For my own part the encouragement I have always met with from another quarter, the Europeans, from my youth, has more than compensated me for the sneers of my countrymen. Seeing me busily making arrangements for leaving home, my daughter and friends were given to understand that I was preparing for a sojourn at Nowsaree, a place about 150 miles distant from Bombay. Thus, every one being on the wrong scent, I often proposed in jest that ten or twenty of our club should go to the Delhi assemblage, to which they made answer: 'It is not for us to encounter such difficulties, even if we could go to Delhi, we females would not be able openly to enjoy any of the sights.' This simplicity made me laugh but responding in the same strain I would say, 'Ah yes, a trip to Nowsaree or Gandevi is all that we women can hope for while our husbands roll in luxury and deny themselves nothing, so, in spite of our being reputed of higher culture than many of our sisters, we lead the same dull and tasteless life.'

In due time all was ready and our party of seven comprising my husband, his old aunt of the comic disposition, our two sons, my brother Heerjeebhoy and an old tried servant of the house, took our departure from Bombay on the 22nd December. As my husband's business affairs did not allow of a very long absence it was necessary to have my brother's company during our tour after the assemblage was over. He expressed his inability to meet the expenses of such protracted travels, but on my indignantly demanding 'Who asks anything from you?' he made up his mind to escort me. The manager of my husband's firm had been very unwilling to spare him and was only persuaded to do so on condition that he (my husband) should return, in case urgent business compelled his being telegraphed for. This my good husband kept to himself, lest by his inability to remain with us the whole project should be upset. At the last, feeling sore at the thought of enjoying so much without my daughter sharing it with me, I asked her to come with me, but she again refused on account of the difficulties and troubles into which she thought I rushed willingly. It seemed unnatural to be without her, as she had till now always accompanied me in all my pleasures, I willingly defraying all expenses, but my husband's company kept up my spirits. He took the management of everything and right well did he discharge the self-imposed duty. He wrote to his cousins in Delhi to secure suitable accommodation and make all suitable arrangements for the reception of a European friend and his family whom he would accompany down to Delhi. He also wrote to his two friends, Shapoorjee and Jamsetjee Eduljee Chinoy, who were in the service of the Nizam's late uncle, Amir-e-Kabir, co-regent of Hyderabad, and held in high estimation; these two gentlemen were intimate with my husband and had frequent intercourse with him in Bombay and they were also given to understand that a European and his wife were coming, thus the secret was kept to the last. I wrote to Bai Sakerbai, wife of Set Manekjee Rustomjee, at Calcutta, informing her of my intention to sojourn there for a time after the Durbar at Delhi and requesting her to hire lodgings for me. An intimate friendship had sprung up between us while she stayed for about three years in Bombay. She had honoured us by her company at my daughter's marriage and we frequently visited each other at that time. Through this letter the fact of my intended visit to Delhi became known to friends in Bombay, two or three days before our departure, for the daughter-in-law of my friend in Calcutta, extremely surprised by this unexampled proceeding on my part, at once wrote to her mother and brother in Bombay asking if the news could be true. The brother in his turn interrogated a Hindoo teacher, who came to my house to instruct my two sons; he, however, was quite in the dark as to our intention and could not satisfy the gentleman's curiosity. Meanwhile I received a favourable reply from Bai Sakerbai, kindly inviting me to stay with her while in Calcutta. Before setting out on this tour, I paid a visit to my kind friend, Lady Sassoon, and on informing her of my projected journey she could not at first give credence to my words, but on being assured that it really was so, she expressed herself pleased, saying she also would have gone if she could have found suitable lodgings there. Here I met Lord Kilman, brother of the late Mrs O.T. Burne, wife of the Private Secretary of H.E. the Viceroy of India, who also expressed himself pleased with my going to Delhi, but he did not know that I was the only Parsee lady who should be there. On the 22nd December we started from the Boree Bunder. Amongst many loungers at the station were Set Dhunjeebhoy Framjee Patell and other members of the Panthakey family whose surprise on seeing our tickets to Delhi knew no bounds and they asked how we could venture to go into such immense crowds as would be assembled there, especially as no other Parsee female would be there. At 5:30 the train started, and on reaching Byculla my daughter, who had escorted us so far, alighted. Next day our departure for Delhi came to be generally known by an announcement of the fact in the local papers. This brought many congratulatory letters from my well meaning friends, but it cannot be denied that many others were much incensed against me; however, I would not allow their envy and folly to deprive me of one iota of the enjoyment placed within my reach. We reached Jubbulpore the next evening at 9 p.m. and on alighting, my husband as he apprehended received a telegram, calling him back to Bombay on urgent business. This was extremely dejecting, but my husband comforted me somewhat by promising to hasten after us if his affairs allowed; he therefore parted from us, taking his youngest son who desired to go back to Bombay with his father. We continued our journey and next day at 7 a.m. reached Allahabad; this railway station was then considered the largest and finest in India. We break-fasted there and spent the day in the city. We hired a carriage and drove to the fortress which to me presented a grand and imposing appearance. There was a regiment encamped in it and there was much life about the place. At a particular spot near the fortress there is a spacious subterranean cellar which we also visited; sacred rites and ceremonies are performed here by the Hindoos. We saw human skeletons hanging here and there, it looked dark and gruesome and I would not venture far, though other members of our party went with lighted tapers and saw the whole vast extent of the place. Thence we went to the Bazaar, which is held in an open space without roof or structure of any kind. Of the fruit of this place the pear is a speciality; it has a sweet, delicious taste and is four times the size of those we get in Bombay; it has a small collection of stones like those of the date or greengage in the middle. We next proceeded to the confluence of the Ganges and Jumna where many Hindoo devotees were bathing in the holy waters with their clothes on and performing various religious ceremonies—all this is worth seeing. After this we went through the streets and saw houses and shops of curious architecture and plan. The dust, however, was the prevailing element and sadly annoyed us. At dusk we returned to the station and partook of a meal prepared by our own servant, then rested a little and started again on our way at 9 p.m., reaching Toondla next morning. At all the stations the station masters and hotel keepers rendered us every possible assistance and attention; they unanimously declared that thousands of passengers had passed through their station on their way to Delhi during the last two months, but that they had seen no Parsee lady till I came. The English passengers freely commented on my appearance till they became aware that I could talk their language, thus many new friendships sprang up in the course of this journey. At this station two new passengers entered our carriage, one of whom was a barrister practising at Cawnpore, the other was the Principal of the Martiniere College at Lucknow. The amusing conversation which they carried on together caused me to smile, whereupon the man of learning whispered to his friend of the long robe that he thought I understood what they were saying, the other retorted that such a grown up Parsee lady was certainly not so accomplished; this created much merriment and we soon were chatting together and feeling quite at home with one another. The schoolmaster showed me much consideration by rendering me assistance whenever he could. The nearer we approached Delhi the more the number of passengers increased, so that the crowding and bustle of the last hour were such as to throw into oblivion the troubles of the three preceding days' journey; however, by God's grace we arrived safely at our destination. At the Delhi station the great concourse of people, the shouting and excitement made me think that the timorous folk in Bombay were not so far wrong, that this was really no place for a native female to be in, especially without her husband. But I caught sight of my husband's cousin, Mr Eduljee Cowasjee Jamsetjee, hurrying towards us, and my courage revived. This gentleman carries on the business of my late father-in-law under the name of Jehangeer and Co., a name well-known throughout the Punjaub and Cabul. This 'friend in need' had made all fitting arrangements for the reception of an English lady and gentleman, whom my husband was to accompany, and had come to the station to await them. He was glad that his exertions had been made on my behalf and he skilfully steered me through the great crowd and drove me to the small bungalow in the compound of the United Service Hotel which he had secured for the supposed English couple. Though the miniature bungalow was cabin-like in its dimensions, it was nicely furnished and answered all our requirements, but the cold was so severe that I was glad to bring into requisition the extra bedding we had brought with us. Early on the morning after our arrival, I was awakened by some one knocking at the door. This turned out to be a Hindoo clerk in the service of H.H. the Amir-i-Kabir, co-regent of Hyderabad; the poor man had been on our track all night and was glad to find us at last. The explanation of the matter is that, on my husband's return from Jubbulpore, he had telegraphed my coming to his kind and good friend Mr Shapoorjee, but the message arriving too late he had failed to meet me at the station, and had employed this clerk to find out my whereabouts. Shortly afterwards, his brother, Mr Jamsetjee, followed in his carriage. He insisted on our leaving the Hotel and making use of the beautiful tents which they had erected for us. I thanked him kindly but had resolved to stay where we were. On the 26th I had a long drive in Mr Shapoorjee's open mail phaeton drawn by a pair of beautiful studs through the principal thoroughfares of the city, and wherever the eyes were cast dense crowds of people were to be seen, to whom the sight of a Parsee female was a novelty, thus we reached the large open space studded with innumerable tents. Here we saw two of those tents, which Mr Shapoorjee had so kindly provided for our use, they were most comfortable and inviting, supplied with every convenience and our heartfelt thanks were offered to our hospitable friend, but I excused myself from accepting the accommodation on account of the extreme cold which would have been experienced in such an open and unprotected plain. Returning thence we re-entered the city by the high spacious Cashmere and Lahore gates, once no doubt grand and imposing but now falling into decay. Proceeding through streets teeming with people we came to Chandni-Chowk, flanked on each side by houses and reminding me of the Bhindy Bazaar or Parell Road of Bombay. We saw a great many Hindoos and Mahomedans, a few Baboos and a very few Parsees. They were taken by surprise on seeing me drive through this city of antiquity in an open carriage and the gaping crowd that gathered round the carriage made it a matter of difficulty to proceed. I heard several passing their opinion as to my identity; some said I was a European, some took me for a Chinese, some for an Egyptian, a Turkish lady and so on, but very few knew me as a Parsee, as they did not believe a Parsee lady would venture through such populous thoroughfares in an open carriage. It was exceedingly droll to listen to the rejoinders made by my old aunt to these openly expressed opinions; she did not hesitate to scold back the curious crowd saying, 'If you want to see persons like us come to Bombay.' The general astonishment with which we were beheld wherever we went in this city was due to the gaily coloured sarees we wore and to the fact that none of the native females had ever been seen in an open carriage before, but according to custom they never appear in public nor go from one place to another without being caged up in a carriage with all venetian blinds and shutters fast closed. At 4 in the afternoon of this day Mr Shapoorjee again came to take us sight-seeing, I took my place on his open mail phaeton and my aunt with my son and brother on that of his brother. We met several Princes and Rajahs with their retinues, as also some of the handsome four-in-hand coaches of Englishmen. Of these, the turn-out of the Lieutenant-Governor attracted most attention for its novelty. The State carriage was drawn by six camels ridden by grooms in gorgeous livery much bedecked with gold fringe and silver lace; in the carriage, which was a large open brake, a number of beautiful young ladies were seated. This unique show was very striking to us, but apparently more so to my old aunty who in the exuberance of her delight showered down blessings on me for having afforded her such enjoyments at her advanced age. On our return we saw several old buildings, the most remarkable being the fortress of gigantic magnitude. The strength and stability of this ancient fortification, most part of which has been destroyed by war, prove that the architects of old understood the secret of setting time and decay at defiance. We had a grand view of the Jooma Musjid, the largest mosque in India. Proceeding further we had to make our way through streets literally teeming with people whose smiling faces turned towards our carriage wherever we went. The clouds of dust somewhat marred our enjoyment although the roads had been so plentifully watered as to present a monsoon appearance. A cold breeze and thick fog came on the accompanying darkness rendering it necessary for us to return home by 7 o'clock, Mr Shapoorjee and his brother making their way as best they could to their tents, carrying with them our grateful thanks for the delightful and interesting drive. After taking some tea to keep off cold we mixed in the company at the Hotel, where I found some acquaintances, and in animated conversation the time passed pleasantly. Amongst them was Mr Dadabhoy, son of the late worthy Maneckjee Nowrojee Setna. Before retiring to rest, I offered prayer and thanksgiving to God for having allotted me a share in such rare enjoyment. On the morning of the 27th we started for an early walk but had to beat a hasty retreat. The cold was more than we could bear. After dressing ourselves in warm woollen garments, one above the other, and I enveloping myself in a long over-coat such as European ladies wear, we ventured forth again and took a brisk walk which soon made us warm and comfortable. Returning at 10 o'clock we took breakfast, afterwards taking a drive in a wagonette. We arranged with the Hotel-keeper to have a carriage and pair retained for our use, besides which Mr Shapoorjee placed a carriage and horses at our disposal. Everything was procurable for money, but I found the prices little in excess of those usual in Bombay and below what report had led us to expect. I met another old acquaintance here, Mr Hormusjee Shapoorjee Bookbinder, for many years clerk in my father-in-law's firm in the Punjaub; he left this service and had set up a Hotel, known as the Prince of Wales Hotel, a coach factory and livery stable at Lucknow and had in a short time amassed great wealth and become a leading citizen. He was to be seen driving about with great pomp here in Delhi, his fine carriages and horses and English coachman attracting much attention. On seeing me, he began to eulogize my husband under whom he had once served: 'It is with heartfelt joy,' he would say, 'that I see my patron's family here and my pleasure would be enhanced if I could execute any of your commands.' And he also desired us to make use of his horses and carriages. To Mr Sorabjee Mody, Manager of my late father-in-law's firm, as also to Mr Eduljee, I was indebted for many kind services and much assistance and consideration. This evening we again drove in an open carriage to other celebrated quarters of Delhi, but it grew cold and foggy as on the preceding day, so we returned early to our apartments. On Thursday, the 28th we bent our steps early in the morning towards the garden of the city where the tombs and monuments of rich nobles who flourished in the past are daily strewn with fresh flowers and fragrant herbs. At 11 a.m. I started in company with my brother to pay a visit to the Hon'ble Mrs Burne in the Viceroy's camp; we unfortunately forgot to take the guide book of this vast encampment and had therefore much trouble and unnecessary fatigue before we could find her tent. I was most kindly received by Mrs Burne, who invited me to a supper party and also asked me to come and be presented to Lady Lytton in the evening. She further invited me to take a glass of wine or a cup of tea or coffee; for all these civilities I expressed myself, as I felt, deeply obliged. Returning home, I selected suitable garments for the visit to Her Excellency and at half past four drove with my son to the Viceroy's tents in a splendid carriage and pair lent for the occasion by the forementioned Mr Hormusjee, but in consequence of the circuitous route which had to be taken the appointed hour was long past when we reached our goal and Lady Lytton and Mrs Burne had gone out. So we had to return in disappointment. On the way we saw several Rajahs with their retinues and had an opportunity of learning something of the intricacies of the vast encampment. The streets were more crowded than ever, indeed every day seemed to increase the number of the populace. While sitting reading the newspaper of the day in which was detailed everything going on in Delhi, a trooper rode up with a note from the Viceroy's camp. It was from kind Mrs Burne regretting having missed my visit and hoping I would fix another time for being presented to Lady Lytton.

My Ascent in a Balloon

Next morning I heard that a balloon was to ascend from the Trocadéro (the Exhibition), and that any one who liked could enjoy the novel pleasure of an aerial sail. My hotel friends were surprised to hear that I ardently longed to go up in the balloon and asked me, whether all the Parsee women were a bold, intrepid nature like myself. I had to dispel this very erroneous idea by telling them that a few years ago Parsee women and even a few of the men were frightened at Europeans, and would run away if they saw any approaching them. I, however, by my early associations with Europeans had imbibed their tastes and some of their courage. These remarks pleased my American friends, who again urged me to visit New York, most hospitably extracting from me a promise that, when I did so, I should go to no hotel or boarding house but stay with them. Dressing myself in warm clothing and carrying with me in a handbag some note paper, wine, biscuits and a piece of iron to which to attach any missive I might wish to send down to the people below, I set out for the place from which the ascent was to take place. Here there was an immense crowd, whose amazement at seeing me amongst the aeronauts was most amusing to behold. On payment of a sum of Rs. 10, I took my seat. This balloon being merely intended for pleasure excursions, was attached to the earth by a long rope. There were in all fifteen passengers, three of whom were ladies. I did not allow my son to accompany me for fear of an accident. At 5 p.m. we began gently to ascend, and I saw the earth receding from beneath us. Presently the panorama that spread itself out before us, as we hovered over the splendid city was most strange and fantastic; the people whom we had left below might have been taken for a swarm of bees, the river Seine with its stately bridges, the gardens with their flowers and ancient trees, the fountains with their feeble jets of water vainly trying to reach us, the proud monuments, the magnificent buildings and their tall spires, the majestic Opera House, the thousands of boats darting like fishes hither and thither on the water, the Exhibition from which hundreds of flags were gaily waving, and the innumerable other places of interest in this wonderful city formed a scene which bore resemblance more to the fabled abodes of genii than to anything sublunary; indeed, might we not say that it seemed a faint reflex of the unfading lustre and undying joy of Paradise itself! How long will my wealthy sisters shut themselves up in their old habits and prejudices, shunning the healthy and ennobling pleasures which lie alluringly at their very door! Why do they cling so tenaciously to their idle crude custom, and know no higher ambition than to glide along in the same groove as their ancestors, instead of proving themselves worthy of the times they live in by basking in the free air of enlightenment! Awake, dear sisters, ere the stealthy hand of Time rob you of youth and opportunity to learn wisdom? To die in the hope of entering Paradise is blessed, but thrice blessed is he who, living a life of piety and virtue, learns something of the world he lives in, and of the other races of mankind who share it with him. But to return to the point—as the balloon rose higher and higher, the cold became more intense, and as I began to shiver, I had to take a good draught of the wine I had brought with me. I offered some to a lady who looked very delicate and who felt grateful for the offer. We had now risen to the full height allowed by the rope, namely 700 metres, and I experienced an exhilarating sensation of pleasure in soaring like a bird above the earth— a pleasure enhanced by the knowledge that we were securely tied to mother earth and that all precautions were taken to preserve the balloon in its upright position. As we began to descend, Paris which had dwindled into an insignificant speck, gradually assumed her own graceful dimensions and we were soon deposited again on terra firma, after an aerial flight of forty-five minutes. A medal commemorating our ascent was presented to each passenger. Oh! for words to describe this exciting adventure. As the gardens of the Tuileries had attracted my notice from the balloon, we went there and found much to admire. It covers a large area and is rich in flowers, lawns, avenue, trees, statues and fountains; an old-fashioned stately atmosphere pervades the place. The palace has been in a state of dilapidation since the Franco-German war but is imposing in its very ruins.

On the 16th August, after writing letters to Bombay, London and Germany, we went to the Exhibition and spent the whole day in looking at the fine collection of pictures, but it would have needed a full month to see them all thoroughly, so immense was the number. Some of the pictures were valued at from a lac to a lac and a half of rupees—almost incredible to our Indian mind. On the 17th I went to a jeweller's and ordered some ornaments to be sent out to me to India and returning heard from my son of his having accidentally met a gentleman of the firm of Messrs. Fallek, after we had given up all hopes of seeing any one of that firm. Messrs. Fallek, while in Bombay ten years before, were in the habit of coming to our place to negotiate, through my husband, for the purchase of pearls. The gentleman was much pleased at our being in Paris, and invited us to spend the evening at his house. Then we went to a photographer's and had ourselves photographed.

On the 18th, after breakfast, I started by train for Versailles, which was reached in half an hour. This was a national fête-day, an anniversary on which the fountains play and crowds of people flock to see them. Within an enclosure, the beautifully designed garden lay in its smiling beauty, interspersed with alabaster equestrian statues. Proceeding along the avenue, we came in sight of the celebrated palace—a building worthy of such surroundings. As I was entering the spacious hall, an Englishman, named, as I afterwards learnt, Mr Cuthbert, politely enquired if I had been there before and as it was difficult to see all the places of interest in the palace without guidance, he most kindly offered assistance and I most gladly availed myself of it, thanking God, Who in every emergency, anticipated and even exceeded my wants. The palace is divided into many suites of apartments, each in the charge of an official, who conducted the visitors through the suite and gave an account of everything contained therein, Mr Cuthbert kindly translating to me as we went on. The ancient furniture was so beautifully polished that it looked quite new. There were splendid old picture in all the rooms, and the entire walls of several others were hung with tapestry, representing battle scene. The palace itself is a noble building, and contains so many interesting objects that we were worn out with the very looking at them. The ceiling of the dining hall is exquisitely painted with figures of fairies in gold and silver.

There were four other equally splendid palaces standing at a mile distance from each other in the garden. The extent of the garden can be judged from this fact, but its beauty must be seen to be believed. It is a terrestrial Eden and has a number of cool retreats and shady arbours. There are also undulating pieces of ground covered over with luxuriant grass, romantic lakes lying at the foot of hills and swiftly flowing streams meandering through the lovely landscape. In short, nature and art have combined to produce a masterpiece. We saw a number of carriages here which had belonged to Louis XIV and Napoleon Bonaparte; they were richly gilded and painted with birds, the seats were covered with velvet and hung with gold and silver tassels. Each carriage was valued at 100,000 francs. Proceeding further, Mr Cuthbert exclaimed: 'Here is the centre of attraction!' And so it was truly. We stood before a large pond or reservoir of water in which about a hundred fountains were playing in the most fantastic forms. Some represented a tree with its trunk, branches, twigs and leaves, others assumed a thousand fanciful shapes as they rose and fell, while the largest, which only plays once a year on this day, represented Neptune, the God of Water. In this one figure, there must have been at least a thousand jets at play, the air around was thereby rendered as moist as in the rainy season. There were seats arranged as in a theatre down to the very margin of the lake for the convnience of the numerous spectators. It is impossible to convey to my readers an idea of the marvellous beauty of this enchanting scene. Taking leave of Mr Cuthbert, we hired a carriage and returned to our hotel at 6 p.m.

On the next day I saw Sir Albert Sassoon after a lapse of six years and found little or no change in him. We had a pleasant conversation on the past. Afterwards Messieurs Fallek came and took me to see their house where we had a pleasant tiffin and a merry chat. They afterwards took me to see the Grand Hotel which was considered the best till the Continental was built.

The 22nd of August being my birthday, I rose early to pour out my thanks to God for his mercy in having granted me the fulfilment of my long-cherished desire, namely, the visit to England, and for having, in addition, enabled me to see the great Exhibition and be a lodger in the best, though none the less expensive, hotel in Paris. After breakfast I went with Mr and Mrs Kirby and their daughters to the Bon Marché, one of the most fashionable shops in Paris, in size and magnificence a veritable palace. It was difficult in the midst of so many beautiful things in the shop to make a choice, but at last I selected some silks, fans, handkerchiefs and woollen fabrics. One of the superintendents kindly showed me over the entire establishment, saying that their shop was never before graced by the presence of a lady of my race and dress, and the entire staff therefore had stopped work to have a look at me. Again on the 23rd and 24th I visited this shop and made some more purchases. Two days were spent in leave-taking and making preparations for our departure, and on the 28th I went and bought Cook's Tickets for myself and son, and then went to have a last look at the Exhibition and saw what I had seen hurriedly before. Returned again after dinner to the Trocadéro and took a sorrowful farewell of this unparalleled Exhibition, which had been the main incentive for my crossing the ocean. The last evening at the hotel was spent in the company of my friends; we pledged each other's health and spoke of meeting again ...

Closing Reflections

Here I conclude the story of my life, leaving the indulgent reader to judge for himself or herself what has been accomplished during the half-century and over that I have engaged myself in the field of women's education and of social progress. To enable the generation of the present day to realize the condition that was prevalent at the time I entered that noble arena amidst the vortex of controversy and opposition, I give the following extract from the issue of an old Indian journal, *The Bombay Courier*, dated the 19th August 1842:

The United Service Gasette of Tuesday stated that a young Parsee lady has been placed as a pupil in Mrs Ward's seminary, but that the Editor was unable, owing to the lateness of the hour at which the intelligence reached him, to state the father's name; and adds with great truth: 'The Courier will rejoice at it when he knows it.' We assure our contemporary that we do sincerely and unaffectedly rejoice at it. We consider the man, whose mind is sufficiently enlarged to admit of his taking the initiative in breaking down the prejudices of country and of caste, in so good a cause, not only deserving of our humble applause, but of the approbation which he is sure to obtain of the whole civilized world. There was a time, a period of European History when a premium was offered to ignorance—when reading and writing were left to clerks and considered badges of vulgarity by the Sovereign and his Feudal Chiefs—when the proud Peers themselves could only make their marks, or impress their signature with a stamp. But this was in the time of barbarians, when the human intellect lay fettered—when bodily strength and dexterity in the use of arms constituted almost the sole pretentions of a gentleman. Happily, knowledge superseded ignorance and a brighter day has dawned on the intellectual horizon. *Ex Oriente lux*. In the East arose the sun of human enlightenment, it travelled Westward, and confers that power which consists in knowledge. We of the West are bound, therefore, and feel the obligation to return to its Eastern source, as far as files it our power, the blessings of enlightenment. The dissemination of knowledge over the whole earth is a paramount object with the philanthropist of every clime.

The Parsees, of all the inhabitants of this portion of the globe ought peculiarly to appreciate and prize the cultivation of the mental faculties, for to their education is to be attributed in a great degree, if not altogether, their wealth, their liberality, and their acknowledged influence. They know this and they prove their knowledge by the pains they take, and the expenses they incur, in the education of their male children. Why they have so long neglected their female offspring, can only be accounted for by their blind subserviency to the usage they found established in a country which afforded them protection. The fear of ridicule, the censure of the common herd, the dislike to innovation have deterred many of even the master-minds of our own country from departing from the established usages of their fatherland, and it required the exercise of the most transcendant moral courage to break the bonds of prejudice and senseless reverence for time-hallowed and established usage. In considering the sacrifice which this Parsee gentleman has made of early prejudice, we do not regard it as an occurrence of ephemeral interest, but as a type and forerunner of superior intellectual advancement amongst the class to which he belongs; and we hail it as a happy omen of what may be accomplished even in our own day. It will not be disputed that the happiness of life principally depends upon the enjoyments of our home—that the enjoyments of home principally depend upon that sex, in this country hitherto debased and degraded by the profoundest ignorance—that a woman's powers of pleasing mainly depend upon her capabilities to participate in feelings and in objects common to both her husband and herself—that man of education can have but little community of sentiment with women whose knowledge is confined to the acquirements fitting them merely for the household drudgery of superior domestic slaves. The experience of the world teaches us, that from such an ill-assorted association, nothing but disgust must eventually ensue and mutual estrangement is commonly the result. This in Eastern nations evinces itself, in a toleration of plurality of wives, and concubinage. When the freshness of youth and beauty have faded, the woman has lost the only charm that once attracted, and in the absence of the beauties of the mind, she has no resource but to conform to her lot, and become in her husband's house the principal domestic. From such a fate, from such a degradation, from such a prostitution of the ends and objects of marriage the liberal minded Parsee bids fair to rescue his child. We heartily wish him life and health, to reap the reward of his devotion to his daughter's true interests. This is a theme so grateful to us to descant upon, that we could write upon it by the mile as Coroner Wakeley writes verses, out until the name of the Parsee reaches us, with a confirmation of the fact, we think it would be premature to say more than that we fully expect his name will be handed down to posterity, as a benefactor of the humane race, on the same page with that of Sir Jamsetji Jijibhoy—different traits of the same liberality of sentiment, and nobility of mind, are exhibited in the conduct of both—they are a step in advance of the age they live in—and will be proudly recorded in the living page of England's History.

The *Courier*, however, has erred in one respect which is most essential to rectify. It mentions that I was educated by my father. This is a mistake, as at the time I was being educated my father was not living, but had died four years previously. Thus the mother alone was my sole guardian, and as such evinced great care and solicitude in looking after me. It was a very courageous step that she took in placing me in Mrs Ward's Seminary at the tender age of ten. In this wise the plaudits belong to my late revered mother Bai Meheribai only, and in justice to her memory I have rectified this error of the *Courier* even at such a remote date as 70 years after the event.

In the evening of my life it is gratifying to notice that Mr M.M. Murzban, Bar-at-Law, a Parsee author of remarkable ability, who is translating Mademoiselle Menant's French work 'Les Parsis' into English, points out that at page 339 of that history, Miss Menant in a footnote observes as follows:—'It is but fair to note here the effort of Mrs C.J. Jessawalla (Bai Dosebai, wife of Cowasji Jehangir Jessawalla), actively co-operated in the work of Maneckji Kharsetji, on behalf of English education for Parsee girls.' I have emphatically to contradict the statement of Miss Menant inasmuch as I had never had anything to do with Mr Maneckjee or any member of his family. I have always held my own course irrespective of any of them. On this point I should like to refer my readers to the correspondence which was published on the subject in the *Bombay Gazette* as far back as 1887 soon after the death of Mr Maneckji Kharsetji, wherein the correspondent said that no small credit was due to Bai Meheribai for championing the cause of women's education. He has referred in detail to the difficulties she encountered at the hands of her co-religionists. The correspondent in good faith pointed out that Mr Maneckji was not the gentleman who took the lead, but the germ was first laid into the soil by the hand of a woman (Bai Meheribai) who had the courage and foresight to take the initiative. The writer who supports the cause of Maneckji candidly admits that he (Mr Maneckji) had at a considerably subsequent period engaged the services of a governess but did not send his daughters to the school conducted in those days by ladies like Mrs Ward. I have no desire to enter into discussion on this point as it is too well-known to the public, especially those of the old generation, as to who the originator of this movement was. But since people ignorant of the actual state of things have come forward authoritatively to throw into obscurity the claim of my revered mother, I have thought fit as a loyal and dutiful daughter to stand on her side and place the historical facts publicly on record. The perusal of this humble work will amply convince my readers how matters stood in the early days with regard to women's education. Just a week before I started on my tour round the world, a short sketch of my life was published in the *Times of India* in May 1907 and several well-known leading Gujarati papers. These accounts were also published in several leading papers of London, and none has dared to refute one iota of those long and truthful accounts. I have to thank Mr Murzban for inserting the whole of the article above referred to in the *Times of India* in his translation. It clearly indicates that Miss Menant was probably misinformed or else the note under discussion would not have appeared.

Thus comes to an end the story of my humble yet eventful life. In spite of the various difficulties that intervened, I have at last been able to place it before the world; and it only remains for me to thank the Almighty God for having spared me to see the desire of my life accomplished, and to express a confident hope that the coming generations of women in my beloved Motherland will emulate whatever of good and noble and beautiful they may gather in these pages.

—*The Story of My Life* (1911)

Toru Dutt
(1856–1877)

Mrs E.F. Chapman, in her *Sketches of Some Distinguished Indian Women* (1891) tells us that Toru's writings first appeared in print in the *Bengal Magazine*, to which she contributed an essay on the poetry of Le Conte de Lisle, a writer with whom she was much in sympathy.

He was a Creole, born in Mauritius and, as we may judge from the following extract from the article, she felt that in some respects his case resembled her own: 'The faults generally attributed to all Asiatic or half-caste poets, writing in the languages of Europe, are weakness, languor, conventionalism, and imitation. From most of these defects Le Conte de Lisle was singularly free. He is wonderfully vigorous and very often thoroughly original. Not only is he very well read, not only has he mediated much, but he has that gifted poetic eye, which can seize at once, and extract poetry from the meanest object.' Toru was quite clearly a prodigy. She wrote in English and French with equal fluency, and was learning Sanskrit in the hope of being able to translate from the language, when she died. Even at fourteen she was deeply interested in French politics, and translated French poetry and speeches she admired, particularly those of Victor Hugo.

Mrs Chapman also mentions the appearance of Toru's first book in 1876. The story of *A Sheaf Gleaned in French Fields* is, by now, well known. It was badly printed and when, at the *Examiner*, it was forced on the famous critic Edmund Gosse for a review (it was the dead season for books) he thought that this 'shabby little book of some two hundred pages, without preface or introduction, seemed specially destined by its particular providence to find its way hastily into the waste paper basket'.

He opened the book, read a little, and then wrote: 'What was my surprise and almost rapture to open at such verse as this ...! When poetry is as good as this, it does not matter whether Rouveyre prints it upon Whatman paper or whether it steals to light in blurred type from some press in Bhowanipore.'

The young Miss Dutt could also play the piano, was a good horsewoman, and could hold her own in conversation with the great men and women she met. Harihar Das documents an incident where Lord Lawrence, Viceroy of India (1864–1867), once told Toru and her sister Aru that instead of reading too many novels, they should opt for histories. While Aru didn't reply, Toru answered for her sister by saying, 'We like to read novels'. When questioned by Lord Lawrence about her choice, she smiled and replied: 'Because novels are true, and histories are false.'

Toru's literary influences were many. The Dutts were Christians, baptized in Calcutta in 1862. They were known to missionaries from her great-grandfather's time, and had deep-rooted connections with English literature as the *Dutt Family Album*, a compilation of works by family members, reveals.

As for Toru's own work, it includes *A Sheaf Gleaned in French Fields: Ballads and Legends of Hindustan* with an introduction by Edmund Gosse (1882), a novel in French entitled *Le Journal de Mademoiselle D' Arvers*, (1879), published in Paris, and *Bianca or The Young Spanish Maiden*, an unfinished novel in English, published posthumously in the Bengal Magazine between January and April 1878.

Her most famous poem, *Our Casuarina Tree* is a frequently anthologized piece of work that stands apart from her other poetry. It reveals a deep feeling for nature that can also be seen in the work of other writers such as Krupabai Satthianadhan (also featured in this volume).

In her letters that were mostly written to an old friend in Cambridge, Mary Martin, Toru comes across as a lively, warm, caring person who felt as deeply about life and living as she did about the work in which she was constantly involved. After the death of both her brother, then Aru, from consumption, Toru's own poor health was put into perspective in her poetry, as she struggled to rise above the physical: 'I knew in such a world as this, no one can gain his heart's desire, or pass the years in perfect bliss; like gold, we must be tried by fire.'

Toru died at the age of twenty-one, leaving behind only a suggestion of what she could have accomplished had she lived longer to further develop her skills. In the *Life and Letters of Toru Dutt*, Harihar Das quotes the French writer and critic James Darmesteter who said of her: 'This daughter of Bengal, so admirably and so strangely gifted, Hindu by race and tradition, an English woman by education, a French woman at heart, poet in English, prose-writer in French; who at the age of eighteen made India acquainted with the poets of France in the rhyme of England, who blended in herself three souls and three traditions, and died at the age of twenty-one, in the full bloom of her talent and on the eve of the awakening of her genius, presents in the history of literature a phenomenon without parallel.'

Letters to Miss Martin, January 1876–December 1876

Calcutta
13 January 1876

My dear Mary,—I received your welcome letter on Sunday last. I have not been able to answer it sooner, on account of being very busy copying out my book for the press and correcting the proofs. The book consists of about one hundred and sixty pieces of French poems translated into English. I shall send you a copy as soon as the book is out. It is to be printed only, not published, and it will be ready about the end of February.

Many many thanks or your kind wishes, and for the Christmas card; it will be all the more precious as being made by yourself. I should indeed very much like to have a sketch or two of your own drawings, if it is no trouble to you.

I have sent off a packet to your address, containing three photographs of our garden at Baugmaree. I hope you will receive it safely.

The Prince left Calcutta on Monday last. We had capital opportunities of seeing him, though we did not go out with the fixed purpose of seeing His Royal Highness. Once we were out driving in the forenoon, on the Strand, and we saw him driving down to the *Serapis*, to lunch. We were going rather slowly, and his carriage was also going at a slow rate, so we had a good look at him. Our carriages passed each other, and I had a good view of his pleasant and rather handsome face and his merry blue eyes. I suppose you have seen him, have you not? He has very beautiful auburn hair, though he is a little bald near the forehead. Russell described him, when he was going to be married to the Princess, in the well-known lines of Scott, only varying one or two words for the occasion.

> *Blue* was his eagle eye,
> And auburn of the richest dye
> His short *moustache* and hair.

We saw him again on the morning when he was going to open the Chapter for conferring the honour of knighthood on several of the big-wigs here. Papa saw him very well at the Belgachia entertainment given to him by the native community of Calcutta. We have also seen some of the Rajas and the Maharajas who came down to Calcutta during the Prince's sojourn there. The Maharaja of Cashmere had a *pugree* (head-dress) on his head, which was at least worth forty lakhs of rupees, so bejewelled it was. He has given a great many very valuable presents to the Prince, amongst which are hundred and one Cashmere shawls of the best material and the most 'cunning' workmanship, a *hookah* of gold set with diamonds and precious stones, a gold tea service, a gold dinner service, a silver bedstead, a tent of Cashmere workmanship with silver posts, and I do not remember the others: besides presents for the Princess. The Prince is now in Lucknow; at Benares a rich zemindar presented to him a crown worth six lakhs of rupees.

There is a good deal of talk at present about a Bengali gentleman and a pleader, Babu Juggodanuno Mukherjee, because he permitted the Prince to see his Zenana. All the papers conducted by natives are loudly crying out against this 'Outrage on Hindu Society'. The Prince did not visit any private gentleman at his own house, and only went to Babu Mukherjee's because he was promised that he would there be shown a real Zenana of native ladies of high position. This 'Scandalous behaviour', as the papers say, of the above-named Babu, is unpardonable in the eyes of the greater number of Hindus. The *Daily News* of Calcutta had a very sensible article on the subject. It said that if the Babu means to bring out his family, as in English society every European does, and let his friends visit and mingle with his family, as behoves civilized men and manners, he is a very well-meaning man, and his aims are very laudable; but if he has only made an exception for the Prince and his suite, and means to 'lock up' his wife and family, as all Hindus do, his allowing the Prince to visit his family is a bit of flunkeyism, quite unpardonable, and worthy of the highest disapprobation. Is not this sensibly and fairly put?

Lord Carrington, who is with the Prince, is very unlucky on horseback; he had a fall from his horse at Bombay, but fortunately escaped; he lost some of his teeth, while out on a shooting-party near here, by the handle of a spear, with which he had speared a boar, striking his mouth, and now he has had another fall, during the last shooting-expedition, which has dislocated his collar-borne. He will be alright in a fortnight or so, the papers say. Lord Hastings, who also accompanied the Prince, died of jungle fever at Madras. He was very young, being only twenty-one years of age. It must be sad for his family, who sent him away on this pleasure trip, full of youth and hope; it makes me sad to think of it.

Our Governor-General, Lord Northbrook, has resigned. He will be a great loss to India; he is greatly liked both by the native and European community. He will leave in the spring. Lord Lytton, son of the famous author of that name, is to succeed him. Lord Lytton is a poet himself; his *nom de plume* is Owen Meredith. Lord Northbrook's horses are to be sold by auction on Saturday next, which is a piece of rather interesting news to me! The *Serapis* and the *Osborne* are open to the public, but we do not care much to go and see them.

I am very sorry to hear that your father has been so ill; I am very glad that he is better now. Is the winter very severe and trying this year? Our winter is now very pleasant: imagine the warmest day of spring with a cloudless blue sky!

One of my aunts, who was a Hindu and a widow, and who used to live next door to us, died very suddenly, about a fortnight ago, of heart disease. She was subject to sudden and severe attacks of pain near the heart, but she did not think them anything serious. On the night of the 27th December (the night of the Belgachia entertainment) she returned at about eight o'clock from witnessing the street illuminations; at four in the morning she was taken ill with one of her attacks of pain, and in half an hour she died. Her death was so sudden and unexpected that her daughter (who was staying with her at the time) had not the time to send for a doctor. She sent word to her two brothers soon after her mother was taken ill, but when they arrived they found her dead. She was taken to the Ghaut, and burned the same day, according to the Hindu rites.

A rather amusing story is told about the Prince. While at Bombay he visited some school (I forget the name). On seeing a prismatic compass lying on the table, he asked the school boy nearest him what it was; the boy (somewhat agitated I suppose at being questioned by Royalty itself) answered, stammering: 'A royal com—com—com—pass, your prismatic Highness!' At this the whole company could not help smiling, and the Prince himself burst into a hearty laugh.

There is another amusing story about the Duke of Sutherland. He did not come to Calcutta from Madras with the Prince, but came a day later and by rail. His train, though, was three hours later than the appointed time, and the carriages sent from Government House to receive him at the station, tired of waiting, as they well might be, returned. When the train arrived, the Duke, finding nobody waiting for him, told the station master to get him a 'cab'. The hackney coachman refused to take a *sahib* he did not know; he had fears about his hire. He was told that the *sahib* was the *burra-sahib's* (Governor-General's) brother, but he held out till a policeman got up on the coachbox and obliged him to carry His Lordship to Government House.

We went to see the horses at Chitpore, a place three miles from here, where annually, in the cold season, horses are brought down from the upper provinces and from the Government studs for sale. There are a great number of them this season. Beautiful cows and sheep are also brought down from the upper provinces for sale at Chitpore. The cows and calves are extremely handsome; some have ears quite drooping, and hiding their pretty faces: they also give more milk than the Calcutta cows. My own Jeunette and Gentille are doing well. I often apply to them (when speaking of them to any one) the words which M. Seaufflaire, in Hugo's *Les Misérables*, applied to his horse, when recommending him to a purchaser: 'Elle est douce comme une fille, elle va comme le vent.' My uncle used to pride himself on the swiftness of his horse, but my Jeunette and Gentille beat his horse twice; and since then my uncle does not mention the speed of his galloway!

I am very very sorry to hear all what you say about dear Mrs Hall. I am afraid that in your next letter you will announce her death. Poor lady! We all used to like her very very much.

I am glad to hear that you met Mrs Cowell. Please give her my love and Mamma's when you next meet her. I daresay the book she has promised to lend you is *Govinda Samanta*, for Professor Cowell had, I know, very kindly undertaken to correct the proofs and to do the needful.

How is Mrs Baker? I have not yet any answer from her to my note. I hope she is quite well.

All the drainage works in and near our house are finished. I cannot describe the relief we find at this! When are you going to have your likeness taken? I hope very soon, and please to send me one as soon as you can.

I have not been reading anything lately; indeed I have entirely been taken up with my book for the last week. The printer makes such dreadful mistakes sometimes. In one of Victor Hugo's *chansons*, where the lines should have run,

> If there be a loving heart
> Where *Honour's* throne is drest,

they printed as follows:

> If there be a loving heart
> Where *Horror's* throne is drest.

And again in another piece: 'The Mother's Birthday,' the children, addressing their mother, say:

> Then to please thee in our duties,
>   We shall try to do our best,
> Never lift our heads while praying,
>   Just before we go to bed.

The printer has it thus:

> Then to please thee in our duties,
>   We shall try to do our best,
> Never lift our heads while *prying* (!)
>   Just before we go to bed.

Mamma had one of her attacks of pain a week ago; but she is quite well now, I am happy to say. I am pretty well at present; the cough is there still, a little more troublesome than it was in the summer, with blood-spitting off and on; but, on the whole, I am better now than I was in January last, a year ago.

We are going on with our Sanskrit lessons. When we have finished the book we are reading now, we shall take up Valmiki's Ramayana. My uncle has followed our example, and has commenced reading Sanskrit also, with another pundit.

I hope you will be able to decipher this scrawl. Please give our kindest regards to your father and mother. Mamma sends you her love, and with best love from myself—Believe me, yours very affectionately.

Toru Dutt

Calcutta
February 1876

25th. I had the first mangoes of the season from our Garden for breakfast just now. They were delicious. I wish I could send you one with this letter!

What beautiful cold weather you are having at present! I wish I was there!

Do tell me which of the pieces in my book your papa and your dear mother like? You see I am full of my book! *Entre nous*, I confess I *am* a little proud of it! Though I see its faults as well as its merits.

I am quite as rich as you are, dear! For I have got in the Savings Bank about the same sum as you have in the Cambridge Building Society. If I was not afraid of people calling me extravagant, I would spend the whole amount in buying a splendid stud of horses!

What *shall* I write about? Our cow, one of our milch cows, that is, did not give any milk for two days running. *Voici pourquoi*: a servant had the stupidity to introduce a large owl into the dairy; the cows got so frightened that they ran out quite wild from the shed, and it was a whole day's work catching them! And though this happened about five days ago, the cows do not on any account approach the shed, and we have been obliged to keep them in another. One of our best hens, with a pair of young turkeys which she had hatched, was run away with by a jackal, to Mamma's great sorrow and dismay! Are not these very interesting items?

The Maharaja of Pattialla died a few days ago at Simla of apoplexy. His infant son succeeds him.

I am sure you will like *Wives and Daughters*. It is a very well-written and interesting book. All the Brontës were rather inclined to the sensational in their works, but they are wonderfully interesting. *Wuthering Heights* treats of the supernatural, I have heard, for I have never read the book; I have only read *Jane Eyre* by Charlotte Brontë. Though the *moral* is not very high (for the authoress favours bigamy), the work is written with a masterly power, and shows a gift of discerning characters, which is wonderful in a woman. If you once commence the book, you will not be able to sleep unless you finish it! Have you read any of Thackeray's works? They are very good. I must stop my chatter for a while to read the paper.

26th. My grandfather has hired a house and garden near ours, where he intends to stay with his family for three or four months. We went to see them yesterday; they will remove to-day, and we are to go and see them this evening in their new home. I wish you knew my grandmother; a kinder, or gentler, or more loving woman never breathed. How all her dear face lights up when we go to see her! I wish she would become a Christian. She is so much better than many who profess to be Christians, but whose conduct is anything but so. And she is so fond of me and so proud of me, is my grandmother! She thinks me the handsomest, the best, and the most accomplished girl that ever breathed! She would spoil me quite, if I lived with her a week! And she is so proud of Papa! You know that Hindu mothers-in-law generally do not talk with their sons-in-law. Isn't that funny? When Mamma was ill she came and stayed with us, keeping awake two nights running. ...

I have just been turning over a collection of Shirley Brook's poems, which have been chosen out from his contributions to *Punch* by his son. I have come on a piece which I cannot help writing out for you. It is entitled *Dagon* and is on the death of Nicholas, the Emperor of all the Russias, in 1855. It appeared in *Punch* and created a great sensation at the time. It is finely written and is full of spirit.

Smitten—as by lightning—smitten
Down, amid his armed array;
With the fiery scroll scarce written
Calling myriads to the fray.
There—but yesterday defying
Europe's banners, linked and flying
For her freedom—see him lying
Earth's Colossus—earth's own clay.
Let no triumph-shout be given,
Knee to earth and eye to heaven!
God hath judged the day.

Ark of Freedom! lightly-spoken
Vows to thee vain kings have said,
Many an oath thy priests have broken,
Many a flight thy guards have fled:
But thine ancient Consecration
Sealed as oft by stern libation,
Lifeblood of a struggling nation,
In the foeman's doom is read.
Still, O Ark! the hand that gave thee
Strikes, in peril's hour to save thee
Here lies Dagon—dead!

Have you read any of Bulwer Lytton's novels? The *Last of the Barons* is very interesting and well-written, in the Walter Scott style. He once attacked the Laureate in a satire in Pope's style, calling the Tennyson school, 'Miss Alfred'! The Laureate answered him in verses which were anything but school-girlish and which appeared in *Punch*. Lord Lytton attacked him under the *nom de plume* of the *New Timon*, and the Laureate, after alluding to Shakespeare's *Timon of Athens* says:

—here comes the New,
Regard him: a familiar face;
I *thought* we knew him. What, it's you,
The padded man that wears the stays;

Who killed the girls and thrilled the boys
With dandy pathos when you wrote;
A Lion, you, that made a noise,
And shook a mane *en papillotes*.

.   .   .   .   .   .

> What profits now to understand
> The merits of a spotless shirt,
> A dapper boot—a little hand,
> If half the little soul is dirt?

I quote from memory, so you must overlook mistakes if you find any.

It's dreadfully hot to-day, even the crows seem oppressed by the heat and keep silent, except now and then, when a very thirsty one utters a parched 'caw'! The grass on the lawns has assumed a dry burnt-up appearance, which is never seen in England. In the streets, horses are often falling down, smitten by heat apoplexy. The other day we saw one: poor animal! It seemed to suffer terribly; it was unable to rise, and dashed its head against the pavement in vain efforts to do so; water, large bucketfuls, was thrown over it to relieve its pain, but to no purpose. I am afraid and never allow my Jeunette and Gentille to be driven during the middle of the day for fear of their getting sunstrokes.

Please give my love to A.L. when you write to her. I am sorry to hear that your dear father has not recovered quite from the effects of his last illness, but I hope he will with the warmer weather. I am keeping well myself; so is Papa and Mamma. My grandmother has made lots of chutnies, Indian jams, &c., which are exceedingly palatable, I can tell you, notwithstanding their extremes of being either too acid or too hot, &c. Best love to your dear self, and love and kindest regards from all to your father and mother.

12, Manicktollah Street
Calcutta
26 June 1876

Your nice long letter of the 22nd May I received on Saturday, that is, the day before yesterday. I could not answer it sooner as I had just recovered from a slight attack of fever and felt very weak.

Your letter is very interesting indeed. Of course the Rama of Sita is the same whose name occurs in the Sanskrit couplet inserted among my notes. Do read *La Femme dans l'Inde Antique*, or even *The Iliad of the East*. I should so like to hear what you think of my country's legends and heroes and heroines. I am glad to hear that you are enjoying the May gaieties of Cambridge.

As for the state of demoralization of English society, I shall neither be surprised at nor afraid of it. Calcutta is the very sink of iniquity. Not only among the Hindus (in the midst of whom there are many respectable and nice people), but even among the Bengali Christians, the *moral* is so execrable. And the saddest thing is, that Hindus have a very bad idea of Christianity and only think it a cloak which some people take to commit under its cover a multitude of sins. But let me stop here; the manners of Bengali Christian Society (with a very few exceptions) are such as would sadden the merriest heart and dishearten the most hopeful.

Did I ever tell you about the Syrian gentleman on board our vessel when we were coming to India? He only spoke French, and knew English very imperfectly indeed. Well, one day, dinner was over, and the dessert had just been put on the table; he helped himself to some fruit; and as the steward in taking away his plate asked him if he would take 'anything else, Sir?' he answered 'Nothing', but he pronounced it 'Nutton'. The next minute the steward (a little surprised at the request) brought him a plateful of roast mutton and potatoes! Our Syrian was a good deal taken aback; but as he saw that explanations would only make matters worse, he contented himself with muttering below his breath, in a sad desponding manner, 'Est-ce là qu'on appelle "nothing"'?

You are indignant at the way some Anglo-Indians speak of India and her inhabitants. What would you think if you read some of the police reports which appear in the Indian daily papers? I shall tell you of a case which I read some months ago, and which impressed me then very much. I do not remember the details, but I shall tell you all that I can remember about it. Several soldiers went out for a holiday, having their guns with them. In a village they chanced to spy some peacocks, and they began shooting at them. The birds were the property of a Bengali farmer; of course he protested. He was told to 'be off and be—!' He called his neighbours. From words they came to blows; one soldier was severely beaten; the others decamped, leaving *nine* Bengalis *dead* and some seven Bengalis wounded. The case was brought before the magistrate; and what do you think his judgement was? The villagers were fined each and all; the soldiers acquitted: 'natives should know how precious is the life of one British soldier in the eyes of the British Government—.'

Yesterday a horse of one of our neighbours was struck with heat apoplexy. It had been taken out to exercise in the afternoon (when it was very hot), and when it came home the groom turned it in the stall without dressing or cooling the tired animal. The consequence was it rushed madly out of its stall and fell in a neighbouring tank (or pond), just behind our house. After a great deal of trouble it was got out. I saw it this morning from the roof of our house. Poor animal! It had been left lying on the damp mud, behind the owner's stable, with not a single man nigh to allay its sufferings. Isn't this cruel and inhuman? After some twelve hours it was lifted up by bamboo props (and a free use of the lash and administration of buckets of cold water into its nostrils and eyes!) and conveyed inside the stable. It is a Waler, that is, an Australian horse. I do not think that it will live. Jeunette and Gentille are well and in excellent condition. Jeunette is very fond of bread; she would follow me about anywhere in the hope of getting some. Gentille prefers sugar came and other sweet things. They have just thrown off their winter coats and are now sleek and 'satin-skinned' in their new summer ones. I wish you could see them!

Papa was telling me of some of the events of the Mutiny of 1857, the other evening. I was only a year old then. Papa and my uncles enrolled themselves as volunteers, and each bought a gun, the first they had ever handled. He remembers one evening, at some entertainment at Government House, as he was going up the broad staircase, the sort of 'saisissement' he felt as he looked in at the large hall, where a small English guard was going through the evolutions, 'Shoulder-arms!' &c. We had an old Sikh porter, who had formerly been a soldier. It was he who first brought us the news of the outbreak at Barrackpore. We were at that time in the Garden. When questioned about it he used to shake his grey head and say sadly, 'Ah! the English have mismanaged the whole affair! If they had explained and smoothed away the matter, all would have been well. But now—they have all gone' (meaning the Indian troops), 'all gone! The best, the bravest, the strongest!'

27th. The poor horse over the way! During the night it had somehow or other got out of the stable, and is now lying in the mud, all covered with dirt, and with not even a kindly hand near to frighten away the crows which come to pick its quivering flesh! The eyes are very intelligent still. When it hears the pawing of its stable companions in their stalls it turns a wistful eye towards the stable, as if it longed to get in there. It should have been shot, and put out of this misery. It is sad to see it lift its head as if to rise; then, seeing the attempt vain, let it fall hopelessly on the ground. It was a fine animal, of a dark grey almost turning to black. Australian horses suffer very much from the heat; hundreds die of congestion and sunstrokes during the hot season of Calcutta. The stud-breds are more inured to the climate, being born and bred in India. If the horse, which is now dying, had been properly and kindly treated from the first day of its illness, it *might* have lived.

You see we have removed from the Garden to our town house. The reason is, the rains have commenced. To-day it rained in the middle of the day, and so the late afternoon has turned out cool and fine. It pours continually for weeks sometimes. I was very sorry to leave the Garden; I used so to enjoy exercising Jeunette and Gentille.

We shall be going to Baugmaree again at the end of the rains, that is, in the beginning of November.

I have not read much lately. The *Revue des Deux Mondes* has been my only solace for the last week. I was reading an article on Baron Stockmar's book, by Saint-René Taillandier. A very ably-written article it is, and gives you the whole of the Stockmar memoirs in a condensed and interesting form, truly delightful.

The papers say that lord Lytton will resign and return to England by the end of the next year. It is said that he thinks India is very unhealthy. He has been suffering from constant bilious complaints since he has gone to Simla. He liked Barrackpore pretty well when he was there, for he wrote in a telegram to Lady Lytton that he found the above-mentioned place very charming indeed, just like an English country seat.

We were so amused the other day with reading in the *Illustrated London News* that the Prince of Wales created 'Bullen', 'Smith', 'Degember', 'Mitter', as Companions of the Order of the Star of India. 'Bullen-Smith' is *one* gentleman, and not two, as 'Bullen', 'Smith' would seem to imply, and 'Degember Mitter' is ditto! By the by, we saw Babu Degember Mitter to-day as we were taking our morning drive at five o'clock.

The afternoons now turn out generally wet and cloudy, so I am going to take my drives in the morning instead of the evening. I got up at half-past three this morning to be ready for my drive before five. The morning was cool and fine, and I enjoyed the fresh air very much. I wish you were with me, bowling smoothly along at the rate of fourteen miles an hour, with the fresh breeze blowing in your face, and Jeunette's and Gentille's wavy black manes glancing [sic] in the sun, just visible if you lean forward to look at them. The streets were very quiet; not a soul, except the policemen, was to be seen.

Where shall you go this summer? To the Lakes again? I am sure you would enjoy a trip to the Continent, and who knows if you venture as far as Italy that you might not embark at Brindisi, and just lengthening your voyage a little come to Calcutta! Ah! dear, I long to see you again. I feel a little lonely sometimes. In England life was so much more active and free; here, on the contrary, I lead a rather solitary and sedentary life, but not in the least do I feel it dull, *au contraire*, it is a quiet peaceful sort of life.

28th. The poor horse is dead. I am glad it is out of its misery at last, for the way it was maltreated by the wretches (I mean the grooms) was simply atrocious.

—*Life and Letters of Toru Dutt* (1921)

Pandita Ramabai
(1858–1922)

A.B. Shah, who edited *The Letters and Correspondence of Pandita Ramabai* (Maharashtra State Board for Literature and Culture, Bombay 1977), describes Pandita Ramabai as 'the greatest woman produced by Modern India and one of the greatest Indians in all history. Her achievements as a champion of women's rights and as a pioneer in the fields of women's education and social reform remain unrivalled even after a lapse of nearly a century since she first appeared on the scene.'

Sister Geraldine, who originally compiled these letters, belonged to the Community of St Mary the Virgin at Wantage in England. She came to India in 1878 as Sister-in-Charge of St Mary's School, Poona, and it was here that she came to know Ramabai and her infant daughter Manorama.

Perhaps the most impressive quality of the letters of Pandita Ramabai to Sister Geraldine and to various other correspondents, is the single-minded insistence on accepting only what she wanted to accept of Christian dogma (she was baptized a Christian in England in 1883) instead of being bound by any particular Christian church. Needless to say, such an attitude resulted in some acerbic exchanges.

That also explains, in a way, the ambiguous position Pandita Ramabai occupies in the pantheon of Indian literature, as she was never completely forgiven for her conversion. Included here is one of Ramabai's central works, *The High Caste Hindu Woman* (1887). It is unique simply because it makes us privy to the perspective of a woman who knew Hindu scriptures better than most men of her time.

Also included here is Ramabai's *Famine Experiences* (1897), which is noteworthy not just for the autobiographical details it provides, but also for her scathing criticism of the way British officials dealt with the famine. It is poignant in parts, when she describes her father's decision to drown himself to escape starvation, and how she and her brother buried themselves up to their necks in sand to escape the winter in Punjab, or how they survived by eating wild berries and swallowing hard stones too.

From her childhood, Ramabai's life was an arduous one. Her father was persecuted for trying to educate his wife Laxmibai. To escape this persecution, the family set out on a long pilgrimage during which Laxmibai taught Ramabai Sanskrit. At twenty, Ramabai was publicly honoured by the Shastris of Calcutta as a Pandita. In 1880, Ramabai married a Brahmo lawyer, Bipin Behari Das Medhavi, but he died of cholera two years later, leaving Ramabai with her infant daughter Manorama.

Ramabai travelled to England in June 1883 to study medicine. She travelled at her own expense but made arrangements to stay with the nuns at Wantage. She was to earn her living there by teaching Marathi to nuns who would be sent to Western India as missionaries. However, for reasons of poor health, she had to settle for studying English, Math and the natural sciences instead. After three years in England, she went to the US where she was lionized. She lived there from 1886 to 1888 and, in 1887, published *The High Caste Hindu Woman* to help pay her way back. When she returned to India in 1889 she opened the Sharda Sadan for destitute women in Bombay, moving it to Poona later when it became too expensive to manage.

She was reputed to be the first woman to have read the Vedas in modern times, and carried out her work in the face of vehement opposition from nationalist groups. In 1898 she entered politics and, along with eight women delegates, attended the Fifth National Meeting of the Congress.

Ramabai wrote in both, English and Marathi. Her writings in English include *The Cry of Indian Women* (1883), *An Autobiographical Account* (1883), and *Indian Religion* (1886), all published in England, as well as *Famine Experiences* (1897), *A Short History of Kripa Sadan or Home of Mercy* (1903), *A Testimony of Our Inexhaustible Treasure* (1907) and *The Word-Seed* (1908).

Letter to Sister Geraldine

Ladies' College, Cheltenham,
May 12th, 1885

Dear Old Ajeebai,

Last night as I came back from Bristol, I received your long letter. I did not write to you the other day that I was going to Bristol to see a friend who was once my teacher of Bible in Cachar, when my husband was living. I was too much excited and felt too tired to write in detail about my journey to Bristol or rather to Clifton. I was so pleased to see my old friend again, you may have heard about him from me. His name is Rey Isaac Allen. He was staying with Mr and Mrs Glover, a Baptist Minister of Clifton. Mr and Mrs Glover who knew me long since through him had invited me (last term) to pay them a short visit, but then having no time to spare I refused to do so. This time, Mr Allen who was staying with them asked me to go there and see him. He is not very well, his health broke down in Cachar, so he had to leave that station and come home in order to save his life from the malarial fever. I enjoyed my visit to Bristol very much. On my arrival there on Saturday afternoon Mrs Glover took me to the Arnos Vail Cemetery to see the tomb of Raja Ram Mohan Roy. On Sunday I attended the Annual Meeting of the Baptist Sunday Schools where Mr Jones, a missionary who has returned from Agra spoke about mission work in India.

Yesterday I went with Mrs Glover to see the portrait of Raja Ram Mohan Roy in the Bristol Mission, and the Bristol Cathedral, and came back to Cheltenham at 7 p.m. Here ends my three days' history. Now to turn to your letter, I will first reply to to-day's letter and then go back to that of yesterday.

Do you ever really think, my dear Ajeebai, that I could be otherwise than a true friend to you? We may more than thousand times differ in our opinions and must be separated by unavoidable temporal difficulties, but it does not in any way follow that we must be enemies or indifferent to each other; even in barbarous countries and people it is a shame to be false to a friend who has put confidence in any person, how much more it is (or at least ought to be) so among ourselves who profess to be the members of civilized countries and followers of the true religion and perfect love. At the same time it does not follow that because we are friends we ought not to have our own judgment and mind, but on the contrary we are to agree in everything; as all that is ordered for us by the Most High is *for the best*, and we must always accept the order of the circumstances and the will of those who have authority to speak as expressing His will! It seems to me that you are advising me under the WE to accept always the will of those who have authority, etc. This however I cannot accept. I have a conscience, and mind and a judgment of my own, I must myself think and do everything which GOD has given me the power of doing. You have, perhaps, known that on the eve of my leaving India for England, a priest had told me that it was not according to GOD's will that I should start for England. But it so happened that my mind told me it was GOD's will that I should *then* go to England, and I did so. Although priests and bishops may have certain authority over the church yet the church has another Master Who is Superior even to the bishops. I am, it is true, a member of the Church of Christ, but am not bound to accept every word that falls down from the lips of priests or bishops. If it pleases you to call my word liberty as lawlessness you may do so, but as far as I know myself, I am not lawless. Obedience to the law and to the Word of GOD is quite different from perfect obedience to priests only. I have just with great efforts freed myself from the yoke of the Indian priestly tribe, so I am not at present willing to place myself under another similar yoke by accepting everything which comes from the priests as authorized command of the Most High. At the same time I am not willing to offend anyone or to do wrong. But can you or your friends prove that giving lessons to boys is a wrong thing? You must have misunderstood me if you think that I have told you I began to lecture in public in obedience to the Syndicate or the Englishmen, in your words the 'Elders of my people' for I have never told you so. On the contrary I told you that at first my brother and I were invited by Pandit Tara Nath into a large meeting of Pandits where a Pandit (the Principal of Sanskrit College of Calcutta) having seen me was interested in me and introduced me to Mr Fauny and Mr Croft (I do not know the exact spelling of their names). When in the college, they with the assistance of the said Pandit examined me in Sanskrit, kindly gave me the title of 'Saraswati'. I did not tell you that the Syndicate suggested or commanded me to lecture in public, for they never did so, etc. I have also told you (if you remember) that it was the example set by the good Brahmos which kindled my spirit and made me able to plead the cause of women before my countrymen. It is true, it is not necessary for me to be a teacher of men, but when either in India or England I can get women as well as men for my pupils there is no reason why I should not teach both. It is not a general custom in India for ladies to teach men, it is true because there are scarcely any among ladies who can teach. It surprises me very much to think that neither my father nor my husband objected [to] my mother's or my teaching young men while some English people are doing so. You can call some of my countrywomen 'hedged' but you cannot apply this adjective to Marathi brahmin women. You have yourself seen that Marathi ladies are neither hedged nor kept behind thick curtains. Even in the days of the Mussulman rulers they never used to be so. It is true they do not mix as a general rule with men as you do in England, but you cannot say now some of them do not [do] so, I am one of those 'some' and am not afraid of men. Why do you say (if you trust me) that to address mixed audiences is quite different from giving lessons to young Englishmen? I have not addressed only mixed audiences but most of them (especially in Bengal and North-West Provinces, where no Hindu lady is allowed to come before men) purely composed of men, and have also given lessons to young men at different times. But then it did not seem to take away my influence with my country people, and why should it be so now, I cannot see. I am not anxious to give lessons to young men, but I am anxious to do away with all kinds of prejudices which deprive a woman in India of her proper place in society. Can I confine my work only to women in India and have nothing to do with men? I do not think so. To help the women to come forward in the society I must first of all urge open men, and teach men of poorer classes. Then when men are convinced of the necessity of elevating the condition of their women, I shall have access to their Zenanas. Unless I begin to have a regular and pure intercourse with men, I shall in vain hope and try to help my countrywomen.

I do not think I shall say anything on behalf of my liberty. You have yourself misunderstood this my word, [and] give sermons about it. As far as I know from the time I have had a real liberty, I have not acted as a lawless woman, and never want to do so. When people decide anything for me, without consulting with me about it, I of course call it interfering with my liberty, and am not willing to let them do it. Suppose you were in my place and as unknown bishop were to advise your friends to decide a thing for you without telling you about it, and your friends did so, what would you think of it? Would you feel bound to accept every word or rule which comes from the bishop as the expression of the will of the Most High. Perhaps you would. I am not quite sure about it, but I do not, and will not. I am not going to act against Miss Beale's promise or your decision at present, but I do not want to ask or follow the opinion of the bishops before whom you are going again to put this matter. My conscience does not trouble me in this matter and that is quite enough. It will be impossible for me to follow others in every single act and to be always pleasing them and never to think for myself.

With love and honour to you,

I am,
Ever yours faithfully,
Mary Rama

Letter to Canon Butler

Ladies' College,
3rd July 1885

Dear Canon,

Thank you very very much for your kind letter. I am sorry if I have imagined falsely what you thought or said about my being under the influence of the Devil, but I will give you the reason that led me to imagine so. Last time when I saw you at Wantage, I suppose you remember that your conversation with me opened with a parable of a sick man, his good friend and his enemy, and when I asked you the meaning of it, you said it was about me and my good Friend the Saviour, and the Devil my enemy (I do not put here your words exactly what they were but they were something like these).

And why did you open your conversation in such a manner? Because I had felt some doubt (and even now I am not free from it) about the doctrine of our Saviour's Deity; and you imagined that this doubt was not mine own but the Devil, my enemy, was encouraging me to think that our Lord was not God Almighty, and according to his (the Devil's) advice I began to ask this sort of questions, and would not accept humbly what the church or rather church people taught me.

Let me tell you (and I say it from the bottom of my heart), my dear Canon, I am indeed very grateful to you for all your kindness, and to others who are like you to me in Christ. I have not forgotten the lessons which my dear parents had taught me in my childhood *i.e.* to honour and be grateful to those who led me to the life immortal. I honour and am grateful to those my parents first, and next to them, I honour those who are my spiritual parents and who brought me to Christ and to God. But at the same time, I should never (at least ought not to) hesitate to ask them some questions and to tell honestly to them that I could not agree with them in every point of faith. I must be allowed to think for myself. God has given me an independent conscience, not to accept everything slavishly that other people say, but 'hear and see' for and by myself. May I not then ask some questions and discuss about matters which I do not quite understand? It is indeed very true that we do not understand everything; we are to accept some supernatural things which pass our limited understanding, with faith; but still we are bound to consider things and consult with the Scriptures, before we accept them fully. This freedom of thought I honestly say I was not allowed to have by my Wantage friends. The moment I asked any questions they would either mistake me or say that I was sinning against such and such commandment of God. Consequently, I dared not to ask you or Sister Geraldine any question concerning the doctrines taught by the church, and so laboured for a time, and underwent many afflictions of my troubled conscience. After I came here, I found a friend in Miss Beale, who has gone through many such difficulties and who could therefore sympathize with me, so I placed my difficulties before her, which I had never mentioned to Sister Geraldine or to you before, fearing that you would mistake me. These my questions reached Sister Geraldine through Miss Beale, and from her to you. Now Sister Geraldine imagines (for she told me so) that I accepted the faith of Christ because I was impressed much with the holy unselfish life, which the followers of Christ—the Sisters—lead; and had not any difficulty in believing in such a faith which makes [one] so unselfish and holy. But after I accepted it, I wanted now to prove it, and make sure of its truthfulness, so I am experiencing these difficulties, etc. but at the same time should accept humbly what the church people say. This is her opinion. I held my silence when I heard this, thinking that it was not of much consequence to discuss upon such points of question but now I see that the misunderstanding is growing too formidable not to be corrected.

I was indeed impressed with the holy life of the Sisters, and their sublime unselfishness, and am so impressed to this moment, but I must say for the sake of truth that their life was not the cause of my accepting the faith of Christ. It was Father Goreh's letter that proved that the faith which I professed (I mean the Brahmo faith) was not taught by our Veda as I had thought, but it was the Christian faith which was brought before me by my friends disguised under the name of Brahmo religion. Well, I thought if Christ is the source of this sublime faith, why should not I confess Him openly to be my Lord and my Divine teacher? And so I did, and do confess Him my Saviour. I believe Him to be the Son of the Most High and His Messiah. But this confession does not mean that I believe also all the doctrines taught by other people, unless they be proved to be true from Christ's own teaching. Yet to ask questions to my Wantage friends was something dreadful, because it led them to think that I was sinning against some commandments of God, so I was obliged to keep silence while I was staying there, and even now I shall not ask any questions to them unless I be convinced that they do not mistake me.

When Miss Beale told Sister Geraldine that I was experiencing some difficulties in accepting the whole faith taught by the English Church, she thought that these difficulties are newly arising in my mind, and perhaps led you to think so. And when I came to see you, my thought was confirmed when I heard your parable that it was no use asking questions to my Wantage friends, either directly or indirectly. They would always misunderstand me.

You, my dear Father in Christ, and Sister Geraldine, and my other Christian friends, are too learned, too spiritual, too wise, and and too faithful to your faith which you profess from your childhood, to understand my difficulties in accepting wholly the religion taught by you. You have never gone through the same experience of choosing another religion for yourself, which was totally foreign to you, as I have. You, wise and experienced and old as you are, you cannot interpenetrate my poor feelings. You will, I trust, not be offended if I say so, for no man is omniscient. You do me injustice if you apply such parables to me as you did last time when I ask you question and say in a roundabout way (or lead me to understand so) that I was not humble and in a teachable spirit when I came to you. If a Hindoo theologian—however learned and holy and good he may be—comes and tells you that your religion was a false one, and that you were to accept humbly everything that he taught, could you do it?

If every question that I ask and everything that I say to you lead you to think that I was not humble and that I did not come to you in teachable spirit, how could I ever ask you, and even dare to mention anything to my friends about this? So I thought it better to hold my tongue than to run such a risk as to lead you to make mistakes.

I am very sorry to observe that even my common speeches of no consequence lead people to think otherwise. For instance, the other day I was talking with some of my friends about my hand-writing or something, and I said to silence a friend who brought a charge of imperfection against me (and in joke too) that no man can be perfect in this world (and I believe it is true, for St. Paul says he is not perfect, but is pressing on towards perfection). But my dear old Ajeebai (Sister Geraldine) took this speech of mine and wrote a very dogmatical letter which was too learned for me, saying that I was very wrong in saying so, and that I was not as earnest to glorify God as I used to be in the early days of my conversion, and that she was not surprised at my conduct, because (she thinks) the Devil is always trying to get hold of us, i.e., me, etc., etc. This remark sounded in my ear just like the echo of your parable of the sick man, etc., which you were kind enough to apply to me, and I wrote a letter in answer to Sister Geraldine's letter, that it was not right of you to say or imagine that I was under the influence of the Devil—to say these words under the disguise of a parable!

This I say without fear, and without any such suspicion as exciting your displeasure towards me. If you lead me by such reasons to believing that you or Sister Geraldine are determined to misunderstand me, you and she must never expect that I should ask any questions or say anything to you about my faith or of my difficulties. But for all this, my respect, and love, and grateful feelings towards you are not the less, and please God, it may never come to this end. Let me again tell you plainly that I believe in Christ and His God, and as one of His disciples—though least—am bound to do and believe in His teaching, as I have promised in my Baptism. But at the same time I shall not bind myself to believe in and accept everything that is taught by the church; before I accept it I must be convinced that it is according to Christ's teaching that you teach me.

And as long as I am led to think that my asking questions to you leads you to misunderstand me, I shall not say one single word to you about it, but shall read the Bible by myself, and follow the teaching of Christ. I have full faith that the Holy Spirit of God will lead me on toward the true faith.

With all honour and love to you,

I am,
Your humble child in Christ,
Mary Rama

Please do not misunderstand my words. I have written to you very plainly what I thought, and without any intention to offend you, and I trust you will excuse my freedom in speaking to you.

—*The Letters and Correspondence of Pandita Ramabai* (1977)

Widowhood

We now come to the worst and most dreaded period of a high-caste woman's life. Throughout India, widowhood is regarded as the punishment for a horrible crime or crimes committed by the woman in her former existence upon earth. The period of punishment may be greater or less, according to the nature of the crime. Disobedience and disloyalty to the husband, or murdering him in an earlier existence, are the chief crimes punished in the present birth by widowhood.

If the widow be a mother of sons, she is not usually a pitiable object; although she is certainly looked upon as a sinner, yet social abuse and hatred are greatly diminished [by] virtue of the fact that she is a mother of the superior beings. Next in rank to her stands an ancient widow, because a virtuous, aged widow who has bravely withstood the thousand temptations and persecutions of her lot commands an involuntary respect from all people, to which may be added the honour given to old age quite independent of the individual. The widow-mother of girls is treated indifferently and sometimes with genuine hatred, especially when her daughters have not been given in marriage in her husband's lifetime. But it is the child-widow or a childless young widow upon whom in an especial manner falls the abuse and hatred of the community as the greatest criminal upon whom Heaven's judgment has been pronounced.

In ancient times, when the code of Manu was yet in the dark future and when the priesthood had not yet mutilated the original reading of a Vedic text concerning widows, a custom of remarriage was in existence.

Its history may be briefly stated. The rite of child-marriage left many a girl a widow before she knew what marriage was. Her husband, having died sonless, had no right to enter into heaven and enjoy immortality, for 'the father throws his debts on the son and obtains immortality if he sees the face of a living son. It is declared in the Vedas, endless are the words of those who have sons; there is no place for the man who is destitute of male offspring.' The greatest curse that could be pronounced on enemies, was, 'May our enemies be destitute of offspring.'

In order that these young husbands might attain the abodes of the blessed, the ancient sages invented the custom of 'appointment' by which, as among the Jews, the Hindu Aryans raised up seed for the deceased husband. The husband's brother, cousin or [any] other kinsman successively was 'appointed' and duly authorized to raise offspring from the dead. The desired issue having been obtained any intercourse between the appointed persons was thenceforth considered illegal and sinful.

The woman still remained the widow of her deceased husband, and her children by the appointment were considered his heirs. Later on, this custom of 'appointment' was gradually discouraged in spite of the Vedic text already quoted, 'there is no place for the man who is destitute of male offspring.'

The duties of a widow are thus described in the code of Manu:

At her pleasure let her emaciate her body by living on pure flowers, roots and fruit; but she must never even mention the name of another man after her husband has died.

Until death let her be patient of hardships, self-controlled, and chaste, and strive to fulfil that most excellent duty which is prescribed for wives who have one husband only (*Manu*, v, 157–8).

... nor is a second husband anywhere prescribed for virtuous women. (*Manu*, v, 162).

A virtuous wife, who after the death of her husband constantly remains chaste, reaches heaven, ... (*Manu*, v, 160).

In reward of such conduct, a female who controls her thoughts, speech, and actions, gains in this life highest renown, and in the next world a place near her husband.[††] (*Manu*, v, 166).

The following are the rules for a widower:

A twice-born man, versed in the sacred law, shall burn a wife of equal caste who conducts herself thus and dies before him, with the sacred fires used for the Agnihotra, and with the sacrificial implements.

Having thus at the funeral, given the sacred fires to his wife who dies before him, he may marry again, and again kindle the (nuptial) fires.

... And having taken a wife, he must dwell in his own house during the second period of his life. (*Manu*, v, 167–9).

The self-immolation of widows on their deceased husband's pyre[s] was evidently a custom invented by the priesthood after the code of Manu was compiled. The laws taught in the schools of Apastamba, Asvalayana and others older than Manu do not mention it, neither does the code of Manu. The code of Vishnu, which is comparatively recent, says that a woman 'after the death of her husband should either lead a virtuous life or ascend the funeral pile of her husband' (*Vishnu*, xxv, 2).

It is very difficult to ascertain the motives of those who invented the terrible custom of the so-called *Suttee*, which was regarded as a sublimely meritorious act. As Manu the greatest authority next to the Vedas, did not sanction this sacrifice, the priests saw the necessity of producing some text which would overcome the natural fears of the widow as well as silence the critic who should refuse to allow such a horrid rite without strong authority. So the priests said there was a text in the Rig-veda which, according to their own rendering reads thus:

Om! Let these women, not to be widowed, good wives, adorned with collyrium, holding clarified butter, consign themselves to the fire! Immortal, not childless, not husbandless, well adorned with gems, let them pass into the fire whose original element is water.

Here was an authority greater than that of Manu or of any other law-giver, which could not be disobeyed. The priests and their allies pictured heaven in the most beautiful colours and described various enjoyments

[††]It should be borne in mind that according to the popular belief there is no other heaven to a woman than the seat of mansion of her husband, where she shares the heavenly bliss with him in the next world if she be faithful to him in thought, word and deed. The only place where she can be independent of him is in hell.

so vividly that the poor widow became madly impatient to get to the blessed place in company with her departed husband. Not only was the woman assured of her getting into heaven by this sublime act, but also that by this great sacrifice she would secure salvation to herself and husband, and to their families [up] to the seventh generation. Be they even sinful, they would surely attain the highest bliss in heaven, and prosperity on earth. Who would not sacrifice herself if she were sure of such a result to herself and her loved ones? Besides this, she was conscious of the miseries and degradation to which she would be subjected now that she had survived her husband. The momentary agony of suffocation in the flames was nothing compared to her lot as a widow. She gladly consented and voluntarily offered herself to please the gods and men. The rite of *Suttee* is thus described:

> The widow bathed, put on new and bright garments, and, holding kusha grass in her left hand, sipped water from her right palm, scattered some tila grains, and then, looking eastward, quietly said, 'Om! On this day I, such and such a one, of such a family, die in the fire, that I may meet Arundhati, and reside in *Svarga*; that the years of my sojourn there may be as many as the hairs upon my husband, many scores multiplied; that I may enjoy with him the facilities of heaven, and bless my maternal and paternal ancestors, and those of my lord's line; that, praised by Apsara I may go far through the fourteen regions of Indra; that pardon may be given to my lord's sins whether he have even killed a Brahman, broken the laws of gratitude and truth, or slain his friend. Now I do ascend this funeral pile of my husband, and I call upon you, guardians of the eight regions of the world, of sun, moon, air, of the fire, the ether, the earth and the water, and my own soul. Yama, king of Death, and you, Day, Night and Twilight, witness that I die for my beloved, by his side upon his funeral pile.' Is it wonderful that the passage of the Sati to her couch of flame was like a public festival, that the sick and sorrowful prayed her to touch them with her little, fearless, conquering hand, that criminals were let loose if she looked upon them, that the horse which carried her was never used again for earthly service? (E. Arnold)

The act was supposed to be altogether a voluntary one, and no doubt it was so in many cases. Some died for the love stronger than death which they cherished for their husbands. Some died not because they had been happy in this world, but because they believed with all the[ir] heart that they should be made happy hereafter. Some, to obtain great renown, for tombstones and monuments were erected to those who thus died, and afterwards the[ir] names were inscribed on the long list of family gods; others, again, to escape the thousand temptations, and sins and miseries which they knew would fall to their lot as widows. Those who from pure ambition or from momentary impulse, declared their intentions thus to die, very often shrank from the fearful altar; no sooner did they feel the heat of the flames than they tried to leap down and escape the terrible fate, but it was too late. They had taken the solemn oath which must never be broken, priests and other men were at hand to force them to remount the pyre. In Bengal, where this custom was most in practice, countless, fearful tragedies of this description occurred even after British rule was long established there. Christian missionaries petitioned the government to abolish this human custom, but they were told that the social and religious customs of the people constituted no part of the business of the government, and that their rule in India might be endangered by such interference. The custom went on unmolested until the first quarter of the present century, when a man from among the Hindus, Raja Ram Mohun Roy, set his face against it, and declared that it was not sanctioned by the Veda as the priests claimed. He wrote many books on this subject, showing the wickedness of the act, and with the noble cooperation of a few friends, he succeeded at last in getting the government to abolish it. Lord William Bentick, when Governor-General of India, had the moral courage to enact the famous law of 1829, prohibiting the *Suttee* rite within British domains, and holding as criminals, subject to capital punishment, those who countenanced it. But it was not until 1844 that the law had any effect upon orthodox Hindu minds.

That the text quoted from the Veda was mistranslated, and a part of it forged, could have been easily shown had all Brahmans known the meaning of the Veda. The Vedic language is the oldest form of Sanskrit, and greatly differs from the later form. Many know the Vedas by heart and repeat them without a mistake, but few indeed are those that know the meaning of the texts they repeat. 'The Rigveda,' says Max Muller, 'so far from enforcing the burning of widows, shows clearly that this custom was not sanctioned during the earliest period of Indian history. According to the hymns of the Rigveda, and the Vedic ceremonial contained in the Grihya-sutras, the wife accompanies the corpse of her husband to the funeral pile, but she is there addressed with a verse taken from the Rigveda, and ordered to leave her husband and to return to the world of the living.

'"Rise, woman," it is said, "come to the world of life, thou sleepest nigh unto him whose life is gone. Come to us. Thou hast thus fulfilled the duties of a wife to the husband, who once took thy hand and made thee a mother."'

'This verse is preceded by the very verse which the later Brahmans have falsified and quoted in support of their cruel tenet. The reading of the verse is beyond all doubt, for there is no various reading, in our sense of the word, in the whole of Rigveda. Besides, we have the commentaries and the ceremonials, and nowhere is there any difference to the text or its meaning. It is addressed to the other women who are present at the funeral, and who have to pour oil and butter on the pile.

'May these women who are not widows, but have good husbands, draw near with oil and butter. These who are mothers may go up first to the altar, without tears, without sorrow, but decked with fine jewels.'

It was by falsifying a single syllable that the unscrupulous priests managed to change entirely the meaning of the whole verse. Those who know the Sanskrit characters can easily understand that the falsification very likely originated in the carelessness of the transcriber or copyist, but for all that the priests who permitted the error are not excusable in the least. Instead of comparing the verse with its context, they translated it as their fancy dictated and thus under the pretext of religion they have been the cause of destroying countless lives for more than two thousand years.

Now that the *Suttee* rite, partly by the will of the people and partly by the law of the empire, is prohibited, many good people feel easy in their minds, thinking that the Hindu widow has been delivered from the hands of her terrible fate; but little do they realize the true state of affairs!

Throughout India, except in the Northwestern Province, women are put to the severest trial imaginable after the husband's death. The manner in which they are brought up and treated from their earliest childhood compels them to be slaves to their own petty little interests, to be passionate lovers of ornaments and of self-adornment, but no sooner does the husband die than they are deprived of every gold and silver ornament, of the bright-coloured garments, and of all the things they love to have about or on their persons. The cruelty of social customs does not stop here. Among the Brahmans of the Deccan, the heads of all widows must be shaved regularly every fortnight. Some of the lower castes, too, have adopted this custom of shaving widows' heads, and have much pride in imitating their high-caste brethren. What woman is there who does not love the wealth of soft and glossy hair with which nature has so generously decorated her head? A Hindu woman thinks it worse than death to lose her beautiful hair. Girls of fourteen and fifteen who hardly know the reason why they are so cruelly deprived of everything they like, are often seen wearing sad countenances, their eyes swollen from shedding bitter tears. They are glad to find a dark corner where they may hide their faces as if they have done something shameful and criminal. The widow must wear a single coarse garment, white, red or brown. She must eat only one meal during the twenty-four hours of a day. She must never take part in family feasts and jubilees, with others. She must not show herself to people on auspicious occasions. A man or woman thinks it unlucky to behold a widow's face before seeing any other object in the morning. A man will postpone his journey if his path happens to be crossed by a widow at the time of his departure.

A widow is called a 'inauspicious'. The name 'rand', by which she is generally known, is the same thing that is borne by a Nautch girl or a harlot. The relatives and neighbours of the young widow's husband are always ready to call her bad names, and to address her in abusive language at every opportunity. There is scarcely a day of her life on which she is not cursed by these people as the cause of their beloved friend's death. The mother-in-law gives vent to her grief by using such language that, when once heard, burns into a human heart. In short, the young widow's life is rendered intolerable in every possible way. There may be exceptions to this rule, but, unhappily, they are not many. In addition to all this the young widow is always looked upon with suspicion, and closely guarded as if she were a prisoner, for fear she may at any time bring disgrace upon the family by committing some improper act. The purpose of disfiguring her by shaving her head, by not allowing her to put ornaments or bright garments on her person, is to render her less attractive to a man's eye. Not allowing her to eat more than once a day, and compelling her to abstain from food altogether on sacred days, is a part of the discipline by which to mortify her youthful nature and desire. She is closely confined to the house, forbidden even to associate with her female friends as often as she wishes; no man except her father, brother, uncles and her aunt-cousins who are regarded as brothers) is allowed to see or speak with her. Her life then, destitute as it is of the least literary knowledge, void of all hope, empty of every pleasure and social advantage, becomes intolerable, a curse to herself and to society at large. She has but few persons to sympathize with her. Her own parents, with whom she lives in case her husband has no relatives, or if his relatives are unable to take care of her, do, of course, sympathize with her, but custom and religious faith have a stronger hold upon them than parental love. They, too, regard their daughter with concern, lest she bring disgrace upon their family.

It is not an uncommon thing for a young widow, without occupation that may satisfy mind and heart, and unable [any] longer to endure the slights and suspicions to which she is perpetually subjected, to escape from her prison-home. But when she gets away from it, where shall she go? No respectable family, even of a lower caste, will have her for a servant. She is completely ignorant of any art by which she may make an honest living. She has nothing but the single garment which she wears on her person. Starvation and death stare her in the face; no ray of hope penetrates her densely-darkened mind. What can she do? The only alternative before her is either to commit suicide or, worse still, accept a life of infamy and shame. Oh, cruel is the custom that drives thousands of young widows to such a fate. Here is a prayer by a woman doomed to lifelong misery, which will describe her own and her sisters' feelings better than any words of mine. It was written by a pupil of a British Zenana missionary, one of the few Hindu women who can read and write, and one who has tasted the bitter sorrows and degradation of Hindu widowhood from her childhood.

Oh Lord, hear my prayer! No one has turned an eye on the oppression that we poor women suffer, though with weeping, and crying and desire, we have turned to all sides, hoping that someone would save us. No one has lifted up his eyelids to look upon us, nor inquire into our case. We have searched above and below, but Thou art the only One who wilt hear our complaint. Thou knowest our impotence, our degradation, our dishonour. O Lord, inquire into our case. For ages, dark ignorance has brooded over our minds and spirits; like a cloud of dust it rises and wraps us round, and we are like prisoners in an old and mouldering house, choked and buried in the dust of custom, and we have no strength to go out. Bruised and beaten, we are like the dry husks of the sugarcane when the sweet juice has been extracted. All-knowing God, hear our prayer! Forgive our sins and give us power of escape, that we may see something of thy world. O Father, when shall we be set free from this jail? For what sin have we been born to live in this prison? From Thy throne of judgment justice flows, but it does not reach us; in this, our lifelong misery, only injustice comes near us.

Thou hearer of prayer, if we have sinned against Thee, forgive, but we are too ignorant to know what sin is. Must the punishment of sin fall on those who are too ignorant to know what it is? O great Lord, our name is written with drunkards, with lunatics, with imbeciles, with the very animals; as they are not responsible, we are not. Criminals, confined in jails for life, are happier than we, for they know something of Thy world. They were not born in prison, but we have not for one day, no, not even in our dreams, seen Thy world; to us it is nothing but a name; and not having seen the world, we cannot know thee, its maker. Those who have seen Thy works may learn to understand thee, but for us, who are shut in, it is not possible to learn to know Thee. We see only four walls of the house. Shall we call them the world, or India? We have been born in this jail, we have died here, and are dying.

O Father of the world, hast Thou not created us? Or has perchance, some other god made us? Dost Thou care only for men? Hast Thou no thought for us women? Why hast Thou created us male and female? O Almighty, hast Thou not power to make us other than we are, that we too might have some share in the comforts of this life? The cry of the oppressed is heard even in the world. Then canst Thou look upon our victim hosts, and shut Thy doors of justice? O God Almighty and Unapproachable, think upon Thy mercy, which is a vast sea, and remember us. O Lord, save us, for we cannot bear our hard lot; many of us have killed ourselves, and we are still killing ourselves. O God of mercy, our prayer to Thee is this, that the curse may be removed from the women of India. Create in the hearts of the men some sympathy, that our lives may no longer be passed in vain longing, that saved by Thy mercy, we may taste something of the joys of life.

A Hindu gentleman contributes an article entitled 'The Hindu Widow', to *The Nineteenth Century*. I quote from this as testimony from the other sex, of the truthfulness of my statement, lest I should appear to exaggerate the miserable condition to which my sister-widows are doomed for life:

The widow who has no parents has to pass her whole life under the roof of her father-in-law, and then she knows no comfort whatever. She has to meet from her late husband's relations only unkind looks and unjust reproaches. She has to work like a slave, and for the reward of all her drudgery she only receives hatred and abhorrence from her mother-in-law and sisters-in-law. If there is any disorder in the domestic arrangements of the family, the widow is blamed and cursed for it. Among Hindus, women cannot inherit any paternal property, and if a widow is left any property by her husband she cannot call it her own. All her wealth belongs to her son, if she has any, and if she has nobody to inherit it she is made to adopt an heir, and give him all her property directly when he comes of age, and herself live on a bare allowance granted by him. Even death cannot save a widow from indignities. For when a wife dies she is burnt in the clothes she had on, but a widow's corpse is covered with a coarse white cloth, and there is little ceremony at her funeral. ...

'The English have abolished sati (suttee), but alas! neither the English nor the angels know what goes on in our houses, and the Hindus not only do not care, but think it good!' Such were the words of a widow; and well might she exclaim that 'neither the English nor the angels know, and that the Hindus not only don't care, but think it good'; for Hindus as I am, I can vouch for her statement that very few Hindus have a fair knowledge of the actual sufferings of the widows among them, and fewer still care to know the evils and horrors of the barbarous customs which victimizes their own sisters and daughters in so ruthless a manner; nay, on the contrary, the majority of the orthodox Hindus consider the practice to be good and salutary. Only the Hindu widows know their own sufferings; it is perfectly impossible for any other mortal, or even 'the angels', (as the widow says) to realize them. One can easily imagine how hard the widow's lot must be ... when to the continuous course of fastings, self-inflictions and humiliations is added the galling ill-treatment which she receives from her own relations and friends. To a Hindu widow, death is a thousand times more welcome than her miserable existence. It is no doubt this feeling that drove in former times many widows to immolate themselves on the funeral pyres of their dead husbands. (Devendra N. Das, *The Nineteenth Century*, September 1886).

There is a class of reformers who think that they will meet all the wants of widows by establishing the re-marriage system. This system should certainly be introduced for the benefit of the infant widows who wish to marry on coming to age; but at the same time, it should be remembered that this alone is incapable and insufficient to meet their wants.

In the first place, widow-marriage among the high-caste people will not for a long time become an approved custom. The old idea is too deeply rooted in the heart of society to be soon removed. Second, there are not many men who will boldly come forward and marry widows, even if the widows wish it. It is one thing to talk about doing things contrary to the approved custom, but to practise [it] is quite another matter. It is now about fifty years since the movement called widow-marriage among the high-caste Hindus was started, but those who have practised it are but few. I have known men of great learning and high reputation who took oaths to the effect that if they were to become widowers and wished to marry again they would marry widows. But no sooner had their first wives died than they forgot all about the oaths and married pretty little maidens. Society threatens them with excommunication, their friends and relatives entreat them with tears in their eyes, others offer money and maids if they will consent to give up the idea of marrying a widow. Can flesh and blood resist these temptations? If some men wish to be true to their convictions, they must be prepared to suffer perpetual martyrdom. After marrying a widow they are sure to be cut off from all connection with society and friends, and even with their nearest relatives. In such a case, no faithful Hindu would ever give them assistance if they were to fall in distress or become unable to earn their daily bread; they will be ridiculed and hated by all men. How many people are there in the world who would make this tremendous sacrifice on the altar of conscience? The persecution to be endured by people who transgress established customs is so great that life becomes a burden. A few years ago, a high-caste man in Cutch (Northwestern India) ventured to marry a widow, but to endure the persecution which ensued was beyond his power, and the wretched fellow was soon after found dead, having committed suicide.

Re-marriage, therefore, is not available, nor would it be at all times desirable, as a mitigation of the sufferer's lot. So, the poor, helpless high-caste widow with the one chance of ending her miseries in the Suttee rite taken away from her, remains as in ages past with none to help her.

—The High Caste Hindu Woman (1894)

Anapurna Turkhad
(b. 1823d.)

Anapurna Turkhad was married to the Vice Principal of Baroda College, Harold Littledale. She was the daughter of Dr Atmaram Pandurang, who was one of the founders of the Prathna Samaj. Rabindranth Tagore stayed with the family before he went to the U.K. Anapurna was slightly older than he was, and also fairly anglicized. She asked Tagore to write a poem for her. Tagore did that and also wrote about her in a book of childhood memories.

The letter included here was first published in the Spectator in Britain on 22 October 1881, then reprinted in the *Times of India* soon after. The letter was entitled 'The Mental Seclusion of India'. Anapurna Turkhad died in 1891.

The Mental Seclusion of India: Letter to the *Spectator* and *the Times of India* (1881)

Sir,—Will you kindly allow me, though quite ignorant of the art of writing to the papers, to make a few remarks upon your interesting article on the above subject which appeared in the *Spectator* of October 22nd?

I am only a Hindu girl (though my husband may, I think, be classed among your 'few cultivated Europeans who ever lived *happily* with a native wife'), and I fear that you will think that my 'mental seclusion' has not allowed me to give you a very clear view of my opinions on the subject; but such as they are, I offer them for your consideration.

The question is,—Why do Europeans fail to see *through* the Indian mind, why cannot they solve its 'elements of the unknown or the capricious'? In the first place, I think that there are Europeans who, in their limited circles of Indian friends, have penetrated this veil of reserve; but India is too big a place for such men to generalize about 'the natives' as though they were homogenous from Peshawar to Cape Comorin, and men do not often care to write books about their immediate circles of friends merely. Leaving such Europeans out of the question, you must make allowance for the abysmal ignorance of India and things Indian in the English mind 'at home'. Most Europeans are full-grown before they think of coming to India at all; there is little *practical* recognition (there is plenty of talk) of the moral responsibility of England to attain to some serious knowledge of her great dependency.

Next, looking at the mass of Europeans in this country, and their social relations to the native, what do we see? Speaking as a native, I can say generally that natives regard Europeans with a sort of respectful awe. They can be and are free-spoken among themselves—in fact, they pride themselves upon not being burdened with social conventionalities like the Europeans—but they never dream of being as free in their intercourse with those people as among themselves. Our friend Vishnupant, for instance, may hold as high a position (financially) as Mr Brown, but Vishnupant would never think of taking any liberties with the latter, or of laughing and talking as freely with him as he would unhesitatingly do with his subordinate clerk, Govindrao. Europeans, he would say, if asked, 'are not of us—how do you expect them to understand us'? Even the children know that a Saheb is a different sort of being than a native. If a Saheb comes to see their father, the children are told to be 'chup' ('shut up'). 'A Saheb has come, take care!' they are told, and so a fear of such people is instilled from infancy, which fear gradually develops into a sort of respectful awe as the child grows into the man.

You say, truly, that the natives are shy of speaking of their thoughts or feelings; that what encouragement have they had from Europeans for them to be otherwise? As an illustration, let me speak of a considerable class, the so-called 'reformers', or adaptive natives, men and women, who are ready enough to accept such crumbs as they are offered of Western habits and Western thought. Brown Saheb may call on Vishnupant, but is Brown Madam Saheb with him when he calls? Of course, Mrs Brown will say that Vishnupant's wife cannot speak English, and she cannot speak Marathi; granted, but even if Vishnupant, like many another Hindu gentleman of modern days, has had his wife taught English, would Mrs Brown care to make her acquaintance? Except, perhaps, in very few cases she would not; 'for,' she would say, 'what is the use of calling on a native lady?' Mrs Vishnupant and she could not have much in common; they could not converse upon any practical topic, they could not invite each other to tennis or dinner. Mrs Vishnupant's cocoa-nut-oily baby would make Mrs Brown shudder; there would be no necessity for calling. And poor little Mrs Vishnupant, on her part, would not see the necessity of knowing English, and would wonder why her husband had made her learn the language; and Mrs Brown's formality (if she did call) would strike a worse chill into the poor little impulsive heart, and make her more shy and reticent, make her hide herself more within herself than ever. One must be educated to a certain degree to have any opinions on any subject. How can Indian women, child-wives as they often are, talk about politics or science, or fashion, or domestic economy, or 'going home', or even 'men' or the price of beef as English-women do? Very few of them read newspapers, still fewer understand them. Poor souls! Their conversation is but simple and homely,—of Yamuna's coming marriage, of the expenditure of the house, of children and the round of common duties; and even then no opinions are given, such as 'I think it right' that such and such a thing should be done, but all facts are given simply and plainly without the Ego being once visible. And their hands are full of work, not elegant trifling with crewel or crochet, but hard domestic drudgery. They have not idle time to 'kill' with light amusements.

Very few Europeans care enough for Indians to be anxious to know anything about their inner lives. They 'live on the spot with them and work with them', because they have to do so, but as for genuine affection and uncondescending friendship, I doubt whether there is much of either. A few European ladies may, perhaps, take a sort of patronizing interest in women like Vishnupant's wife, but would they ever unlock their hearts to such? Is it, then surprising that towards Europeans our minds are 'kept in a casket', as you say? If the Anglo-Indians could like and mix with the Indians more, if they could shake off a little of that *I am the salt of the earth* air which is so infinitely amusing to the 'quiet humerousness' which you have recognized in the Hindu, there would be some chance of opening the casket and revealing its contents; as things stand, it is unlikely that such an event should occur when there is so much of constraint on both sides. There is much in the Indian character which but few Europeans know; one main feature of it is its sensitiveness, intensely acute sensitiveness (a faculty closely allied to the humerousness you speak of), which makes us often times fancy slight or ridicule where neither slight nor ridicule is meant. Perhaps Vishnupant, being a 'reformer', may wish his wife to go out with him, and will insist on her covering her pretty little bare feet with brand-new English boots; the poor wife, with true Indian-wifely obedience, would go out with him thus compositely attired; presently they come across Mrs Brown with some English companions. Mrs Brown, perhaps, thinks or even whispers, 'what a guy!' and though Mrs Vishnupant has not heard the whisper, she has read the look, and (we are all sensitive about our appearance when we've got new clothes on) will at once feel that she is being laughed at. Mrs Brown had been fairly friendly to her Indian acquaintance when alone together; she may be a kind-hearted woman in her way, but, before other Europeans the fear of ridicule overpowers her good intentions, and that feeling which in private betrayed her into an approach to cordiality, is in public chilled into the stiffest formality, if not shamed into actual rudeness. I have said that Europeans talk of 'natives' as if they were of a single nation and a single type. The absurdity is so obvious, that one would hardly think it worth recurring to, if it were not so often committed. I am a Maratha, and can speak of my own people only; distinct as they are to me, to the English eye they come under the same broad classification which groups all Indian races and creed, more numerous and diverse than all the nationalities of Europe put together, under the one term 'natives'. And what natives does the average European see? His low-caste servants, or his official dependents? The former he loathes for their savageness and uncleanliness; the latter he despises for their obsequiousness and their indolence. Of true Indian *life* of the 'homely joys and destiny obscure' of the million of non-official natives, he knows, as you say, next to nothing. And so long as he thinks— or lets the natives fancy that he thinks—that he is *condescending* in his attempt to pluck out the heart of their mystery, he will fail; the mild Hindu will not wear his heart upon his sleeve, for even Sahebs to pluck at.

I have spoken somewhat of myself already, and I will be so egotistic as to say a word more. I have lived as a native, with native ways, and I live among Europeans and in their ways. I do not feel now that my being a native makes the least difference in the way in which I am treated; I have many dearly-loved English friends, even in India, but this has not been my experience from the first. Some years ago, long before I married, I used to feel myself an alien from every one. English ways were less known then than now among my countrywomen, and they neither understood me nor sympathized with me. Still more was I alien to English men, because there was no feeling of equality to be got from them, and I did not want patronage. I used to long and long for a friend in those days!

You will consider this very one-sided, but you will, I think, welcome even an *ex parte* statement on the native side, though only from a woman's pen. I am quite aware that the natives are at fault, being so sensitive (the conquered are ever so, and magnanimity is not an Anglo-Indian virtue); the caste system imposes many restrictions justly repugnant to English notions of social intercourse; and the subjection of women, the result of child-marriages, retards progress towards a better state of things. But still I say if England wishes to understand India, England must begin. 'Peace has her victories,' and these have yet to be won.

I am, Sir,

Yours respectfully,

Lotus Flower

—Vishrabdha Sharda vol. I (1972)

Krupabai Satthianadhan
(1862–1894)

Krupabai Satthianadhan's parents were among the first converts to Christianity in the Bombay Presidency. Apart from being one of the earliest women medical students in India, Krupabai was also involved in contemporary feminism.

Her novel *Saguna: A Story of Native Christian Life*, happens to be the first autobiographical novel in English by an Indian woman, making it extremely important from a socio-cultural perspective. First published serially in the Madras Christian College Magazine in 1887–88, it can be credited with introducing the Indian heroine into English fiction by Indian women. It also pioneers the writing tradition of the 'Indian New-Woman' in English, in the autobiographical mode.

Published posthumously as a book, by Srinivasa, Varadachari and Co., Madras, in 1895, *Saguna* was presented to and read by Queen Victoria who then requested any other work by the author. It was, along with Satthianadhan's other novel, *Kamala: A Story of Hindu Life* (1894) also translated into Tamil in 1896. Both were popularly read and reviewed in India as well as in England when first published.

The excerpt from *Saguna* provides the reader a glimpse into Satthianadhan's unveiling of social codes and customs. It exemplifies her style of writing, her memories of an idyllic childhood, her love of nature, and her unique views on friends and social customs. There is also a subtle use of irony.

The novel concludes with Saguna dedicating her life to God and her husband, Samuel. It remains a compelling account revealing, at one level, the combined effects of a hybrid religion and culture and, on another, the simple truths of what it meant to be a woman caught in the tumultuous years that would initiate a movement leading to India's independence.

Satthianadhan's novel *Kamala: A Story of Hindu Life* was also first published serially in the *Madras Christian College Magazine* in

1894, before being published posthumously the same year. It documents the life and times of a humble Hindu girl in rural India, recounting her experiences as a child-wife, mother and, eventually, widow in an orthodox society.

It also occupies a special place in Indian fiction in English as it is among the earliest instances of an Indian woman being the protagonist. Her experiences as a child-wife are social documents that not only speak volumes about existing conditions of women at the time, but also about Satthianadhan's private beliefs and attitudes towards gender and the female identity.

Interwoven with Kamala's personal struggle for independence are the lives of her friends and other young wives caught in their own struggles in confining homes. The novel, as a whole, thus becomes a powerful critique of the orthodoxy of Hinduism and its many social institutions. Kamala's innocence and portrayal as a child of nature before marriage is in sharp contrast with her future experiences. The farce surrounding the actual ceremony is exploited by Satthianadhan to full effect. It depicts Kamala's inability to comprehend the concept of marriage, while the 'playful' customs and traditions after the ceremony come as a rude shock to Kamala, who takes her first step towards complete subordination.

The novel ends with Kamala turning to a life of austerity as a widow which, we are told, makes her a saint in the eyes of society.

Irrespective of what its heroine eventually chooses, the novel must be credited for the stance it adopts and its examination of the options and realities of the lives of women in Satthianadhan's time.

Chapter V

It was when we were spending our summer days in our mountain home that I first had glimpses in the early life of my parents. The scenery around and the associations of the place bore so striking a resemblance to the old home where my father had spent his life, that my mother was unconsciously led to revive past scenes, and my brother, Bhasker, in his walks, to dwell with characteristic enthusiasm on the particulars of my father's life. I loved to draw from my mother's lips the little incidents of her childhood. I loved to dwell on them, and picture them to myself, and when the pictures were incomplete, with love and veneration, I tried to fill in the gaps. Our father's name was always mentioned with reverence, and the recollection of his face haunted our minds and produced in us a glow of pride and emulation which made us exclaim— 'Oh! we must walk worthy of our noble father.' But childhood is a wonderful period, the influences are exaggerated, the impulses are strong, the heart is full of fire, and there is no room for dull apathy or indifference. It is contact with the cold, selfish world that damps the fire of good impulses and compels the once noble soul:

> To linger on the ignoble plain,
> To truckle for a soulless gain,
> And learn the tricks and shifts of trade.

The summer visit came to a close all too soon. A cart journey was arranged for. My brothers were anxious to leave the place, and eagerly looked forward to the excitement of the journey. But as for me I could not leave without a pang the place where I had spent so many happy days, and where each day I had discovered a new loveliness in everything around me, where the rocks and the trees, the mists and the shadows seemed friends, and where each new and varying phase of the mountain scene found a corresponding place in my heart. I remember well the last day when Bhasker and I got up while the stars were still shining, and stole to the mountain haunts to have a last look at the dear place. There was nothing to be seen at first as far as the eye could reach, except small and great hills and peaks all around; but soon the scene changed. As we ascended the hill in front of our house we seemed to be leaving the world, and piercing the region of the unknown, so thick was the mist round us; and when we reached the highest point we were startled by the dim majesty and grandeur that burst upon us. We seemed to be looking down on mortals below from another world. The shadowy cloudland, dark and gloomy, like a large bird with spreading wings hovered overhead, and the great world sleeping in mist lay below in its purity and whiteness, like a huge sea stretched at our feet. The billows in it heaved and rolled in silence. It was the silence of eternity linked to the world for a moment. A soft starry dreamland light enwrapped and overspread all. Above the ocean of mist the neighbouring peaks, distant and dark, mysteriously loomed like fingers pointing to heaven. The strangely transformed world, the heavenly beauty and purity of the scene bound us fast, and when I looked up my brother seemed strangely excited. He turned to me and said: 'It was in this place with such a scene before me some years ago that I determined that my life should be pure and holy. Oh! how our lives are wasted. Promise me that yours will be devoted to God's glory—wholly to God's glory.' We were alone, alone with God on the mountain top, and we fell on our knees and prayed. The tension of feeling was too great for me to bear; I rushed down at the first sign of the dissolution of the magic scene. I could not bear to watch the mist clouds rise like giants from the earth, or be driven hither and thither, a fantastic mass of light and colour. When I reached the valley below I received a broad shining smile and a merry laugh from the stream I knew and loved so well. How it used to tempt me with its reeds, its flowers, and its pure gurgling water! There were the groves and the singing birds, and each note of their sweet voice went into my heart like the tones of a departing friend. Strange, they seemed sad notes today, the stream seemed gentle and quiet, and the wind that thrilled all the leaves and wrapped itself round me so softly seemed to speak to me. I listened for its voice and felt its sad meaning in the low moan that fell on my ear through rocks and trees, and childlike I felt that the winds and the birds were sorry too. My brother Bhasker was near me. I knew he sympathized with me, but whilst my thoughts were childish, his were grand and sublime.

At home the boys were all excitement and in high spirits. They made huge bundles and stowed away all sorts of delightful things in the carts. They revealed to me, as a great secret, a bundle of glittering quarts which surely contained gold, but which was unfortunatley destined to be thrown away by the indignant driver as making the cart too heavy. Soon I fell into the spirit of the adventure. It was a delicious novelty. I had often longed to be driven in a cart, and the broad white road in front of our house, as it curved round the hill, crossed the bridge near the valley and shot down, a long arrowy streak of white in the midst of sloping hills and broad waving trees, losing itself in what seemed interminable stretches of the blue distant country, had a great attraction for me. I hate the bustling, hurrying smoky trains in which everything seems to fly past me when in motion, and everybody to stare at me when at rest; and the busy stations in which crowds of hurrying people jostle one another amid the deafening din of voices and the creaking of wheels. But what delight do these primitive cart journeys afford! What a wild breeziness and what freedom from restraint there is about them! We feel that all men are akin to us. The weary wayfarer, the peasant toiling in the fields, the chatty old dame that tells of her affairs loudly and walks briskly on, the sturdy farmer returning loaded with drooping sheaves of corn, their smiling faces a study in themselves,—all seem one with us. Safely we jog on in our two-wheeled clumsy vehicle, safe from any interruption, safe to enjoy our days and nights. The bullocks walk on at a uniform pace, and the driver now nods at his post, and now with a start, and with a sense of neglected duty, applies his hand vigorously to twist the tails of the patient animals. Once the village and the limits of human habitation are passed, the straggling fields and solitary temples soon disappear, and we are face to face with nature in all her wild grandeur. The soul catches a responding note of wild, joyous freedom. Sometimes idly dreaming and watching, we seem to see in the sky-mingling distance fairy castles gently take shape and rise, revealing in the nearer view some ancient fortress of a ruined Mahratta power. Then we find ourselves surrounded by hills, dark and frowning and melting into blue in the hazy distance. Then suddenly as if by the touch of a fairy wand the scene changes, and a smiling river, green fields, villages embosomed in clusters of trees, and waving cornfields rise in the place of rugged, barren uninviting scenes. The sound of waters is in our ears. Large spreading trees extend their gigantic boughs, which meet overhead and form a long cool alcove, through which light comes in fitful gleams. The chattering monkey and the soft notes of birds fill the air with a pleasant din. A little further and the forest disappears; we emerge in the sunlight, and look with a mysterious, superstitious dread on the dark avenue left behind. Before us rise shrines and temples hewn out of solid rocks, solemn and solitary in the midst of twisted, stunted, trees. The rocks and stones grow more numerous, till it seems as if all the stones in the world have been thrown in picturesque heaps by the roadside. The sun sets, and its yellow rays light up the stones and the weird trees into brown, gold, and red. Night falls, and we are alone in the silent solitude of stars. Somewhat like this was the journey to our city home.

Our house was in a narrow street with a broad tank in front. At the further edge of the tank was a temple, with a few stunted trees peeping over a broken wall and overshadowing the steps of the tank. Our little home was the smallest in the street. It was built differently from the others. It had a balcony in front and a covered staircase at the side. The neighbouring banyan sent its long branches right in front and almost hid the house from view, and then a hardy creeper covered the balcony all around with a light green drapery, so that we seemed in a real bower in rain, storm, and thunder, and looked out into the world through twinkling leaves and tufts of flowers. At night the stars peeped through and the moonlight danced on the leaves. In front of the house was a little compound. Bhasker had planted plantain trees there, and under their shade we worked, and tended our jessamine and roses. The little hall, which was our drawing room, had windows on all sides. In continuation of a portion of the hall was a small study and a narrow passage. My room was next to the hall. Then came a bedroom, another passage, the place where the fireplace was, and lastly the small pipe room.

Soon we had settled down and the daily routine of work commenced. My brothers went to school, and my mother to her work of preaching. I sewed and read and helped my mother morning and evening. But how dusty, crowded and palling seemed all around me now! How dejecting the view of a seen of houses from my window! What a sickly light seemed to be cast over it all! The plants where they grew had a tendency to wither as if a blight had fallen on them. The only cheering sight in the midst of all this was the tall coconut trees with their graceful crowns lifted here and there above the mass of houses. The sky was an old friend, but seen under a new aspect it appeared somewhat dull. It laid aside its brightest blue and its gayest colours, as if unfit for a place like this, and wore our hue—a greyish neutral tint. The sight of the tank, a broad sheet of water in front of our house, was, however, always refreshing. I had a peculiar satisfaction in thinking that the huge stones by its sides were real rocks, something like the ones that I had left behind me. I clothed them with verdure or left them barren and blank, and in my imagination I placed the tank amongst hills, so that it seemed a real lake, with living springs, reflecting clouds and surrounded with hills with their ever-varying colours. I felt they were all with me, those hills and rocks, fields and flowers. I had only to shut my eyes and see them all. I soon took a greater interest in everything round me; my lessons became quite a treat. ...

—*Saguna* (1895)

Shevantibai M. Nikambe
(b. 1865)

In an essay published in *Women in Modern India*, Shevantibai Nikambe writes about Pandita Ramabai and her own work for women: 'My own work for married ladies began when I joined Pandita Ramabai's staff in Bombay. When she moved her school to Poona, I remained in Bombay and gradually developed the Married Women's School which has now been in existence for sixteen years, during which time 1000 women have taken advantage of the school courses: amongst whom have been child wives and widows in large numbers, also the wives of many professional men.' Shevantibai ran the special school for married ladies from 1912 to 1934. Her special interest in the education of married women finds expression in the only novel she wrote, *Ratanbai*. Ratanbai is nine years old when she is married. Her father insists on sending her to school while her husband is studying for his BA, then goes to Britain, to return via America, Japan and China. The husband too insists that the girl be educated, despite the opposition from his widowed mother and the women in Ratanbai's family. By the end of the novel one infers that it is Ratanbai's education that gives the couple a basis for a happy and equal relationship. However, the novel tells us little about the actual quality of Ratanbai's education. We know she takes lessons in English and a few other subjects. She is asked to recite a verse from the poem 'Casabianca.' But the focus is generally on the customs of the Brahmin families. The novel has its heart in the right place, but cannot compare for instance, with, Krupabai's handling of the same themes.

Nevertheless, Shevantibai is as remarkable for her times as are many of the other women included in this anthology. She was an Indian Christian, born in Poona in 1865, and educated at St Peter's School in Bombay, from where she matriculated in 1884. She visited Europe and America in 1896, and studied Christian work and methods. In 1913, she visited Europe again, studying educational and social work on the Continent. At Aden Girls' School from 1885 to 1890, she also served as the first headmistress of the students' literary and scientific societies, the proprietress and headmistress of the English School for Indian Girls, and inspector of Girls' Primary Schools in Bombay. It is a pity she did not write about her experiences. These bare facts are all that could be found about her. Even her novel is difficult to find: a copy was eventually located through the British Library in London.

The footnotes are from the original text.

Early Reformers

... With the help of the Sisters of the Wantage Mission she came to England at last. A slight defect of hearing made it impossible for her to take the course in medicine that she had contemplated. At Cheltenham College she formed a life-long friendship with that pioneer educationalist, Miss Beale; and here she perfected her knowledge of the English language and published a book, *The High Caste Hindu Woman*.

Ramabai went next to America, where her book had a wide circulation. American women, with their charm, eagerness and love for women of other lands, gave a great welcome to the Pandita, and took her to their hearts and homes. She stood before them, a fragile little woman clad in the spotless white flowing garb of ancient India, whither she proposed to return to work for the emancipation of widows.

Finally, equipped with funds and experience, Ramabai arrived in Bombay and opened an educational institution, the Sharada Sadan in a bungalow at Chowpatty, Bombay. There were present on this auspicious occasion many friends of female education, amongst whom were the most prominent of the Hindus. The entrance to the house was decorated with plantain trees, and yellow-flowered garlands told of emancipation for the oppressed widows for whom educational facilities were now provided.

It was the privilege of myself and my husband to be there that day and I well remember what a wonderful sight it seemed. The Pandita stood as hostess garbed in the white muslin of a Dakshini lady. Her hair was cut short, she wore no bangles on her arms, and her feet were clad in Brahma shoes without stockings. We were chiefly struck by the intellectuality of her brow, by her beautiful grey-blue eyes, and by her charming happy smile. She was true, she was noble, she was great. On this day, she was surrounded by grave Pandits, among whom were Rao Sahib Mandik,

Rao Sahib V.A. Modak, The Hon. Mr Justice K.T. Telang, Dr Bhandarkar, Mr Chandavarkar, and others, all of whom were keenly interested in the cause of women's education.

The Sharada Sadan was so called from one of the names of the Goddess Saraswati, the Goddess of Learning and Wisdom; to this House of Wisdom came numerous high-caste girls and persecuted young widows. After having become a Theist, the Pandita had adopted Christianity and the Sadan became a Christian institution.

Great as its work was, it still seemed circumscribed to the Pandita's great spirit. With the terrible famine of 1896 came a vast extension. She had herself suffered terrific privations from famine during her wander years. She had begged food for her dying mother, and had lived with her brother on roots and wild berries. She departed now for the stricken area. The first sight of three little famished skeleton-like forms determined her in her resolve to admit into her institution all the destitute girls who needed refuge. 'The Lord has put it into my heart to save three hundred girls out of the famine districts and I shall go to work in His name. The funds sent to me by my friends in America are barely enough to feed and educate fifty girls and several people are asking me how I am going to support all these girls who may come from Central India. But the Lord knows what I need.' Her helpers at the Sadan received loyally the burden of their new charges—wild, undisciplined, illiterate girls. When the Pandita returned, she organized at Khedgaon, near Poona, the Mukti Sadan, or House of Salvation. It meant an almost complete retirement along with these girls, from the active intellectual stimulus of life at Poona. But as the Pandita said, 'There is no room for murmuring.'

In time, all the work was concentrated at Khedgaon. The Sharada Sadan was transferred there as part of the larger project. It continued its work of providing higher education for girls who could take advantage of it. But the reach of the Pandita's compassion was henceforth unlimited. A third department was opened, the Kripa Sadan or Rescue Home.

In 1900, with the Gujerat famine, came a new time of trial and test. Twenty of her helpers went out to the area, 'Eight of them women who had been saved from starvation in 1896'. When she had had resources in 1896 for fifty girls, she had admitted three hundred. Now she had resources for five or six hundred, and she admitted thirteen hundred and fifty, bringing the total population at Mukti up to nineteen hundred, 'with over a hundred cattle'. With the help of a hundred and fifty devoted young women, she dealt with this new situation. A school was organized with over fifty classes and teachers. Four hundred children were occupied in the Kindergarten. A Training School for Teachers was opened, and an Industrial School with garden, fields, oil-press, dairy, laundry, departments for baking, sewing, weaving and embroidery. For those who could only do very coarse work there were grain-parching, tinning culinary utensils, dyeing.

It was a wonderful piece of organization. We are told that the Pandita's day began well before four o'clock in the morning, during the last twenty-two years. One can well believe it. Never were the gates of the Sadan shut to any who were in need. And yet in this vast work of organizing, she never lost her serenity and her spirituality; no sign of bustle or worry marred the repose of her beautiful spirit. Her nights were spent in prayer and vigil; her great aim was to bring joyousness and blessedness into the lives of these girls, often so untrained, sullen, gross on their first admission. She never forgot this in the detail of management of this large scale work. Through the busy, bustling life of the place moved the slight serene figure with the great brow and the wide grey eyes, her spirit soaring above age, sorrow, labour, till at last she was called in 1922 to the rest she had always denied herself.

My own work for married ladies began when I joined Pandita Ramabai's staff in Bombay. When she moved her school to Poona, I remained in Bombay and gradually developed the Married Women's School which has now been in existence for sixteen years, during which time 1000 women have taken advantage of the school courses; amongst whom have been child-wives and widows in large numbers, also the wives of many professional men.

The married woman in India presents a problem. As a rule she is not given much chance for education as she is bound by caste and tradition and she is called upon to fulfil solemn duties and responsibilities long before she is fit for them. Homes being sacred temples, the Hindu woman is in the right sense of the term a Priestess in her own house.

Home is also the first school of every child, the mother being the child's first teacher. It is therefore very important to bring enlightenment and a fitting training to the married women, so that the foundations of home life may be truly built. Every girl's natural ambition is to possess her own home, but if she should become a widow her life can be consecrated to some special service for her country, such as has been rendered in the West by sisterhoods or cloisters. Widows have been sent for specialized training in Colleges or Hospitals where they learn to be teachers or nurses.

The work of my school has met with support from both Government and the general public. The success of this work in Bombay proves, I think, that special schools for married women might well be attached to every Primary or High School for girls in which general and special courses of study are being followed.

Educated women are waking up to their real responsibilities in public matters and, provided there is right guidance and proper organization, there is hope that some of the crying problems which affect women may be solved through an improvement in public opinion which has been brought about by extended education. Women who have become alive to the needs of their sisters are seeking opportunities for helpfulness and efforts are being made to break the bonds of custom and caste. In such work lies a most important sphere for the married women and the widow. If educated on proper lines these women will prove to be the fit ones to solve all the great and small problems that involve the progress and prosperity of our land.

This call then is to the married women and widows. Let them in their leisure hours take up their duties, let them form committees and organize and open classes and special schools for widows and married women and as far as is possible let the teachers in such schools be married women. Education has so far advanced that it is possible for the married woman to spare her leisure hours for this important work.

There is no need to wait for Government or Municipalities to take the lead. It is the duty of individual women to start such work and Government and Municipalities should supplement the Funds.

Public bodies however do not need educated women on their committees as much as those are needed on the committees of homes and families. It is in the Home that the prime duty of the mother and wife lies.

Let us then seek out those and give them educational relief and then mark the changes which will follow.

Two royal ladies, one a Maharani and the other a Navab Shah Begum have come forward to take the lead and it is hoped that many others will follow them.

No structure dare be built without a solid foundation and that foundation is brave wives and mothers; therefore let us offer as many facilities as possible for the married women and widows that they may advance along the right lines and fulfil the needs of that noble domain the HOME with its many responsibilities.

—*Women in Modern India* (1929)

Chapter III

One evening Ratanbai on returning from school, rushed into the house, and embracing her mother, said: 'Mother, dear, Mrs B—, who visits our school, has invited us to a party at her bungalow next week; and the teacher told us to-day all those who come regularly to school, and do the lessons well, will be taken to this party: so you will let me go every day, won't you? pleaded the child. The mother promised; but Kakubai, who was near, said: 'Why do you want to go to the English people's houses? They will give you something to eat, and defile you.' And, turning to Ratan's mother, she added: 'Anandi, you had better tell Ratan that she must not eat anything there.'

Ratanbai. Is there any harm in eating the fruits?

Kakubai. No; you may have fruit, but do not touch anything else.

The day of the party arrived, and Ratan, who was regular at school, came home early to dress. Her mother arranged her hair, and dressed her in a quiet but costly sari, allowing her no extra jewels except a nose ring. The girls were to start exactly at a quarter to four from the school, and Ratan was in the midst of the excited and happy party just ten minutes earlier. The carriages came one by one to the door, and the girls, in groups of five and six, took their seats, and drove up to Malabar Hill, to one of those beautiful bungalows which command a splendid view of the city and its surroundings. It was nearly eight o'clock when Ratanbai returned home, and after she had hurriedly thrown her shawl on the 'chowphala',[1] she sat down before Kakubai and began relating the evening's history. As Ratan began, Tarabai, who was in the inner apartment, drew closer to the door, and listened intently to her bright happy niece: 'There were twelve carriages, and in each about six or seven sat. When we came to the house, Mrs B—and her daughter received us, and first we were taken into the cloak-room, where our shawls were kept, and each of us had a *veni* (flower-wreath) given by her, which we put in our hair. Then we went upstairs into the *Diwankhana.* It was so pretty with mirrors and curtains, and pictures and piano. There were silk and satin sofas and chairs, and photographs were kept in silver frames. After a while we were told 'tea was ready.' At this the girls simply rose to their feet and said: 'No tea for us.' But Muktibai came near, and assured us that we were to have fruit and not tea. Then we went downstairs into the dining room. It is a large, beautiful room, with pretty pictures and mirrors, and any amount of glass things. There was a large table in the middle, and on it was a beautiful white cloth, and on this the plates, knives, forks, and glasses were arranged. There were fruits—mangoes, figs, grapes, oranges, plantains, custard apples, pineapples, and *pumbalows.* Beside these were *pedhe*[2] and *barphi*[2]. All round this large table were chairs, and when we were told to

[1]Swing.
[2]Native sweets.

take our seats it was such fun! We had never in our lives sat at table
before, and at first we were all backward to do it; and when we did sit
some of us made mistakes. Kamaliabai and Nanibai sat together first on
one chair, and we did laugh; Gangabai, while cutting a mango, cut her
finger, and Balajipant, the Brahmin, had to take her outside to tie it up.
Some girls sucked the mango instead of cutting it, and the juice all ran
down over the clean white cloth; and one of the girls, while helping
herself to an orange, hit a glass, which fell into bits on the floor.'

Kakubai. Then you caused much damage to the poor, kind madam?

Ratanbai. But she was most kind. First, we told her that we could not sit
at the table and eat, but she would not listen, and so we did our best.
There were so many kinds of fruits, and the table looked so pretty with the
flowers; and Balajipant was there to serve, so it was a regular Hindu repast.

Kakubai. After eating, how did you manage about the water?

Ratanbai. Oh, then we were taken outside to the pipe, and Balajipant
gave us water, and then we went into the playground at the back and
had games. We played one or two English games, but the girls enjoyed
'*zhima*'[3] and '*phugadi*'[4] most. After a little rest we went again into the
Diwankhana, and heard singing and playing. Mrs B—played the piano,
and Miss B—sang. When Miss B—began I thought she was crying, but
we were told afterwards that that was the way English ladies sing. After
the singing, Mrs B—taught us a new game called 'Thimble,' and then I
was asked to recite 'Meddlesome Matty,' and Dwarkabai and Manjulabai
played a duet on the piano. When it got dark we were anxious to return
home, and as we rose to go, Mrs B—came near and told us that we must
go and spend such evenings with her often, for it had given her much
pleasure to have us there. She told us to be good girls and attend school
regularly, and before long there will be another party for us. Sonabai
then carried in the tray of flowers which we had brought from school,
and I put the garlands round their necks. They were glad—but so
surprised! Then one of the elder girls came forward and said a few simple
sentences in English to thank the ladies. After this we sang the Queen's
'*stotra*'[5] and came downstairs. Mrs B—shook hands with us upstairs, and
when we got into our carriages she came down and saw us again. She is

[3]*Zhima*, is a game constantly played by girls. Four stand in a group, and they move on
backwards and forwards in a circle, clasping one another's hands, and making a sharp noise
with their finger and thumb. When the game is played fast, with many groups, it looks very
graceful.

[4]*Phugadi* is played by two girls who stand opposite, their feet touching one another.
They cross hands, and holding tightly, balance backwards and whirl around.

[5]Hymn.

so kind and beautiful, and her house is simply a little palace. The punkahs, the carpets, the curtains, and the mirrors were so pretty.

Here Ratan's mother said: 'That will do now; have some supper, and talk about your party afterwards. The whole night will not suffice for you to tell about it all.'

'I have had so many fruits and sweets today,' said Ratanbai, 'that I do not feel much inclined to have supper. But I will try a little rice and "sambarè"'.[6]

As Ratan rose to go, Kakubai, with a disturbed look on her face, began, 'I cannot think what enjoyment the girls find in going to parties. Why do we want all this? It is not so very essential. Did we have these enjoyments in our days? And yet we grew up and prospered. Where did we go to school? Did we even handle a book? We went to the temples daily and worshipped Māravti. We did household work, and attended to 'veni phani'.[7] The girls of these days want to go to school, to parties, to sabhās, and eat fruits from the 'mlench'[8] hands. It is true the Brahmin served, but it was in the house of English people. We are Arya, but our Aryanism is getting all defiled. People are mad after English. Who are these English? Are not they incarnations of monkeys? Only the tail is not allowed them. What if they are rulers? We must not forget our caste and religion! Truly sin is raging, and the world is coming to an end. Oh Narayan! do thou open the eyes of the people!' Thus talked Kakubai; and giving a deep sigh, she stretched herself on the floor for a nap.

Ratan went to sleep rather excited and tired that evening.

For six weeks all went on as usual. Then came the 'Shravana' month. It occurs about in August, and every young Hindu wife is then kept very busy.

The first day of the month fell on a Saturday. Everyone in Mr Vasudevrav's house was up at an early hour. ...

—*Ratanbai: A Sketch of a Bombay High Caste Hindu Wife* (1895)

---

[6]A very tasty dish made of the juice of lentils.
[7]The toilet.
[8]unclean.

Maharanee Sunity Devee C I of Cooch Behar
(b. 1864)

Perhaps the best-known fact about Maharanee Sunity Devee, daughter of the reformer Keshub Chunder Sen, was that her marriage into the Cooch Behar royal family split the Brahmo community into liberal and conservative factions in 1878.

Mrs E.F. Chapman writes, 'The prince was the head of one of the most ancient royal families in Bengal, which, however, had the disadvantage of belonging to a low caste, the Sankoche Kettry caste ... the principle they professed with regard to caste prevented any objections being raised on that ground, but they vehemently opposed the project, both on the score of the youth of the contracting parties and also on that of the religion of the bridegroom.' Sunity Devee was fourteen at the time, and her husband sixteen. In the extract from *The Autobiography of an Indian Princess* (1921) included here, Sunity Devee records the events that led up to the marriage which, as in the case of some other ruling families, was actually brokered by the British.

Also included here are stories and anecdotes from one of her earlier books *Bengal Dacoits and Tigers* (1916). Sources list *The Beautiful Mogul Princess* (1918) as one of her works, but no trace of this text could be found.

Speaking about Sunity Devee, Gayatri Devi her grand-daughter writes in *A Princess Remembers* (1995): 'When the storms came the insects and the snakes often took shelter in the palace. Almost every sort of snake and insect known in India is found in Cooch Behar, and my grandmother, Sunity Devee, catalogued over a hundred varieties of flying insects alone.'

She also makes another interesting observation: 'Sunity Devee was a genteel and affectionate presence all through my childhood. Outside the state she worked diligently to encourage the emancipation of women in Bengal, but for some reason she did not attempt to put an end to *purdah* in Cooch Behar. Although she moved freely during her visits to Calcutta and other places in India, in Cooch Behar she lived in the *zenana* quarters, where none of the other women had even seen the front of the palace.'

In the chapter from her autobiography, reproduced here, Sunity Devee writes about the many discussions and arguments that lay behind her betrothal, also adding that she fell in love with her husband almost at first sight. She admits that her father initially refused to let her marry the Maharaja: 'In one of his letters he said that I was neither very pretty nor highly educated, and therefore I was not a suitable bride for the young Maharaja.' Even though Keshub Chunder Sen was censured by his peers for agreeing to the marriage, he steadfastly refused to mention why he eventually agreed.

Another chapter describing her first visit to England includes a number of anecdotes about English customs, her meeting with the Queen—'Her conversation was simple and kindly, and every word revealed her queen, woman and mother'—and even her refusal to dance with the Prince of Wales. The Maharanee documents an evening when she was introduced by her husband to the ex-Kaiser, then Prince William at Buckingham Palace. Apparently, the young prince 'bent down and kissed my hand. I blushed and my throat grew dry; my hand had never been kissed before by a man. After the prince left us I tried to scold my husband in Bengali, but he laughed, and said: "Sunity, it is a great honour that your hand should be kissed by the future German Emperor, you ought to be feel proud."'

My Romance

My happy home life continued undisturbed until I was thirteen. Indian girls of that age are more advanced than their Western sisters, but I was still very much a child, thanks to my parents.

My father's name is for ever associated with the Civil Marriage Act, as it was entirely owing to his exertions that the Government passed this wise measure fixing the marriageable age of men and girls at eighteen and fourteen respectively.

The fairy prince in my romance was the young Nripendra Narayan Bhup Bahadur, Maharajah of Cooch Behar, who had been a ward of the Government since his infancy, and carefully educated to be a model ruler. Colonel Haughton wrote: 'Ever since I have become Commissioner for Cooch Behar, the honour of the young Maharajah, his future happiness, and the welfare of the State have been my anxious care.'

This Indian prince's family records show that he was descended from one of the oldest ruling families in the country. According to popular tradition his race had been founded by the love of a god and a maiden, and through successive ages strife and love have been associated with the dynasty of Cooch Behar, whose chiefs are always great rulers, great lovers, and great fighters.

The first wish of the Government was to prevent any palace interference with the baby Maharajah's upbringing. When his father, the late Maharajah, was a ward of the Government, the Maharanis had been very hostile to the idea of a foreign education, and similar opposition was what the Government now wanted to avoid. Therefore, for this and other private reasons which can easily be understood when it is remembered that the late Maharajah left many wives, the Maharajah was removed, when he was five years old, to the Wards' institution at Benares, near which the members of the Cooch Behar Raj family lived in several houses know as the Cooch Behar Palace.

When he was eleven, the Government removed him from Benares to Patna, where he became a student at Government College, and Colonel Haughton's anxious instructions to Babu Kasi Kanto Mukerji, who was in charge of the boy, were 'to watch over his conduct and the management of the household: to see that strangers and unauthorized persons have no access to them: and generally to discharge such duties with regard to him as a good parent is bound to do.'

In 1872 Mr St. John Kneller became his tutor and guardian. The Maharajah remained in Patna for five years, during which time he and Mr Kneller visited the North-Western Provinces, Oudh, and the Punjab, and in 1877 the Maharajah attended the Durbar at Delhi, when the Queen was proclaimed Empress of India. The Viceroy, the late Lord Lytton, received the young ruler most cordially, and presented him with the Kaisar-i-Hind medal. Now for the first time the Maharajah was saluted with thirteen guns, and had a European guard of honour to attend him.

So far the experiment of training the ideal ruler for the ideal state had succeeded beyond the highest expectations of the Government. The Maharajah had become a clever young man and a keen sportsman and, as Mr Dalton remarked at the Chaurakaran ceremony at Cooch Behar in 1876, 'His Highness is fond of his native soil and the people, and enjoys himself thoroughly, taking an interest in everything.'

But now arose the question of the future. To ensure final success for the Government's scheme, it was necessary that the young ruler should marry an equally advanced girl, who would second him in his (and incidentally the Government's) efforts for Cooch Behar.

The difficult problem then arose as to whether an educated wife would agree to the polygamy hitherto customary with Maharajahs, and to adopt the many old-fashioned ideas and ways of a Hindu Court. The Government was keenly alive to the fact that marriage might make or mar their experiment, and they were determined to do all they could to prevent failure.

But as it is a principle of the British not to interfere with the marriage question in India, it was necessary for them to be very discreet in their plans, which required great tact to carry out with success.

Mr Jadab Chandra Chuckerbutty, the Magistrate of Cooch Behar, was deputed to make confidential investigations and find if possible the enlightened girl whom the Government could approve as the Maharani of Cooch Behar. He carried out his mission with discretion; but none of the girls whom he found came up to the required standard.

It was absolutely necessary for the question of the Maharajah's marriage to be settled without further delay, as his visit to England was in contemplation. This journey was a very sore point with the Palace ladies, and Sir Richard Temple, the then Lieutenant-Governor of Bengal, had discussed it rather heatedly.

'During my interview with the Rajah's mother and grandmother,' wrote Sir Richard, 'these ladies expressed anxiety regarding the Rajah's visiting England, which they deprecated on the grounds that after seeing Europe he would never care for such a place as Cooch Behar nor for such quiet, homely people as his relatives. I explained that it had not been decided whether the Rajah should visit England; but that, if he did, it would only be for a short time, enough indeed to enlarge and strengthen his mind, but not enough to make him forget his home and kindred; and that, while giving him the benefit of an English education, we should take every pains to train and prepare him for the duties he would hereafter have to discharge as the Head of a Hindu State.'

These arguments somewhat pacified the ladies, but they maintained that only as a married man could the Maharajah go away from India with any degree of security. At that time they had not realized that the hope of the Government was that the Maharajah would take one wife only when the time for his marriage came.

The party from Cooch Behar in search of a bride at last arrived at Calcutta, and Mr Chuckerbutty went direct to Prosonna Babu, one of my father's missionaries, for advice and help. After several interviews and discussions Jadab Babu spoke of me. But Mr Chuckerbutty said: 'It is too much to expect that the Minister's daughter will be our Maharani.' Still they thought they would try.

When the marriage was first suggested my father was very surprised.

He never gave a thought to worldly or family affairs; his mind was too full of his religious work; and he refused the offer. But the Government and the representatives of the State would not be discouraged. They continued writing to my father, interviewing him, and sending messages urging that the marriage of the young Prince and myself was most desirable. My father repeatedly refused. In one of his letters he said that I was neither very pretty nor highly educated, and therefore I was not a suitable bride for the young Maharajah.

This unexpected opposition was a set-back to the plans of the Government, and they determined it must be overcome at any cost. Those in authority were clever enough to understand that they must discover my father's weak point and work upon it, as it was evident the worldly advantages of the match made no appeal to him.

The messenger went backwards and forwards several times, for Jadab Babu and others would not hear of any refusal. My father with a troubled mind prayed and prayed until at last he obtained light from above and realized that the marriage would be for the spiritual good of the country. Thus he became in the end persuaded that such a union was a Divine command, and if he allowed me to marry this young ruler he would be fulfilling the will of God.

Of course the matter was not mentioned to me, but one day my second sister Bino remarked confidentially: 'Father and mother are talking about marriage, aren't they?' 'Oh no,' I answered, 'it's nothing particular, probably one of the young missionaries is going to be married.' 'Well, let me tell you, it's no missionary, but someone far more important.' 'It doesn't matter to me,' I said, and I thought no more of it.

Later one of the missionaries remarked with meaning in his voice: 'You will be surprised in a day or two, Sunity. Some very important people are coming to see the school.'

'So much the better,' I assured him, 'for now you have told me I can study hard and tell the others to do the same.'

The day before the officials arrived from Cooch Behar, I fell ill with fever. After a restless night, I awoke to find my father and mother standing by my bedside.

They looked to each other. 'Have you told Sunity?' asked my father.

'No,' replied mother, 'it is better you should.'

'Listen, Sunity,' said my father. 'Has Prosonna Babu mentioned some visitors who are expected to-day?'

'Yes, he said that some Englishmen are coming to see the school; and, father,' I faltered, 'I can't get up.'

'Sunity,' answered my father in that loving voice which always made us children thrill with affection, 'it is not the school. These gentlemen are coming to see you.'

'To see me!' I cried. 'Why?' 'Sunity,' said my father in a gentle voice, 'these people are coming to see you, and if we all agree, perhaps some day you will marry a handsome young Maharajah.'

I hid my face in my pillow. I could not speak. Marriage was to me an undiscussed subject. I had never considered it. I felt so shy I became quite red in the face.

After a few hours I was told to get ready. Mother gave me some lovely jewels which looked beautiful on my mauve and gold sari. My hair was dressed. We drove over to dear Miss Pigot's school-house, where I usually had lessons. I was very nervous, and through fear and ague combined I trembled like a leaf.

I rested a little while on the verandah. While I was there I was given a strong dose of quinine. I shall never forget the unpleasant taste of that special draught.

Then I was taken to the drawing-room, where Mr Dalton and the Bengali officials awaited me. Mr Dalton looked kind but critical.

'Won't you play to me?' he asked.

I obediently seated myself at the piano and played a simple piece of music. Mr Dalton watched me up to the piano and back to my seat and as I talked to him; and wrote a full description to the young Maharajah afterwards. 'Very nice,' he said, in such a charming way that I did not think he was examining me. He seemed favourably impressed, and so it proved, for in one of his letters to my father he wrote: 'I thought your daughter a very charming young lady, and in every way a suitable bride for the Maharajah.'

Letters passed and repassed between Cooch Behar and Calcutta, but nothing was settled until the 27th of January 1878, when Mr Dalton wrote as follows:

'My Dear Sir,

'The Lieutenant-Governor has at last decided that the Rajah is to go to England in March, and, looking to the desirability of perfecting his bride's education, it is better that he should be married before he starts. Mr Eden at first saw difficulties in the way of a match with your family, but our arguments in favour of the proposal have at length found weight with him, and he has given his consent.

'The Rajah has expressed his distaste to being married at all, as I told you in a previous letter, principally because he was averse to being worried about the matter, and partly because he knew that he was not to be permitted to live with his wife at once and wished to remain single until of an age to do so. But he has come to see that an educated bride is not to be procured at all, and is now eager for the alliance with your daughter, the idea of which was always pleasant to him, provided he could secure his mother's consent. This consent I have at length secured with great difficulty, on terms which Babu Jadab Chundra Chuckerbutty will explain to you, and which I hope you will agree to.

'I know it will seem difficult to you to arrange for a wedding on the 6th of March, and also that the idea of marrying your daughter before she has completed her fourteenth year is repugnant to you. But consider the circumstances, and that in fact the marriage will not be a marriage in the ordinary acceptance of the term but a solemn betrothal, the Rajah proceeding to Europe immediately after the ceremony.

'I have read through your memo. There are some paragraphs which I think we can hardly consent to in their entirety, but by a little concession on both sides, I have no doubt that, if you are really well disposed to this marriage, we may come to an agreement which will suit both parties.

'One of the Rani's conditions is that one of your relatives, not yourself, should give away the bride.

'The objection to you is principally based on the fact that you have been to England. I imagine that, as you will be actually present (or may be, if you like), it will not make any great difference to you should a brother or uncle actually repeat the formula. This is a condition on which great stress is laid, and I hope you will not arrest negotiations *in limine* by refusing to accede to it. Remember that we on our side have had great difficulties to smooth away, and that we have already conceded almost all that we have the power of conceding.

'Remember, also, that if you care about this alliance, it is a question of now or never, for nothing short of the urgency of the case (the Rajah going to England in March and the Ranis in despair at the idea of his going unmarried) would have brought Mr Eden to change his mind, a thing he rarely does.

'With my regards to yourself, etc.'

Observe how in this letter, Government smoothed away all my father's objections. The marriage was to be merely a 'solemn betrothal', and *hey presto*! the age difficulty vanished. Concessions were certain so far as his religious scruples were concerned, but the words 'now or never' throw a curious side-light upon the Government policy. The Cooch Behar-Sen alliance was necessary to them, and my father was to be finally 'rushed' into giving his consent. That such was the case is shown by the following telegram from the Dewan to Babu Chuckerbutty:

'Deputy Commissioner says can't wait too long even if matter not published. Must have private assurances of Keshub Babu's consent without delay. Remember preparations. 27-1-78.'

Then the delight of Babu Chuckerbutty found expression in this letter to Prosonna Babu:

'My Dear Prosonna Babu,

'Such has been the pleasure of God! and I am amongst you to re-open the question of marriage.

'Mountains and oceans stood as barriers before us, but thanks to the great Remover of all difficulties, we have managed to get over them all.

'Should we not see in all this, the hand of Him who dispenseth of everything human? We have all done all we could: it now rests finally with you as to the remainder. I have just now arrived here. I left Cooch Behar at midnight day before yesterday, and have come in at once. My present address is 6, Bhobani Dutt Lane, and my man will lead you to my house. I hope that our Maharajah is here.

'Yours, etc.,
'Jadab Chunder Chuckerbutty.'

The Maharajah wrote to my father as follows:

'My Dear Sir,

'I have been asked to let you know what my honest opinion is on the subject of polygamy.

'In reply I beg to inform you that it has always been my opinion that no man should take more than one wife, and I can assure you that I hold that opinion still.

'I give below a statement of my religious views and opinions. I believe in one true God and I am in heart a Theist.

'Yours truly,
'Nripendra Narayan Bhup.'

—*The Autobiography of an Indian Princess* (1921)

A Punjabee Dacoit

In a railway train several Punjabee ladies sat on the lower berths of a second class compartment, laughing and talking gaily. They were, with one exception, all richly dressed and each of them wore a quantity of jewels. The exception was a capable, good-looking woman, of about twenty-five. Her short hair, neck and arms bare of jewellery, and plain white *saree*, proclaimed her a widow. But like the others she chatted merrily, and a listener would have learned from their conversation that they had been attending a wedding, and were now on their way home. Witty remarks about the guests, criticism of the looks of the bride, and comparisons of this wedding with others, passed from one to another, and whiled away the hours of the journey as the train sped onwards.

Night fell, and the ladies became silent. They rested against each other and dozed at intervals. The widow sat on a trunk at the end of the carriage and silently told her beads. The train slowed down and stopped at a little station. Then the bell clanged and once again they were on their way.

The little station had not been left far behind when a dark figure appeared on the footboard of the ladies' carriage, and a man's head was thrust in at one of the windows. A startled exclamation from one of the party drew the attention of all to the intruder, who was pulling himself up into the carriage. He was very fierce-looking, wore a huge turban, and had a bushy black beard. In one hand he held a knife and with the other he assisted himself into the compartment, in spite of the ladies' protestations.

Some of them began to cry but one or two bolder spirits ventured to argue with him. In answer to their questions and objections, he said roughly: 'It is a long while before you will reach another station. I have come for your jewels. If you give them to me quietly, I will not hurt any of you; but if not ...' and he looked very expressively at the knife in his hand.

After some few minutes, the ladies, who were inclined to oppose him, yielded to the tearful advice of their more timid sisters, and one by one they began to unclasp necklaces and belts and hand them over to the dacoit together with bracelets, bangles and rings. The ruffian, finding them docile, did not hustle them in any way but stood leisurely receiving the spoil. Then he carefully folded all in a rich *saree* and was knotting the ends together when the train suddenly stopped, and an Englishman pushed open the door of the ladies' compartment and sprang at him with the exclamation, 'You scoundrel!'

The sudden surprise and assault threw the robber off his feet, and he fell sprawling on the carriage floor, with the Englishman on top of him. In the meantime, the guard and others arrived and the thief was secured and his hands and feet were bound together with his own *pugree*, and he was removed to the guard's van.

The widow was the heroine of the adventure. As soon as she saw the man entering the carriage, she realized his purpose. Slipping into the lavatory she climbed through the window there on to the footboard, and pulled herself along by the carriage rods to the next compartment where the solitary occupant, an Englishman, sat reading.

He was amazed to see a woman clinging to the window of his carriage, but fortunately he understood the language; and when she said 'Help, thief in the next carriage', he opened the door and got her into his carriage without any delay. In a few words, she acquainted him with what was happening in the next compartment. He immediately pulled the alarm cord to stop the train, and hurried along the footboard to the assistance of the ladies. They were profuse in their expressions of gratitude to him, but he insisted that they owed their lives and their jewels to their courageous friend.

—*Bengal Dacoits and Tigers* (1916)

Cornelia Sorabji
(1864–1954)

'Always picturesque and striking in appearance, the legal
champion during the past forty years of the purdah-enwrapped
aristocratic women, Miss Cornelia Sorabji has been a notable figure
as the first Indian woman Barrister, the historic Indian Portia,
one of a number of notable sisters who all dedicated themselves
to serve their day and generation. Yet she has been before her
time. Her father was a Parsee, her mother a Hindu; they fused
through conversion to Christianity. Miss Cornelia was the product
of the Protestant sect of English Christianity and has seen her
own country and presented it to the non-Indian world through
those lenses in the individualist career she has carved out for herself
and in which she has brilliantly shown the pioneer woman
moulded by Western institutions.' Thus writes Margaret Cousins
in *Indian Womanhood Today* (1941).

If guile was Portia's weapon, tact and humour were Cornelia
Sorabji's. She needed these to deal either with wily priests who
advised gullible purdah women, or usurpers ready to poison and
murder to get their way, or women ready to try out the most
dangerously ignorant forms of 'healing'. In the middle of all this
travelling, and dealing with cases, Cornelia Sorabji still found time
to be one of the most enduringly significant writers India has
produced. She used her experience to craft both fiction and non-
fiction. She also wrote a play, and stories for children. Her stories
are invariably touching, sometimes amusing, always memorable.
'Making a Hindu Will' from *India Recalled* (1936) is probably one
of the funniest descriptions of the byzantine world of legal procedures
one is likely to come across.

Cornelia Sorabji was no stranger to byzantine procedures. A
few years before she went to college, her father, Sorabji Kharsedji,
Post Master at Belgaum, wrote asking the University of Bombay
whether his daughter Phiroze could appear for the Maharashtrian

examination. This letter, written in 1875, created a crisis, as no such request had ever been received before. The Syndicate finally told the Post Master that it had no powers to decide whether any woman could or could not sit for the examination, and the Post Master had to accept this decision.

However, some enlightened members of the Syndicate thought they needed to do better than that. Eight years of deliberations followed, after which women were allowed to take the examination. Cornelia Sorabji benefited from this decision. She became the first woman in Western India to attend a college, and was awarded the BA degree with a First Class at the convocation of 1888. The Senate of the University then passed a resolution: 'that words in the masculine in the rules of the University shall for the future include the feminine'.

In 1889, Cornelia Sorabji went to Oxford to study Law. Here again there were problems because women were not permitted to become barristers, but Benjamin Jowett, Master of Balliol and Vice Chancellor of Oxford conferred a special degree on her in 1893 allowing her to take the Law examination. In England through Jowett, she met many of the leading figures of the day including Gladstone, Balfour, Max Müeller, Lady Carlyle, and Florence Nightingale. She was also received by Queen Victoria.

Cornelia Sorabji's parents were both converts to Christianity—her father from Zoroastrianism, her mother from Hinduism. Both, her parents and her sister Susie, contributed a great deal to education by opening schools, teaching imaginatively, and encouraging girls to be educated.

Cornelia Sorabji came back to India to work for women and when, in 1922, women in England were finally allowed to become barristers, she returned there and qualified in 1923. Some of her books are concerned with her work as Government of India Legal Adviser to the *purdahnashins* of Bengal, Bihar, Assam and Orissa, a post to which she was appointed in 1904. Before that, however, there were other frustrations. Her Oxford qualifications were not accepted in India and she had to appear for the LLB exam. She finally retired in 1929 and settled in England.

Cornelia Sorabji's publications include *Reminiscences and Experiences, Love and Life Behind the Purdah* (London: Freemantle and Co., 1901), *Between the Twilights: Being Studies of Indian Women by One of Themselves* (London: Harper and Brothers, 1908),

Therefore: An Impression of Sorabji Kharshedji Langrana and His Wife Franscina (Oxford University Press, 1924), *Susie Sorabji: Christian Parsee Educationist of Western India* (Oxford University Press, 1934), *India Calling: The Memoirs of Cornelia Sorabji* (London: Nisbet and Co., 1934), *India Recalled* (London: Nisbet and Co., 1936), and *The Purdanashin* (Thacker, Spink and Co., n.d.).

In the first chapter of *India Calling* (1934) Cornelia Sorabji tells us something about her family background: 'My father owed his personal thinking in an orthodox Parsee family to his English tutor, George Valentine. My mother owed her education and ideals to her adoptive mother, Lady Ford, the wife of Sir Francis Ford, an Englishman in command of a regiment stationed during her childhood at the place in the Hills where her parents lived. We were therefore 'brought up English'—i.e. on English nursery tales with English discipline; on the English language used with our father and mother, in a home furnished like an English home. *But* and this is where the parents showed their wisdom—we were also compelled to learn the languages of the peoples among whom we dwelt. We were told tales of our ancestors in Persia, and of our forbears and immediate family in the Parsee community in India. We were made proud of that community; but from our earliest days we were taught to call ourselves Indians, and to love and be proud of the country of our adoption; while the history of our parents made us love also the people and country to which George Valentine and Cornelia Ford belonged.'

Cornelia Sorabji also tells us how at the age of eight or so, she decided to be a lawyer. A *thakurani* who visited her mother told her of her troubles. After the thakurani left Cornelia's mother said, 'There are many Indian women in trouble in that way. Would you like to learn how to help them?' When little Cornelia said she would, her mother said, 'Then, when you grow up and are able to choose the special thing you want to learn, ask to study *the Law*. That will show you the way to help in this kind of trouble.' Cornelia Sorabji continues, 'And that was her secret and mine, fostered openly from time to time, when we talked of careers. I was going to be a Lawyer: and my littlest sister was equally determined to be a Doctor.'

The Fire is Quenched!
A Sketch in Indian Ink

I

[Introductory Note—Under the early Zoroastrian law, contact with a dead body meant contamination, for which the penalty was ten thousand stripes, *i.e.* death.

The Zoroastrian idea of worship is the keeping the sacred fire perpetually alight on the altar. It must never be allowed to go out. There is no greater sin than neglect of this duty.]

The town was ecclesiastical—of this there was no doubt. It was not your peculiar faculty for seeing which disclosed this to you,—indeed you have yet all to learn concerning this special kind of eccelesiasticity,—but there was an air of quiet, hushed sanctity abroad, which somehow thrust the conviction upon you.

It is a picturesque type of sanctity, too. The hour is six in the evening. Look at the women, sitting with their faces west-wards, weaving, weaving, and praying silently the while. They are all daughters and wives of the priesthood; and those pretty and costly silk draperies would be becoming, you reflect, to faces even less pleasing and cultured than those which meet your eye. The head is bound with a white fillet, typical of the subjection of all actions and imaginings to the bondage of the law; and among the draperies is visible a finely embroidered white lappet—a garment every square inch of which has some religious significance. ... But the women weave and weave; and it looks so uninteresting this thing which they weave—neither the soft delicate-tinted silk, nor even the white linen embroidery, but just lengths of cord no thicker than ordinary packing twine. It is the Zoroastrian *kusthi*, the sacred cord: there are seventy-two gossamer-like strands woven into it—seventy-two, for the seventy-two angels; and as she weaves, the good Zoroastrian lady will say prayers for all the future generations who may use that sacred *kusthi*. One day it will pass through the fingers of some pretty, careless girl, or may be a feather-headed boy, who will tie the knots with flippancy and reel off the ancient zend in meaningless levity. But, and if the weaver be but faithful enough, perhaps those incessant short prayers of hers will act as a charm against all future contingencies.

'That I shall ask Thee, tell it me right, O Ahura!

'How arose this present life?

'By what means are the present things to be supported?

'O righteous Mazda! Be their guardian, to ward off from them every evil: Thou art the promoter of all life.

'In every being which beholds the sun's light, may Armaiti, the spirit of piety, reside.

'The good of the good mind is in Thy own possession, O righteous!

'The voice of the law, it is *Thy* voice, O Ahura Mazda!'

Thus old Avemai, as she bends to her task in the open doorway of the high priest's house. She is worn with years and with disappointed hopes—a little crooked old woman, but with character and determination proclaiming itself from every furrow of the wrinkled face.

Khursud, the high priest, is her son, and she lives with him and his pretty wife Makkhi in the house which had been his father's and grandfather's before him. At this stage of existence her affections are busy over little Khutti, aged five, the grandchild. Such a winsome child it is, too—the most delicate of limbs, dark brown curls, and eyes to match, and a mouth made for laughter. Listen! you can hear a little joyous peal this very minute. Khutti drives her goat-cart home from the pleasure-house by the water; and Siddi, the small negro attendant, has been acting zany for her amusement.

'Do it again, Siddi,' she says, 'and again. Show me how the big fish eat the little fish, and how it slipper-slippered down his throat.'

'I can do better than that,' said Siddi; 'I can show you how a fish can slipper-slipper down Siddi's own throat. But that will be another day, after I have had a chance of dodging that long-limbed old cook in his hot-weather garment. This evening you shall hear all about why your grand-aunts send you so many fish—big and little—on your birthdays; and why the mai, who sweeps the house, paints them, the lucky things, all over the doorsteps and pavement; and why, in short, a fish always means that good things will happen.'

And so he told her, in his own whimsical way, a legend of his own devising—touching the Parsee exodus from Persia, and how, when mermaids and devils would have tempted the exiles out of their course, a great scaly fish, with a waving tail, swam before them, to land them, and the sacred fire they guarded, with due safety in their Indian refuge.

And when it was ended—'There! isn't that pretty?' said he. 'But here is the scolding ayah. I must get beyond reach of her bangle-laden arm!'

'Eh! Siddi! Ever filling my baby's ears with infidel tales. *Pshu!*—begone, I say. I will tell the bai sahib of you some day.'

'Oh ayah!' said Khutti, 'he has told me lovely tales, about fishes, and things in the sea, and big ships.'

'Pooh! lies, lies, all lies! Son he is of a sow-eared mother,' replied the woman. 'Yes! Makkhi bai sahib—baby coming to supper and bed.'

Through the hot hours of the next day Khutti played in her luxurious little nursery, requisitioning whatever playmate her imperious fancy suggested, and always getting the right one too—solemn father, or bonny mother, or fond, wrinkled old grandame.

And she told them all her fish story and they had to act and re-enact it a hundred times: now she was the smiling maiden, and now the red coral gnome, and now again the great big fish with his leering slit of a mouth and winking eye.

But, after her usual evening drive, she sought the old Ave, once more at her accustomed weaving, and—'Oh, Avemai,' she said, 'my throat here, it hurts so.' No one knew how it happened—a bad drain, perhaps a little cold. Who could tell? Ayah said Siddi had bewitched her; and Siddi was tied up and whipped, in the servants' regions, and made to go through the most gruesome of ordeals, although indeed he barely felt the pain of the lash as he sobbed his small heart out for grief that his little mistress was ill.

But neither this, nor the spells of any caste, or class, or religion, worked the longed-for improvement. And at last—it was but a chance—'Take her to the hills,' said the doctor, 'the fever may abate, at any rate.'

II

It was five in the morning at a quiet Indian railway station. The booking clerk was asleep—the full length of him—on the table in the office, with a red-and-green woollen comforter round his neck, his official cap neglected on the dusty floor, and over his legs loose white folds of quasi-petti-coat, which, with his imitation English coat, gave him a strangely hybrid appearance.

'Ding, dong! ding, dong! ding, dong! Train left last station,' shouted the porter, thrusting a drowsy head momentarily into the booking-office. The clerk rose and yawned, and cracked the knuckles of his bony fingers, and proceeded to deal little green tickets to the greasy crowd behind the railing. Applicants there 'were of every description—applicants with bundles on their heads or their backs, and with ten days' provisions in their wallets. Sometimes the bundles were heard to scream—human screams; and often they were seen moving recalcitrant little limbs. (To carry a baby in a sling over your shoulder is a favourite Eastern device.) Of licensed vendors at this early hour there were but few; but the lean hungry Brahmin priest, with his collection-box—'For the preservation of the Cow'—and his bribe of cut flowers, was already walking the platform, and small boys carrying unappetising trays of sickly Indian sweetmeats were being patronized at the third-class compartments, while the messman's assistant made his customary proffer of tea and coffee.

From a luxuriously reserved carriage issued a Parsee lady, dressed in pale blue silk draperies, falling gracefully into the lines of her slight figure; in her arms she carried a child loosely clad in a red crimson vest—the rich colour whereof lighted up the little face. And it needed that: for, notwithstanding the slight smile about the lips, its suggestion of stillness, somehow, struck a cold chill to your heart.

Servants, of varying degree, were in attendance—offering garrulous and obstrusive aid; but the lady refused to be relieved. 'A carriage, Marothi, quick!' she commanded, 'and bid them drive to the kitchen door. The household is not to be disturbed.'

Arrived unobserved at baby's nursery, Makkhi—for it was she, the mother of the erstwhile joyous little Khutti—barred the door, and flew instantly across to the dawning light at the window.

'They must never know that she died in the train,' she reflected. 'And in my arms too, poor darling! The grandame would say 'twas contamination. What is the penalty? Beating with ten thousand stripes! Ah! it would mean death. And yet, without my Khutti, what came I for life? But—and I must be sadly callous—my heart is like the marble stone which I shall soon lay her. Not a tear can I shed. It is well, perhaps; no time is there for weeping. I must lay my plans. ... Even ayah fancies she is asleep. Well! in half an hour I must send for the dying slab, and lift her on to it. My grief will be sufficient excuse for the barred door. At eight, when the granny is through her usual duties, I will bring her in and show her the cold little body. Oh! that I could warm it! Khutti mai—wake up! wake up!' she wailed, clasping the little thing tight against her own warm breast, a world of yearning in her voice and attitude.

Oh! irrevocable death!

Meantime Ave had been very busy. It was her husband's 'day'—the anniversary of his death, and there were special dishes to be cooked, and there was his room claiming attention. Daily through the long years since his bones had dropped through the grid, in the Tower of Silence, had provision been made for the possible wants of his spirit: fresh changes of raiment were placed ready for him, and his favourite dishes, and the little snuff-box handy on the arm of his long chair. The snuff never diminished, and the clothes looked strangely unrumpled, and there was no perceptible difference under the covers—but spirits have odd ways. Perchance were the things not there, he would miss them.

On his great day Avemai came herself to look after the arrangements; his fullest priest's robe it must be to-day, and that conical white hat, and the most elaborate of his sandals. She was so particular about everything that it was quite eight o'clock before she encountered ayah. She was on her way to the wine-cellar to get a bottle of the oldest brew—for in those good days bottles of wine were buried at the birth of each child in a Parsee household, giving quite respectable antiquity to the consumable fluid in the cellars of some of the old families. She encountered ayah then—and

'You here!' she said. 'You *have* startled me! Have you returned for aught?'

'Khutti mai got worse,' said the woman; 'the bai sahib brought her home. She is mad with grief. I have sent for the doctor sahib, and the bai has locked the baby's door, and watches the child on the dying slab.'

'Fool!' said the old woman. 'Why did you not call me?'

'Who bade me call you?' queried the menial, with the irresponsibility of the Indian servant.

Ave hurried, with tottering steps, to the nursery door. 'Mi! Mai! Makkhi mai! let me in,' she said—and could say no more.

But the door was ajar, and there was Makkhi at a discreet distance from the little dead form on the cold white marble. But the tension had snapped in the still solitude of the death-watch, and she was sobbing now, sobbing healing tears.

'No,' thought Ave. 'I may not even touch the child, to test the truth of what I see. The bearers must do the final rites.'

It was the weaving hour, when a long white-robed procession of high priests and priests of lower degree, walking two abreast—a spotless handkerchief unfolded between each pair—followed, in silence, the death-bearers to the distant Tower of Silence. Something there was, not altogether without hope, in the absence of the solemn black, which is the outward and visible sign of Western mourning. Yes! not without hope—albeit the death-bearers must mount alone the steps to those high shelves in the turret, and leave there the dainty little burden to the rough talons and sharp beaks of the hungry vultures.

And, at home, Ave wept bitter tears into the names of the seventy-two angels—(for nothing excused that sunset duty)—and the wives of the white-robed mourners sat in long rows on the verandahs, and chatted nothings or tactless somethings to the broken-hearted mother.

III

Midnight, and a bright moon overhead. Makkhi has had a wretched evening, sleepless and anxious, and aching with longing for the impossible; and, at last; she has crept noiselessly to the darkest corner of the fire temple. There is Khursud, her husband, reciting the classic zend, in his monotonous voice. Distinctly came the words of the old Gatha.

'I ask from Thee, O Homa! who expellest death, that I may stand forth at will, powerful and successful upon earth; putting down trouble and annihilating the destructive powers. I ask from Thee, Homa! who expellest death, who grantest strength and vigour to those who, mounted on white horses, run in the race—I ask that I may stand forth as victor and conqueror in the battle upon earth. Strike a deadly blow, O yellow Homa, at the body of the disturber of righteousness, who binds our thoughts to earth and earthly things, and makes us forget the sacred religion of Zarthushta. Strike the blow, O yellow Homa! Strike!'

How he had loved the child! And this duty, keeping the fire alight—must it not weigh on his soul to-night? Yet he did it! Ah! they knew how to cling to duty, those two—Khursud and his old mother—and they clung fiercely, as if in that alone lay life, salvation.

Could she tell them? And if not she, who would? It was her own secret, whispered a voice within. Even the doctor had not been in time, and there was no one to suggest the hour at which death had in reality supervened.

But to keep a secret, how impossible! And a secret of her own wickedness, too! Ah! she must speak, if she would buy peace of mind and strength to live.

They were loving too, those two—so tenderly loving—perhaps they would show her how to expiate; and at worst, 'twas only *Death* which could come. ... Besides, it was her *duty* to tell. This last was the thought which would recur most often with the memory of Ave and her weaving at her heart, and with the sight of Khursud burning the sacred sandalwood before her eyes in stern unmovedness.

But she was so young, and life was still sweet, and the love of her husband sweeter still—how *could* she confess! No, let her have time to think. So it prolonged itself—the struggle—for a succession of nights; the fiercest part of the battle always fought in the far corner of the fire temple—and the result always problematical. Till—the merest chance brought decision. The evening and the morning were the seventh day; and Kursud, walking the empty room at the close of his nightly vigil, found, to his surprise, Makkhi lying against a stone pillar, asleep through sheer watching and fatigue,—while she, startled past discretion, and touched by his kind thoughtfulness for her, obeyed her best impulse, and told him all.

There never was any doubt as to the sequel. Ave issued the mandate. The book said ten thousand stripes; ten thousand—be it ... and Khursud must administer them.

IV

It is midnight once more; but the moon has veiled her light, as it were in pity for the cruelties of good men's tender mercies.

There is silence, the silence of expectation, in the long, low fire temple; the faint sweet odour of burning sandalwood is in the air; the red light glows on the altar. Is it the only live thing within the walls? Presently the priest's private door opens noiselessly, and there enter together the little, old, bent Avemai, the stern embodiment of the Zoroastrian Leviticus, and (picturesque foil!) the young pathetic—faced mother—beautiful, but still criminal—criminal, because she loved much; because the mother's heart in her would not let the dying child smile its last smile into a strange face; because, as long as the world lasts, the voice of ignorant man will always outshout the inspirations of the all-knowing God.

At a little distance behind the women followed Khursud, the high priest. His spotless robes carried the suggestion of something awful and unapproachable; and yet, did he raise that bent head of his, you would see that he was only a poor crushed creature, not intoxicated by a sense of duty, like his stern old mother—conscious but that his loved child was where the vultures were gathered together, and that the only thing which made life livable would soon be there also. Self-despoiled! childless! wifeless! inexorable fate! Truly was the law his taskmaster!—but to bring him, where? to what?

Then spoke old Ave, the daughter, the wife, the mother of the Zoroastrian priest-hood. 'My son! that which thou hast to do should be done quickly! and it should be done here, before the altar. Let the Holy Prophet know 'tis done in his name. Bare thy back, my Makkhi. I have loved thee much; but we must all perforce love the law and the prophet more. To this end were we born, and to prove this have I tarried on earth so long. ... Here is the lash: *ten thousand stripes*, says the book. Perhaps—fewer ... will ... suffice.'

An owl screeched in the coconut palms. 'Ha!' thought Khursud, 'how my pretty Khutti used to shudder at that noise.' Then, oddly enough— 'The coconuts will be ready for tapping this month. Shall we go and drink an early glass of the sweet white juice at the palm groves by the sea? Makkhi, *little* Makkhi! what was it you wore the day we exchanged the betrothal ring? ... Good God! *I can't*!'

'Come, Khursud,' said the unwavering voice of the law. 'She is ready *now*! ... The wisdom of the prophet must be justified of her children.'

The old woman lay on her face, beseeching God—(not the fire, nor the seventy-two angels, nor yet even Zoroaster himself this time; she wanted something, someone, beyond and above these)—beseeching God with all the powers of her lean, limited soul to accept this expiation—to send the pain be not very great—oh! to interpose, to end it all, *somehow*.

One, ... two, ... three, ... they came unflinchingly; the lash rising and falling on the silent night air. How the long minutes passed they knew not, and no one counted the strokes—till—

'My son! my son! the fire on the altar, it is dead! *dead*! DEAD! and for the first time since our fathers brought it across the waters! Oh! who will expiate *now*? We have punished the lesser sin—but the greater?'—

So spoke Ave, at sight of the neglected altar; there followed once more a silence, and once more 'twas broken by a shriek—but a shriek piercing and awful in its hopeless unrelievable horror. And this time it came not from the owl in the palm tree.

The law of Zoroaster, the wisdom of the prophet, is she justified of her children—now?

—*Love and Life Behind the Purdah* (1901)

The 'Squirrel Lady'

... It was when I was immersed in the Cross-eyed Boy's affairs, that a messenger came from the Panch Mahal's several miles distant, riding an ambling pony, and wearing the crooked little Kathiawar sword in his spotted muslin *kamar-band* (waistband), demanding audience.

The servants brought him to me where I sat, outside my tent door in the cool of the evening.

'Will the *Huzur* have an elephant for a client?' asked the man, making the triple sweeping salaam of the district, back bent.

'But of course,' said I; 'what has the elephant done?'

'It is not what he has done, but what has been done to him,' said he. And he told his story.

A Thakur, grandfather to the man on the *gadi*, had a favourite beast, an elephant, to whom he left by deed a large plantation, together with a respectable sum of money for the support during the elephant's life of himself and his *Mahout* (keeper).

Through the reign of the donor's son, the elephant uprooted and consumed the sugar-palm trees of his estate, in lordly ease. But the grandson, then on the *gadi*, said, 'A foolish waste. I have need of that valuable plantation for myself. The elephant can go get his food in the jungle.'

News had reached the elephant, however, concluded the man, of my presence in the neighbourhood: and he wanted to know if I would accept a 'brief' for him! The bearer of the message was the *Mahout*, whose income was of course also involved. I have not cited the actual words he used, but the purport thereof.

He laid a scroll at my feet as he finished speaking. It was a valid document, and duly executed.

I said, yes—we could bring an action on the deed; in the name of the

·elephant. But it would have to be in the Durbar Court, against the Thakur-Defendant who was also Judge in the Court, and he might not grant me a *Sanad* to appear.

Oh, yes, he would!—he himself had sent the *Mahout* to find me, had offered me hospitality, and had said that I might choose a day convenient to myself for the hearing.

I accepted the last courtesy, but refused the hospitality. I would plead my case, said I, and return to my camp.

In due course arrived a carriage and pair, and outriders with drawn swords. The Thakur had said that as the District afforded no public conveyances save a palanquin, he begged that I would use the Durbar carriage which he had sent, to save myself discomfort on the long journey.

Extraordinarily decent in an adversary! But then the medieval manners of Raj States are like that; and I was only too glad to escape the palanquin-coffin-on-poles, especially as we were in the middle of the hot weather.

Arrived at the Palace, the Prime Minister and other Durbar officials met me: and there was my client, dressed in green and gold standing in the courtyard. He wore his 'dress clothes'—a long emerald green cloth, heavily embroidered in gold; his forehead was painted in ancient devices in the same colours, so were his tusks, which were also fitted at the points with filigree gold metal: the lobes of his ears were tasselled with little ear-rings in gold and precious stones, and long 'bobble-d' ear-rings of twisted silk in green and gold were slipped round his ears and hung to his feet. He had 'rings on his fingers and bells on his toes'—to wit, heavy gold anklets with pendent tinkling bells.

Even his sturdy tail was adorned with circlets and pompoms of silk at intervals, down its entire length. He stood as tall as a house, and his trunk was upraised in the Raj Elephant's salute.

Never in my wildest fairy-tale dreams had I conceived such a client. He should be served with the best I had to give!

'What is the hour fixed for the hearing?'

'As Your Honour pleases,' said the P.M.

'But when does the Court sit?'

'When Your Honour pleases. Will Your Honour first partake of refreshment? It is ready at the Guest-house.'

No. 'Her Honour' would not—thank you.

Then, when would I like to go into Court?

Immediately.

'I will inform the Raja Sahib,' and he departed, while I talked to my client, and told him to cheer up, his case was four-square, and he should eat sugar palms of his own 'slaying' to the end of his days—lordly elephants such as this wind their trunks round the trees and bring them down, insert a tusk, sniff, and if the result is satisfactory, carry off the tree, rolled into their trunks, to the bedding-out place to be savoured at ease.

Presently the P.M. returned.

'The Raja Sahib is in Court. The Durbar Hall where the *Huzur* sits, is up those steps.'

Steps and steps, gleaming white in the fierce sun, led from the courtyard, a story high; and on the top step, at the threshold of the Court, sat a thorough-bred English bulldog, looking very fierce and blue-blooded, his mouth open, and his tongue hanging out to cool itself.

I love all dogs, and automatically stopped to pat him as I entered. He licked my hand, and followed me to Counsel's table, curling up on the hem of my garment. The 'Court' sat, very lightly clad indeed in a white muslin *achkan* (like a long shirt), on a roomy swing, hung with strong iron chains from the ceiling. This was apparently the Bench. Under the seat of the swing and attached to it was a musical box. As the Court swung to and fro the musical box played. 'Champagne Charlie is my name' was the tune that greeted me: and the Court beamed upon me.

'That which you have asked is already granted.' Any lawyer will realize my disgust at a win of that kind.

'But do you not wish to hear me plead my case?'

'Without doubt. Did my messengers not beg you to choose your own day and hour so that the hearing might be convenient? But, your demand is already granted ...'

In the half-hearted way in which one would plead a cause, compliance already thrown at one, I proceeded to justify my plea. The elephant must not be disturbed in his tenure. The terms of the deed must be observed.

'They shall be,' said the Court, without calling upon Counsel for himself! And then, to the official, who in that Court wrote the orders of the Court:

'Write,' said he, 'whoever interferes with the grant of the plantation to the elephant 'Heart Emerald' under his deed, shall be trampled to death by wild elephants.'

The musical box still played, another tune now.

The Court turned to me. 'Are you satisfied?'

I said, 'Quite!' and bowing to the Bench left the Court, the dog conducting me to the exit.

Down the steps again, the P.M. following, obsequious, smiling and massaging his hands.

'That was very clever, Miss Sahiba.'

'What was clever?' I said sulkily. 'The Court gave me no chance to be clever. Success was thrown at me, even as I entered.'

'Oh! but it *was* clever to make friends with the dog.'

'Now, whatever do you mean?'

'Did your honour not know that *the Dog* decides the cases in this Court? When the Thakur-Sahib became Raja and Judge in the Durbar Court, he made this plan. He knew no law, and cases were long and tiresome. He devised a remedy. This favourite dog of his should sit at the door of the Court and decide all questions brought before the Durbar. Whomever the dog likes, to him the Huzur gives whatever he desires, even, as you saw, against himself and his own desires.' ...

—*India Calling* (1934)

Making a Hindu Will

I have said that Hindu women have rights of disposition of property by deed or will. And I propose to insert here an experience of my own, in 1933, which seems to me to tell more about orthodox Hindu purdahnashins (not alone in this relationship, but generally as to 'setting' and spiritual horizon) than could be conveyed by talk 'about it and about'.

It is a great undertaking when an orthodox Hindu purdahnashin, sonless and widowed, settles to the making of her will. That she may make one at all is due to enactments of British rule; but these enactments simply give sanction to disposal by testament of that over which she would ordinarily have control in dispositions known to the law of her race and her religion. So she is absolutely free to make her will in the vernacular— in every sense.

She arrives at the decision then that a will must be made. 'I have lived thirty years; this is old age. I may die any moment, and my gods would be unprotected if I did not make provision.' Relations are a secondary consideration, but not unimportant, since, they might believe themselves to have an interest in her death, and might hasten that event. To provide against this possibility she gives them as much as she can while still alive, trying to emphasize the importance of a *living* donor. But they do not always, these countless relations, interpret her actions a right. It is therefore necessary that the important document should be made and registered *and broadcast to the family.*

So it is indicated that a will shall be made. The next step is to find an auspicious day on which to visit Benares and assure herself of the needs and condition of the family idols: do they get enough to eat in the temples already dedicated to them? Are the pilgrims who visit these temples sufficiently cared for? Should her benefactions be for these or for other gods and goddesses? ... And when she does get to Benares, more delays. The auspicious moment for investigation has to be found: the priest, who alone knows the wishes of the gods in question, may be ill or on a journey. But at long last that stage is overpast, and the possibilities, duly listed, are carried back home to the Raj, for submission to her personal spiritual adviser.

Meantime, he also has been holding durbars. The whole district knows that the Rani is making a will, and applicants besiege him. Next in importance to the gods come worthy charities: 'The diseased cows in a certain *taluka* (district) fed hitherto by a pious Hindu, are without a patron. The Hindu has died, and his bounty with him.' Or (from the more enlightened): 'The village where the Rani was born has no school for boys and girls.' Or, again (from social organizations and English foundations): 'The town in which the Rani lives has no hospital for women, and the general hospital lacks an X-Ray department, and a maternity ward'—thus and thus might the Rani do, and make her name great!

Her entourage for miles around is interested in the will, and travels to headquarters with suggestions. Nor is this resented or deemed impertinent. The making of a will is a family concern (in the feudal sense). Not to be interested would be a mark of unfriendliness, even of hostility. 'All contact between us is severed. I have not asked to whom she means to marry her neice, and I have made no suggestions about the disposal of her property,' would be almost a declaration of war. It would cut the gentle Rani to the heart; and she would send discreet emissaries to discover how she had offended. No! the suggestions are 'common form'; and, the claims of the gods having been dealt with, as has been said, in the Sacred City, the Rani returns to tackle the domestic items.

Death ceremonies. 'Set down that my father-in-law's *shradh* must be commemorated by the feeding of twelve priests at Buddh-Gaya, on the anniversary of his death—the priests to be paid according to the amount they consume. They must feed to repletion.'

I have seen such a feeding. The priests fast for days beforehand, and sit cross-legged on one of the stone platforms at the beautiful and ancient city of Buddh-Gaya (of special sanctity for death ceremonies), overlooking the ruins and the great-leaved tree under which Buddha, the conqueror of the flesh and all fleshly impulse, attained Buddhahood. In the near distance is the monastery of the caste Hindus, who through this shradh ceremony have acquired rights, at the Buddhist stronghold of the men who deny caste. The pink-robed priests go in and out of the curved white arches, and the little green parrakeets stagger in and out of the eaves, having buried themselves in the cups of the blood-red flowers of the cotton tree and drunk to intoxication ... it all comes back to mind, with talk of a shradh at Buddh-Gaya.

'For my mother-in-law there must be shradhs at Benares, in the temples she has founded. So many priests must be fed, and so many pilgrims also; and so many cows, and the pigeons who frequent the courtyard.' He the Personal Spiritual Adviser intervenes: 'Is it remembered by the Presence that it is unlucky to turn away any who come to a shradh festival! May it not be as well to say, "Spend so much money on feeding priests and pilgrims, cows and pigeons," rather than to limit the number?'

And it is thus that the clause written: 'For me lord (husband) there must be a seven years' shradh, and then a fourteen, and then a twenty-one years' shradh the duration of the shradh increased by seven years, upon the expiration of each term.'

This rather staggers the P.S.A. 'Huzur', he says gently, 'have you considered about the money needed to carry out this command? We have only that which will be left by yourself. No son is there who will see to it that these wishes are fulfilled, and will add to the money left by you when it is exhausted. The heirs of 'the 8-anna share', the heartless ones, will think of their ancestors alone, and of their own 'brother-ties', and will give never a pice to us and our needs.'

'Well! set in down for now,' says the Rani, 'and tell the *vakil* to find a way.'

With her own shradh she deals summarily: 'Five thousand rupees are to be spent annually upon my own shradh on the anniversaries of my death; and better write also that no more than ten thousand rupees be spent on my funeral ceremonies. You must take me to *Kasi* (Benares) to die, or if the gods are angered with me, and I die before I get there, I must be taken to Benares to be burnt. Jagdish Babu will know about arranging for a special train.'

The 'worthy charities' take months for consideration. But before she arrives at these, some family friction has made the Rani remember that family expectations must be slain forthwith. So the brothers and nephews and nieces and cousin-brothers (especially the cousin-brothers of the third and fourth remove) are summoned to a *Bhojan*—a feast in the Raj palace. The Rani, being purdah, may not be present at the feast; her guests are fed in her name, and at her expense. The morning after the feast the Rani, having bathed and worshipped and consulted her astrologer about the exact hour when she should meet her relatives, comes to the house-of-reception in her palace and sites behind the purdah, her mother and sisters, her brothers and maternal uncles, may be in the reception house beside her; and the others—the remoter relations, her brothers-in-law or nephews-in-law, all the relations of her husband—must be in the outer room. They may neither see her face nor hear her voice. The P.S.A. sits beside her. The officers of her household and her men lawyers sit in the outer room with what an English-knowing member of the family describes as 'the homoeopathic relationships'.

The P.S.A. opens the proceedings: 'The Rani Sahiba has summoned you together because, as you know, she is making her will; and she would take you into confidence. The will is not yet complete; many clauses remain to be written, and the god clauses and the shradh—clauses are not yet formulated. But she would have you hear one clause which is complete.' And he reads: 'For my relations in whatever degree I have made provision and will continue to make provision during my life. They are to get nothing in any shape or form whatsoever under this will. I lay this command upon my trustees.' 'Now,' said the Rani Sahiba to one who sat beside her, as the depressed family members shuffled away—'now is my mind easier. I shall be allowed to live!'

It was four years from the date when the will was first taken in hand that the lawyers were told to put it into legal form, and yet another year before it got any further. From the vakils it went to the barristers to be 'settled', then back again to Benares to an orthodox Hindu barrister who had retired to the Holy City in expectation of death. Many changes did he make, each change having been made on an appropriately auspicious day, and each change in turn being submitted to the testator on a day which had to be equally propitious. When complete the draft was a most diverting document—a delightful mixture of legal formality, of Hindu orthodoxy, and of the mannerisms of my purdahnashin.

The appointment of executors and trustees was a shrewd and cautious proceeding. It included the priesthood for administration of the temple lands and direction of the temple services—it included the least obnoxious of the 'family members', the head of a collateral branch, who was sufficiently rigid in orthodoxy to fear disaster from outraged or hungry idols; and finally (this by the Hani's express command) it included the representative of an English firm of chartered accountants whose duty it would be to check accounts and to see that the priests and 'family member' applied her money to the appointed uses. All trustees were removable upon the vote of the majority—all except the chartered accountant. 'For, of course,' said the Rani, 'if I did not so provide they would remove him and defeat my precaution.'

In final shape the 'god-provisions' were most elaborate, etiquette being carefully observed as to the numbers of *shris* (a term of respect) preceding the name of any god—'*Shri, Shri, Ramji*' or '*Shri, Shri, Shri, Shri, Shri, Kaliji*' (her particular goddess). Provision was made for installation of new gods and goddesses, for repair and upkeep of temples, of temple precincts and priestly dwellings; for feasts to pilgrims and *Kasi-basis*—men and women who had come to live in Kasi (Benares) in expectation of death; first-aid was to be given to sick or moribund temple-goers; schools were to be provided for young children accompanying them. All was carefully regulated and prescribed to the minutest detail, even to the number of temple beneficiaries who were to be of any particular Brahmin sub-caste: '24 *Mithila* Brahmins,' '12 Buhiyar Brahmins,' and so on. The pilgrim's ration of rice and grain was set down; *and his thumb impression was to be taken as a receipt for the 2 annas per head* which was given to this fugitive journeyman to the gates of Death! Social service demand had not gone unheeded. (There's progress for you!) The hospital got its maternity ward and X-ray apparatus, and generous provision was made for 'the *he* and *she* schools' (to quote the English-knowing family member aforesaid).

And now the draft, finally settled, was ready for engrossment. But an unexpected hitch occurred. The P.S.A. advised upon consultation of the astrologers had discovered that the will as drafted was unlucky: the last clause represented an even number; that could not be allowed. The lawyers obligingly readjusted the numbering of clauses. The P.S.A. then declared that, upon like consultation, it was obligatory that the will should be in manuscript, written by a man who had two thumbs to his right hand; if one could be found with double thumbs on both hands the auspices would be the more favourable. By great good luck a maternal uncle could answer the 'most favourable' requisition, and was set to copying the will under the eye of the private secretary and the family vakil.

It was now time to warn the lawyers and witnesses that a certain month would be appropriate for the execution of the will. The actual day could not be announced until the family astrologer returned from a tour upon which he had most inconsiderately set forth, without revealing either his route or the auspicious day. As will be imagined, sorrowful chances such as these are most hazardous to the punctilious legal adviser, who realizes all that may be at stake in disappointing his client. In this respect the kasi-basi legal adviser is best off. For once a kasi-basi, always a kasi-basi. You may never leave Benares once you have entered that sacred city *with intent* to await death: not even the most prematurely depressed victim of influenza may claim exemption from this rule. There is no exit door to the theatre of the kasi-basi. So the kasi-basi of my purdahnashin's will escaped hustling. I myself (not being a kasi-basi) was not so fortunate. At the moment of the astrologer's return and disclosure of a date I was at a place five days' distance by rail from the maker of the will: I had to travel post-haste in response to a telegram which said that a day—the sixth from the receipt of the telegram by myself—was declared to be the *only* auspicious day for execution within the next twelve month! I arrived in time, breathless, to be met by a further shock: the only fortunate hour on that day was, it appeared, the hour of my arrival! ... All necessary parties had been collected, save a doctor. Would I 'collect' the English civil surgeon and a mind of the executant? This was duly arranged, and the great moment arrived. I sat beside my purdahnashin in the inner chamber. In the outer sat a large company of lawyers, officials, the civil surgeon, and material witnesses.

Let no one imagine that a will rightly executed is the secret and almost clandestine proceeding which we make of it in the West. What is there to hide, if intentions are honourable! The will was read aloud to the Rani by the scribe sitting close up against the purdah so that the company in the outer room might also hear. I was then asked to explain the will clause by clause to my purdahnashin in language which she could understand, and clause by clause to ask her if her wishes were therein embodied—explanation, question and answer to be audible, in like manner, to 'the outside'. Then the four-thumbed man wrote at the foot of the will once more that that paper represented the last will and testament of the Rani Sahiba. It was peremptory that the document and his hand as he wrote upon it should be visible to the men in the outer room—though *no more than that* was to be visible. And the civil surgeon, for one, confessed to me afterwards, that the sight of that moving double-thumbed hand was the weirdest thing he had ever seen.

I had then formally to identify my purdahnashin, who affixed her signature to the *first* page of the will. She was also required to sign every other page, but the first signature was the validating one. 'As she signed, her hand and the document had, as with the scribe, to be visible to the groups of people in the outer room. The civil surgeon was the first witness. He was admitted to the inner room, where he examined the lady, discreetly veiled, as to her mental capacity, the independence of her action, etc. Followed the signatures of other witnesses; and we breathed freely when 'The Keeper of High Action' declared that all had been concluded within the time required by the horoscope.

The final formality was registration. The registrar of wills came to the house: identification, signatures, and thumb marks, a new catechism to elicit how far the lady was a free agent—all this had to be faced over again. And a will which had been five years in the making was carried away to safe custody.

—*India Recalled* (1936)

Susie Sorabji
(1868–1931)

Susie Sorabji, sister of Cornelia Sorabji was born in Sholapur. She was the Principal of St Helena's, Poona, described as an international and co-educational school with children of seven nationalities. She also supervised and controlled the two vernacular schools known as St John's. She visited prisons, hospitals, poor-houses, and the Soldiers' Home. She also served on the committees of the Bombay Presidency Council of Women, the Temperance Union, the League of Mercy, the All-India Educational Conference, and other bodies.

Cornelia wrote about her sister Susie in a book entitled *Susie Sorabji: Christian Parsee Educationist of Western India*, published by Oxford University Press in 1934. *The Life of Susie Sorabji* by Humphrey Milford appeared in 1932, also published by Oxford University Press. The road on which St Helena's School stands is named after Susie Sorabji.

Shrimati Ramabai Ranade

Ramabai Ranade the founder and president of the now famous Seva Sadan of Poona, was born in a little hill-girt town, in the Satara district, of a family whose faithful service to the Peshwas had won for them a *jagir* in Devarashtra.

We picture the little Brahmin maiden, sitting on her father's knee, listening wide-eyed, to his stories of saints and gods, and spirits, or watching her mother who was skilled in the knowledge of herbs and plants, distilling remedies for the villagers who came to her to be cured of their ills.

It was in such a wholesome unselfish atmosphere that Ramabai learned her first lessons of love for her fellowmen. No wonder that Justice Ranade found in her an apt pupil, when he began to prepare her (the little thirteen-year old bride, whom he had been compelled by his father to wed) for this great work that she was to do in Poona, after his death—a work that stands today a magnificent monument, showing what a good woman can achieve, if she will but yield herself, a willing instrument, to God's Omnipotent Hand.

We have illuminating glimpses of Ramabai Ranade's early life, in her *Reminiscences*—one such is peculiarly interesting. Her father was going to Poona—that wonderful town of which he used to bring home great stories to amuse his little daughter, as they sat under the shade of the dark trees in the hot afternoons, or beneath the feathery bamboos when the harvest moon rode high in the cloudless sky. For very long Ramabai had coveted a doll—a beautiful doll, such as he told her was to be purchased in the wonder shops, patronized by English people. Now she ventured, as he bade her goodbye, to whisper her wish to him, and obtained a ready promise that when he returned he would bring her what she so desired. For days she went about hugging her delightful secret. At last, to make matters doubly sure, she thought she would breathe her hopes to the tutelary Deity of the house, when she did her morning *pooja*. No one else should know about it! Oh no, it must be a secret between her father, herself and Shiwa the Omnipotent, who was able to make her dream come true! So it was with a certain shock of surprise that she heard her brother say, 'So father is bringing a doll home, for you!' 'How did you know?', asked the little maiden. Was it possible—but not it could not be!—the silent Shiwa would never have betrayed her! Seeing her mystification the teasing brother would not tell her that the simple explanation of her puzzle was a letter he had received from his father, that morning. It is natural incidents like this that help us to see *why* Mrs Ranade understood children so well, and was so loved by them. She never forgot, when with them, that she had once been a child, and so their little troubles and joys were always shared with a sympathy that was as natural to her, as it is rare with others.

When Justice Ranade decided to educate his girl-wife he set himself a task in which he had many opponents in his own household. From the time Ramabai, in the sanctuary of her learned husband's own room, made her first obeisance to the god of learning (Ganesh), to the day when she made her first speech before Sir James Fergusson, the Governor of Bombay, in the Town Hall, in Poona, regarding the necessity of establishing a High School for Indian girls, she had to suffer quiet, but bitter persecution, from the orthodox old women, in her own house. But she allowed nothing to deter her from the course her husband had laid down for her. The bitter taunts she heard, downstairs, could not damp the joy she felt as she sat upstairs, and recited Sanskrit *shloks*, or read Meadow's Taylor's thrilling

Tara or *Sita* aloud to the Judge. What did it matter if, after a joyous afternoon at one of Pandita Ramabai's lectures, on coming home she was outcasted, so to speak, and not allowed to help in the kitchen work with the women of the family, until she had had a bath of purification? Even the water for the bath had to be drawn, (so said the scandalized ladies) from a well outside, not from the fountain, *within* the sacred precincts of their home. Patiently the brave-hearted girl, bent on learning all her husband wished her to know, and on attaining his ideal of an educated wife, pursued her course,—unmurmuringly. Quietly would she pick up the brass or copper vessel given to her, and go out to the dark well to draw water for the ablutions that would fit her to sit amongst her women relations again.

But this dark water brought on a fever which confined her to her bed for many a day. Then it was that Justice Ranade discovered all that she had been enduring, and put his foot down on the petty persecutions that had been going on, under his own roof, of the little girl-wife.

One cannot help thinking that it was thus that Ramabai Ranade learned the lesson of tolerance, and acquired that broadmindedness and sympathy which so fitted her for the presidentship of an institution that aims at giving to Indian women, every opportunity for self-realization and self-expression, and helps them to develop every God-given faculty. In the bracing atmosphere of her Seva Sadan she was able to give to her countrywomen what the human soul craves so ardently, and what is, in fact, its birthright.

Happy days, however, were in store for her—the Judge was appointed to Nasik, and there, at last, Ramabai had the joy of managing her own house. The golden memories, stored up in those days, helped immeasurably in brightening the dreariness of the ones that followed her husband's death. Whether in the house attending to the duties that every wife loves to perform, the duties that constitute the mysterious art of home-making (and are of an intellectual as much as of a social character), or in the garden which she so loved, where she coaxed the fragrant mogra, or the stately rose to grow, Ramabai's heart sang merrily.

She used to tell of how, when the Judge, in order to test her practical knowledge, asked her what sum she need for the household monthly expenses, she who had never been allowed in Poona to know anything of the inner working of the domestic arrangements, named a figure below what was actually needed, and how, as the end of the month approached, when it hardly seemed possible that the little sum would last out the time, she was overcome with anxiety and shame, because she feared the emptiness of the household exchequer was due to her lack of economy. She would not speak, however, of the trouble, and tried to eke out the sum, till the true state of affairs was discovered by the kind Judge who assured her she had done splendidly, and that he had only been waiting for her to ask him for more money. The next household budget was, you may be sure, more accurately and more generously drawn up.

In Nasik, where some of the happiest days of her life were spent, Ramabai found a family that seemed a link, between the old orthodox world that had tried to hold so tyrannical a sway over her, and the new progressive world that was beckoning to her to come and taste the joys of freedom, education, culture and reform. This family were keenly interested in social service, and, encouraged by their example, Ramabai began taking part in activities that had the good of others as their object. She presided, at a school prize-giving, about this time, and was much interested in the school-children to whom she distributed the prizes.

But life is made up of sunshine and shadow, and the clouds gathered over Ramabai's horizon, when Justice Ranade in the course of his duties contracted cholera in a cholera-infected district. In a public resthouse the faithful young wife nursed him. Who can describe the agony of mind through which she passed in that lonely vigil by the sick man's bed. The local doctor declared his pulse was failing, and in her anguish she felt she must seek comfort in prayer, and so she stole out into the gathering darkness and made her way into the little temple in the courtyard, where sad and weary pilgrims for scores of years had sought and found relief in their despair, bowing, not surely as much to the little stone image there, as to the great God Who bids us seek His face; and to Whom the heavy-laden, stretching forth imploring hands into the darkness, cry 'Have mercy on me!' There, in the dimly lighted temple, the weeping women fell prostrate and poured out her heart to him Who alone could help her, and felt a sudden peace steal over her. Somehow she knew her prayer had been answered, and she stole back to her post at the sick man's side, comforted and strengthened. Mr Ranade recovered, and it was not till 1901, that he passed away.

Smitten, and well nigh overwhelmed, Ramabai shut herself up for a little; but then came the thought of the suffering womanhood around her, and it was in that temporary seclusion that she consecrated her life to the service of her country-women. Forgetting, or rather laying aside, her own sorrow, she went forth to minister to others in like trouble and to lift their eyes to the great fields of labour, the golden harvest of opportunity that awaited their sickles. New vistas opened before them, where hitherto they had seen nothing but a blank wall. Yes, to these hopeless and despairing ones she, like her friend Pandita Ramabai, came with a message of hope, of possibilities of service and usefulness, and bade them rise, and follow her. Together they ministered to the captive women in prison, to whom she took the sympathy and cheer they so much needed, to keep them from despair. They visited the little lads in the Reformatory, who were being given a chance to make good, and fit themselves for honest citizenship. Nor was the bedside of the sick and dying forgotten; and the hospital where lived the mentally afflicted ones. Around her she gathered a band of women who used to gather, week by week, to listen to lectures on how to render First Aid to the injured, to work for the poor, and to hear accounts of women in other lands who served their fellows.

Where did she dream that beautiful dream of a Home of Service, where would come as helpers all those whose hearts God had touched with love for the great suffering world? One cannot tell, perhaps, as she sat at the feet of her husband, that prince of reformers, listening to his inspiring words; or in those dark days, where a simple English or Sanskrit lesson was taken in her husband's room; or when attendance at a lecture given by her friend Pandita Ramabai would bring down a storm of opposition and reproach. At any rate the dream became a reality, and one wonderful day, she formulated her plans, organized the work which has grown, so marvellously, into the colossal Institution, known as the Poona Seva Sadan, with its branches all over the Presidency of Bombay.

How does the mighty oak grow from the little acorn. Who can follow the miraculous process? One can only watch, and wonder, and rejoice.

As early as 1904, at the all India Women's Conference in Bombay, Mrs Ranade outlined the nature of the social service she proposed should be carried on by those whose motto, she declared, was to be 'Life is a sacred trust.' How fully she herself realized her trusteeship, every day of her selfless life proved.

The great Seva Sadan had its inaugural meetings in Mrs Ranade's own house (that home where her husband had brought the girl-wife whom he was to train for service. From a small attempt on the part of the members of 'The Hindu Ladies Social and Literary Club' to educate women by means of regular classes and institutions, started to impart instruction of a religious, literary, medical and industries character, the work gradually grew into the splendid organization it is, and was at the time of Mrs Ranade's death.

In a brief review, written by her ten years after she began, she set forth some of the principal objects of the Seva Sadan. These were:

(a) To teach and educate women by means of regular classes and to impart instruction of a religious, literary, scientific, medical, and industrial character. To teach them the principles of First Aid, Hygiene, Sanitation and Domestic Economy.

(b) To widen the range of women's knowledge by means of libraries, lectures, publications, books, magazines etc., and by tours, excursions, and other popular methods.

(c) To enable women to participate intelligently in all domestic, social and national responsibilities, and to inculcate in their minds, the principles of self-reliance and mutual helpfulness.

(d) To train women to render in a patriotic spirit, educational, medical, and philanthropic service to the motherland, and to their brothers and sisters in specially backward areas.

(e) To help in the promotion of national work in all these, and similar ways for the social, material, and educational uplift of Indian women.

(f) To promote greater fellowship amongst the women of India.

(g) To start institutions for the promotion of these objects and ideals, and to affiliate those that are working for them.

(h) To adopt such measures as will be conducive to the furtherance of these objects.

(i) To work directly to promote the all-round well-being of Indian womanhood.

Everyone of these objects, this brave worker kept in view throughout the fifteen years she presided over the destiny of this Institution.

One of Mrs Ranade's greatest achievements was the establishment of the Seva Sadan Nursing and Medical Associations. It was due to her inspiration and influence, alone, that high caste Hindu widows and girls volunteered to take up a work, that above all others, is crying set to be done, in India. What marvellous forces she was harnessing for the service of the women and children of India when she took her first batch of probationers to the Samona Hospital Nursing Department, even Mrs Ranade did not know! But all through the coming years, there will be a stream of women pouring into the hospitals, to be equipped for service to the suffering women and girls of this land! It was her hand that unlocked the door that will and *must* remain open, as long as there are pain and suffering in our land.

The ordinary social worker, surveying the field of work before her might easily have been discouraged, but Mrs Ranade's incurable optimism saw no obstacles saw indeed only the greatest opportunities for service and seized them. There was hardly a phase of work to which she and her workers did not turn their attention. To the Home with its wide open doors, came widows, who sought hope and comfort, and found it in serving others; young girls with aims and hopes, and a longing to fit themselves for a wider life; little children who needed protection and love; the sick and sorrowful who claimed aid and advice. For all and sundry the Seva Sadan had help, and to all Mrs Ranade, the loving mother and sympathizer, opened her heart. In the world of education, her help was claimed on text book and similar committees; she was the leader in Poona of an agitation for compulsory primary education for girls. Her reputation as a writer was established by the production of her book *Reminiscences*, now regarded as a Marathi classic.

In politics, the versatility of this wonderful woman was evidenced when she threw herself heart and soul into the campaign begun to obtain the vote for Indian women. Surely a new era dawned for India, when she presided over a gigantic meeting of women who crowded (twenty or thirty deep) round the courtyard of the Seva Sadan, up to the second or third story and even on the roof, to listen in rapt silence, to the eloquent speeches of those, who like their western sisters, were awakened to their duties and privileges as citizens.

Sir H. Lawrence, a member of the Executive Council, declared at the excited debate on the question of Woman's Suffrage, that he would consider it an honour to serve on a Council of which Mrs Ramabai Ranade was a member.

She anticipated members of Council who to-day are introducing bills regarding a widow's title, or the lack of it, to her husband's property, by organizing lectures and debates in order to educate public opinion, to demand the alteration of the law to suit present day conditions. Before she could accomplish much, however, she died.

A few years before her death, she was asked by the Poona Municipality to undertake the care of the thousands of women pilgrims and their little children, who attend the Annual Fair, at Alandi. With her faithful band of workers, who seemed, from the very first, to have caught her spirit of love and devotion, she set forth for the sacred place, and there in the temple courtyard, day and night, she and her co-workers stood, organizing the women's visits to the shrine, taking charge of the infants while some weary pilgrim slipped in, to lay her offerings and her prayers, at the feet of the god. Through the hot days, they would deal out cool draughts of water to the poor thirsty ones, and so really and materially did they improve the condition of these countless frightened hordes of women, that they came and fell at Mrs Ranade's feet in gratitude for the very real help rendered them.

Since her initiation of this great branch of Social Work, the Seva Sadan has been asked to work in co-operation with the provincial Committee in organizing National Health, and Baby Sections, in the Exhibition that is held by the Municipality, for the benefit of the pilgrims that flock to Alandi from all over India.

One of her outstanding characteristics was her inability to see that there was anything extraordinary in her undertakings. Some one said to her one day, 'Dear Mrs Ranade, how wonderful it is, that you should be able to do so much, and such great things for God!' 'Oh no!' she exclaimed quickly, 'there is nothing wonderful in what I am doing. I was fortunate in being the instrument that happened to be lying nearest God's Hand; and so He picked me up, and used me!' 'There lies the secret,' answered her friend, 'It is because you lie so near His Hand, that He uses you.'

Soon after her husband's death, when in her utter misery she shut herself up for a little, there went to her an English friend, one who divined that the only consolation for Mrs Ranade lay in consoling others. 'Come with me,' she said, 'and let us carry a ray of sunshine to those who are shut out, alas, by their own wrong-doing, from the world.' And so she carried her off to the captive women in Yeravda Jail. With that wonderful gift of sympathy that she possessed in such limitless measure, this good woman became the 'prison angel' to these unfortunate women, throwing herself, heart and soul, into the work she continued so faithfully for over twenty years.

Nothing deterred her from those fortnightly visits to the jail, not the length, and loneliness of the drive out there nor yet the apparent hopelessness of the task before her. Summer or winter rain or shine, her brougham used to be seen driving up to the big iron gates, behind which were so many miserable sin-burdened souls. Her gentle sympathetic inquiries about their health, and comfort soon drew a crowd of women round her; and then, when they had all gathered, generally about two hundred, in the open courtyard, she would read aloud an Abhang of Tukaram's which she would translate into simple language, explaining the uplifting thoughts, and sentiments, to those who had wandered so far—so very far—alas, from the path of righteousness. And as she read into the hard faces would steal a softness as new as it was beautiful, and eyes, unused to tears, would grow moist and wistful, as new thoughts and aspirations and longings were aroused by the gentle pleading of the one whose visits made the prison less dismal, and their lot less intolerable.

Is it surprising that away in far-off Africa a dying Indian woman on being told she could not live much longer, gathered her new-born babe to her breast, and made up her mind, in her agony of fear, to cross the (to her) terrible ocean, in order to lay it in the motherly arms of her friend Ramabai Ranade? How faithfully she tended the helpless infant, till the boy grew to manhood, is a story by itself.

Then came the end. It was a hot April afternoon, when the Angel of Death hovered over the chamber where the great woman lay dying. For some days she had been ill—in agony, but oh so brave, so uncomplaining, so calm, even to the very end, thinking of others, rather than of herself. It was not, however, till the western sun had dipped behind the ghats, and the sudden darkness of the oriental night had settled down, upon the crowded city, that her soul took its flight to God.

They laid her in the large hall that bore her name—a noble beautiful figure she lay there, wrapped in her snow-white draperies, and covered with the fragrant roses and mogras she had loved so well to weave into garlands to adorn the life-sized portrait of her husband that always held the place of honour in her simple room.

The news of her passing, soon spread through the city and they came, one and all,—men, women and children—an endless procession, to file in silent reverence, past her who had been a mother to her people, Ramabai, the friend the enthusiast, the worker! She had spent her years in the uplift of her people. She had blazed the trail for them in a practically trackless wild! Who, who would follow her? Thank God, there are many—many noble women, from her own dearly loved Seva Sadan, who have taken up the torch her dying hands dropped, who are now carrying on the glorious work she started and who are adding to their ranks every day, devoted, well-equipped, enthusiastic workers whose one object in life is to strive for the uplift and betterment of suffering humanity.

—*Women in Modern India* (1929)

Dr Rukhmabai
(1864–1955)

Rukhmabai was born in Bombay in 1864, and while her early education was at home, her further education was in England. She studied at the London School of Medicine for Women and at the Royal Free Hospital. She was the Medical Officer for Women in Surat for twenty-two years, Zenana Medical Officer for Women's Hospital in Rajkot for twelve years, and the first secretary of the Arya Mahila Samaj. She retired from active service in 1930. Sudhir Chandra in his book on the case *Enslaved Daughters* (1998) remarks in a footnote that Rukhmabai was the first doctor to be given charge of a dispensary established at Surat under what was popularly known as the Countess of Dufferin Movement (the National Association for Supplying Female Medical Aid to the Women of India). He writes: 'Such was her dedication to her work, and the popularity she won, that the dispensary, named after Sheth Mararbhai Vijbhukhandas, the donor who provided money for it, continues to be popularly known as the Rukhmabai Hospital even today, a hundred years after she joined it. Significantly, the local legend does not remember her as a martyr to the cause of women's emancipation.'

Although *Who's Who of Women in India* carries an entry on Rukhmabai, it makes no mention of the case that actually brought her fame—her refusal to go to the home of the man she had been married to as a child. To quote Sudhir Chandra once again: 'I was browsing through Malabari's *Indian Spectator* when I saw a report about a young woman of twenty-five who told a British Indian High Court in 1887 that she would willingly endure a maximum punishment it would accord to her but would not obey its command to go to a husband whom she disliked.'

Among Rukhmabai's most famous supporters were Behramji M. Malabari (1853–1912), Henry Curwen (1845–1920), editor of the *Times of India* and grandson of Wordsworth, and Pandita Ramabai. Rukhmabai herself wrote several letters pseudonymously to the *Times of India*. Eventually Queen Victoria intervened, dissolved Rukhmabai's marriage, and commuted her sentence. Rukhmabai then went to England to study medicine and returned to India to head a Hindu hospital in Poona. Rukhmabai was married at the age of eleven to Dadaji Bhikaji and lived with her parents and studied in school. When her husband decided it was time for her to go to live with him, she refused to do so.

Cornelia Sorabji discusses the case in *India Calling* (1934). She writes: 'About the time of which I write, *Rukhmabai's Case* has stirred the Zenana to its depths all over the Bombay Presidency ... She went to prison. "Was the World coming to an end?" said the Zenana. Not a quiver of sympathy from "the Inside" greeted her courage. The newspapers of the day wrangled over her, varying in direct ratio to their Hindu orthodoxy. Rukhmabai never read the papers, and cared nothing. She had found herself. That was all there was to it—an unusual and fine character, silent and almost stolid. She did not want to marry anyone else, or indeed to marry at all. She wanted to study; to be a doctor. ... In due course Rukhmabai returned as a doctor to India, and has served her country with ability and dignity. Throughout her active professional life, she remained unemotional, and untouched by the hysteria of politics or "Women's Rights", nor—and this seems to be her greatest achievement—has she suffered for this at the hands of the progressive hysterical women of later days. "No Patriot"—"Betrayer of Your Country"—the jibes thrown at the steady workers who refused to be entangled with the moment's politics—have never been thrown at her.'

Letter to the *Times*, 9 April 1887

Bombay, 17 February 1887

My dear Madam,—I would thank you very much for the interest you so kindly take in my unfortunate trial, and in my native sisters in general. I learn from my friend ... that you would like to know the particulars of my still pending case more minutely than I had written to you in my first letter.

Before explaining my own troubles, I should like to state a few facts concerning our disastrous child-marriage custom, which has enslaved the daughters (and even sons to a certain degree) of India for centuries. In our vast country, right from the Himalayas to Cape Comorin, it has become a rule that every individual must be married be it a lame, blind, or diseased one. And by this rule it has become customary to betroth every child, male or female, at the age of five or six but in higher classes at the minimum of one or two years of age and sometimes (girls) even before they are born. Among the Hindoos only there are more than a thousand different castes, and inter-marriages even between the sects of slightest differences are strictly prohibited. This being the case and by the pressure of child marriage, every parent is obliged to marry its child within the limit of the age and within the limit of its own caste, be it a fit or unfit match. In this way a robust promising youth gets a rickety consumptive wife, while an intelligent girl gets an inferior husband. Now for the Sastras and the Hindoo laws. It is clearly stated in our religious books that a boy should be entitled by the moony or thread ceremony to become a regular student from the age of eight years. After that he should study for twelve years, and then after having a good experience in the world for four years more should be allowed to marry at the age of twenty-two with a girl of suitable age and with his own accord. Well, for girls also it is stated that they should be allowed to marry if they become of age and with their own choice, though nothing has been said for their education. We find in ancient history marriages taking place between the boys and girls of mature ages and with their own liking. But these good laws have ceased to be observed and other pernicious customs have taken their place, the results of which lie before us if many horrible forms. As for castes, no more than four distinct classes—the Brahmins, the Kshatrias, the Vayshias, and the Sudras—are mentioned in our religion. But during the past two or three thousand years there has been a growing tendency to split up these four classes into many divisions, so that in some castes there are scarcely a few hundred people. By this fact it is clearly difficult for parents to find suitable and reasonable marriages for their children. Both the father of the boy and of the girl in looking for a husband or a wife for his child pay greater attention to the respectability and standing of the family than to the personal attributes of the child itself.

Lately, by the descent of India's fortune stars, all the worthy commands and precepts of our sacred religion were disobeyed and uncared for through ignorance and superstition, the consequences of which have proved deadly fatal, and India's material, physical, and spiritual condition has been totally ruined, and now she has piteously and helplessly to look to foreigners to get through the folly of her own people.

Now for my own misfortunes I belong to the second class of castes, in which, fortunately, widow re-marriage is allowed. In 1867 my own father died, leaving me, an orphan of two-and-a half years of age, in the care of my mother (then seventeen years of age) and my maternal grandfather. Six years after that my mother was re-married with a celebrated doctor in Bombay, who proved an unusually kind stepfather to me. He protected and loved me as his own child throughout his life, but by the will of the Almighty his useful life was cut short, and for these twenty-two months, dear lady, he rests very far from us, leaving his widow and five children behind lamenting in vain. Well, according to the above-mentioned facts, I was married at the age of eleven years (an age rather beyond the limit of the fixed marriageable age in girls) with a boy of nineteen, on conditions that he should thoroughly be provided by us, but that he should study and become a good man. To these conditions he, his mother (who died a few months after the marriage), and relations had quite agreed. However, in a few months after the marriage in 1876 ... he began to neglect his duties, leaving the school, and, disobeying my father and grandfather, fell into bad company. I should rather say the consequence of which was that he fell sick, and was attacked with consumption, confined to his bed for three continuous years, in such a state that he was not expected to live another season. But by God's grace he recovered a little day by day ... Now, as for myself, being of much reserved disposition from childhood, I had a great liking for study while a great disgust for married life; and though not fortunate enough to attain school after the age of eleven years to complete Marathi studies, I began to learn English at home after leaving the school. I used to ask a number of pronunciations and meanings of English words at a time whenever my European lady friends happened to call. Day by day my love for education and social reform increased, and I continued to pursue my studies as much as I could; but in this country it is very hard for women to study at home. But constant association with the people who had tried to devote their lives to the social reform of India, and by the aid of the little education which I had been able to gain I began seriously to consider the former and present condition of our Hindoo women, and wished to do something, if in my power, to ameliorate our present sufferings. On the other hand, the ... habits of the man with whom I had been given in marriage added more to my natural distaste for married life. However, my father, considering his constitution, habits, and unfitness for any work, resolved not to send me to his house to live as his wife. He also seemed indifferent to the matter ... but by some former disputes between the leaders of our castes and the constant instigations of wicked people (very common in India), and in the hope of getting my little money, he was induced to file a suit to make me go and live as his wife. On the 19th of March 1884, he filed it in the Bombay High Court, thinking that by this action my father would be afraid of losing his reputation (because to have a suit of this kind in a Court is considered a greatest disgrace among us Hindoos), and would quietly send me to his house with all that I possessed. Our party, having resolved long before never to send me to his house, did not care for his suit in that point (but, of course, money matters and the result of the suit were the points of deep interest), and so we began to prepare ourselves for the defence as it became necessary. On the 21st of September 1885, the humane decision was given in my favour by Mr Justice Pinhey without taking our offence. The decision, if it had been supported, would have altered the fate of millions and millions of daughters of India, and the longed-for freedom would have been easily secured. In the same way Mr Justice Pinhey's name would have been made immortal. But it seemed the will of God that it should not be so; for the man appealed the case, on which it was decided on the 2nd of April 1886 by the Chief Justice, Sir Charles Sargent, and Mr Justice Bayler that the first decision should be reversed, and that the case should be sent back for re-trial. Since then it is still pending in the Court.

In our matrimonial laws, or rather in the prevailing customs, a man can marry any number of wives at a time, or whenever he chooses to do so, keeping all of them with him, or driving away those for whom he does not care much; while a woman is wedded once for all. She cannot remarry even after the death of her first husband, nor can she deny to live with him even on reasonable grounds. He may ill-treat her, beat her, drive her away a thousand times, keep her without food, but she must submit to her lot and stay with him (if he keeps her) till she dies a natural death or is killed by him, her sole lord and master. Is it not inhuman that our Hindoo men should have every liberty while women are tied on every hand for ever? If I were to write you all about this system of slavery it would require months to complete it; but I refrain from doing so as everybody, even in England, is aware of it to some extent. The only thing I can hope is that it should be amended some day. Oh! but who has the power to venture and interfere in the customs and notions of such a vast multitude except the Government which rules over it? And as long as the Government is indifferent to it I feel sure that India's daughters must not expect to be relieved from their present sufferings. From some of the quotations in our old religious books I find it stated that women may marry in case of following five misfortunes:—(1) if she is a child-widow; (2) if her husband has become a saint; (3) if he is wanting in manhood; (4) if he has converted; and (5) if he is a leper. None of these suit me in my misfortunes; but I also find that a woman can deny to become his wife before the consummation of marriage. However, these quotations are not unfortunately *reckoned* in the English book on Hindoo laws.

It seems to me to be an inevitable duty of the present Government (in spite of our old laws and customs) to have the most urgently required reform, suitable to the present age and state of the country. Everywhere a law needs revision in at least a few centuries, to suit the prevailing ages; and how is it possible that our Hindoo matrimonial laws, formed about thousands of years ago, suit the present age (an age half-Europeanized)? The only way to face the difficulties is the law reform. For many years social reformers are trying to eradicate these pernicious customs, struggling hard in vain. Lately Mr Malabari (a Parsee gentleman) and his colleagues have roused the whole of India through their formidable efforts among innumerable opponents and few advocates; they have created a great stir throughout India to abolish child marriages and enforced widowhood. But alas! what can one person do without unity and support? By their continuous perseverance and requests the Indian Government was kind enough to make inquiries into the matter, asking the opinions of many influential Hindoo gentlemen: but to the greatest dissatisfaction of every reformer, the numbers of the opponents to the intended reform surpassed that of advocates, and all the aspirations of anxious reformers were thus at an end.

Everywhere it is considered one of the greatest blessings of God that we are under the protection of our beloved Queen Victoria's Government, which has its worldwide fame for best administration. If such a Government cannot help and unyoke us Hindoo women, what Government on earth has the power to relieve the daughters of India from their present miseries?

This 50th year of our Queen's accession to the most renowned throne is the jubilee year in which every town and every village in her dominions is to show their loyalty in the best way it can and wish the Mother-Queen a long happy life to rule over us for many years with peace and prosperity. At such an unusual occasion will the mother listen to an earnest appeal from her millions of Indian daughters and grant them a few simple words of change into the books on Hindoo law—that 'marriages performed before the respective ages of twenty in boys and fifteen in girls shall not be considered legal in the eyes of the law if brought before the Court.' This mere sentence will be sufficient for the present, to have enough check on child marriages, without creating a great vexation among the ignorant masses.

This jubilee year must leave some expression on us Hindoo women and nothing will be more gratefully received than the introduction of this mere sentence into our law books. It is the war of a day if God wished it, but without His aid every effort seems to be in vain. So far, dear lady, I have dwelt on your patience, I which an apology is necessary. With best compliments, I remain, yours very sincerely.

Rukhmabai

—*Enslaved Daughters* (1998)

Purdah—The Need for its Abolition

It is an extraordinary thing what unnatural cruelties can be perpetrated all over the world under the crushing weight of long-established custom and superstition. Open air and sunlight may not be denied to plants and animals if healthy growth is to be secured and yet, under strict Purdah conditions, they are denied to women young and old all through their lives. From the time they attain puberty, numbers of young girls, Hindu and Mahomedan, often just children in instinct and feeling, retire into seclusion. They see no men except those of their own household; they go out veiled or in closed and curtained conveyances when they do go out at all; and even this degree of liberty is denied them under the stricter Purdah conditions.

Purdah, the seclusion of girls who have attained puberty, is a Mahomedan institution more rigidly enforced in north India. In that part of the country, it has been frequently adopted by the Hindus, especially in Rajputana. It does not prevail at all among south Indian Hindus; or among the people of Maharashtra and a large section of Gujarat, or in the Madras and Bombay Presidencies. As a result of this, it is less rigid among the poor Mahomedans of South India. Unfortunately there is a tendency, even at the present day, for communities that have not originally adopted Purdah to do so as a mark of growing social status and prosperity. The Kathiawaris, for instance, have adopted it only in the past fifty years; and doctors working among them have already felt the deplorable physical results of this adoptions, the increase of tuberculosis and of early maternal mortality.

Purdah differs very much in the degree of seclusion practised in various parts of the country. At its best and especially among the poor classes, women can move about on the public road and go about their outdoor work with a veil over their faces. If rich they can use curtained conveyances, and social intercourse of a restricted kind is not denied them. Even under such conditions the system is an infliction on the natural dignity of womanhood, and, on the purely physical side, results still in a deplorable lack of air and exercise that will lead to the physical deterioration of the race. On the other hand Purdah may be so rigid that a woman may, among the poor, be confined to a small house, practically windowless or with openings high up in the walls, and she may not leave the house even to fetch water for household purposes. However poor the household, she can take no share in the work, except for the cooking which she can do indoors. It has been said that a Rajputani may not leave her house to fetch water though the house may be in a jungle and the well in front of it. The experience of doctors working among these *Purdah nashin* women is a tragic revelation of numberless cases of tuberculosis, stunted growth, disease, both among the women themselves and their children.

Purdah has pressed least hard on the very poor and the rich. For the rich there could be alleviations, air and light were not denied them, in the physical or in the cultural sense. There have been in Indian history, many very cultured Moghul and Rajput princesses. They had spacious gardens, they painted and read. For the poor the demands of hard necessity often raised the veil, though less so in India than in other Moslem countries and much less so in North than in South India. The conditions of modern town life have also intensified the worst physical evils of Purdah.

If in the richer houses, especially the household of those princes and zamindars who have adopted Purdah, there is less suffering from lack of the elementary essentials such as air and sunlight, the mental effect is still often disastrous. Because of the restrictions on education, companionship, and the development of outside interests, women are thrown for companionship on the society of female servants, and the atmosphere is often clouded with domestic gossip, jealousy, intrigue. Undoubtedly numerous instances may be quoted of Moghul and Rajput ladies, cultured in the arts and music, living within Zenana walls a free and liberal life. But these instances are not numerous enough to be considered any real alleviation of the system and assuredly they are not a justification of it.

Women of the wealthier classes and of the aristocracy have in other countries contributed considerably to social and philanthropic work. Purdah has been a restriction on the activities of a considerable body of women similarly situated in India, and the country has suffered thereby. Voluntary social enterprise has lagged behind in India as compared with other countries and in India itself those provinces where Purdah prevails are far behind those where women have been able to do organized social work.

Progress is being made, though with painful slowness in the attempt, to increase the spread of education within Purdah. Even as this paper is being written one reads of a Girl Guide Rally held at Secundrabad under Purdah, of a Women's Conference on Educational Reform to be held at Ajmere-Merwera in Rajputana, the stronghold of Hindu Purdah, the conference in its agenda laying considerable stress on the need for physical training. One reads of Purdah Clubs with facilities for games and social intercourse. In all these cases, 'under Purdah' implies the absence of men from the proceedings. The Women's Political Conference recently held at Meerut was more militant in spirit! There the Purdah arrangements provided for the ladies were strongly resented by them, and it was not until all the screens and curtains were removed that they would enter the pandal!

The attempt to educate girls while still maintaining Purdah conditions has led to many comic anomalies. An Urdu primary teacher may often have to take her normal examination in the practice of teaching under a male Inspector of Schools. In that case both the teacher and the class may be in Purdah, while the Inspector sits outside behind a screen, with the guidance of a senior lady teacher inside who affords assistance by remarking, 'Now the teacher is writing on the black-board,' 'Now the class is doing an exercise.' The unfortunate man on his part has been known to complain of being stifled, as the windows on his side are firmly closed, so that no chink of light may assist him to glimpse behind the curtains.

A sweeping change through legislation would finally be a simpler matter than cautious attempts at compromise. Turkey has completely abolished Purdah by such legislation.

A very slow and laborious method has often been suggested and occasionally followed of attacking this institution by education, by a method of house-to-house visiting in order to teach Moslem girls, and by holding classes under secluded conditions and at times when it is possible for these girls to leave their domestic work. But the method is slow, laborious and very costly in proportion to the results attained. These attempts, though praiseworthy, are an ineffective means of dealing with the strongly conservative influence of the older women of the house. And this influence is often a very strong factor in the Moslem Purdah household. Such women have no outside interests, and have often a dominating personality. With adult natures and no general interests or education, this personality is a considerable reactionary force in all domestic affairs, against which the invasion of the house-to-house visitor is ineffectual. If schools are provided, it is practically impossible to enforce regular attendance. In fact it has been stated ironically by an educational authority that, 'It would be as easy and far more profitable for a provincial Government to legislate against child-marriage as to enforce the regular school attendance of girls and prolongation of such attendance after puberty.' This applies to Purdah as to child marriage. Under such conditions, the adoption of compulsory primary education for Moslem girls becomes almost impossible.[1]

Surely the work lies in the hands of the younger women who have energy and enthusiasm to work decisively for the immediate abolition of this deplorable custom, which by causing unhealthy conditions for mothers drains the national vigour, and which degrades India in the eyes of the world.

—*Women in Modern India* (1929)

[1]A beginning in compulsory education for Moslim girls had however just been made in some Municipal Schools in Bombay City—*Editor*.

Maharani Chimnabai Gaekwad II of Baroda (b. c 1870)

The Maharani Chimnabai Gaekwad II of Baroda, Dr Muthulakshmi Reddy and the Rani of Mandi were among the women who were concerned with the practical aspects of women's lives and their uplift. Muthulakshmi wrote about Health, the Rani of Mandi busied herself with Education (she wrote several articles on the subject), and the Maharani of Baroda with employment, both for women inside the home and outside.

In her Preface to *The Position of Women in Indian Life* (1911) she says, 'During the course of several visits to the West, both to Europe and America, I was naturally struck by the difference between the position of woman in English and in Indian public life, as represented by her share in the organizations for human welfare in the two countries. The cooperation which exists between Western men and women in public affairs is practically unknown in India.' Anxious to use her experiences abroad for the benefit of Indian women, the Maharani of Baroda decided to write about them 'with the hope that some of the organizations might be adapted to the conditions of my native land.' In this she was helped by S.M. Mitra who shared her preoccupations.

In his Note S.M. Mitra says the book is an account 'not of the present status of the female sex in India, but of some Western feminine institutions, the adaptation of which to suit Eastern requirements is likely to help Indian women achieve a higher position in public life than they at present hold.'

The Position of Women in Indian Life includes chapters on Matrons and Superintendents, Women Inspectors, Hotels, Shops, Arts and Crafts, Domestic Science, Philanthropic Work and so on.

Commenting on the book Margaret Cousins writes in *Indian Womanhood Today*: 'Nor can the influence of Her Highness the Maharani of Baroda be under-estimated. Her book *The Position of Women in Indian Life*, published in 1911 is a classic on the Women's Movement and Ideals of thirty years ago. All her life she has lead women into new spheres of freedom, and it was entirely due to her initiative and courage that the All-India Women's Conference in its first session, which had been called to discuss Educational Reform, immediately started a social reform agitation for a Law against Child Marriage.'

Margaret Cousins' note on the Maharani reads: 'One born to rule. As much at home in the courts and capitals of Europe as in India. When she was sixty, after lunching me off a gold plate, and showing me the artistic Parisian setting of her pearls, she briefed me as to how I might put the case before the late Gaekwad for reformed inheritance rights for women, and for the initiation of such laws in Baroda. And then she brought me to her tennis court and played three spanking sets of tennis with tip-top tennis players. She had led Indian womanhood with spirit and vision since she published her book in 1911. But now she deplores the way modern women are interesting themselves in politics. Though she has retired from public life she is still 'La Grande Dame' and retains the old fire and 'the grand manner'.

Married in 1885, the Maharani was the second wife of Maharaja Sayaji Rao Gaekwad of Baroda. She travelled to Europe with her husband who was keen on her helping him bring progress to Baroda. Writing in 1901 in the journal The Nineteenth Century, her husband said that it had been her influence that convinced him to encourage his subjects to educate and emancipate their daughters. In 1907 an Anglo-vernacular school for girls was established in Baroda.

Her daughter Indira married the Brahmo heir to the throne of Cooch Behar, the son of Sunity Devee. Indira's daughter Gayatri Devi of Jaipur wrote A Princess Remembers (1995).

Intellectual Callings

'God has placed no limits to the exercise of the intellect he has given us on this side the grave.'—Bacon.

There are countless ways now in which a woman may exercise the powers of her busy brain. She may go in for chemistry, and, like Madame Curie, give to the world some fresh discovery—such as radium—as the result of her scientific research. As a woman doctor she may perform skilful operations with unflinching nerve. She may enter the realm of literature and win distinction as authoress or journalist. Or she may follow a path in which she is universally admitted to stand unrivalled—the teaching of the young. All these main roads with their many side-tracks are open to her; but as the secrets of success in these callings have been publicly discussed so often, we propose to pass them over and to treat of only one or two in which the women of India will be perhaps on less familiar ground. The first of these is LECTURING—a field which might prove highly interesting for the intellectual woman who has a gift for speaking and a love of imparting information. Here, as elsewhere, the cardinal rule is specialization, but specialization on top of a broad general knowledge. Choose a special topic, one for which you have a particular love, make yourself thoroughly mistress of it, and your enthusiasm will communicate itself to the audience. In England the University Extension Societies do much to encourage lecturing by organizing courses on different subjects at various centres, and, by applying to these bodies, a woman who possesses a university degree or its equivalent, and some testimonials as to qualifications for lecturing, may be appointed on their list of lecturers. She is required to give a test lecture before the University authorities before her application can meet with success.

In connection with art, music, literature, nursing, hygiene, domestic science, social schemes, there is an infinite variety of subjects to choose from, and if lecturing-tours on an extended scale were organized and carried out by eloquent speakers, they might become a feature of women's life in India which would do much to broaden their mental outlook. Science is a subject of which women of all classes are mostly very ignorant. Physiology, too, is a domain in which they badly need instruction. The woman lecturer who organized a series of interesting addresses on such themes would probably meet with an enthusiastic reception, and her audience would find the facts of science put in attractive fashion even more enthralling and much more practical than most general literature. A popular lecturer on art, science, etc., could earn a considerable sum, while those who undertake the work merely for the love of it will find it a valuable intellectual training. The effort necessary to systematize one's information, to present it in the clearest and most pleasing form to the audience, is a splendid method of mental culture for the lecturer herself. Immediately after a University Extension Lecture is finished there is a certain time set apart for answering any questions the listeners may like to put, also for returning papers which they have written on the subject-matter of the previous lecture. Such discussion is most helpful in bringing different points of view before the notice of both lecturer and audience. Anyone who wishes to become a good public speaker should take every opportunity of practising the art of addressing others, so as to gain confidence and ease of delivery, not forgetting that simplicity and earnestness are the secrets of eloquence.

The profession of lecturer has the advantage of not monopolizing the whole time of the woman who devotes herself to it. It can be carried on in addition to her household duties, and so need entail no sacrifice of home interests. Undertaken as a social work, it is a valuable means of imparting knowledge on medicine, cookery, etc., to the poor. Even to take one branch, hygiene, and institute a course of lectures throughout the country districts, would do a great deal to awaken a sense of the necessity of fresh air, light, and pure food among the crowded dwellings of the lower classes. To the poor the spoken word always comes with greater force than the written message, and in a country like India, where so large a proportion of the population is illiterate, it seems absolutely the only expedient to reach them at all. In this way, viewed as a philanthropic work, as well as a paying profession, lecturing by women to women might achieve great results.

In England the Women's Imperial Health Association has already done much good work by its health caravan-tours, during which lectures are given to children and adult women in poor districts which would otherwise be out of reach of medical addresses. At present this society is organizing a national crusade to promote the care of the teeth among school-children, and is arranging a series of 'talks' with children at various centres, when an eminent dental surgeon will demonstrate to the young people the importance of the subject from the point of view of health. Such 'tooth-talks,' as they are called, will doubtless do much to impress and interest the children, and the idea is capable of being developed.

The next profession which we shall deal with is ADVERTISEMENT WRITING: and as this has scarcely been touched as yet by women, even in England, the best thing will be to show Indian women the method by which their masculine predecessors in the field have gone to work to climb the ladder of success.

Advertising is not a modern art. It was known to ancient Rome. Our primitive ancestors, too, had recourse to various methods in order to make a fact known to their neighbours. In England the muffin-man's bell was perhaps the first advertising medium used by the forefathers of the present Briton. In our own country, the blowing of a conch-shell announced to the neighbours that they were expected to divert their attention to something unusual that was taking place. It may be noted here that both the muffin-man's bell and the conch-shell have survived the inroads of the more elaborate contrivances of civilization, both in the East and in the West. But although advertising is of such ancient origin, yet the systematic employment of advertisement writing as a means of earning a livelihood is quite a recent development. An enormous amount is now spent yearly by the public in advertisement, and the placing of these sums of money with the different newspapers and other advertising media affords occupation to a large number of advertising agents.

Before starting anything so ambitious as an agency, it is necessary to have a thorough knowledge of the principles that govern advertisement writing, which in itself would constitute a lucrative profession for women. Good advertisement writers are badly wanted, but one must have a gift for the subject, so that the advertisement may catch the public eye and pay the advertiser well by bringing increase of custom. Originality is essential, also a knowledge of trade, and the power to look at things from the purchaser's point of view. The writer must have the faculty of making the commonplace interesting, he must have a literary style, concise and to the point, a knowledge of printing processes, of the costs of reproduction, of the nature of the different magazine, newspapers, etc., and of the various classes of advertisement which will appeal to them. In a word, the more general his knowledge, the greater his chance of success. Training for such a post is best attained by studying the style of successful advertisements, always bearing in mind that originality is the goal after which to strive. Those who take up a magazine of, say, twenty years back, cannot fail to notice the difference between past and present modes of advertising. The way in which the modern advertisement writer seems to take the public into his confidence and address the reader individually is a feature of present day publicity.

As well as newspaper advertising, there are pamphlets, circulars, and other advertising matter to be studied. Sometimes such examination may suggest innovations, and novel ideas may be submitted to the firm in question, who will probably be quite willing to pay for a new suggestion. Thus a connection may be formed, and the foundation laid of a more ambitious career as advertising-consultant or advertisement agent. Advertising-consultants are experts whose advice is sought as to the best methods of conducting huge publicity schemes. Naturally it would take a long time before a woman could hope to command sufficient confidence to direct such large undertakings; but everything has a beginning, and she might start by first acquiring a practical knowledge of advertisement writing, advertisement illustration, typesetting, and proof reading. Then by degrees she might set up an office with a small staff under her. She will have to possess a thorough acquaintance with all the journals, and their methods of doing business; she must know the cost of advertisement in each, and the public among whom they circulate. She will have to be a thoroughly practical woman, proficient in accountancy, with a clear head when it comes to entering into contracts with advertisers or papers. At first she would probably have to be a general factotum and supervise all sections of the office routine.

Advertising agents usually buy a certain amount of space in various leading journals, which they then fill to their own advantage. The custom in England is for the newspaper to give the agent a percentage on the worth of the advertisement sent in to them, but of this commission the advertiser in his turn usually expects a certain proportion to be restored to him. The buying of space alone and then the passing on of the advertisements as they are secured to the newspaper will not bring any very great prosperity to the agent. If she acts on a more ambitious scale and organizes the whole scheme of advertising for her clients, she will naturally be able to command a much higher rate of remuneration for these advertisement campaigns than when merely acting as a broker between the advertising public and the publisher.

After taking an office, a connection is worked up by means of public advertising, private issue of circulars, by letters, and by diligent canvassing. Much, of course, depends on the personality of the aspirant, and push is indispensable. An advertisement writer in India must pay special attention to caste rules. She must keep herself quite familiar with the Hindu and Moslem almanac, for religious fairs, regulate the demand for particular articles. Nor should the 'wedding seasons' be forgotten. To make the most of occasions such as these and to be alive to every opportunity is the only way to succeed.

—*The Position of Women in Indian Life* (1911)

Mrs F.K. Patuck
(b. 1874)

Mrs F.K. Patuck is one of the more important figures connected with the women's movement, especially as it concerned Zoroastrian women. She started the Parsi Women's Class in 1890, founded the Women's Zoroastrian Association in 1903, and helped to start an industrial institute for Parsi women, the Ratan Tata Industrial Institute which is still in existence. She was Honorary General Secretary of both the associations and the institute from their inception. Born in 1874, Mrs Dinbai F.K. Patuck was educated in Gujarati and English to Matriculation in Girton High School, Bombay. The speech included here is on the work of the Women's Zoroastrian Association and was published by the organization as part of a jubilee volume, *The Stree Bodhe and Social Progress in India*, in 1908.

'Stree Zarthosti Mandal'
(The Women's Zoroastrian Association)
How we came to form it.

Nearly four years ago the Women's Zoroastrian Association was first started. And it was not too soon that such an Association came into existence at the time, to do its work of sympathy amongst our working people. The idea was suggested in the first years of the plague, when people from close houses and chawls and infected quarters were sent out to stay in temporary segregation camps. Those were also days of scarcity; the mills worked short hours and paid smaller wages, so it was altogether a very hard time for those whose monthly income came from our mills and factories.

A visit now and again to the segregation camps brought us into close connection with the occupants and so face to face with their troubles, small and great. In some instances the dread plague had claimed the bread-winners of many a happy little family for its victims and perhaps an aged parent and young grand-children, or a young widow with several small mites were left to shift for themselves as best they could. And their best at the time seemed a dull despair with no prospect, no future, nothing to look out into. In other cases scarcity of work and the dearness of food-stuffs meant scanty fare to live upon for those, who at the best of times never had very sufficient to boast of.

The Parsi Panchayat came forward with its help in several ways,—as it always does at a crisis—and private individuals also freely helped. But the passing time works its own changes, whether you would or not: and it had brought about a great change in the conditions of life, and the old time methods of dispensing and through the Parsi Panchayat did not seem very efficient when tried by the altered conditions. Besides, temporary help, or for the matter of that any help from outside could hardly do much lasting good where the cases were so desperate,—and there is always involved a certain danger, in indiscriminate giving, of rendering the helped more helpless than before. Help had to come from within to be lasting. And with that end in view,—that is by way of helping them to help themselves,—we deemed it advisable to start a work-room, as a beginning, where women could be taught to earn a living. For one rather noticeable feature of those cases was, that whereas the family could scarcely make both ends meet, the young girls, who had left schools and had not much to do at home, often frittered away their most precious hours, the most critical period of their lives, in idle gossip. Because, time had already wrought a great change, in that girls did not marry so early as they did in the old days. Now, were they employed to do some handiwork, in the intervening space between leaving school and marriage, they might materially help the home finances, besides acquiring a craft and educating their own minds.

Hence the starting of the Parsi Women's Work-class. Here the girls could come; here also wives and mothers and widows, who could not leave their homes altogether, could attend after doing their household work and cooking of a morning, and after the men folks and children had gone to their several works and schools—here they could work all day and return home about 5 or 6 in the afternoon. At this Work-class they are being taught to do all kinds of plain needle-work, and to cut out and make up garments of ordinary every-day wear, for which there is a constant demand. They are also initiated into the mysteries of all sorts of fancy work, which is found to be more paying than the former. The idea of course being new, did not appeal to many at first, as the discipline and method entailed in the training were irksome to them. But then some needed to earn very badly, perhaps to feed their own children, and these remained steadily at work, and in time more and more came, until at one time there were as many as a hundred and fifty women taking advantage of the work-room. They are paid according to the work they turn out, and after acquiring the necessary skill they have been enabled to earn as much as Rs. 25 a month, the usual monthly wages of an ordinary clerk or turner or fitter.

The work-room brought us into more direct and daily communication with the workers. We found that in 50 per cent cases the constitutions of the young women left much to be desired. They suffered from one complaint or another, at the bottom of which always lay general debility, and cases of weak chests leading to phthisis were getting numerous. The medical advisers were of the opinion that it was all the result of close surroundings, smoky rooms, no exercise in the open air and scanty food. Such a state of affair was sad to see, especially when we felt that a little judicious treatment at the right time could be the saving of many a young woman, mother of the future, from early, untimely decay. A change into healthier surroundings, with strengthening tonics and nourishing food at the critical moment might ward off the germs of many a disease from taking root and make all the difference in their lives. Again, there were many men and women very willing to work, and on whose labours the family depended for subsistence, but unfit to do so on account of their weak physical condition; a little timely change could set them up again, whereas without it they would be dragging along an aimless existence, making their lives a burden to themselves and to others. A convalescent home, we believed, might in a good measure supply the need. Mrs Sherenebai M.D. Cama, who also had seen the great want of such an institution, now opened one—a Convalescent Home for Parsi women, a home of rest for the ailing, and the weak and the suffering—on a pleasant mount in a suburb by the sea. Mrs Cama herself undertook to look after the inmates, women and children, and give them all the advantage of fresh sea-breezes with nourishing foods and tonics.

About this time, famine in the mofussil villages drove innumerable families into our city to seek means of livelihood. When these people could not find such means all at once where scarcity of work and food already prevailed, some of them took to begging, not openly of course, but in various ways, which in the long run, amounts to the same thing. This moral degradation was another new phase of Parsi life—and a very sad one too. For, has it not ever been the pride of the Parsis that they have no beggars in the community? But the old self-dependence, the old pride, the old sturdy forbearance seemed to be lagging behind. A part of the community seemed to be losing its standing ground,—also, that self-assurance and backbone, which had stood them in such good stead in an alien land for so many centuries! Such a sorry plight of physical decadence and moral poverty could not but strike many an onlooker with horror. Many an educated Parsi woman was ready and anxious to help, but did not feel quite sure where to begin. The time seemed ripe for them to form a body, and to frame rules and regulations for their guidance in order to meet such a situation, or rather as far as they could reach it. A meeting of Parsi ladies was called, which was readily responded to, and here-after some interchange of views, it was agreed that they should form themselves into a band of workers—henceforth called 'the Women's Zoroastrian Association'—as their line of work was purely based on the tenets of the Zoroastrian creed. The chief aim of the Association was to try and improve as far as possible the moral, material and physical condition of that particular class of people that had come to accept doles of charity, to subsist anyhow on the scanty and precarious means of such charity, and to let mind and body undergo a deterioration; also by a little timely assistance of the right sort to help many a deserving person to help herself.

Rules of the Association

Any Parsi lady of the age of twenty-four or more may join the Association as a working member by paying a monthly fee of Re. 1, which is used for the work of the Association.

Any Parsi lady who sympathizes with the work but cannot take an active part in it, becomes a helping member, by paying a monthly fee of Rs. 2.

Groups of two members each are told to visit specified chawls in certain streets at least once a week. Their duties are:

(a) To get parents to send their children to school, where they do not do so already, by impressing on their minds their duty of educating them; and in cases where free schools are not within reach and the parents really unable to pay the fees, to pay for the schooling as well as books from the Association funds.

(b) Where the young girls have no definite duties at home, to induce them to join the work-rooms and put them in the way of leading useful lives.

(c) To find such service for their mothers as they can attend to with their own house-hold work, or supply them with work which they may do at home.

(d) To get medical advice for those women and children, who may be unable to go to work or school on account of uncertain health; to induce them to go to hospitals, sanatoria or the Convalescent Home as may be necessary in order to help them to get fit again for their duties; or to supply tonic or other medicines to such as need these only to set them up again.

(e) To try and get work-rooms opened in such quarters where there may be a large working population.

(f) To take the women working in the work-classes and elsewhere out for a change and rest for a fortnight every year, or to make arrangements for their so going out.

(g) To give or to arrange for lectures and readings on moral and religious subjects once a week, in some central place in Parsi quarters, and to encourage wholesome reading generally by lending good books.

The members meet on the first Saturday of every month to give an account of their work during the month, to discuss difficulties and make plans for any special cases, etc.

There are twenty-two 'working' and forty-five 'helping' members in the Association now. It has been gratifying to find Parsi ladies of all classes in sympathy with the movement. From all parts of the country they have expressed their willingness to join, and even those who have not given their names to the list of members have readily helped in various ways.

During the four years the Association has been in existence it has been able to do the following work:

Ninety-three children have been sent to school and their fees paid from the Association funds.

Eighty-two young women have been got to join the work-classes.

Forty-six aged women were supplied with materials to make twine at home.

Fifteen young women were sent out to cooking service and to learn nursing in hospitals.

Sixty-five were given glasses for the eyes.

Nearly a hundred were sent to hospitals, sanatoria and the Convalescent Home, the largest number to the last place. Of these some were broken-down teachers and others suffering from chronic fevers, weakness, etc. Most of these were able to do work after some months at the Home.

By far the largest number, nearly four hundred and fifty persons, have been supplied with tonics and nourishing foods. Of these, here is just one example. A poor mother with 8 small children had long been ailing from some chest complaint. She received about five rupees a month from the Parsi Panchayat, and on that miserable pittance and a little help from her widow mother managed to live somehow with her children. The doctor advised that she needed maltine with cod-liver-oil and milk to strengthen her chest. We gave her these for two months, and as soon as she was able to get about induced her to join the work-room. There, by degrees, she has been enabled to earn about Rs. 15 a month. Her children have been put to school, but we have to continue the maltine and the milk in her case, for those are found to be most essential for her. She has been at the work-room for 3 years now, and works pleasantly chatting with others all day *and has nearly forgotten her old complaint* and the old miserable days.

But the Association hopes to extend the scope of its work further. The present number of its working members is insufficient to meet the demands on its activity. We want women of enlightenment, but of real sympathy for the work and with those amongst whom they have to work, to join as working members; for, without this sympathy as also some insight and understanding, it is not possible to do much good,—and that way lies the danger of doing harm to the cause. After all there is no very great gulf between them and us, and as for certain virtues of natural kindliness of heart, and a real greatness of nature, we have often found them surpass us. For, where we would hesitate and let reason guide, they allow an impulsive kindly instinct to step in and act—which seldom fails to do the truest thing, although the world may not regard it as the most correct one. In fact there is no such great distinction of class and class among us as one sees in Continental countries, in Christian lands. A Christian minister was once anxious to meet and see some of our poorest people. He was taken amongst them, and was most agreeably surprised to find them so superior to the same class of people he had met with in England and elsewhere. That coarseness of nature, and vulgarity of mind that leave their own indelible marks on the physique were not discernible in these, nor could he see traces of any such inferior breeding in manners and conversation.

One of the reasons why they are so superior is that until now we have not kept them apart as beings belonging to a distinct or different order. Thank Heaven! We have no Belgravia, neither have we an East-end. We have honoured and respected the god-given heritage of manhood and womanhood in them, which no distinction of worldly estate could give or take away. For this reason we want members with sympathy, women who can see beyond the surface-film and honour the nobility of a pure soul, so self-less and loyal as we often find it, enshrined within the worn and weak and outwardly insignificant frame of many a humble working sister.

Then we would extend the scope of our work so far as to be able to pay visits to the women's wards of our hospitals, also to girls schools, and widows' homes, and the chawls and Parsi quarters we are not able to reach now on account of the limited number of our members. The widows' homes, especially, we should like to see managed as such institutions are in European countries. Again we would have some more of such institutions opened, where women could be engaged in such work as would in nowise injure their constitutions nor take them away from their homes altogether to the detriment of home-life. The art of washing and dyeing silks could be introduced with advantage for them. And above all we would that we might be able to instil into their minds the nobility comprised in honest labour and in self-reliance, next to their reliance on their Maker.

Dinbai Patuck

Stree Zarthosti Mandal,
Bombay

—*The Stree Bodhe and Social Progress in India* (1908)

Herabai Tata
(b. 1879)

Herabai Tata who was born in Bombay was educated in Bombay and London. She was engaged in educational and social franchise work. She was Honorary Secretary and Treasurer, WIA Bombay Branch. She wrote both in English and Gujarati.

Geraldine Forbes in *Women in Modern India* gives us an account of Herabai Tata's work for franchise for women. She says that though the WIA sent Annie Besant and Sarojini Naidu as representatives, Herabai 'was the real soldier in the campaign'. An early influence on Herabai was the granddaughter of Ranjit Singh of the Punjab, Princess Sophie Duleepsingh who met Herabai in Kashmir. However, Madame Bhikaji Cama (1861–1936) suggested that they work for India's political independence, and all other rights would follow. Discouragement, however, did not prevent the women in favour of franchise from continuing their struggle.

A Short Sketch of Indian Women's Franchise Work

The awakening of India to her rights as a great nation, which has proceeded so rapidly during the past few years, has not been confined to the men of India. When in the year 1916 the national movement progressed with such swift strides, the women of India by no means lagged behind their men, but knew and felt that they, too, should assert their right to be represented in any scheme of reform that was to be given to the Indian people.

In the following year Mr Montagu, Secretary of State for India, went to that country to investigate and study the conditions there, and in December a deputation of Indian women, in which all the Province were represented, waited on the Viceroy and the Secretary of State, and spoke on behalf of their Indian sisters. The chief promoters of this deputation were a group of Indian University women, helped by two ladies who had been ardent workers for the Suffrage in England, Mrs Margaret Cousins and Mrs Dorothy Jinarajadasa.

The first demand made by the deputation, and those whom they represented, was that 'when the terms of the Indian Franchise were drawn up the word "people" should be understood as including women, and that the whole should be worded in such terms as will not disqualify our sex, but allow our women the same opportunities of representation as our men.'

The next step came in the form of a resolution in favour of women's suffrage which was, for the first time, placed on the Agenda of the National Congress, held that year at Calcutta. Unfortunately, this resolution, owing to lack of time, was not brought before the Congress.

In April 1918, the women of Bombay sent a requisition to the Bombay Provincial Conference, asking it to move a resolution in favour of the removal of sex disqualification from the Reform scheme. This resolution was moved by an Indian lady, and was carried unanimously.

Similar requisitions were sent by the women of Madras, when the Madras Provincial Conference was held in April 1918, and Suffrage resolutions were put forward by the ladies of the Presidency. In the same year the Malabar District Conference received the demand of the women of the district with sympathy, and again a lady had the honour of moving a resolution on the question, which was carried unanimously. These requisitions were signed by a large number of women's societies and by prominent ladies in the Presidencies.

Women's suffrage resolutions were further passed by the Provincial Congress Committees of the Bombay and Madras Presidencies, the Central Provinces, Panjab and the United Provinces, and by the Andhra Provincial Conference, which met in the same year and decided unanimously in favour of the women's suffrage resolution moved by an Indian lady during its session.

The Muslim League, which represents the whole Muslim opinion of the country, voted at its meeting in September 1918, in favour of the franchise for Indian women, and the Special National Congress held in Bombay in September 1918, discussed the whole question at great length, and passed by a three-fourths majority a resolution in favour of women's suffrage. Several Indian ladies took part in the proceedings of the Congress, and spoke in support of the resolution.

In December of that year the Delhi National Congress received proposals from the women of the Province to consider a resolution in favour of the enfranchisement of Indian women. This resolution was again moved by an Indian lady, and supported by other lady speakers.

These Congresses were the representative bodies of all India where the delegates, including men and women, came from all the Provinces of India to voice Indian aspirations and desires for the progress of their nation.

The purport of all the resolutions is 'that the word "people" or "persons" should be taken to refer to both men and women, instead of to men alone, and that women should not be put on par with children, foreigners, and lunatics in any scheme of reforms to be given to the country'. Further, 'that women possessing the same qualifications as are laid down for men in any part of the scheme shall not be disqualified on account of sex'.

The Secretary of State, after making his investigations over all parts of the country, drew up with the Viceroy of India a scheme of reforms (which has now passed into an Act), and which was generally known as the 'Montagu-Chelmsford Scheme of Reforms for India'. Among the suggested reforms was one for the larger representation of Indians on the Legislative Councils, and the widening of the electorate. When the Montagu-Chelmsford scheme came out, no mention of women was made, the question of their rights was just ignored, in spite of the representations and the resolutions passed by the various Conferences and Congresses advocating the giving of the Franchise to Indian women. Two Committees were appointed to investigate the suggestions put forward in the reform scheme and place them on a workable basis. The Committee appointed to deal with the question of elections was called the Southborough Franchise Committee.

Before the Southborough Franchise Committee started its work, a member of the Bombay Legislative Council undertook to move a resolution in the Legislative Council to the effect that women in the Bombay Presidency should be eligible to sit as municipal councillors. The women of Bombay did all they could in support of this action, and created considerable public interest in the question, with the result that the Bombay Legislative Council in 1918, under Lord Willingdon as its President, passed the resolution by a majority, many Government officials voting in favour of it. The principle was granted by the resolution, but it was left to each municipality to do as it thought fit with regard to putting it into practice.

In 1919 a resolution to the same effect was moved in the Corporation of Bombay. A public meeting of women in Bombay had been previously organized at which speeches were made in the vernaculars and English by Indian ladies, asking the Corporation to pass the resolution. Many women attended the meetings of the Corporation when the matter was discussed, but on account of some unfortunate misunderstandings, it was thrown out. The principle, however, being granted, the women felt assured that the right to vote and to take active part in the affairs of their country would soon be theirs in actuality.

The Southborough Committee was, as everybody knows, appointed by Government to discover Indian opinion on the question of the Reforms, and, as stated by the Secretary of State for India, to collect for the information of the British Parliament all available criticism on the Franchise proposals. The women of India recognizing that the time was critical, took every available opportunity of bringing to the notice of the Committee all possible evidence which showed the need for including women in the new Electorate.

The Southborough Committee toured India, and when they visited Bombay, a Requisition signed by about 800 educated women of the Presidency was submitted to them, asking that women, as a sex, should not be excluded from the Franchise proposals.

In addition to this, Requisitions expressing the strong and widespread claim of Indian women to be included in the Franchise, were presented by the members of the earlier *All India Women's Deputation* to the Southborough Committee, by the *Women Graduates' Union* in Bombay, the forty branches of the *Women's Indian Association, the Women's branches of the Home Rule League, the Bharata Stree Mandal*, and other bodies to the Secretary of State for India. Two Indian ladies also appeared personally as witnesses before the Southborough Committee to express the views of the Bengal and Panjab Provinces.

For over fifteen years the women of Bombay have enjoyed the Municipal Vote, and have experienced no difficulty in exercising this function, the women going to the polling booths just as the men do, and recording their vote. Even Lord Southborough's Committee had to admit that Bombay women used their rights in this respect with intelligence and diligence.

Yet when the Report of the Committee made its appearance in April 1919, the claims of Indian women to exercise the power to vote were entirely ignored, the recommendations of the Committee being the total exclusion of the sex irrespective of qualifications of education, property, or social position, from the Franchise. It was understood that the members of the Committee based their recommendation on the views they held as to the social customs regarding Indian women, which, they alleged, made the granting of the Franchise premature.

Only two gentlemen in office upheld the claims of the women—Mr Hogg, one of the members of the Southborough Franchise Committee, advocated giving Indian women the franchise; and Sir Sankaran Nair, in the Government of India, also urged that qualified Indian women should be given the vote at this juncture.

The grounds for refusing the suffrage were felt by the thinking Indian women to be untenable, for the social customs vary considerably in different parts of India. In July 1919, the women of Bombay assembled in a public meeting to protest against the indignity put upon their sex, and to express their deep regret at the recommendations of the Southborough Franchise Committee (and the acceptance of these recommendations by the Government of India) not to include Indian women as a whole in the Franchise proposals.

Protest meetings were also held in other parts of India by the combined women's Associations, and Resolutions were passed asking the Secretary of State for India to carry out the expressed wishes of the Indian people, both men and women, to give a certain measure of franchise to Indian women in the Reform Scheme which was under consideration.

No less than 11 cablegrams, giving the text of the unanimous resolutions passed at a public protest meeting, were despatched to prominent persons in England, urging the need for the inclusion of women's franchise in the Reform Bill. The text of the resolution, which was sent through the President of the meeting, was as follows:

> As President, women's public meeting, Bombay, July 12, 1919, have the honour to submit resolution passed unanimously for sympathetic consideration and support. 'Public meeting of the women of Bombay protests against the recommendation of the Southborough Committee and the Government of India disqualifying women for franchise in Reform Scheme on grounds that social conditions in India make it premature and impracticable to grant it. This meeting begs to draw attention to the fact that women in Bombay Presidency and other parts of the country already exercise franchise intelligently in municipal and other elections. It urges there is no reason to consider it premature and unpractical for qualified women to exercise higher vote and requests that their sex should not disqualify them. The meeting considers the postponement of this question a distinct grievance and the denial of due rights to women likely to deter their progress. It earnestly urges the Government of India and the British Parliament to reconsider the question removing sex disqualification.

In July 1919, after the Introduction of the Government of India Bill into Parliament, the Joint Select Committee of members of both the Houses was appointed to take the evidence of the representative Indians on the suggested Reforms and to place them on a workable basis. All the Indian deputations which came to London to give evidence, composed of educated and thinking Indians, without exception showed their desire to give votes to the qualified women of India. We did not ask the votes for all women, as for some time to come universal suffrage may not be practicable in India, but we do claim that women who possess the same qualifications as are laid down for men, should not be debarred from the enjoyment of the right to vote on account of their sex.

When at the end of July 1919, the women of Bombay read the astounding evidence given by Lord Southborough before the Joint Select Committee, to the effect that Indian women do not themselves desire enfranchisement, a meeting was at once called, and the following resolution passed, and cabled to the Secretary of State in the name of Mrs Jaiji Jehangir Petit, who presided thereat.

> Bombay women favouring women's suffrage have read with pain and surprise Lord Southborough's evidence before your committee stating franchise to women in India not desired by women themselves. That belief is not founded on fact. Largely attended Indian women's meeting recently held in Bombay enthusiastically claimed franchise; similarly various women's representations were submitted to Southborough Committee. Women ask no favour, but claim right and justice. If the vote is denied it will mean serious check to women's advancement in India.

The Bombay Presidency Social Reform Association further sent a cablegram through its President, Sir Narayan Chandavarkar to the Joint Select Committee to the following effect:

> The Bombay Presidency Social Reform Association desires me as President to represent to you respectfully the Association's great disappointment at recommendation of Southborough Committee against franchise to women in India in Reform Scheme; cause of social reform much discouraged thereby, and among women in India and large class of social reformers also there is growing feeling of dissatisfaction. Franchise to women will greatly help cause of sanitation and education on which India's future greatly depends. Educated women by reason of intelligence and sound practical sense more deserving of franchise than uneducated classes to whom Southborough Committee have recommended elective right.

From the forty-five branches of the *Women's Indian Association* the following cablegram was sent (by the General Secretary, Mrs Dorothy Jinarajdasa) to the Joint Committee, asking the votes for the women of India:

> Forty-five branches Women's Indian Associations controverts Southborough's evidence; they claim votes, protest against sex disqualification.

The immense propaganda work by speaking and writing, carried on by Mrs Annie Besant and the members of the All-India Home Rule

Deputation, and by the various other Deputations who came to London in the summer of 1919, to give evidence before the Joint Committee, has stirred up in England a widespread interest in the views and the efforts of the Indian people for reforms, which the weekly journal, UNITED INDIA, started by Mrs Besant in October 1919, exists to foster and augment.

On 6 August 1919, Mrs Sarojini Naidu handed in a paper to the Joint Select Committee in London supporting the women's franchise in India. A deputation consisting of prominent Indian ladies and gentlemen waited upon the Secretary of State at the same time to urge the cause of woman's suffrage in India.

A woman's committee, consisting of twenty prominent ladies of the Bombay presidency of different communities, was formed, and on 1 August 1919, a woman's public meeting was held in Bombay to send their representatives to England to work for women's franchise.

On 2 August 1919, Mrs H.A. Tata and Miss. M.A. Tata, started for England as deputies with Sir Sankaran Nair.

Public meetings were held in many parts of Great Britain and many women's associations in England showed sympathy and took interest in the cause of Indian women.

Resolutions to this effect were passed by the public bodies, and meetings, and were sent to the Premier, the Members of Parliament, the Secretary of State for India, and the Joint Select Committee:

'That the Women's Associations of Great Britain approve the principle of equality in the citizenship of men and women, and urges that the proposals in the present Bill for India for the enfranchisement of men should be extended to women possessing the same qualifications so that popular Government in India may start without any sex disability.'

At the request of the Joint Select Committee a statement was supplied by Mrs H.A. Tata and Miss M.A. Tata on 13 October 1919, as there was no time left to take their evidence.

Let me note, in passing, that from time immemorial the Indian woman has been considered the equal of man. India is not a new country, but has a magnificent past to inspire her for future progress. The highest honour which the Indian people can give to a person, the Presidentship of the Indian National Congress, was given in 1917 to a venerable lady, Mrs Annie Besant.

The vote improves the status of women, elevates them socially, morally and intellectually, so that man may not see in a woman an inferior being but his co-partner in weal or woe.

In the progressive and advanced countries we see women enjoying freedom of life; equal opportunities are given to them for the franchise, women take their part in the political life of the country, and in movements for social and economic reforms.

The self-development of women affects the growth of the country with the result that there is a good educational system—fine schools to which every boy and girl must go up to a certain age. The children are generally well and strong, and the death-rate among them is low.

It is the inevitable consequence that where women take their responsible share in national life, a very much better condition of life exits than where the women do not have any responsibility outside their own home. So the position and status of women counts in the National development of a country.

The Joint Select Committee decided to leave the question of women's franchise for India to be settled by the future Legislative Councils of India for each Province.

When the franchise rules are being framed in the near future under the Reform Act, we hope that the Indian Legislative Councils from the beginning will start in the right direction and will include qualified women in the rules.

Thus we hope that ere long the growing understanding by British men and women of the hopes and aspirations of their Indian fellow subjects, will hasten the realization that, in India as in England, responsible and satisfactory Government can only be achieved when men and women each bear their share in electing their representatives, and give the results of their experience and knowledge in service on public bodies.

—*A Short Sketch of Indian Women's Franchise Work* (n.d.)

Lady Mehri Dorab Tata
(1879–1931)

Lady Dorab Tata: A Book of Remembrance, published in Bombay in 1932 is a book commemorating the life of Lady Mehri Dorab Tata. It contains a life sketch, tributes and condolences from India and abroad, and a section on her speeches and letters, which attempts to explain India succinctly to audiences abroad. Equally remarkable, as Life Sketch by K. Natarajan points out, 'was the letter she wrote to Miss S.M. Cursetjee, who had tried to get Lady Tata interested in a Parsi orphanage, and on the subject of Parsi charities'. Some expressions in this letter may sound rather harsh and perhaps Lady Tata could have given more credit to the munificent donors of these charities for their earnest desire to serve their community. She was, of course, perfectly right in her contention that these charities, as often administered, were sources of demoralization. Lady Tata wanted more of these charities to be spent in educating young Parsis to enable them to stand on their feet. This is now being gradually recognized as the only true form of charity.

Lady Tata was one of the pioneers of the women's movement in India. A note on her in *A Quest for Roots*, a collection of biographical notes tells us that in 1904, 'six years after her marriage, Mehribai went on a tour of Europe, and was much struck by European women's commitment to social work. In 1905 she organized an exhibition of women's crafts as part of the Industrial Exhibition in Bombay. In 1917 she led a large delegation of women to the Viceroy to protest against the condition of indentured labourers in the colonies. She blamed purdah, caste differences and lack of education for the divisions between women and their inability to associate with each other and produce social change. Both at home and abroad, her presence carried weight, and under her aegis the National Council of Indian Women was formed in 1929.'

She was passionately interested in sports, particularly tennis. She played and won in several tournaments, and she played in a sari. She wanted to fly and her ambition was gratified at Baden-Baden where she went up for a couple of hours in the Zeppelin 'Victoria Louise' stationed there.

Letter to Miss Serenbai Maneckjee Cursetjee

Esplanade House
Bombay
3rd March 1931

My Dear Serenbai,

In accordance with your desire that I should write to you as a result of our talk about Parsi poverty in general and the stupid attitude of poor Parsis, both men and women, of refusing to do manual work to earn an honest living, I am now writing to you. I am sorry I have not been able to attend your meetings, but I am very much interested in this question. It is very essential that the foolish charities that are being doled out year after year and have caused this deplorable condition amongst the Parsi poor should now be stopped being given in this way and should be co-ordinated and reorganized so as to use these large amounts of monies to the best advantage.

One way of changing the attitude of the poor is to make them feel ashamed of it and to create a sense of self-respect in them and to teach them the value of the 'dignity of labour'. It is not disgraceful or shameful to earn an honest living even if it be that of breaking stones on the road or doing any other hard manual labour and earning a living thereby. It is truly shameful and disgraceful to go from house to house as beggars begging for help and to live on charitable doles which unfortunately are so much available to them. One of the worst things that Lloyd George did for England was to introduce the 'dole' system. It has made the working classes in England refuse to work as the doles they receive are sufficient for them to live on and consequently the unemployment in England is increasing daily and a steady deterioration in the working classes is being encouraged by this wretched dole system. The same thing has been done here by these foolish and ridiculous Parsi charities. In order to bring home to those poor Parsis, who are able-bodied and refuse to work, to take up any profession such as cooking, boot-making, carpentry, or any other profession, is to start an organized campaign by which earnest and dis-interested workers with the real missionary spirit in them should be collected amongst our people, both men and women, and they should then be asked to visit every Parsi centre, such as colonies, chawls, settlements, poor dwellings, orphanages, etc. and have regular personal talks with them, an hour or so once or twice a week, and keep on reiterating to them the necessity of self-respecting honest work and the disgrace of living on charity alone, until some impression is made. By so doing gradual public opinion may be created in favour of work and against the disgraceful and indolent life led by these people living as beggars or on charitable doles. Such talks can be given in the open, outside the buildings where these people live. At first they may not receive much encouragement, but even if half-a-dozen people collect to hear what is being said that will be something. The volunteers who come forth to undertake this kind of visiting must be prepared at first for much unpleasantness. They may be insulted or ridiculed or treated with indifference, but they must have the determination to persevere with the knowledge in their hearts that they must ultimately succeed in moving these people in the right direction and thus gain the great satisfaction of having done a great and good work.

To illustrate the meaning of the 'dignity of labour', which in Europe and America is treated with the greatest honour and respect, I shall give you a few illustrations of instances I have personally known. Nearly everybody knows that Mr Perin, the Consulting Engineer, who came out to organize and start the Tata Iron and Steel Works at Jamshedpur was being paid by the Company a sum equivalent to Rs. 20,000 a month. I should like to tell you of his early training before he reached this high position. He is the son of a doctor and belonged to a very old and honoured family in America. After he finished his university career at Harvard, which is one of the best universities in America, he decided to go in for Mining Engineering and studied in the School of Mines for four years and then in order to gain practical knowledge in every department he signed on as a common labourer in a large Iron and Steel Works belonging to one of his father's friends. At these Works he started at the very lowest rung of the ladder, coal-stoking. For one whole year he did nothing but shovel coals into the furnace like a common navvy during the day time. For the next year he did the same work during the night time, that is for 365 nights without a single holiday he shovelled coals into the furnace. After these two years he went into the workshops and worked there for several months, and so on he went through every single department working with his own hands and brains until he got a thorough knowledge of every detail connected with Mining Engineering and the conduct of Iron and Steel Works. This took him more than five years. Was it not, I ask you, a most praiseworthy action of his to voluntarily undertake all this hard manual labour although he was a university graduate and the son of one of the best families in America? Does he not deserve all the honour and respect we can give him? And what was the result of this splendid training he took? He soon became well-known as a Consulting Engineer and as I have said above, he ultimately reached such a position as to earn as much a Rs. 20,000 a month which is far more than the Viceroy of India receives.

Now another instance. When our Tata Iron and Steel Works had been started we visited the Works in company with Mr Perin and Mr Sahlin, who was his colleague, in order to see the Works. One evening we visited the furnace when the molten iron was being run out of it into the moulds for making pig iron. We saw amongst others a hefty young man in his short sleeve opening up the furnace, letting the molten iron run out and finally closing the furnace. After it was all over this young man put on his coat and came and mixed with all of us with a cigarette in his mouth and talking to us as our equal. Sir Dorabji and I were a little surprised at this and inquired who he was. We were told that he was the son of a man who owns three such Works in America, but that he had preferred to come out to our Works to sign on as a common labourer in order to become familiar with all the various departments of the Works. After some years this man, Mr Tutwiler, became the Manager of these very same Works and remained so for many years.

When we were in America in 1927 we had occasion to go to the great Sanatorium there at Battle Creek. We saw several instances there of how young men and women, sons and daughters of respectable families but who could not pay for their college careers actually worked for their college training. There is a large college at Battle Creek run by the Battle Creek Sanatorium people. At the time we were in the Sanatorium there were about 600 patients in it. But during the summer time, I was told, the number of patients goes up to over 2,000. Every day at each meal for lunch and dinner we were served by about a hundred girls from the College who acted as waitresses, and in that way earned their college training. How many Parsi girls, I wonder, who are attending the colleges here would care to do such a thing. The fact that these girls waited on us as waitresses did not lower them in our eyes but raised them immeasurably and they became our personal friends. Similarly the boys also do such work in order to gain their college training. One afternoon the Head of the Sanatorium, Dr Kellogg, took us for a drive in his motor car. The young man acting as his chauffeur was the son of a friend of his, a doctor in the neighbouring town. The young man preferred to earn his college training by his own efforts rather than be a burden on his father. So he acted as Dr Kellogg's chauffeur in addition to studying at the college and thus paid his way through. When we said good-bye to Dr Kellogg we shook hands with the young man, the chauffeur, who commanded our respect by this action of his. Similarly, we heard of hundreds of such instances where young men and women of respectable families in order to pay for their education would, during the vacation months, go into New York and work as waiters and waitresses in the big hotels and restaurants in that city and, with the monies they earned in those few months, they would go back to their colleges and pay for their training which enabled them to earn an honest living later on. College students even work as shoe-blacks and newspaper boys in the streets in order to pay for their education. Schwabe, the Headman of the Carnegie Steel Works, now earning a salary of £100,000 a year, began life as a shoe-black and newspaper boy and he learnt everything he knew by this means.

When, a few years ago, one of the Directors of the Taj Mahal Hotel approached the Petit Parsi Orphanage boys in Bombay to take up the profession of cooks and waiters at the Taj Mahal Hotel, there was not a single boy found willing to do so although they are all penniless and helpless orphans. Their one desire is, like so many thousands of others in India, to become clerks on Rs. 40 or Rs. 50 a month and to remain so all their lives. Whereas by taking up such professions they could ultimately earn Rs. 400 to Rs. 500 a month or even more. The Head Chef of the Taj Mahal Hotel is generally paid Rs. 1,000 a month with board and quarters. It is very deplorable that in the training given at this orphanage no attempt is made to impress upon them the valuable understanding of the dignity of labour and the honourable and respectable position of a man who earns his own living by his own hard and honest work. Such instances should be repeatedly told to those people who refuse to work and prefer to live on charity. If out of the many thousands of such people ten or twelve could be won over to this point of view and a beginning made in their change of vision of an honourable and respectable life something will be gained.

Another instance comes to my mind. When I visited with a friend one of the large Drapery Stores in Oxford Street, London, two years ago, we were surprised to find a young sales-woman there who recognized us. She said she had been in Bombay not very long ago and had stayed as a guest of one of the Governor's A.D.C's who knew her well. Owing to the death of her father and the impoverished condition of her mother she was obliged to take some sort of service and had become a saleswoman in these stores. It is no joke to be a sales woman in such a big shop. It means standing on one's feet from 9 a.m. to 6 or 7 p.m. with very little rest in between. It also means a great mental strain as they have to be invariably polite and obliging and well-mannered, no matter how aggravating some of the customers are, who can be very inconsiderate and troublesome and sometimes even vulgar in their speech, from amongst the hundreds of customers that pass through daily. Where necessity must and there is no choice left one has to make the best of things and to undergo any hardship in order to earn an honest living rather than be dependent on relations and friends or receive doles from any charitable concern or individual. There is not only indolence in our Parsi poor but also a sense of false pride and snobbishness in refusing to take up any work or profession which should be severely knocked out of them. As against the above instance, I may quote from my personal knowledge an instance that happened here about three years ago. An aunt of mine appealed to me on behalf of the widowed niece of one of her tenants saying that she was left penniless and required help. I asked my aunt if she would take service as a companion to one of the Dowager Lady Jamsetjees and she said yes, so I spoke to Lady Jamsetjee who agreed to see the girl with a view of engaging her. When I sent word to the girl about this, to my amazement and disgust her uncle-in-law in whose house she lived refused to let her take 'service' anywhere as it would be a great shock to the 'abroo' (respect) of his family who though poor were 'very respectable'. This same uncle and his niece did not think it at all derogatory to their 'abroo' to come and beg of me to give her some assistance every month. I was so annoyed and disgusted that I refused absolutely to give her any assistance, and told them they ought to be ashamed of themselves for this attitude and that they should never come to me again for any help.

With best wishes,

Yours sincerely,
Mehri D. Tata

—*Lady Dorab Tata: A Book of Rememberance* (1932)

Kitty Shiva Rao
(n.d.)

Kitty Shiva Rao served on many education boards and committees, including the Delhi University Board and the All-India Education Fund Association. She carried out a detailed study of child education, and spent many years teaching in progressive schools both in Europe and in India.

Child Education

All the world over an intensified interest in the development of the child and its education has been manifest during these last thirty years, and one might well ask oneself what are the reasons that have focused the attention of educationists and psychologists on that problem in particular.

To start with, the process of intensive industrialization in the West and with it the increasing number of women going to factories necessitated the opening of creches, nurseries and children's schools by the thousand to relieve working parents of the anxiety of having to leave children at home without supervision. Large numbers of children assembled day by day to spend most of their waking hours in those children's schools and homes where they played, ate their mid-day meal, rested and only went home in the evening after the factories were closed. Difficulties of adjustment and peculiarities of individual behaviour soon cropped up, and the nurses or kindergarten teachers were confronted with problems that had never arisen on such a scale when the majority of children spent their time at home or in the streets, and when every mother dealt with her own children or in the alternative left them to their own devices.

The adjustment of the child to organized society—that is to a group of other children and adults in an organization—had not been experienced as a problem until the child went to school. Even there, however, it arose only particularly because the old-fashioned school was determined to teach in the narrow sense of the word, and concerned itself very little with the individuality of the child or his problems. The day was divided into a specified number of periods when children sat and listened to the teacher or were questioned by him. Problems only arose when children 'could not or would not learn' which the teacher sought to solve by punishment. Some children submitted to that punishment and others did not or not quite—they became the 'unmanageable ones' or the 'duds' and there the problem ended for the teacher.

The educationists in the children's schools and homes, however, could not get away as easily as that. In the course of the day's work and play, of eating and resting, of tears and laughter, the child gave evidence of his unmistakable individuality, his fears and hopes and his reactions to the world of people and things. Children brought their home problems to the teacher as we adults take our problems very often to those who are our friends but not related to us and therefore are more impartial. Teachers, on the other hand, finding themselves ill-equipped to solve all these varied problems looked around for help and guidance; and thus was organized a comprehensive effort to do research work on Child Development and the Education of the Child on the part of educationists, psychologists and educational field workers.

Subsequently, other factors also added to the zest for Child Study, such as the realization that maladjustments in later life, nervous breakdowns, insanity and crime had more often than not their roots and origin in events that occurred early in a child's life but never received adequate or proper attention:

On further investigation it was found that in the course of growth, physical, mental and emotional, every child had to pass through certain phases which, while being natural and beneficial at that particular phase, become unnatural and harmful at a later phase and therefore tended to obstruct growth. Thus, if a child at the age of one sucks his finger we take it as natural; but when a child of 10 or even 6 still sucks his finger, we feel something has to be done about it. Similarly it is natural for a child to rely and be dependent on his mother for all his needs, bodily and emotional alike. But if this dependence continues to an age when he ought to be self-dependent and emotionally more or less mature, the matter becomes serious. We then find an adolescent or an adult who has refused to grow up and therefore instead of being an asset to society, is on the contrary a liability.

Child Education, therefore, has to concern itself with the 'safe passage', as it were, of the child from stage to stage. This passage starts from the day the child is born upto the pre-adolescent age, that is up to the age of 10 or 12. Needless to say, the passage goes on even after that until the adult emerges, but we are not concerned with it here. In an arbitrary and general way, parents and teachers have complied with this necessity by threats and punishments more or less successfully. Who has not heard a parent say 'I shall cut off your finger if you do not stop sucking it' or 'God will punish you if you hurt others'. While Child Psychology has given us an explanation for the validity of such a threat by explaining the necessity for a child to overcome his pleasures and impulses, it has at the same time shown us that the method adopted has not always been so helpful.

Let us consider for a moment what are the agencies through which the child is educated in the larger sense of the term. His entry into the world probably means an intense discomfort, leaving an environment where he was surrounded by liquid matter in an even temperature to one which is solid with a changeable temperature. The process of feeding, more or less continuous in the pre-natal period, has now to be limited to strict intervals, which in the case of an enlightened and determined mother cannot be altered even by the most heart-rending crying. The modern mother also braves the baby's crying during the night for perhaps two or three weeks without yielding to the temptation to take him up and console him, because she realizes that once that is done, the child will not get used to sleeping through the night which is ultimately so necessary for his well-being. We thus have already two agencies influencing and educating the child: the environment and the mother.

As a child grows, both these agencies continue to function in increasing measure and other agencies are added. There is the father to be reckoned with, who adds his weight and influence to that of the mother and there are the sisters, or brothers, or both, with whom a definite relationship has to be established—in fact the family begins to assert itself in no uncertain measure. The next agency is the kindergarten or school with the teacher and the children therein. In other words, the teacher and an organized little group of society definitely begin to make their demands. We thus count five agencies by the time the child has entered school: the environment, the mother, the family, the teacher and society.

The question, however, still remains, how these various agencies function and impose their demands on the child. Why does the child accede to the mother's demands in spite of his obvious discomfort and reluctance? Why does the child obey rather than pursue his own pleasures and inclinations? Why does he ultimately abstain from taking other children's toys? There is one answer to all these questions: that being dependent for his food, his comfort, his emotional and social needs on all these agencies he can only do one of two things—he can defy them and risk discomfort, disapproval and loss of affection and security or comply with their demands (more or less unwillingly) and assure himself of his needs and position being safe-guarded. However strong may be the impulse to follow his inclinations and pleasures in a normal child, the impulse to be loved and protected and accepted in society is even stronger and ultimately tips the balance. The process is a long and continuous one and has many stages. In those cases where a child fails to make this adjustment and cannot give up his impulses and desires even though he realizes the consequences, we are faced with what is called maladjustment leading in some instances to delinquency and crime.

One may ask where the responsibility of the parent or the teacher rests, since a child in the majority of cases decides to accept imposition from outside of his own accord; also, why the modern educationist lays so much stress on the minimum of force and restriction being used on the child and insists that the child must be given every possible opportunity for spontaneous expression and a great latitude in the choice of his activities.

The responsibility, in fact, is all the greater since we have begun to understand better the working of the human mind and have realized that there is such a thing as the 'subconscious,' which, though not visible or measurable, influences our conscious make-up and behaviour. We may or may not agree with many of the theories of Professor Freud, but the fact that there is such a thing as a subconscious state of mind, which has been examined and described by him in great detail, has now been widely accepted. This subconscious state is mostly built up during early childhood, and no thinking educationist knowing that would deny a certain responsibility in its formation. You may say these are 'new fangled' ideas but they are there in every branch of science and life. The modern surgeon does not amputate a gangrenous limb by just cutting it off with a knife without using an anaesthetic, nor does he disinfect it with boiling tar as was the practice in olden days. In the same way the modern educationist would not dream of handling children as they were handled a hundred years ago—convinced that he knows better now. There is also another point we have to take into consideration, and that is the various demands society makes of the individual, implying a greatly increased nervous strain. The modern educator also realizes the need for greater individual responsibility and independence of mind as well as of a certain balance of emotion if a new outlook is to be evolved.

Modern Child Education, therefore, aims at allowing the child to grow as spontaneously as possible and imposing a minimum of restrictions on his conduct compatible with the elementary requirements of habit formation and discipline. It stresses acquisition by the educator of a deep understanding of the processes of growth and an attitude of respect for the individual's integrity and the personality of the child. To his original function to teach there is now the added function to learn, to understand, and to give effect to this new understanding in his relationship to the child and in his teaching.

The greatest contribution to this approach and its practical application we no doubt owe to Dr. Maria Montessori. She has been a pioneer amongst educationists and has taught us to recognize and respect the integrity of the child: 'To realize the needs of the child and to satisfy them in order that his life may unfold itself to the fullest—that is the basis of the New Education.' She has pointed out to us that in the past the one aim of education was to 'prepare the child for the life he will have to lead in the future as an adult', and that was why we attempted to induce him to submit 'his striving to the yoke of obedience, his creative energies to that of imitation' ... 'to mould him into the pattern of our culture and behaviour we thought indispensible'. And not until this process was completed, she pointed out, was the child considered a personality at all.

Not only has Dr. Montessori fought for the recognition of the integrity of the child, but she has also shown us ways and means of putting that recognition into practice. Her method is based on the fulfilment of the needs of the child at various stages and the Montessori School is a place where the child finds an environment specially prepared for him and in which he can function as an adult functions in the environment he has created for himself.

In addition to Kindergartens, Montessori Schools and Homes for children of the pre-school age, there have also sprung up scientific research bureaus, children's clinics, child laboratories, all with a view to giving training to those entrusted with the upbringing of the young and to enable them to discuss such problems with specialists in various fields. It is not possible to give a specialized training to every teacher, but he must have the opportunity of advice from those who have made child study their life's work.

In India, the question of child education has hardly been touched, except in big towns where a few Montessori schools and kindergartens have come into existence for the well-to-do and a few schools have been opened by owners of factories for the children of their workers. Teachers have banded themselves together to work for the education of the child but, on the whole, the effort has been sporadic and unorganized, and the question of research has not yet begun to arise. This is quite natural in a country where even elementary education is not compulsory and where literacy does not cover more than 15% of the whole population. The Women's Sub-Committee of the National Planning Committee has, if I remember rightly, laid great stress on the need for the education of the pre-school child. The Sargent Report on Post-war Educational Reconstruction more recently has recommended pre-basic education on a large scale.

The first step towards child education will have to be the training of teachers—preferably women teachers and subsequently the opening of children's schools amongst all classes of people. I would like to stress here that in the interests of the child, the economic position of the kindergarten or school teacher must be safeguarded. No woman—or man for that matter—can give her best and her whole attention to the child if she has to struggle to make both ends meet. She must have a certain amount of security if she is to give security to others.

I can foresee many new problems arising in India which are different from those of the West. It is true that human needs and human growth remain essentially the same all the world over; yet there are climatic conditions, perhaps too, cultural traditions, that may have a determining influence. For one thing, the span of childhood to all appearances seems to be shorter in India than in the West. That is to say, the average child of three in India seems less developed physically, emotionally and mentally than a child of the same age in the West. The child of ten or twelve, however, seems better developed here than his opposite number in the West. That would mean that the child in India takes more time over the initial stages of growth, but more than makes up for it later. If research were to bear out this fact, the whole basis of training and the curriculum in the school would have to be suitably adjusted.

A long childhood is considered an advantage from the point of view of development. It has been established beyond doubt that the higher developed an animal is, the longer is the span of his immaturity. Personally I have noticed in my own experience that in India girls, for instance, who go to school from the age of 5 or 6 retain their childhood much longer than girls who are only sent to school at the age of ten or even later. The difference is very striking, especially when they happen to come from the same family and have the same background. It may well be that with compulsory education from the age of 5 or 6, with its regular routine work and play, the general span of childhood of the average child will be prolonged. I have mentioned this problem because I think it is a real one and will need investigation.

With regard to the cultural background, I should like to mention one of the problems that I have come up against very frequently in India and that is the relationship of the child to his parents and his elders generally. Every child is taught reverence for his elders, whatever else he may or may not be taught. This reverence goes so far that even when the child has grown into an adult, he would rather obey a command even though he disagreed with the wisdom of it, than follow his own judgment. This is somewhat strange when one considers side by side the cult of Sri Krishna, the worship of God in the child and the child in God; but it is an anomaly which is found in many faiths and religions, including Christianity. This reverence for and obedience towards the elders may also have its roots in olden times when a guru accepted selected students—chelas—who sat at his feet and gathered from him not only knowledge, but also the wisdom of a saint, because that is what a guru was supposed to be. Times have changed, however, and with mass education it is impossible for every teacher to aim at such a position. Hence the relationship must become a less exalted one; and, in fact, almost a reverse process must set in.

An actual incident in a children's school I was working in opened my eyes to this aspect. One night, after all the children had gone to bed—their ages were between 5 and 7—I went on a round of the rooms to see that they were properly covered, for it was a cold winter night in Benares. To my surprise I found three children in a room, standing near the open window in their night pyjamas without any warm clothes on, looking at the moon. I asked them to go back to bed and added that they might catch a cold. One little boy replied, 'No, we won't catch a cold and we don't want to go back to bed.' I insisted that they would get ill and would have to be segregated in the sick room and that if they wanted to look at the moon, they could do so from their beds. The children went back to bed reluctantly, and I thought the incident was closed. Three or four days later, however, they came to me and said: 'We have been standing near the window without warm clothes every night since you talked to us, and we did not catch a cold as you told us we would. How do we know that the other things you tell us are true when this was not true?' How indeed? And yet to the old-fashioned teacher or parent, a straight question like that is abhorrent. How dare a child question the authority of an adult? It is a difficult adjustment, but it has to be made wherever the problems of child education have been tackled. When the process is completed, we may produce a younger generation whose outlook is very different from that of the present one—that at least is the hope of every educationist.

Another step towards Child Education on a large scale is the production of books for children in the different Indian languages. School books there are today, but they are dull and unattractive, the print is bad, and they aim at teaching facts without stimulating thought. Children are keen readers once they have mastered the art of it and should be provided with books on a variety of subjects, including elementary Botany, Geology, Science and other subjects of interest, apart from stories.

Last but not least, artistic expression has to be stimulated. It is painful to see the amount of 'copying' of designs that is being done in schools and the scarcity of original drawing, painting, modelling, paper-cutting and other handiwork, and that in a nation which has such an exquisite sense of colour and design and where handiwork and cottage industries have flourished for centuries past. There is a great deal of talent, but it is being squashed and superimposed by the art of copying which should not be considered an art at all. The same is true of writing original stories and plays and acting them, along with making costumes and setting up a stage.

In fact, the modern school for the child must open its doors to all activities that can be brought within the horizon of the child's understanding and capacity.

We have so far mostly dealt with the Kindergarten and the school and not with the home. However important the education of the child in the Kindergarten and the school may be, whatever expert treatment and teaching they may provide and whatever may be their influence on the child, the influence of the home will be equally great or greater! The co-operation of the parents with the school is an essential necessity, as otherwise the authority of the teacher and the authority of the parents may clash in very essential matters, and how is the child to judge who the real authority is? I should like to cite here a little incident which occurred in one of the Montessori schools in Berlin many years ago. A child of four came to school as usual one morning and told her best friend, a boy of 5, that the stork had brought her a little sister the previous night. The boy who had been told by his mother how children were born, told his little friend that she was mistaken and that the stork did not bring babies into the house, but that they came from the womb of the mother. He asked the teacher whether he was right in this belief and she confirmed it. The little girl was upset and said she would ask her mother again on her return home. The next day she came back to school and asserted that her mother maintained it was the stork who brought babies. After arguments backwards and forwards the teacher was called in again to arbitrate and she bore out the boy's version, whereupon the boy said to his friend: 'Did I not tell you? My mother and the teacher know how babies are born, but your mother must be very stupid if she still thinks that it is the stork that brings babies!' It is not a happy thing for a child to feel that his mother is either stupid or untruthful.

The home also has to give the child the necessary training in orderliness and discipline if it contributes anything at all beyond food and shelter. Routine and orderliness give a child a sense of security which is essential to his self-confidence and are not to be underrated. I have given here only a very few instances of the way the home influences the education of the child; but there are many more factors which it is difficult to mention here. Suffice it to say that in any organized effort to further the education of the child, the home has to play its part.

In conclusion, let us hope that India will apply herself to this fundamental problem of Child Education which must be the basis of all higher education, whether technical or academic. Those who may be entrusted with its planning and organization will, we hope, take into account the psychological as well as the physiological factors and enable field work to go hand in hand with research, without which no educational reform can succeed.

—*Education of Women in Modern India* (1946)

Sakinatul Fatima Wazir Hasan
(n.d.)

Sakinatul Fatima Wazir Hasan's paper 'Indian Muslim Women— A Perspective' is from *Our Cause: A Symposium by Indian Women* (1938). The symposium included talks by Cornelia Sorabji, and Sakinatul as part of the 'Retrospect' section, by Nilima Devi on House Decoration and Furnishing, by Vijayalakshmi Pandit on Children and Their Upbringing and sections on Health, Education, the Arts, Industry, Rural Life, Social Evils, Marriage and Divorce, Legal Rights, Political Struggle, and the Future of Indian Women.

The Editor, Sham Kumari Nehru writes: 'It is not our aim to present an abstract picture of Indian womanhood or to paint a Utopian future. We have, on the other hand, attempted to examine the question in a scientific and practical spirit with a historical background; basing our conclusions on facts as they are, and to suggest a way of progress on the basis of complete equality in the social, political and economic spheres.'

Indian Muslim Women—a Perspective

Fifty years ago, the condition of Muslim women in India perhaps constituted one of the most pathetic of all the social problems which existed in our country. Following the ruin and disorganization of the Muslim upper class in 1857, all culture and education even among the women of the privileged sections of our community either died out completely or existed only in a stereotyped and formal state. The little education that was doled out to 'ladies' of the upper classes before this collapse of culture, was of a very limited nature. Women's place even in these high spheres was a subordinate one—she was allowed to study literature and theology so that she may become a better 'ornament' in the household of her master-man. As to the millions of other Muslim women belonging to the so-called 'lower' classes, they lived and toiled in the towns and villages of India, just like the women of any other community.

When Sir Syed Ahmad Khan began his movement for education, on Western lines, of the Muslims of India, he made it quite clear that he did not include women in his scheme. He was a firm opponent of female education. And we can well understand the general state of the Muslim mind at this time, if we remember that even the proposal of men's education on modern lines met with strong opposition. The advocacy of female education branded a man with apostasy in orthodox circles.

But with the spread of modern ideas voices began to be raised about the necessity of bringing some kind of education inside the household. The gentlemen who were educated in colleges and universities, or who returned after several years stay abroad found the *zenana* steeped in the profoundest medieval obscurity. They could, of course keep their women hidden behind the *purdah* away from the vulgar gaze of an all too critical a public. But the necessities of an up-to-date modern household demanded that the lady of the house-hold too, should, to a certain extent, be modernized. With the introduction in our homes, of sofas, couches, and easychairs, made in the most third rate European style, and their installation in a room, to be known henceforth as the drawing-room, the necessity of a wife to fit in these surroundings, began to be increasingly felt.

Muslim reformers began to write books, exposing the credulity, ignorance and stupidity of old-fashioned ladies. Molvi Nazir Ahmad and Hali pleaded for the education of women—they preached obedience, fidelity, and the virtues of efficient housekeeping to the new Muslim woman. Of all the Muslim writers of the late nineties Hali went the furthest, and in a magnificent Urdu poem called 'Homage of Silence', traced the role of women in society, and pleaded not only for their education, but for an altogether different attitude towards them.

Very soon practical shape was given to this tendency, and in 1896, a group of advanced reformers launched forth the bold scheme of starting schools on modern lines for Muslim girls. As Muslims would not send their girls to be educated in non-denominational schools, these reformers thought of starting purdah schools for Muslim girls. The Muslim parent, none too enthusiastic to educate his girl, had to be assured about the absolute moral and intellectual security of the new institution, before he could be persuaded to allow his girls to leave home for a few hours a day. As was to be expected, these reformers met with the strongest opposition from a large section of the community; and for a long time they could hardly gather more than a few scores of pupils in their institutions. The two earliest of such institutions to be founded, Muslim Girls' School,

Aligarh, and Muslim Girls' School, Lucknow, are flourishing to-day, but there is still very strong opposition in the Muslim community not only to these institutions and all they stand for, but to female education in general.

Just as in the field of education so in the political and social sphere of our national life the part played by Muslim women has been very small. Among the upper and middle classes purdah is still the rule, and orthodoxy which seems to have found its last resort amongst the Muslims of India, is firmly entrenched. There is no other Muslim country in the world where in social matters like the purdah, marriage, and status of women generally, so much dull-witted reaction prevails as in India. It would seem that the modern women of Turkey, Egypt and Central Asia—Bokhara and Samarkand—have hardly anything in common with us. They have already achieved political equality with men and in social matters they are well on the way towards overcoming all the moral and intellectual backwardness caused by centuries of ignorance, dependence and helplessness.

Why is it that Indian women in general, and Muslim women in particular have lagged behind in the race of world progress? The only plausible answer seems to be that it is due to the backward condition of India as a whole—the main features of that condition being the political subjection of India and the terrible poverty of her people. We have inherited from our medieval past many social institutions, customs and beliefs, which have lost all their significance to-day. In the modern age they are just dead forms which help to crush all that is vital and dynamic in us. The disabilities from which Indian women suffer are due to this fact. This lack of harmony between form and content in our social life is, at bottom, the result of our present day economic and political institutions. It is because these latter have outlived their utility; because the historical conditions which gave birth to them have changed; because they no longer satisfy the needs of millions of Indians that our society is threatened with catastrophic changes. The forces of reaction have gathered on their side all the foul paraphernalia of obscurantism. Because men's minds are still in the grip of worn-out ideas; because they are still chained to dead social institutions, it is in the interests of the reactionary party to keep these institutions intact, and thus ward off the day of their doom.

Indian society will tend more and more to be divided in two camps— the camp of reaction and the camp of progress. It will be a division that will cut through the communal divisions—where men and women of all communities will be ranged on both sides according to their own particular interests. And the struggle between these two sections—one that of progress, strong in number, to-day down-trodden and without power—the other that of reaction with all the power in the world, but weak in numbers and moral stamina will be a struggle not only for political and economic emancipation but on the fate of that struggle will depend also the final solution of all our social problems. The measure in which women—Muslims and Hindus—take part in this struggle will also be the measure of their social emancipation. It is only through constant activity on a national plane, in diverse spheres of work of national, organization—that Indian women's emancipation can become a reality. A superficial tinsel of modernity should not satisfy the Indian woman. If she belongs to the upper classes and has had the good fortune to be among the two per cent, educated women of India; she can best emancipate herself and win her inalienable right of equality with men, by identifying herself with those millions of women who have been denied not only all educational enlightenment but also the possibility of a decent living, those women who bear the burden not only of overwhelming physical work, but also of the cruelty and selfishness of man, demoralized by ignorance, poverty and disease.

There is no doubt that if the educated Indian woman chooses this path she will be face to face with enormous difficulties—specially if she happens to be a Muslim woman. Privation and want, social opprobrium and calumny will pursue her with a mercilessness like that of fate. But if she can go through all this without breaking, she would have given to the Indian woman a personality and a soul of her own, and a great step forward would have been taken towards our national regeneration.

—*Our Cause: A Symposium by Indian Women* (1938)

Sarojini Naidu
(1879–1949)

Poetess, political activist, feminist, ardent nationalist, Nightingale of India—Sarojini Naidu lived up to all these roles with equal elegance. She was born in Hyderabad in an environment shaped to a large extent by her father Aghorenath Chattopadhyay, a brilliant scientist, linguist and respected scholar. He established the Nizam's College in 1878, a pioneering women's educational institute.

His daughter, on the other hand, decided she wanted to write poetry: 'One day when I was eleven, I was sighing over a sum in algebra. It wouldn't come right; but instead, a whole poem came to me suddenly. I wrote it down. From that day my poetic career began.'

A young Sarojini had first-hand experience of the suffragist campaign in England, before coming back to India and being drawn to the Congress and Gandhiji's Non-Cooperation Movement. She contributed greatly to the women's movement, lecturing all over India, along with Annie Besant, on the welfare of youth, dignity of labour, women's emancipation and nationalism.

About those years, Margaret Cousins, in *Indian Womanhood Today* writes: 'Dogged by ill-health, she has performed miracles of physical endurance—with all the refined sensitiveness of a supreme singer of lyrical verse, she endures years of ear-splitting committee meetings and bone-shaking travel on Indian railways.'

In 1924, Sarojini travelled to Eastern Africa and South Africa in the interest of Indians there, and became the first woman president of the National Congress the following year. Her anti-British activity earned her a number of prison sentences. She also accompanied Gandhi to London for the second session of the Round Table Conference for Indian-British cooperation in 1931.

A deep love for her country and affection for Nehru and Gandhi are obvious in her writing. Also evident is a love for nature as this excerpt from a letter written to Nehru in 1925 shows: '... bravely I have deserted my post for a few weeks because my soul needed and cried out for an atmosphere of beauty, burgeoning trees, nesting birds, lyric poets, the children and dogs and old friends and a little leisure from the constructive programme and the self-destructive programme of our so-called politics.'

Other letters suggest that Hindu-Muslim unity and a secular India were the main mission of her life. Between 1917 and 1919, also considered the most dynamic phase of her career as a public figure, she rallied public opinion on the Khilafat issue, Rowlatt or 'Black bills', Montagu-Chelmsford Reforms, Sabarmati Pact and the Satyagraha pledge. She went on to become Gandhi's most faithful lieutenant when he launched the Civil Disobedience Movement on April 6, 1919, and continued the work after he was imprisoned. Some of her other letters reveal how she would also gently tease him when he was being impractical. In a letter to Nehru in 1937, she writes: 'The Little Man (refers to Gandhiji) is sitting unconcernedly eating spinach and boiled marrow while the world ebbs and flows about him breaking into waves of Bengali, Gujarati, English and Hindi.'

With Independence, Sarojini Naidu became the first Indian woman Governor of the United Provinces (now Uttar Pradesh), and retained the post until her death on March 2, 1949. She published four collections of poems, all in English—*The Golden Threshold* (1905), *The Bird of Time* (1912), *The Broken Wing* (1917), and *The Sceptred Flute* (1937). She was also elected to the Royal Society of Literature.

An interesting and little-known fact is that many of her early poems were published by Kamala, the second wife of Samuel Satthianadhan. Samuel was initially married to the author Krupabai Satthianadhan.

Sarojini Naidu is represented here by a couple of letters written by her to Pandit Jawaharlal Nehru. On her death, the latter said: 'Here was a person of great brilliance ... She infused artistry and poetry into our national struggle.'

She remains a compelling figure who, apart from her contribution to Indian poetry in English, can be looked upon as an integral part of a group responsible for shaping a new independent India.

Letters to Jawaharlal Nehru

[This letter was written on the birth of Indira Gandhi]

Madras
17 December 1917

Dear Jawahar,

I have not one single moment since hearing your good news to sit down and send a word of congratulation to you and Kamala or a blessing for my new niece. I do both now in a half second snatched from a day *filled*—as usual—with engagements. Madras has gone *mad*—O quite mad!—and insists on sending me mad also.

If you are going to Calcutta you will find me at 7 Hungerford Street: so don't fail to look me up. I am sending you a copy of the Soul of India which is my contribution to the Montagu bombardment.

Love to all and a kiss to the new Soul of India.

Yours affectionately,
Sarojini Naidu

Taj Mahal Hotel,
Bombay, June 13 [?1923]

Dear Jawahar,

Cheerio! We shall weather the storm bravely—and fulfil the advice to let our work be a battle and our peace a victory. I think the idea of a full conference about Bakr Id is quite sound and the meeting place should be Allahabad in preference to Nagpur for various reasons. The idea is to have also a joint meeting of Khilafat and Congress Working Committees.

The Nagpur-Satyagraha is well organized and the only drawback is that local people do not take part. The Jubbulpore Satyagraha is really more genuine from that point of view and, on a close inquiry, I discovered that Jubbulpore had been badly let down by the very people who had instigated it and also backed it officially by sanctioning a grant of Rs. 15,000 towards it!! However, I have asked them to stop all Satyagraha in connection with the Town Hall by the 20th. In view of the commitments made under the impression that they were acting with the blessing of the old Working Committee, they could not in bare justice be ordered to stop all once.

Old Rajagopalachari is behaving shockingly and with [sic] deviation from the exact 'cross-your-heart' kind of truth!!

The Swaraj Party here is about finished and Patel is, I hear setting up some rival candidates against Swaraj Party candidates. C.R. Das is making matters pretty desperate by his speeches in the South.

However let us go on churning the ocean till we do evolve some supreme gift of Harmony—but first let us tide over Bakr Id which *Inshallah*, we shall do!

Love from your loving sister

Sarojini

The Golden Threshold,
Hyderabad-Deccan,
11 May 1925

My dear Jawahar,

I am writing from the Golden Threshold sitting on my own carved blackwood couch with Ras. Taffari, Pavo Nourmi, Nicolo Pissano and Dik Dik Mahjong—the four-footed rulers of the House luxuriously stretched all round me, the sun-birds and honeybirds making music in the garden among the flaming Gul Mohurs and Scarlet Roses. Mina is in the throes of packing books and boots and dictionaries for crossword puzzles because we are going out camping to Osman Sagar this evening. Padmaja is in thrills over the new Fiat that has just arrived from Bombay. Govind is praying in his heart while he feeds on a belated lunch of *bhaigara baingan* and *falsa sherbat* that the Exalted One won't spoil his holiday among the rocks and waters of our intended destination.

In a word, I am at home having my first holiday since 1921, a real holiday with every snake shut out from the paradise in the guise of outside cares, responsibilities and duties. Basely but bravely have I deserted my post for a few weeks because my soul needed and cried out for an atmosphere of beauty, burgeoning trees, nesting birds, lyric poets, the children and dogs and old friends and a little leisure from the constructive programme and the self-destructive programme of our so-called politics. I shall return duly to neglected duties and responsibilities but meanwhile I wish you could share the delight—the real delight of being in Hyderabad boating on the Mir Alam, of lounging and loafing around and meeting the most truly cosmopolitan society in India, which needless to say haunts The Golden Threshold even unto 4 generations beginning with the generation that was my parents—almost pre-historic!—and ending with the smallest tiniest generation that sits on the floor and shares its cakes with the cat and upsets its sherbat on its clothes. Why don't you too go on strike and hide here? I will ask Shuaib to come on strike too but I do draw the line at your other colleague. Lord save the mark!

I am not attending the Working Committee at Calcutta. I have been ill for weeks and I need the change of environment and occupation, mentally even more than physically. Besides, the agenda does not call loudly for my brain-wave except perhaps the 'Present Situation' as created by Deshbandhu!

I hope that Papaji and dear little Mamaji are well, that Kamala is quite strong again and that Indu is still like Atalanta, fleet of foot with the sun-rise in her eyes.

Padmaja sends her love to all, especially to Betty of the Beautiful Eyes. Leilamani has got re-absorbed into the Oxford atmosphere and is quite happy.

Au revoir. I send you all my renewed joy of life to share.

Your affectionate sister,
Sarojini

Bombay,
15 October 1926

Dear Jawahar,

I had a wire from Papaji this morning to say that quite inadvertently he had omitted to write to any of you in time to catch tomorrow's mail and that I was to write and let you know that he was 'convalescent and rapidly recouping. Others well.' Papaji was wonderfully well after his prolonged rest in Mussoorie before he went to Simla. Since then he began to languish—that I think is the right word for it, for mental even more than physical reasons: the wretched political situation, the internal quarrels, the wholly unworthy and disintegrating moves and counter-moves on the part of men whom he had trusted and worked with. ... Besides of course the strain of his tours. But now I think he is really getting better after the last sharp attack of fever. The elections are bothering him unduly. I think of the whole the situation is not nearly so gloomy for his party as was feared. I shall be glad when the next few weeks are over and there is a relaxing of the purely artificially produced and deliberately sustained tensions—communal, internecine, personal and all sorts.

I hear all sorts of nice rumours about you—things that please me of your restored *joie de vivre*. I am so glad that you have had such a prolonged vacation from the torpid horrors of Indian life. For you Europe must have been a fresh revelation of yourself and a real recovery from the ills of the soul. I hope Kamala is progressing. I wonder if she likes the Swiss air and the Swiss people. I am not very fond of Switzerland though I adore the green slopes when they are enamelled with Autumn flowers. Indu is a young mademoiselle by now jabbering in French with a real Swiss accent. Betty I hope is enjoying her holiday. Sarup and Ranjit I am told have had a superb time. Hélas! I would I were away across the seas! I have had a most strenuous time touring and settling quarrels. Just now I am somewhat ill. Padmaja is very well but Leilamani had a serious operation and is still only convalescing. The Hedaji Hajis came back rather fed up. The Maulana is very vocal and verbose against Saud. Shuaib does not seem too happy. Hie is seriously thinking of doing business in Bombay. Ansari has been more or less a dry nurse to royalty all these months. He looks bored stiff—he is imprisoned practically with thermometers and gargles and bandages as his only companions in bondage. ...

Umar's death makes Bombay a nightmare to me ... poor Umar royal-hearted Umar! I wonder if his unhappy soul has found peace. How he loved you!

I wonder if you can read my scrawl. My wrist is stiff with pain. 'Main sar-a-pa dard hun' to quote Iqbal literally.

Good Night, dear Jawahar. How I rejoice that you are out of India and that you soul has found its chance to renew its youth and glory and the vision of the Eternal Beauty. My love to the girls—mother and child.

Your loving sister,
Sarojini

Lucknow
29 September 1929

My beloved Jawahar,

I wonder if in the whole of India there was yesterday a prouder heart than your father's or a heavier heart than yours. Mine was the peculiar position of sharing in almost equal measure both his pride and your pain. I lay awake until late into the night thinking of the significance of the words I had used so often in reference to you, that you were predestined to a splendid martyrdom. As I watched your face while you were being given the rousing ovation on your election, I felt I was envisaging both the Coronation and the Crucifixion—indeed the two are inseparable and almost synonymous in some circumstances and some situations: they are synonyms today especially for you, because you are so sensitive and so fastidious in your spiritual response and reaction and you will suffer a hundred-fold more poignantly than men and women of less fine fibre and less vivid perception and apprehension, in dealing with the ugliness of weakness, falsehood, backsliding, betrayal ... all the inevitable attributes of weakness that seeks to hide its poverty by aggressive and bombastic sound. ... However, I have an abiding faith in your incorruptible sincerity and passion for liberty and though you said to me that you felt you had neither the personal strength nor a sufficient backing to put your own ideas and ideals into effect under the turmoils of so burdensome an office, I feel that you have been given a challenge as well as offered a tribute: and it is the challenge that will transmute and transfigure all your noblest qualities into dynamic force, courage and vision and wisdom. I have no fear in my faith.

In whatever fashion it is possible for me to help you or serve you in your tremendous and almost terrible task you know you have but to ask ... if I can give no more concrete help, I can at least give you full measure of understanding and affection ... and though as Khalil Gibran says: 'The vision of one man lends not its wings to another man,' yet I believe that the invincible faith of one's spirit kindles the flame of another in radiance that illumines the world ...

Your loving friend and sister,
Sarojini Naidu

Taj Mahal Hotel,
Bombay,
20 November 1929

Dear Jawaharlal,

This is called the pursuit of friendship under difficulties. Padmaja and I are on the threshold of departure and both of us being vulgarly popular people we are besieged with 'miscellaneous fellows' of both sexes every moment. Padmaja is terribly excited over her first voyage and her first escape from domestic thraldom. I hope the trip is going to give a new turn to her health and spirits. I had to make up my mind very suddenly almost between two heart-beats whether I would go or not to Africa. But they are in difficulties and their S.O.S. was urgent ... and Padmaja's longing to go to Africa was one of the sub-conscious influences that decided me.

Good-bye, dear Jawaharlal. I am coming back in time for your Congress on the 21st December. Please see that Papa President sends a cable to daughter president by 6th December to Nairobi with a message to be read out at the opening of the Congress.

Au revoir. Padmaja and I send love to all at Anand Bhawan.

Your loving
Sarojini

The Mahatma's Camp,
Calcutta,
13 November 1937

My very dear Jawahar,

I am writing from the modern version of the Tower of Babel. The little Man (Gandhiji) is sitting unconcernedly eating spinach and boiled marrow while the world ebbs and flows about him breaking into waves of Bengali, Gujarati, English and Hindi. Bidhan and his colleagues are in despair over his stubborn indocility as regards his health. He is really ill ... not only in his brittle bones and thinning blood but in the core of his soul ... the most lonely and tragic figure of his time ... India's man of destiny on the edge of his own doom ...

To you the other man of destiny I am sending a birthday greeting ... It will not reach you in time because of intervening eyes that must scan your correspondence. I have been watching you these two years with a most poignant sense of your suffering and loneliness, knowing that it cannot be otherwise.

What shall I wish you for the coming year? Happiness? Peace? Triumph? All these things that men hold supremely dear are but secondary things to you ... almost incidental ... I will wish you, my dear ... unflinching faith and unfaltering courage in your *via cruces* that all must tread who seek freedom and hold it more precious than life ... not personal freedom but the deliverance of a nation from bondage. Walk steadfastly along that steep and perilous path ... if sorrow and pain and loneliness by your portion. Remember Liberty is the ultimate crown of all your sacrifice ... but you will not walk alone.

Your loving
Sarojini

—*A Bunch of Old Letters* (1958)

Rokeya Sakhawat Hossain
(1880–1932)

Rokeya Sakhawat Hossain was born into a Bengali Muslim upper-class family in the north of present day Bangladesh. While her two brothers were educated at the prestigious St Xavier's College in Calcutta, Rokeya and her sisters, Karimunessa and Humaira, received a traditional education at home comprising popular books on proper 'feminine' conduct.

They were prevented from learning Bengali and English in order to pre-empt their being 'contaminated' by radical ideas from outside. Luckily, Rokeya's eldest brother was in favour of educating women, and secretly taught her English and Bengali at home, while everyone else slept.

She was married at the age of sixteen to a widower, Syed Sakhawat Hossain, who firmly believed that the education of women was the cure for society's ills. He encouraged his wife to write and even set aside 10,000 rupees to start a school for Muslim women. Eleven years after their marriage, he died and Rokeya started a school in Bhagalpur in his memory. In the face of opposition, the Sakhawat Memorial Girls' School reopened in Calcutta a few years later and, by 1930, evolved into a high school where Bengali and English were regular courses. Rokeya then entered the world of civil affairs and founded the Anjuman-e-Khawatin-e-Islam, Bangla (Bengali Muslim Women's Association) in 1916. She continued to be an active supporter of women's advancement, and was working on an essay entitled *Narir Adhikar* (The Rights of Women) when she died.

These humble beginnings are what make the witty fantasy *Sultana's Dream* (1905) so special. It was first written in English, then translated by Rokeya into Bengali. Never before had anyone created fiction where women controlled the state and men stayed confined to the '*murdana*'. A Utopia without war or crime, it is a place where horticulture is serious business, cooking is a pleasure, and science is used to serve humanity. For someone who constantly fought the '*purdah* of ignorance,' this short story must have been cathartic, to say the least.

To cite an example, the queen of this wonderful land meets Rokeya and explains to her why her land can't trade with countries where women are kept in *zenanas*: 'Men, we find, are rather of lower morals and so we do not like dealing with them. We do not covet other people's land, we do not fight for a piece of diamond though it may be thousand-fold brighter than the Koh-i-Noor, nor do we grudge a ruler his Peacock Throne.'

Selection from *Sultana's Dream*

One evening I was lounging in an easy chair in my bedroom and thinking lazily of the condition of Indian womanhood. I am not sure whether I dozed off or not. But, as far as I remember, I was wide awake. I saw the moonlit sky sparkling with thousand of diamond-like stars, very distinctly.

All of a sudden a lady stood before me; how she came in, I do not know. I took her for my friend, Sister Sara.

'Good morning,' said Sister Sara. I smiled inwardly as I knew it was not morning, but starry night. However, I replied to her, saying, 'How do you do?'

'I am all right, thank you. Will you please come out and have a look at our garden?'

I looked again at the moon through the open window, and thought there was no harm in going out at that time The men-servants outside were fast asleep just then, and I could have a pleasant walk with Sister Sara.

I used to take my walks with Sister Sara, when we were at Darjeeling. Many a time did we walk hand in hand and talk light-heartedly in the Botanical Gardens there. I fancied Sister Sara had probably come to take me to some such garden, and I readily accepted her offer and went out with her.

When walking I found to my surprise that it was a fine morning. The town was fully awake and the streets alive with bustling crowds. I felt very shy, since I was walking in the street in broad daylight, but there was not a single man visible.

Some of the passers-by made jokes at me. Though I could not understand their language, yet I felt sure they were joking. I asked my friend, 'What do they say?'

'The women say that you look very mannish.'

'Mannish?' said I, 'What do they mean by that?'

'They mean that you are shy and timid like men.'

'Shy and timid like men?' It was really a joke. I became very nervous, when I found that my companion was not Sister Sara, but a stranger. Oh, what a fool had I been to mistake this lady for my dear old friend, Sister Sara.

She felt my fingers tremble in her hand, as we were walking hand in hand.

'What is the matter, dear, dear?' she said affectionately.

'I feel somewhat awkward,' I said in a rather apologizing tone, 'as being a purdahnashin woman, I am not accustomed to walking about unveiled.'

'You need not be afraid of coming across a man here. This is Lady-land, free from sin and harm. Virtue herself reigns here.'

By and by I was enjoying the scenery. Really it was very grand. I mistook a patch of green grass for a velvet cushion. Feeling as if I were walking on a soft carpet. I looked down and found the path covered with moss and flowers.

'How nice it is,' said I.

'Do you like it?' asked Sister Sara. (I continued calling her 'Sister Sara,' and she kept calling me by my name.)

'Yes, very much; but I do not like to tread on the tender and sweet flowers.'

'Never mind, dear Sultana. Your treading will not harm them; they are street flowers.'

'The whole place looks like a garden,' said I admiringly. 'You have arranged every plant so skillfully.'

'Your Calcutta could become a nicer garden than this, if only your countrymen wanted to make it so.'

'They would think it useless to give so much attention to horticulture, while they have so many other things to do.'

'They could not find a better excuse,' said she with [a] smile.

I became very curious to know where the men were. I met more than a hundred women while walking there, but not a single man.

'Where are the men?' I asked her.

'In their proper places, where they ought to be.'

'Pray let me know what you mean by "their proper places."'

'O, I see my mistake, you cannot know our customs, as you were never here before. We shut our men indoors.'

'Just as we are kept in the Zenana?'

'Exactly so.'

'How funny,' I burst into a laugh. Sister Sara laughed too.

'But dear Sultana, how unfair it is to shut in the harmless women and let loose the men.'

'Why? It is not safe for us to come out of the zenana, as we are naturally weak.'

'Yes, it is not safe so long as there are men about the streets, nor is it so when a wild animal enters a marketplace.'

'Of course not.'

'Suppose, some lunatics escape from the asylum and begin to do all sorts of mischief to men, horses and other creatures, in that case what will your countrymen do?'

'They will try to capture them and put them back into their asylum.'

'Thank you! And you do not think it wise to keep sane people inside an asylum and let loose the insane?'

'Of course not!' said I laughing lightly.

'As a matter of fact, in your country this very thing is done! Men, who do or at least are capable of doing no end of mischief, are let loose and the innocent women shut up in the zenana! How can you trust those untrained men out of doors?'

'We have no hand or voice in the management of our social affairs. In India man is lord and master. He has taken to himself all powers and privileges and shut up the women in the zenana.'

'Why do you allow yourselves to be shut up?'

'Because it cannot be helped as they are stronger than women.'

'A lion is stronger than a man, but it does not enable him to dominate the human race. You have neglected the duty you owe to yourselves and you have lost your natural rights by shutting your eyes to your own interests.'

'But my dear Sister Sara, if we do everything by ourselves, what will the men do then?'

'They should not do anything, excuse me; they are fit for nothing. Only catch them and put the into the zenana.'

'But would it be very easy to catch and put them inside the four walls?' said I. 'And even if this were done would all their business—political and commercial—also go with them into the zenana!'

Sister Sara made no reply. She only smiled sweetly. Perhaps she thought it useless to argue with one who was no better than a frog in a well.

By this time we reached Sister Sara's house. It was situated in a beautiful heart-shaped garden. It was a bungalow with a corrugated iron roof. It was cooler and nicer than any of our rich buildings. I cannot describe how neat and how nicely furnished and how tastefully decorated it was.

We sat side by side. She brought out of the parlour a piece of embroidery work and began putting on a fresh design.

'Do you know how to knit and do needlework?'

'Yes; we have nothing else to do in our zenana.'

'But we do not trust our zenana members with embroidery!' She said laughing, 'as a man has not patience enough to pass thread through a needlehole even!'

'Have you done all this work yourself?' I asked her pointing to the various pieces of embroidered teapoy cloths.

'Yes.'

'How can you find time to do all these? You have to do the office work as well? Have you not?'

'Yes. I do not stick to the laboratory all day long. I finish my work in two hours.'

'In two hours! How do you manage? In our land the officers, magistrates for instance, work seven hours daily.'

'I have seen some of them doing their work. Do you think they work all the seven hours?'

'Certainly they do!'

'No, dear Sultana, they do not. They dawdle away their time in smoking. Some smoke two or three cheroots during the office time. They talk much about their work, but do little. Suppose one cheroot takes half an hour to burn off, and a man smokes twelve cheroots daily; then you see, he wastes six hours every day in sheer smoking.'

We talked on various subjects; and I learned that they were not subject to any kind of epidemic disease—not did they suffer from mosquito-bites as we do. I was very much astonished to hear that in Ladyland no one died in youth except by rare accident.

'Will you care to see our kitchen?' she asked me.

'With pleasure,' said I, and we went to see it. Of course the men had been asked to clear off when I was going there. The kitchen was situated in a beautiful vegetable garden. Every creeper, every tomato plant was itself an ornament. I found no smoke, nor any chimney either in the kitchen,—it was clean and bright; the windows were decorated with flower garlands. There was no sign of coal or fire.

'How do you cook?' I asked.

'With solar heat,' she said, at the same time showing me the pipe, through which passed the concentrated sunlight and heat. And she cooked something then and there to show me the process.

'How did you manage to gather and store up the sun heat?' I asked her in amazement.

'Let me tell you a little of our past history then. Thirty years ago, when our present Queen was thirteen years old, she inherited the throne. She was Queen in name only, the Prime Minister really ruling the country.

'Our good Queen liked science very much. She circulated an order that all the women in her country should be educated. Accordingly a number of girls' schools were founded and supported by the Government. Education was spread far and wide among women. And early marriage also was stopped. No woman was to be allowed to marry before she was twenty-one. I must tell you that, before this change we had been kept in strict purdah.'

'How the tables are turned,' I interposed with a laugh.

'But the seclusion is the same,' she said. 'In a few years we had separate universities, where no men were admitted.

'In the capital, where our Queen lives, there are two universities. One of these invented a wonderful balloon, to which they attached a number of pipes. By means of this captive balloon which they managed to keep afloat above the cloud-land, they could draw as much water from the atmosphere as they pleased. As the water was incessantly being drawn by the University people, no cloud gathered and the ingenious Lady Principal stopped rain and storms thereby.'

'Really! Now I understand why there is no mud here!' said I. But I could not understand how it was possible to accumulate water in the pipes. She explained to me how it was done; but I was unable to understand her, as my scientific knowledge was very limited. However, she went on,—

'When the other university came to know of this, they became exceedingly jealous and tried to do something more extraordinary still. They invented an instrument by which they could collect as much sun-heat as they wanted. And they kept the heat stored up to be distributed among others as required.

'While the women were engaged in scientific researches, the men of this country were busy increasing their military power. When they came to know that the female universities were able to draw water from the atmosphere and collect heat from the sun, they only laughed at the members of the universities and called the whole thing "a sentimental nightmare!"'

'Your achievements are very wonderful indeed! But tell me, how you managed to put the men of your country into the zenana. Did you entrap them first?'

'No.'

'It is not likely that they would surrender their free and open air life of their own accord and confine themselves within the four walls of the zenana! They must have been overpowered.'

'Yes, they have been!'

'By whom?—by some lady-warriors, I suppose?'

'No, not by arms.'

'Yes, it cannot be so. Men's arms are stronger than women's.'

'Then?'

'By brain.'

'Even their brains are bigger and heavier than women's. Are they not?'

'Yes, but what of that? An elephant also has got a bigger and heavier brain than a man has. Yet men can enchain elephants and employ them, according to their own wishes.'

'Well said, but tell me please, how it all actually happened. I am dying to know it!'

'Women's brains are somewhat quicker than men's. Ten years ago, when the military officers called our scientific discoveries 'a sentimental nightmare', some of the young ladies wanted to say something in reply to those remarks. But both the Lady Principals restrained them and said, they should reply, not by word, but by deed, if ever they got the opportunity. And they had not long to wait for that opportunity.'

'How marvellous!' I heartily clapped my hands.

'And now the proud gentlemen are dreaming sentimental dreams themselves.

'Soon afterwards certain persons came from a neighbouring country and took shelter in ours. They were in trouble having committed some political offence. The King who cared more for power than for good government asked our kind-hearted Queen to hand them over to his officers. She refused, as it was against her principle to turn out refugees. For this refusal the King declared war against our country.

'Our military officers sprang to their feet at once and marched out to meet the enemy.'

'The enemy however, was too strong for them. Our soldiers fought bravely, no doubt. But in spite of all their bravery the foreign army advanced step by step to invade our country.'

'Nearly all the men had gone out to fight; even a boy of sixteen was not left home. Most of our warriors were killed, the rest driven back and the enemy came within twenty-five miles of the capital.'

'A meeting of a number of wise ladies was held at the Queen's palace to advise [as] to what should be done to save the land.'

'Some proposed to fight like soldiers; others objected and said that women were not trained to fight with swords and guns; nor were they accustomed to fighting with any weapons. A third party regretfully remarked that they were hopelessly weak of body.'

'If you cannot save your country for lack of physical strength, said the Queen, try to do so by brain power.'

'There was a dead silence for a few minutes. Her Royal Highness said again, "I must commit suicide if the land and my honour are lost." '

'Then the Lady Principal of the second University, (who had collected sun-heat), who had been silently thinking during the consultation, remarked that they were all but lost; and there was little hope left for them. There was however, one plan which she would like to try, and this would be her first and last efforts; if she failed in this, there would be nothing left but to commit suicide. All present solemnly vowed that they would never allow themselves to be enslaved, no matter what happened.

'The Queen thanked them heartily, and asked the Lady Principal to try her plan.'

'The Lady Principal rose again and said, 'before we go out the men must enter the zenanas. I make this prayer for the sake of purdah.' 'Yes, of course,' replied Her Royal Highness.

'On the following day the Queen called upon all men to retire into zenanas for the sake of honour and liberty.'

'Wounded and tired as they were, they took that order rather for a boon! They bowed low and entered the zenanas without uttering a single word of protest. They were sure that there was no hope for this country at all.'

'Then the Lady Principal with her two thousand students marched to the battlefield, and arriving there directed all the rays of the concentrated sunlight and heat towards the enemy.'

'The heat and light were too much for them to bear. They all ran away panic-stricken, not knowing in their bewilderment how to counteract that scorching heat. When they fled away leaving their guns and other ammunitions of war, they were burnt down by means of the same sun-heat.'

'Since then no one has tried to invade our country any more.'

'And since then your countrymen never tried to come out of the zenana?'

'Yes, they wanted to be free. Some of the Police Commissioners and District Magistrates sent word to the Queen to the effect that the Military Officers certainly deserved to be imprisoned for their failure; but they never neglected their duty and therefore they should not be punished and they prayed to be restored to their respective offices.'

'Her Royal Highness sent them a circular letter intimating them that if their services should ever be needed they would be sent for, and that in the meanwhile they should remain where they were.'

'Now that they are accustomed to the purdah system and have ceased to grumble at their seclusion, we call the system "Murdana" instead of "zenana".'

'But how do you manage,' I asked Sister Sara, 'to do without the Police or Magistrates in case of theft or murder?'

'Since the "Murdana" system has been established, there has been no more crime or sin; therefore we do not require a Policeman to find out a culprit nor do we want a Magistrate to try a criminal case.'

'That is very good, indeed. I suppose if there were any dishonest person, you could very easily chastize her. As you gained a decisive victory without shedding a single drop of blood, you could drive off crime and criminals too without much difficulty!'

'Now, dear Sultana, will you sit here or come to my parlour?' she asked me.

'Your kitchen is not inferior to a queen's boudoir!' I replied with a pleasant smile, 'but we must leave it now; for the gentlemen may be cursing me for keeping them away from their duties in the kitchen so long.' We both laughed heartily.

'How my friends at home will be amused and amazed, when I go back and tell them that in the far-off Ladyland, ladies rule over the country and control all social matters, while gentlemen are kept in the Murdanas to mind babies, to cook and to do all sorts of domestic work; and that cooking is so easy a thing that it is simply a pleasure to cook!'

'Yes, tell them about all that you see here.'

'Please let me know, how you carry on land cultivation and how you plough the land and do other hard manual work.'

'Our fields are tilled by means of electricity, which supplies motive power for other hard work a well and we employ it for our aerial conveyances too. We have no railroad nor any paved streets here.'

'Therefore neither street nor railway accidents occur here,' said I. 'Do not you ever suffer from want of rainwater?' I asked.

'Never since the "water balloon" has been set up. You see the big balloon and pipes attached thereto. By their aid we can draw as much rainwater as we require. Nor do we ever suffer from flood or thunderstorms. We are all very busy making nature yield as much as she can. We do not find time to quarrel with one another as we never sit idle. Our noble Queen is exceedingly fond of Botany; it is her ambition to convert the whole country into one grand garden.'

'The idea is excellent. What is your chief food?'

'Fruits.'

'How do you keep your country cool in hot weather? We regard the rainfall in summer as a blessing from heaven.'

'When the heat becomes unbearable, we sprinkle the ground with plentiful showers drawn from the artificial fountains. And in cold weather we keep our room warm with sun-heat.'

She showed me her bathroom, the roof of which was removable. She could enjoy a shower bath whenever she liked by simply removing the roof (which was like the lid of a box) and turning on the tap of the shower pipe.

'You are a lucky people!' ejaculated I. 'You know no want. What is your religion, may I ask?'

'Our religion is based on Love and Truth. It is our religious duty to love one another and to be absolutely truthful. If any person lies, she or he is—.'

'Punished with death?'

'No; not with death. We do not take pleasure in killing a creature of God,—specially a human being. The liar is asked to leave this land for good and never to come to it again.'

'Is an offender never forgiven?'

'Yes, if that person repents sincerely.'

'Are you not allowed to see any men, except your own relations?'

'No one except sacred relations.'

'Our circle of sacred relations is very limited too, even first cousins are not sacred.'

'But ours is very large; a distant cousin is as sacred as a brother.'

'That is very good. I see Purity itself reigns over your land. I should like to see the good Queen, who is so sagacious and far-sighted and who has made all these rules.'

'All right,' said Sister Sara.

Then she screwed a couple of seats on to a square piece of plank. To this plank she attached two smooth and well-polished balls. When I asked her what the balls were for, she said, they were hydrogen balls and they were used to overcome the force of gravity. The balls were of different capacities to be used according to the different weights desired to be overcome. She then fastened to the air-car two wing-like blades, which, she said, were worked by electricity. After we were comfortably seated she touched a knob and the blades began to whirl, moving faster and faster every moment. At first we were raised to the height of about six or seven feet and then off we flew. And before I could realize that we had commenced moving, we reached the Garden of the Queen.

My friend lowered the air-car by reversing the action of the machine, and when the car touched the ground the machine was stopped and we got out.

I had seen from the air-car the Queen walking on a garden path with her little daughter (who was four years old) and her maids of honour.

'Halloo! you here!' cried the Queen addressing Sister Sara. I was introduced to Her Royal Highness and was received by her cordially without any ceremony.

I was very much delighted to make her acquaintance. In [the] course of the conversation I had with her, the Queen told me that she had no objection to permitting her subjects to trade with other countries. 'But', she continued, 'no trade was possible with countries where the women were kept in the zenanas and so unable to come and trade with us. Men we find are rather of lower morals and so we do not like dealing with them. We do not covet other people's land, we do not fight for a piece of diamond though it may be a thousand-fold brighter than the Koh-i-Noor, nor do we grudge a ruler his Peacock Throne. We dive deep into the ocean of knowledge and try to find out the precious gems, which nature has kept in store for us. We enjoy Nature's gifts as much as we can.'

After taking leave of the Queen, I visited the famous universities, and was shown over some of their manufactories, laboratories and observatories.

After visiting the above places of interest we got again into the air-car, but as soon as it began moving I somehow slipped down and the fall started me out of my dream. And on opening my eyes, I found myself in my own bedroom still lounging in the easy-chair.

—*Sultana's Dream* (1905)

Nalini Turkhud
(n.d.)

Nalini Turkhud was an actress with Prabhat Studios in Poona in the 1940s, and one of the films she starred in was called *Chandrasena*. S.A. Subnis who wrote the Foreword to Nalini Turkhud's novel *The Jagirdar of Palna* (1935) tells us that the novel is 'the handiwork of a young girl still in her teens.' He finds the plot of the novel 'catching', and it is. It can be called a melodramatic plot, with the real *rani* and her son being displaced by usurpers, except that such melodrama was an ordinary part of life at the royal courts of India. But it is told very briskly, and that gives the novel some energy. S.A. Subnis tells us that 'Miss Nalini has steered clear of everything that is iconoclastic and revolutionary ... and has staunchly adhered to the old, time-honoured ideas. Gouri Dutt is the old, venerable type of Indian girlhood, and although educated on the modern pattern, refuses to go ahead with the vanguard of European civilization and fondly clings to the old traditions. The fate of Sushila is meant to be a warning to all such as are disposed to defy the traditional sex law and succumb to temptations which ordinarily come in the way of beautiful and young girls.'

The Foreword makes no mention of Nalini Turkhud's foray into films, so presumably her renown as a novelist was followed only much later by her stardom.

Chapter XIV

The next day arrived. The evening found me with Elsie in her charming suite at the Metropol Hotel.

'Why! Haven't you brought your bag and baggage?' she asked.

'I only came for tea,' I answered.

'That means you are not coming with me?'

'Of course, I am.'

The tea was brought in. Elsie closely surveyed me. 'Why are you so pale, child?—Are you not well?'

'Am quite well, thank you. You are always making an unnecessary fuss about me.'

'Not at all! You need somebody to look after you.'

'I am not a baby. Twenty long years have passed.'

'That makes no difference. You are yet a child;—too innocent to face this deceiving world.'

'I may have been—but I am not now. Experience has awakened—no, it has roughly shaken me out of the illusions of my childhood.'

'Your case seems to be something like mine, Gouri,' Elsie said pouring the tea. 'Wait, let us finish tea. We will then sit in the quiet outside gallery, and I will narrate to you my surprising tale.'

Tea was over. Elsie beckoned me to the tiny, circular veranda-like gallery. A servant placed two wicker chairs. We sat down.

For a considerable time, my usually jovial and talkative companion was silent and grave. She blankly looked towards the distant scenery.

'You think me happy, don't you? It is a pretence. There was a time when I was like you; innocent, trusting and guileless, but instead of making me happy, my innocence made me suffer.

'Don't look so tragic, Gouri. Listen to me with a smile. My tale may be bitter, yet it will be a warning to girls like you. Have you heard the name of the Earl of Randolf?'

'You mean the owner of Eastborne Castle?'

'The same. He is my father.'

'Your father!,' I ejaculated. 'Do you mean that you are the Honourable Miss Elizabeth Manners?'

She nodded. 'That's me! Four years ago, I was engaged to Philip Esmond. Papa was against it, and I was then just like you,—too simple-minded to understand that I was loved, only as an heiress and not for myself.

'Philip flattered me. He was a perfect and adoring gentleman. Handsome, obliging, with pleasing manners he seemed all that a girl could desire. He proposed, and in the great enthusiasm of my first love, I accepted him. The marriage hour arrived, a pale miserable-looking woman came to see me. I saw her. What do you think she revealed? She was the wife of Philip Esmond. With tears she told me of the ill-treatment she had received at the hands of her apparently sleek and polished husband.

'As soon as I came to know of it, my would-be bride-groom disappeared. Everything that was only a few minutes ago joyous and festive became suddenly gloomy and funeral. My papa cursed and swore; some guests enjoyed the fun; others pitied me. Gouri! had you been in my place how would you have felt? It was a bullet through my ignorant heart and a shock to my simple faith. I gave up attending social functions for I hated the crowd. It pained me when people intently questioned me about my wedding fiasco. Solitude became my sole companion. I brooded; my health rapidly gave way, and I suffered more and more mentally and bodily.

'Every day poor papa anxiously surveyed his only child. He begged me to forget the incident; to occupy my mind in something else. He, then gave me his long-asked-for consent, to appear on the stage. For two years I did theatrical work; it helped a great deal to heal my wounded heart. Then I appeared in three British films; these demanded much of my attention and had more or less revived me from semi-insane state. About this time, Captain Lawton was organizing a dancing revue. I joined him. We travelled all over and were successful. The Indian trip then came. We had a very strenuous time in Bombay and Southern India, and now I wanted a rest, so I decided to take a two months holiday in some quiet, healthy place. I was suggested this, and seeing the place, I liked it and decided to come here.

'Well, Gouri, are you astonished to know my real position in life?'
'Certainly I am.'
'Do you feel ashamed of being a dancer's friend?'
'Of course not! but still I cannot understand how you took a fancy to a poor girl like me. It is a puzzle to me.'

She smiled. 'I do not know that myself, but I believe it was the first impression which drew me to you. If any other person had been bitten that day, she would have got angry and cursed me—but you! You only offered an anguished smile, and angelic civility. It astonished me, and I wanted to know more of you. Then in the hospital, from his manner I thought the doctor to be some relative of yours. His rudeness had hurt me much. The next day when I wrote to you, I had very little hope of a good reply—but it did come. Written in a peculiar, yet striking hand, it again established your good nature. Days passed by, you told me little things about yourself and I gathered from them, that you had also suffered. Here I saw in you, myself as I was before the shock of Philip Esmond's deceit, and I felt that at last I had found a real companion. For those who have undergone agony of this nature can only realize what it is. Is it not so, Gouri?'

I nodded.

'Well, let us drop the curtain now. Have you notified your doctor that you're leaving?'
'Not yet, though I hinted to him about it.'
'Why only hinted? You should have told him straight off.'
'I will tell him now.'

'I must wire to Lawton to engage two passages instead of one.'

'Do you mean on the steamer?'

'Yes.'

'How can I manage about going to Europe? I am so ignorant, foolish, besides, I have not even decent clothes to wear.'

'Oh, leave that to me child. You may be a Hindoo girl, yet to me you are, as a younger sister, and I should like you to feel the same towards me.'

'It is so good of you. How in the world will I be able to repay your wonderful kindness!'

'Only by not mentioning it,' remarked Elsie.

The clock chimed eight o'clock. 'Is it so late?' I asked surprised how quickly the time had passed.

'Yes, it is eight o'clock.' Elsie declared. 'Dinner must be ready and oh! I forgot to tell you to change your sari into a nice little one which I have brought for you.'

She ushered me to the dressing-room and showed me a beautiful crimson, silk-embroidered sari of some very fine material. 'And this one,' she said revealing another cream coloured one of the same pattern, 'I have brought it for myself and you must show me how to wear it. Which colour do you like? I thought the red one will look better with your olive skin'.

'But both the colours will suit you well.'

'What of it? I am not going to wear saris always. I brought this just for fun.' She put the yellow sari in its box. 'Quick! wear this; we will be late for dinner.'

'Please excuse me now. I have not told Mrs Sinha. She will be waiting for me.'

'Let her wait. Who cares!'

'No Elsie, please let me go. It is the last night. From to-morrow I am with you till you get tired of me.'

'I suppose you are anxious to say farewell to your Orphanage kiddies, the hospital staff, and your blessed doctor; are you not?'

'Of course, I am.'

'What time shall I send the car for you? Will one hour be enough for you to finish your parting bye byes?'

'When are we leaving?'

'At 6.30 to-morrow morning.'

'Send the car for me at half past nine.'

'Come with your bag and baggage; no changing your mind now.'

I departed and arrived at Manor Hall.

Mrs Sinha had dined, so I took my meals alone.

Somehow, I was unhappy at the thought of leaving. Three years had sheltered me here, in peace and security; but woe to my wandering luck!

Mrs Sinha's room was closed. I wanted to wish her good-bye and offer my humble gratitude for the kindness which she had shown me. I asked Mary. She said, 'Her ladyship would not like to be disturbed.'

'Where is the master?' I asked.

'Upstairs, in the library. On his return from the hospital he enquired if you were in.'

'At what time?'

'Eight.'

I went to my room; packed my few things in a newly bought leather suit-case. Then I departed to the doctor's library. I knocked.

'What is that?', came the doctor's stern demand.

'It is me, Sir—Gouri.'

'Enter.'

I did so.

'Well, what has brought you here?'

'I have come to bid you goodbye and thank you for all the goodness and kindness you have shown to a friendless girl.'

'Anything else?'

'No, nothing.'

'Where are you going?'

'To assume duties at my new post.'

'You are determined to leave?'

'There is no other alternative.'

'What if I make one?'

'My word is given.'

'You must be very happy to leave such humiliating surroundings?'

'No, I am not,—in fact I am sorry to leave.'

'Do you know what will be the condition of one man, when you leave?'

I did not understand him. I was mute.

He continued 'You will be degrading him;—taking your own words you, who have lifted him, will be dragging him down to perdition.'

'I do not understand you'.

'Of course you will not.—You are too innocent to know a man's deep feelings.' Suddenly his face became extremely stern. It means Gouri Dutt, you cannot go.'

'Everything is settled.'

A book was in his hand. He threw it on the table, got up, pushed his chair aside, and came towards me.

'Nothing is settled! Go and write a refusal to your master or mistress whoever it is.'

'I cannot do it.'

'Why not?'

'Because when your bride comes she will not like my presence here.'

'Who has told you so, and who is my bride?'

'The Rajkumari of Mena.'

He laughed.

'My little girl, what baseless information you have.'

'It is not baseless Sir. I have received it from a reliable source.'

'May I know the reliable source?'

This perplexed me.

'Go on, out with it,' he demanded.

'Mrs Sinha has told me Sir.'

'And she has also told you that my bride will not like your presence here?'

I bent my head and kept my eyes on the mosaic-covered floor.

'Speak! for God's sake speak!'

I did not speak.

For a moment he stood before me and then he fiercely turned towards the door.

'I will ask her,' he savagely growled.

I quickly moved forward, and caught the sleeve of his coat.

'Please don't,' I begged, 'it will cause me greater unhappiness.'

'Yes, and what about me—my life? Have you no thought for it? For years I have waited for my ideal;—a woman who would combine the East and West; who, with all her modern ideas and habits would lend them the grace and modesty of the ancient Hindu girl. I looked all over for her; sometimes I thought I had a glimpse of her, but ere I moved another step, I found myself mistaken for, either she would be too westernized or too shy and stupid. I gave up hope altogether of finding my ideal woman when, it was fated that I should save and bring an unknown wanderer home. She looked weary and travel-worn and as I carried her in my arms, dripping wet, a queer sensation came over me. I felt that something entirely new was entering my life. I left her in Manor Hall and went on my village cholera-tour.

When I returned she was better, and was given the Orphanage Matron's post for a trial. Here, this frail, shy-looking mistress's superb mode of teaching satisfied—no, it astonished me. I was at once struck by her reserved and quiet nature, and studied her more closely whenever I got the opportunity to do. She was shy, yet she offered a bold and daring glance; she was modern in outward appearance yet there shone within her the bright star of venerable, time-honoured, civilization. I tried to see more of her but whenever she could she always avoided me. Then one day an incident took place; little by little those close petals opened and displayed the interior beauty of the flower. She became my sacred power; my holy altar, whereon I found perfect peace and happiness. Outside my work, she alone occupied my thoughts.'—He tried to shake my hands off his coat-sleeve. 'Let me go,' he demanded, 'I want to ask my mother as to why she wants to rob me of my only happiness.' He faced me; my eyes met his. 'Gouri, I want to know why she told you all this—.'

I interrupted 'She has done it for your good; she knows her son's welfare and what is best for him.'

'Stop your philosophy and let me go,' he again angrily demanded.

'I won't, and cannot let you go. Kill me if you like. I will not leave you unless you promise me that you will not utter,—nor question Mrs Sinha about any such thing.'

'What if I do go and tell her? What is your delicate strength against mine! If I want to go I can,' so saying he wrenched himself free.

I stood defiant. 'Go!—Give me my last parting shock. It must come. I am afraid it is fated to come. I must quietly swallow the bitter pill of anguish which you are forcing on me. Three years hard labour has earned me your mother's good will and now you want to lower me in her eyes—,' but I abruptly changed my tone. I must not lose my temper; I must not get excited. 'I am sorry', I commenced gently 'I forgot, that I could never get rid of the disgraceful and cruel accusation;—it is like a contagious obstinate disease, and can only be shaken off by death alone. I happen to have, not a very pleasing past, so naturally your mother resents my staying here any more, because she came to know of this only yesterday,—from the Ranisaheb of Mena. No mother would like her son to associate with a girl of a doubtful character. Mrs Sinha has been too good to me but—,' I stopped and a sigh of agony escaped my lips.

From the door the doctor had listened intently but as I stopped, he came to me and caught my hands—. 'Who accuses you? Who declares your conduct is culpable? Bring the persons to me. I will deal with them.'

'There is no need Sir. What is destined must happen, so what good is there in my blaming the world!'

He patted my hands—. 'My poor Gouri, how sadly you seem to have been misunderstood.'

'My outward appearance has deceived them.'

'It could not deceive me.'

'You may be mistaken.'

'I never am. My judgment is always accurate.'

I tried to draw my hands away.

'No Gouri, let them remain. Poor and unworthy as I am, I entreat you to accept me as your husband.'

'Sir!' escaped my dumbfounded lips but he unheeded me and continued, 'let me shelter you from the pitfalls and dangers of this cruel world. Queer and whimsical I may be, yet I will try to wash away sorrow and its every trace from your life. Quick! My tender flower. Say yes.'

Bewildered I stared at his face.

'Gouri!' he recommenced 'Gouri, why are you so terrified? Speak to me, tell me that you will accept me.'

'Are you trying to mock me?'

'Mock you! What for?—You distrust my words?'

'Entirely.'

'May I know why?'

'Because you are engaged to, and must marry the Rajkumari.'

'Why are you harping on the Rajkumari?' he vehemently asked. 'I tell you I am not engaged to her, neither will I ever be. What love or respect do I entertain for her?—She has physical attractions no doubt, but her heart is barren no light shines through the windows of her soul. She is nothing; merely a beautiful doll.'

'Your mother desires you to marry her.'

'May be, but I am not going to sin against my own soul just to fulfil her desire.'

'There is no such thing—.'

'Of course,' he interrupted, 'When she desires me to marry a woman just for her family and rank, while my bleeding heart will lie at the feet of another. What greater transgression could a man commit! If I marry, it will be you; otherwise, through darkness or light, through joy or sorrow, I will remain as I am, a bachelor.'

'If you marry me, do you know that it will be a heart-breaking shock to your dear mother?'

'Never! If I ask her she will not go against my wish—my happiness.'

'She may consent outwardly, but in her heart she will keep brooding on what she will consider a misalliance. No mother would like an ill-reputed, beggar girl to become her son's bride.—No! If I had been in her place, I would not have liked it.'

There was a knock at the door. 'What is it?' hoarsely the doctor asked.

'Dr. Brownsab has sent me to tell you that the A. Ward patient has been taken to the operation room.'

'For heaven's sake go, I am coming,' was the doctor's ferocious reply. His face was agitated and strange lustrous gleams shone from his eyes.

He studied my face. 'Well?' with that penetrating, yet agonizing look he asked.

'Let us bid goodbye, for we may not meet again,' said I.

He left my hands.

'Never,' said he, as he bent his head, 'never will I touch those hands in farewell. Offer them to me as my bride.'

He spoke with a queer gentleness which broke me down; tears came to my eyes.

He then strode to the door but abruptly stopped and faced me.

'Gouri Dutt,' he began with a strange force, 'remember you leave me here in anguish, in pain, but let me tell you that you may go even to the other end of the world, still a day will dawn when God will drag you to my side, then you will come to me with faith and trust.—You will offer your love nobly as my bride!' and with a last tragic look, he banged the door and departed.

Unhappily I gazed at the swinging door. I heard the doctor's heavy steps descend the stairs. How I longed to call him back, to consent to become his bride. I loved him; he understood my inner feelings; he had offered me comfort, a home, an honourable name, and last of all his heart. They were proffered with nobility, yet I could not accept them.

Mrs Sinha commanded my respect and I was not prepared to repay her kindness by ingratitude. She would, I knew—feel extremely degraded to have me as her daughter-in-law.

I went downstairs, Mrs Sinha's room was open; she was seated in the arm-chair and was as usual, dressed in a plain white mull sari, which made her look exquisitely divine. I entered, knelt at her side.

—*The Jagirdar of Palna* (1936)

Dr S. Muthulakshmi Reddy
(1886–1968)

In her *Autobiography*, Dr S. Muthulakshmi Reddy writes: 'When I was four years-old I was admitted into a pial school in Pudukottah where I learnt Tamil alphabets. When I was admitted into the pial school I distinctly remember my father telling them to teach me just enough Tamil so as to enable me to keep milk and dhoby accounts.'

As the years passed, Dr Reddy went on to become the first woman to study medicine in Madras, the first woman to be a member of the Madras legislature, the first Alderwoman in the Madras Corporation and the first woman Deputy President of the Madras Legislative Council.

Muthulakshmi Reddy was born in the princely state of Pudukottah. Her father was the Principal of the Maharaja's College, while her mother came from a family that had traditionally danced in temples. The latter wanted her daughter to be educated, only marginally. As Muthulakshmi Reddy says, though her mother was pious, pure, religious and loyal to her father, she would later tell him that her daughter's education had to be stopped in order to get her married off. 'My mother never could see any value in the education of girls. Though not an educated lady, she could efficiently manage the home and bring up her children with good habits. In those days absolute obedience and loyalty to the husband was a virtue by itself.'

When Muthulakshmi applied to the Maharaja's College in her home town at the age of eighteen, the Principal and Diwan turned down the application alleging that her presence would 'demoralize' the boys. Intervention by the Maharaja himself made it possible for her to join.

About her later years of study, she writes, 'The photograph of Smt Kamala Satthianadhan and her sister, Krishnamma (Telugu Brahmin converts to Christianity) dressed in the graduate gown in a magazine sent to my father from Madras made a deep impression on me.'

In 1914, Muthulakshmi married Dr. T. Sundara Reddy. She served women and children as a visiting doctor in the Widows Home and in the Social Service League. In 1925 she went to England on a government scholarship to specialize in the diseases of women and children. Her main contribution to social service was during her tenure as Legislator from 1927 to 1930. During this period she succeeded in abolishing the *devadasi* system of temple prostitution, in 1929. Writing about it in her *Autobiography*, she discusses why she wanted the devadasi institution abolished, while looking for a possible remedy. Her passionate plea is ample proof of the importance she attached to the issue: 'Now I appeal to you in the name of humanity, in the name of justice and on behalf of the thousands of our young innocent girls who are sacrificed on the altar of immortality and vice, that Madras may take the lead in enacting a permanent measure to put a stop to this evil as even it has taken its first place in the granting of political rights to its women, a status unequalled in the history of any other nation in the world.'

Muthulakshmi Reddy also piloted social and moral reform acts, including the Sharda Act which increased the marriageable age for boys and girls. In 1930 she managed to have the Act for the Suppression of Brothels and Immoral Traffic, passed in Madras. Close to Gandhiji, she also worked towards securing political emancipation for Indian women. She visited the US in 1933 and attended the International Women's Conference in Chicago. In 1931 she presided over the fifth meeting of the All India Women's Conference in Lahore and continued to be its president and vice president till 1935. She was also awarded the Padma Bhushan.

The extract from *My Experiences as a Legislator* (1930) illustrates her qualities as a feisty fighter for the causes in which she believed. She wrote several books both in English and in the vernacular: her *Autobiography*, *Works of Mrs Margaret Cousins* and *My Experiences as a Legislator* to name a few. She was also deeply religious and believed in the dictum of Avvai—there are two castes, the selfish and unselfish.

Writing about Muthulakshmi Reddy, Margaret Cousins, in her book *Indian Womanhood Today*, says, 'She sacrificed a lucrative practise to act as the first woman member of a Provincial Council and Deputy-Speaker of the Madras Parliament. She was meticulous in studying the subjects on which she secured reform legislation. It annoys her that women in public life do not read newspapers sufficiently to be up-to-date on topical subjects. She got a great reception in America, and after travelling all over India with the Hartog Commission on Education, she could have been an All India Leader, but she has limited herself to building fine charitable trusts in Madras, the Avvai Home for Orphans and Destitute Women. In politics she's a born independent.'

Cousins goes on to mention Muthulakshmi's husband and highlights his role in her life thus: 'Her husband says he has taken a new degree since he retired from the medical college. He is now P.A. Personal Assistant to Muthulakshmiammal! A noble pair devoted to the poor.'

The independence of spirit that Cousins mentions is plain in *My Experience as a Legislator*, where Muthulakshmi talks about women's institutes, examines ways and means of improving them along with the quality of women's education in India and also, interestingly, gives us her reasons for initially wanting to refuse the post of Legislator: 'When the Women's Association pressed me to accept the honour and the high responsibility of that office, I hesitated; my reasons being, firstly, that as a medical practitioner of fourteen years' standing, and commanding a wide practice I thought that Council work would interfere with my medical work; secondly, having then recently finished a course of post-graduate study in diseases of women and children in England and having learnt the most-up-to-date methods of treatment, I did not want to exchange medical and research work for politics. Thirdly, I felt that I had not enough experience of public life. In short, I was neither a politician nor was I interested in the politics of the country except what directly concerned the women's life even though, subsequently I found that whatever concerns men, equally concern women and all Acts and Laws should affect both men and women alike.'

How I Became a Legislator

It was only at the beginning of the third Madras Provincial Legislative Council, that is about the middle of 1926, that women were granted the right to be elected or to be nominated to the local Council.

Therefore there was not much time before the election date for women candidates to do any canvassing among the electorate. In spite of the shortness of time our sister in S. Canara, Mrs Kamaladevi Chattopadhyaya, now in Yerwada Jail, had the public spirit and the courage to announce her candidature in the press and to face election with the gentlemen candidate in her constituency, but unfortunately she was defeated by a narrow majority of votes.

Therefore, there was no other alternative for women but to be appointed to the Council through nomination. The premier Women Association in the city, namely the Women's Indian Association, that not only secured franchise for Indian women but also secured for them the right to sit in the Council, chose and sent up to Government a few names of well-known women workers (including mine) for nomination to the local Council and thus the Madras Government conferred on me the honour and the privilege to represent the women of this presidency in the local Legislative Council.

When the Women's Association pressed me to accept the honour and the high responsibility of that office, I hesitated; my reasons being, *firstly*, myself being a medical practitioner of fourteen years' standing and commanding a wide practice I thought that Council work would interfere with my medical work; *secondly*, having then recently finished a course of post-graduate study in diseases of women and children in England and having learnt the most-up-to-date methods of treatment, I did not want to exchange medical and research work for politics. *Thirdly*, I felt that I had not enough experience of public life. In short, I was neither a politician nor was I interested in the politics of the country except what directly concerned the women's life even though, subsequently I found that whatever concerns men, equally concerns women and all Acts and Laws should affect both men and women alike.

However, when the Women's Indian Association pleaded that I should accept nomination to represent my sisters' cause in the Council, I could not but yield to their wishes. Therefore, with many misgivings and fears I entered this new sphere of public activity.

Hereafter the records of the local Legislative Council which lasted from December 1926 to June 1930, will speak for themselves.

Election of the Hon. President

On the 14th December 1926, the new Council assembled when the election of the president took place. Rao Bahadur C.V.S. Narsimha Raju Garu was unanimously elected to the chair, on which he was congratulated by all parties in the Council. Being the only woman member in the House a few of my brother councillors desired very much that I should also address the Chair on that occasion. I had not known the president before, I had no other women friend in the house to consult on that matter and I must confess that I felt very nervous, with all eyes turned towards me, when I stood up to speak. Here is an extract from my speech:

> 'Sir, I have great pleasure in congratulating you on the very lofty position that has been assigned to you by the unanimous vote of the House. I am the only lady member in this assembly, even though one half of the population are women. You know, Sir, that our position in society is still backward and we have many grievances one of which is that only two women out of every one hundred are able to read and write. So, you will side with me in all my attempts to ameliorate their condition realizing that no country or nation will prosper without the active support and co-operation of its women.'

Now I rejoice to state that the president did come up to my expectations of him and readily and willingly helped me in all my attempts to better the condition of women in this presidency as the following records will show. The Council then adjourned to meet again on the 24th January 1927.

Meanwhile it was brought to my notice that in the Chengleput District Board, in the seat vacated by a woman member, a gentleman was nominated by the Government and I immediately felt called upon to ventilate that grievance on the floor of the Council; I gave notice of certain interpellations (interpellation is the parliamentary term for question) which appeared with the Government replies on the agenda paper of the 24th January meeting.

Questions

1. Will the Hon. Minister for Education and Local Self-Government be pleased to state:

(a) whether any proposal has been received from the President of the Chengleput District Board or the Collect or of Chengleput for filling up the vacancy caused by the resignation of a lady member of the District Board; and if so; when;

(b) whose name was recommended to the Government;

(c) if the name of a lady member has not been proposed, the reasons given by the recommending authorities therefor:

(d) what attempts were made to get a lady nominee for the place vacated by the lady member; and

(e) whether Government will be prepared to consider the desirability of appointing a lady member in that vacancy?

Answer

(a) to (d) The President, District Board, Chengleput, submitted proposals in July 1926 for the nomination of a lady resident in Madras in the place of Mrs K. Satthianadhan resigned. As the nominee was entirely unconnected with the district, the President was asked to suggest the name of a lady of the Chengleput District. He submitted a nomination accordingly in September 1926. The Government however considered it desirable to fill the vacancy otherwise on that occasion.

(e) The Government will consider the question of appointing a lady member when an occasion presents itself, as stated in answer to clauses (e) and (f) of question No. 19.

Question

Sir, with reference to the answer to the question (a) to (d) may I ask the Hon. Minister for Local Self-Government on what grounds the government have set aside the nomination of the President of the District Board and appointed a gentleman in the vacancy caused by the resignation of a lady member?

Government reply:

The *then* Government thought that the Board would be better served by the nomination of the gentleman.'

Question

Does the Hon. Minister presume that the lady member recommended had not the requisite capacity?

Reply

I never said anything of the kind.

We women are grateful to the Hon. Dr P. Subbarayan who did keep up his promise to the Council by nominating women to the District Boards, Educational Councils and Municipalities in the Presidency.

However, I found, later on, that owing to my shy and sensitive nature, questioning and replying was not a very agreeable task for me though the Government Members were always polite and considerate in their replies to me.

Election of the Deputy President

After the question time on that day the election of the Deputy President took place. As all the parties had already made up their minds to elect me, when my name was proposed by Mr P.T. Rajan of the Justice Party and seconded by the Zamindar of Seithur, the whip of the Ministerialist Party, it received the unanimous support of the whole House and the Hon. President announced that I was duly elected.

I very much wished that such honour and responsibility had fallen upon older and more experienced shoulders, but even then, my natural reserve and shyness prevented me from speaking out my mind, though on the previous day, I had pleaded with my friends my incapacity and inexperience for such a high place. However I became conscious that the Council had conferred on me a great honour and a heavy responsibility and that I should discharge my duties to the best of my ability so as to bring glory and honour to my sex. Many a time I have since wished that I were only an M.L.C. and not the honoured Deputy President of the Council not because I experienced any difficulty in the discharge of my duties but because I was aware of my inexperience in parliamentary work. On the same date I spoke in support of a motion for a grant to a scheme of extension and improvements for the Government Women and Children's Hospital, Mangalore.

Here is an extract from that speech:

'I am of opinion that all the district hospitals for women and children should be properly equipped and staffed on the most up-to-date lines so that the women and the children of those districts may have the benefits of the most up-to-date treatment for their ailments because we in Madras very often get cases from the mofussils that have been badly handled and treated, also you know as well as I do, that any money spent on the health of women and children is an asset to the State.'

Which speech I noticed was well received by the Council.

The Council reassembling on the 25th January, the President announced amidst loud applause that His Excellency has given his assent to my election as the Deputy President of the Council, when Dewan Bahadur M. Krishnan Nayar expressed the following sentiments:

'May I say one word Sir, with reference to the election of Dr Muthulakshmi Reddy as Deputy President? I wish to convey my hearty congratulations— I am sorry she is not here—and also I convey the congratulations of the whole House to Dr Muthulakshmi Reddy. The Madras Legislative Council has given the lead to the other Legislative Councils in India in the matter of giving privileges to women. It was this Council that first passed a resolution giving the right of franchise to women and some of the other Councils in India followed the example of this Council. It was again this Council that first passed a resolution enabling women to stand as candidates for election and to be nominated as Members of this Council. I believe this is, so far as I am aware, the first instance in which a woman has been elected to preside over the deliberations of a Legislative assembly in the whole world. I know, Sir, that there have been women governors in some of the States that form the United States of America. We know also that there have been women members in the Cabinet; for instance, in the Last Labour Cabinet in England there was a woman Minister; but I believe there has been no instance in the world in which a Legislative Assembly chose a woman as a person to guide its deliberations. I believe it is the proud privilege of this House to have bestowed that honour upon a woman.

If I may be permitted, Sir, to strike a personal note, I may say that I have had the privilege of moving both those resolutions in this house—the resolution to get franchise to women, and the resolution to give the right to women to stand as candidates and as nominees to the Legislative Council. With these observations, Sir, I congratulate Dr Muthulakshmi Reddy and in all humility, this Council also.'

During the above proceedings I was not present in the Council as I was detained in a private house that morning by an urgent delivery case.

In the Chair

On the 27th January 1927, the Hon. President announced that the Hon. Deputy President would take the chair for the first time. The Deputy President who was taken by surprise by such an announcement, before occupying the chair, addressed the Council as follows:

'Before taking the chair I wish to express my heartfelt thanks to the Council which has conferred on me this unique honour so unanimously, and so whole-heartedly. My elevation to this seat I consider is not so much an honour to me personally as to the whole of Indian womenhood. This Presidency so far as the women's cause is concerned, has been very unique in many a respect. It was the first in granting the franchise to women, and then in admitting one of them to this Council. It has now earned the unparalleled distinction of electing her to the post of Deputy President of this council unsolicited and unasked, thereby authorizing her to guide its deliberations. I hope and I am sure that our Presidency will take the lead in initiating many reforms conducive to the welfare of my sex. Such action on your part speaks very highly of your wisdom, statesmanship and magnanimity and above all of the honour and esteem in which you hold your women. You have demonstrated to the world that you have rightly understood the power and influence of women not only in the inner life of your homes but also in the wider sphere of your public activities. In conclusion, I wish to express to the Hon. Members of this Council that I have accepted the onerous responsibilities with the full hope that I can always count upon your sympathy, co-operation and support which has already been assured to me by your unanimous vote. With these few words, I take the chair.' (Applause).

I found that the Presidential Chair was too big for me and I simply sank into it, but realizing very soon that I was there to preside over such an august body composed of the Members of the Madras Cabinet, the Hon. Ministers, the ex-Ministers, Zamindars, Rajas, Landlords, District Board Presidents, Advocates, Lawyers, overcoming my nervousness I listened gravely and attentively to the speeches of the Hon. Members. It would interest others to know that I was not then feeling very comfortable in the chair, as these thoughts were passing through my mind in rapid succession that I have accepted too much responsibility, that I might not do full justice to that high office, that the public might be disappointed in me, that I might not bring honour to my country people but on the other hand by my failure to come up to their high expectations of me, I might lower my sex and my country in the estimation of the whole world. During that first sitting itself, I was called upon to give a ruling. The discussion was on the amendment of the Kumararaja of Venkatagiri to the Madras Famine Code. I gave the ruling which was accepted by the Council and I learnt afterwards that my ruling was correct. I now record with a feeling of pride and gratitude that whenever I was in the chair, the Council was most courteous and considerate towards me.

—*My Experiences as a Legislator* (1930)

Hansa Mehta
(b. 1897)

Hansa Mehta was one of the first women to join Baroda College and to graduate from there. Her reminiscences of those days are taken from *The Baroda College Jubilee Commemoration Volume* (1933). The editor of the column describes her reminiscences as 'too true ... Fortunately things are far better now.'

Hansa Mehta wrote in Gujarati and has published plays, stories for children, and written for magazines. She was also the President of the Co-operative Society Mandal, a member of the Bombay University Senate, Educational Member, Karve's University, President, Bombay War Council, Chairman, MPWC Management Committee 1930–31, a member of various social work committees, a member of the Educational Committee, Vanita Vishram, and Secretary, National Council of Women.

My Reminiscences of Student Days in Baroda College (1913–17)

Some nineteen years ago three forlorn females timidly knocked at the door of this great seat of learning called the Baroda College and found admission. One was my sister Mrs Raiji, the other Miss Clarice Acquino, who alas! is no more and the third myself.

Daily had I passed and repassed this great awe-inspiring structure, little dreaming that one day its portals would be opened to me. For in those days very few women at least in Baroda thought of joining a man's college!

Our colleges in this Presidency are meant mainly for men; they cater for men. Women are admitted there on sufferance. That is what we felt when we three freshers were shown to a poky little room—six by ten would be a generous estimate—a small space partitioned off on the landing, called the Lady Students' waiting room! There was no peace or privacy in this shelter, as the partition was such that we could see innumerable feet marching up and down the passage all the time. As the room was on the landing near the stairs this procession of feet seemed never ending! There were three other women students besides ourselves, so that the room was quite a tight fit when we were all there! Later on as the number increased we asked for a larger room and got it, but the authorities did not know how to furnish it! However, no amount of discomfort was going to deter us from our determination to seek knowledge!

It was indeed a difficult search! In the first three years we hardly exchanged a word with our professors. We were very shy, but some of the professors were shyer still. They could hardly look at us in the class! A very funny incident happened to Miss Acquino once. Going to her French Class she had to pass through the room of our professor of Algebra. While returning she saw him sitting there and thought she would ask him about some difficulty in Algebra she wished to be solved. She approached the unwary gentleman with that purpose. But he got such a start and looked so scared that she bolted. We laughed and laughed when she told us about her adventure and the discomfiture of poor 'Xns square' as we called him!

The other Professor of Mathematics, however, was quite a different being. He was supposed to be a misogynist. We had heard such stories about him that we expected to see an ogre! We found him, however, a very good teacher. Geometry was my favourite subject and I really enjoyed his lucid way of teaching the subject. His fault was that he was strictly impartial. 'No favours to the fair sex' was perhaps his motto! He had the hardihood to ask us questions in the class! Once he reduced Miss Acquino to tears by cross examining her so much that she got confused and sat down to the great glee of the students and the professor! How we imitated his lisp by way of revenge in the privacy of our room!

Sanskrit poets are so embarrassing! They have abused their poetic license by wallowing so disgustingly openly in Shringar Ras! They little dreamt what difficult situation they would create for our poor Shastriji who had to read their poetry aloud in the class in the presence of women! As a rule we ourselves remained absent when we expected such passages. One day, however, we forgot to remain absent as we had not gone over the text beforehand. As we were preparing to attend the class our Shastriji waylaid us and begged us not to attend!

We women students were expected to remain on our dignity all the time that we were in the class. Like three owls we sat. The only human expression that we occasionally allowed ourselves was a fleeting smile! If there was any joke we avoided each other's eyes. Once we were in our room, however, we threw aside the mantle of dignity and our suppressed feelings would come out in bursts of laughter. I wonder what the professors and men students would have said if they had seen the three blue stockings—as I am sure we appeared to them—holding their sides with laughter!! One day, however, we did forget ourselves in the class. It was a History period. The professor was supposed to teach us Indian Administration. With a dull and monotonous voice the Professor read from the Gazeteer. He always managed to produce a very somnolent atmosphere. I used to draw caricatures and pictures in my notebook in order to keep awake. One day a student was found sleeping very peacefully while the Professor read on. He may even have snored, for the students started stamping their feet and clapping their hands by way of diversion. The Professor saw the cause of this noise, sleeping peacefully, and was purple with rage. He asked some one to wake up the culprit. When the unsuspecting student woke up, the angry Professor instead of shouting 'Leave the class!' shouted 'Left!' At this we who had with difficulty kept calm, burst out like the rest of the students with laughter. That, I believe, was the unkindest cut of all! The Professor looked very much crest fallen and could hardly look up for some time!

The only professor with whom we really came in touch was our Professor of Philosophy, Mr Widgery. He encouraged his students to read the latest books on the subject and lent his own books, for alas! the College Library was anything but up-to-date. He invited his students and his colleagues to his home, where Mrs Widgery always welcomed us with a smile. But it was not for a discussion on lofty philosophical subjects but to eat and play. It was a treat to see our staid and sober Professor Trivedi [sic] playing badminton with us!

One of our English professors known as the champion of Indian womanhood used to tell us that the presence of women students in the college was having a great cultural influence on the men students. If we did exert such influence, we at least were not aware of it! In spite of our co-educational Institution we hardly saw much of our co-students of the opposite sex till perhaps the final year. I believe they had nicknames for us—one lady with a huge knot of hair was called the college dome!—But so had we. But there was no real contact. I remember once there was a strike in the college. We were not told anything about it; and came to know there was a strike when we went to college in the morning. Yet they put it in the local paper that we were also with the strikers. The late Professor Masani who was our Principal came to us in surprise and asked us if we were in it as he had seen it in the paper. We told him that we were not and we were going to contradict it in the paper and so we did. It was a cheek on the part of the men students to take us for granted and expect us to join a strike without knowing the reason why. Had we been consulted beforehand we would certainly have decided on the merit of the issue.

Somehow we did not participate in the college life as such, with the men students. They were always anxious for us to take part in social gatherings or in college debates. Our number was so insignificant that we had not the courage to take part in these activities knowing full well that the least we did was ever an object of criticism. Once when we were in the final year, a fellow student read a paper on the 'Duties of Indian Women.' I have no idea if the paper was to provoke a rejoinder from us or the student really believed in what he wrote—I pity him if he did. Our men seem to know such a lot about the duties of women. It is a wonder how they forget their own duties! We were expected to reply, but we thought it futile when we were so few against so many. But I did give a rejoinder later on when an opportunity came. It was my turn to read a paper before another society of students. At first I thought of reading a paper on 'Duties of Indian men.' However, I changed my mind and read a paper on what we conceive to be our duties. It was to be my maiden speech. I remember I was very nervous and had to equip myself with throat lozenges! My two comrades were equally nervous. They felt it was the woman's cause and my failure to read the paper well would mean the failure of all women in general! I have no idea how I acquitted myself. My comrades were pleased and so I was happy. That was my first speech and last as a student.

My debut on the platform emboldened me to become a writer and for the first time I contributed to the college magazine. It was a very live problem in Philosophy that I had dramatized and called—'Revolt of Sciences.' The professor who edited the magazine, however, compared it to the well known parable in the Esop's fables, viz. the quarrel between the 'Belly and other parts of the body.' I felt that the editor by making this comparison showed great ignorance. The problem was as to what place Metaphysics will have in the scheme of knowledge when sciences were advancing with such rapid strides and explaining away things so long unknown, and hence in the sphere of Metaphysics, in their own light. My thesis was that Metaphysics will retain her position so long as the riddle of the universe remains unsolved! But professors are learned beings and cannot be in the wrong, at least that was the feeling in good old days when I was a student at Baroda College.

—*The Baroda College Golden Jubilee Commemoration Volume* (1933)

Ruttie Jinnah
(1900–1929)

Ruttie Jinnah, the daughter of Sir Dinshaw and Lady Dinbai Petit was sixteen when she met Jinnah, but she had to wait till she was eighteen to marry him as her parents were against the marriage and took a High Court injunction against the marriage and any contact with Jinnah.

Kanji Dwarkadas, a friend of both the Jinnahs writes in his book *Ruttie Jinnah: The Story of a Great Friendship* (n.d.) that Ruttie remained capable of spirited behaviour throughout her young life. He relates an incident in which Ruttie was introduced to Lord Chelmsford at the Viceregal Lodge in Simla. 'She did not follow the British custom of curtseying before the Viceroy. Instead she followed the Indian custom and folded her hands after shaking hands with the Viceroy. Immediately after dinner the ADC took Ruttie to talk to the Viceroy. Lord Chelmsford pompously told her: "Mrs Jinnah, your husband has a great political future, you must not spoil it. In Rome you must do as the Romans do." Mrs Jinnah retorted quickly: "That is exactly what I did Your Excellency. In India I greeted you in the Indian way." That was the first and the last time she met Lord Chelmsford.'

But the book is finally concerned most with Ruttie's interest in 'life beyond the physical.' The letters reflect this.

Chapter XXII

In December 1924, the Theosophical Convention was held in Bombay and among those who participated and spoke at the Convention were Mrs Besant, J. Krishnamurti and Jinarajadasa and this gave me an opportunity to help Ruttie. At my request Mrs James Cousins saw her and had a long talk with her. Ruttie wrote to me on 28th December 1924:

'I was delighted to meet Mrs Cousins and I feel that as I owe you the pleasure I should thank you for having given me the opportunity.

'She is a charming woman and was very patient and helpful though of course what I am after is a seance controlled by some experienced medium—professional—or otherwise; as I am most anxious to get a personal experience of this matter in which I so passionately believe.

'Mrs Cousins very kindly took me with her to the Theosophical Meeting at which I listened to a most inspired address by Mr Jinarajadas. What a charming wife he has, by the way! Looking into her face (it is one of those faces one looks into and not at) I understand for the first time what is meant by a 'radiant face'. I must confess I fell for her absolutely and I hope that you will try and arrange so that I may meet her some time when she happens to be in Bombay.

'Do come and see me soon so that we may resume our chat of the last occasion.

'What is your opinion of *Towards the Stars*? I only wish it hadn't been marred by the waggish self-assurance of the author. But more of that when we meet. Until then let me thank you once again for having brought me into contact with a very charming and rare type of womanhood.

'I am afraid it is too late to get this posted now. So I should have dated in 8th. However it hardly matters!'

South Court,
7th April 1925
Midnight

'My dear Kanji,

'Yes, I know of the dream travels of which you speak. But I do all my dreaming in my waking hours. I am not being waggish. There is nothing I would welcome with greater rejoicing than an experience of the sort to which you refer in your letter, but in my heavy drug like sleep there is no redeeming feature and besides the five or at most six hours rest it ensures a restive mind, and a correspondingly restless physical state it has *no* value. I don't dream excepting very rarely and then I wake up only to the consciousness of having dreamt, and no more.

'My soul is too clogged! and though I aspire and crave, God knows how earnestly! how intensely, my researches remain uncrowned—even by thorns! I am feeling peculiarly restless and wish one with psychic powers could come to my assistance.

'My proud soul humbles before the magnitude of this subject and in my estimation those of us with Second Sight and other such psychic powers should rank with the world's poets and songsters for their gift if more intelligible is also more divine. The seers and the saints should stand among the world's prophets. After all we are at present too blind and unseeing to comprehend what the psychics would reveal to our half demented senses. But what the mind often revolts at, and refuses to accept, the intrinsic self within us admits with certain ease which makes the more thoughtful ponder; as though it had some ancient and original knowledge of its own.

'There is much to clear away, and almost as much to mend, before I can dare to feel disappointment, because certain signs and manifestations for which I long and contrive do not occur. But I am weak and spoilt by indulgence, and to drive myself is a task to which I don't impose a time limit for obvious reasons.

'I have written much, but I feel confident that it is in the sympathetic hands and they will be understanding eyes that read what I have said.

'As I have already told you, you have but to let me know by phone or a written word when you are free to come, and you will be more than welcome.

Yours sincerely,
Ruttie.'

South Court,
12th April 1925

'My dear Kanji,

'Thanks for the books. I have been wading through them. But they are nothing as exhaustive as H.P. B.'s *Secret Doctrine*. The number of points that book has elucidated for me is remarkable. I have a very confusing mind as one should have in serious matters of this sort and though I have often referred to standard authors on the subject, they have not given a particle of the help H.P.B. has, and yet if I take up the Secret Doctrine, it is more often than not that I have to put it down in utter bewilderment. It is so supremely elusive! And though I have read quite a respectable lot on the subject, I have never come across anything quite so easy to *follow* nor yet quite so hard to *grasp*. I wish I could get hold of somebody to guide me on such matters as puzzle me, one whose knowledge could save me when I stumble. By the way, do let me know whenever there are any lectures etc. to be heard on the subject worth the hearing as also if there is any journal to keep one posted with the latest development. "Light"—I of course know of—but has it an Indian counterpart?

'I am slowly, but surely drawing J's interest into the matter and by alternate bullying and coaxing I got him to read that book *The Spirit of*

Irene, of which I had spoken to you at the time of lending you *Towards the Stars*. I wished to give it to you but could not find it at the time. It is really the most conclusive piece of evidence that has come my way ever since I first interested myself in Spiritualism. However, J. had to admit that it was remarkable and irrefutable. There is no other feature to recommend it. Neither refinement of thought nor any marked literary ability and though it does provide a solid bit of evidence it is not of a nature to appeal to one who already believes. Besides the result of the whole experiment is such that it can hardly be expected to appeal to those of our way of reasoning. The incident deals with the tracing of a murder and the ultimate bringing to justice of a murderer. I think judgment would be better responded. There is a notorious crime known to criminal annals as the Boscombs Murder and it revolves round a poor girl—a cook—who was decoyed from London to Boscomb and then done to death, the details of the crime are horrible, it having been a crime of lust. The police being baffled by the cunning of the man, were at their wits end, or you may be sure they would not have consented to hold seance. Anyway they got the needed clue and the evidence was of such a nature that the unfortunate man was hanged.

'The book gives the names and designations of the respective witnesses and as the book has now gone through two editions without calling forth any word to the contrary either from the police officials therein mentioned or any others. I suppose that one may reasonably surmise that the author speaks with knowledge. J[1] was, not at all events, [sic] able to find any flaw in the case.

'It doesn't look as if we were going to Kashmere after all, as J is engaged in the Bawla case. So it is more than likely that we shall remain in Bombay. With K. regards.'

'P.S. I have written to Chatterjee, the artist, for whose address infinite thanks. I have asked him to do three reproductions for me in varying sizes. I am awaiting the answer with impatience and hope that he accepts the commission.

'By the by, I am very excited and equally happy as at last I have two manifestations, one was a most extra-ordinary luminance—a sort of perpetual flash suspended midway at the corner of Hughes Road and Sandhurst Bridge.'

—*Ruttie Jinnah: The Story of a Great Friendship* (n.d.)

---

[1](Ruttie used to call Jinnah 'J').

Mithan Choksi
(1901–1987)

An educationist and the first editor of the NCWI Bulletin. She was also joint editor of *Women in Modern India* (1929).

Some Impressions of Indian Women's Colleges

When under the deadening influence of long wars and foreign invasions the old education systems had died out and the whole cultural inheritance of the Hindus and Mahomedans was at a low ebb, a new system heralded by Macaulay's famous Minute came into being. And the new system entirely ignored the question of women's education. There was a tacit and wholly gratuitous assumption that the schools and colleges were intended only for boys and men, and that there was no demand for women's education in any part of the country. The educated gentlewomen of nineteenth century England had their counterpart among the Brahman and Mahratta women of the higher classes. But the women's High school and College movement being still in its infancy in England, it was natural that the scheme initiated by the British Government made no provision for women's education. This was confirmed by the country's own tendency, especially at this period of degeneration, to confine unduly the sphere and activities of women. But such a state of things could not persist; as the country revived from torpor, province after province took in hand the question of education for women. Among the first was Bombay. Here as elsewhere private teaching and then educational institutions for girls under private and missionary agency gradually began to make headway; and in time these educational institutions became the regular girls' schools, that slowly stepped into line with boys' schools. In 1883, the Bombay University roll shows the names of eight girls who matriculated. But collegiate education for women was in general yet unthought of and if the idea was entertained, the ridicule of commonsense at the imposition of additional burdens upon the frail feminine mind must have effectively negatived any tentative proposals—even as in Victorian England.

Hence when in 1886 a Parsi gentlemen of Bombay wished his daughters to have the advantage of college education, he found great difficulty in procuring admission for them in the Arts colleges of the city. He was considerably assisted, however, by the encouragement of Dr Mackichan, the principal of Wilson College—then known as the Free General Assembly's Institution.—Dr Mackichan admitted them and later got the University authorities to enact that the word 'he' wherever it occurred in the university Calendar should also mean 'she'. These were along the first girls to enter college. In 1926, forty years later, the returns for the different colleges affiliated to the University show a total of 450 women students, among them being candidates for degrees in Arts, Science, Medicine, Teaching, Law, Commerce and Agriculture. A short comparison may be drawn concerning the state of things in the different provinces. In the Madras Presidency, the figures for 1927 show 550 women students in the Arts Colleges and about 140 in the Medical Schools, the largest total of the different provinces. The first woman was admitted into the Medical College, Madras, in 1878, but the real advance did not commence till the establishment in 1914 and 1915 of two women's colleges in Madras city with bright surroundings and residential quarters, followed by a third at Trivandrum.

At Calcutta there are two women's colleges—one of them Bethune College dating back to 1849, the first Government institution for girls in India,—and about 300 women students, including those studying at the medical and men's colleges.

At Delhi is an All-India institution, the Lady Hardinge College for women, founded in 1916 with accommodation for 100 medical students and its own hospital attached. Its students are largely drawn from the Punjab, the United Provinces and the Central Provinces with a few others from all over India. In practice it has been found that the large cities, like Bombay and Madras cater for their own women medical students.

At Lahore are two women's colleges with about 70 students; at Mysore, two Intermediate colleges and one constituent college, the Maharani's College, with a total of about 30 students.

In most provinces in India, where women are studying in any number, the principle of separate women's colleges has been accepted. In every case, at the commencement, women were admitted into men's colleges, but it was found that the establishment of separate colleges attracted a much larger number of women students. In Bombay, however, the principle of co-educational colleges seems by now to have been definitely accepted and preferred to separate colleges. The evidence given recently before the

Bombay University Commission seemed to show that separate colleges, in Bombay city at least, would if anything be considered a retrograde step. This may be ascribed to the influence, at the outset, of the Parsi community, and later of the Marathi.

The figures given above will show that the real advance is confined to Bombay and Madras. Bombay will be taken here as a fair index of the forward movement in higher education for women.

To turn our attention first to the intellectual aspect of this movement. It has often been said that the standard of attainment in Indian universities is low compared with that in those of the West: the remark applying with greater force to women. It is true: the achievements of women's education are less than they might have been; yet, in justice, two great mitigating causes may be suggested.

The difficulty, inseparably connected with Indian education at its present stage of evolution, that of teaching through the medium of English rather than the vernacular, pursues one into the college course with complications equal to those created in the High Schools. As a result of the methods of teaching English, the vast majority of students come to college with a very imperfect, fragmentary, and incoherent ability either to speak or write: it may be added that in general the women are far better than the men. Where all the advanced teaching is in English, considerable emphasis has to be laid on the student's capacity for expression in speech and writing; yet often that gives a very unfair impression of even the students' actual reading and still less of his intellectual maturity. I have often, after discussing a piece of literature with students, found their appreciation very incoherent and immature; later, in an informal talk with the students in the vernacular on the same subject, I have been surprised to find how much of the apparent immaturity was due to the utter incapacity for felicitous or even consistent expression in English. The problem is fraught with added perplexity when we consider the many vernaculars of the Presidency.

This difficulty of teaching through the medium of English is also a potent factor in the limitations of the High School curriculum, which is the other mitigating factor. In the average Indian school more periods in a week are devoted to the actual teaching of the English language than are given to any one subject in schools in England or Europe; naturally, therefore the time spent on other subjects is much more restricted: with the result that the High School courses, having English as their centre, are elementary and incomplete and leave too may loose ends. The students feel quite rightly that it is not possible to stop short at such a point: for many of them the natural requirement is a further two years of High School with a course which even if elementary is better rounded-off and complete in itself. Few of them have the more speculative and specialized interest that would fit them for college work, nor the independence of mind that would enable them to dispense with school-room methods of teaching. All these are compelled to come to the colleges if they desire to follow up the fragmentary education the schools provide, and consequently the colleges have to adapt themselves to suit their needs. Elementary and incomplete as are the courses, a further difficulty is evident in that they offer to the callow student the fruits of an alien culture, that can only be assimilated by a riper intelligence. This state of things has led to reiteration of the cry that it is impossible to lecture to the students of a college, till the schools equip them with greater capacity for reading and understanding books and a better grasp of the aims and methods of private study. From all sides one hears with increasing insistence the complaint that college students are doing higher Secondary school work—for the Indian educationalist has no illusions: no one is more alive to the limitations of our educational achievement.

Much has been said in India as elsewhere on the subject of alteration of the curriculum to suit the special needs of women. Such an alteration would certainly be an asset in the High schools, where a curriculum on a much broader basis is necessary to suit the varied needs of a large number. But it is doubtful whether a university can so circumscribe cultural aims as to propose and equip women as house-keepers, wives or even mothers. Its great aim should finally be to produce accurate, far-reaching and critical thought.

An account of women's colleges would, however, be incomplete without mention of a very interesting development in what may be called the intermediate stages of collegiate education. This is the institution at Poona, known as the Indian Women's University, initiated and supported entirely by private agency. Its most interesting feature is the endeavour to teach collegiate subjects through the medium of the vernacular. Professor Karve, the founder, an intensely practical educationalist, felt strongly the necessity for some means of rapidly bridging over the widening gulf between the cultural achievement of men and women in India. If women's education was to show both rapid advance and diffusion, it was necessary to resort to the natural method of teaching in the vernacular. The importance at the same time of English as 'a language of world wide culture, and of special importance to India on political and national grounds, was recognized by including it as a compulsory second language. Among other compulsory subjects are Psychology. Study of the Child Mind, Biology, Sociology and History. The standard aimed at in most subjects is not higher than that of the Intermediate examination of other universities. Though objection has been taken to the name as marking out an unnecessary separation in the higher education of men and women, the importance of the work as an experiment conducted on sound and practical lines is being recognized. There is an increasing number of girls' schools in the Presidency affiliated to this institution, the figures for 1926 show 7 High Schools and 8 Middle Schools, most of these staffed by women who have graduated from the institution. This is rapid advance for ten years—the University was founded in 1916—and shows that it has succeeded in one of its aims, the rapid diffusion of education among girls. On the other hand the actual numbers in the three Arts colleges is very small compared to those in women's colleges conducted on the usual lines, being in 1926, 17, 8, and 7. In general, the establishment and progress of this university seems to show that the question of higher education in the vernacular is by no means finally settled and there is room and indeed necessity for such an experiment; though a wholesale adoption of the vernaculars as the media of instruction in collegiate subjects does not seem immediately possible when even the recent committee on University Reforms in Bombay has declared that 'the introduction of the vernaculars as media of instruction is not in the interests of the higher education of women.'

However, though education, collegiate and otherwise, is hampered considerably by the vexed question of the vernaculars, there is a brighter side to the picture. While these difficulties minimize the intellectual quality of the colleges, the production of accurate and keen habits of thought is promoted by opportunities for varied social intercourse. An account of some of the debates in a Bombay college at which the writer was present, may be of some interest in throwing light upon the activity of mind of the Hindu girl. At the outset it may be mentioned that all formal rules of debate were rejected as comic encumbrances by the practically minded Hindu girl: the debates were in the nature of informal discussions and were conducted with much more vigour and understanding when they dealt with social rather than literary questions. A vigorously contested subject, that might be of interest of European readers, was that 'the Joint Family System should be suspended.' The arguments relating to the hardships of the system have been too often repeated to need mention. But the ably contested defence was an interesting proof of the often forgotten fact that the ameliorative factors of a system are always far less apparent to an outsider than its hardships. Much was made of the far brighter and joyful childhood that was conditioned by the congregation of so many children under one roof—the games, festivals, flower-wreathings, outings, surprise meals, and treats in which nine children participated being contrasted by one speaker with the childhood of her more westernized friends brought up in homes containing two or three children. It was amusing to hear Crichton-Miller and western psychology quoted as a defence for the joint-family system, the speaker's point being that inhibitions, daydreams, brooding, and so on, were impossible to the child with the companionship of so many of its fellows. Another pathetic picture was of a worn-out middle class mother attending, servantless and irritable through overwork, to the needs of her baby, who would have been much better looked after among the profusion of aunts and female relatives in a family of the older system, where the older women could provide the experience to deal with the baby's illnesses and the younger women the leisure and health to occupy his playfulness.

These debates were of considerable interest to me, a Parsi, one of a community among whom the system is not prevalent except among sections of the poor: that is why I quote it at some length, as having a similar interest for those who have no intimate acquaintance with the inner working of Indian domestic life. Another debate was on the proposition that 'marriage by arrangement has done less harm to Society than marriage by Choice,' the slightly humorous phrasing of the proposition being the work of the most thoughtful among them. The students of the senior year were particularly keen about it, having studied during the year a course of Modern English Literature, which had provoked much discussion and thought. This was drawn upon considerably by the defenders of the proposition. Scathing references were made to the women of western novelists who 'took life-long vows of marriage, met men they liked better than their husbands, waved good-bye and went'. The tone of the debates showed a marked difference from what it would have been in the past. The best and the most thoughtful of the students were now critical of, if not distinctly antagonistic to, the wholesale adoption of things foreign. Fifteen years ago it would have been a different matter; students of this type would have been among the most anxious to urge adoption of western modes of thought. But the war and its aftermath produced a far more critical attitude towards western civilization, an attitude which was assisted by the natural reaction towards the earlier attitude and by the growth of national consciousness. Most people European and Indian will agree that even if often aggressive and intolerant, this was a much healthier frame of mind than in the days when, it is said, the fascination of western civilization was so great that prominent Bengalis prided themselves on even dreaming in English instead of Bengali.

These casual glimpses of a critical attitude towards western modes of thought are given partly as an indication of the considerable tension that prevails in the mental life of the universities. For there is room for criticism of the curriculum on far more radical lines than the inclusion of a few subjects dealing with mothercraft and home-hygiene for women students. It is a criticism that concerns both men and women, and no paper on collegiate education, can ignore it. This is the complete ousting of the national culture in the universities by the study of the English language and western science. Where separate courses exist for the study of oriental learning, they are on lines meant only for the antiquarian and the specialist. Hence the resulting effect on the Indian university student; the disquiet and excitement of the few under the stimulus of a foreign culture unassimilated with their own and the stagnation of the many at the imposition of a culture so alien.

A brief historical sketch may throw light on the question. As an example of the pursuit of learning before the adoption of modern western methods, we may turn to the life of Anant Sastri, the father of Pandita Ramabai whose life has been already narrated. Learning was the passion and vital principle of his being. His life was spent in wandering and contemplation in pursuit of learning. He sought it in the courts and libraries of Rajas at Mysore and Nepal and wealth and patronage (which meant nothing to him) were showered upon him. He sought it in pilgrimage throughout the length and breadth of India. He sought it finally for twelve years in the wilderness, building a little hut in the heart of the Ganganule forest where an *ashram* of devoted students gathered round him to be taught by him and his wife. But this learning and speculation that he pursued with such intensity of devotion was purely religious and philosophical. Much of it would be characterized by western educationalists as hair-splitting. It was remote from all the concerns of life, understood by the average westerner as practical wage-earning business. It produced great subtlety of intellect, but in particular fields of speculative thought. As such the more positive spirit of his daughter as a Raja Ram and the early reformers rebelled against it. They welcomed the new fields of knowledge and culture opened out by western thought. And western science and thought superseded it completely; with western modes of the spread of education the high school for the forest ashram.

The result included much positive gain. Western education gave a profound stimulus both to industrial development and the cause of social and political reform. It left a permanent tincture, a positive cast in the Indian mind. Many of the students of our colleges fail to realize how much of their cast of mind, their individualism, their ideas of evolution, of democracy, of self-determination were due to the complete absorption of the western modes of thought, which they so often and so strongly criticize.

But there was also much loss that counterbalanced this gain. Much was lost in spiritual content by the divorcing of education from religion and the home, the two great vitalizing forces. A state of things was produced where, according to an educational authority, 'Students could write a better

English essay on Chaucer than on Tulsidas and Tukaram, where Indian homes of educated people resembled third-rate English suburban lodgings or, at their best, contained English period furniture ordered wholesale from reputed English furniture-dealers. Instead of national culture, language study occupied a disproportionate part of school and college life—English being studied for utilitarian purposes as the key of entrance to Government service or to the professions. It is not to be wondered at that higher education could achieve so little. Behind the practical difficulties imposed by teaching in a foreign language was the intense mental confusion imposed by the struggle of two cultures with widely differing schemes of values and standards of life. These have so far been antagonistic rather than fused. For the Indian student coming to college from a village home where three sets of values, the one arbitrarily taught in schools and colleges, the second, the standards prevalent in the traditional outlook of often illiterate homes; and the third, the ideal of which the second was the practical reflection which he faintly glimpsed in the lost national culture that had been ousted from his normal life. With the passion for coherency of the Indian mind it is not to be wondered at that higher education produced stagnation in the mediocre, dissatisfaction and restlessness in the able. The Indian mind cannot be content with an acceptance of the fragmentation and disharmony of personality, or the struggle-for-life principle, such as seem possible to the English and the American.

The exploitation of the sources of wealth is one of the greatest achievements of the nineteenth century to the westerner. It is touched with romance and heroism. But it leaves the Indian cold. The exuberant enthusiasm with which even a Babbitt can redeem the grossness of his material pursuits is denied to the Indian. And in spite of increasing reform in social and political adjustments, the secret of happiness seems to have been lost and the universities cannot provide it. Is it so impossible to achieve a fusion of the two cultures? At Santiniketan is a school and college, a women's college and hostel and Research Institute, a School of Art and Music and finally an Institution of Rural Reconstruction, all closely associated, whereby is promoted a vigorous and full intellectual life with great possibilities of assimilation.

In the meantime, in spite of the depression of spirit produced by a survey of the immense difficulties that stand in the way of a full and free type of University education, there is still much practical achievement and progress in the development of this higher education. Even our brief glimpse within an Indian college may suggest the vividness and buoyancy of spirit which can characterize college life, and in which lies much source of hope for the future of women's work in India.

On the social side particularly beneficial have been the results of the spread of college education among Indian women, especially in the co-educational colleges. I wonder if colleges in any country have done so much for the breaking down of barriers between the sexes, castes, communities and classes as the Indian women's colleges and even more, the co-educational colleges. This is an important factor in a country which is almost a continent and which has communities with such different traditions, as well as numerous castes within the community.

Indian High Schools are usually more distinctly communal; and the college-going age is particularly suitable for the development of enthusiastic friendships and sympathetic co-operative work. The colleges started by private Indian agency and by Christian missions have both done a great deal to promote the best and wisest sort of co-operation, which consists in agreeing to differ.

In a Bombay hostel for university women one may meet with the interesting and refreshing spectacle of a number of young college students of different traditions, customs and castes, sitting in happy fellowship in the same dining-room but with different kinds of food served to them. Though the complications and perplexities of the housekeeper must be endless—she has to see for instance that not even the eggs penetrate into the 'vegetarian' kitchen—she can and usually does feel that she has helped towards the achievement of the spirit of mutual forbearance and understanding that is one of the most tangible results of college education for women in India.

Finally, one may express the conviction that despite the limitations, the lowness of intellectual standards and its attendant ills, it is this college education that has both by corporate influence and individual achievement made possible new movements, has opened out new vistas of social thought and action for the many and in general has helped the amelioration of woman-kind in innumerable, incalculable ways. On the one hand, the corporate influence is revealed in a body like the Women Graduates' Union. These unions which have been formed in the main Presidency towns, have always taken an active part in initiating or assisting all movements connected with women's amelioration: they now form the Indian branch of the International Federation of University Women. On the other hand, individual achievement is expressed by creative and constructive work, though not original, in many fields—social, medical, educational, and even political. Take as an illustration, some of the writers in this book. Add to this that the colleges turn out an increasing number of Indian women of mature abilities, some of whom go on to complete their education at the foremost British and European universities. Again men have not been slow to recognize the partnership of women in affairs: for a Mahomedan university has as Chancellor, the Begum of Bhopal—

perhaps the only woman in the world to hold an office of this nature: and the universities of Bombay and Madras have women sitting in their Senates.

And viewed relatively, collegiate education has shown a more substantial advance than either Primary or Secondary. The achievement in the past thirty years has been swifter, more varied, more vivid than the corresponding achievement in mass education. The advance however, has not been all over India: Madras and Bombay making a disproportionately large contribution. But the future of mass education for girls will lie very much in the hands of the increasing number of young and enthusiastic women that the colleges turn out.

—*Women in Modern India* (1929)

Ela Sen
(b. 1899)

In her Foreword to *Darkening Days: Being a Narrative of Famine-Striken Bengal*, Ela Sen writes, 'This book is admittedly written from a woman's point of view. If on this account over-emphasis is laid on the vicissitudes faced by women during the dreadful days of last year it is not for want of appreciation of the sufferings of men. The short stories which make up the major portion of the book have all been culled from real life. Names have been altered, but the facts remain.'

Ela Sen has written two other collections of short stories, *A Child is Born and Other Stories* (1943) and *Midnight on the Lakes and Other Stories* (1943) both published in Bombay. *Testament of India* (1939) is a collection of essays on major figures such as Subhas Chandra Bose, Jinnah, and also on subjects like 'The Younger Socialists' and 'Terrorism'. *Wives of Famous Men* comprise short essays originally published in *The Statesman*, on Kasturba Gandhi, Eleanor Roosevelt, Madame Stalin, Madame Chian Kai-Shek, Mrs de Valera, Else Einstein, the Empress of Abyssinia and others.

Ela Sen also published biographies of Mahatma Gandhi and Indira Gandhi. As a freelance journalist, she contributed to all leading Indian national dailies between 1938–1945. From 1946–54 she was Special Columnist for the *Hindustan Times* contributing to Indian, British and other overseas broadsheets. She now lives permanently in London. She also translated Tarasankar Banerjee's *The Eternal Lotus* (1945), and Premendra Mitra's *Kaleidoscope: A Novel* (1945).

Taken from *Gunpowder Women and Other Stories* (1943), the essay, 'A Woman of Spain,' included here, is about Dolores Ibarruri, the woman called La Passionara by her people, and documents her fight against Fascism. She is described by Sen as 'the unconquerable spirit of Spain, personifying its fiery courage and heroism.'

Also reproduced here is the Preface from *Darkening Days*, a passionate outpouring against the government's inability to ease suffering during the great famine that swept through Bengal: 'One does not take advantage of a national calamity to bring a greater plague, but one seeks leadership that will knit the hungry millions into one strong force that will demand of a corrupt government the death penalty for the hoarder, proper rationing and price control and considerable planning to safeguard the future.'

The short story, 'The Queue,' from *Darkening Days*, focuses on a long queue for food formed by victims of the famine, and shifts perspective from one person to another while the line constantly moves forward. As one woman loses her baby, another sells herself for food, and yet another gives birth, the queue moves endlessly on, stopping for no one. Based on situations in real life, the technique effectively evokes pathos, making the stories all the more powerful.

Who's Who of Women in India volume tells us that Mrs Eila (sic) Sen was a Bengali Brahmo educated at home and at Loreto Convent, Calcutta. She was one of the promoters of the Stri Sammelani Management Committee Blind School, a member of the Provincial Child Welfare Committee and the Lady Stevenson Hall Management Committee.

Her name has been variously spelt: Ela, Ila, and Eila.

A Woman of Spain

The land of romance and music, Spain is also the land of the miner and the peasant. Under its outer gilding little was at one time thought of Spain that was not connected with its decadent aristocracy, but now it is linked immortally with those working people, who, against overwhelming odds, struggled to save their country from Fascism, and among them is Dolores Ibarruri, a miner's child, who was destined to play a great part in the evolution of her country.

The leader that she was, she proudly claimed for herself first the title of 'A Woman of Spain', which signified the greatest of all aristocracy to her, while the people named her La Passionara, for she had the fire and passion of old Spain, which she infused into her people during their struggle.

La Passionara's Spain was the Spain of stricken women, orphaned and shell-shocked children and mutilated men. The womanliness in her rose up in horror at the sorrows of her sisters; the mother love of her heart gathered the young ones under her wing, while the love of humanity sent her to the aid of her brethren fighting in the trenches.

La Passionara fought Fascism with her spirit, her eloquence and complete championship in a cause she knew to be right and therefore not lost. Patriotism for her was not just something which embraced those in her near vicinity, but it was a cog in that vaguely spoken of thing known as internationalism. To her it was not vague at all, but vitally tangible. Coming of a stock that had learnt its lessons from life's hard school, her analysis of war and its subsequent effects went further than surface value.

As a personality, Dolores Ibarruri's pseudonym La Passionara, was correctly descriptive. Untutored in the way of politics, her driving force was an immense sincerity and genuineness of feeling for the suffering people of Spain. There was nothing impersonal about her, the million afflictions of her country were like personal bereavements to her. It was a calmness of spirit, wholly consonant with the fiery gifts of oratory which was hers, that helped her to fight the odds that were against her. Her philosophy accepted defeats, but it did not make her so passive as to lose all fight and to the last she struggled and she exhorted her people.

In appearance there is nothing particularly outstanding about Dolores Ibarruri, for she is a typical Spanish matron, full-bosomed and well-built. But her beautiful eyes carry in them a multitude of impressions and expressions. What she feels in the heart is conveyed through her eyes as they flash in battle, grow sombre in sorrow, calm in repose and smile in hopeful joy. Sun and shade ripple across their depths as upon a deep and secluded mountain pool. The eloquence of her eyes find their counterpart in her sensitive mouth and the liquidity of her speech. The words she strings together, not in studied oratory, but out of the spontaneity of her heart, convey by their very sound and delivery a sense of what she means even when one is foreign to the language she uses. It is impossible not to be moved by her manner of speaking, for it strikes at the root of all one's feelings for humanity and stirs into life all the decency of which man is capable. This part of the secret of her sway over the Spanish masses was the reason why Franco ordered her exile, confiscated her belongings and would like to have her securely under surveillance, for while she is at liberty, she is dangerous to all Fascist elements. By her very honesty of purpose, by the very sponsoring of the cause of her own class of people, La Passionara has earned the respect and love of all peoples and is feared by those who would crucify her class. She remains one of the champions of a lost cause, but it were sad for the world if that cause were truly lost, for Spain is but a sample of what awaits the world under totalitarianism.

This latter fact as far back as 1937 La Passionara spoke to the people of Europe when she was going from country to country on the Continent, begging help, not for Spain alone, but for the world. It was then that she told the people of what was awaiting them were Republican Spain to fall: she implored them not to look upon Spain's struggle as merely internecine but as Fascism's trial of strength. In no unsure words she outlined and prophesied all that has befallen Europe and threatens to engulf the world, if Spain were to be refused assistance in her crucial hour. Those who would not believe laughed at her, and those who did had little power to give substantial aid.

Time and again, La Passionara warned France and the French people in particular that if Spain were to become Fascist a similar fate would await France. As far back as that date she told them of Fascist agents amongst their own people and was scoffed at by the then Government of France. Though she succeeded in creating a spirit of agitation amongst the French people, the reactionary elements in power classed it as part of the 'Red' bogey. If ever an ambassador of goodwill and peace existed it was La Passionara when she was going from capital to capital in Europe, begging them to protect themselves and Spain. But there were few who were forewarned, and there must be a great many who rue the day when Republican Spain was left forlorn and alone.

She cried out:

'Democrats of France, democrats of Great Britain, democrats of the whole world fight to organize the forces of peace. Compel your governments, in conjunction with the great Soviet democracy, to build a barrier against the insolence of Fascism, to prevent it launching against mankind a wave of destruction and barbarity.'

That was in the end of July 1938; much that she pleaded for has happened, but, alas, as are the ways of this world, it has come at too late a stage to prevent the massacre and destruction she foresaw.

Earlier than this she spoke at a meeting in Paris, where the majority in the audience were French and had little Spanish, but the flashing of her eyes and her impassioned oratory left not one person unmoved. They saw before them the spirit of Spain, defiant, militant and idealistic, and realized that once more its great tradition and culture was raising its head to demand recognition, help and co-operation.

'We know that in Spain the future of Europe is at stake—Comrades of France, you must not remain passive in face of the Fascist menace, irrespective of whether it is directed against your country or another country. If we are crushed France will soon suffer the convulsions of counter revolution, as the armed conspiracy of the "Cagoulards" and their criminal plans show. ... In France the Bastille has been destroyed, but if a misfortune should happen and Spain be defeated, bear in mind that the reaction will erect in France a new Bastille, as it would like to erect one in every country.'

It was five years ago that La Passionara asked the people of France, nay the world, to choose and the Fascist plan has deviated little from the path she foreshadowed.

La Passionara was essentially a woman, and she never forgot that in human society little attention is paid to her sex. The recognition of her own merits was but an individual case, and she strove for its recognition amongst the masses of her kind. As she stood for every underdog, so she never forgot that no class has been so exploited as the womanhood of a nation. Her own capabilities and her own personality she utilized to prove that women were not inferior and well able to occupy positions of equality and responsibility. Many Spanish women, inspired by her courage and example, fought in the ranks with the soldiers. They shared every hardship with the men, kept up their courage so that the men should not falter, and La Passionara pointed out that women deserved to be recognized as thoroughly responsible for all undertakings. She demanded that they must be promoted to responsible positions, and fought against the reactionary role relegated to them.

'Woman must not be regarded as a mere female and drudge to wait on husband and children; woman should be the friend and comrade of her husband, share his joys and sorrows, his victories and defeats in the struggle. Women must become independent in the material sense as well, for women will become free only when they are in a position to earn their livelihood.'

Through all the strenuous days of her work, while she exhorted her own people on to the struggle and pleaded the cause before the people of Europe she was characterized by a gloomy foreboding of the coming struggle of which Spain was the first phase. Even while, on behalf of the women of Republican Spain, she sent her greetings to the women of the Soviet Union on the anniversary of the International Women's Day, she could not resist this thought, born of admiration and love for the Soviet women.

'You can indulge in rejoicing and laughter, working and protecting the security of your country, on which are cast the avaricious glances of the Fascist butchers who are dreaming of flinging the world back to the gloomy days of mediaeval slavery.'

And there was a tragic note when speaking for the women of Spain, for she emphasized that though they were prepared to die for the sake of the country, they wanted to live and make Spain the real fatherland where the outward merriment and the sound of the guitar would penetrate to the enslaved women workers and peasants and would no longer merely serve to conceal their age-long sufferings.

Through La Passionara one comes to know of what the Spanish women are capable, how they courted death rather than live in slavery. She gloried in them, she discovered them and revealed the spirit of liberty which was native to them. With them and for them, no less for the men who were their comrades, La Passionara went from battle front to battle front, and wherever she went her pride in her own sex soared higher. It was long long ago that Byron wrote of the Spanish maiden:

> 'Her lover sinks—she sheds no ill-timed tear:
> Her chief is slain—she fills his fatal post.'

What he said then remains true to this day.

'We dye our colours in honour of you, dear women comrades, who march into battle together with the men'—thus spoke Dolores Ibarruri.

So great was her faith in the natural integrity of woman-kind that she felt and rightly, too, that if their appeal were heard it would make a far better world. She felt that no woman voluntarily tolerates destruction and slaughter; if she appears to do so, it is because she has become the unthinking machinery of a system that does not encourage freedom of thought. So to the women of far countries she appealed for sympathy and understandings, and above all she wrote to the women of South America, upon whose Spanish descent she counted for sympathy to her cause.

Dolores herself is a mother of several grown-up children, who are no less dear to her because she has wept for the children of others. And her thoughts were always with them, however pre-occupied she might be with her numerous duties. In writing to them she was like a thousand other mothers who try to instil what they feel to be the best in their children. At a time that was most difficult, yet most exhilarating for youth, she advised her son Ruben to learn to work, to understand political questions, and to study. But he must at the same time be ready to 'fight without weakness, sacrifice yourself to the end on behalf of our cause.' So vast was the work she had embraced that it meant long separation from husband and children, and there is rather a pathetic line in her letter to Ruben, saying: 'I have no news from your father because communications have been cut.' It brings home a little of what war does to individual lives.

Again on International Youth Day, she writes: 'I want to spare some time from my work to write to you, my children, who become dearer to me everyday.' But after having indulged in her maternal solicitude, she turns to the stern resolve that completely fills her, saying: 'I want to remind you of the past when poverty and privation was your lot. I want to tell you a little about the present and to show the future prospects that face our youth and our people.'

Of such material is Dolores Ibarruri, who could make her home and public life both compatible and synchronizing. From her one has a great deal to imbibe of all that is expected of the modern women; from her one can learn the lesson of balance and integrity, of the art of welding the personal into public, without sacrificing privacy or becoming an automation. This miner's child, this leader of the Spanish people, is first and foremost a woman, and has sacrificed nothing of her feminine qualities but rather embodied them in service.

Within her there lives a flame which will one day rekindle in her country the smouldering fire of anti-Fascism. She remains a symbol of all that the common men and women have stood for and endured in the world through the ages. A woman of Spain, La Passionara is also the unconquerable spirit of Spain, personifying its fiery courage and heroism.

—*Gunpowder Women and Other Essays* (1943)

Preface

A storm blows over the countryside, little eddies of dust rise up to meet it and are whirled away to sink back to the ground somewhere else far away. The storm passes, the clouds lift but the fallen tree by the wayside, the roof of some wretched hovel lying prostrate and derelict, and the stray garbage floating in the little streamlets that have appeared in the pathway cannot be as easily disposed of or ignored. A famine came to Bengal in the midst of plenty, and has left in its wake broken minds, damaged bodies and crushed hopes. No longer does the sight of a good green crop bring exultation to the hearts and a smile to the lips of the agriculturist, for no longer does it spell security from at least hunger for him. He greets it apprehensively and with reservation, for much of it is already mortgaged to his landlord, who in his turn has sold it to the smooth-spoken merchant from the cities. There has been a bumper crop but the hands to harvest it have, alas, been few—most of the male population has perished, many have grown decrepit through eating offal, others are stricken with malaria and all have been weakened and debilitated by malnutrition and starvation. The soil of Bengal has not been false to those that tended her, out of her womb she has brought forth ample, but who shall garner in the wealth of her gifts? Gaunt skeleton hands stretch out for the sickle and feverishly eyes grown bright on the sharp edge of hunger's rawness watch greedily over this promise of new life. Parched lips that have forgotten to smile crack and part to leer hideously and a sob bursts from the throat as memory of those lost ones brings overwhelming desolation. Lamentation echoes from hilltop to plain, it pierces even into the concrete houses of the rich whose walls are not as impervious as their hearts, and it reaches the ears of the profiteer and hoarder—and does he still smile? This is the resultant aftermath that has to be faced and combated.

How shall I characterize the spirit of this spectral population of Bengal? Out of such starvation and exploitation revolutions have been wrought in other countries when hunger-maddened crowds have rushed upon death to endeavour to bring forward a change of rule or government. But these people whose sufferings have exceeded all human realization have only had recourse to lamentation. There have been no curses, no abuse, no desire to feed themselves at the expense of the rich, but just passive tears. This acceptance, this terrible passivity has been the curse with which we have watched our people develop cunning and a beggarlike importunity which they would have held in horror at one time so much had they prized their respectability. With a tragic realization one has watched the utter demoralization of spirit, as they floated about begging a morsel, without leadership and without a leader. If they had risen in a body, however disorganized, and *demanded* food instead of *begging* for it, one could have hoped for an organization growing out of it whereby their voices would have been heard. Instead they moaned, they begged for a handful of rice they had grown by their labours and they were denied it. Bitterness grew in a hardened crust round their simple trusting peasant hearts, and the insensibility of the world crushed whatever hopes and beliefs they might have had. Had there been leadership, concrete and strong, to help them out of this fatalistic inertia, their souls would have been saved, but now they wallowed in the quagmire of superstition, *karma*, and predestination. They welcomed the pipes of death playing their bitter sweet melody, and shut their eyes to the importance of living. Even in the days when they had dragged their debt-laden lives on from year to year and had existed without actually boasting of life, there had been compensations in the contact of man and woman, in the birth of a new child, in the laughter of children and the celebration of festivals—but now they were faced with hungry mouths clamouring for food that could not be found, thin hands upraised for one morsel, parents forgetting parenthood in the scramble for food, wives selling their chastity for it and children falling by the wayside with eyes glazed in death. What incentive could such a people have for wanting to carry on this hideous nightmare of life? With them was dying the future of Bengal's agriculture: the little hands that would one day have grasped the plough and the little maids who would have brought forth peasant children were lying inert, uncaring, piled insensitively on the same funeral pyre. Leaderless and lost, all thoughts of nation or country drowned in the vital, gnawing, primeval pains of hunger, the population floundered on in a spirit of reckless bitterness. Many and sundry tried to minister to their bodies, but nobody thought of the shrivelling up soul.

A strong imperialism triumphant within and a virile and powerful foe at the gates is no time for revolution, since it can but result in the unnecessary killing of innocents and the installation of chaos. One does not take advantage of a national calamity to bring a greater plague, but one seeks leadership that will knit the hungry millions into one strong force that will demand of a corrupt government the death penalty for the hoarder, proper rationing and price control and considerate planning to safe guard the future. It will also warn fearlessly that they are pro-Fascists who do not urge and labour ceaselessly for death to profiteering in the food grains of a people. The prosecution of war upon Japan would have been hastened and become more efficient if Bengal's eighty millions had not to face this food crisis. This leadership would call upon all who style themselves anti-Fascists to eradicate the black market in rice so that greater co-operation, greater war effort and production might be demanded of the people.

Instead the accredited leaders of the Indian people are imprisoned—and they have no contact with the people who shift about lost and unguided—a prey to fifth column and imperialist propaganda; the purchasing of new crops has been made over to the hoarder; rationing in cities has done little to ease the situation in the villages; people have lost all purchasing power and no alternative occupation is planned or found for them. The shadow of another famine hovers in the background and the Jap invader is at our gates. Bengal's tragedy must be viewed from an all-India angle before there can be a correct focussing of its urgency—for it is true that upon the development of her situation depends the life of India. She is the spearhead of the war against Japan, and the prosecution of any war is hopelessly hampered by a hungry, discontented and epidemic-ravaged population. All the men and materials which the United States and Great Britain can pour in can be of no avail unless Bengal's internal and vital affairs are handled from the point of national interest. The war is unnecessarily lengthened and ultimate ends jeopardized thereby. Imperialism has failed to adjust its perspective as it is inevitable that it must, but we the Indian people, too, have failed to bring this disaster and imperialism's failure to the anvil of our national needs. The leadership that consolidates such moments into the momentum of a movement has been wanting, and all efficacy of public agitation and thought has been lost in the alleyways of policies and controversies. Caught in the midst of conflict, the people flounder and suffer hopelessly.

Japan came openly into the war in December 1941, and Rangoon fell in March 1942. From that time a whisper rose that the Burma rice had gone and India might be faced with a food crisis. Japanese invasion of India seemed imminent, there was panic, evacuation and general confusion. War industries were being speeded up, and in certain big concerns factory workers were being given a dearness allowance from 5 to 6 per cent. It was during this period of confusion that the profiteers went quietly about and began to buy up rice all over Bengal. If the Government knew it did nothing about it; if it was not aware it can only be adduced that it had given way to panic. About April 1942 there was a general stir that the price of rice was rising, from Rs. 5 per md. it had gone up to Rs. 10. Much was made of the loss of Burma, until it was found that only 5 per cent of Burma rice was imported into Bengal, and a quantity of fine India rice used also to be exported to Burma. People who had begun to think of India on a war time basis begged for rationing to be enforced, for the selling price of rice and paddy to be fixed—and a result of this agitation was the controlled shops which instead became nests of abuse, profiteering and graft. At that stage there began the first exodus from the rice producing villages into the cities—a strange anomaly of position. The granaries of the villages stood empty and lonesome, the godowns of the merchants were full and overflowing. Rice released for the consumption of the people was three times too little as compared with the crowds that clamoured for it. Strange things began to happen that had never occurred before—a trade in gravel sprang up for mixing with rice and thus shortening the weight of the actual grains. No longer could people choose what rice they would eat, they had to take whatever was given to them, which was quite often a mixture of two or three types of grain. In many markets *goondas* took over the distribution in controlled shops, and appropriated one-third of the grain for black marketing purposes. Graft became rampant from petty to high officials. The price of rice soared up to Rs. 40, except in the controlled shops whose stocks gave out within a few hours. The streets of Calcutta resounded with the cry of people that were hungry.

This was the beginning of the vast procession that trod unknown paths to come to the city to look for food. They were unaware of the tragic significance that their hands had sown and garnered the very food they sought in the gaunt by-ways of the city, hitherto it was they who had fed the cities—to-day they were destitute and crying for food as for charity. Droves of them—men, women and children—flooded the country roads, jumped trains and somehow footsore and weary found their way into the cities. And what sort of welcome did they get? The pavement became their homes, they forgot that once they had possessed a home for had they not sold the roof over their heads for the price of thatch to buy food? They took possession of the city, and in their begging and importunity the cry of the villages came home to the city dweller. One could not open one's door but there was a whole family sitting silently importunate, gaunt and hungry-looking. One could not lift a morsel to the lips of one's children but there through the window looked in the hungry-eyed children of the poor. They were ever at one's elbow, emaciated and hungry, and as spectres they rose to embitter the luxuries of the well-to-do. Their reproachful look followed one about as they hunted amidst garbage for some forgotten morsel of food, or sat on the pavement opposite one's comfortable and hospitable mansion and deliberately ate grass and offal. They died, too, as uncomplainingly as they had lived, and with eternal hunger in their bellies there was little time to be wasted on sorrow. When they could wander about no longer, they just stopped by the wayside anywhere and lay down to die. The passers-by made a great deal of fuss, talked of ambulances etc., but the dying child gazed resentfully at them as with a whimper its troubles ceased for ever. The mother, with her shrunken breasts, watched immovably while death stalked near her. There was nothing she could do about it, who was she to complain? The little one was at least at peace from their wanderings and the fire in its belly that had fast consumed all the flesh.

Out of this ghastly panorama there emerged one beauty—motherhood. Emaciated, broken in body, with a baby in her arms and three others clustering round her ragged remnant of a *sari*, she trudged miles every day looking for food for the hungry little mouths. They whimpered, they cried themselves to sleep and she would spread her rags over them and look after them as tenderly as under ordinary circumstances. Through all the abnormality of her life the woman never forgot or grudged her motherhood. Wherever she went she kept her brood close at her heels; whatever she found was first for them though often she looked on with wolfish hunger in her eyes. Untiring energy, undaunted love and greatness characterized these simple peasant women who had become destitute of all worldly possessions. There was hardly a case where a mother deserted her children, though there were many women left to their fate by their husbands. Through the most dire trials and needs they begged food and clothing for their children first, and were more grateful for any care lavished on their little ones than for anything one could do for them. Many of them were pregnant and this too they bore with a quiet pride, though so many had to make the pavement their place of *accouchement*. It is an eternal tribute to motherhood that in the midst of death this tiny spark of newborn life had the gift of brushing a smile over the lips and a still-born child had still the power to bring a tear from eyelids sore and heavy-laden with trials and sorrows. In the midst of this primeval cry for food the gaunt and spectral mother with her brood of skeleton children epitomized the spirit of Bengal's women—undaunted and alive in the midst of death, pure as a flame amongst garbage. Was it a newer edition of Niobe that greeted one? Or could it have been yet another version of the Madonna?

One question rises naturally from this—how then did they sell their children? How then did they become victims of prostitution? Those women who sold their children did it only as an extreme measure, when they felt that no longer could they do anything for them and that it was better they should get a proper life with somebody who could. It is not surprising that their perspective should have gone awry, where they only focussed their eye on the choice between life and death and be unaware of the vast question mark—what after that? They passionately wanted their young to live, and for this they sold or 'deserted' their children in such convenient places where they felt they would be taken care of. The immediate urgency of their need made them easy prey to those who take human flesh in slavery. A large number of women became bereft of their senses through privation and want, and rather than watch their children die slowly and in pain, they would put them out of their misery—in the same way as an animal will not allow a decrepit offspring to live. It is true also that the ranks of prostitution swelled and this was due to two reasons—mainly because young and middle-aged women were won by the chicanery of procurers who lured them with smooth promises of food and shelter, which to the destitute meant heaven itself; and because unwittingly mothers sold their young daughters to the agents of brothers promising to look after them in a good home.

Free canteens and cheap canteens sprang up in every corner of the city, and the destitute were made welcome to the food. The citizens of Calcutta responded eagerly to the call of the starving but while they attended to the need of the moment how many thought of the future that was to come or the past that had been? The Indian heart responds easily to deeds of charity, which are of avail in a God-given disaster but in a man-made one there are other things that are of greater value. The idea of service for the needy inspired individuals to action but very few gave thought to the idea of after this what now? Hoarders and profiteers eased their consciences by releasing a small fraction of the food grains for the use of those that had laboured to produce them. They became charitable, benevolent, but the black market prospered. They donated money to canteens and there was no public conscience that rose up and flung their filthy lucre in their faces ostracizing them for trafficking in the staple food of a people. Through all the magnificent aid given by individuals and organizations this spirit of 'outcast the hoarder' was absent thus exposing those they wanted to benefit to exploitation by the profiteer. Where public spirit failed was in not indicting those who had been guilty of profiteering and who were still keeping the black market alive, in not plucking the viper from their bosoms to be trod to death under the weight of a public conscience. These their brothers had asked for bread and had received stones—for all their service and charity was lost if the real cause could not be located or isolated. It is no use blaming a government, for no government can last on misrule if the weight of united public opinion demands that hoarders, however powerful, be summarily punished and examples made of them. Therefore I say that in spite of the daily, hourly, great service that the people of Calcutta gave, they failed to do the maximum.

Then the Viceroy came down to Calcutta and found the streets of the city converted into public latrines, the drains flowing with filth, people crowded together and huddling for food—the population of Calcutta swollen abnormally. The destitutes held the city, and the citizens were at their service. He realized with a great shrewdness that people cannot bear to see misery but once it is out of their sight they become forgetful and callous until finally they lull themselves into thinking that it does not exist. It was also bad for the morale of British and American troops who had the famine-stricken spectres before them and had begun to ask awkward questions of what was wrong where. Journalists were, in spite of heavy censorship, making good capital out of the state of affairs. Bengal's famine had become India's show piece, and foreigners from all over the country came to see what it was like. The people of India responded from their hearts in donating for Bengal relief—it was something that had touched them vitally and found a response that all the Red Cross and War Savings Certificates had not. Therefore Lord Wavell decreed that the destitutes must be repatriated, the streets of Calcutta must be cleared and if the provincial government was unable or unwilling he would get military help for this purpose. Then began the sweeping of human garbage off the streets of Calcutta—the culminating tragedy of a shocking spectacle.

Fear shook the destitutes as they saw police vans, A.R.P. vans with uniformed attendants picking up people at random and taking them away. Where? Rumours were rife, and as a breeze whispers sprang up: 'Let us run away, back to our deserted villages, rather to die there than be sacrificed here.' Mothers weeping for their children were forcibly picked up and carried away in these vans; when in desperation they tried to escape, rough hands tied them by their hair in their places. Children, perhaps left by a mother gone in search of food, were taken away sobbing bitterly for their mother. Thus husbands, wives and children were separated through official inefficiency to handle the situation and their general unwillingness to secure the co-operation of the public who had the confidence of the destitute. It is true that the citizens of Calcutta wanted the streets cleared but not in this high-handed fashion that caused them to range themselves on the side of the destitute, giving them shelter and hiding them from the official vans. Hiding under bridges and culverts, or in the back porches of indulgent residents, they would creep out by night feeling secure in the darkness. They whispered together fearsomely crouched in the darkest corner of what they were to do. Horror and despair overwhelmed them aggravated by the wanton official behaviour and circulation by rumour-mongers of the probable fate of those who had been picked up by the vans. Then the great exodus began and to escape forceful repatriation nearly 80,000 men, women and children faced the rigours of the journey back and the probability of starvation at the end. It had never been explained to them as to the real reason, where and how they were being taken and when some explanation was given they just did not believe the police or civic guards or any official source. Wherever the people of the locality intervened, the result was usually a meek compliance with their request, but the majority began their trudge on foot. The road back was increasingly dreadful, for they saw neither hope nor promise at the end. To what were they returning? True a new harvest was ahead of them—but prematurely aged men and women, fallen prey to the evil effect of malnutrition had little left that was promising. Many of them had sold even the roof of their huts, their eating vessels, and in the case of tradesmen their articles of trade such as looms etc. They were penniless—what was there for them to look forward to? Thus a silent band of weary travellers went on and on, trickling back to their villages much the worse for their absence. When they arrived at their destination, a feeling of home overcame them, and tears rolled down their cheeks, but quite soon the tragedy of their village lives was unrolled before their eyes. Described, roofless hovels, in some places nothing stood that had been there before—those that had stayed behind were dead, and so many of those who had gone forward had also perished. Only on both sides rose the paddy, tall, green and golden—all that remained to speak of the hands that had planted and tended it. The luscious crop swayed gently in the breeze, welcoming them back—but was it theirs? They did not dare to think but wept in the utter desolation of all that had once been so familiar and dear to them.

The loss of Burma rice having been exploded as not being extensive enough to scarcity [sic], and the cyclone and floods having been found to be responsible for 15 per cent loss, the disappearance of the remaining 80 per cent can only be put down to hoarding and profiteering. Hoarders can be subdivided into three classes of criminals—the big trader who buys from the agriculturist at say Rs. 9 a md. and sells to government for Rs. 15 this is to-day when there is rationing—but previously these traders were sending millions of rupees worth of rice underground for the black market so that rice could not be found in the open market. Long after the cyclone and floods had come and gone, came the long awaited *aus* crop last August, but that passed underground and no relief was felt in the situation that prevailed. In fact, only after the repatriation of destitutes and enforcement of rationing such as it is, the hoarded *aus* rice began to be unloaded in the village market. This was proved beyond a doubt by the fact that the harvesting of the *aman* crop (December) was not over, yet rice that had disappeared began to trickle into the open market. But alas for the destitutes bereft of all buying capacity; they had not the wherewith to buy this rice—thus even with it on sale in the open market the people suffered starvation.

The second class of hoarder, who has been created by the demands of the big trader is the agricultural landlord, who holds back rice from the normal channels of trade to be able to get a better price from the profiteer. In fact, his misfortune is also great because he sold off even his seed grains at what he thought a very profitable price, but when he wanted to buy rice for his family, leaving aside the question of seeds for the next crop, he found it had gone from the open market and could only be had at abnormal price (at one stage Rs. 40 to Rs. 60 a maund) in the black market. His greed in trying to make money at the risk of starving his landless labour, and in believing the smooth-spoken words of the city merchant, constitutes his guilt.

Also aggravated by the abnormal conditions introduced by the big hoarder, the upper class householders turned panicky and in their turn began to hoard rice. Afraid that a day might come when no longer at any price would rice be available, they purchased in the black market, kept large stocks in reserve for their consumption, thus in their turn helping the black market to function. These people are in our midst, among our relatives, our aunts and uncles, and their actions give actual proof of how little the consciousness of a national calamity had penetrated. It showed a want to conscience and a desire to safeguard their own interests, without realizing that as long as this scale of profiteering continued and the majority starved, they with all their hoards were not safe; ultimately it would reach out to them also in many ways. Such a type of hoarding showed up the anti-social mid of the upper class public as well as a want of realization of reality, and was as contributory and as dangerous to the general situation as the afore-mentioned two classes.

Thus the misfortunes of Bengal, aggravated as they were by cyclone and floods, became a thousand times more inflamed by indiscriminate and merciless hoarding and profiteering. These may be constituted as the main reasons as to the destitution of the people of this province. Let it not be imagined as it was once remarked that 'the Bengal famine was made by Bengalis'—far from it, it was engineered by Hindus, Moslems and British alike, and the guilt lies heavy on each one of them. The profiteer was in the midst of them all, like vampires upon the bosom of Bengal.

What were the repercussions of their deeds—that is the greatest indictment upon those who allow the black market to still flourish and to engulf not only our food grains, the clothing off our backs, leaving our children naked and shivering during the cold winter days, the drugs and medicines which are needed for the fight against epidemics, but our women as well. That is the sum total of Bengal's tragedy. Who suffered most? To answer that question briefly, one would have to say—they who were the weakest either physically or economically. In this, to take, a general census, one finds that the severest repercussions fell upon the women, who are in a body to-day faced with social disintegration Next on the list one would place certain classes of men such as landless labourers, the weavers, the fishermen and the potters. These people had to depend for their food on the agricultural landlords, who having sold out to the hoarder left this class of men free for exploitation. The resultant effect of this is terrible. The landless labourer forced to migrate with his family to the cities, unable to find employment between the two harvests, sold even the last of his possessions to be able to buy food—but even so all his assets were not sufficient to secure food for himself and his family. Malnutrition and actual starvation, coupled with malaria in epidemic form, caused such an undue strain upon their physique that many just perished, while those who were tougher perhaps gradually became decrepit and weak, therefore useless unless restored to a proper and balanced diet. The weavers sold or mortgaged their looms during the crisis for these were their only valuable assets; as such, those who have weathered the storm find themselves without a trade or employment and families—in fact, whole communities—are faced with ruin. Little large-scale effort is being made by the State to reinstate them in their trade by buying looms for them or by taking out those that are mortgaged, and hand-weaving which was a speciality of this province is seriously endangered thereby. Large areas are affected, yet neither adequate loans nor co-operative planning is forthcoming. Fishing, too, was an important industry, since there was a ready market and the rivers and tanks abound in a large variety of fish, but this famine has just swept the fishermen out. Many of them have died, being dependent for their food grains upon the local landlord and having few assets to realize; others that live are ravaged by epidemics to which their condition of debility has made them susceptible. This is applicable also to the potter whose resources are as limited and totally dependent on others and therefore these economically dependent people were sold unmercifully to the hoarder.

The question of how vitally it affected the women is wider—because their suffering was from all sides, economic as well as moral. It is strange to relate that a far higher percentage of men and children perished during these times that women for somehow in spite of the odds against them they clung tenaciously to life and were not willing victims of demoralization. The men suffered a queer psychological reverse on their reduction to beggary, and their mortification and humiliation was so great at having to revert from honest toil to begging that they rather welcomed death than continue the struggle for existence. Women fought against this apathy and instead of allowing the whirlpool to drag them down they struggled to get out of it. It left them worn, battered and bruised, mere wraiths of their former selves, but they lived. Thus there came into being a vast army of white-clad women—widows young and old-and an equally large number of guardianless girls. In shoals they went back to their homes—to find what? Alone, homeless and workless, often with emaciated young ones in their arms. The situation was fraught with tragedy and left them open to the designs of those who take advantage of any situation to traffic in human flesh. Since rice had reappeared in the market free kitchens closed down, but these women had neither money nor work, so they just had to starve unless. ... Some persevered and sought whatever work they could find, others resisted all blandishments until the fire in their bellies and the constant demand for their bodies made them reckless enough to be susceptible to the all-winning promises of food and shelter. Thus prostitution or death became the twin possibilities for these women, and the presence of the military provided greater opportunities for a strange and new black marketing—in women. Thus family life which was the keystone of all stability for them was gradually becoming disintegrated, until it has assumed such alarming proportions that Bengal's entire womanhood stands menaced. The ground is being cut under their feet. The villages are far and secluded, so people may think that this poison will not appear on the surface, but they are also the nucleus of city life, therefore sooner or later the cancerous growth will eat into the vitals of society and all security will vanish.

Shall we then blame those who had struggled to life out of the chaos of those critical days to find that they were truly destitute, that there was no planning for them, no provisions and the crossroads facing them were towards death whose soothing voice they had spurned so long or to the wide and shaded avenue of prostitution? They wanted to live, to labour and to perform their share of national life, and they were condemned to the penal servitude of brothels. The inability to prevent this has branded shame across the hearts of Bengal's patriotic children—yet why are they powerless to prevent these innocent people being sacrificed into the ever-widening maws of prostitution? Because food and the people of Bengal have been made a pawn in the game of power politics, and until the public conscience is powerful enough to acknowledge this, we shall go on from one phase of degradation to another.

Ministries came and ministries went while lamentations and cries for food rose up in a black cloud of general indignation. But men still intrigued, still fought to keep a ministry or unseat it. The people and their food were utilized on platforms for such purposes. The public cursed whoever was in power, but were totally unable to handle a situation that was being tossed about between a handful of power-seeking politicians. But the tragedy has lain in this that this atmosphere of vilifications has been utilized by bureaucracy to interpret the utter incompetency of Indians to handle provincial autonomy. Every cry raised against the existing ministry, however well-merited, was a blow redirected by imperialism to prove India's unfitness for freedom. It is true that the provincial governments were totally incapable and not sufficiently disinterested to compass a solution of the tragic developments, but an equally heavy share of guilt rested on the Central Government, the Viceroy and the Secretary of State for India. It was the core that was rotten and therefore the flesh had grown poisonous, but never was the attention of the world once focussed in this direction, it has been diverted upon the unfortunate provincial government. But bad as it is, no government could have existed at this time that could succeed in the only solution of this problem because of the rot at the Centre. Much has been spoken of autonomy and national government—but the falseness of such phrases is borne upon any student of contemporary Indian politics with the national leaders of the Indian people in imprisonment. The Congress still remains the greatest power in Indian affairs and while it is bureaucracy's aim to discredit Indian leaders and provincial governments, it is the blindness of the people who do not see through this game—or is it perhaps the self-interest of a few?—and rise up in a body to demand a government that will be truly national in character. The entire edifice of imperialism must be destroyed and democratic rule established if such tragedies as Bengal has experienced are to be avoided. In the final analysis it is correct to characterize this famine as not 'an act of God' but a political failure.

The Queue

There was a stir of life upon the pavement, and in the half light of dawn they looked a ghostly crew conjured out of another world. Somebody kicked somebody else, and a child cried out. That seemed to be the general signal for awakening, and there they were twittering and babbling under the trees and folding up their ragged clothes. The atmosphere was foul with the smell of filth in which they had sat the whole day and whole night, defiling the freshness of the morning.

Shyama roused her mother-in-law, and tried to quieten the whimperings of two-year-old Batu. They had arrived too late yesterday to get a favoured position in the queue; and after having trudged over miles of dusty road their disappointment had been keen. What a journey it had been! In her eagerness to reach the city where rice was available, people had said, after days of starvation it had seemed that the old people walked too slow and the little ones held them back. Shyama had imagined the city as a kindly mother welcoming them, full of promises in the depths of her maternal bosom, so she had clasped her old mother-in-law by the hand and picked up Batu in her arms and tried to hasten the progress. But they had arrived too late, and halfway down the line the rice had given out. Her mother-in-law fatigued and hungry had beaten her forehead and wept, her husband had just squatted on the ground resentful and sullen, while Shyama herself dully wondered if instead of an *el dorado* she had wandered into the witch queen's domain. Everything round her was foul— the people mouthing curses at each other, fighting with dogs for a scrap of something that had been discarded as refuse, women with a brutal and vicious look in their eyes and children that cried and cried.

Last night the little family, like numerous other little families around them, had spread themselves out on the pavement to await tomorrow's distribution. Shyama had been amazed at how these people who had once had stability had become used to the life of vagrants. They felt no shame in sitting upon the pavement and picking lice from each other's hair, or that their children played about in the gutter and fouled the place indiscriminately. They made not the slightest effort to move off but clung grimly to their places in the queue. Those who had been able to obtain something cooked it and shamelessly ate it before the hungry eyes of the others. One woman had cooked grass with shrimp shells which she and her children had devoured greedily. Shyama had shuddered wondering if she too would become like that some day, and had lain down while the fire in her belly played havoc within her.

It was morning now and the amber sunlight picked out the filth and grime of their condition. The rush had begun. Shyama dragged her mother-in-law along, her husband was already in the men's queue. For a second she paused to look back at him—gaunt, unshaven, with the watchful, furtive look of those in want—and she wondered if it was really him or his wraith? Had she too changed as he had? Sorrowfully she thought that everything had changed—what did it matter about two insignificant units like themselves? People were trying to push her out, sensing that she was new to it, but Shyama struck out with her elbows and found a position for herself and her mother-in-law. The old woman, hardly able to stand, clung to her sturdy daughter-in-law's waist.

Solitary, like a desolate island amidst a sea of human beings, Kusum sat on the pavement. She held her child in her arms, she hugged him fiercely, but he remained still and unresponsive. Somebody, passing by had flung callously at her: 'He is dead!' But she could not believe it—how could it be? It was only last night that his feverish hands had clung to her, when that horrible whisper had first come to her ears: 'He is dying because you cannot give him nourishment. Come with me and you shall get all you want.' At first, she had resisted, but finally the whimpering of her child had made her frantic. He had been such a bright merry creature, not many days ago, full of life and mischief, but there he had lain, only an occasional whimper showing that he still lived. Kusum felt she could not lose him, she had lost them all—they had all fallen by the wayside and this last one she must save at any cost. Where was the man who had promised her every thing—he was at her elbow and slowly she followed him.

Dully, with a queer pain searing her heart and brain, she wondered how she had done it and how any man could have found any pleasure in her filthy, wizened body. Hunger had drained all sex out of her. But there had been so many of them who had made use of her woman's body. They had given her food which she had eaten ravenously as like ghouls they stood round her waiting for their pleasure. Their faces were lost in the delirium of those awful moments, when she had wanted to rise up and claw at their throats. But the thought of her child who must be saved had withheld her, and she had allowed them the use of herself as if she were just refuse too. If her soul had been anywhere about, it had wept in shame and humiliation, but her body had remained motionless, dead, her thoughts intent on the money she would get to buy food and medicines for her little one. Would he ever forgive this defilement when he grew up? With this came the thought—would he ever attain manhood? As she looked down at him, she acknowledged dully but without resentment that he never would.

Kusum had stared greedily at the two rupees they had flung at her—it was hers, she had torn out her soul and sold it but the money was hers. In the morning she would get all that was necessary for the child, and as she crept back to the pavement she clutched the money feverishly in her hands. Her head was reeling, she felt weak and bruised, but somehow she stumbled to her place under the tree where the heap of rags told her that he was safe. Nobody saw her as she slid wraithlike back from where she had risen and lay down exhausted. But the morning had brought the awful truth to her—she had been lying beside a dead child. It was unbelievable and even now she tried to infuse the warmth of her own body into his.

Somebody was calling to her: 'Hey, Kusum, aren't you going to queue up for rice?'

She shook her head, what was the use? They wanted to live but she had died last night, died when the last vestige of her womanhood had been torn from her. Who would want to carry this burden of shame for ever? She who had once been the loved wife of an honest ploughman—what was she now? With what anticipation her parents had named her Kusum or blossom; she was indeed a faded flower that lies upon a dung heap. Gradually everything had been stripped off her until she stood shivering in the nudity of her destitution. They had robbed her physically and morally. Her hard-earned rupees slipped from her grasp and fluttered on to the ground. Eyes that had been greedily watching them slid a hand round clawing at one of the notes. Kusum spied it and dealt a hard smack upon the skeleton fingers, the man turned upon her with a foul epithet and retreated disappointed.

Kusum felt that she had to do something with the stiff little body in her arms. Still numb from the shock of her experiences and the futility of what she had done, she could not readjust her mental equilibrium sufficiently. Therefore still with the child in her arms she rose up unsteadily, and started floundering forward realizing that it was up to her to act. She saw nothing and heard nothing of the squabbling and fighting over rice; she looked on curiously detached. What was it all about? Why did they desire to live? What could they expect of life? Had they still some expectations? Then they were not like her, she was empty, her body was a husk out of which the best had been squeezed out. She staggered and nearly fell over a prostrate figure that groaned and writhed. Kusum looked about her and found that she had come away from the market-place, and the clamour of voices came in a muffled roar. She paused for a second to stare unseeingly at the form lying across her way, and then deliberately she picked her way and passed on.

Sukhi saw her go away, clasping a bundle of rags in her arms, and even though she cried aloud in agony nobody stepped near her even out of curiosity. Even in the midst of her pain she tried to cover her shame with her inadequate rags. The searing pain had come on just after midnight had struck from some nearby clock, and it had lasted in spasms. Her husband had sat helplessly by her side until she had forced him to go and take his place in the queue. He had not wanted to leave her, but what good would that do? They had to eat, and she hated being a burden upon him at this time. She had been very near her time when they had left their village home, and her mother-in-law had said: 'I don't think, *Bowma*, you had better come. You are very near your time and might have an accident on the way.'

Afraid of being left alone Sukhi had said: 'I am very strong, mother; I promise you I'll not be a burden upon you. And I shall starve if you leave me.' Her children too had clung to her saying: 'Mother, mother, you must come with us,' and her husband had clinched all arguments by saying: 'She can't be left here to starve. She is my wife; I shall take her with me.' Her mother-in-law had muttered angrily that it was unseemly for a woman so far gone in pregnancy to come out in the open, but had not dared to interfere further. Since yesterday morning she had taken her two grand-children and gone exploring to another side of the city, and thus when the pain came on, Sukhi had been alone with her husband and his helplessness moved her to tears. She assured him that she was all right, that such pains were inevitable, yet she fancied she had seen tears in his eyes and a grimness about his mouth. With his help she had staggered to the back of the market, away from lewd and irreverent eyes and sent him to his place in the queue. His wife lay there and nobody could help her, and she had to bear her pains alone. But when they came in searing waves she dug her nails into the ground and beat her forehead. She screamed too, and even in the midst of her agony she looked round ashamed in case anybody had heard her. If they did, they had no time to stop and speak to her. It went on and the waves came in rapid succession and she felt she was drowning. Hopelessly over-whelmed, unaware of her surroundings, she just battled with the pain. Her mind was set that it must be combatted, beyond that she knew nothing. Gradually the mist cleared, her eyesight came back and she returned to reality and utterly worn out she wanted to sleep. But at the back of her mind there was a haunting thought that something more she had to do. Of course, she sat up hurriedly and experienced an emptiness, there was the child. She looked down, its breath was coming in pitiful gasps; with experienced hands she slapped its buttocks and the infant burst out into a loud cry. Sukhi tried to pick it up in her arms and found it was still attached to the cord. Wildly the woman looked round wondering what to do, and then like an animal she bent down and with her strong teeth bit it through.

Like birds that seek their roost at sunset, the destitutes were returning to the pavement to take up their positions for the night. Shyama was one of them. Their one meal over, there was nothing left for the family to do but brood for the rest of the evening. The men sat back sullen, unsatisfied, hopeless, they somehow lacked the study faith of their womenfolk. They hated themselves for having been reduced to beggary. They felt they were dishonest and chafed against it. The children had fallen asleep in the luxury of some ballast in their stomachs. Night was creeping in, soft-footed, soothing and comfortable. It brought a sense of friendliness in shrouding their destitution, it hid their wretchedness from the eyes of the world. Yet the feeling of surging turbulence persisted, and whispers sprang up all around. Shyama stretched her body on the pavement and a feeling of rest crept over her. A tiny breeze fanned her brow, and brought relief to the heaviness of her tousled and matted head. She slept. When she awoke it was with the touch of a hand on her legs, which she thrust aside. The hands were creeping over her, up to her breasts, fondling them, she cried out in horror. Her husband woke up with: 'What is it? What's happened?' Sitting up she said: 'I don't know, somebody was trying to paw and handle me.' He looked round fiercely and ran after a shape stumbling in the darkness. The faint sound of a scuffle and oaths floated back to her and she held herself taut until he returned: 'The swine will have a bruised face to get home with now!'

Simultaneously came shouts from the other destitutes:

'For God's sake shut up!'

'Look after your woman—can't you? without disturbing others.'

Somebody moaned: 'Even at night we cannot be left in peace.'

'Why don't they keep their rows to themselves?'

'The woman is to blame—bloody bitch!'

With a muttered curse and a warning they turned over on their sides and slept. Shyama clung watchfully to her husband's hand, shamed and mortified at her experience.

—*Darkening Days* (1944)

Vijayalakshmi Pandit
(1900–1990)

Born on August 18, 1900, Vijayalakshmi Pandit was the daughter of nationalist leader Motilal Nehru, and sister of Jawaharlal Nehru, the first prime minister of independent India. She grew up to become the first woman President of the United Nations General Assembly, in 1953. She was also the first woman ambassador, not merely in India but in the entire world, as well as the first woman minister of British India.

In 1921, after receiving private education in India and abroad, she married Ranjit Sinh Pandit, a fellow Congress worker who died in 1944. In keeping with her family tradition, she was an active worker in the Nationalist Movement, for which she was imprisoned thrice by the British.

From Ministry to Prison, reproduced here, gives us a vivid, day-by-day account of one of her spells in prison. The small notes take into account everything from the politics and corruption she encountered while she was there, to the quality of prison food, lack of humanity, and the daily tragedies that befell poor young Indian women arrested for crimes of various kinds.

After Independence, she distinguished herself in a diplomatic career, taking on the role of India's High Commissioner in London from 1954 to 1961, and Spain from 1958 to 61. She was also Governor of Maharashtra from 1962 to 64, and a member of the Lok Sabha from 1964 to 68.

She played an important role in the All India Women's Conference, having been its President from 1940 to 1942. In 1979 she published *The Scope of Happiness: A Personal Memoir*. She spent the last few years of her life at Dehradun, till her death in 1990. Nayantara Sahgal one her three daughters is an eminent writer of our times.

Vijayalakshmi Pandit has been described as an 'aristocrat and proud if it. But she was not feudal, and it is an important difference.' Some of the situations she describes in *So I Became a Minister* are still painfully recognizable: the memorial meeting for Maxim Gorky in which 'many learned people appeared on the platform and read papers in which they compared Gorky to every other author living and dead ...'

From her understanding of the woman's situation, she also comes across as an extremely modern woman who knew that she and her kind were being closeted in a manner more subtle than obvious: 'Woman has been taught to hide her feelings behind a mask. She must not try to see things as they are, or give expression to the urges within her. The name given to this mask is "womanly instinct", and if any woman growing bold should try and discard it, a cry of protest is raised by old people of both sexes. They beg woman not to throw away her modesty and become unsexed and shameless. They entreat her in the name of India's past glory not to discard those virtues which, it is said, made the woman of a past age great. What these people really wish to preserve is neither virtue nor chastity, but that ignorance which has kept woman enslaved through the ages and which is now giving place to the light of knowledge.'

Epitomizing her belief in the power of womankind, and the zeal with which she undertook everything assigned to her in her various capacities, she admits that 'The greatest satisfaction of all has been the thought that, in however small a way, one was helping to dispel the age-old tradition that woman could not do man's work.'

So I Became A Minister

I wonder how far people realize that one gets out of life just what one puts into it, and it is because so many people do not put in what is best in them that the return they get is poor, resulting in a constant state of dissatisfaction and boredom.

I am one of those fortunate individuals who have always been able to get a thrill out of life, and I can honestly say the occasions when I have been bored have been exceedingly rare. Difficulties, opposition, criticism—these things are meant to be overcome, and there is a special joy in facing them and coming out on top. It is only when there is nothing but praise that life loses its charm and I begin to wonder what I should do about it!

Joining the Ministry with this outlook on life, it seemed fairly obvious to me that whatever the difficulties in doing work for which I had no training or previous experience, I was going to get something very satisfying out of it. Because of this, and also because I knew there would be many who would question my ability to handle such an important and difficult task. I did not hesitate unduly in accepting the responsibility of Ministership. Somewhere, way back in my genealogical line there must have existed an ancestor (or was it perhaps an ancestress!) who loved a fight, and this fighting blood has certainly been transmitted to me and rejoices whenever there is a chance to prove its mettle. So I became a Minister.

My knowledge of a Council in action was confined to a few occasions when, as a girl, I had sat in the Visitors' gallery in the Assembly Chamber in Delhi or Simla during the days when my father led the Swaraj party opposition in the Assembly.

I had an exceedingly vague idea of the duties of a Minister when, on the 18th July 1937, I entered my office-room in the Civil Secretariat for the first time. A young man presented himself and announced that he was my Personal Assistant. I wondered what that meant and decided to seek information later. Meanwhile I was more interested in the room where I would, in future, have to spend a good deal of my time. There was a large writing table in the centre of the room and an equally large leather covered sofa against the wall. The rest of the space was occupied by innumerable chairs, small tables and book-shelves and looked like a second-hand furniture dealer's shop. A perfectly impossible pink carpet struck a discordant note against the apple green distemper on the walls and a layer of dust covered everything. I stood in the doorway and surveyed the room with a sinking heart. However could I sit here and concentrate on important matters? Very hesitatingly I asked the Personal Assistant if it was possible to remove some of the unwanted furniture and was relieved to hear that this was permissible. Straightway I took my courage in my hands and started giving orders.

The pink carpet was quickly removed and by dint of a few compliments to the dear old man who was caretaker, a delightful beige and bluish-green one was substituted. The angles of the writing table and sofa were changed, unnecessary chairs and book-shelves sent to the godown, and a couple of restful blue-green curtains obtained from my house and hung up. Things began to look much better. I felt I could now spend some time in this room without being oppressed—yet something still seemed lacking—of course, flowers! I sent for a green 'Khurja' bowl from the Arts and Crafts Emporium across the road and asked for it to be filled with roses, which I had seen growing in profusion in the Secretariat Gardens as I passed through. My request was met by a horrified silence. Eventually, the caretaker summoned up his courage. 'But Madam you can't have flowers in here, it has never been done before.' 'Hasn't it,' I said with well feigned surprise, 'then it's time someone began. I think I shall go down to the garden and pick some now.' This was too much. The idea of a Cabinet Minister, armed with a pair of scissors, cutting roses in the sacred precincts of the Secretariat garden, was not to be borne. Hastily the caretaker went out promising to bring the roses himself, and from that day it has become the established custom for a bowl of flowers to brighten my office.

Last year during their visit to Lucknow Lord and Lady Samuel came to see me. Seeing him look at my green bowl, filled that day with lovely crimson roses, I felt slightly nervous and began a sort of apology for having flowers in an office—Lord Samuel cut me short—'What lovely roses,' he said, 'always surround yourself with flowers, they are such a help!'

And so having arranged the room to my satisfaction I turned my thoughts to more important things. There were a large number of files on the table. How on earth should I tackle them? Evidently it was no one's business to initiate me into the mysteries of reading a file. I had better teach myself. I looked through them and chose one that looked less complicated than the rest and began to read from the first page. It turned out to be interesting—soon I was engrossed in it and by the time I had read it through, felt quite competent to pass an order. Without hesitation I put down my opinion. After this I went on with greater confidence to the next file and by the time the afternoon was over I had learnt the proper method of reading a file and had also dealt with several important matters. Not a bad day's work!

My second trial was when my department Secretary introduced himself to me. I have always had an inferiority complex when confronted by tall people, and I was not pleased when a giant six-feet odd in height—came into my room. Never was I more conscious of my lack of height than when I stood up to shake hands with him. Good heavens! I thought—do I have to give orders to this exceedingly tall Englishman—however shall I manage? But manage I did, and if his opinion is to be believed, I managed very well!

My Parliamentary Secretary was the next obstacle in my path. I had not met him before, though I knew him by reputation. I had scarcely got used to daily dealings with the Departmental Secretary and the Personal Assistant when this third man loomed threateningly on my horizon. Why were all these men necessary—life, I felt, was going to be difficult after all. But once again fortune came to my aid. The Parliamentary Secretary soon fell in with my ways and after the first few days of adjustment, we were able to work in a smooth and satisfactory manner.

Inevitably there must be a softening of the angularities when men and women work together, and in a very little while it was apparent to me that the notes submitted by my various Secretaries were couched in gentler and more chivalrous language! My experience in preparing my first budget will illustrate this point.

During the days preceding the presentation of the Budget in the House I seemed to be surrounded by figures. I swam in a sea composed of noughts and my very dreams were disturbed by them. Never having learnt sufficient arithmetic in spite of the efforts of the best masters this period was a sore trial for me, and in a mood of despair I wrote to my Parliamentary Secretary as follows: 'These figures alarm me, Will P.S. kindly explain?' Swift came the reply 'Figures alarm you? I cannot believe it. I know H.M. is prepared to face battalions and mould the destiny of nations. I can only take her note as an encouragement to me in my work'—an explanatory note was attached! The figures certainly seemed less alarming after this!

My experiences in the Assembly itself would fill a volume, and it is difficult to choose from amongst them. It was impossible for me to look upon the Assembly with the seriousness it deserved. From the Treasury benches I saw before me men whom I had known from childhood as clients and, in many instances, friends of my father's. I couldn't suddenly begin to think of them as dangerous opponents. Besides, they weren't dangerous— not to anyone but themselves. The views they represented belonged to a comparatively small group and their rather limited vision, so it seemed to me, would, in the long-run injure them more than the policy they opposed in the Assembly. And so the Council Chamber also presented to me its humorous side.

Came the day when I had to make my maiden speech. The first Government resolution rejecting the Government of India Act and demanding a new Act to be framed by a Constituent Assembly was to be moved by our Premier. Unfortunately he was ill and confined to bed and for some reason his choice fell on me, and I was informed that I should have to move the most important resolution of the session.

I was not new to public speaking, but I had never before spoken in the Assembly and felt slightly nervous as I sat waiting for the Speaker to call my name. Suddenly I remembered what my father always used to tell me. 'Don't ever be nervous,' he would say. 'Prepare your speech, then forget it, and address your audience as if they knew less than nothing.' I suddenly felt brave. After all I knew what I wanted to say. Why should I feel nervous of people whom I had known from childhood? I stood up and spoke. The speech went smoothly and so vanished the last remnants of stage fright.

My first Civic Address gave me an insight into the way things were managed in the 'ancient regime'. I was due to visit a certain town and had consented to receive an address from the Municipal Board. Imagine my surprise when, a few days before my visit, I received a copy of the Municipal

Board's address together with suggestions for the reply I had to give. I rubbed my eyes. Surely things didn't happen like this outside a story book. I felt annoyed and sent the reply back to the authorities concerned with the remark that I felt capable of giving an adequate reply to any address I might receive, and have always continued to speak *ex tempore* at all public functions including replies to civic addresses.

It has been an interesting, even fascinating, task familiarizing myself with various Acts and points of law. There has been pleasure in the working up of a difficult case and in the ultimate passing of an order one felt right and just. The greatest satisfaction of all has been the thought that, in however small a way one was helping to dispel the age-old tradition that woman could not do man's work. And as I look back on the last two years I see them full of a rich and very varied experience which has added to my understanding of life. There have been times of disillusion and distress and a feeling of helplessness in face of tremendous odds, yet this period of Ministership cannot ever be entirely wasted. The lessons I have learnt have been of value and their worth will increase as the years go by and I find myself faced with other and perhaps more difficult problems.

From where I sit and write I see before me range upon range of purple mountains stretching in an unending chain, their peaks almost merging with the blue of the sky above. Such it seems to me is the never-ending progress of human thought and activity, each thought current slightly bigger than the one before until one more perfect than the rest changes the world and a new conception of an age-old principle takes shape. One such thought current has been born in our midst today, and as it goes onwards in ever-widening circles, I feel that we are moving daily nearer to the fulfilment of our hearts' desire, an independent India.

On Being Interviewed

In the days when politics were to me only a name I used to read with earnest attention the various interviews which appeared from time to time in the press. I swallowed every word as gospel truth whether it fell from the lips of statesman, sportsman, or cinema star, and it seemed to me that no job in life was quite so enviable as that of a journalist—the man who had access to all great people and whose words of wisdom he was privileged to present to an unsophisticated world. Since that time many things have happened, and although, counted in years, it is not so long ago, yet I am today a wiser and perhaps a sadder person than before.

The political game is full of rapid ups and downs, and having entered the political field I now find myself amongst those people who are the legitimate prey of the journalist and whose utterances are inflicted on a sorely tired world from time to time. How have I fared and what have my reactions been? They may be summed up in one word as unfortunate. If you care, you may read on and be warned in time!

It is my opinion that the two greatest pests in the world today are the telephone and the journalist. The telephone can, however, be disconnected when your nerves are frayed, but the journalist cannot be so easily dealt with. He is everywhere, irrepressible and eternally optimistic. What would discourage an ordinary individual only spurs him on to greater effort, and a snub is but so much water on the back of the proverbial duck.

'How is it you have accepted a seat in the Cabinet after your opposition to acceptance of office?' And, utterly disregarding my reply, the papers next morning announce: 'Mrs Pandit forced to accept Ministership ...'

I am due to speak at a meeting, and enthusiastic young journalists come to ask for an advance copy of my address. I explain politely that there is no copy and I hope they will endeavour to give a correct report. They assure me this will be so, and I go to the meeting with a light heart. Little do I think that what strikes me as important will be passed over by these bright youths, while special emphasis is laid on what, in my ignorance, I look upon as trivial. But this is actually what happens, and those people who read their morning paper and follow my career through its columns must be often bewildered at the many contradictory things I am supposed to have said. Quite recently, while speaking to some girl students, I said that they must not let themselves be influenced by what prejudiced persons said about women and their duties, as it is usual for those who resent modern thought and advancement to oppose it on the plea that the goddess of the home must not be corrupted. In this connection, I referred to a letter published that day in a local daily on the subject of divorce for women, in which the writer had opposed the idea on somewhat similar grounds. Later I read my talk as interpreted by the press. 'Mrs Pandit, supporting divorce for women, said "You must cease to be goddesses and become human beings, etc. etc."' I have since been flooded with letters of criticism and advice. Had my bright young journalist friend left my talk unreported, I should have been saved a lot of unnecessary work.

During my recent visit to Europe my experiences of being interviewed have, if possible, been even more disastrous. Descending from the plane at Croydon late at night, I had to face a battery of cameras and a crowd of excited journalists. Interviews were, however, postponed and time given for them at a later date. It was my first experience of women journalists, and I can honestly say that among journalists, the female of the species is certainly more deadly than the male!

A young woman comes into my room. She is smartly dressed and pleasing to behold—'How do you do, Mrs Pandit. It's such a pleasure to

meet you. Can you give me some information about the women of India?'
... We have a talk, and I endeavour to answer her questions to the best of
my ability. As she leaves she says quite casually—'What do you think of
physical culture?' I answer without thinking—'Oh yes, I am a believer in
it—specially the Indian variety'. Next morning a popular daily announces
to the London public, 'Woman Minister begins 18-hour-day by standing
on head!'

Another bright young thing is anxious to interview me. She is not
quite so hard boiled and is therefore, slightly nervous, but taking her courage
in both hands she begins, 'Did you meet your husband in prison,' she asks.
I tell her I had been married for ten years before I went to jail. She smiles
and says, 'but you wouldn't mind if I said you met him in prison. It sounds
so much more interesting from the public point of view.' In vain I explain
that it will be difficult, not to say embarrassing, to reconcile the fact of
a fifteen-year-old daughter with this statement. She goes on her way
undaunted, and later on her paper gives various interesting and incorrect
details of my life, including a romantic meeting in jail which later on is
supposed to have led to marriage.

But yet another lady comes to see me. 'Don't you get frightfully tired of
office work, Mrs Pandit? I expect you long to do ordinary things about the
house.' I innocently reply that I enjoy doing ordinary things just as much
as the extraordinary ones. The report published next day informs those
who are in search of news that 'Indian woman Minister darns husband's
socks.'

The men journalists also have their innings. They want information
about the Indian woman. Yet the questions they ask leave me wondering
what there is in my appearance which gives them the idea that I am
mentally deficient. The interviews these men journalists produce generally
begin with a description of my dress which varies with every account
according to the mood and politics of the writer. If he is of the socialist
school of thought, I am dressed plainly, due emphasis being given to some
aspect of my work. If, however, the writer represents either the popular
press or the conservative view, I am clothed with all the magnificence of
the Orient, form the 'red enamel caste mark' on my forehead to my 'scarlet
lacquered finger and toe nails'. I have wondered often what conclusions
the English public actually come to after reading these conflicting reports.

I think of the interviews I have seen my brother give. What straight,
clear and intelligent questions are put to him, and yet I, who also attempt
to do public work, am treated as if my interests were confined to clothes
and children and those petty social activities in which the lady of means
and leisure engages in order to allay the prickings of her conscience.

Tradition dies hard and the world moves slowly; but slower still is the progress of human thought. Woman, though theoretically now the equal of man in most countries, is still regarded in fact as the lesser being even by those whose public utterances would make it appear that they had accepted an equal partnership. But the advancement of woman cannot now be kept back in this way. She is now going forward, not because of the courtesy or chivalry of man, but because it is an accepted fact that in her advancement alone lies the future progress and prosperity of the world.

—*Vijayalakshmi Pandit* (1983)

From Ministry to Prison

12th August 1942

I woke up with a start and switched on the light. Binda was standing at the foot of my bed. He told me the police had arrived and wished to see me. It was 2 a.m. My mind was a confused jumble of the events of the preceding twenty-four hours. The shots fired on the students' procession were still ringing in my ears and before my eyes I could only see the faces of those young men whom I had helped to pick up and remove to hospital. I was utterly weary in mind and body and more than a little dazed.

The girls were asleep on the veranda and I did not wish to disturb them. Both Lekha and Tara had gone to bed exhausted after what they had been through the day before. They had seen sights which would not easily be effaced from their memory and were bewildered and unhappy.

I went out to the porch. The City Magistrate the Deputy Superintendent of Police and half a dozen armed policemen were standing waiting for me in the darkness. I switched on the light and was amazed to find the grounds full of plain-clothes men some of whom had actually come up on to the veranda. This annoyed me and very curtly I ordered them off into the garden before speaking to the City Magistrate. He was ill at ease and said he had a warrant for my arrest. 'Why is it necessary for so many armed men to come to arrest one unarmed woman at this amazing hour?' I asked. A search was also take place, I was informed I told them to go ahead with the search while I got ready for prison.

I had not expected to be arrested and was taken by surprise. There was no one with the girls, no possibility of making satisfactory arrangements. Indira had arrived from Bombay a few hours earlier. She was tired so I ran upstairs to say good-bye to her. After a kiss and a few hurried instructions to Indira I woke the girls and broke the news. They were brave as always and immediately grasped the situation—no useless questions no fuss. All three of them helped me to pack and Lekha hurriedly put together a few books for me to take along. Rita looked at me with big eyes heavy with sleep. Looking at her my courage began to ebb. She was so little and the world was so big—who would take care of her? As if sensing my thoughts she smiled at me. 'How wonderful to live in these days Mummie,' she said, 'I wish I could go to jail too.' I felt suddenly that there was no need to worry and with a lighter heart I bent down to kiss her. 'Let's say good-bye to you outside Mummie, Tara and I want the police to see how we take these partings.' They came out with me and at the porch we said good-bye. 'Darling Don't worry. Everything will be fine. I will look after the kids,' said Lekha, giving me quick tight hug. 'Bye-bye Mummie darling,' said Tara, 'we shall keep the flag flying,' Her eyes were bright and she held her head high. Rita clung to me for a minute but her voice was firm as she said, 'Mummie darling, take care of yourself. We shall be fighting the British outside while you are in.'

By this time some of the servants had arrived and I was able to say good-bye to them. They were not as brave as the children and some of them had tears in their eyes. I walked down the drive to the gate and was surprised to find it locked as usual at that hour. How had the police come in? Evidently by the side wicket. We went out the same way.

There or more police lorries were lined up on the road outside. In the darkness could not make out the exact number. More armed men appeared out of the shadows. I was asked to get into the first lorry. The D.S.P. took the wheel. The City Magistrate and some others got in behind and we started.

The city had been in the hands of the military for several hours—martial law was everything but name and a curfew order in force [sic]. We drove in an atmosphere of extreme tension. As we travelled along the familiar road to Naini my mind was full of many thoughts and before my eyes like some film in a cinema were pictures of other journeys—dozens of them from 1921 onwards. We reached the Jumna bridge, heavily guarded and were challenged by the sentries on duty. Even after the words 'Friend' and 'Police car' were shouted, the vigilant sentry was doubtful about letting us proceed—what terrific loyalty the British inspire in those who serve them!

Arriving at Naini I was informed that the jail authorities had not been intimated of my approaching arrival. Orders had, apparently, been communicated late at night to the police and the jail staff did not expect me. After half an hour's wait, the door of the Female Prison was opened and the matron in the manner of all jail matrons, came rushing along panting and puffing and very much out of breath.

I was conducted to the old familiar barrack. It was 3.45 a.m. I spread my bedding on the ground, was locked in, and a new term of prison-life began. My head ached badly and the throbbing in my temple prevented sleep. I lay thinking over the events of the past two days. I was worried about Lekha and felt she would land up in prison. The previous evening as she was going to bed I talked with her and tried to get her reactions to events. She spoke with great bitterness. 'It will take a long time for me to forget what I have seen Mummie, and it will be longer before I can root out the hatred which is growing in my heart. We can't think in terms of normal life any more—there's no going back for us. We must go on straight to the end, whatever the end may be.' Of course, she is right—we must go on—to the end. At last I fell asleep.

13th August 1942

My first thought on waking was of the girls. My head continued to ache and I lay in bed until the *lambardarni* announced that she wished to sweep the barrack.

There are few of the old familiar faces left and the new ones look at me like something out of a museum. There is no water, no sanitary arrangements—in fact nothing at all. I walked in the yard for half an hour then I got a little water from the convicts bathing tap and washed my face. About seven the matron came and said she would send me some tea from her house as the jail was unable to supply rations until 10 a.m. I had no desire to accept the matron's tea but my head continued to throb and I thought perhaps the tea would help. It didn't. I spent a miserable day.

Towards noon some raw rations arrived, but still no coal, so cooking was not possible. Later, with the help of one of the convicts, I made a small fire of twigs and made an attempt to cook but it was a failure as the fire would not light. I read and slept and finally got up at 4 a.m. to start this diary. It is now six and lock up takes place in a few moments.

Here comes the matron followed by the usual procession of wardresses to lock up and so ends the first day in my third term of imprisonment.

After lock up the matron came back again in half an hour and announced that she had orders to leave my barrack open and that I might sleep outside if I wished. I was glad of this concession. Before leaving, she enquired what I was having for dinner and was horrified when I said I had nothing to eat at hand. She wanted to send me something but I refused.

I walked in the yard for a while. It was fairly cool and my head felt much better. As I walked I almost forgot that I had been away from here for nearly a year and half. It seemed as if this was just a continuation of the previous imprisonment. I put my bed outside in the yard and lay down to read—but my mind wandered and I could not follow the book. Every now and again shouts of '*Inquilab Jindabad*' and other slogans came to me over the wall. I felt less alone after that, and in a way, happier. The stars were out and I lay looking up at the sky for a while, then went back to my book. At 9.30 I put out the light as hoards of insects were making life impossible by crawling all over me and getting into my hair.

I woke up at eleven to find myself wet and the rain coming down in torrents. By the time I had brought my bed in, I was soaked and had to change. After the rain it was cool and I had a peaceful night.

14th August 1942

I woke up in the morning feeling fresh and prepared to be civil to the world, but when by 8.30 a.m. there was no coal and no tea I found myself losing my temper. I think hunger had something to do with it also. The matron had not been [sic], so I wrote and informed the Superintendent that since I had been admitted to the jail no food had been supplied to me and if it had not been for the matron's kindness in sending me some tea from her house I should have starved completely. I mentioned that if the jail was short of raw rations I might be given the cooked food served to the convicts. This note brought the matron running and out of breath—full of apologies for the slackness in the arrival of my rations.

Shortly afterwards some raw rations and vegetables arrived and a bundle of firewood. Earlier I had, with the help of one of the convicts built a *chula* in the portion the veranda which is to serve as a kitchen. I cleaned up some vegetables and cooked a simple meal. Being really hungry I enjoyed it.

15th August 1942

Food is an overrated subject. One realized this most forcibly in jail. It is all right if one is in pleasant surroundings with the right people and the food is well cooked and well served. It is certainly possible to enjoy a meal in such a setting. But when one has to cook in the most primitive fashion and the heat is making one ill and the rations are mildewed, it is really a doubtful pleasure. I have decided to give it up and shall try to confine myself to bread and tea.

Prison tea has to be seen to be believed! My experience of tea is fairly varied, ranging from the exquisitely perfumed and delicate varieties that Madam Chiang sends me to the nondescript syrupy stuff one is obliged to swallow during election campaigns—but never have I seen or tasted anything like jail tea. I am convinced it is some special and very deadly variety of leaf grown for the poor unfortunates who are in prison. Not having any tea of my own I took this decoction once and nearly passed out. It would give me a tremendous thrill if I could make all jail officials live for one week on jail rations. We should not have quite so much talk about the 'well-balanced and wholesome diet'. I wonder why we are always able to plan well-balanced diets for others but for ourselves we generally try to get the most tasty, forgetting the balance part entirely.

I am going to read a fascinating book Indu has lent me an anthology of 'The World's Great Letters'. I am looking forward to an interesting evening. I like to keep myself occupied at this hour because, above all others it is the hour when I grow reminiscent and a little-homesick. I have no idea how long this term of imprisonment is going to last. I had better shake off such weakness and settle down!

16th August 1942

The first thing I learnt this morning was that there had been firing in the city twice yesterday. The information is not from a source I consider reliable, but nevertheless it has disturbed me. It is terrible to be shut up there when others are exposed to daily dangers.

I was interrupted by the matron who seemed to be in a mood for a chat. Having nothing to say to her I sat silent while she told me the story of her life. There was also a running commentary on the various Superintendents under whom she has served and the Inspector Generals of Prisons she has seen and spoken to. It is amusing to compare notes about jail administration as seen by different matrons. Some day I shall write a book about 'Jails and Matrons I have Known'. It should make amusing reading. If my term of imprisonment is long enough I should be well acquainted with prison politics—though I seem to have more than a passing knowledge of them already. They are not intricate to any one who tries to understand a little the workings of the human mind.

I spent an hour last night reading 'The Letters'. Some of them are really beautiful. 'Letters are always interesting—specially if they are other people's.' Voltaire has said, 'The post is the consolation of life,' and some one else has added, 'As long as there are postmen life will have zest.' There must be very few people who have not at some period of their lives recognized the truth of the above sayings. Most of us have waited in breathless suspense for the post which was to bring the one letter we wanted most—may be it was news of a child far away from us—a friend from whom we have been parted—money on which many things depended— or just a love letter—one of those silly epistles which all lovers write full of the pleasant nothings which the beloved waits for with so much eagerness and which she imagines are hers alone—forgetting that the same words and sentiments have been shared by all lovers since the beginning of time.

Today the matron has permitted one of the convict girls to come over and help me with my cleaning and cooking etc. Her name is Durgi and she belongs to the potter class. From her history-ticket I see she is twenty-six years old and is serving a sentence for the murder of her husband. She has already done eight years. She is very dark but has good features and pleasing manners. Like all other convicts she wears a pair of tiny drawers and an upper garment which has no special name. The regular jail uniform—skirt and bodice is too heavy and hot for use in the summer and is only worn on inspection days. Durgi has nice limbs and they are seen to good advantage in her abbreviated costume. I think she and I will be good friends.

There has been a hard shower of rain today and it is cooler at last. The sky is dark with clouds so there will be more rain tonight. The barrack is leaking so badly that there is no spot where my bed can entirely escape. I have chosen a place where my head is safe but where my feet will get a bath! The insects have increased and it is almost impossible to keep the light on—but I do not intend to be beaten so easily. It is only 7.30 p.m. and I cannot possibly go to bed yet—so I shall seek forgetfulness in my book and read Heloise's beautiful letters to Abelard.

There are rigid social conventions in prison as outside. The woman who is in for abduction is on the lowest rank of the social ladder, then come the counterfeiters of coins, thieves and finally the women who are serving a sentence for murder. These are the leaders and they are tremendously proud of their position. It is usual when a quarrel takes place for a woman to say—'Don't dare to treat me as if I were a common thief—won't stand for it—I am in for murder.' During my first term of imprisonment in 1932 I was a little afraid of this type in the beginning. But soon one recognized how after all any one of us might commit an act of violence in a moment of anger of through sheer force of temper—it wouldn't necessarily degrade us to the level of the human being who commits daily in cold blood acts such as thieft, abduction and the like.

17th August 1942

It has rained in torrents since last night. My barrack looks like a lake and the bed an island—the only spot where one can have a degree of safety from the elements. Yet somehow the weather has helped me. It is in keeping with my mood and I do not mind it. I think if the sun had been shining today I would have felt more depressed.

The day has dragged on and I have felt no inclination to do anything—I asked Durgi to make me something to eat thinking in my ignorance that it would be a fairly simple thing for her to do. The dish she presented to me looked like dirty porridge and tasted worse.

Charcoal is not supplied as on previous occasions and the smoke from the damp wood makes cooking very difficult. The rations are of the poorest quality and mixed with grit and dirt, tiny stones and even an odd spider or two thrown in for good weight. After cleaning the dal and rice one finds that the quantity has appreciably diminished. I am keeping the dirt I have taken out of my ration until inspection day and will show it to the doctor. The ghee supplied is dark brown in colour and has a funny smell. There is so little of it, it seems useless to bother about the quality.

Lack of news is irritating. Rumours of course, come in—a jail is sort of whispering gallery and the whispers have a habit of echoing and re-echoing round the place, one can't help hearing them, but rumours are not enough and one craves for some real authentic news especially at a time like this. I find myself fretting and losing my temper quite unnecessarily.

—*Vijayalakshmi Pandit* (1993).

Kamaladevi Chattopadhyay
(1903–1988)

Born in 1903 to a wealthy Saraswat family of South Karnataka, Kamaladevi Chattopadhyay was educated at a Catholic convent and St Mary's College in Mangalore. She married young— becoming a child-widow while still in school—before breaking with orthodoxy to marry the poet Harindranath Chattopadhyay, the brother of Sarojini Naidu.

She later left for the U.K. with her husband, and studied social service at Bedford College, London. The couple also travelled to Europe and a number of places, learned dramatic production, and produced a number of plays after returning to India. Kamaladevi played lead roles and was involved in a lot of pioneering work on stage.

She was an ardent nationalist and among the foremost leaders of the women's movement in India, actively participating in the freedom struggle and the emergence of the nationalist women's movement of the 1920s. During this period she served three prison terms at Theraveda, Belgaum and Vellore, and later went on to court arrest a number of times.

Margaret Cousins in her essay entitled 'Vignettes of Indian Women Leaders,' writes about Kamaladevi and says that it was largely owing to the latter's intense study of Political Science, Economics and History, during the Civil Disobedience imprisonment, that she became a convinced socialist and the organizer-founder of the All India Congress Socialist Party.

As a leading socialist figure, Kamaladevi set up labour organizations and extended her fullest cooperation to the formation of the All India Women's Conference in 1926, where she served as Secretary and, later, as President.

In her memoirs, *Inner Recesses, Outer Spaces*, she reminisces about the many people who influenced her, mentioning luminaries like Pandita Ramabai, Ramabai Ranade, Premlilaben Thackersay, Maharashi Karve, Sri Aurobindo, and even Gandhi who, learning of her initial doubts about the success of non -violence, sent her a card 'in which he expressed his apprehension' and asked her not to join the movement if she didn't have faith in non-violence.

Her research and concern for women is also obvious when one reads *The Awakening of Indian Women*, where she takes the reader through a gamut of facts, statistics, and hard-hitting truths about the condition of women. 'It is class that determines the fate of women, not sex,' she says, adding 'While men seek new pastures to enliven their idle hours and take to intellectual pursuits, they deny entrance therein to women. Woman is thus reduced to the status of a reproductive machine, and while man's sphere keeps expanding, hers keeps contracting.'

While discussing the man-woman relationship, Kamaladevi notes, not without sarcasm, that 'The greater her submission to man and more the suffering at his hands, the surer and quicker is her road to heaven.' She also attacks what she calls the 'double standards of morality' that create severe codes for women as the preservers of social morals, while men are allowed to be as fickle as they choose to be.

Kamaladevi was interested in empowering villagers by reviving traditional handicraft industries. She interacted with them, helped redesign traditional handicrafts to make them marketable, and was actively involved in developing the Cottage Industries Emporium as an outlet for crafts. Many claim that the acceptance ethnic traditional weaving enjoys today is largely due to the work of people like her.

This interest in building up sections of society, economically, was a well thought-out plan, if her chapter on Imperialism and Class Struggle is anything to go by: 'The economic motive is one of the strongest in the human element and it is through the economic demands that a programme that they can visualize as freedom can be built up and out of this struggle will rise the great struggle for political power by the masses.' She became Chairman of the All India Handicrafts Board in 1952, and was also Vice President of the All India Designs Centre and World Craft Council. She also wrote ten books on various issues, and received a number of awards including the Watumull Award (1962), Magasaysay Award for community leadership (1966), the Padma Bhushan and, later, the Padma Vibhushan from the Government of India.

Imperialism and Class-Struggle

The birth of the Socialist Party in the Congress marks an important epoch in Indian politics, though few perhaps have realized its significant role. People in their ignorance merely regard it as a symbol of revolt against Gandhiji and Gandhism, an indiscriminate importation of inassimilative western notions. There are some who are sympathetic, but regard its appearance as premature. All these betray a lack of historical knowledge and historical sense. The majority takes its stand on the ground that our struggle today is against a foreign power and the talk of class-war confuses the issue and gives rise to internecine fights. This shows that a great many people have not understood the nature of Imperialism or the characteristics which a struggle against it ought to develop. Unless we get a clear understanding on that, it is not possible to get a correct perspective of India's struggle or of the role of the Socialist Party in it.

Imperialism is the outcome of capitalistic production, that is, production of commodities sold at the highest profit; hence its need for a constant expansion of market to maintain a level of prosperity. It also means export of capital from an industrialized country to undeveloped tracts, thus reaping heavy dividends. Such capital is employed not in industrial development, for that would necessarily mean limiting the imports coming from the 'Home' market. So it goes into the development of the means of transportation. And so far as the exports go, the expansion is only illusory. No real expansion is possible unless production also increases and this is not possible except through improved means of production, which again has no chance in a colonial country. So, the high rate of profit that the foreign creditor derives from investments in colonies is raised by the continuous exploitation of the masses by depriving them of even the little surplus they might otherwise have saved. Thus the heavy taxation in India represents the high interest rate paid to the foreign creditor.

Now let us examine the relationship between this Imperialism and its Indian allies, such as the princes, landlords capitalists, middlemen, moneylenders etc., for, then we shall have realized the class-basis of the Indian anti-Imperialist struggle. For the efficient working of Imperialism an Indian agency is indispensable, because without some such social basis it would not be possible for it to maintain its hold. The landlords, the capitalists, the middlemen in India are the creation of Imperialism. When the East India Company came in, they found a country where the old order was passing away, but trade had already become an important social factor, though the industry was of pre-capitalist mode. This was a stumbling block in the path of a free importation of cheap manufacture for which a ready market had to be created somehow. So the handicrafts were ruthlessly destroyed, throwing hundreds of thousands out of employment and abruptly converting the country into a purely agricultural one. This was also in the interest of Imperialism, for the 'Home' country had to be assured of an unlimited supply of raw material for its factories.

Left to itself the social process of evolution from semifeudalistic society and pre-capitalistic industry would have worked itself out as in other countries. The decaying feudalistic order would have been destroyed by the rising bourgeois and industry would have passed into the capitalist mould. Instead, the foreign intervention brought in a chain of events entirely different in character. The old feudalistic absolutism was overthrown as a political power and in its place a whole lot of tax-farmers was created from among the contractors, the highest bidders being made the overlords of several villages and invested with full proprietary powers, over and above the keeping of puppet princes. They were to be the 'pillars of Imperialism' in India. The pre-capitalistic form of production was also maintained as its retention as an integral part of colonial capitalism prevents the rise of mass prosperity which must necessarily bring in its wake industrialisation. Here we begin to see the link between Imperialism and this ballast of feudal conditions and why it is impossible to overcome the one without overcoming the other.

Let us now understand this semi-feudalistic condition which Imperialism maintains as its handmaid. About 75 per cent or about 260 millions of the Indian population live on agriculture. Of these nearly 12 millions live on the rents they receive as landlords or ruling chiefs, their income being estimated at nearly 180 crores. This class leads the typical parasitical existence living on an unearned income. Nor is this income spent for productive purposes. It is mostly diverted to urban areas, squandered on degenerate luxuries or spent abroad. The rural areas are left starving for finances for general improvement and the same is the fate of industries. Nearly one-third of the cultivated area is owned by this class and all this vast tract of land and the millions that toil on it are doomed to a dark gloomy existence.

The rest of the land is owned by the Government. The fate of these areas and of those who cultivate them is hardly any better, though they are formally free from feudal bondage. All agriculturists, whether they be petty land proprietors or tenants, are practically a proletarianized mass, for, they do not in either case possess the land they work upon. They are completely at the mercy of the land-owner. The living they eke out is more in the nature of wages than an independent income. In addition there is the money-lender to whom their produce is mortgaged.

The intense overcrowding on the lands due to the absence of industries to absorb the surplus population now struggling on the land, the primitive methods of production which do not give India a chance of competing in the world-market and merely making the life of the villager an unrelieved drudgery, all these are accountable for the utter pauperization of the peasantry. This continuous exploitation, frustration of every effort, a futureless horizon, have killed the incentive in them, filling them with a despairing fatalism.

The solution of the agrarian problem is, therefore, an essential condition for India getting out of this vicious rut. It alone will lead to successful industrialization which must necessarily lead to the general prosperity. This will relieve the pressure on the land, raise the purchasing power of the masses and give India a place in the worldmarket. But, to bring this about, a radical change in the social structure is essential. If antiquated modes have to be replaced by newer and more scientific ones, the feudalistic system must give place to a more just and equitable system of land tenure, the pre-capitalistic mode of production to mechanisation, then surely the overthow of Imperialism must also mean the abolition of landlordism. This will releaze the peasantry from its present economic slavery and open up the land for intense cultivation by modern methods and all the wealth which now runs into unproductive channels will be available for fostering industries. This will mean great stimulation of the general economic life of the country.

Lastly, there are the middlemen who are also partners in this Imperialistic game of exploitation. In the absence of any sound credit system, usury offers an attractive opening. In the absence of any marketing facilities the middlemen plunder the poor peasantry. Thus, under the pre-capitalistic mode of production, the middlemen have a good stake and they will not be a willing party to the abolition of this system of economy which is the inevitable prelude to normal industrialization. Now the question may be raised how this historic task of abolishing the feudalistic system cannot be done by the bourgeois in India as has been the case in most other countries. For the obvious reason that the Indian masses today are in reality the slaves of capitalism, for Imperialism is the ultimate phase of capitalism, the semi-feudal conditions are maintained by Imperialism as part of its function. The Indian bourgeois is, therefore, an instrument of capitalism in the exploitation of the masses. Imperialism has buttressed itself behind the upper classes. Whenever a peasant struggles against excess rent or tax, a worker to better his condition of living, or the subjects of the native states resist the absolute powers of the Princes, the Imperialist forces appear as protectors of the exploiters. Thus, when the toiling masses who form nearly 90 per cent of the population fight for complete national independence they must necessarily fight Imperialism in all its strength, that is, together with all its allies.

Indian capitalism has grown as a by-product of Imperialism and is linked up with Imperialist trade and industry. Due to its own contradictions, British Imperialism, though unwillingly, is forced to give some economic and political concessions to Indian capitalism and other upper classes to maintain themselves and allow them to grow, though the normal development is chequered. The capitalist class is more than satisfied with its condition. Its existence is therefore, conditioned by the continuance of Imperialism, whereas by the overthrow of Imperialism its life is endangered. Under the framework of Imperialism whatever political reforms are granted, the condition of the masses cannot improve. In fact, by the new constitution or any similar reform, the alliance between Imperialism and the Indian bourgeois will be tightened, leading to greater exploitation of the toiling classes. The classes that will fight Imperialism are those whose condition will deteriorate by the presence of Imperialism. It is only those classes who have 'nothing to lose but their chains and a world to gain' that will fight—and these are the workers, the peasants and the lower middle classes.

In a colonial country, class-struggle inevitably coincides with the struggle for national freedom, for the anti-Imperialist movement is also a struggle against capitalism and landlordism. The same arguments apply to Indian conditions. The Indian capitalist will throw in his lot with the national struggle in so far as his interests conflict with those of foreign capitalism. But with the concession of facilities to improve and develop his capitalist investment in indigenous industrialism, he automatically turns into copartnership with the very force against which he was ranged in opposition only a little while ago. Both draw upon cheap Indian labour and cheap raw material. It pays capitalism, whether white or coloured to keep native labour at a low ebb.

The post-war chaos that capitalism had to face, induced British Imperialism to change its colonial policy. The purchasing power of the Indian peasants being at a very low par, some effort had to be made to raise the standard of living in order to stimulate trade. So, a limited scheme of industrialization was launched upon and high tariffs set up. This meant a renewed field for investment and the sale of heavy machinery and a demand for engineering experts, all for the benefit of the foreign creditor, and the 'Home' country and the Indian bourgeois, all ready instruments in working out this scheme of a more direct exploitation of the Indian masses. For this would mean larger surplus value of a big dividend to the share-holders. The Indian capitalist was to be lavishly fed on high tariffs to meet the budget deficits. But in this declining stage of capitalism its last desperate effort to reinstate itself is failing. While the prices of finished goods rise, thanks to the tariffs, the price of the raw material falls and the purchasing power of the masses goes down bringing in its wake greater chaos. The acute distress caused by this is creating a spirit of revolt in the masses which is leading to a closer union between the British and Indian capitalist. To retain this support British Imperialism is launching upon political reform, a few make believe concessions that only mean the strengthening of the chains. For, without an appreciable expansion in the productivity of labour, the Indian capitalist can only profit by further exploitation of the Indian proletariat and that is what we are witnessing to-day.

The crisis created by the contradiction of Imperialism cannot be overcome unless by the termination of Imperialism. Thus alone can India save herself from destruction. Reformism cannot find a foot-hold under present conditions. It has a place only under capitalist prosperity when concessions could still be wrung from it. Normal social, economic and political growth being impossible under these circumstances, because, they are inherent in a colonial system, the system itself needs to be changed. The progressive undermined state of national economy means progressive contraction of the purchasing power of the masses. An expanding market is the basic condition for industrial development. And this is impossible with a declining purchasing power. Hence, even though there is plenty of labour power going waste, there cannot be industrial progress. Our internal market can expand only when the Indian peasant is spread a little of his surplus produce instead of being wiped clean by rents, taxes—direct or indirect—and usurious interest. This is not possible in the present property relations within the framework of Imperialism. The present state is an expression of Imperialist domination. The radical changes it needs to undergo before any appreciable benefit can be derived, cannot be effected by Indianisation of services, responsibility at the centre, or fiscal autonomy. That would only mean drawing a larger Indian element into the vortex of the Imperialist machinery and the Indian bourgeois being given a junior partnership in the business. The power will still remain in the hands of a small minority and not transferred to the people and the old game of exploitation will continue.

In order to mobilize and harness the mass energy to the anti-imperialist struggle there must be political consciousness in the masses. This is possible only through the economic fight built out of demands for a few immediate items. The economic motive is one of the strongest in the human element and it is through the economic demands that a programme that they can visualize as freedom can be built up and out of this struggle will rise the great struggle for political power by the masses. Roughly these demands will work out as follows:

1. Higher wages and better conditions of labour;
2. 40 hours' week;
3. Insurance against unemployment, sickness, old age and adequate protection for women workers during maternity;
4. 50 per cent reduction in rent;
5. Annulment of the indebtedness of the peasants, workers and artisans;
6. Complete exemption of rent of uneconomic holdings;
7. Control of usury;
8. Abolition of all indirect taxes;
9. Free and compulsory primary education; and
10. Freedom of press, platform and association.

In the course of their struggle for these concessions they will learn by experience that even the few crumbs have ceased to fall from the Imperialist table, and the solution as well as the salvation lies in a radical change of the entire system. And the struggle on their immediate demands will develop into the struggle for political power. It is after the realization of this struggle that the National Constituent Assembly comes into being. We thus find that the composition of the Constituent Assembly is determined by the class-basis of the national movement and the constitution by the social composition of the Constituent Assembly. The talk of convoking it at this stage with the sanction of Imperialism is sheer delusion. It would be anything but a Constituent Assembly. In fact, it will be a positive danger, for under the name of Constituent Assembly, a puppet of Imperialism will come into being to lead to further strengthening of its domination. Moreover, it will lack both the mass sanction and composition. An analysis of the nature and function of Imperialism and the anti-imperialist struggle, the reasons for the rise of the Socialist party, answer themselves. The Indian struggle is unique in its own way. Historically, it ought to be democratic, but in view of the world-conditions, the decaying condition of capitalism and the class-basis of the entire structure, it assumes the features of a socialistic struggle.

It is stupid for people to imagine that class-struggle is a creation of the socialists. Class-struggle is a historical fact. It has existed from the time primitive communist society ceased to be. One may ban the use of the term 'Class-struggle' as the word 'Sex' was tabooed in the 19th century. But from merely abstaining from mentioning a fact, the fact does not cease to be. As long as the means of production remain in the hands of the few, labour remains a commodity for exchange which the owner of the productive machinery converts into huge profits for himself, as under capitalism and feudalism. Under modern capitalism production is socialized. Labour is collectively performed and is an indivisible unit. But the means of this production—land, factories, mines, railways, banks, ships etc.—

are owned by a mere handful who have nothing to do with actual production. The minimum human requirements are not satisfied; millions starve, hence the obvious conflicts between the two classes, owners and the toilers. This contradiction can be overcome only when collective ownership of the means of production is established, that is, when the producers also become the owners of the means of production.

In conclusion, I wish to impress upon you the necessity of rallying round the Congress and making it the chief organ of the anti-imperialist struggle. There are historical reasons why the Congress should be the real anti-imperialist platform. Ever since 1921, it is the only organization which has been fighting Imperialism. No doubt, the leadership is either bourgeois or the people who have the bourgeois ideology. It represents however the objective strivings of the masses, that is, freedom from foreign domination, and the politically conscious people are in the Congress. The content of the Congress is not bourgeois. Therefore to create any petty-bourgeois anti-imperialist platform outside the Congress and to try to duplicate it would be wrong. It will become the sham replica of a working Class Party and cannot embrace the entire petty-bourgeois anti-imperialists. All class-conscious working-class elements and the true anti-imperialists, rather than running away from the Congress, calling it bourgeois, should in fact enter it and clarify the issue of the masses, placing before them the correct programme so that the class differentiation that is taking place in the country may be reflected inside the Congress. Then alone shall we be able to capture the Congress movement and prevent the leadership from converting it into a bourgeois party, thus stealing from us the Congress heritage.

—*The Awakening of Indian Women* (1939)

Blossoms, Light, and Music

It has become quite the fashion, especially in Western circles, to speak of the Japanese women as oppressed and exploited, and as objects of pity. It is even more amusing to read in modern Japanese propaganda books a description of the Japanese woman of today, which sounds more like wishful thinking on the part of these male writers when they describe her as subdued, delicate and very domesticated, content to walk behind the man with the baby strapped to her back, while he strides ahead in all his masculine glory, for one sees rather a different picture of her in the Japan of today!

In no Oriental country, and certainly not in all countries of the West, do the women enjoy the opportunities and facilities that the women of modern Japan do. It seems like a land of women. One sees them everywhere—in offices, shops, restaurants, hotels; as bus, tram and train conductors—as police and auxiliary in the army; on the screen and on the stage, and in every type of entertainment—in industries and all types of professions (except the diplomatic and higher political). Not a mere handful scattered here and there as in India, but in remarkably large numbers. Nearly 30 per cent are in professions. Out of 5 million hands in factories, 2 million are women. They dabble in business enterprises too, provision being made to train them for the same through special colours. I found a whole chain of the largest beauty saloons in the country run by a most charming woman who insisted on my accepting her hospitality in the shape of a beauty massage! The present education in the country actually makes the growing women tough, hardy, self-reliant and adventurous, although their education code says that it aims at the development of 'womanly virtues' and 'national morality'. They are taken out like boys on all manner of odd jobs in the fields, in the workshops, on the road side. It is a familiar sight to see them jumping in and out of transports, buxom, uniformed figures with the ruck-sack tied to the back and caught in front with a strap. It is even more breath-taking to see them pearl diving, performing ju-jit-su—and even more amazing—wrestling and fencing. Gymnasiums, play grounds, summer camps are provided for their physical development.

Japan's sudden and electric change from a completely isolated, ruralized country to a highly industrialized State, has meant violent changes in the outer expressions of the life of the entire nation, including the women. Moreover, her expansionist policy, compelling her to remain on a war footing through many decades with a limited population (though unusually large for the little island), has meant the absorption of a very high percentage of manpower, leaving very vital gaps to be necessarily filled by women. I wonder if any country in the world is so dependent for its everyday routine on the support of women as Japan? Were the women to withdraw completely into their domestic shell—as perhaps the men wish were possible—the entire national machinery would undoubtedly collapse. Yet the picture is not as simple as all that. We have already seen how the old feudal spirit is sought to be retained, in spite of the vast material changes. The man is still the head of the family, all the other members being subordinate to him irrespective of their sex. The family has struggled to retain itself as an integrated unit through these upheavals. Its background of social sentiment is still powerful. Socially, therefore, woman is not considered on an equal par with man. She is denied all civic and political rights. The doors of some of the bigger universities are still closed to her. The man does not always share his social life with his women folk. One is surprised to see how small is the sprinkling of women in a social gathering or a meeting. Yet women are no more mere ignorant, helpless dependents leaning on the male prop. They are all educated, thanks to the compulsory education scheme. Japan was the first Oriental country to have a university for women. Often, they are trained for professions and are becoming increasingly earning members. True, they don't always enjoy the fruits of their labour independently as Western women do, as their earnings are often made over to the head of the family. How far this weighs on them as a hardship, their social outlook being what it is, is hard to gauge. Outsiders, especially Westerners speak, for instance, with derision of the dormitory system for factory girls, entirely ignoring the local social conditions which probably makes this an attractive arrangement for most of them who have been closely knit elements in the family pattern, giving them a sense of extension of the home.

We, thus see a picture in which every attempt is made by reactionary forces to keep the women socially inferior while circumstances are compelling those very elements to break down the walls and to push them into every field of activity. Like in all aspects of social life, this contradiction is glaring. The Japanese woman like the Japanese man has shown herself strongly tied in her sentiments to that old world tradition, exhibiting little element of revolt. After all, the women's revolt can only be part of a general social revolt. In the days when the social forces were rising, the women did band themselves together to assert and gain their rights. But with the abating of that wave the feminine ripple seems to have faded out also. Although, I tried to probe the ex-suffragist leaders, I found it to easy task to get a correct idea of their reaction to the present state of affairs. When their reserve and silence did wear down I was conscious of a dissatisfaction beneath the stereotyped mannerism and habitual serenity. This was particularly true of some of the younger women, especially the foreign-educated. But my contacts were few and limited. It would be dangerous to generalize.

One thing was obvious, they had, one and all, developed the habit of subordinating to authority. The Emperor, the State, the Family. Today Japan's supreme need of the hour, her present mission, in plainer words, the war of expansions, comes first with them. This is neither surprising nor unusual. One has witnessed these trends in suffragist movements in other countries, particularly in England during 1914 war, where the movement was more militant and widely organized. The Japanese women leaders assured me that the present period is not a setback for the movement, that it has its points. They pointed to their daily widening opportunities and the growing dependence of the State on them. They were being increasingly associated in national consultations and schemes, far more so than in the past. 'We shall have become so strongly entrenched it won't be possible to dislodge us easily,' they said in assured tones. 'But it has happened with others, why not you'? I challenged sceptically. 'Then we will fight,' came the answer after hours of hedging round and about. 'We won't give up our places. But we are confident that it will not come to that.' That confidence, time and history alone can justify. My scepticism still remains knowing the masculine love of power and its ways.

History, however, tells us that the position of women in Japan was socially on a par with men until the coming of feudalism, which has been mostly the case in all countries. Matriarchy once prevailed in Japan and the fact that the Emperor claims his account from the Sun Goddess is a proof of it.

What is so amazing, however, is the way the Japanese women with their pronouncedly feudal background have adopted themselves in so short as a period of time to a very modern Japan and its heavy exactions. They have shown initiative and skill in slipping so successfully into new roles and performing new functions. Unlike our women, those who go into professions and jobs, have not only adopted Western clothes but even the quick, efficient Western methods and mannerisms. They are far more alive, alert and intelligent than the men-folk of Japan, and decidedly more pleasing, for they combine their brisk ways with a rare charm and grace.

The traditional training every woman is given, aims at teaching her how to please, a definite feudal trait. But formalism that sits so rigidly on men, sits delicately on women. One aspect of this training is the meticulous care they take of their appearance. A woman should always look her best. Even in these days of 'severities' much attention is paid to hair, skin, nails, etc. This explains the wide patronage given to beauty salons which are looked upon as necessities rather than as luxuries. There seemed as big a run on them as on the theatres!

Every little detail in Japanese life is traditionally fixed like a ritual: how to arrange a room, how to enter it with which foot first, how to sit, how to speak, how to hand out and handle things, etc. Etiquette is spelt in very large imposing capitals. These found their highest expression in the tea-ceremony and the flower arrangements. Entertaining of guests is elaborate. The scroll or picture on the wall must be selected to suit the guest, so also the flowers in the vase. I had practically strayed into Japan unplanned, unpremeditated. I was bewildered by the deluge of letters (in Japanese) that flooded me, on an average a 100 a day. They were literally Greek to me. Finally, I sought the aid of a young Japanese man to set up a regular office. Patiently we plodded through them, mostly messages, greetings, invitations from every nook and corner, all evoked by the announcement of my arrival in the Press. They were excessively polite and some times contained quaint sentiments that were revealing like: 'We hope you will become the queen of India when India becomes free.' In Japan every one seems to read the daily paper and listen in to the radio. The leading newspapers have a circulation approximating 7 millions! I never could miss the radio news. The woman who attended on me was always sure to transmit the items to me everyday regularly, with particular care to pick up any reference to India.

With the artists of Japan I found a natural abode. They were like a window in the putrified atmosphere, at last revealing the azure heavens, the dreamy clouds, the enchantment and fascination of this land of the cherry blossoms, its exquisite artistry, the fineness of its aesthetic sense, its worship of art—the finer spirit of Japan which is covered over today as by a pall of suppression and militarism. In this atmosphere alone all barriers vanished. Here was warmth and friendliness without formalism. Artists hold a very honoured place in Japan. I cherish as one of my rarest memories a social given by some of the leading artists, especially women, when the musicians sang, the dancers danced, the actors did short pieces, the writers read from their writings, and as a memento gave me an exquisite fan with their autographs and a few lovely lyrics specially composed for the occasion inscribed on it! *The genius of Japanese culture consists in achieving the richest effect with the minimum of details.* Limitation of space is no doubt mainly responsible for this. A single vase of flowers, yet its arrangement has behind it centuries of trial and experience; a single picture or scroll, yet it must express, with perfection, the mood of the occasion; a tiny garden that carries the fulfilment of a large lay-out. Miniature plants are another aspect of the same, all expressions of that unique genius.

The inner core of Japan's culture has not been quite lost, for Japan was never dominated by foreign rule. A Japanese home is Japanese in every characteristic. Even where Western objects like furniture are introduced, they are not mixed up into one outrageous medley as we do, but confined to one room in the house. So the house remains Japanese in its setting, its atmosphere, its quality, in its spotless cleanliness, its mirror-like matting. All out-door foot-wear is discarded within the house, as in India. But instead, various sets of slippers are provided, each for a different purpose such as the sitting room and the bed room, the bath room, etc., which is hygienically very sound. Spitting all over is scrupulously avoided, spittoons being provided everywhere, especially in railway carriages—one in front of each seat.

Where Westernism has been introduced, it has been to add to the general comfort without detracting from the innate beauty of the Japanese setting. Most of the modern hotels provide both, the Japanese and the Western modes. The innumerable mineral springs offer relaxation and comforts in the way of baths to all classes of people from the richest to the commonest. Up-to-date hotels are built around some of these health-giving waters and fitted with luxurious baths of jade and lapis lazuli, amber and pink marble lit with colour like fairy lands, each with an exquisite name such as dream-pool, rainbow-fountain, etc.

Original and stimulating are some of the Japanese modes of entertaining guests. *Kakayachai* or painting and glazing of pottery is one. It is literally a 'bright' job to hold in the hand an unbaked dull and drab piece, draw designs on it, splash it with colour and see it transformed by our fingers that seem to burn with a new magical quality. Then set up electric ovens with refractions ready to heat up to the required degree. When ready, each piece is presented to the one who painted it. Lo! You have acquired a new art, learnt how deft your fingers can be! Equally exciting is it when at a party an artist's easel is set up and each one makes a single stroke with a brush on the rice paper, some straight, some curved, some circular, some criss-cross. Then finally the artist—with a few swift strokes—converts this erratic play into a thing of beauty, a human shape or a landscape. This is varied by putting dabs of clay in each hand; the sculptor then guides the faltering fingers to mould the shapeless mass into firm contours and curvatures. Such entertainments have been introduced on Japanese boats and form such a contrast to the monotonous mechanical gadgets scattered all over the American boats, down whose gaping mouths coins are always being pushed by bored passengers on the off chance of luck returning them with a small interest; or kindergarten type of games like the toy horse-racing or bingo. Equally original and interesting are the sort of Vaudeville shows skilfully improvised by the Japanese crew. And where else except from a Japanese boat would you be able to watch the unbelievable display of sky rockets and fireworks in the sky in mid ocean?

Very colourful are also the Japanese festivals, especially the seasonal ones. Festival of Fresh Green on 7th January; festival of Peach Blossom on 3rd March which is also known as the Girls' Day or Dolls' Festival when girls are dressed up and dolls are decorated and sent up, and friends pay calls and celebrate. Festival of Sweet Flag or the Boys' Day on 5th May when the boys have their turn; the Festival of Stars on 17th July and the Festival of Chrysanthemums on 9th September.

While some of their old world customs are pleasing, some are boring. It is certainly gracious for the guests to begin a meal by saying 'Itamakai Masu'—permit me, and end up with 'Gochiso Sama Deshita.' It was a nice meal. It seems more appropriate to start the Japanese way than by mechanically invoking the deity while one's heart is intent on the delicacies in front, or by taking the first sip over the latest scandal or race-results. But it is decidedly boring every time you meet some one instead of a simple 'How are you?' or the more modern and snappy 'Hallo' to plunge into a long series of set formal exchange that cover the participants' health, their last visit to each other, health of their family members, etc., etc. All this does seem unnecessary in this fast moving, informal world of today.

An exchange of cards when two strangers are introduced to each other, is understandable. But if you are in company, to have cards passed round to every body, seems like overdoing it. It becomes rather ridiculous when every new entry means an exchange of cards with the new arrival by all present and *vice versa*. In short, every social contact is a card-collecting-distributing affair! If you stop someone on the road to seek directions, he promptly brings out his card and presents it to you over an elaborate bow, and naturally expects you to do the same.

Although the essence of Japanese culture may be said to have survived, its outer expressions have undergone much orientation under the impact of the West. This is particularly true of music, painting and sculpture with few exceptions like the classical theatre music. Ordinarily, the music one hears at musical concerts is as much Japanese as the jazzified New Theatre's music is Indian. It has become completely orchestrated on Western lines even where Japanese instruments are used. But apart from this, a genuine love and understanding of Western classical and modern music prevails and one can listen to as good a symphony concert in Tokyo as in any Western capital.

One is even more amazed to see the deep inroads Western art have made on modern Japanese painting and sculpture. When I was visiting an exhibition in Tokyo, I felt I was at an art exhibition in New York or London, except for that lovely delicacy of touch in the moulding and the exquisite pastel shades so characteristic of Japanese art. Yet the Japanese never tire of telling how untainted they are by the Western influence!

Japan's most outstanding achievement is Theatre. Like the Indian and the Greek, the Japanese play is also believed to have a divine origin. When the Sun Goddess hid herself in the cavern the world was plunged into utter darkness, so the Gods assembled before the cavern to entice her out by performing a dance play. It was the women of Japan who took the lead in the development of the dramatic art which once again points to early matriarchy. The famous *Kabuki* drama was started by a woman O'Keni by name. She married a famous actor and together they performed. Later, as feudalism took grip and woman's status deteriorated, the Government forbade the appearance of women on the stage. After this, the stage went through periods of severe persecution by the authorities who treated it like a criminal. That it should have not only survived this persecution but even grown to such heights of achievement is a tribute both to the vitality and power of the Japanese artist and the rare love of drama amongst the common people. In a way, this very struggle sharpened the skill and wits of the performers. The acting had to be of a very high order and the drama exceptionally good, to maintain its hold on the people. The drama was designed to appeal to the common people. That was its hope of survival! Gradually the different actors came to acquire traditional roles, very much as in India—such as the Villain, the Fool, the Buffoon, the Old Man, Old Woman, etc.; stage-craft made rapid strides, and one of the chief innovations was the revolving state which came into Japan a whole 100 years before it appeared in Europe!

An intriguing factor which shows the deep love and respect for the art of acting is the effort made to perpetuate the name of a great actor through worthy successors. If one is found in the son well and good, or, if the son has no talent, then through some other actor who proves worthy. Thus the name goes on from generation to generation. Fifth Danguro Ichikwa, the Fourth Hanshiro Iwai, the Third Kikumoto Segawa and so on. Those who succeed to the illustrious title must not only give promise of perpetuating the title by maintaining the standard but must add to its quality by even better performance. This is quite different from the common custom of transferring name and fortune to the next kin regardless of his ability.

The advent of Western influence after the Russo-Japanese war led to the Free Theatre movement. This was followed by the Tsukji or the Little Theatre—an experimental movement aimed at using any new knowledge pertaining to the stage and producing new plays. It thus came to be known as 'The Laboratory of Drama.' It put on plays from Ibsen to modern impressionists. When the socialist movement raised its head, this theatre went Left. With the abating of that wave the Little Theatre has settled down to more accepted social forms.

The dramatists of this period were not satisfied with the Kabuki plays which, though called modern to distinguish them from the classical, dealt solely with the Edo period that is 1603–1868. They thought that even a grafting upon it was impossible. So they created new dramas. In recent years, however, the tendency of some of the modern dramatists is to take over some of the Kabuki elements in the creation of the national dramas.

With the coming of the new age, women trekked back to the stage, but formed their own troupes. This was easy enough particularly for the *Geisha* girls who from tender years were trained to please by words, talk, song, gesture, dress, coquetry, etc. And although mixed acting has long come into vogue and pioneering women in this direction like Ritsuko Mori, Kakuko Murata, Yako Mizutani have become loved and respected household words, the women-troupes still continue their individualistic existence—the Moon Troupe, the Cherry Blossom Troupe are some of the well known and popular ones. They put on Nipponized versions of Vaudeville and Follies Bergere. Gorgeous, colourful, and modern varieties, but very Japanese, nevertheless.

Japanese stage is modern in all its equipment and use of scientific apparatus but there is nothing hybrid about their presentation as in India. For sheer aesthetic beauty, the Japanese stage has few equals. Its popularity is stupendous. One has to book seats for the theatre far ahead, so crowded are the houses from day to day. A very large percentage of people are absorbed in this profession. Each troupe has—on an average—about 100 performers,—sometimes twice as many. The theatres are very elaborate and provide a degree of comfort and privacy to the actors which is entirely unknown in India. It shows a sensitive appreciation of and genuine respect for the artist.

Most famous and unique to Japan is the Noh Play. Bernard Shaw after his visit to Japan said that Noh interested him more than almost anything in that country. Although it is formalized and set its artistic quality is startling, its beauty refreshing. Everything about it is traditionally fixed: every object on the stage, every movement of the actor, every article of costume, every line and shade of gesture. One interesting thing about it is the large mirror that is hung in the ante-room in which the actor gazes at himself before going on to the stage to make sure he is quite ready for his appearance, and get himself into the character he is to represent. Another unique character is the construction of the stage, the way it is projected into the auditorium, with a narrow space covered with pebbles between it and the auditorium, so that the audience sees the play, not as a picture in a frame, but rather, as something happening as part of themselves. One of the most distinguishing marks of Noh is the use of masks. These masks are very elaborate and expressive and have become a traditional art in themselves. The make-up is also unusual. A warrior going into battle does not wear armour, nor a Chinese mandarin necessarily appear in his colourful native strappings. A beggar is not disgraced with rags. Noh does not aim at 'realism' in the sense of copying, but rather at depicting of character. So a Noh actor is more a creative interpreter like the Indian singer, since the characters are all fixed by tradition. Noh dramas are also standardized. They are composed of 'God Piece' praising the deity, 'Battle Piece', 'Wig or Woman Piece', 'Lunatic Piece', 'Revenge Piece'. A complete Noh play includes all the five pieces. But commonly 3 to 5 of these pieces are presented with a couple of Commediettas thrown in to relieve the emotional tension, which used to be a feature of the old Indian stage.

The Kabuki stage is also unique in having an approach to the audience called Hanamichi 'Flower Way' a kind of an extension of the stage. This naturally extends the scope of acting as well.

No mention of the Japanese theatre would be complete without reference to the Puppet Play which once ruled the hearts of the people, so much so indeed that the Kabuki absorbed some of its important characteristics including its music. Stage music developed along with the drama, chiefly played on the Samisen, drum, flute and hand-drum. Most dramatically effective is the Samisen, along with vocal compositions. The music is suited to the action of the play, reflecting the mind of the various characters and is performed by separate musicians. Schools of music developed along the lines of the musicians themselves or according to special type of music such as Jorjuri, the music of the Puppet drama.

—*Japan* (1939)

Zeenuth Futehally
(1903–1992)

In her Preface to *Zohra* (1951) Zeenuth Futehally writes, 'Amongst our people, fiction, and specially romantic fiction, is deprecated. But I have put aside my misgivings on this score as it is only through ordinary human emotions that one can best convey the lives of people. And no society, however strict or conventional regarding its women, is yet free from emotional entanglements.'

Rummana Denby, Zeenuth Futehally's daughter explained (in conversation) that the word 'romantic' here means a story that broke taboos. Zohra, married to Bashir, falls in love with his brother Hamid, and he with her. Zohra dies in the end of cholera contracted when she goes to help a poor family. Was that an easy ending? Not really, because helping people is part of Zohra's life.

In the Preface, Zeenuth Futehally also expresses dissatisfaction about her achievement and says that the story was revised many times. Rummana Denby says her mother remained dissatisfied with the book even after it was published. They discussed possible revisions over the years, and Rummana Denby has now prepared a revised version. The extracts included here, however, are from the original.

Zohra was widely and favourably reviewed when it appeared in 1951. Savita Bhatt, in an article on Zeenuth Futehally tells us that Zeenuth travelled to Japan and Manila with her husband, and it was while she was abroad that she first thought of writing the book. Ms Bhatt, who interviewed Zeenuth, and has included excerpts from the interview in the article, says, 'No special influence of any writer was in her mind but she say "Ghalib, Tagore, and Sarojini Naidu were in vogue in that circle"' but Jane Austen was her special favourite. Zeenuth is quoted as saying, 'While she leaves politics completely aloof, I was and am greatly interested in it.'

Interestingly, some of the reviews mention Zeenuth Futehally and Venu Chitale together, though one is not entirely sure how to take *The Sunday Standard* (date not given) article which says, 'Hind Kitabs deserves to be complimented for encouraging new authors. But they must beware lest they be accused of giving preference to women. The first author they publicly honoured was Venu Chitale, every inch a Maharashtrian.'

Chapter XX

When Bashir could move about a little, it was arranged that he should go to a friend's country-house for convalescence.

Zohra was naturally to accompany her husband, but it was also considered advisable by the elders for Hamid to go with them. For, the cottage, although only ten miles from the city, situated at the foot of Mir Mahmood's Hill was rather isolated.

When Safia heard of this, her attitude towards Zohra, which had softened somewhat during Bashir's illness, hardened again, although Zohra had had nothing to do with the plan.

Hamid himself felt rather uneasy, but he had no choice in the matter.

One evening, when they had been nearly a week at Mir Mahmood, Zohra, who was taking a stroll in the garden, met Hamid returning from the city.

'You are late this evening,' she greeted him.

'There was the Taskers' Poetry Society meeting, didn't you remember? I wish you could have come.' They both started to walk towards the house.

'Was it interesting?' she asked.

'Yes quite—refreshing,' he answered.

'Who were present?'

'Oh, the usual people,' he answered. 'The Nizam's brother was naturally seated with the Regal-looking Lady Hydari, while Hydari *Sab* in his genial manner, was exchanging greetings all round. He enquired affectionately after you and seemed genuinely sorry you were not there. He also wanted to know how *Bhaijan* was.'

'Yes, they are a large-hearted couple full of warmth and friendliness— especially for the younger people,' said Zohra, pleased at the recollection of the affection always shown her. 'But who else was there?' she asked.

'Yes, who do you think was the surprise of the evening? Our poetess Sarojini Naidu!'

'I didn't even know she was here,' remarked Zohra.

'Probably she has just come to say goodbye to her people before she is again imprisoned. The songs of 'India's Nightingale' may be hushed under the burden of politics, but still poetry is her first love. ... Besides, she is very friendly with the Taskers.' Then knitting his brows, as if switching off to another world of thought: 'It's really amazing, how so many of the personal friendships have not suffered at all. Gandhiji's *Ahimsa* is wonderful. There is no room in it for petty rancour and bitterness; for he has taught us to look upon the British Government as a thing apart from the British people.'

Resting his hand on the pillar near the steps, where they had stopped to carry on the conversation before going in, he said: 'But here, the Taskers' own response is remarkable too.'

'Yes, and I think they have a real feeling for Hyderabad and the Hyderabadis,' she said looking at him. The light from the top of the steps was falling on them. 'But the most incredible thing to me, is that Gandhiji's lieutenants, of such widely divergent views and backgrounds, should have accepted this creed so whole-heartedly. He indeed wields a miraculous power.' Her eyes shone with a devotional fervour.

'No prophet in his lifetime has had such a large and devoted following,' affirmed Hamid emphatically. 'And Sarojini Naidu is one of Gandhiji's staunchest lieutenants.'

'But how was she? Looking at all depressed?' asked Zohra, placing one foot on the step, as if starting to mount, then halting.

'On the contrary, she was as vivacious as ever, sparkling with wit and humour. Padmaja, looking charming as usual, was with her. And Hydari *Sab*, like most others, was hard pressed dividing his attention between the mother and daughter!'

'And Leilamani?'

'Why, I feel I am doing a Society column!' laughed Hamid. 'I hope it's in the right style?'

'Perfect.' Exclaimed Zohra, responding to his laugh. 'And what next?' she asked with mock gravity.

'Yes, and Leilamani, in her forthright manner made a bee-line for Lady Hydari, who embraced her in her gracious maternal way. She really treats her as if she were her own daughter.'

'And then ...?' asked Zohra, in the manner of carrying on a pleasant game.

'And then ... when all the notables were gathered, Lady Tasker got the proceedings duly started,' responded Hamid keeping up the style into which their conversation had now lapsed. 'By special request Leilamani recited one of her mother's poems. She did it beautifully in her resonant voice. And so I come to the end of my column. But seriously, the Naidu family was in great form, and no one could ever dream that Mrs Naidu was preparing for sordid gaol life. She is really wonderful.'

Hamid's pale face glowed with enthusiasm as he shook back the lock of hair that had strayed on to his forehead.

'Yes, in her own way, she is the most wonderful woman,' admitted Zohra. 'She can never forget a face, and her circle of friends is boundless. She has a soft corner for you too, hasn't she?' She asked with a mischievous gleam.

'You are jealous,' he remarked thoughtlessly, but at once a self-consciousness fell over them both. In an effort to get over it, she said:

'There was a message from *Ammijan*. *Apajan* has had twins.' She sounded thrilled at her sister's performance.

'*Mubarak*! It sounds exciting!' he exclaimed with the smile that was always boyish when he was enthusiastic.

'It's the first pair of twins in the family. It must be nice having twins; saves such a lot of trouble,' she said.

'You mean, it's nature's labour-saving device for women who desire large families?' He gave an amused questioning glance, but she evaded it. She remembered how she had been longing for twins when Shahedah was born.

'But I don't think Apajan will be pleased. She already had five—these make seven.'

'An error of judgment on nature's part!' A shy smile lurked in his eyes causing the swift colour to rise to her face which even in that artificial light he could observe.

But suddenly she became grave as she thought of her sister. Mehrunnissa's husband, a weak character, had started keeping mistresses in the house together with the children he had by them. Mehrunnissa, at first jealous and rebellious, had now fallen into a lethargy. She no longer delighted in clothes or ornaments. Her figure was wholly ruined. Her children, never well cared for, were now entirely neglected.

Hamid and Zohra started to go in now. Hamid wondered why Zohra desired more children. Anyway, it was good for the race if women like her had more children, he reflected with a queer feeling.

As the days went by and Bashir gained strength, he became more and more absorbed in work. He had few real friends who would care to visit him.

Zohra's friends and relations also came rarely, as women did not like to go long distances without a male escort, even in private cars. Zohra was therefore often lonely. She read a great deal, but even that she sometimes found tiring. She tried to paint, but somehow the mood did not possess her. She was often nervous and fidgety. Safia's attitude, too, continued to hurt her. She never came once to see them, nor did she send her child with the other two children when they visited Mir Mahmood.

Hamid was making use of this opportunity to finish what he had been writing for some time now. He retired into the round pavilion, away from the house, to work in quiet. He knew this was the only way he could go on staying there. He did not return to the house even for his midday meal, but had coffee and toast sent to him. Even Zohra dared not disturb him. His friends sometimes visited him, bringing news of the bookshop. Whenever Khorshed called, he asked Zohra to join the party. He now knew for certain that he could not marry Khorshed, and wanted to give her no chance for further misunderstanding. He felt a cad for the way he had once encouraged her. But Zohra sensed that Khorshed resented her presence, and was therefore reluctant to join them. Yet, Hamid insisted, and she could not refuse. Altogether relations among the three of them were becoming strained and awkward.

Zohra had named Hamid's pavilion the 'Hermit's Cell'. It was open on three sides and overlooked the clear lake and green vistas studded with blazing red-and-orange Gul-Mohor trees.

Once, early in the evening, she strolled out into the garden, and was tempted to walk past his retreat. At sight of her he called out: 'What are you doing?' His voice was friendly.

'What are you always doing?' she questioned in return. She strolled up and leaned against the wooden pillar.

He laughed with a hesitant gleam in his eyes. He had not yet confided to her the nature of his writing.

'Trying to decide the fate of two young people.'

'That sounds God-like,' she laughed.

'Come in and I'll show you,' he said on an impulse. 'Perhaps, you can help me out of the dilemma.'

Zohra went in. Hamid, offering her his own chair, moved towards the wooden settee.

'What is it—a novel?' she asked, sitting down in front of the table.

'It's a kind of socio-political tale. It's more an effort to rouse Muslim Nationalism against Communalism. But, as you know, a romantic interest is essential, especially to hold women's attention.' He tried to chide her.

'It sounds good; but then I am only a woman!' She laughed a little self-consciously. 'But what is the setting for your story?'

'It starts in Hyderabad. Two young people, although very much in love, decide to postpone their marriage and to go and join the *Satyagraha* movement. Their romance is thus disrupted for the time being, and. ...'

'But romances don't exist in Hyderabad,' she interrupted with an impatience wholly unnecessary to the occasion.

'What do you mean?' he asked, startled by her vehemence.

'Oh, you know. ...'she faltered, then continued hastily, 'people get married first and then ...' She wished she had not so impulsively launched on such a delicate subject. She did not now know how to proceed.

'And yet most marriages here are successful,' observed Hamid in an impersonal tone, trying to keep away sarcasm from his words. 'But I was not writing of arranged marriages, in any case. One has really to understand the psychology of persons entering into such marriages before attempting to write about them.' There was a hint of questioning in his voice.

'Oh girls are brought up to expect their parents to arrange marriages for them.' She spoke with an affected carelessness. 'It is seldom that any other ideas enter their minds.'

'It's amazing. Any girl and any boy, and yet they live happily ever after!' Hamid's voice was controlled; it was as if he were only in search of knowledge.

'Not any girl and any boy!' She tried to laugh, but an undercurrent of something else was now quite apparent. 'The parents in their own way usually take great pains to find a suitable partner.'

Hamid, his handsome head inclined towards her, was nervously playing with his pencil. Seeing her falter, he encouraged her with: 'Yes?'

'I can only speak for girls,' she said quickly. 'They are brought up to look upon marriage in the same way as they look upon birth and death. In none of these do they expect to have any voice.'

'But what happens if a girl rebels?'

'You should know that a girl openly rebelling is almost unheard of in our strict Hyderabadi society! Why, don't you know that marriage is a forbidden subject between girls and their parents?' She was getting more worked up than the occasion demanded.

'But, according to the Muslim law, a girl's voluntary consent is essential,' he argued, on an irresistible impulse to probe her mind on the subject. 'She can withhold that.'

'Where have you been living, really?' she chided him, as her soft voice rose to rather a high pitch. 'A Hyderabadi girl would no more think of questioning her parents' right to arrange a marriage for her than she would of questioning God's right to dispense birth and death.' The subject evoked from her this spontaneous outburst.

'So that God and the parents between them can dispose of all the three fates?' he asked with a strange look in his eyes. 'And a girl is ready to accept the parents' choice, and offer her husband love and loyalty as naturally as she bestows affection upon her God-chosen parents. Is that the idea?'

'You have summed up the case beautifully,' she answered quietening down.

'But marriage is such a personal affair.' His eye-brows were knit close together now, as he tried to focus his attention on his pencil. 'Mutual attraction I should have thought was essential.' He was still avoiding her eyes.

'The *purdah* system is a great saviour,' she was roused to say. 'This mode of marriage can hold good only in a *zenana* society, where there are no standards of comparison. Difficulties would arise if the girls started moving about in mixed circles.'

Throughout the conversation she had tried to keep up an impersonal tone; but it was obvious she was trying to suppress something very deep. 'But tell me more about your plot. How do you propose tackling your problems?' she asked hastily, as if trying to get away from that something.

Hamid gave her a brief outline of the story. As she became interested, he promised to let her read the whole of the yet incomplete manuscript. 'I am wondering whether to give it a sad ending or a happy one.'

'What is more usual in life?' Her soft eyes were now raised to him questioningly.

'Tragedy, or quasi-tragedy. Disillusionment.' He was trying to sound detached.

'But for that very reason, people might wish to see a different ending to a book.'

'I have already changed it once. I first started giving it a happy ending, then altered it to tragedy. Now, again, I am uncertain.' He laughed in deprecation of his own indecision.

'It had never struck me before how easy it was for a writer to play with the fates of his heroes and heroines,' she commented.

'Yes, in a few strokes one can change their destinies completely! It is fascinating.'

'I wonder if God also enjoys playing with our fates in this fashion,' she said gazing in the direction of the lake.

'Sometimes I feel it's all a deep plan preconceived. At other times, I feel things just happen as we go along. Anyway, life is not always an amusing game,' he said casually; but the look in his eyes was earnest.

'Problems could be solved more easily if one were only single-minded,' she observed, alluding to his indecision regarding the ending. 'But life tosses one this way and that with such swift jerks, that it becomes difficult to keep one's balance.' She did not quite know herself why she made this remark; it was just forced out of her.

'Problems are like the Hydra of old, as soon as we solve one, two crop up in its place.' Hamid made a gesture that seemed to dismiss everything. A silence fell over them both.

Hamid too had marked with concern Safia's antagonism towards Zohra. He had even tried to speak to Safia about it, but had only received offensive replies, with dark implications, warning him against her spell. This had strained the ties between Safia and her once-beloved brother. Hamid was even sorry that Zohra had given her the child. Now looking at Zohra, he wondered how much of her present restlessness was due to that. For, he had noticed that in spite of her ardent love for nature, Zohra seemed lost as if she did not know what to do with herself. Her husband had at first demanded her attention, but now he was once again becoming absorbed in his own work. Hamid, though he realized his own difficulties, still thought it his duty to help her.

'Zohra, why don't you do some sketching here?' he suggested.

'I did try,' she said, 'but somehow I can't.'

'Will you illustrate this?' he asked impulsively, wanting to give her an incentive, but even as he said it he wondered if he had spoken wisely.

'I? Why, I find I can't do a thing. I'll probably make a mess of it!' But the idea was exciting to her.

'I have seen some of your old sketches,' he said, 'you could do it if you tried.'

'Anyway, it's an idea to keep me occupied. Then you can burn them all and make a blazing fire, or throw them into the waters there,' she said, pointing to the lake.

A strange exhilaration came upon her at the mere thought of sharing something with Hamid. She started on the illustrations that very night and soon became engrossed in them.

Bashir was pleased to see her thus occupied. He now spent his mornings and late afternoons in the garden to get the benefit of the sun when it was not too hot. One day, he noticed a small boat tied up by the water's edge. Both Zohra and Hamid were with him.

'Why don't you two go boating? Hamid, you can teach Zohra to row. It's really not good for her to be tied up to a semi-invalid all the time.' He spoke in his smooth voice.

Chapter XXI

A couple of days later, after Zohra had struggled to row the boat smoothly, she put down the oars and looking at her palms, unaccustomed to such exercise, and rubbing them, said: 'Let's glide along in peace for a while.'

Hamid merely nodded.

The countryside all around was scattered with black boulders of various sizes and shapes, often balanced one on top of the other as delicately as the brass water pots on the heads of Maratha women.

In the dazzling sunlight the bare rocks appeared dark and ominous. Although shrubs and green grass that sprouted through the crevices, gave them in places a mellowed look. Hamid, watching them, mused: Under the burning rays of the southern sun how quickly these rocks absorb and radiate heat. And at the close of day how quickly again they cool down and everything seems fresh and inviting. ... How closely in this, do they mirror the moods of Hyderabad's ruling class. For, are not the emotional Muslims quick to flare up and as quick to calm down? Warm and exuberant in their hospitality and affection, they take offence easily and as easily cool off. ... Or, thought Hamid, these multitudinous boulders, might well symbolize fecundity, for so abundantly are they scattered about the landscape—these offspring of Mother Earth. ... And he remembered, how it was said, that thousands and tens of thousands of years ago, the earth had opened up in violent and spasmodic convulsions, and thrown out streams of lava which had through the long ages congealed into these hard, black rocks. ... These thoughts passed through Hamid's mind in a disjointed fashion, for, while he was consciously trying to muse over what his eyes beheld, a deeper and a more pressing current of thought threatened to overpower him. All around he could also see, in small clusters, green trees—*ber* and *sitaphal*, the latter with sweet and luscious fruit, named after Sita, the devoted wife of Rama, who on her long wanderings with her exiled husband, had found them delicious and sustaining. Also, here and there stood tall, spreading Gul-Mohor trees with sprays of dazzling red-and-orange flowers that shimmered in the evening light.

Gradually, the sun started disappearing below the western horizon and the golden light cast a warm glow on their faces. The chirping of birds greeted their ears; they still glided along in complete silence till at last Zohra said: 'You appear to be absorbed in yourself.'

'So are you. Human beings are really solitary creatures; and their thoughts are the only faithful companions they have in this world,' Hamid countered, passing his fingers through his hair. 'But I confess I sometimes feel like running away—escaping from them also.'

'You feel like escaping from everything and everyone—your friends, your admirers; whilst they are only waiting for you to lift up your little finger to gather round you. You are never lonely by compulsion.'

'What you mean is, I am not alone by compulsion, but I can be lonely all the same.' After a pause, he added, 'In the ancient days of leisure, philosophy had a much larger place in our lives.'

'Isn't our climate also conducive to such pursuits?' she asked.

'Anyway, the present-day bustle in alien to the Indian temperament.

We should once more cultivate the habit of contemplation.' Then casting a swift glance at her: 'If I had any say in the matter, I'd introduce the study of Yoga in our educational system: it gives one both mental and physical poise. I myself would like to take it up more seriously.'

'This place is ideal for meditation,' remarked Zohra.

'Perhaps some day I shall retire alone to some such place, at least for a period.'

'You're always wanting to escape from life. What you really need is a wife, a soul-mate!' She laughed, but her heart gave a queer tug. Hurriedly, she quoted Ghalib:

> Impossible is it to pass life without love;
> But thou hast not the strength to bear the sorrows of love.

Suddenly and for the first time, Hamid now fixed his intent gaze on her: 'Zohra!' his voice was soft with the richness of love yet unprofessed, 'don't you realize that I love you?'

To Zohra it was as if all her life she had waited to hear those three simple words from Hamid's lips. They were like the 'open sesame' to the meaning of life for her. Sunlit with love, she glowed in every fibre of her being. Not knowing how to look him in the face, she dropped her eyes, in wild confusion, and fidgeted nervously with her hands. Hamid, still watching her intently, said:

'Zohra,' there was exhilaration in his voice, 'you care for me too, don't you?' She could only give a faint nod. Hamid became silent, tense. After what seemed to them a long, long time, with a jerk of his head and pulling his hair, Hamid said: 'Let's go somewhere and talk.' Zohra acquiesced.

Hamid took up the oars again. Gaining the opposite bank he got down first and offered Zohra his hand. She was shy and nervous, and in her embarassment would not let him touch her. She jumped down by herself, her sari getting caught under her foot and being torn. In the queer excitement that overcome her she lost track of everything save the man she loved. Hamid tied up the boat and came to Zohra.

'Let's sit there,' he pointed to one of the smooth, black boulders that stood there like a platform, and cool in the evening breeze, looked inviting, as if it were a stage set for a sylvan play. They sat down a little apart. Zohra embarrassed, had drawn the *pallau* closely over her shapely semi-bare arms, that now tightly encircled the raised knees. The soft folds of her sari, draping her graceful figure, were trailing right over her feet. As she sat thus, to Hamid, there appeared to be a nymph-like quality about her. She looked strangely withdrawn. Hamid stretched out his legs and leaned back with his hands resting on the ground. Each seemed to be in awe of the other.

Zohra rested her forehead on her knees, to hide the emotions that had so suddenly overtaken her.

At last he called, almost reverently: 'Zohra!'

Startled, she raised her head and turned towards him without looking at him.

'Zohra, how lovely you look! I could sit and gaze on you all my life!' Hamid spoke jerkily. 'But, why don't you speak? Say something!'

'Something!' repeated Zohra, catching hold of the last word as her saviour, lest she be drowned in silence. They laughed; she shyly, he amused. This gave Zohra a little more self-confidence.

'Did you know that I loved you?' His dreamy eyes had now a shy reticence.

'Yes,' she murmured.

'I loved you from our very first meeting. Only, I did not like to admit it, even to myself. You remember your throwing that garland round my neck like in a *Swayamwara* of old, and our eyes meeting in confusion— or was it recognition? I had never seen anyone more graceful; and how embarrassed you looked. ... Do you remember, Zohra?' He was smiling his fascinating smile, through which his white teeth gleamed.

'Can I forget it?' she asked softly, her eyes half raised to him. She dared not meet his eyes.

'You reminded me of a daffodil; I think it's the way you hold your head, with a proud but graceful bend, on a long shapely neck. But, Zohra, when did you first realize that you ... you ... cared for me?'

'I don't know. But I feel I've loved you all my life,' she said hesitatingly, in a tone that was like the murmur of water. Hamid had to strain his ears to catch her words.

'But we had never even met until my return!' He burst into his boyish laugh.

'I know, but ...' she faltered and could not proceed.

'But what?' he encouraged her with a smile. He wanted to take her hand in his, but controlled himself, for he did not know what her reaction would be.

'In my heart I had idealized love and romance,' at last she forced herself to say in a low, tremulous voice. 'Only, I thought they were just a poet's dream. Some people did try to make love to me even here, in Hyderabad, after my marriage. But I warded them off. When you arrived ...' she hesitated not knowing how to express herself.

'I filled that place!' He laughed in happy self-derision. 'This is all very flattering. Only, don't idealize me. I have more than my share of human weaknesses.' He spoke with a shy earnestness, his eyes focussed as if on some far-away object. 'My only virtue is that I love you as I have never loved before, nor had ever expected to love.'

Their eyes met for the first time, and held, each other as if in a shy embrace. They could not speak. It was Hamid who first broke the silence. They talked happily, excitedly for some time.

It was growing dark; Hamid was the first to realize it. 'It's late, and we must get back. Brother will be waiting.'

It was their first touch with reality that evening. They felt no guilt at their love, but to face Bashir was embarrassing; they were both self-conscious and could not talk to each other as they had done before the confession. Hamid also felt a pang of jealousy which he tried to suppress.

The next morning Hamid retired into his shed very early without greeting Zohra, but everything he tried to write was surcharged with her: 'Zohra', 'Zohra', 'Zohra', ran through his mind. How would she like it? When would she read it? How would she look? His eyes constantly wandered towards the house, trying to catch a glimpse of her. He could do little with his mind so obsessed, but he was determined not to go in.

Zohra tried to paint, but with every stroke, it was Hamid smiling, Hamid talking, Hamid lingering beside her. How could she work? Instead of a grey stroke she put a streak of blazing red. She looked at it and smiled in amusement. Her mind was so full of happiness that she saw everything in bright colours.

The whole day they consciously avoided each other; but her eyes strayed constantly towards the shed, even though she could not see Hamid.

That evening Zohra selected a golden-coloured sari and dressed herself with special care; yet she was doubly careful not to do anything that would betray her either to her husband or to Hamid.

When the three met that afternoon in the garden for tea, she could not meet Hamid's eyes, but watched him stealthily. They waited till Bashir had gone in and they were once more alone in the boat. There was the joy of reunion. Again they rowed out to the opposite bank, and went and sat on the same boulder.

'Are you glad Zohra that I spoke?' asked Hamid; he could see plainly that there was no need for the question.

'What do you think?' She looked up shyly at him.

They recalled a number of past incidents which had made them aware of each other. They were like carefree children, happy in their newly-acquired joy. At the moment they wanted nothing more from each other but the knowledge of each other's love.

'Why do people say it's wrong to love? How can an emotion that leads to such exaltation be wrong?' she asked with a tender gleam in her eyes.

'There is nothing wrong in love, but you belong to another.' A sudden hopelessness came over him.

'But what are we doing? That is ...' she faltered, not knowing how to express herself. 'That is ... marriage,' she at last dragged out of herself in a subdued tone, 'but this is love—the expression of one's deeper self. It cannot be acquired.' Her tone conveyed that the other thing could be acquired. As Ghalib has said:

> There is no compulsion in love, for it's that fire,
> O Ghalib,
> Which can neither be ignited, nor quenched
> at one's will.

'My dear, all that is true, but love will demand other expressions— fulfilments.' He spoke guardedly, not knowing how she would take it. At that moment, she looked so uplifted that it seemed almost a sacrilege to hint to her of physical love.

'But ... but, we know that ... that is impossible.' She faltered, not daring to look at him.

'I know, and that is why I have suddenly started wondering whether we were right in igniting it. So long as we were silent, there was a veil of inhibitions between us.'

'Is it a sin to love? To feel the ecstasy of the heart?' she asked in a hushed voice.

'There is no sin in loving. Personally, I feel even physical love when accompanied by an emotion as deep as ours is ennobling. It's the culmination to everything else. According to the Sufi philosophy, it is through union with the belove that one tries to reach oneness with the Divine. Love is the most beautiful thing, but what are we to do in our present circumstances?' he asked, tortured, in his agitation frantically pulling at his hair.

'But love is more a quality of the mind; it is the stirring of one's imagination; it is the fulfilment of one's spiritual self.' She looked intoxicated.

'Let's hope that it brings us happiness!' He sounded pessimistic, for already he was feeling an overwhelming desire to touch her, to hold her hand, but he dared not.

'Let us make the best of what we can get—be happy in each other's company,' she murmured softly.

'Zohra, you—a married woman—talk in this innocent manner? You should know better!' He sounded almost irritated.

She could not reply. Her lips quivered.

'My dear, I'm not sure if we can go on with this. My courage fails me.

I cannot come with you alone, day by day, and not be tempted. ... I am afraid of myself. You remember once I told you not to awaken the sleeping devil in me.' He was pulling out grass from the crevices as he spoke.

'Have I done wrong in loving you?' she asked timidly.

'Sin only lies in the consciousness of sin,' he answered earnestly. 'It's one's own approach to a thing that makes it right or wrong. Wine may be the nectar of the gods to one, but poison to another. Hafiz says, 'What devil seeks happiness in wine? It is only a moment of forgetfulness that I crave, night and day!'

'In my imagination I had placed love on the highest pedestal, as something unattainable. I had deified it.' She spoke with a quiet, devotional fervour.

'Yes, one may enter a shrine like a devotee, to worship, or like a sceptic, merely to admire the form and scoff at the spirit,' he commented sadly.

They were silent for a while. He then burst out almost in anger against himself: 'Oh, had I come back from England immediately after my studies, instead of loitering around, seeking God knows what, probably we should have been married. Safia always talked about it. But it was not to be!' He gave a shrug of despair.

'Oh, why did you not come back!' Her voice came like a wail. 'As for my marriage ...' she spoke hesitantly, as if struggling to have her most intimate thoughts reach out to him. 'I had a foreboding. You can never know what tears I shed on my wedding day. I had looked forward to love, where two spirits could commune with each other, and what I felt was the funeral of all my dreams. But after the marriage your brother was so good to me, that I was happy and contented, or at least so I thought until I met you. In a way, I even created an illusion of love for him, but now I know the difference. I now know why my heart ached and why I wept so bitterly that day. ...' Even as she said this, tears welled up in her eyes, for she knew that on that day she had forfeited her freedom, her right to choose.

Hamid, tortured and compassionate, gazed at her and under his gaze she gave way, and burst into violent sobs. Without pausing to think, he drew her head on to his shoulder, and though he was himself greatly disturbed, held it down gently. She was vaguely conscious of this tender gesture, and troubled by it. And she wept all the more bitterly. Gradually, as the sobs subsided, she lifted up her head in embarrassment and alarm. As she fumbled for a handkerchief, Hamid offered her his, then walked away. After a few minutes, feeling somewhat calmer, he came back to where she still sat in utter bewilderment. And sitting down, he said:

'Zohra, today your head rested on my shoulder. It just happened. It was natural in the circumstances. Tomorrow something else may happen.' He spoke quietly. 'One thing leads to another. When two people are so fatally attracted, they have either to belong to each other wholly, or to part.'

She said nothing, but involuntarily caught hold of his sleeve, as if she could never let him go. They sat together a little longer. Then, on a sudden, Hamid realized the time. 'It's late and the clouds are gathering. We were too absorbed to notice.'

They hurried back. As they entered the sitting room, Bashir turned sharply in his chair to confront them. He had not the same control over his temper as before his illness. Addressing Zohra, he said: 'It's chilly, with the damp monsoon air blowing. You might easily have caught a cold. Sometimes, ... sometimes, you still behave like a young girl!'

'Perhaps I feel like one,' she answered, sitting down near the window and trying not to take his displeasure seriously.

Hamid felt a wild desire to shout at him, 'But why are you always after Zohra? Why can't you let her lead a normal life? Since when has she been so susceptible to colds?' But with a sudden pang he realized he had no right over her, whilst Bashir, as her husband, had every right. The thought was maddening. He stood fidgeting with the back of a chair.

'I know you love boating,' Bashir now continued in a more normal voice, 'but there should be a limit to everything. Look, it has already started raining; you might have got drenched! The lake is small enough. Where were you all this time? I couldn't see the boat. I wanted to signal to you.'

'Oh, we got down at the other end.' She spoke carelessly. 'We were just talking. ...'

'But what on earth were you talking about that you should forget the time and place—and the threatening clouds?'

They became self-conscious, wondering if he suspected anything. Hamid realized that it was for Zohra to decide what she wanted to tell her husband; he turned to her. He saw her pull herself up. There seemed to be a quiet determination about her, an honesty of purpose that hated taking shelter behind lies. It seemed as if she would tell him everything, if only he were to ask, and face the consequences. She had no time to consider what its effects upon him would be, whether there was no kinder way. Hamid felt a wave of admiration for her courage rise within him; only he knew it would be foolish to wreck his brother's peace of mind as well as their own. What would they gain by it? Strange, he thought, how nervous she was when speaking of love, but faced with a situation where real courage was needed, her spirit rose undaunted to meet any challenge.

Whilst the two were expecting an explosion from Bashir, the latter merely continued:

'Hamid has nothing to talk about these days save the Congress, Gandhi and his *Satyagraha* movement. He could talk all night long and forget the time. He does not realize that women don't have his khadi *sherwani* to keep off the chill!' Turning to Hamid, he observed sarcastically: 'Yes, by wearing the coarsest of *khaddhar* and by submitting to violence in the sacred name of non-violence, you will indeed get your *swaraj*!' Then in a more normal tone he added: 'It's amazing how anyone can have faith in non-violence!'

Hamid, controlling his temper with an effort, said: 'Last time it almost succeeded. It united the Hindus and Muslims as seldom before, at least, since the British *Raj*. Why, even you were worked up then.'

'But we have seen that it failed.'

'That was not a failure.' It was Hamid's turn now to turn sharply on his brother. 'You cannot uproot anything so firmly embedded as Imperialism at one wrench but it has had its foundations badly shaken. It only requires one more effort. There is no other way. Non-violence is not only best suited to our conditions, but it is also the most civilized way. It certainly is the highest form of courage to suffer and not to hit back,' Hamid flung at him vehemently and sat down. 'Only the land of the Buddha could have produced the Mahatma. It requires the courage of one's convictions; control over the spirit of vengeance. ... Non-violence is not a creed for the weak; it is a creed for the bravest.'

'We fight in the open battlefield,' said Bashir with cold finality. 'This method is certainly not suited to our Muslim genius.'

Hamid, losing all self-control, burst out: 'Why do we have to talk of the Muslim genius and the Hindu genius? After all, the majority of us come from the same stock. We are mostly converts, and have the same background of thought.' He banged the chair with his hand for emphasis.

'Even so, once converted, our social order has changed radically. We in Islam have complete equality. With us, there is none of that inhuman caste system. You cannot shut up human beings in tight-fitting compartments in the name of religion. It is against the very spirit of Islam. The servant can rub shoulders with his master in the mosque. Before God, they are equal. But a Harijan may not even enter a caste-Hindu temple. A Brahmin will not allow even the shadow of an untouchable to pollute him. What indeed is there in common between us?' Bashir asked exasperatedly.

'I do not claim that Hinduism is free from abuses. But who is crusading more strongly against them than Mahatma Gandhi himself? And look at the tremendous effect of it even among women. You can see Nalini for yourself. She never ate with us before because her elders would not allow it. Now the elders just have to accept it. Then, again, is Islam free from such abuses? Look, look at the way we have kept our women in the darkness of *purdah*. Is that human? Are we following the laws of the Prophet?' Hamid's voice rose as his temper got out of control.

'Certainly, there are abuses in Islam too. I am all for reform, but you cannot deny that the *Shariat* accords women more rights than any other religion does. The laws of marriage, divorce, widow-remarriage, inheritance, they are all in favour of women. With the Hindus, on the contrary, child marriages and the plight of child-widows are positively inhuman.'

Hamid squirmed, he felt like shouting: 'But how many of these rights you boast of are translated into practice? Can a girl really marry of her own free will, or get a divorce on any reasonable grounds?'—But he controlled himself and said:

'Hindu philosophy is one of the world's oldest and greatest. One has to study that in order to understand the Hindu mind. It's no use attacking a system without even knowing in what it is rooted. And Hindu and Muslim cultures did reach a synthesis in the glorious days of Akbar. Look at the Nehrus; aren't they the products of this synthesis? It's their Kashmiri heritage. Look at Jawaharlal, isn't he the idol of everyone? Is there any Muslim to rival him?'

'Yes, handsome and impetuous, performing dare-devil feats like a cinema star, he is at least the idol of all women,' commented Bashir coldly. He was forgetting himself in the heat of the argument; for he had often confessed that Jawaharlal was the only Hindu leader whom he could understand.

'I didn't know there was anything wrong in being idolized by women. I am sure we should all like it,' said Hamid in an equally cold voice. 'Only, Jawaharlal is idolized by men, women and children, all alike. He has that magnetic personality which is made for hero-worship. Radiating electric sparks. Quivering with sensibility. ...'

'This is just another form of idolatry', broke in Bashir pungently. 'If you cannot have a stone deity you must have a clay one.'

'If that deity symbolizes some ideal, some perfection, then I for one, see no harm in it. We are all doing it in one way or another,' returned Hamid, as the picture of Zohra floated before his mind, even though his eyes were sedulously averted from her. Then he added hurriedly: 'But speaking of culture, look at our own Kishen Parshad Bahadur. Can you deny that he symbolizes the best of both cultures? He has a Muslim wife, and you know, the children by her are Muslim. Members of the best Muslim families are eager to marry them. What greater unity or tolerance could we expect?' His hand hit the chair again in a vehement gesture.

'The Maharaj Bahadur is an exception,' said Bashir drily. 'He does not belong to the common rut of men. But his culture is more Muslim than Hindu, the graciousness of life, the large-heartedness.'

Did Bashir imagine he possessed these qualities? wondered Hamid impatiently. Aloud he remarked: 'Yes, they don't squander money foolishly as we do. They have greater depth. I only wish, however, we would stop talking about different cultures. The differences are more provincial than religious. Religion is now being exploited only for power politics. The British used it in their policy of *divide et impera*. We were foolish enough to play blindly into their hands. And the way certain Muslim leaders are talking now, I dread to think of the future. ... We *must* all unite and fight the battle of freedom. Youth is mostly on our side.' Hamid's eyes were burning; his face quivering.

'Yes, you can always rely on youth to get excited over anything revolutionary. They are carried away by your Gandhis and Nehrus and their slogans. It's just mass hysteria!' said Bashir in his monotonously dry voice.

'What country but India could have produced a leader like Mahatma Gandhi, a politician who is also a saint?' asked Hamid aggressively. 'As for Jawaharlal, although he is more understandable, he is head and shoulders above all other men; a fighter, an idealist, a humanitarian, an intellectual, a nationalist who is at the same time a great internationalist. Actually, the father, Pandit Motilal, too is an outstanding personality, but the son has caught the public imagination. He symbolizes the youth— the India of the future, at least, as we would wish it to be.'

Bashir, leaning back more comfortably, gave his brother a cold stare. It provoked Hamid still further: 'To me, Hindus and Muslims are one, possessing a common heritage, belonging to a common Motherland, fighting common battles,' he said. 'We are intermingled, living together side by side. 'Surely, you cannot divide up each little plot of land and say this is Hindu India and that is Muslim India? To me that sounds like a graveyard!'

'I don't say that we have to divide the country up.' Bashir spoke in a hard metallic voice, as if he were dispensing judgment. 'I only say that there is justification for what some Muslims have started saying. ... In a democracy we shall always be under the Hindus. We cannot tolerate that. We belong to the race of conquerors.'

'History never shows a race of permanent conquerors,' said Hamid with an impatient gesture.' 'Besides, Muslims can have their majority provinces with safeguards at the Centre. British Raj cannot last indefinitely. World opinion is already against them. And on the same basis, Hyderabadi Muslims have no right to rule the Hindu majority. We must all be prepared for changes.' Hamid spoke with intense conviction.

'The Hindus were not born to be rulers, they are Yogis,' Bashir asserted with equal conviction. 'The Muslims never accepted British domination easily. Don't forget that we were the first to strike a blow at British rule.

The Mutiny of 1857 was our attempt at freeing India. We fought an open battle, and not this Ahimsa—non-violence. Even the Hindu diet is all wrong. No one can be strong on mere vegetables!'

'I don't agree with you there,' said Hamid with a jerk of his head. 'But anyway, in a free India, nobody is going to tie you down to sectarian habits. Even amongst them, there are many non-vegetarian sects.'

'Altogether, it's their way of life against ours—the two can never meet. How can we come closer to each other when they won't even eat with us?'

'I am not defending Hindu conservatism, but I cannot defend Muslim narrowness either,' said Hamid heatedly.

'Muslims are not narrow.' Bashir was emphatic.

'That's our difficulty. Like the camel we can never see our own hump.' Hamid gave a despairing shrug.

'You have no right to call yourself a Muslim!' Bashir's tone was so offensive that Zohra, no longer able to control herself, suddenly burst out: 'It's people like you who make one almost wish one were a Hindu. There should be some toleration, a spirit of give and take. We all have Hindu friends, and what is the difference? Except, perhaps, that they are cleverer!'

'Hamid has been undermining you. I don't think his influence is good for any susceptible young person.' Bashir's voice was scornful.

'A little while ago you asked me when I would stop acting like a young girl. I should now like to know when you will stop treating me like one,' she asked haughtily, rising from the chair. 'If I am susceptible, you cannot change me. I shall be influenced by whomsoever I like!' With a proud toss of her head, she left the room. She had never talked to him like this before. Bashir, angry and hurt, and no longer able to bear his brother's company, soon followed her.

—*Zohra* (1951)

Krishna Nehru Hutheesing
(b. 1907)

Though she was the youngest sister of Jawaharlal Nehru, there is surprisingly little known about Krishna Nehru Hutheesing, though her older sister Vijayalakshmi Pandit is still a recognizable figure in India's political history.

A small paragraph in Nehru's will and testament reads: 'In the course of a life which has had its share of trial and difficulty, the love and tender care for me of both my sisters, Vijayalakshmi Pandit and Krishna Hutheesing, have been of the greatest solace to me. I can give nothing to balance this except my own love and affection which they have in full measure.'

She married Raja Hutheesing, and wrote a number of books including *Shadows on the Wall* (1948), *Nehru's Letters to His Sister* (1963), *We Nehrus* (1968), and *With No Regrets: An Autobiography*, from which excerpts are reproduced here.

The writing is natural, informal, yet controlled. She cites a letter from Jawaharlal Nehru written to her shortly after the death of their father Motilal Nehru, in which he tells her, 'We are children of our father and have something of his great strength and courage, and whatever the trials and difficulties that may come our way, we shall face them with resolution and with the determination to overcome them.' She goes on to admit that 'though Jawahar does not know it, innumerable times when I have been overcome by despair or have been down-hearted, this letter written twelve years ago has given me courage to face life's problems.'

Another interesting extract depicts her spirited nature and sense of fair play which, one can assume, was shared by her sister Vijayalakshmi Pandit as well. It is about an English Superintendent's visit to the jail where she was imprisoned for a while, on account of her participation in the struggle for freedom. 'One day a friend of mine and I were rather late in appearing outside our cell. As soon as he saw us he shouted, 'Hurry up, hurry up, I can't wait here all day for you. A tennis tournament is on which I must see and I am held up here in this most unpleasant place.' I was very annoyed too. So I retorted back, 'We find this even more annoying than you do as everything is so filthy here. And as for missing the tennis tournament, why should you not miss it one day when we are missing it daily?' The Superintendent went almost livid, but fortunately said nothing further.' Like her sister, Krishna Hutheesing also documents the tragedies of women in prison. 'Little do we know, living a life of ease and surrounded by the care of those who love us what temptations our less fortunate sisters are faced with.' She specifically mentions the case of a young friend of hers called Bachuli, who was sentenced for the murder of her husband.

Another chapter reproduced here is of interest because of the light it throws upon Kamala Nehru, the wife of Jawaharlal. 'Kamala was an ardent feminist and many were the battles she fought for the rights of women amongst her friends and workers. Often she landed herself in trouble with the menfolk, because they said that their wives had been listening to Kamalaji and imbibing her views which did not suit them at all! She had a spirit that was most independent and which no hardship or sickness could conquer.'

Chapter IX

'The fairest things have fleetest end,
Their scent services their close;
But the rose's scent is bitterness,
To him that loved the rose.'

—Francis Thompson

The first time I saw Kamala was at a party given by my father at Anand Bhawan. I was quite a little girl and not allowed to attend the party, but I could watch it from the verandah, which I did. It was an aunt of mine, I think, who pointed out Kamala to me and said, 'Do you see that girl and do you think you will like her? She is going to be your sister-in-law.' I looked in the direction my aunt pointed out and saw a tall, slim, exceedingly pretty girl sitting with some others at a table. I could not quite understand what a sister-in-law meant, but I guessed she was coming to live with us. I thought it would be nice to have another sister, though I wished she had been younger and nearer my age! I have never forgotten that first picture of her and the utter youthfulness and freshness that was Kamala's when she was seventeen.

Some months later Jawahar's wedding took place in Delhi and Kamala came to live with us. I remember well the pride my parents took in showing off their beautiful daughter-in-law; she was not only pretty, she was the picture of health. Looking at her, one would never have prophesied that she was to spend most of her life on a sick bed. Marriage seemed to start off well for Kamala and Jawahar. The future looked very bright and no clouds darkened the horizon, and a few years of happiness passed. Then suddenly changes started taking place. Politics took hold of Jawahar and also of my father, and many drastic changes took place because a thin half-starved looking man came into our lives and also into the lives of many others to change the whole course of events. That little man was Gandhiji. Kamala like the rest of our family gave up all luxuries and became one of his most devoted followers. He had very great affection for her and she for him and the cause he had made so dear.

Kamala had never known hardship or sorrow. Before she got married and afterwards she had led a life of security and ease with no fear of what the morrow would bring. Suddenly all this changed and it became one of uncertainty, of separation and heartaches and also many physical discomforts. With an unflinching courage Kamala confronted everything smilingly. Not once did I hear a word of complaint or dissatisfaction— no grouse against fate as most of us have when things do not work out the way we want them to. When Jawahar dedicated his life to his country, Kamala did not hesitate a second to fall in beside him. If ever India had a super-soldier with thoughts only for the country and none for self, with an energy that never flagged and a courage the like of which one rarely comes across, that soldier was Kamala. Little is known of Kamala, and as a friend of mine has written about her, 'her life was like the luminous flame of an oil lamp. It wavered, it brightened, it grew in intensity all the time and then quietly when the oil got drained the flame flickered and died.' It is said that 'whom the gods love, die young' and this must be so, for no one could help loving Kamala or admiring her pluck. Living as she did, over-shadowed by strong personalities like her husband's and father-in-law's, she still made a place for herself in politics, and might have attained much fame if death had not snatched her away so cruelly. She was frail to look at, but her character was strong and true. Few people except those who knew her very well, knew the strength that lay behind those gentle eyes or quiet manner of hers. She had many virtues but many faults too. She was child-like to a fault and never seemed to have grown out of her girlhood days. At times she was terribly neglectful of her health and no amount of good advice given, would make her take more care of herself. Inspite of many illnesses which almost cost her life, she never seemed to age. Till the end she retained the sweet girlish looks and figure that she had when she was married. Ill-health caused havoc with her body internally but externally she barely changed during all the years I knew her.

For years after Kamala's marriage I saw very little of her. She, as a new bride, was always being feted and later on, she was kept occupied with social activities, as my father entertained a great deal and mother being more or less an invalid, Kamala acted as hostess for him. In 1926 when we were together in Europe, I really got to know Kamala well and we became great friends. We used to have long and sometimes very heated discussions on various things in life that concerned us or on what we had read or heard about specially on women's rights, but they always ended pleasantly. She was confined to bed most of the time in Europe. The few months of companionship we had together when she was able to travel about were grand. She was always eager to see new things, to learn something new. She enjoyed a picnic or a party to the fullest extent and never acted like a spoil sport, no matter how weary she felt. She never complained, however grave the provocation might be. On our return from Europe we came closer together for we both took an active part in politics and worked together. Here again I marvelled at Kamala's energy. I, who was far more healthy than she, often gave in to fatigue or weariness and stayed at home, but not she. At 5 a.m., on a cold winter's day, she used to be up and ready as we had to have drill for the women volunteers at that hour and then from 8 a.m., our daily work of picketing foreign cloth shops started. Throughout the cold months of winter Kamala continued the usual routine and worked all day long. Then summer came and she still kept at her post inspite of the blazing sun and the terrible heat. Many of us did the same but we often grumbled and felt tired and disheartened. Not so Kamala, whose faith and spirits never seemed to flag. But tiring herself out in this manner she hastened her end, for though her spirit was strong her pain-racked body could not stand the strain and in the end death conquered.

Though a very quiet and unobtrusive person, Kamala had very definite views on life and once her mind was made up, she acted with a determination which ill-health would not shake. She was naturally overshadowed by Jawahar to some extent, but not entirely so, for she had a personality of her own.

Kamala was an ardent feminist and many were the battles she fought for the rights of women amongst her friends and workers. Often she landed herself in trouble with the menfolk, because they said that their wives had been listening to Kamalaji and imbibing her views which did not suit them at all! She had a spirit that was most independent and which no hardship or sickness could conquer. She was proud of the fact that she had been able to play even a small part in her country's struggle for Independence, and was happy in the knowledge that Jawahar was the beloved of millions. She never grudged him his fame and was never jealous of his admirers.

From 1934 onwards Kamala's health deteriorated rapidly. She was sent to a sanatorium in Bhowali. We spent many anxious days hoping and praying for the best, but she gradually got worse. Jawahar was once again back in prison. This time he was in Almora and was allowed to visit Kamala now and then at given intervals. How much she must have looked forward to them and how fleetingly the hours they spent together must have passed by! At last the doctors suggested that Kamala should go to Switzerland. Raja and I had gone up to Bhowali to be with her for some time before she left. I had a son hardly two months old and Kamala was even more overjoyed to see him than my mother had been! She threatened me then that on her return she would take my little son away from me and bring him up if I myself did not do so properly!

On the day fixed for her departure Jawahar was allowed to come from Almora Jail and see her off. What thoughts kept passing through his mind on that agonizing day I cannot say; but to watch his face was heart-breaking. His eyes held all the sorrow which he tried in vain to hide by a stern expression. As the moment came to bid farewell he and Kamala did so, each with a brave smile. Then her car took her down the hill to the train which was to take her to Bombay. Jawahar after embracing mother and me, with unshed tears in his eyes, got into the waiting car that was to take him back to the Almora prison! As he turned his back on us and walked away, he suddenly seemed to have lost the spring in his walk and the energy he always had. He looked utterly worn out and much older than a few hours ago. Some months later Jawahar was released and flew to Europe as Kamala's condition was bad and on 28 February 1936 she died in Badenweiler, a small town in Germany, with Jawahar and Indira by her side.

Chapter XXVIII

... Jail life had not been pleasant, but it had been a great experience and I for one, was very glad to have been able to make friends with some of those convicts who were considered a menace to society, but who were far better specimens of humanity than many of the people we come across in our daily life. I was glad to be going home, but it hurt to know that these poor creatures were to be left behind for many long years and when released they would have no home to go to, no shelter, no helping hand to guide them to a new life. Nothing except the cunning that they had learnt in jail to help them eke out an existence for themselves until, condemned by society and knocked about from pillar to post, they would at last in desperation commit some crime. This they would often do in order to relieve their hunger, driven by necessity. Then, back in jail once more, perhaps for the rest of their lives.

We read so often in the newspapers about young girls being sentenced for some terrible crime, of women who had murdered someone or other, of others who had been sentenced again and again and we shudder to think that such things can happen. Little do we know, living a life of ease and surrounded by the care of those who love us what temptations our less fortunate sisters are faced with. We are ready and willing always to show a righteous horror when we hear or read of a ghastly crime, but I wonder how we would act if we lived under the same circumstances as those who are forced to do such things. We were in a juvenile prison and all the convict girls were under twenty-one years of age. It was strange how sensitive, affectionate and understanding most of these girls were whom society considered a menace. They were frank and open hearted if treated with kindness and friendship. And yet these poor girls were condemned to long terms of imprisonment because life had been unkind to them and in a moment of anger they had given way to certain murderous instincts that a great many of us feel, but are too civilized to give in to. It made me a little sad to leave these new found friends of mine behind. I felt ashamed of having so many of the good things in life when they had nothing.

I had become very fond of one of the girls called Bachuli. She was a fair, grey-eyed girl, plump and not quite five feet tall, with hair down to her shoulders, matted and coarse. Yet, inspite of her rough clothes and none too clean an appearance, she made a pretty picture when I saw her for the first time against the grim prison walls trying to learn to crochet. She looked so very young and had such an innocent expression that I wondered why she was in jail, or what great offence this mere child could have committed. When I walked up to her she was humming a song, one of those sad haunting melodies one hears in the mountains of Northern India.

'What is your name?' I asked her. She looked at me suspiciously and asked in her turn very gently and hesitatingly, 'Who are you and how did you get in here?' 'I am a prisoner too,' I replied and she burst out laughing. 'What are you in for?' she asked again. I told her I was a political prisoner and though she nodded her head wisely, I think she but vaguely understood what it meant. Anyhow she decided I was trying to be friendly and being satisfied that I was no jail official, she told me her name. Shyly she looked up at me with a very lovely smile and then with a sigh resumed her work. 'Why are you here, Bachuli?' I asked. A pair of large frank eyes looked straight into mine and she said simply, 'for murder.'

'For murder?' I asked incredulously and she nodded her head to confirm it. I could hardly believe my eyes or ears. This child still in her teens could not possibly have murdered anyone. There must be some mistake.

'Bachuli, why did you have to murder someone?' I asked. 'You are so young. Perhaps you did not know what you were doing. It may have been an accident.' She raised her head slowly and looked at me again. The laughter had gone from her eyes and in its place came a look of fear and hatred which hardened her usually soft expression.

This is her story:

'It was my husband I murdered,' she said slowly. 'He was very cruel to me and beat me and locked me up very often. He also made me starve and though there was always enough to eat in the house, he would take my share away from me and give me very little of it, eating the rest himself or throwing it away. Every now and then he would invent some new way of causing me pain though I tried hard to please him. He was very good-looking and when I married him I was only fourteen years old, but I liked him and I vowed to the gods and goddesses that I would be a good wife to him, serve and obey him, as my mother had told me to, and feed him well. But a few months after our marriage he suddenly started being cruel, and it gave him pleasure to see me being afraid of him. He told me that he teased me because it amused him and I was terribly afraid. For nearly a year I suffered. My husband would not let me go back to my parents though I begged him to do so. Each day I became more and more unhappy. Inspite of all this ill-treatment, I tried to make him like me, but nothing I could do would help or please him. One morning he gave me a thrashing because I had not washed a coat of his that he wanted to wear and after the thrashing he went out, leaving me in agony. Some hours later he returned, dressed in new clothes with a bright red-silk handkerchief around his neck. I was doing some work and did not turn round when he entered. So he called to me, 'Come here, you little idiot,' he said, 'and admire my new clothes. Do I not look handsome in them?' I did not reply, but looked at my own clothes which were dirty and torn. 'Speak up, can't you?' he shouted 'Or are you jealous of my new clothes?' I still remained quiet. So he came up to me and slapped my face twice, holding my wrist so that it hurt me terribly. 'Let go of me,' I cried, 'or I shall kill you one of these days. Why should I admire your clothes when you eat all day long and starve me. Why ...' and before I could finish or say any more, he took his stick and abusing and cursing me, he hit me again and again till I nearly fainted and then he flung me aside. 'Now try and kill me if you can,' he said and throwing away his stick he calmly lay down and soon fell off to sleep. After some hours had elapsed I tried to move, but all my body ached and I lay down again. Suddenly I saw my husband fast asleep in a corner. He had taken off his new clothes and hung them up, but the new silk handkerchief was still round his neck. As I looked at him I hated him and all of a sudden I felt I should kill him and be done with him. But how? I looked around and found nothing with which I could hit him. Then my glance fell on the bright, red handkerchief. I do not know how it happened but I was up in no time, tying the handkerchief tighter and tighter round my husband's neck. He woke up at the first pressure, struggled and tried to shout, but I just went on tightening the handkerchief till his eyes nearly came out of their sockets and then he went limp. I let go and being utterly exhausted I fell back in a daze half expecting my husband to get up and give me another thrashing. But he did not and I lay there beside him unable to move. That is how someone found us the next morning. He discovered my husband was dead and sent for the police and ran hither and thither telling all our neighbours. I was still dazed, unable to believe that I had really killed my husband.

No one came near me till a policeman arrived and I was taken away to prison. After my trial I was sent to this prison and so here I am. I was too young to be hanged and women do not usually get a death sentence. I got life imprisonment. That is all.'

I had listened to this strange tale in silence with my eyes on Bachuli's face. I still could not believe what she had told me and yet it must be true as she was in prison.

As though she had told me just a story, Bachuli resumed her work. She was not curious to know what effect her story had had on me. To her it was an incident which in her innocence and simplicity she believed the fates had willed. She submitted to her life in prison as a matter of course, something which could not be averted and so why worry?

As I looked at her bent head my heart ached for her. She was so young, still very immature and looked anything but a criminal. Why had the fates dealt with her so harshly? What was her life going to be? Should not, I pondered, such cases be tried differently and a different punishment given? A life sentence is not a joke! It means twenty years if not more, behind prison walls. With no knowledge of the outside world, no one but criminals around one, hearing nothing but the coarsest of languages, seeing nothing but the lowest of God's creatures and learning such cunningness inside the jail as one may not learn outside in a dozen years. Bachuli was fifteen years old. She would be thirty-five when she left the prison. Having spent all her youth in prison, would she remain as sweet and untouched as she was now? Or would she become a hardened criminal who would be shunned by her fellowmen and live a life of evil which would inevitably lead her footsteps back to jail?

My thoughts were confused. I stroked Bachuli's head and said 'I hope I see you again, Bachuli. You must work well and get a lot of remission, then you can get out of the jail quicker perhaps.' A bright smile lit up her face. 'Oh yes' she said 'they tell me if I give no trouble and work hard I shall get off much sooner and will not have to do my full term. I shall go to my parents and it will be so lovely. My home is in the mountains and I do love them so.' I walked away sadly, hoping that her courage and optimism would never falter through the long years she was to remain in prison. A child of the mountain, this young creature, was used to trees, flowers and the fresh air. How would she stand prison life on the plains, or the intense heat of the summer? These were the doubts that assailed me and yet she seemed fairly contented and resigned to her fate. I could not but admire her spirit.

I looked round once again and saw her completely engrossed in her work. A year I spent with little Bachuli in that prison. I often longed for the outside world, but when the day dawned for me to go, I felt unhappy. There would be no bright-eyed Bachuli with me to while away the hours with her talk and mountain ditties, and the thought of leaving her behind, made me most miserable. The day dawned which was the last in my prison home and I went round to my comrades bidding them farewell. Suddenly two arms were flung round me and I saw beloved Bachuli, her large eyes filled with tears standing mutely beside me. I embraced her and making her look straight at me I said 'You must be brave, Bachuli, and try and be happy. When you come out, you must let me know and if you want to come to me you can do so.' 'You will not forget me in the great world outside?' asked Bachuli, 'For they tell me here that no one likes to remember convicts once they are in the great big world?' I stroked her head and assured her that it would not be so, and though many years have passed, her memory is still very fresh and will remain thus for a long time.

As I, together with some of my comrades who were also releazed the same day, walked out of the prison yards and through the prison gates, I sent up a prayer that Bachuli and other young people like her would not spend their lives in jail, but that some kind fate would restore them to their homes and to a life of peace and happiness.

I turned back once to have a last look at the prison with its grim and forbidding wall which held captive dozens of young offenders, all in their teens, and which had been my home for a year. The large gates were slowly closing and through them I still should see the young girls assembled in the yard to bid us farewell. I waved and quickly turned my head away so that my comrades should not see the tears in my eyes, but they did and laughingly asked the whether it was breaking my heart to leave them. They little knew for whom my tears were shed, for they had not learnt to know these young convicts as my sister and I had done. They had remained aloof from them and could not understand our feelings for them. My tears were not shed because I was leaving jail, for jail had not been a bed of roses for any of us. They were shed because I was leaving behind a few helpless little girls in their teens, girls who were sentenced to long terms of imprisonment for crimes committed in ignorance and unhappiness, and who, through sheer misunderstanding and cruelty were made to commit such acts which they never would have committed had poverty, neglect and cruelty not been their lot. It was for these little creatures who had been so human, so childlike and affectionate that my heart bled and I was loathe to leave them. I was going back home, to loved ones and friends, all waiting to welcome me while they, what of them I wondered? I dared not think.

—With No Regrets: An Autobiography (1943)

Sucheta Kripalani
(1908–1974)

'To start with, I was a very dull student. My elder sister Sulekha was very fair, vivacious, restless and an attractive child. My younger sister Hemani was a very lovely child with a mass of curly hair, sparkling intelligent eyes, and full of mischief. In between these two extroverts, I was dark, dull and agonizingly shy. Mother's friends used to say, "You talk of three daughters but where is the second daughter? We never see her."'

No one reading this paragraph could have associated it with the life of Sucheta Kripalani. Born into a liberal Brahmo family, she was first influenced by the Russian Revolution, later becoming a staunch follower of Gandhi. She toured affected areas during pre-Partition communal riots, mobilized women during the Quit India movement, and was jailed in 1940 and 1944.

In the midst of it all, while teaching at Banaras Hindu University in 1929, she met Acharya J.B. Kripalani and married him in 1936. Her husband's enthusiasm enabled her to work tirelessly for the country. After working with Dr Rajendra Prasad for flood and earthquake relief in 1939, she went on to establish and became Secretary of the Women's Section of the Congress. She also became a coordinator of the Kasturba Gandhi National Memorial Trust, and worked with Jai Prakash Narayan, Ram Manohar Lohia and Aruna Asaf Ali.

Sucheta Kripalani also became the first woman Chief Minister of India on October 2, 1963—a post she held until March 1967—and can be credited with the organizing and building of an effective administrative service in Uttar Pradesh.

The present selection of her work includes a long autobiographical essay, another one on the poet Langston Hughes, and her thoughts on the role of creative writers in society. The writing shows a deep love for Gandhi, India, the freedom struggle and those who were involved in it. Even when she was ten-years-old, she wrote that she 'could understand enough to feel great anger against the British. We vented our anger on some Anglo-Indian children who played with us, calling them all kinds of names.'

There are descriptions of Lahore during its turbulent times, a touching account of the funeral procession held for Bhagat Singh, Raj Guru and Sukhdev, accounts of her time spent with Gandhi and the appeal he made persuading her not to get married. Later in her life, while speaking about the role of the creative writer at the P.E.N. Conference of Lucknow on October 10, 1964, she said with disarming honesty:

'... whatever I may say, some of you might think that I was treading on grounds which should be out of bounds for a politician, particularly for a politician in office. So, there is a risk that I shall oscillate between banality and impertinence. But I assure you that the offence, whether it is of banality or of impertinence, will be a brief one.'

The Partition made a deep impression on her, and Sucheta toured troubled areas with Gandhi, trying to prevent bloodshed. It is said that in those days she carried a phial of arsenic with her at all times, with which to take her life if the need ever arose.

An Unfinished Autobiography

When I look back over the long years of my life it strikes me as very full, interesting and, on the whole gratifying. I do not seem to have much to regret.

My childhood days were happy and carefree. We had a simple uncomplicated family life. My father, Surendra Nath Mazumdar, came from an old Brahmo family. My grandfather, Dinanath, born in a well-to-do zamindar family of Bengal, voluntarily left his home and embraced a life of hardship and poverty, though perhaps one of much spiritual and psychological satisfaction to him. As a young man on a visit to Calcutta, he attended a meeting of Keshab Chandra Sen, the leader of the Brahmo Samaj, purely out of fun and curiosity. But the eloquence of Keshab Chandra so moved him that, then and there, he decided not only to be initiated into the Brahmo faith, but to dedicate his life to its propagation.

Keshab Chandra had twelve close disciples or associates who organized the work of the Samaj and took its message to different parts of India. My grandfather Dinanath was one of them. He was deputed to work in

Bihar. Later, he carried on his activities to the Punjab and Sind. He, therefore, used to be out on prolonged tours. My grandmother struggled as best she could to look after the large family.

My father, after matriculating from Patna, studied in the Lahore Medical College and, later, joined medical service in the Punjab. We, brothers and sisters, were born and brought up in the Punjab.

Pujas and Hymns

We were a happy, boisterous family. Father was indulgent to his children, jolly, witty and ready to share with us some fun, when he was not too busy. Mother was strict; scoldings and occasional slaps came from her. But she ran the home well. A hard worker herself, she made us share the household chores. Father and mother started their day with prayers in the small puja room. In the evenings, mother gathered her children round her for a hymn and a short prayer, suited to the children. In this we followed the true Brahmo tradition. I am afraid, by the time we reached college, somehow or other the evening prayer had been discontinued. Mother was a good singer with a melodious voice. In the evenings, when my parents had no outside engagements we would all sing together, mother playing the organ. By the time I was in my teens, I would take mother's place when she was not there. I was fond of singing. My youngest sister had the sweetest voice of all. She went to Santiniketan to get trained in music. She did well and, till her marriage, did radio programmes from the Calcutta station.

Our education was very chequered. Due to Father's frequent transfers, I must have changed a dozen schools by the time I matriculated. To start with, I was a very dull student. My elder sister Sulekha was very fair, vivacious, restless and an attractive child. My younger sister Hemani was a very lovely child with a mass of curly hair, sparkling intelligent eyes, and full of mischief. In between these two extroverts, I was dark, dull and agonisingly shy. Mother's friends used to say, 'You talk of three daughters but where is the second daughter? We never see her.'

In school I was a headache for the teachers. I would not stand up to answer their questions. My sister, only a year and a half older than me, a bright student in her class, tried to give me whatever protection she could. We were very close friends but that did not stop us from having occasional bouts of fighting. For my emergence from a dull to a bright student, I owed much to Mrs Roy who taught me for some months.

My elder sister Sulekha and myself and been sent to study in the Loreto Convent in Simla. Here she fell ill with a rheumatic heart. We were both then brought down and kept at home. Sulekha was seriously ill for a long time. Mrs Roy, a friend of the family, offered to teach me. She constantly gave me encouragement. I soon came to like my studies and worked hard at them. From then onwards I steadily improved. When, after a few months, I was sent to a boarding school in Allahabad, I was counted among the top students to the class. After a year in this school, Sulekha, who had by then recovered, and I were sent to the Queen Mary's School in Delhi. We stayed in the boarding house there till we matriculated.

We had a happy time at school. It was run by two missionary ladies, Miss Jerwood and Miss Fenn. Miss Jerwood was keen to give her charges a good, sound eduction, and awareness of the society and the country and a sense of obligation towards them. They organized for us small service activities in school such as the needle work circle, to make baby clothes for the poor children. We raised funds for various causes like flood and famine relief. In our Domestic Science course, besides what we were taught in class, we got practical training, while training in Baby Care, for example, we bathed and cleaned the slum babies who were brought to us by their mothers. We became bold enough to adopt a newly born baby from the hospital, but this experiment did not last long.

We have a good library and were encouraged to develop a taste for reading. We also ran a kind of a weekly wall-newspaper. Miss Jerwood, the Principal, was a strict disciplinarian. She stood tall, thin, straight as a martinet; her sharp eyes missed nothing. We held her in awe. Later, I realized how good she was. She drilled into us neatness, good behaviour, punctuality, steady habits and many sound qualities. The Vice-Principal, Miss Fenn, was just the opposite. She was a mathematics Tripos from Cambridge and a Wrangler. In fact, she was too highly qualified to teach elementary mathematics to schoolchildren. She was kind, forgetful and untidy, her mind often wool-gathering somewhere else.

Bitterness against the Raj

I must go back a few years to recount how strong nationalistic sentiments penetrated our home. I have vague recollections of the agitation in the house over the Jallianwala Bagh and the subsequent Punjab incidents. Shortly before this, Father had been posted at Saharanpur. Many of our friends and relatives, who were in the Punjab at that time, came away and stayed with us till things quietened down. A wave of indignation and wrath swept through our house, when they recounted to us their harrowing experience. I was about ten-years-old and could understand enough to feel great anger against the British. We vented our anger on some of the Anglo-Indian children who played with us, calling them all kinds of names.

The next impact came when, in 1920, Kripalani left the Banaras Hindu University with a batch of about two hundred students and joined the satyagraha movement. One of the students in Kripalani's batch was Dhiren Mozumdar, my cousin, who was then studying in the Engineering College. Dhiren visited us frequently. He used to regale us with the stories of their life in the Ashram, their experiments in village work, the production and sale of khadi, their jail life and, of course, their remarkable leader 'Dada' (Kripalani). Through him we came to know the main workers of the Ashram. We got all our khadi from the Meerut Ashram. They could, in the beginning, only produce plain white Khadi of small width which was very coarse. We made saris out of them by stitching two pieces together and embellishing them as best we could. I remember our joy when the first printed sari of adequate width was produced!

I have no clear recollection when I first saw Gandhiji. In all probability, it was in 1924 when Gandhiji was fasting in Delhi. Dhiren took some of us to have Gandhiji's darshan. We waited, all elation and excitement, in a crowded room having a look at the great man! Little did I then imagine how close to him I was to get one day!

This was the year when Sulekha and I appeared for our matriculation examination. We got through the examination both getting a first class, my sister getting four marks more than I. We stood first and second among the girl students. We both secured scholarships.

In Defence of the Gita

We joined Indraprastha College, Delhi, for our Intermediate but as Father was soon transferred to Lahore, we changed over to Kinniard College. It was a nice well-run college. Students were not many, about 20 to 25 girls in the class. Enough individual attention was given to us. At this distant time, I do not recall much except one incident. In the Bible class, which was compulsory, the teacher, an Indian Christian lady, in her enthusiasm one day said some disparaging things about Hinduism, particularly citing the loose ways of Krishna's life. The Hindu girls were hurt and annoyed but we could not give her a proper answer.

Sulekha and I came home fuming. Father sat with us the whole evening coaching us on Sri Krishna's teachings from the Gita. He marked out the passages and prepared us well. Next day in the Bible class, we challenged the teacher and started reading texts from the Gita, quoting Sri Krishna's true teachings. The teacher was quite unprepared for all this attack from chits of young girls! However, she had the grace to say that, if that was the real teaching of Krishna, she had nothing more to say. After that, she never referred to Hindu religion in her class! But we were no longer *persona grata* with her. This was reflected in the marks she gave us in the other subjects she taught us!

A few months before our examination, Sulekha caught a chill; this developed into her old ailment of rheumatic fever and heart condition. For the next four or five months, we were just in and out of the hospital, Mother, Father and myself taking turns to nurse her. But all our care was of no avail. On May 4, while I was in the midst of my Intermediate examination, she died. This was the first death in our house. Our parents grieved the death of their first child deeply. Father's health started to deteriorate from then on.

But for this tragedy we had a happy life in Lahore. We had a wide circle of friends who could roughly be divided into three groups—Father's professional friends, doctors and their families, the Brahmos and the Bengali community in Lahore. With the Brahmo Samaj as the nucleus, several religious, social and cultural functions were organized, in which we participated. The Bengalis had their own social and cultural functions.

I passed my Intermediate examination in first class and stood first among the girl candidates, which incidentally brought me a gold medal and a scholarship. I did not like to go back to the Kinniard College without my sister. I, therefore, did my B.A. in the Government College for Women. My two years there were uneventful.

An incident I remember here is of a strike we organized in the college. Those days, strikes, particularly in girls' institutions, were extremely rare. Our principal, a stodgy Englishwoman, whom none of us liked, made some disparaging remarks about the Indians. This set us moving and we organized a mini-strike. She was quite unprepared for this! She fretted and fumed, but nothing came of it till she called all of us to the assembly hall and tendered some kind of an apology and withdrew her remarks.

The carefree days of my young life were about to end. My father suddenly feel seriously ill in December 1927. It was diagnosed as T.B. About a year earlier he had been transferred from Lahore. Some of us, studying either in the colleges or schools, could not leave Lahore. A flat had, therefore, been rented for us. A friend of my parents, one Miss Sen, the principal of a school, had agreed to stay with us. Our real guardian, however, was our old cook who had been in our service since before my birth. He was like a member of the family. Because of his sudden illness father was brought to this flat in Lahore. My mother was in weak health as my youngest brother had been born only a few weeks before Father fell ill. She looked after Father in the day and we two sisters, myself and Hemani, took care of him at night. It was a most anxious time. The entire household was disrupted. Mother had to wind up her household in haste, sell the horse and carriage and all the heavy furniture before coming back to Lahore. There was the constant hustle and bustle of the doctors coming and going. Father's medical friends were greatly helpful. After a couple of months, his conditions stabilized and he started to improve. Our examinations were on top of us. Hemani was appearing for Inter, and I for B.A. We had hardly touched our books. Mother decided to take Father and the younger children away to Simla for the summer and leave a little early, to give us two to three weeks' time to study.

Close-knit Brahmos

After the examinations we had a few happy months in Simla, as father was steadily improving. Our social life mainly centred on the Brahmo Samaj. We had rented a house in the spacious grounds of the Samaj by the Mall. That year, the Maharani of Mayurbhanj, a daughter of Keshab Chandra Sen, was also visiting Simla. Father was happy to meet her after many years. The early Brahmo families who had lived and suffered privation with Keshab Chandra Sen were bound together in deep bonds of affection. We could see how close Father and this lady felt to each other. When our results came out we had both passed but missed first class. However, my marks were high enough to get me a scholarship.

From Simla, we decided to shift to Delhi. Hemani and I got admitted in the St. Stephen's College. There were then hardly half a dozen girls in the St. Stephen's College. We had a small girls' retiring room attached to the house of the Principal, Mr Mukherjee. We went into the classes along with the teachers. St. Stephen's College was then in the old building in Kashmiri Gate, located on the fork, between two roads. Across one road was the hostel and the Maitland House, where some of our professors resided. Our tutorials were also held there. Across the other road stood the Hindu College. In the M.A. Class, as university students we had to attend classes in both the colleges.

I was a student of History. Our Head of the Department was Dr Spears, an excellent teachers, popular with the students. He expressed in those days, great admiration for Gandhi, Tagore and other Indian personalities which endeared him to us. My first days in St. Stephen's were a little bewildering. I had been taught before by English women but never by men. For three or four days I could not follow their lectures, as their pronunciation and intonation sounded strange to me. But soon I got over the difficulty. My second worry was how to keep up my end against the boys. The boys naturally watched the only girl in the class very critically. There was also a certain amount of sniggering and loud remarks about me. All this made me more nervous. Before our first house examinations were to be held, I went to Dr Spears and asked for exemption on the plea of preoccupation at home due to Father's illness. He sympathized but insisted that I appear in as many papers as I could. In all the papers I took, except in one, I stood first. I heaved a sigh of relief. I had no longer to bother about the sniggerings of the boys. My reputation in St. Stephen's was established.

When I was in the sixth year, father's health which had till then been steadily improving started to decline. We took him to Simla. But, in spite of all our care, he passed away after a severe haemorrhage towards the end of June 1929. Then followed the most distressing period of our lives. Grief-stricken, bewildered, in financial difficulties, we had to change our entire mode of living. We returned to Delhi and rented a very modest flat near the college. My younger brother had then joined the Hindu College. The house was depressing. We had never lived inside the city in such a congested area.

We curtailed all possible expenditure except on education. Mother struggled valiantly to see that our health and education did not suffer. We were greatly helped by three good friends, my cousin Jotin who lived in New Delhi, Mr Mukherjee, businessman and a close friend of my father, and Dr Basu, a class friend of my father, who lived near by, and who acted more or less as our guardian.

Mr Mukherjee and Dr Basu played the role of uncles to us in our distress. Our relatives felt somewhat apprehensive about getting involved with us. They knew we were a big family and father had not left us too well provided. Mother in any case was too proud to ask any one for help, and we, her children, were also determined to make good on our own. That year, none of our elder relatives cared to pay a visit to us except Mother's youngest brother who was a barrister practising in Kuala Lumpur in distant Malaya. His short visit heartened my mother greatly.

Academic Successes

All these months I had paid scant attention to my studies, and was mentally very disturbed. Our Principal, Mr Mukherjee, therefore, suggested to me to skip that year and take the examination the next year as, he said, my teachers did not want me to miss a good position. But I could not afford to wait a whole year. I, therefore, started working, somehow dragging my harassed mind to the studies. Two of my younger sisters and one brother were also to appear for the B.A. and Intermediate examinations. We all got through but none did too well.

I had topped the list of students in the History group. I was happy and relieved at not having to do the examination over again. This also brought me a gold medal.

After leaving college I worked for some months in a newly started school in Lahore. It was on the whole a pleasant experience. A noble incident of this period, which remains vivid in my memory, was the reaction in Lahore over the execution of Bhagat Singh, Raj Guru and Sukhdev. People were anxious to see if the efforts of Gandhiji would succeed in saving their lives. Then came the news that they had been taken to an unknown destination and executed. The relatives of the three victims, after a frantic search, discovered the place where their bodies had been cut up in pieces and burnt with petrol. The remains were brought and a mighty funeral procession wound its way through the streets of the city to the banks of the Ravi. I have rarely seen such an emotional upheaval! All of us spontaneously went and joined the procession. Anger against the Government was intense. The whole of Lahore seemed shaken by a storm.

I did not stay long in Lahore. I wanted a college job. During the vacation, I got offers to join either my old college, the Lahore College for Women—a Government job with a good pay scale-or the Benares Hindu University where the pay was even less than what I was getting in the school. But it was a National University. I chose the latter.

In the thirties, the atmosphere was surcharged with strong sentiments for the freedom struggle. My keen desire to join the movement was checked by my obligation to help Mother. Working in Benares would be some satisfaction. In July 1931, I joined the women's college as a lecturer in History. The Principal was Miss Asha Adhikari. Later, as Mrs Aryanayakam, she and her husband were the pioneers in carrying out Gandhiji's experiments and research in Basic Education at Wardha. We took to each other immediately.

The university was very much in the mainstream of the struggle. We had frequent strikes and political demonstrations. Though the staff was in full sympathy with the strikers, they had to make an effort to hold classes. The girls would, of course, join the strike, but they were in these days not bold enough to go out and take part in the demonstrations along with the boys. I told them that whenever there was a hartal or a strike, I would not take regular classes but give them a talk on the significance of our freedom struggle. This succeeded admirably; not only my own students but girls from the other classes flocked to my room. We used to have lively discussions and the students got a lesson in current History.

My younger sister, Hemani, got married that year to a young professor at St. Stephen's. Dr Sarvadaman Chawla, a brilliant mathematician. He joined the Benaras Hindu university for a while. It was nice to have them there.

During this time, I came in greater contact with Acharya Kripalani. He and Dr Verrier Elwin were touring UP. When they came to Benares they came to call on me. They were going to visit Sarnath and invited me to join them. I went along with them and enjoyed myself greatly. Their company was exhilarating. Both of them were men of sharp intellect and deep learning. Their conversation was racy, full of wit and humour. From then on whenever Kripalani came to Benares, he called on me. He came fairly often as the university was a good recruiting ground for volunteers for the political movements.

On 15 January 1934, North India felt a severe shock of earthquake. In Benares, the shock was so severe that we could see our houses tilt at an angle for a few seconds. The next day we got news of the terrible havoc in Bihar. The disaster had affected an area of 77,000 sq km. A population of a crore and a half had been affected. Some towns in North Bihar had been razed to the ground. Big fissures and chasms had occurred, throwing up water and sand. Thousands of acres of land had been rendered uncultivable. Lacs of people had become homeless and thousands had been killed or injured.

Contact with Gandhiji

The British Government, unable to cope with a disaster of this magnitude, released Dr. Rajendra Prasad from jail to organize the relief operations. Gandhiji camped at Patna. Congress workers, big and small, from all over India came to help in the relief work. When my classes were over and the students were preparing for the examinations, I took leave from the university and went there. This was the first time I came in close contact with Gandhiji and the Congress leaders. I was encouraged in this venture by Kripalani who was then spending all his time in Bihar. He had in the last few years become a very close friend of mine.

I was assigned to go and work in a village called Rampur Hari in Muzaffarpur District. Another lady and a young boy of about 16 formed our unit. We had to survey 10 villages and help the people of the area.

Jamnalal Bajaj came to like me very much and wanted me to leave the university and join the Mahila Ashram in Wardha. He had started this national institution to educate and train women for national service. At his invitation, I went on a short visit to Wardha. The Mahila Ashram was located among a group of buildings on a big compound. One was occupied by Gandhiji and his party. The life of the students appeared to me somewhat harsh and rigid. However, as Jamnalalji was pressing me, I was half inclined to take it up. Vinoba Bhave was, I think, the Chairman of the Board and had to approve of me. When I was taken to see him, he was fasting to expiate for the sin of two young people living in the ashram complex who had fallen in love with each other! These two were going about the ashram with hurt faces. The whole thing appeared to me rather atrocious. Vinoba's rigid attitude and extreme self-mortification somehow put me off from joining the Mahila Ashram.

In the last few years, Kripalani and I had been getting closer to each other. We exchanged letters regularly. His letters were wonderful, revealing the yearnings of a soul dedicated to freeing India from poverty and degradation. There was much in common in our ideas and outlook. This gradually developed into a strong attachment.

We decided to marry but the impediments were many. There was a great difference in age and he lived a life of extreme austerity and hardship. Mother was opposed as she wanted a life of ease and comfort for me, i.e., the life of a normal housewife. On the other side, his only sister Kiki reacted very strongly against the idea of her 'Sadhu' brother marrying at so advanced an age. He was in his forties at that time. She thought he would lose his reputation and all his life's work would be destroyed. She was a well-known and respected Congress worker in Sind.

'You will Break my Right Arm'

She wrote to Gandhiji. Gandhiji himself was opposed to the marriage. He was generally against his lieutenants and workers marrying. He thought family responsibilities diverted their attention from the work before them and weakened their ardour for the struggle. Gandhiji sent for me. I went to see him, a little afraid. But he had a wonderful capacity of putting people at ease. Further, no subject was taboo for him. So the talk was not the ordeal I thought it would be.

Early in the morning, while taking his walk, he spoke to me in a leisurely way, persuading me to give up the idea. He finally said, 'If you marry him, you will break my right arm.' I asked him why did he not think that, instead of losing one political worker, he would gain two. But he just brushed aside the idea and said: 'I have seen many cases. They just got embroiled in family and household.' I returned to Benares without arriving at any decision.

The marriage was delayed also because of Jawaharlal's long imprisonment. Kripalani and he were close friends then. He could not think of marriage while his friend was in prison. During this waiting period of over two years, Gandhiji called me two or three times to Wardha. Finally, I bowed to his wishes and agreed to give up the idea. Then he said: 'You have to give him up in thought, word and deed, have no contact, no letter even.' To that too I agreed. Then the next day, he came out with something more. He said, 'If you remain unhappy, it will hurt Kripalani. So you must marry someone else.' At this, I turned round and told him that what he was proposing was wrong, it would be unjust and immoral to do so. He had no answer to that. That ended our discussions.

Jamnalaji's sympathy was with us; he did some canvassing with Gandhiji for us. However, some time in early 1936, Gandhiji sent for me and told me that he had no objection to our marriage, but he would not be able to bless us, he could only pray for us. We were satisfied with his prayers. In April 1936, we got married according to Brahmo rites in Benares. From there we went to Allahabad where Jawaharlal's mother Swaroop Rani warmly received me with the gift of a very nice sari. At a wedding reception held in Anand Bhavan, our marriage was registered with Jawaharlal as one of the witnesses.

Kripalani had become the General Secretary of the Congress in 1934. The AICC Office up to this time was a modest affair, a mobile office shifting with each President to his home town. Kripalani built a proper office at Swaraj Bhavan with different departments, a library, etc. The General Secretary was responsible for the day-to-day running of the office. The President paid only occasional visits and was kept in touch by phone and by correspondence.

Yearning For Political Activity

Kripalani was living in a couple of rooms in Swaraj Bhawan in utmost austerity. He had hardly any belongings; he was doing mostly his own cooking. I joined him in this grand household of his! With my coming, things changed somewhat. I did not give up my university job for another two years I used to be in Allahabad only during the holidays. During the week-ends, whenever possible, we used to visit each other. This continued till April 1938, when I took one year's leave and came away to Allahabad. I resigned from my job in 1939.

Politically these were rather quiet years. I was keen to start political work. I used to feel small before all these veteran jail-goers as I had not graduated through jail life. Kripalani was not too keen for me to enter politics, he wanted me to do any work of my choice, not necessarily politics. He was not only my husband but also my political guide. Living close to him, I imbibed often unconsciously his way of thinking, of assessing situations, and even of public speaking. In the course of years, I have developed my own style of speaking and functioning but his early influence has left its indelible impression on me.

In Allahabad, I started doing political work at the lowest rung of the ladder as a worker of the ward Congress. But this little work at the ward level did not satisfy me. I, therefore, started working in the AICC Office. The Foreign Department had been started but there was no one to look after it. I took up the work. We published a fortnightly bulletin and sent it abroad to sympathizers of our freedom struggle, to newspapers, and various other bodies. We also published news of political struggles in other parts of the world in the Indian papers. We received and disseminated a good deal of news about the Chinese resistance. At that time, we felt great sympathy for the Chinese. Jawaharlal had developed friendship with Chiang Kai-shek. During the visit of General and Madame Chiang Kai-shek to Allahabad we held a reception in their honour.

After I had worked as Secretary of the Foreign Department for some months, Dr Rammanohar Lohia joined the AICC and took charge of the department. He was a brilliant young man recently returned from Europe. The Congress then thought of organizing a regular women's department in the AICC as well as at the provincial levels. I was asked to take up the work. This meant not only office work at Swaraj Bhavan but a good deal of touring. After a few months of sustained work, a structure was built with branches in all the Provinces.

The quiet life at Swaraj Bhawan was coming to an end. The Second World War had started. As soon as England declared war on Germany, the Viceroy, on behalf of India, committed our country to the war. The Congress Working Committee declared on 14 September that a 'free and democratic India would associate itself with the free nations for mutual defence against aggression.' They invited the Government to declare their war aims and their views on democracy and how they would apply to India during the duration of the war and after. But the Viceroy was unable to give any assurance of freedom in the future. The Congress then declared that India could not participate in the war effort and asked the provincial ministries which had come to power in 1937 to resign.

In March 1940, at the Ramgargh (Bihar) Session of the Congress, which was held in the midst of heavy rain and storm, it was decided to launch Individual Satyagraha. Gandhiji took a few months to prepare the country and then started Individual Civil Disobedience, instead of a mass movement. He selected a list of satyagrahis who had to go and address public meetings asking people to withhold support to the war effort of the Government. The satyagrahis have previous intimation to the District Magistrate about the time and place of the meeting [sic]. Vinobaji was chosen as the first satyagrahi.

Keen to Court Arrest

I was very keen to court arrest. So my name was sent early to him in the UP list. I offered satyagraha in December from Faizabad district. I came and stayed in Faizabad for some months and organized this work. On the day previous to my arrest, Kripalani and myself reached Faizabad and stayed with a friend, Shri Vishnu Narain, an old student of Kripalani belonging to one of the leading families of the town. I had informed the magistrate of my intention to address a public meeting the next day at 5 p.m. But early in the morning, while it was still dark, I woke up to the sound of heavy boots marching near the verandah. The police had arrived. Kripalaniji and Vishnuji accompanied me to the jail. My trial was held within the jail and I was awarded one year's imprisonment and a fine of Rs. 200.

Soon I was transferred to Lucknow Central Jail where women political prisoners were concentrated. We had barracks in separate yards for the political prisoners. Life was more interesting. We kept ourselves busy reading, writing, sewing, gardening, etc. I used to teach some of the younger girls. Most of the other women had three to six months' sentences. So they came and went.

The most oppressive thing in jail is the uniform drabness of the surroundings unrelieved for months. Our troubles with the authorities were mainly over shortage of rations which were mostly stolen in transit. But somehow we managed, as we cooked the food ourselves. We had a common kitchen and took turns at cooking. We, at least, thereby had the satisfaction of eating clean food. The letters were another source of irritation. The fortnightly letter due to us was usually badly mutilated and sometimes held back by the censors. Towards the end of my term, I was left alone, the others having been releazed. My health was not good. I was suffering from amoebiasis and low temperature. But the jail authorities had brushed aside my complaints as malingering, though I had lost 16 Ib!

On my release after a year, I stepped into a different political atmosphere. Feeling against the Government ran high. We were, therefore, constantly out touring the country. I resumed my work in the Women's Department, but I received frequent invitations from the different Provincial Congress Committees to attend their functions and undertake propaganda tours. By this time, I had become a fairly fluent speaker in Hindi. So I was kept very busy.

The theatre of war had now shifted to Asia. The British administration started to withdraw before the advancing Japanese forces. We were faced with the possibility of the British retreating, leaving us unprepared to face the Japanese invasion. They had already taken steps to implement the scorched-earth policy on the eastern borders and in the Provinces of Assam and Bengal. Means of communication had been disrupted. Even boats, bullock-carts and cycles had been destroyed. Standing crops had been burnt. Our leaders were anxious to be invested with political power in order to organize the defence of the nation against the threatened Japanese invasion.

Churchill, who did not want to 'preside over the liquidation of the British Empire' under pressure from Roosevelt and the British Labour Party at last agreed to negotiate a settlement with the Indians. He sent Stafford Cripps with a formula for a settlement. The formula was suspect in the eyes of our leaders in several respects. Their scheme did not hold out a promise of Independence in future. There was also the possibility of dividing India into segments. A veto was being given to the minorities. The proposed ministers were being offered no real power for the defence of the country. Gandhiji soon saw through the hollowness of the scheme and said so frankly to Cripps. The Working Committee, however, pursued the matter hopefully a little longer. The failure of the Cripps Mission aggravated the situation. It also decided to hold the next meeting on 7 August in Bombay.

The intervening months were used by Gandhiji to educate the people about the need to build up national resistance against the Japanese and the desirability of the withdrawal of the British to enable us to defend ourselves.

On 7 August 1942, we all gathered in Bombay at the historic AICC meeting. My husband and I were the guests of Sardar Patel at his son's flat on Marine Drive. On 8 August the famous Quit India resolution was passed. Gandhiji exhorted us to 'Do or Die'. The session lasted till late in the night. Early in the morning, at about 3.30 a.m., the doorbell buzzed loud and persistent. We woke up with a start and knew that the police had arrived. The leaders were not expecting arrest so soon, as Gandhiji had kept the door open for further negotiations. Later events indicated that preparations had been made all over the country for the arrest of all important Congress leaders and workers with severe repression to follow. We tried to telephone Gandhiji and others but found that all the lines had been cut.

Sardar and Kripalani were arrested and taken away. I tried to get some last-minute instructions from Kripalani but all that he could say then was to try to continue the struggle from Bombay. We rushed to Birla House and were told by Pyarelal and Kasturba that Gandhiji had also been arrested, so also all the other big leaders. The whole morning, news of arrests poured in from all quarters. We soon learnt that all the Bombay leaders as well as the leaders in other States were in jail. Then news came that Gandhiji and his party were detained at Poona and taken to the Aga Khan Palace. The train with the other members of the Working Committee had gone further South to an unknown destination. For about a fortnight, we had no news of these leaders. Then we learnt with some relief that they were all together in the Ahmednagar Fort.

Turmoil in Bombay

The whole of Bombay was in turmoil. Attempts at holding meetings and processions were thwarted with lathi-charges and tear gas. Meanwhile, a few others and I met privately to chalk out our future course of action. Sadiq Ali was then the Office Secretary. Some members of the AICC staff were also in Bombay. We decided to run an underground office. Between the whole lot of us, we had about Rs. 300 (our bank accounts were frozen). The AICC Office in Swaraj Bhawan was sealed, so also the BPCC Office where the money for current expenses had been deposited. Dayabhai, Sardar's son, and some other friends agreed to raise funds. My husband's nephew Girdhari left his home and work at Nagpur and joined me in Bombay.

The pent-up feelings of the people burst forth in nationwide demonstrations and protest meetings at the news of the sudden arrest of Gandhiji and all the leaders. Government's violent repression was answered with violence. All known workers were arrested; only those of us, whose warrants were issued in their home States but happened to be out of the State at that time, could go underground and continue the movement. Our AICC Office was located in a few houses. We lived scattered in different places and met secretly.

We soon started gathering news and issuing bulletins. As for instructions, people did not wait for them. In their anger in the first outburst, they did just what they liked. There was extensive sabotage of Railway and other Government property, particularly in Bihar, Bengal, some parts of UP and Maharashtra. In a few days' time, our office was organized. A number of friends, who had no previous connection with the Congress and were, therefore, not under watch by the police, acted as our messengers and couriers. Some of them were smart young men and women belonging to the fashionable set. We established links with all the active groups in the Provinces. Our aim was to bring the Government to a standstill by any method excluding violence. The country had somehow automatically taken to sabotage of government property. Some time later, Lohia, Aruna Asaf Ali and Achchyut Patwardhan, one by one, appeared on the Bombay scene and joined our group.

Underground Broadcasts

Mainly through Lohia's efforts, we succeeded in setting up an underground Radio Station. Usha Mehta, who is now teaching Political Science in Bombay University, was our announcer. We had to shift the transmitting equipment from house to house in quick succession in order to escape the police. All news as banned by the Government was put across by our Radio. It functioned for nearly two months before the police finally broke into the house and arrested Usha while she was announcing. This brave young girl was given a tough time during police interrogation and then thrown into prison for a long duration.

We were trying to send the news of the brutal repression in India to people abroad. Sometimes we succeeded in doing so through innocuous-looking people travelling abroad. Terribly brutal repression had taken place in Bihar, in some pockets of UP like Balia and in Midnapur in Bengal. Some indignant speeches were made in the Central Assembly by a few courageous Indian members. We wanted to publish a book with all the facts and figures. But it was a sizable task beyond our ability. Ramnath Goenka came to our rescue. In the strictest of secrecy in his press in Madras, it was printed in one night and despatched in suitcases to Delhi and Bombay. Some were smuggled out of India. It was a tremendously efficient and brave job by him.

We decided to hold a demonstration in Delhi on 26 January 1943. Police vigilance was very strict and most of the workers were in jail. New batches had to be found for the demonstration. I came down from Bombay to organize this demonstration. As Delhi was too hot for me, I stayed in a humble house in Brindaban as a pious lady on a religious pilgrimage. My young host was an underground worker not yet known to the police. Through him and a few other young men, I maintained contact with Delhi. We succeeded in holding a fair-sized demonstration and sent a number of people to jail.

Gradually, the underground workers were picked up one by one and the watch for the hard core running the Central Office was increased. Warrants had been issued for us in a number of Provinces. The movement was flagging due to severe repression. Properties were confiscated, family members of workers were tortured. I remember one day a tall big UP peasant came to see me. I asked him what he wanted. He just sat down and showed me the soles of his feet. They were scarred and burnt in long ridges! I was shocked and asked him how it had happened. He said he was one of the underground workers, the last link of the chain at the grass-roots level. The police, after capturing him, had tortured him to get information.

Among other things, they made him stand on an iron sheet placed over a fire; even if he curled up his toes unable to bear the heat, they hit his feet with a stick. His soles were badly burnt, but he did not divulge anything to the police. But later he sought me out just to tell me. The courage and sacrifice of the ordinary workers at the lowest level was tremendous. I met this man again, when I was Chief Minister of UP. I am sure in the Tamrapatra racket, his name will not be there since today he is not with the Indira Congress!

Now a controversy arose about the use of violence by the people in their fight against the government. Some of the orthodox Congressmen arrested on August 8 had been released. They disapproved of all that had been done in the first flush of anger by the people, as well as the continuance of the sabotage programme.

At this time, the news came of Gandhiji's fast in the Aga Khan Palace. A time came when we thought he would surely die. He was allowed to see visitors. I decided that I would see him even if I got arrested. I just walked into the room of H.V.R. Ienger (then Home Secretary of Bombay). I had not divulged my identity to his PA but I told Ienger who I was and that I knew there were warrants against me, but I must see Gandhiji. My request to him was that he could arrest me only after I had seen Gandhiji but not before. I did not know how he agreed. Later, reading an article of his, I learnt that he had consulted the Governor who gave me 24 hours' respite. I reached Poona with the family members of a Sindhi friend, Pratap Dayaldas. I too was somewhat smartly dressed so as to be inconspicuous among the smart ladies of his family.

At the interview, Bapu was surprised to see me. He asked: 'Tu kaise aa gayi?' (How did you come?) I just replied: 'I managed to come.' I had thought he would take me to task for the wrong methods used by us as complaints about the underground leaders had reached him. But he did not say anything. He asked a few questions. Anyhow, he was too weak to speak much. That very evening, I left Poona again with the same family group. I had found a family group to be the best camouflage. Once I had travelled with a friend's small baby from Calcutta to Bombay. The baby was being sent and I too had to go. It was a good arrangement. Only a servant travelled to rescue the baby in case I was detected and arrested on the way.

In March 1944, reports came from Bihar that the work was flagging. I decided to go there. I had been to Patna several times. Therefore, there was a risk of my being detected. I travelled with two young children of a friend. They were going to Calcutta, while I was to detrain at Patna. A Communist worker got into the compartment at Kanpur. He somehow recognized me and got it confirmed by talking to one of the children. The Communists were then fighting the 'People's War' in collaboration with the British Imperialists. We used to be as wary of them as of the CID. I detrained at Patna at 2 a.m. I was to stay with a lawyer friend, but I told those who had come to receive me what had happened and asked them to take me to some other house. Sure enough, before dawn, the house where I as to stay was raided by the police. I was in Patna for a week, changing house every night.

My cousin S.N. Mazumdar was a senior ICS Officer of the Bihar Government. My mother and youngest brother and sister were then visiting him. They wanted me to come and spend a night with them. I knew it was risky to do so, but I was utterly tired of underground life. The movement had more or less petered out. With difficulty, we were able occasionally to put up some demonstrations. The controversy over violence and non-violence had also discouraged us. I, therefore, did not care.

I slept there one night. Early in the morning, three or four truckloads of policemen surrounded the house. My poet cousin later got it in the neck from the Governor. I was taken to Patna Jail and kept for an hour with Rajen Babu, as they had to make some suitable arrangements for me. So I posted Rajen Babu with the up-to-date information. I was in Patna Jail for a month and then sent to Lucknow, my old place of detention. The other political prisoners had been shifted overnight to the middle yard. They were told that a 'dangerous prisoner' was coming. They were naturally waiting anxiously to see who the 'dangerous prisoner' was and were shocked when they saw me.

Police Interrogation

There were warrants against me in almost all the Provinces. So police from all these Provinces came to interrogate me I would spent hours in the office with a number of CID men flinging questions at me. As almost all of the original group of workers had been arrested and some of them had made incriminating statements, it was quite a job for me to dodge their questions and, at the same time, give plausible replies. Alone in the barracks, I would ponder over the next day's questions and the answers I would make.

It was a frightening time. I was expecting a trial and a harsh sentence but, after a month, they decided to detain me indefinitely.

I remained in Lucknow Prison till July 1945 when, after the settlement with the British, all the political prisoners were released.

We reached Haimchar, a big village in the district of Tipperah, near Noakhali. Here too there had been rioting. A few terror-stricken Hindus, who were hiding among the burnt ruins of their houses, came out to tell us the story of their sufferings. Two dead bodies lay exposed on a village path. We next visited Choumuhani in Noakhali. It is a railway station, about 16 miles from the main area of trouble, hence it was not affected by the riots. With this place as our headquarters, we walked to Dattapara, 16 miles away, which also was not affected. About 5,000 refugees had gathered in the house of a zamindar, Shri Guha Roy, who had opened his granary to feed them. Harrowing tales were recounted to us by the refugees there. We were told about kidnapping of girls and their forcible marriages to Muslims. We were informed that a girl, Arati, had been forcibly taken away to the house of a Muslim leader of a village and married to his son. The next day, a Deputy Minister and the District Magistrate, an Irishman, Mr Machinery, came to see us. Kripalani and others spoke to them, while I listened to the conversation. When Kripalani told him of girls being kidnapped and forcibly married to Muslims, his cool reply was that such marriages were willing unions between young people who had fallen in love with each other! At this, I flew into a temper and told him that not a single marriage was case of willing union of the young Hindu girls. They were all dastardly crimes against women and I cited Arati's case. My anger somehow stirred him out of his complacency. He noted down the information given by me. Late in the evening he returned and started shouting from the gate of our house, 'Mrs Kripalani! See whom I have brought.' I rushed out and asked, 'Have you brought Arati?' He said, 'Yes, I have brought the girl'. She stayed with us.

Next day he visited the house of the Muslim concerned. He asked the girl if she had been forcibly married. She said 'no' in the presence of the Muslim family. Then a Bengali journalist, accompanying the magistrate, took her aside and told her not to be afraid but to tell the truth, as she was in the presence of the officer. At this, she burst into loud sobbing and said that they had threatened to kill her parents if they did not hand her over to the Muslims. We brought the girl back with us.

The news of Arati's rescue spread like lightning through the little town. This was the first good thing that had happened to the Hindus since the riot broke out.

Our short survey of the riot-affected area was over and we were to leave early next morning for Delhi. But the Hindus of Choumuhani implored us that at least I should stay longer to help them, even though Kripalani must go. I had not come prepared to stay long, and Kripalani had his own misgivings about leaving me there to work alone in this dangerous area. However, we both could not disappoint the people, to whom our visit had come as the first ray of hope.

Kripalani returned to make his report to Gandhiji and inform the country of what the people had suffered. Next day I decided to shift my headquarters to Dattapara. I became the guest of the zamindar, whom I have mentioned earlier. We collected some brave young men, from among the refugees who had gathered there, to form a volunteer corps. They were allocated different duties in this makeshift camp, such as supervision, sanitation, distribution of provisions and kitchen work.

Virtual Prisoners

A group of strong young men and I took up rescue work as well. In each village, there would be just a few Hindu houses, where the families of those who had suffered would be living virtually as prisoners—surrounded by their Muslim persecutors. The belongings which they could salvage, their cattle, even their womenfolk, were crowded into these houses. Many Hindus had been forcibly converted. The men were not allowed to wear dhotis, but were obliged to cut them into two and wear them as *lungis* or *tehmad*. *Sindur* was wiped off the foreheads of married women and their shell bangles the sign that their husbands were living were broken. In short they were leading a life of utter terror and moral degradation.

We started every morning to cover as many villages as possible and to rescue the families marooned among the inimical Muslims. Sometimes, the men preferred to stay with the Muslims and send away their womenfolk. The following account given by a young girl from a rich family who somehow had managed to escape should be revealing:

One morning a group of Muslims came to her house and threatened that, if they were not given Rs. 500, the members of the house would be murdered, their property looted and their house burnt. The money was paid. After sometime, a large crowd surrounded the house. The eldest son of the family tried his best to pacify the mob and was attacked by a long curved knife called a *dao*. The grandfather was thrown on the floor and was belaboured with bamboos. The son was forcibly placed on the prostrate body of the father. The mother fell over the son to save him from the lathi blows and pleaded with the rioters not to kill him. She received a lathi blow that rendered her unconscious.

The girl then rushed out of the room where she was hiding and gave them the ornaments of the family and Rs. 400 in cash to save her parents. The men took the ornaments and the money and yet her father was given a blow which killed him.

There were other similarly harrowing stories. In one case I remember, a solitary well-to-do family was surrounded for nearly a month by the Muslims. The family at last surrendered and was forcibly converted. Their fear was that, during the ensuing Id day, they would be compelled to eat beef. They believed that, once they had eaten beef, all hope of returning to the Hindu fold would be lost. To such depths of superstition has Hindu society fallen! When we reached the gate of the house, the head of the family, an elderly man dressed like a Muslim with a small growth of beard, rushed to me, fell on the ground, with his arms stretched, doing *sashtanga pranam*, and shouted; 'Ma, you have come at last to save us!' He left the house and his property and, along with his family, came away with us.

Ironically enough, a day after reaching the camp, there was some trouble. The old man refused to have food from the common kitchen and said that since he belonged to a high caste he could not eat food touched by all and sundry! I pointed out to him that for nearly a month he had been converted to Islam and was eating food touched by Muslims and here he was objecting to food served by his co-religionists! His cool reply was: 'That was my *apat kalin dharma* (my conduct in distress); now when I am in my own community, I follow its rules.' That is caste logic!

Almost simultaneously with my arrival, a small unit of soldiers under a Muslim O.C. and a young British officer was posted at Dattapara. Unfortunately, most of the soldiers sent were Muslims. I tried to be on ever friendly terms with the two officers in order to get help in the rescue work. They did not directly help me but in the beginning were quite cooperative. At my request, they would organize their route marches along the direction I suggested. I used to cover 15 to 20 miles every day. Sometimes, the soldiers would complain that I was walking too fast! I was driven by my intense anxiety to reach as many isolated and beleaguered Hindu families as quickly as possible.

A People Divided

The soldiers, naturally, were not driven by any such anxiety or urgency. With their coming, killing, looting and arson and had stopped but petty thieving, harassment, terrorization, as also the molestation of Hindu women, continued. The Muslims soon succeeded in poisoning the minds of the Muslim soldiers and they began being nasty and uncoopertaive. I finally decided not to approach them for any help and went on with my work with my volunteers.

On the Id day, which the Hindus were dreading, I decided to call on some of the Muslims. I realized that the Hindus would have to live there without the protection of the police and the army, which would soon be withdrawn. Ultimately, they would have to live on the goodwill of the neighbours in the majority community. Fortunately, Id passed off without much trouble.

From then on came a change in our method of work. We tried to win the Muslims' goodwill, a tough task by any standard. The poison of ill-will and hatred, preached by the Muslim League leaders and the Mullas and Maulvis, had gone very deep. But even those who had participated in killing, looting and arson were afraid of the high officials. The Government of Bengal, under pressure from the Centre, was making some show of a police inquiry into the excesses and crimes committed.

The social order having been destroyed, even the Muslims, especially the poor, had to suffer. All the markets, schools, hospitals and dispensaries had been destroyed. Bullocks had been killed and eaten up and ploughs had been burnt. Even boats and fishing nets had been destroyed. Normal life was totally disrupted. Poor Muslim families were starving. Only the few at the top, who were bloated with looted goods, had gained by the riots. I had to render assistance to the Muslims as well as the Hindus.

No help could come from Delhi. It was plagued with a Government divided in itself. The League representatives were both in the Government and in the Opposition. I set up a committee with local men of influence; one of them contributed Rs. 4,000; grain was contributed by many; the most generous had been the Guha Roys. They had been feeding, as I said, more than 6,000 refugees.

Soon people from Calcutta, leaders, press reporters, representatives of relief societies and a number of young volunteers, girls and boys, started to come. Doctors and medicines also arrived. We started to set up small centres, spread over the whole of the affected area. There was a loose kind of coordination among the different centres. In course of time, a big batch of volunteers started to work with me. I organised 20 centres we did both relief and rehabilitation work. We compelled the Government to give some compensation to the affected people. The assessment of their losses was based on our reports and according to lists submitted by us. The distribution was done under our direct supervision. For some reason, which we did not understand, Gandhiji was not in favour of our getting *ex gratia* grants from Government for our work.

After I had been in Noakhali for about three weeks, Gandhiji was able to come. On his arrival, we met him at Choumuhani. Shri Jogendra Mozumdar, a wholesale grain merchant of the town, was host to him and all who had come with him.

I gave Bapu a report of my work and my assessment of the situation. According to me, most of the Hindus were demoralized. They had lost all hope, and the Muslims, barring very few, had turned into antisocial goondas. Gandhiji, of course, did not agree with me. He never lost faith in the basic goodness of human nature!

He decided to enter the riot-affected area from Dattapara, which was our headquarters, and asked me how many people he should bring with him! I told him to bring a small party, as we were very short of food, since the Government had not yet started supplying it. We had difficulty about water as well. For Gandhiji's tub-bath, we repaired an old hard-pump. From somewhere, the Guha Roys produced an enamel bathtub which we had kept in a small room adjoining his room on the first floor. The water was taken to the bath by several young men standing in a line from the hand-pump to the bathroom. There was no shortage of manpower then!

As soon as Gandhiji arrived, he made a radical change in our method of work. He said we should not try to evacuate people, but gather them in camps. Our workers, singly or in small units, should spread out all over the affected area and do all they could among the Muslims and the Hindus to bring about amity between the two communities.

The Gandhian Way

I would like to relate here a story that shows Gandhiji helped the poor and the needy. He asked me if I gave work to those whom I rendered help. I said No. He said, 'That is wrong. You are depriving these poor people of what is left to them—their self-respect.' I said, 'Bapu, how can I ask a poor woman, with a babe in her arms, to work to get help and what work is there that I can give her?' He said, 'Put a stone in place of your heart and tell her to dig a hole, which may be filled afterwards. But never give the poor free doles?'

Gandhiji addressed the first prayer meeting at Dattapara to a large gathering, where he made this appeal and announced that as an expiation for the hatred and violence indulged in by his 'brothers, the Muslims', but would do *padayatra* over the entire area.

Thus started Bapu's famous tour in Noakhali, his peace mission. Though one or two places came to be regarded as his headquarters, he was constantly on the move. Thousands flocked to his evening prayer meetings. His hosts during the tour were both Hindus and Muslims. His day's route was announced beforehand. Volunteers and villagers would try to prepare the route, filling in the ditches, clearing the undergrowth. But often we would find that the Muslims, who were inimical to his peace mission, had, during the night, dirtied the paths by throwing night soil. They would even spread broken glass, thorns, etc. He bore all his with uncomplaining patience. He even gave up his *chappals* and walked barefoot. One day, I asked him, 'Is it necessary that you walk barefoot?' His reply was: 'Yes, here it befits me to walk barefoot.' These few words of his made me realize the depth of his sorrow over the happenings in Noakhali.

After that, we all spread out in small groups to different centres. I had, as I said, 20 centres under my supervision. With a couple of other workers, I shifted to a village, about five miles from Dattapara, which had been completely burnt by the rioters. All the Hindus families had fled, except a few of the very poor. We occupied a burnt-out house. Nothing was there except the masonry platforms which had constituted the floor. The roofs of these houses were usually of corrugated iron sheets and several of these were lying around half-burnt. With these we managed to put up some shacks—to live and to work in. We borrowed a few utensils from the

Guha Roys and the minimum of bedding. The winter nights were very cold under tin roofs. However, thick spreads of paddy straw served as our mattresses and kept us warm.

The Riots Spread

When I had been in Noakhali for about seven months, disturbing reports of the outbreak of communal riots in the NWFP and the Punjab reached us. It was a time of great distress for all of us who had worked for the freedom of the country. The talks with the authorities, regarding the transfer of power, were not proceeding smoothly. The Muslim League was deliberately fanning the flames of communal hatred and violence. These levers were used by them to pressure a Government which needed no pressure to carry out the wishes of the League. During the last war with Pakistan, Mountbatten said he had been against Partition, but Jinnah had wanted it. The mighty empire which could successfully fight Hitler's Germany was afraid of Jinnah!

In April 1947, during one of my occasional visits to Delhi, I found Kripalani getting ready to visit Kashmir, in an effort to bring about some sort of a rapproachment between the Maharaja and Sheikh Abdullah, who was in prison. Jawaharlal was keen on the release of the Sheikh. Earlier, he had tried to go to Kashmir himself, but on the borders he was arrested by the Kashmir Government. He was released on the intervention of the Viceory, because, as Congress President, he was needed for the talks that were in progress between the political parties and the Government. Everybody was anxious that the question of accession of Kashmir to India be settled. It was thought that if Sheikh Abdullah were released, he might bring his pressure, and that of the people of the Valley, to bear on the Maharaja to agree to Kashmir's joining India. This was a vain hope. String were being pulled by the foreign Government. Neither the Maharaja nor Abdullah nor the people counted.

I decided to accompany Kripalani. We went to Kashmir via Lahore and Rawalpindi. At Lahore, we heard ominous rumours about the Muslim League's activities and its vendetta against the Hindus and the Sikhs. It was said that worse things had happened there than in Calcutta, Noakhali and Bihar. We had talks with the leaders of Punjab. Lahore was in the midst of constant communal rioting. But the two parties, the Hindus and the Muslims, were matched there. There were rumours that something like Noakhali was happening in the rural areas around Rawalpindi. The Hindus and the Sikhs living there were being literally wiped out. We learnt that the Governor and the British officers refused to give them any protection. When approached, they asked the suffering people to go to Gandhiji for protection!

The whole of Rawalpindi was like a vast refugee camp. We heard about the sufferings of the people and visited some villages where not a Hindu or Sikh was left. We saw the village Kallar Dhuberal, where there had been systematic massacre of the members of the minority communities. These villages looked like small towns with houses and space built of pucca bricks.

Everywhere, we saw broken safes lying. This opulence was the result of the two World Wars. It was the area from which Indian Jawans were recruited. The Hindus and Sikhs were fighting men, but what could they do against such odds! We were shown the deep well where a brave Sikh lady, with about 150 of her companions, had jumped to death, after reciting *japjee*, too save their honour. In one house, the Sikh and Hindu children of the village had been collected and burnt alive! One could see the bones of the little ones scattered in the place. We were told stories of great courage shown by men and women, facing imminent death.

After going round for three days, we left of Kashmir. Kripalani's mission there turned out to be a futile endeavour. The Maharaja was virtually a prisoner of the British. His Dewan, Prime Minister Kak, was a British agent, with an English wife. He kept the Maharaja under such a rigorous watch that nobody, who had anything to do with public affairs, could meet and talk to him, except in his presence. We were unable to meet the Maharaja in Srinagar. He was going to Jammu and we had to follow him in haste.

The Maharani, however, was a woman of some spirit. She invited us to lunch and manoeuvred to leave Kripalani and the Maharaja alone together for some time to enable them to talk without the presence of Kak. However, nothing came of the talk, as the Maharaja was too tied up with the British to take any initiative and make any move. The Maharani gave me a cheque for Rs 25,000 for my refugee relief work. This was represented to Jawaharlal by the Kashmir leaders as being meant to deflect us from our mission. Jawaharlal, in those days, was so enamoured of these leaders that he seemed to have believed them and did not ask Kripalani about what had happened during his visit.

On my return to Delhi, I met Bapu and conveyed to him what I had seen and the great shock and horror I had felt. He heard me with great patience and was deeply moved by my report. That evening, while talking to the leaders, he told them that, before reading my report, he did not have a full idea of the grimness and horror of the situation.

I was too mentally disturbed with what I had heard and seen in the

North-West to go back and work in Noakhali. Though the need for work was still there, life and more or less taken on a quiet tenor. There was no active lawlessness and crime.

May and June 1947 were months of great political significance. We were all on tenterhooks to see what would be the outcome of the talks going on between the new Viceroy, Mountbatten and the Indian leaders.

Partition!

It was at last decided to partition India. Therefore, I had even less inclination to go back to Noakhali. I paid a last visit there, to make the necessary arrangements for the continuation of what could be done, under the changed conditions, and then returned to Delhi.

By July, refugees from West Punjab and NWFP started to come to Delhi. It started as a trickle but soon assumed the proportions of an avalanche. Thousands poured into the city, presenting a living picture of torture and outrage of every description. They came in a horror-struck and dazed condition.

As there was no agency to look after the refugees, as Congress President, Kripalani appointed a Relief Committee, with Rajendra Basu as President and myself as General Secretary. Some prominent local Congressmen as well as officers, the DC and the ADM, were also members of this Committee. Thus started our marathon work of relief and rehabilitation of the refugees coming from NWFP, Punjab and Sind.

Our Committee worked for a number of years. We started modestly with a small camp at the eastern end of Chandni Chowk, outside the Diwan Hall and opposite the main gate of the Red Fort. (This place is now occupied by the Lajpat Rai Market.) In a couple of days the camp became overcrowded and we had to find some more spacious accommodation. Another reason for deciding to shift the refugees from the congested city area was that we came to know that some of the refugees were thinking of wreaking vengeance on the Muslims living near by for the misery they had suffered. Some Muslim shops were looted and some Muslims, too, were murdered. In a tense atmosphere, in a situation where it was difficult to maintain law and order, our task was none too easy. We did not want to take the risk of having a large number of refugees, full of understandable resentment, anger and hate, disturb the peace in the capital.

Setting up Camp

The DC, Shri Randhawa, an energetic officer, suggested that we shift the refugees to the old unused police barracks in the Kingsway Camp. These needed immediate repairs and we did not have money for it, as every pie collected was spent on the purchase of food and medicines. I drew Rs 3,000 from my personal account and asked my workers to go ahead and carry out the minimum necessary repairs. But when the barracks were ready, it became a job to persuade the refugees to shift to the place as it was rather out of the way.

For three days, the buses would go to fetch them and return empty, as no one would get into them. Rather, some of the refugees would hold out threats to the workers who went with the buses. On the fourth morning, I went personally and explained to them the reasons for shifting them—the need for more accommodation and to prevent some anti-social elements from making trouble. But nothing could persuade them to shift till I threatened them with police action. Even then, only some of them agreed to go. Once the movement started, however, they all followed suit.

Within a few weeks we had twenty-four thousand refugees in the Kingsway Camp and we had to find another area to accommodate the new arrivals. We then discovered a vacant spot near the Kalkaji Temple and soon a township of tents went up there to accommodate them. Both these places still continue as refugees colonies.

By December, the Delhi administration had set up the Department of Relief and Rehabilitation and were willing to take over the camps. Our newly established Swaraj Government was too preoccupied with political matters to attend to the work of relief and rehabilitation of the refugees. The tremendous task of bringing out the oppressed and tortured Hindus and Sikhs out of Pakistan and sending the Muslims, who wanted to leave for Pakistan, was taking up all our energies. I sometimes returned home at midnight.

Though other relief organizations sprang up afterwards, the most important and well organized was ours. About 300 young men and women were working with me day and night as volunteers. Funds started coming in, as soon as people saw the dimension of our task. Our reception centre was in a building opposite the Railway Station, used for the soldiers during the war. It was known as the Wavell Canteen. We had to run a huge kitchen there to provide the refugees with their first meal on arrival. The warmth and generosity with which Delhi citizens responded to my appeal over the radio for cooked food was most gratifying. Villages would bring chapatis, while dal and vegetables would be supplied by local dhabawalas.

Saga of Service

Once, we got news that the refugees in Kala Camp in Rawalpindi, waiting to be transferred to India, were going without food. We decided to send a planeload of chapatis. I just made an appeal and women from various localities in Delhi in no time contributed four thousand chapatis and dal, to be flown over to Rawalpindi. The large-heartedness and affection with which people helped the sufferers constituted a veritable saga of service!

The refugees had gone to other places too, so we spread our activities, though on a smaller scale, to East Punjab, Rajasthan, UP and Madhya Pradesh. Two of our work centres, with local help, were established in distant Bangalore and Madras, where some refugees had managed to reach. We organized handicraft centres to provide work to a limited number of men and women. At one time we gave employment to more than two thousand men and women in the Kingsway and other camps in Delhi.

Another piece of work we took up on a large scale was house building. After some months, the tents were becoming torn and ragged and we were not able to get enough replacements from the military. Vinoba Bhave came to Delhi and addressed our committee. While discussing the housing problem, a suggestion was made that we start building some *kachcha* houses for the refugees. This was because whenever we approached the Central PWD, even for putting up temporary barracks, they refused to undertake the work, on the plea of shortage of building materials—bricks, cement, etc. We then started the manufacture of *kachcha* bricks in the Kingsway Camp. Soon we were able to secure pucca bricks, cement, etc., and used these for new constructions.

Corruption!

Work in this new field brought us varied experience. We acquired direct knowledge of the graft that goes on in the Public Works Department of the Government. Their work is done through contractors and approved and certified as satisfactory by the officials of the Department. Strangely enough, our buildings were also required to be certified as fit by official engineers and overseers of the Department. Normally, before certifying and buildings as fit, the officials had to be given some gratification. The Relief Committee had neither the intention of encouraging the corrupt system, nor the money to pay. The result was that every time a building was ready, I personally had to move the highest authorities in the Department, sometimes even the Ministers, to get the necessary certificates of fitness for our buildings.

I recall an interesting episode of this period. A few months later, Lady Mountbatten, along with some fashionable ladies, the wives of high Indian officials, started a Refugee Relief Committee. She wrote informing me that I could apply to her Committee for any help I needed. I could only smile at such ignorance and assumption of superiority in our foreign rulers. I took the letter to Gandhiji, who told me to ignore it.

Election to up Assembly

In the winter of 1947, I was elected a member of the Legislative Assembly in UP. Since I was still mostly engaged in refugee work, my attendance in the Assembly was not continuous. Though work in the Assembly kept me away from Kripalani, he did not mind it. He never wanted me to hover around him. He always said that I must live my own life.

I was soon elected a member of the Constituent Assembly from the UP assembly constituency. I could not attend its sitting regularly. But whenever I was in Delhi for some time, I took interest in the work. I had taught Constitutional History as a lecturer in the Women's College of the Benaras Hindu University.

The Constituent Assembly was soon transformed into India's first Lok Sabha. Since 1946, my main preoccupation had been the refugees. I spoke in Parliament on the Refugee Question. Thakurdas Bhargava, Dr Choitram Gidwani, Lala Achintram, a few other members and I formed group in the Lok Sabha and espoused the cause of the refugees in the House. In the beginning, Jawaharlal was opposed to giving any compensation to them, for the losses they had suffered for no fault of theirs, and was willing to make some *ex-gratia* payment only. However, we fought such a pitched battle inside and outside Parliament that he finally gave in. A scheme of paying compensation on the basis of properties left and lost by the refugees in Pakistan was evolved. I soon found myself on almost all the important committees appointed by the Government, for dealing with the multifarious problems of the refugees.

Influx

When there were communal riots in East Pakistan and Hindu refugees started to pour into Assam, Bengal and Bihar, a Parliamentary Committee, with myself as Chairman, went out to tour the area, to assess the losses the refugees had suffered and to suggest measures for their relief and rehabilitation. But though the Bengali refugees were living in camps, there were no proposals for their permanent settlement, as Jawaharlal thought that they would go back. The problem of their permanent settlement remained hanging for a long time.

—*Sucheta Kripalani* (1993)

Story of a Negro Genius

An American friend had taken me to the Afro Arts Exhibition in Harlem (New York) where I was told I would meet a most interesting group of cultured and progressive Negro men and women. I expected to meet among them Mr Langston Hughes, the Negro poet of whom I had heard much. My disappointment, therefore, was great when I found that he had not come. After spending a couple of hours at this interesting show, as we were going I saw a gentleman walk quickly across the pavement towards us, and I found myself looking up at a lively brown face with large expressive eyes which had a mischievous twinkle and a hint of smile in them. This was Mr Langston Hughes, the poet. A conversation full of humour and banter sprang up at once between him and my companions. I saw before me a man of strong and marked personality with a clear and alert mind and a fund of humour. Perhaps there was also just an imperceptible hint of shyness in the presence of a stranger like myself. I met him again a few times at the house of a highly cultured Negro family. But these gatherings were usually crowded, and I was too preoccupied in my attempt to understand the problem of the coloured people in America, to get a chance really to know Langston Hughes or the other very interesting personalities I met there.

What I missed of Langston Hughes in America I got perhaps in full measure when I read his autobiography, *The Big Sea*. 'Literature is a big sea full of many fish. I let down my net and pulled. What I caught was amazing.' Thus ends the narrative of Langston Hughes' life—a fascinating book which holds one's interest from the first page to the last. It is not only the story of a young genius who chose to lead a life of dangerous adventure in preference to one of stability, quiet and security, but through the pages of the book is unfolded the poignant story of the Negro life in America—their struggles, humiliations, and aspirations, their patriotic love of America, the only country they know, and a nostalgia for the unknown mysteries of Africa, the land of their forefathers. The book is more fascinating than a novel because the hero, a friendly, humorous and attractive personality, tells in a charmingly simple style the most interesting story of his own experiences. His restless spirit takes him across three continents, America, Europe and Africa, as a student, a sailor, a waiter, a cook, a bus-boy, a teacher of English, and in several other capacities. But wherever he goes he somehow manages to get into the circle of artistic, literary and musical people and swings along a merrily in and out of these groups. Often he has to starve but he does this with a merry twinkle in his eyes and a witticism on his lips. Through all these ups and downs his genius for writing develops and he steadily keeps on writing one book after another. First come his poems: *Fine Clothes for the Jew; The Weary Blues; The Dream Keeper*; then his novels and short stories: *The Way of the White Folk* and *Not Without Laughter*.

As a young rising poet he finds himself the centre of the Negro Renaissance in Harlem. In 1920 there came a time when Negro art and entertainment was the fashion of the day. American aristocracy and patrons of art and literature flocked to Harlem. Their sophisticated and blasé tastes sought novel and curious forms of entertainment and amusement. A kind of Negro Art and Literature sprang up full of the so-called Negro sentimentality and clownishness. This was the consequence of a conscious attempt to please the white patrons. But it humiliated the self-respect of many of the race and spurred the young intellectuals among them to seek a new creative expression untainted by white patronage. A group of artists became the spear-head of the Negro renaissance. Langston Hughes was one of them. In a manifesto for the movement of the new Negro poetry he wrote, 'We younger Negro Artists who create now intend to express our individual dark-skinned selves without fear or shame. If white people are pleased we are glad. If they are not, it does not matter. We know we are beautiful. And ugly too. The tom-tom cries and the tom-tom laughs. If coloured people are pleased we are glad. If they are not their displeasure doesn't matter either. We build our temple for tomorrow, strong as we know how, and we stand on top of the mountain, free within ourselves.' The young Negro spirit declared its independence after centuries of slavery. This spirit of triumph and defiance is seen in the pages of *The Big Sea* and the other books written by this talented author. Suffering and humiliation did not crush his indomitable spirit. With remarkable detachment he describes in his books the humiliation that he and his people suffer even in the matter of small day-to-day experiences. He writes of them lightly and with humour but beneath the veneer lurks the pathos of a race that has suffered suppression and humiliation for centuries. All this can best be described in his own inimitable language:

The Negro

> I am a Negro:
> Black as the night is black,
> Black like the depths of my Africa.
>
> I've been a slave:
> Caesar told me to keep his door-steps clean.
> I brushed the boots of Washington.

I've been a worker:
Under my hand the pyramids arose.
I made mortar for the Woolworth Building.

I've been a singer:
All the way from Africa to Georgia
I carried my sorrow songs.
I made ragtime.

I've been a victim:
The Belgians cut off my hands in the Congo.
They lynch me now in Texas.

I am a Negro:
Black as the night is black,
Black like the depths of my Africa

But Langston Hughes is never pessimistic. His brave and joyous spirit is indomitable. He symbolizes the Negro spirit that is full of the hope because of its faith in democratic America. Here are two little Lyrics which may interest the reader.

Youth

We have tomorrow
Bright before us
Like a flame.

Yesterday
A night-gone thing,
a sun-down name.

And dawn-today
Broad arch above the road we came.
We march!

Dreams

Hold fast to dreams
For if dreams die
Life is a broken-winged bird
That cannot fly.

Hold fast to dreams
For when dreams go
Life is a barren field
Frozen with snow.

—*Sucheta Kripalani* (1993)

🔊

The Role of the Creative Writer

[From a speech delivered at the P.E.N. Conference of Lucknow on October 10, 1964]

I am thankful to the organizers of this Conference, and especially to Madame Sofia Wadia, for having chosen Lucknow as its venue. I thank them on behalf of the people of Lucknow and Uttar Pradesh as well as on my own.

This city of Lucknow has an old tradition of art and culture. When the Avadh rule was at its height, eminent writers and artists, dancers and musicians used to gather here under the patronage of the Avadh rulers. Lucknow, therefore, acquired a fame as a city of culture. Since then, Lucknow has passed through many vicissitudes and today it does not occupy a place of eminence in the cultural life of India, but I hope it shall again gradually come to attain that height. I am eager that the cultural life of Lucknow should develop. It was, therefore, a matter of great gratification to me that the P.E.N. chose Lucknow as the venue of their Conference.

Again, it is a great honour to be asked to address a gathering like this, of distinguished writers from all over India—an honour which I deeply appreciate and for which I am duly thankful. At the same time, I am aware that this is a privilege which, though glittering, is not quite free from danger. For, whatever I may say, some of you might think that I was treading on ground which should be out of bounds to a politician, particularly to a politician in office. So, there is a risk that I shall oscillate between banality and impertinence. But I assure you that the offence, whether it is a banality or of impertinence, will be a brief one.

A person who is seriously in politics is by definition a committed person. She or he is committed to the pursuit of certain objectives and certain programmes. Of course, in politics, power inevitably is a common objective, barring rare historic exceptions. But even for one whose sole objective is power for self, its pursuit has to be clothed in some other regarding programme. It is like hypocrisy being the homage paid by vice to virtue. If hypocrisy pays, that is, in the short run, it is so because there are honest people in the world and there is faith in honesty. In a completely dishonest or insincere world, hypocrisy would lose its *raison d'être*.

Role of the Creative Writer

However, attenuated through selfishness or other cause, commitment is a normal condition in politics, whereas in the literature world commitment does not seem to be an issue that is beyond controversy. Because from time to time we hear from a distance echoes of controversial sounds—about the role of the creative writer, whether he should have an ideology, whether he has an obligation to serve certain political or social aims through his writings, and so on.

I should be the last person to pontificate on these questions but I might say a word or two, about what I have sometimes felt about them. In the first place, I have felt that basically these are not literary issues at all, though they have sometimes caused very bitter feuds between literary persons. It was not their literary selves as such, which were involved in these feuds. The protagonists were fighting simply as political partisans.

Creative Writer and Ideology

And of course there is no reason why, a creative writer, like any other person, cannot have a passionate interest in some socio-political objectives nor why he should not make use of this special talent, for consciously serving those objectives. In so many among the great writers of the world, we have seen artistic power matched by passionate interest in some political, social or religious ideal. Was not a great deal of mankind's treasured literary heritage originally written as what could be called 'propaganda'? Do we not regard most of our great literary masters also as great teachers?

It seems to me, therefore, that to ask whether art and ideological commitment are compatible is not a valid literary questions. There is no rule deducible from history by which ideology can be included in, or excluded from, the creative writer's world.

Creative writers are born, they are not made, or if they are made they are made by nature. I do not think it is any use discussing what creative writers should do with themselves. If history is any guide, advice whether mutually tendered among themselves or given by others, will be equally useless for the writers. Creative writers will do as they have always done, that is, go their own respective ways. No, I am not quite right here. They could not always go their respective ways. They were often thwarted but the thwarters never quite got their own ways, either. Throughout history the thwarters were defeated by the artists—in the last resort by destroying themselves in their own ways—of course to mankind's immeasurable loss.

Creative Writer and A Free Society

Therefore, the question to be pondered is not what the writers and artists should do with themselves but what we—society and the State—

should do with them. In a perfect State they would best be left alone. But we are far from that state. At present, we are all too much fixed up. In our present state, I wish most fervently that the creative powers of our writers and artists may be effectively employed towards the furthering of the social, moral, political and cultural objectives that we have placed before us. I think there is nothing wrong in this wish. At the same time, I know—and say with all the emphasis at my command—that this is not a matter of dictation and not even one of planning. For, what is of the very essence of the matter here, is freedom. What, therefore, I wish is just a happy and harmonious conjunction should take in freedom. Freedom cannot be real and durable unless it is based on mutual respect. I do not know what the writers on their side would prescribe as the test of freedom. I can suggest one on the side—society. A free society will not demand conformity from creative writers. In its eyes a creative writer will not cease to be an artist simply because he has gone wrong in his sociology or economics. It seems to me that every creative worker should feel that he has a stake in the building up of such a society.

Tagore—Artist or Propagandist?

Tagore, the greatest artist of the age, who was passionately freedom loving, whom no rules of conformity could limit, being born in enslaved Indian society inevitably voiced the hopes and aspirations of the country and society at that time. He, though not a politician by any chance, always played a part in public movements for the regeneration of his country. Early in his life when freedom movement was taking shape he said: 'away with foreign decorations, foreign dress, foreign food. Though we become poor in worldly goods, we will never be poor in spirit. Whatever we get, we must get with our own brain and muscles; and to this end, let no trial be too sore, no sacrifice too great.'

His writings, prose and poetry, inspired the nation and stirred us on to greater and more courageous action. He along with the people of India dreamt of a free, powerful, prosperous India. His dream of India is embodied in his famous prayer:

Where the mind is without fear and the head is held high;
Where knowledge is free;
Where the world has not been broken up into fragments by
                                narrow domestic walls;
Where words come out from the depth of truth;
Where tireless striving stretches its arms towards perfection:
Where the clear stream of reason has not lost its way into the
                                dreary desert sand of dead habit;

Where the mind is led forward by Thee into ever-widening
thought and action—

Into that heaven of freedom, my Father, let my country awake.'

His intense patriotism finds expression again and again in his songs
and poems. He said:

'Blessed am I that I have been born in this country;
Blessed am I that I have loved this country.'

To me the question is: Was he a propagandist or was he a true artist?
An artist, to my mind, can be true only when he can reflect the urges,
hopes and aspirations, the sorrows and despairs of his times. He should
truly express the emotions that stir the people and society. What is of
essence is that the artist should be free to express his true emotions. No
limits of conformation were imposed on Tagore, yet, he could not be
unresponsive to his times. His poems truly reflect the emotions and urges
of the Indian society. On one side we have the example of Tagore and on
the other hand we see the case of Pasternak where he was inhibited by
bonds of conformation, yet, the true artist in him could not be suppressed.
He broke the rigid bonds and came forth with what he had to say. But
perhaps by the test that I have suggested, namely, the test of freedom, an
artist cannot also be denied the right to be suicidal if he so chooses!

Before I close I cannot help mentioning the great loss that India has
suffered this year in the death of Nehru. He was not only a great political
leader but a writer and a progressive thinker of great eminence. His warm
enthusiasm and support were always with this organization. His absence
will be felt for a long time to come at every turn by people working in
different fields of our national life and activity. What endeared him most
to us was his youthful enthusiasm and hopefulness about everything that
took the country forward towards betterment. I hope this spirit of his
will guide and inform us and our writers in their onward march.

I thank you again.

—*Sucheta Kripalani* (1993)

Aruna Asaf Ali
(1909–1996)

Prominent freedom fighter and social activist, Aruna Asaf Ali was born Aruna Ganguly, in a Bengali Brahmin family. She grew up in Nainital, was educated at Lahore and, refused to comply with her parents' plans to marry her off, and took up a teaching job at the Gokhale Memorial School for Girls in Calcutta.

At the age of nineteen, she broke with convention to marry Asaf Ali, a prominent figure in the freedom struggle who was twenty years her senior. A turning point in her life, her husband's involvement in politics drew her into the National Movement. She plunged into the freedom struggle and social service, was part of Gandhi's Satyagraha movement, and was sent to prison on charges of sedition.

In 1942, with the arrest of top leaders including Gandhi, the All-India Congress Committee's plan to hoist the tricolour at Gowalia Tank Maidan was in jeopardy. It was an important sign that the Quit India movement had begun and, as there was no national leader to unfurl the flag, it was Aruna Asaf Ali who did it, becoming a legend for thousands of youth.

Though the British offered an award for her arrest, she remained free for over three years. She became a radical nationalist, and went underground with her socialist friends in 1943 in order to help channel the fury of angry mobs into disciplined resistance.

Gandhi disagreed with Aruna's tactics and wrote to her asking her to surrender. Despite her reverence for him, however, she ignored his advice, emerging later to be elected President of the Delhi Pradesh Congress Committee in 1947.

This period also marked a transition within her, from nationalism to socialism. She joined the Socialist Party in 1948, broke away two years later, and formed the Left Socialist Group. She served as the first woman Mayor of Delhi in 1958 and, among other honours, was awarded the Lenin Prize and Indira Gandhi Award for National Integration.

The essay 'Bourgeois Feminism is Not Enough' epitomizes her concern for social welfare, especially that of women. She criticizes the 'embourgeoisment' of post-Independence feminism saying that it embodies an attitude far removed from ground realities, as far as the lives of women in rural India are concerned. For example, with reference to the reservation policy, she points out that it is 'no answer to the problems of poverty and illiteracy of the generality of Indian women'.

While citing social evils particularly concerning women, she adds, 'It is strange and sad that the women's movement has not made the liberation of every unwilling prostitute, forced into the profession by family pressure or by her own helplessness because of poverty, a central and insistent demand.'

In his Foreword to Aruna Asaf Ali's book, *Travel Talk: Being a Collection of Articles from 'Janata' Delhi* (Aundh, Aundh Publishing Trust, 1947), Jawaharlal Nehru has some interesting comments to make about the author: '... Aruna is both a disturbing and disconcerting individual to many. She does not fit in easily into the usual pattern, and perhaps she deliberately avoids doing so. She feels that she has a mission and is anxious to live up to it. The real crusaders are always few in number and there is something of the crusader of a cause to which she is passionately attached, about her.'

The book itself is a collection of articles, snippets and small essays that involve the people she met, her meetings with Gandhi, and appeals made to her fellow Congressmen.

The first extract, entitled 'The Return' describes a symbolic yet physical return to her original pledge to serve, where her values are reaffirmed after contact with 'real' Indian people. As an essay it is somewhat verbose; yet it is passionate in this verbosity. 'They had broken through the barriers of my empty urbanity, my cultivated speech, my sophisticated home-spun. If they found it possible to respond to me so humanly, all was not lost. My faith in myself returned. I may yet be an instrument, a means for their ends? They had not disowned me though I returned empty-handed.'

Another extract, 'Seven Weeks in Seven Cities' gives the reader a fairly good idea of the kind of work she was doing, and her constant desire to motivate people as she went from one city to another. She describes an incident where Muslim Leaguers once came to stone her for not joining the League. Her spirit and ability to command is obvious as she reproduces her reply to them. '... "The British can give you Pakistan. If you can fight them, go ahead," I said. "While I am fighting for Hindustan, if you join me and fight Britain for your Pakistan, may be, you will realize that your enemy is not the Hindu from whom you wish to separate. Nizamuddin's League Ministry could not save Muslim Bengalees from dying of starvation—it was a Ministry doing what the British wanted it to." They were silenced. Simple impassioned Indians, Muslims or Hindus follow frank talk and respect fearlessness.'

Yet another extract 'Approach to Personalities' takes an objective look at Gandhi, the man and his idealism.

Among the books Aruna Asaf Ali has written are *Private Face of a Public Person: A Study of Jawaharlal Nehru* (1989), *Resurgence of Indian Women* (1991), and *Fragments from the Past: Selected Writings and Speeches of Aruna Asaf Ali*. She died in 1996 and was posthumously awarded the Bharat Ratna, the third woman after Indira Gandhi and Mother Teresa to win the honour.

Approach to Personalities

Personalities whose activities lend colour and direction to an age are rare. But this shortage in numbers is made good by the influence they radiate. Even in times remote humanity kept count of men renowned for their prowess learning or godliness. They were sources of inspiration to little men in strange, far apart lands. News of kings, priests and saints travelled far and wide. Those however who enjoyed world influence were never many.

Every country and every age has brought into relief men around whom have grown schools of thought and action. And a complex of causes operates to produce these personalities. The wind and tide of circumstance becomes for them a crucible. Biological and environmental factors become the fuel beneath it, while the spiritual instincts of past generations light the fire. Struggling against inherited tendencies, overcoming social handicaps, men who become personalities now come to the selection of values. And this selection grows into a personal philosophy. To the extent to which they succeed in refusing to remain prisoners of their past, they attract the attention of those who fail. The spiritual content however, of the values that stamp their personal philosophies must appeal to the masses' instinctive need for spiritual leadership; otherwise they fail to react. On the spontaneous reaction of the masses to a body of ideas depends the latter's dynamic powers.

Little men build up great men because they feel weak and the great are great because they are either wise, or strong, or clever. When the great are all three together they transcend to Godhood.

Therefore, those who control the organization-life and thought-life of a people are men of intelligence, firmness of purpose and insight. Further, imagination and integrity usually cement their characteristics. To guide a large following of men and women so that the trust reposed by them may not be betrayed, the leaders of men have to be eternally on the watch. *The purpose once fixed, the methods employed to achieve it must subserve the end.* If perfection of means becomes an end, let this be the goal. But if the goal is total freedom from social, political and economic ills, then in the way of its attainment no other interventions should be tolerated.

Watching Gandhiji at the congregational prayers is a valuable experience. Is his struggle twin-fronted? The perfection of the individual receives so much attention that all available energy and material is absorbed in the attempt. Change from within or conditioning through external stimuli is another unresolved poser. At his prayers an attempt is made to combine both the methods. Gandhiji's insistence on the gathering's hymn-clapping in unison is not appreciated by cynics. Some see in it a futile adaptation of a western method, others a deliberate attempt at side tracking spiritual soporifics. Either of these interpretations may be over-simplifications.

As one who knows he is law unto our medieval masses, he may not ignore their psychological urges. And yet as one who has essentially set his heart and so on changing both Indian manhood and its slave environment, he feels the compulsion for a compromise. Tested pragmatically, his method has been amazingly successful, so far. But certain signs do indicate that the method has outlived its utility. Squeezed of its efficacy, it is about to fall into decay. Philosopher-kings and priest-kings have had their day. It is only in our country that Gandhiji has revived the concept in the 20th century. True, in the modern ideal polity, the concept is re-appearing in new form. That is largely because the western man has overreached himself in his quest for material satisfaction. To check this pedestrian philosophy of life the West is turning to the easterners' search for soul perfection as an antidote. While this should be a warning to such of us as seek to imitate the Anglo Saxons slavishly, we cannot afford to be blind to the limitations of the theory and practice of Gandhiji's philosophy.

Daily at his feet through prayers and hymns slave hearts pour out exuberantly their devotion. In advising that they should dedicate all action to God he appears to me to be preaching to the converted. We Indian slaves are so completely absorbed in seeking spiritual solace out of our physical miseries, that Gandhiji's stressing its significance only adds to our ingrained fatalism—so fatal to our growth into freemen. There is of course always a political-social note in his daily discourses after the prayers. These talks again end up, of late, on a note of defeat, that is of submission to our inherent weaknesses and lack of faith in God. His suggestion that only a mastery over the lower self, as purer faith in a deity and greater strength of spirit will break the red ring of ill will and treachery thrown around us by a powerful foreign power acts as a depressant. Even if this be partly true, is it not very much more necessary that some external pressure through organized action be applied to the slack-willed underfed, undeveloped bodymind of our millions stirring them into action for selfgrowth rather than lulling them into an introvert's despair-mood? Is that not what our masses need? In the prayer gatherings men and women come to worship the master rather than follow the leader. Let us have worship in our hearts; but let us demand that we march to our goal and not pray our way to it.

At long last the British have betrayed the trust Gandhiji had in their good intentions. The saint in him is too strong not to admit an error of judgment. He has confessed that his faith has been replaced by 'misgivings' and 'fear'. He is surrounded by darkness and therefore unable to lead and he ascribes his own misgivings to his lack of faith in God! This is the man-of-religion's escape. Smaller individuals see in his confession nothing but naive goodness exploited by an astute opponent. We who cannot forget the inhumanities perpetrated by the British never had any doubts as to their intentions. Manoeuvring for a change of position is no change of heart. Our leaders have been double-crossed. Reactionary allies have helped the British Labour Party to get away with plausible excuses again. They will plead that internecine quarrel stopped them from fulfilling their noble mission. Lao-Tsean humour will help them to prove their case. In his words the British will proclaim:

> The good ones I declare good
> The bad ones I also declare good
> That is the goodness of Virtue
> The honest ones I believe
> The liars I also believe
> That is the faith of Virtue.

Finally after one whole year's effort at freedom struggle we are where we were! One farce had ended. And now a one-act play begins. The audience—a larger one this time—will now witness the Indians' incapacity to think concretely and to act unitedly. In theory we are told the British have quit. In practice they remain just so long as we can't decide amongst ourselves the manner in which we shall loot the treasure house that is India!

In the meantime hungry men and women have started dying. Ill-paid workers have taken to inconvenient ways of getting better wages. Petty tyrants and puppet rulers have dared to check the freedom movements of Congress leaders and Congress revolutionaries. The passion for freedom seeks an outlet everywhere. In Madura men died because Jawaharlal was insulted in Kashmir, a congress Minister's regime notwithstanding! But unless we have the courage to organize their emotional and physical qualities, men will go on dying pointlessly. They will be the subject of pity, not praise. Congressmen everywhere will have to think hard whether they will continue to fight for freedom or discuss what structural shape it *should have when it descends on us.*

—Travel Talk (1947)

Venu Chitale (Leelabai Ganesh Khare) (1912–1993)

In his Foreword to Venu Chitale's *In Transit* (Bombay, Hind Kitabs, 1950), Dr M.R. Jayakar, the Vice Chancellor of Poona University, says: 'It is a socio-political novel depicting Indian family life under the simulations of political and economic ideas covering the important period of 1915–1935. I call this period important, because it was an era when the Indian Nationalist Movement was rapidly gaining in ascendancy in the different parts of the country.'

In Transit is centred on a Brahmin family in Pune, seen as a microcosm of the state and how it is affected by growing nationalism. It also epitomizes progressive Indian families of the period. Spread over three generations, the narrative is more important from a sociological perspective, as it covers, in detail, the way of life, customs, rituals, and events that occur in the family.

One of the extracts reproduced here humorously documents a character's first glimpse of an Englishman: 'She noticed that his face was very red and wondered if he was angry with someone.' It also cover events like a naming ceremony, discriminations between Brahmins and non-Brahmins, and the attitude of some Indians who were part of English social circles.

An undated letter to the author from Mulk Raj Anand follows the Foreword. He seems to have known her in London, and he comments on the strength behind the shyness. He also describes her as having a 'sensitiveness far in excess of your contemporaries', this sensitiveness being demonstrated by 'the way you reacted to the poetry of one of my scripts when your colleagues merely passed it through censorship with the routine expression typical of authorities in such cases'. He goes on to comment on the quality of the book. 'The characterization has obviously been achieved from intimate knowledge of the various households involved. And the narrative is sustained at an even pitch of writing without the purple patch or the deliberate use of lovely words which mars so many novels written in English by Indians who want to show off their mastery of the alien tongue.'

Venu Chitale was educated at Bombay's Wilson College, and University College, London. According to her daughter, Ms Jyotsna Damle, Venu Chitale went to England to study Montessori methods, and stayed on when the War broke out. She was one of Orwell's assistants at the BBC during World War II, and there are some references to her (and a photograph) in *Orwell: The War Broadcasts* edited by W.J. West. Among them is the special Christmas Number of 29 December 1942 in which Orwell asks Venu Chitale to read part of the second chapter of the Gospel of St Matthew. During this period, she edited and transmitted talks by C.E.M. Joad, T.S. Eliot and others, and also adapted Kalidas' plays for radio.

After the War, Venu Chitale worked with the India League in London and attended international conferences at Geneva and Paris as a delegate. She later travelled extensively in India and in 1946 attended the All India Women's Conference in Hyderabad. At the conference she was introduced to Sarojini Naidu.

After her marriage to Mr G.T. Khare, Venu Chitale (now Leelabai Khare) wrote another novel entitled *Incognito* (Sriniwas Cards, Pune 1993), under the pseudonym 'Weenoo'. This is a sequel to *In Transit*, and follows the life of one of the characters, Shesha in her travels around Europe.

Chapter VIII

The women of the family, the relations and the guests gathered in the big room where the naming ceremony was taking place. Little girls roamed about, perfectly at home, but for the young boys there was no special place. They stood against the wall, and too shy to attend the ceremony with the women, waited eagerly for the sweetmeats.

Lopamudra had settled down on the seat next to the cradle specially placed there for her. Awwa brought the baby in, but being a widow, handed it to great-aunt Yamuna, who took it round for all the 'in-laws' present to see and brought it to its mother. It is the aunt's privilege to hold the baby on this occasion. Everybody called for the aunt, and little Mohana was brought in by Daji, with Bal'Baban, the other twin, following. He took the twins, dressed in long trousers and tunic of silver-gray satin, and with embroidered maroon caps titled at an angle, to Lopamudra.

And they, obviously impressed with the dignity of the occasion, sat down solemnly on the seats placed there specially for them. Then to Mohana, the aunt, was given, instead of the baby, a coconut wrapped up in a cape, the ceremonial coconut which always had to be held by someone at the naming ceremony.

Madhav and Bhayya, against the wall at the back of the room, stood on their toes and stretched their necks to see everything that was going on. Mohana and Bal'Baban, who were very hot, and getting more and more bored in their place of honour near the baby, suddenly caught sight of the boys. 'Bhay, Bhay ... Madha ... Madha ...' they called out excitedly. Now disregarding the dignity demanded of them for the occasion, they crawled from their places and wriggled their way happily through the crowd of women and children to the boys.

The afternoon wore on. The cradle was being rocked by the five women guests of honour, all mothers. Their hands were held by those behind them, so that everybody touched the cradle, even though only through a chain of hands. The village ballad-maker, who had travelled all the way from Chinchgao, sang a ballad composed impromptu for the occasion. The bangle-woman had come and presented her gifts. And now lullaby was sung after lullaby by sweet-voiced women from the different *wadas*.

The baby daughter of Lopamudra and Suresh of Indore was named Nalini, 'Dark-Lotus', and her mother's ears tingled with the praises that the village bard showered on her tiny daughter, but the lullaby Lopamudra would remember best of all was the one composed in honour of Tilak, 'the Approved of the People', and written as though sung to him by the land of India, Mother India. Lopamudra had collected many lullabies, from the one in honour of Rama, the epic hero, to the one in honour of Shivaji, the Maratha king, but the one for Tilak stirred her most. 'Home Rule', his watchword, was gradually becoming a household word even among women, and Lopamudra found herself repeating the Tilak ballad as she rocked Nalini.

Deep down in her heart, Awwa had never got over the fact that Mai had not been given in marriage to the ruler of a State. The family were well off, it is true, but after all a Saraf was not a Raja. And so Awwa harboured an ambition. If not Mai, at least one of Mai's children must be married into a State, she said to herself. Dada was her first disappointment, he had married a college girl from Bombay. But Awwa admitted to herself, she would not exchange Vahini for any other wife for Dada, because Vahini was a very queen in all she said and did. Lopamudra was the second disappointment. Bapu and Mai themselves had been the guilty ones, urging

Abba to accept the offer from a fashionable modern Brahmin family of Indore! The women of that family actually wore blouses which came down to the waist instead of the traditional bodice which covered the bust and the arms, and left the body exposed and cool from beneath the bust to the waist.

Awwa counted on her fingers. Now there were left the boys, Daji and Bhaya, and of course the twins, Mohana and Bal'Baban. All of them were still to marry. Her thoughts, however, settled on Mohana, they flew ahead in time and already she saw Mohana seated aloft in the *howdah* on the back of the processional elephant—Mohana as the bride of a prince. And now Mohana was actually twenty-months old, she was getting on.

Mohana was born only twenty minutes before Bal'Baban, and yet those twenty minutes made all the difference, so said the village horoscope-reader. Once, during a visit to the *wada* in Poona, he complained bitterly that city people cared little for foretellers of the future. 'Nobody these days cares about inauspicious or auspicious days for journeys or for commencing important work,' he complained to Awwa with a long face, 'the science of the stars is being lost to us.'

In Awwa, however, the horoscope-reader found a great sympathizer. 'Don't worry,' she said to him in confidence, 'even though Abba doesn't talk much, he knows and he believes, or else he would not have postponed his pilgrimage.'

The twins took up much of the time of the horoscope-reader, but much patience was required on Awwa's part to coax them in turn to sit quietly while she opened the little palms, and said to him, 'Now look, here's the life line and here's the money line, tell me is she destined to wear a crown?' The barely visible lines on the palms of the babies did not worry Awwa.

Bal'Baban's palm indicated little about his future, but to Awwa's delight Mohana had 'Queen' writ large on hers. Of course, only the village horoscope-reader could see that, but that was enough for Awwa. She was determined to see at least Mai's second daughter married to the ruler of a State, and she was determined to assist the stars in bringing it about.

'She was born to rule,' the horoscope-reader intoned as he studied Mohana's sticky little palm. 'She was born to ride and not to walk, to smile and not to weep,' he said with a dreamy look in his eyes. Awwa nodded in confident agreement. 'She was born to ride and not to walk,' she murmured to herself. 'And tell me more,' she spoke to the horoscope-reader, 'when will Dada's wife have a baby?' But the foreteller of the future saw no signs of a child to Vahini. Was she going to be barren, perhaps?

Awwa folded the memory of Mai into her heart. To serve Mai's children with love and care was now the nanny's destiny. She was pleased to see that Vahini had found her feet as a worthy daughter-in-law of the gentle and gracious mistress. But oh, it was now two years since she was married to Dada. Two years! Lopamudra, married a year later than she, already had a daughter four-months-old. Great-aunt Yamuna had already made indirect inquiries whether perhaps the daughters of the Joshi family were late in bearing children. With the slightest indisposition that Vahini had, Awwa would watch her and say to herself, 'Ha! It's on its way now.'

In the servants' quarters there was much gossiping. 'Two years married and nothing yet!' There was constant visiting of the temples to pray for a child for the mistress. 'O Goddess Parvati, grant my mistress a son, and I'll fill Thy lap with a coconut.'

'O Divine Flute-Player Krishna, fill the lap of my mistress with an infant, and I will cover Thy head with a silken cape.'

'O Lord Vishnu, grant the house of my master an heir and I will adorn Thee with a garland of the sacred Tulsi leaves.'

Vahini herself was little ruffled although her childnesses was the focal point of discussion in the inner apartments, and Awwa, whose main activity in life was to handle babies, devised ways and means of impressing on Dada's wife how dusty the maternity room was getting, how little Mohana and Bal'Baban would love to have a nephew to play with, and how delighted the old Saraf would be to see the face of a great-grandson.

The *wada* was concerned with its problems and its disappointments; but while Awwa was worried about the birth of a child to Dada's wife, the whole of India was experiencing the anguish of a new nation coming into being. Peasants hailed Tilak as their king. New slogans such as Passive Resistance, Satyagraha, Hindu-Muslim Unity were being repeated by the enlightened as well as by those who understood little but had been emotionally awakened by the new forces in the nation.

Dada, though much affected by these events, was determined to complete his studies. Little did he know what a pandemonium of prayers was going up in his name for a son and heir for him and Vahini. When his wife told him one day how disappointed everybody was with her for not giving the Sarafs an heir, he said wistfully, 'A day might come when we can't support children.' He spoke quietly, 'Since Father's death our income has gone down, and even the business is not bringing in what it used to. Abba is too old to manage the jewel shop alone and great-uncle is making a mess of the business. He spends more on running the business than the business yields, and then complains that he hasn't enough staff. It is certain that I shall have to start earning soon if we want to stay on in Poona.' He sounded anxious for the responsibilities of the large establishment were great.

'But how can we live anywhere else but in the *wada*?' Vahini asked earnestly.

'You have begun to love Poona,' he kissed her tenderly, and then, 'Yes, we must not be despondent,' he said with assurance.

It was only a few weeks after the twins' third birthday. Bal'Baban had already had his ceremonial hair cutting, the very first time in his life that he had had his hair cut. An auspicious day was then decided upon for Mohana to choose her first bangles. Vahini dressed Mohana in her first 'little-girl's' dress. It was a red silk skirt gathered into a band at the waist and falling down to the ankles, and a short bodice of gold brocade. The skirt hung smooth and heavy with the wide gold border woven into the hem. The design of the border depicted a hunting party with horses and elephants, trees and lakes, birds and animals, while little mangoes embroidered in gold thread dotted the body of the skirt.

The bangle-seller had already arrived and selected a place against a pillar in the verandah-hall where she spread her wares. A servant fetched a seat for Mohana, and drew with her fingers a design in red and white powdered chalk on the floor around it.

The boys and several grown-ups were watching the fun, while Awwa, who had Bal'Baban with her, was examining the tiny bangles carefully. Vahini brought Mohana dressed in her ceremonial splendour but at the high threshold the excited little girl was stumbling over the unaccustomed long skirt. Vahini lifted her up and over the obstacles and placed her on the seat prepared for her and said, 'Sister-in-law, now you may choose the bangles you would like to wear.'

Little Mohana wriggled off her seat to get nearer to the enchanting display of twinkling colours and the tinkling sound of glass as the bangle-woman undid the yarn on which her wares were strung and poured them out in front of her tiny customer. Chubby little hands grasped everything they could reach.

'Which, Mohana-rani, which do you want?' coaxed the old bangle-seller. 'These,' piped Mohana, her hands full of bangles which she immediately dropped to take fresh handfuls to shout again, 'These ... these ... these!'

Completely engrossed, this lovely game would have occupied her for the rest of the day, but Vahini came forward. 'Look, Baby, aren't *these* pretty?' she dangled a dark red pair with gold stars in front of her. Mohana looked up and Vahini was startled once again as she always was to see how grey the child's eyes were, eyes which were habitually half-closed and always looked dark because of those long black lashes. 'Pretty,' the little girl repeated after her, 'pretty.' She had at last made up her mind.

The bangle-woman took Mohana's tiny hand in hers, and according to her usual habit, pressed it gently, pretending to make it supple. She looked at Awwa as she started working the red glass bangles with the circumference of a rupee on to the child's wrist. 'Ah,' she said, her voice husky with feeling, 'she is truly Mai's daughter! Look at this soft little hand, it is her mother's hand.'

The bangle choosing over, Mohana was carried by Vahini first to the family temple to make her thanksgiving and then to show her to all the *wada* in her newly acquired finery. It was her day, and holding up her hands for all to see, she informed everybody 'pretty, pretty', while all applauded.

The excitement was over at last and Vahini handed Mohana to Awwa who took her to be dressed back in her loose, short muslin dress. The little girl's limbs free again, she ran away happily to play with Bal'Baban. But Awwa thinking of the little hands, made so much to today, kept on muttering. 'Yes, her mother's hand, and a hand which has a crown on it. Ah, my little queen, Mohana,' she smiled to herself.

The horoscope-reader's words had made such a strong impression on her, that it became a passion with the old nanny to bring up Mohana as the future wife of a ruler of a State. She knew by heart the names of all the little boys who were being brought up in the palaces of the Brahmin rulers, and she made a point of getting their ages and dates of birth, through priests who visited such homes or had connections with the States. Awwa knew practically all the rich houses of Poona, and the servants there kept her well informed about the family gossip of their masters.

A non-Brahmin servant, belonging to the anti-Brahmin movement, jauntily told Awwa one day that there were two very fine unmarried non-Brahmin princes, good enough to be the husbands of any two girls even if they were Brahmins. Awwa took this as a gross insult to her whole caste. 'Impertinent untouchable!' she said, and a noisy quarrel between the Brahmin and non-Brahmin servants in the *wada* was the result. The older non-Brahmin servants, afraid lest they should lose their bread, quietly withdrew, but peace was not restored until a few black eyes had been exchanged among the younger boys.

'Never mind, the Brahmins will not dare to treat us like untouchables once we get our political rights,' the non-Brahmin' leaders talking to the masses had assured them. The movement of non-Brahmins against the Brahmin claim of superiority of blood and brain, was gradually spreading, and gathering strength in cities like Poona. Abba who had always thought of caste exclusiveness as unjust to the lower castes, nevertheless lacked the courage to mix with them at meals, but Dada was prepared to associate himself actively with reformers who wished to break the caste system. But in the *wada* the Jahagirdar became vocal and violent in his condemnation of non-Brahmins.

'Our daughters to be married into the lower castes! We will rather drown than claim blood from inferiors,' he would shout. He knew however that he could not openly denounce his elder brother's lenient attitude towards non-Brahmins, nor could he answer Dada's arguments against the smugness of the Brahmin caste. And Daji never said much. So it was Bhayya, whose enthusiasm about the national movement and the efforts of leaders towards national unity made him argumentative, whom he picked upon to victimize. Young though Bhayya was, he picked up bits of news and talked about the injustices of the foreign Government and the people who opposed the national leaders, and this gave the Jahagirdar many opportunities to indulge in his favourite habit of screwing the boy's ears as he took him to task. Especially did Bhayya lay himself open to his great-uncle's active displeasure when he brought home with him a non-Brahmin period from school in the afternoons or on half holidays.

'What with servants becoming uppish and children mixing with non-Brahmins, the race of Brahmins will soon die out,' were the Jahagirdar's constant protests.

Chapter IX

It was during this holiday at Mahableshwar that Mohana for the first time in her life saw an Englishman at close quarters. The white faces had frightened her at first when she saw a crowd of them in the big public gardens and around the bandstand. She was only ten and had with Bal'Baban only just begun to learn English. It cost her a great deal of work. To the pure Marathi ears of Mohana words such as 'cat', 'rat' and 'mat' sounded very peculiar. But her surprise grew even more when one day she actually heard English spoken by a real flesh-and-blood Englishman. She noticed that his face was very red and wondered if he was angry with someone. It happened in the market-place in Mahableshwar. Madhav who had accompanied some college friends from Bombay on a cycling tour to the hill-station was visiting the Sarafs for a couple of days. He had met Daji, who had come in from Panchgani, and the children, in Chandu's car on the daily round when they chose a basket of ripe mangoes for the midday meal. While Daji was selecting and buying mangoes and ordering freshly picked strawberries to take back to Kusum, Madhav was keeping an eye on the children. As he was standing on the pavement with his hand on the door lest the youthful battalion should rush out on to the street, he felt a light pat on his shoulder and looked round to find an English lecturer from his College in Bombay standing beside him. The Englishman shook hands with Madhav, a student in his first college year, and looked at the children saying something with a friendly smile.

Mohana who was nearest to Madhav looked up at the Englishman's face and with great courage she smiled back. After all she was learning English too. The lecturer talked to Madhav for quite a while, but oh, what a terrible disappointment! Poor Mohana felt very despondent, for not one word did she understand, and never once did 'cat', 'hat' or 'mat' occur in the long conversation.

Going back home from the market Shashi rode on Madhav's bicycle. The midday meal in Mahableshwar was always a cause of great anxiety to Awwa as the children simply refused to touch any food. Right through the meal it was nothing but mangoes and strawberries and, worst of all, Vahini did not seem to object. 'Let them eat fruit to their hearts' content,' she would say every time anyone complained. Awwa, however, was determined to feed them on their specially cooked rice in the mornings before they started off for their marketing, while great-aunt Yamuna always had a remedy for every illness that she thought of. She made sure that every bowl of mango pulp on the children's dining stools had a pinch of black pepper mixed with it. 'That will prevent them from having stomach-ache.' Besides which she compelled each member of the family to drink a glass of milk before retiring. 'Milk helps to digest the mango,' she had insisted to Vahini whose baby boy was still feeding at her breast.

The midday meal was being served when Bal'Baban came to Vahini and asked her whether he and the other children could accompany Madhav to the I.C.S.'s bungalow. The I.C.S. had invited Madhav for tennis.

'Madhav is going to play bat and ball,' Mohana explained casually as she sprawled on the grass mat on the verandah, where she was trying to make a drawing of the dog Motya with coloured chalks.

While Motya was still making up his mind about a 'tongue in, or tongue out' portrait, Awwa called the children for their meal. Vahini had no peace, the children crying singly or in chorus: 'May we go with Madhav?'

'Are you not going for your evening ride on your ponies today, then?' Vahini asked as she handed her sleepy baby to Chandu.

'Oh, yes, we are going for a ride. But, Vahini, let the groom bring back the ponies and then we can stay with Madhav at the I.C.S.'s bungalow and come back with him.'

To this bright idea of Mohana's Vahini gave her consent and after meals they ran about happily.

As Kusum's mother had come to Panchgani for a few days, Daji decided to stay in Mahableshwar for the afternoon and supervise the swings which were being tied to the Jambul tree, for the children. He was trying out a low swing. Two of the bungalow servants were up the tree and one on the ground, finishing their operations of fixing the ropes for the swings, when suddenly from under the dry leaves on the edge of the compound crawled a long snake. In a moment the place was in an uproar. The servants got their sticks and amidst the din of the childrens' shoutings, advice and suggestions, Daji killed the fearful but fascinating reptile. The serpent then had to be cremated, and the funeral of the dreaded, yet revered creature took place with due respect. The ceremony entranced the children even more than the amazing colours of the snake. They stood around, all eyes looking on with rapt attention. It was when the servant was placing the copper coin in the snake's mouth before cremating it, when all was still and solemn, that Shashi for the first time felt overcome by sheer fright. While the other children were watching the operation with suppressed excitement, she suddenly turned and ran to the house, screaming. Mohana half frightened, half curious, followed her and both reached the unfailing resort of safety and security that was Vahini.

'Bal'Baban is the best rider,' called Madhav from his bicycle to Chandu who was driving slowly in an open car as she accompanied the children on their ponies.

'Yes, among those of his own age certainly, except his twin, mind you. I think Mohana runs him a very close second.' Chandu looked at the twins with pleasure.

'Mohana, you look like a boy,' called out Madhav.

'But I am a boy,' she shouted back. 'Look, I am dressed like Bal'Baban in jodhpurs,' she insisted as she held up a perky little head covered with a Gandhi-cap.

'But she can't ride as fast as we boys can,' called Anant, trying to spur on his pony to demonstration.

Rangi's small brother, a rough lad from Chinchgao, seemed to manage his pony with great skill and Pantoba's son Pandu sat on his small horse, quiet but sure. When they reached the outer gate of the I.C.S.'s compound Chandu turned back and with her went the five ponies led by the groom, while Madhav took the five children, dressed exactly alike and almost of the same height, to the fashionable household of the I.C.S.

The I.C.S. famous for his ultra-western manner of life had a bevy of beautiful daughters. The six Misses Lata (Creeper) ranged from the ages of twenty-eight to nineteen, the youngest being a classmate of Madhav's at the college. Premlata was the eldest and Suvarnalata the youngest. As he came into the porch with the five children he was greeted by six delicate nymphs, dressed in the flimsiest chiffon the I.C.S. could import. It was the first time that Mohana saw such thin saris, sleeveless blouses and queer-looking ornaments, so she decided that the Bombay women must be quite different from the women of Poona. All Vahini's saris had thick borders and her bodices were never sleeveless, and she wore beautiful thick gold bracelets and real pearls for earrings. Mohana started from one to the other and suddenly rubbed her head bashfully against Madhav as she became aware that they were looking at her just as intently. The party trailed from the porch to the front hall and then into the reception room, full of western furniture. The Saraf children, unused to houses furnished in the English manner, did not at all feel at home in the I.C.S. bungalow. They stood holding one another's hands, in spite of Madhav's efforts to make them shake hands with the Creeper sisters whose pretty ripples of laughter were most entertaining to the children, as well as their peculiarly affected anglicized Marathi. The eldest Miss Creeper spoke prettily to Madhav.

'Madhav! well, well, how well this name of Lord Krishna suits you, especially when you have these five Pandavas with you.'

'Aha!' he laughed back, 'but one is a false one.' And he caught Mohana's hand playing with the end of her leather belt.

'Which is the false one?' asked Miss Creeper No. 3. Madhav felt in the highest of spirits and was ready to amuse these England-returned, Paris-returned famous women of Bombay. He made all the five little riders, the four boys and Mohana, stand in a row facing the Creeper sisters. The children immediately played up, but Mohana was desperately anxious. 'If anyone discovers my long plait, whatever shall I do?' was the anxious thought in her mind. She walked backwards to Madhav and held her hands out to him behind her back. She tilted her head back and looked up anxiously into his face as if the whole world would collapse if he did not hide her long, very long pigtail which always gave her away. Madhav immediately guessed her anxiety and rested his chin on her head, announcing: 'Three guesses, ladies! Which is the false Pandava? Or do you think all five are boys?'

The pretty sisters had a number of guesses but failed completely and Mohana emerged triumphant.

'Madhav here?' came the voice of Sir Narayan, the I.C.S., led by his Lady. Lady I.C.S. who usually sneered at everything Indian was strangely impressed by the pure Indian-styled riding clothes of the children. She had even sneered at saris, but when she went to England with her husband she had discovered that dressed in a sari she commanded more respect from her Western admirers and more admiration from her friends than if she tried to wear western clothes. So the I.C.S. household though notorious for its aping of British life and language yet became for chiffon sari merchants a source of constant profit. In a sari, after all, one became *'persona grata*' abroad, in the civilized world of the West, and whatever the West said was law with Lady I.C.S.

Sir Narayan staggered to an easy chair and greeted Madhav saying, 'Madhav, my wife wants you to choose one of the six Creepers for your wife. Don't you, my love?' he turned to his wife. The six Misses Creeper were by now quite fascinated by the 'interesting' Poona children, and anything they said was prettily commented upon as 'interesting'.

The Knight made Madhav sit next to him and asked him questions about his plans for England.

'When do you leave for England, young man?' said Sir Narayan, shaking a cocktail.

'Look at doggy, dear,' said Lady I.C.S. as she knelt in front of a pet dog.

Madhav told Sir Narayan that he did not feel at ease to accept his kind offer to send him abroad. 'Not before I get my degree anyway,' he said nervously. As he was talking, Madhav looked at the lady with her dog and her cigarette holder and was glad the Poona children had gone into the garden. To their *wada* upbringing she was bound to present an extraordinary contrast to Vahini. The lady in question watched Madhav carefully through the lorgnette she had bought in England. 'The boy is very handsome and he's such fun,' she murmured to herself as she sipped her soda. 'If my daughter wants to marry him, Madhav must certainly go to England soon. It was a pity that his sister was such an unlucky girl to be married into that stodgy stuffy household in Poona, most old-fashioned backward lot of political jailbirds.' She was careful not to give tongue to these thoughts in front of Madhav, who was sure to defend his sister promptly. She cast a covetous glance at the boy.

'Madhav, which of my Creepers are you going to marry?' she asked as though she were merely teasing.

'But, my love, Madhav is younger than every single one of your daughters, you do realize that, I hope,' said Sir Narayan himself sipping a whisky.

Madhav laughed bravely and then, regaining himself, 'Well, I'll have to marry them all, I think,' he said boldly.

Sir Narayan threw his head back and laughed as though that were the greatest joke he had ever heard. But his Lady felt annoyed with her husband for making a joke of it.

'Stop it, Naru, don't be cruel, you are just being cruel. Stop it at once!'

Since his arrival in Mahableshwar this was the third time Madhav had heard lady I.C.S. talk in such a manner to Sir Narayan. Again he hoped the Poona children were not listening this time to a quarrel between husband and wife.

'Madhav, my wife has no patience with Chitpawan Brahmins but she loves you, my boy, and that is a great compliment from the Lady,' Sir Narayan tried to pacify his wife.

'That is exactly the reason why I don't want such a nice boy to be wasted on a wretched Chitpawan Brahmin girl. He is too good for those crusty old families anyhow,' she said with assurance.

Madhav was at last relieved to find that the Poona children were indeed out of hearing. The Creeper sisters were playing with them in the garden.

'Will you have a cocktail, Madhav?' asked Sir Narayan.

'No, thank you, Sir, I'd rather have lemon squash if I may. It's very hot, even indoors.'

Sir Narayan placed an enormous lump of ice in Madhav's glass and handed the drink to him. Lady I.C.S. was reminded by Madhav's reference to the heat that even Mahableshwar was too hot for her delicate skin and her general constitution. She liked to look upon the Viceroy as an infallible barometer while in India. Wherever the Viceroy went, the heat of the Indian sun was bound to be tamed. Simla was the place, or may be even Ooty at times. But how could she do it? Sir Narayan's means did not stretch to taking the whole household to Simla, and so she had to be content with Mahableshwar. It was not so bad for, after all, a possible garden party at Government House in this hill-station could make up quite nicely for the loss of so much of the smart society of Simla. She looked sadly at a coloured picture of the Viceroy's residence in Simla and felt an almost unbearable longing to be one of the company of the elite in Simla. Lady Max had promised that one day she would introduce her to the Viceroy and, may be, then there would be a possibility of an invitation from Simla. Lady I.C.S. felt like a fish out of water, torn away from her English friends and Western surroundings.

'Madhav, haven't you yet learnt to smoke?' Lady I.C.S. asked Madhav, whose attention was drawn now to Miss Creeper No. 1 who was calling him from her favourite bower where the fragrant 'Night Queen' grew in rich profusion.

'No, I am afraid I haven't yet taken to it. But Sir Narayan, may I be excused? I think I had better go to the tennis court. I promised a game to all the Misses Creeper.' He ignored Miss Creeper No. 1's call and ran through the rose bed towards the tennis court. Miss Creeper No. 1, however, took a short cut and confronted him at the tennis court gate. She narrowed her eyes and said in a half whisper, 'Madhav, why do you avoid me always? I want to talk to you alone. I am so lonely and you are so cruel.' She put her arm round his shoulders but he, intensely embarrassed, gently removed it.

'I am sorry,' he said, 'I like to play tennis with you all, but I have nothing to talk about with you alone.'

'Madhav, I sent you a note this morning,' Miss Creeper ignored his refusal. 'I was waiting and waiting for you, but you never came. I was alone then.' She looked sweetly at him. 'Won't you stay for supper and then we could sit in my bower and talk. I am so lonely, Madhav.'

The languid-eyed, slim and beautiful Miss Creeper No. 1 frightened the very life out of Madhav. He did not know where to look or what to say. It was very difficult to be a man. When at home in Bombay Chandu and Ayah nearly smothered him with cherishing and spoiling, when in Poona the battalion, of *wada* children drove him mad asking him all day long to play with them, and now these Creeper females surrounded him like tangled undergrowth. Yes, indeed, it was difficult to be a young man. Madhav had just turned seventeen.

The languid Miss Creeper No. 1 might have tried some new means of attack but the children, bored with the stream of questions about Poona, about the *wada* and about Bhayya's prison, had come closer to watch the tennis. They were particularly interested since they had collected balls to play tennis in the *wada*. They asked each other when Madhav was going to play and the mention of his name brought a shower of cries for Madhav from the bevy of beauty on the tennis court. Miss Creeper No. 1 let go of her victim and he ran on to the court with relief.

'Madhav, these children are a perfect psychological study of an old-fashioned Poona Brahmin household,' said the youngest Miss Creeper.

'Very interesting,' chimed in Miss Creeper No. 3.

'Mohana has such lovely long hair,' whispered Miss Creeper No. 1 trying to make conversation. 'How old are you, Mohana?' she asked the small girl in jodhpurs.

'I will soon be nearly eleven years and Bal'Baban is exactly the same, only I arrived twenty minutes before him,' said she, offering all the information she had from Awwa about her birth.

'The twins were born during my sister's wedding, Miss Creeper, and I saw them when they had hardly opened their eyes.'

Madhav played and the children watched. Bal'Baban wondered if Bhayya in the village would ever play tennis like Madhav. Miss Creeper No. 1 who was not in the set walked daintily around the court to look at Madhav. 'Funny boy, why do you run away from me always?' she whispered softly to herself.

That evening Sir Narayan drove his car himself to take the children back to the bungalow. The little boys were exhausted after a long evening and a heavy dinner, and Mohana had fallen asleep on the sofa. Madhav picked her up in his arms and took her home in the car without waking her up.

Awwa tried to take the sleeping Mohana from Madhav's arms saying, 'Dear me, this is a substantial bit of womanhood already. How heavy the child gets when she is asleep!'

Madhav could not help laughing. 'A very substantial bit of womanhood, indeed, Awwa,' he said after her as he tried to unclasp Mohana's arms from around his neck. Awwa carried her away and put her on her own little bed. There was a long sigh and the little girl was fast asleep again.

—*In Transit* (1950)

Amrita Sher-Gil
(1913–1941)

Her father Sardar Umrao Singh Majithia was a scholar and Sikh noble; her mother Antoinette, a musician and opera singer. As for Amrita Sher-Gil, she grew up to be among India's foremost painters, leaving behind works that reveal a powerful and original intellect.

At the age of sixteen, Amrita began to study at the Académie de la Grande Chaumière in Paris, before shifting to the Ecole Nationale des Beaux Arts. She was the first Asian to study there. At the age of twenty—once again a first for an Asian—she was elected an associate of the Grand Salon in Paris.

She married her cousin Dr Victor Egan in 1938 at Budapest, living a life that spanned different cultures, climates and world views. This explains why, when one looks at her paintings, the striking elements of both European and Indian tradition are easily noticeable.

Those close to her called her a passionate artist. Her writings, paintings and letters prove it. Reproduced here, an article by her called 'Evolution of My Art' begins with the statement: 'It seems to me that I never began painting, that I have always painted. And I have always had, with a strange certitude, the conviction that I was meant to be a painter and nothing else. Although I studied, I have never been taught painting in the actual sense of the word, because I possess in my psychological make-up a peculiarity that resents any outside interference. I have always, in everything, wanted to find out things for myself.' As she continues, discussing the Indian art of her time, its trends, and the appreciation of it, what emerges is the portrait of a woman sure of herself, her art, and of what she wanted of it. Interestingly enough, though her self-portraits are not credited with being anything more than mediocre, the personal image she projected was of herself against a flaming red background. Some critics maintain that this reveals her desire to assert her own individuality in a dramatic way.

In a letter written to the critic Karl Khandelavala, in December

1937, she once mentioned a recent experience in India where she was asked to speak on Indian cinema: '... there is quite a controversy raging in the local press as to whether I am an idealist or a visionary or just the reverse; I am also accused of asking Indian producers to be *Photographers* (which I certainly did) instead of being ones "who see with the eyes of the soul" and this is considered quite unforgivable.'

In yet another letter, this time to Pandit Jawaharlal Nehru in 1937, she said that she was always attracted to people who were integral enough to be 'inconsistent without discordancy' and who didn't 'trail viscous threads of regret behind them'. This frank confession can be taken epitomize her approach to art as well as life. Amrita died at 28, on December 5, 1941. In a brief statement on her paintings, A. Ramachandran wrote: 'Unfortunately, after Sher-Gil's death, many Indian painters copied what was genuine in her style—so ruthlessly that ultimately it ended in Vakil's greeting cards. And so, I lost interest in Sher-Gil's painting and avoided thinking of her work as one avoids thinking of Gandhiji when one sees a Gandhi cap.'

Letter to Jawaharlal Nehru

6 November 1937

A little while ago somebody said to me 'You know Jawaharlal Nehru is ill.' I hadn't known it. I never read the papers.

I have been thinking of you a great deal but somehow, perhaps for that very reason, I hadn't felt like writing.

Your letter came as a surprise, I need hardly add an extremely pleasant one.

Thanks for the book.

As a rule I dislike biographies and autobiographies. They ring false. Pomposity or exhibitionism. But I think I will like yours. You are able to discard your halo occasionally. You are capable of saying 'When I saw the sea for the first time' when others would say 'When the sea saw me for the first time.'

I should like to have known you better. I am always attracted to people who are integral enough to be inconsistent without discordancy and who don't trail viscous threads of regret behind them.

I don't think that it is on the threshold of life that one feels chaotic, it is when one has crossed the threshold that one discovers that things which looked simple and feelings that felt simple are infinitely tortuous and complex. That is only in inconsistency that there is any consistency.

But of course *you* have got an orderly mind.

I don't think you were interested in my painting really. You looked at my pictures without seeing them.

You are not hard. You have got a mellow face. I like your face, it is sensitive, sensual and detached at the same time. I am enclosing a cutting that my father asked me to forward to you. It was written by him.

Yours
Amrita Sher Gil

—*A Bunch of Old Letters* (1958)

Evolution of My Art

It seems to me that I never began painting, that I have always painted. And I have always had, with a strange certitude, the conviction that I was meant to be a painter and nothing else. Although I studied, I have never been taught painting in the actual sense of the word, because I possess in my psychological make-up a peculiarity that resents any outside interference. I have always, in everything, wanted to find out things for myself.

With this tendency it is rather fortunate that in 1929 when our parents decided to take my sister and myself to Paris for the study of music and painting respectively, the great French professor Lucien Simon took a fancy to my work and admitted me to his studio at the Ecole des Beaux Arts. Before leaving for Europe I had worked entirely from imagination, and, although I went through an academic phase in the first few years of my stay in Paris, I had never imitated nature servilely; and now I am deviating more and more from naturalism towards the evolving of new, and 'significant' forms, corresponding to my individual conception of the essence of the inner meaning of my subject.

Lucien Simon never 'taught'. He made us think for ourselves and solve technical and pictorial problems ourselves, merely encouraging each of those pupils whose work interested him, in his or her own individual forms of self-expression.

I worked for some time at the Ecole des Beaux Arts and got prizes at the annual portrait and still life competitions for three consecutive years. My work in those days was absolutely western in conception and execution except for the fact that it was never entirely tame or conventional.

I had not in those days learnt that simplicity is the essence of perfection. One sees with such exuberance, uncritically, when one is very young that one is liable to sacrifice the artistic whole to unessential detail, if it happens to be pleasing to the eye. One lacks the faculty of discrimination, so essential to the production of true art.

Towards the end of 1933 I began to be haunted by an intense longing to return to India, feeling in some strange inexplicable way that there lay my destiny as a painter. We returned at the end of 1934. My professor had often said that, judging by the richness of my colouring, I was not really in my element in the grey studios of the West, that my artistic personality would find its true atmosphere in the colour and light of the East. He was right, but my impression was so different from the one I had expected, and so profound that it lasts to this day.

It was the vision of a winter in India—desolate, yet strangely beautiful—of endless tracks of luminous yellow-grey land, of dark-bodied, sad-faced, incredibly thin men and women who move silently looking almost like silhouettes and over which an indefinable melancholy reigns. It was different from the India, voluptuous, colourful, sunny and superficial, the India so false to the tempting travel posters that I had expected to see.

Before leaving for Europe as a very young girl I had been so wholly an introvert that I had never really seen or observed anything round or outside me. I worked entirely from imagination in those days, and living on pictures instead of reality I conceived India through the medium of those unutterably mediocre specimens of fifth rate western art that still abound in the local exhibitions, providing doubtful if not harmful ailment to the artistically under-fed and undeveloped mind. And I 'regret' to say that, not satisfied with the production *ad infinitum* of this type of painting by the Europeans here, it is perpetuated, in blissful ignorance as to its artistic demerits, by a number of Indian artists! I say 'regret', because the paintings can no more be accused of being true interpretations of India than they can be accused of being works of art! When pursued as a form of recreation by amiable foreign amateurs of both sexes, or tourists who wish to conserve, in the form of oils or water-colours that have no pretensions whatsoever of art, souvenirs of their various travels, it is pardonable; but when the essence of mediocrity is adopted to found a school of art to give impetus to a new Indian artistic movement, then it is to be deplored in the extreme. I call this tourist painting, because it has all the characteristics of the tourist mind, being absolutely superficial, both pictorially and psychologically, impressions of impressions, where there is no room for artistic conception, penetration or insight.

—*Marg* (n.d.)

Ramabai, C.T. (Ramabai Trikannad) (b. 1914)

Variously referred to as Ramabai Trikannad or Mrs Ramabai in a few references to her that one comes across, Ramabai C.T. is among the few writers for children whose work could be located. In this list one could also include Santha Rama Rau's *This is India* (1954), a short and simple account of cities, festivals and the like. The folk-tales collected by Shovona Devi in *The Orient Pearls* (1915), are also accessible to children, as are the adventures of dacoits and tigers in Sunity Devee, Maharani of Cooch Behar's book, *Bengal Dacoits and Tigers* (1916).

There were surely more writers for children, contributing to magazines such as *The Children's News*, for which Ramabai wrote for several years. R. Raman, who wrote the Foreword to *Victory of Faith and Other Stories* (1935), says, 'The talented author of this book, Mrs Ramabai, needs no introduction to the reading public of India. Her literary contributions to various magazines and periodicals including *The Children's News*, with which I am associated for the last twelve years, are so frequent and well-known and so much admired by discerning critics that when she requested me out of her own regard for me to write a Foreword to her book I felt small and hesitant ... In India we have not many women writers in the English language and it is therefore a good sign that a band of noble ladies is trying to use the pen with considerable success. Mrs Ramabai is one of them ... Everything coming from her pen is at once fresh, chaste and healthy, full of moral fervour and ennobling ideas. Her manner of writing is so simple, direct and homely that even a boy or girl of tender years can understand it. At the same time it has the mark of a thinker and keen and sympathetic observer of life and its manifold problems although she is only twenty-one years-old.'

It's possible that Ramabai C.T. had some connection with missionaries, as the book was printed at the Basel Mission Press.

The only biographical information available was from the Foreword. An interesting observation one can make while reading the stories reproduced here—The Little Book Binder, Disillusion, and Aunts and Cats—is that unlike most other writers for children, Ramabai takes a particular event or situation, then delves more into the characters' states of mind, than the events themselves.

The Little Book Binder

It was one o'clock on Saturday and Vishwanath had just returned home. So nice, he mused, this half-holiday system on Saturdays. And the following day was a Sunday and holiday too! It gave one the consolation that life was not all work, that the toiling and moiling one had to do in the rotten office was relieved by a day and a half, though once in a week.

Though, sometimes, Vishwanath would muse, it would have been much jollier if the bosses were more considerate and human and made Saturday a complete instead of only a half-holiday. But bosses never understood, this was Vishwanath's usual grievance against them. They thought, perhaps, that men were just hired machines for their office work with limbs that just won't get tired after continuous work in the office.

At these thoughts, Vishwanath's blood would sometimes boil within him. Rotten, dingy little hole of an office, he would think, and rotten bosses to govern over them, who never treated men as human beings like themselves; men who toiled in their offices to fill their own pockets! Well, damn it all, it surely broke one's nerves; it would break the nerves of any fellow—yes, every bit of them. But on this particular Saturday, Vishwanath was in a high mood and quite satisfied and at peace with all the things, bosses and the present state of affairs in the world. And the reason was he had that day just purchased the latest book of that famous author, John Galsworthy, for which he had been hunting high and low until at last he found one in the bookstall at the railway station.

Some people, especially his present neighbours, gave out their own opinion of the book, which wasn't at all flattering to good old John Galsworthy. But Vishwanath did not mind what people said. He liked the book immensely and he was jolly well going to read through his other volumes too.

But amidst all this exaltation his mind was beset with a vague misgiving. And when little, seven-year-old Prema came in to greet him with her usual welcome kiss, he instinctively drew the book closer as if to hide it from her. Prema was his little motherless daughter and, like all children, was extremely fond of pictures.

'A new book?' she asked with sparkling eyes which meant to Vishwanath a forewarning of the approaching danger.

'Oh!' he tried to answer in a careless tone.

'Just a book that was lying in the bookstall that I bought out of curiosity. But it isn't at all a nice book, darling, no pictures, nothing whatever—shh!' He threw it on the top of the shelf with a pretended, disgusted look. But Prema was not to be put off. 'Papa, dear, do hand it over to me, only for a minute.' Putting her arms around his neck, she cooed and, of course, the touch of soft arms about his neck made all his common sense take to wings and Vishwanath took the book down from the shelf and handed it over to her. Little Prema opened the book and exclaimed with a joyful cry, 'There are pictures in the book, it is a very nice one, papa.' She turned the pages over hurriedly emitting shouts of delight as she came upon each new picture.

'Not so roughly, darling,' Vishwanath remarked with an uneasy look. But little Prema had no time to answer. She was busy and absorbed in the pictures.

Vishwanath eyed the book with consternation. Of course, Prema, he knew, was the dearest little angel that ever graced a home and nobody would ever think of denying it. Yet even the dearest little angels often had their drawbacks and little Prema was not an exception. She was so fond of pictures that she had an extraordinary way of handling books that left them wrecked when once they passed through her hands. That was what Vishwanath found most trying. He could never think of buying a new book or novel without the fear of its being spoiled by Prema lurking in his heart. And he would always determine whenever he bought a new novel that this time for sure he wouldn't let it get into her hands.

But how often does a man delude himself into thinking that he could do such and such things which Providence or Fate or a little daughter has designed to be otherwise!

So when smooth and caressing little arms lay clasped about his neck or when winning kisses greeted his return at the end of the day's hard work in the office; where soft little cheeks nestled close against his own and it was whispered into his ear just a 'Papa, dear' by the sweetest little voice in the world that he ever cared to hear;—well, it is no wonder that it should make any fond young father of an only child, as Vishwanath was, lose every bit of his common sense. That was how it would happen in the case of a new novel whenever Vishwanath brought one home.

The rustling of the pages grew louder. The pages began to flash one over the other like lightning.

'Such a nice, pretty book, papa, such beautiful pictures,' said Prema. She raised her eyes bright with delight, and then suddenly bounding, she picked up the book and dashed upstairs, murmuring, 'My new doll.'

The new doll was brought only that morning by Vishwanath. Having forgotten it, while she was absorbed in the pictures, she remembered of it just then and ran upstairs to have it with her.

'Prema, Prema,' Vishwanath called after her, 'just leave the book here, child.'

'Coming, Papa,' Prema answered from above. Vishwanath stood grasping the arms of the chair, his face registering fear, despair and anxiety.

He waited for Prema to come down, all the while glancing at the clock on the shelf. Five minutes passed but there wasn't any Prema to be seen. Still he stood there waiting until the clock ticked another five minutes more.

'Prema, Prema,' Vishwanath called again, his throat now choked with emotion. 'Just bring the book here, child.'

'Will come down in a minute, papa,' answered the sweet little voice above.

And yet another five minutes passed but Prema did not come down. Vishwanath was getting more and more impatient. Muttering an oath he strode up the stairs to fetch the book himself. From the doorway of the room upstairs he saw a sight that set his heart beating wildly with uneasiness.

Prema, with her back to the door, was down on her knees beside a large paper spread in front of her and John Galsworthy's book lay on it while Prema was busy wrapping it with some sort of red paper.

Vishwanath gave a stifled groan. Within two days of his bringing home any new novel, it was sure to get covered with green or red or black paper by Prema when once it passed through her hands. And he knew what the wrapping signified.

With another stifled groan he returned to the drawing room, sank down upon a sofa, and let out yet another groan which he did not try to stifle now. Fifteen minutes later Prema came down with the book in one hand and the doll in the other. Vishwanath sat gazing at her with dumb despair.

'Why, what's the matter, papa?' asked little Prema. 'Are you ill? You look so pale.'

'No, I am quite all right,' answered Vishwanath, 'but Prema, dear, why have you put that nasty red cover on the new book?'

Prema hesitated. Of course, Prema was a truthful little thing and wouldn't ever think of telling a lie; so she broke out.

'Dear Papa, you won't get angry if I tell you, will you?'

'Of course, not,' groaned Vishwanath.

'You won't? Sure you won't get angry when I tell you?' Prema asked again in a doubtful voice.

'Not at all, my dear' answered Vishwanath trying to put on a bright face like the martyr who knows that death is at hand. Prema set down the doll on the table and quickly uncovered the book of its red paper wrapper and held before Vishwanath's eyes its own original cover. The front wrapper of the book was torn a little and in the centre of it lay two pretty little thumb marks. Vishwanath did not speak. He just sat there, staring at the cover of the book with unspeakable emotion!

Prema tripped up to where he sat and stealing her soft arms around his neck, spoke, in a sweet, little trembling voice: 'You aren't angry, dear papa? It happened accidentally. Papa, please say that I haven't vexed you.'

But it would take more than soft little arms around his neck this time to restore Vishwanath from this shock.

'No, no,' he mumbled, while his eyes never left the thumb marks and the torn part which seemed to return his stare with a jeering and mocking look. The little thumb-marks seemed to challenge him: 'Why aren't you happy? You see this is your holiday and tomorrow too. So, why aren't you happy? Why aren't you gay?' And they seemed to grin at him and dance before his eyes like little naughty elves.

'How did it happen?' he asked at last turning to Prema with a stern look in his eyes.

'Papa, I really do not know, I had just finished arranging the new doll in its new dress, and when I took the book up, there I saw the marks on it. O dear Papa, you are angry with me!' saying this little Prema covered her face with her hands and burst out sobbing. Seeing Prema in tears all the vexation of Vishwanath vanished away like the genie in the Arabian Nights.

'Prema, my little darling,' he said, putting his arms about her: 'It doesn't matter at all, my child, not the least bit.'

And often, when Vishwanath goes through all the books in his library, some of which are dog-eared, some of which have marks on them, some of which have little scratches on various pages and again some of which have their pictures cut out—well, when he views all this wreckage sometimes, he often wonders why he can't be more firm and put on a sterner look when Prema, though unintentionally and often carelessly spoils them. That's the problem—why can't he? But the fact is that he cannot.

And all the uprooting of his determinations and resolves is effected by just a single tear that Prema sheds. And when she sheds a lot of them— God!—where is there any further hope for Vishwanath's sternest looks and firmest resolves?

—*Victory of Faith and Other Stories* (1935)

Disillusion

Ah! The dreary days were over and the old happy times had returned. Sushila beheld with joyous eyes her husband—who had died, or whom they had thought dead four years ago—alive and back again. Their two children aged eight and six were clustering around their long-lost father and telling him of their unhappy days without him; the scoldings and beatings they had to bear up at the hands of their master's children.

Sushila herself was preparing refreshments for Madhav, her husband, such as her humble store permitted. How did he come back from the dead—ran her thoughts in wonder at the miracle. She had forgotten to ask. She would ask presently, she thought. He was calling her now.

'Come and sit with me,' he said. 'I will have to go away again presently.'

'Then we too will come with you,' cried the children.

'Nonsense, dears,' chided Sushila, 'your father has come to stay with us permanently. He will never leave us again as long as we live'—'Will you?' she asked turning to her husband. 'No, then. ...' laughed Madhav.

He glanced round the small room in which Sushila at present lived with her children. In one corner was a small worn-out clay-hearth, with most of its clay decayed. Near it, on the ground beside the wall, stood a row of some earthen pots and vessels, which were their cooking utensils. In a nook of the smoke-covered wall was placed a dim lamp, which cast its flickering light in the room. Through a gap of a corner of the old thatched roof drizzled the monsoon rain thereby causing underneath that part of the roof little puddles of water. The half torn and old *tatty* at the entrance, which stood in the place of wooden doors, rocked to and fro as gusts of wind blew and beat against it. It was very cold and their clothes were scanty.

Sushila noticed that her husband took note of all this. And as she looked at him all her past happy married years came into her mind. She who had been the most beloved of her husband had to bear the insults and ill-treatment of strangers! She who had been used to care and comfort had to endure this wretched life! She who had herself been the mistress of servants was now compelled to toil at other's doors!

Sushila saw her husband heave a deep sigh and the tears glistering in his eyes. 'What did you do for a living while I was dead?' he presently asked.

'While I was dead'—how could he come back, Sushila asked herself, if he had been really dead and cremated? But she did not put the question to him and instead, went on relating her and her children's miserable life through the past four years; the continuous days when her children and herself had to go without food. Now she had got a job as a cook in a house two miles from her dwelling place. She had to get up at five; the bullock cart passing the lane by her house and the temple gong woke her up to the time punctually to prepare conjee for her children. Before it struck half past five, she had to be present at her mistress' house; and there she had to toil till twelve in the noon and afterwards return home to prepare their own frugal meal of boiled rice and some curry. Going back again at two she had to return not before eight at night after finishing all the work of her mistress' house, after which their own miserable supper started.

Once she had broken her arm and yet was not granted respite, and so had to work even then. She had remembered her husband every minute and prayed to God to bring him back to her, and God had answered her prayers. She would gladly work now. She could bear anything with him near her. Oh! he must never leave her again!—and Sushila wept in mingled joy and sorrow.

Bending down, Madhav drew her to him saying in his ever tender tones: 'No, no, I shall never go away from you, my dear.' 'At one place my mistress kicked me out,' said Sushila, amid sobs at the sad and humiliating recollection. Madhav wrinkled his brows as if in anger and then said again: 'Never will such days come to you again, my dearest, never will you have to work in other's houses as long as I am alive.'

Again, Sushila mused on his words—'as long as I am alive.' Has he not been dead since four years? How could a dead man live again? Yet he had come back and was now before her, quite alive.

Yes, her miserable days of toil at other people's door for a living, the life of pitiless abuses from her employers, the sicknesses of her children and not a pie with her—all, all those terrible days would end now. She would tell her present mistress that there was no more need for her to work at her house.

While Sushila sat thus, musing on these thoughts, she suddenly felt afraid and crept closer to her husband; afraid of what—she did not know. Was she going to lose Madhav again? Oh, she must not—he must stay!— she put her arms around him and clasped him tightly to her; no, she would not let him go away from her. And then, Sushila shrieked—he was going away. All things vanished from her eyes and she saw a hazy mist before her. O where was he? Where was her Madhav? She shrieked again calling aloud his name.

Sushila got up from her long, long dream, her body wet with perspiration. On the smoke-covered wall the dim light flickered on; in a corner stood the hearth in ruins and beside it, along the wall, the line of earthen vessels. The rain had stopped but, underneath the gap of the roof, still stood the little pools of water—the remains of the recent storm which had actually occurred and of which Sushila had dreamt. The tatty had stopped rocking, the furious wind now having calmed down. The cold was great and Sushila huddled herself upon her bare mat, drawing her two sick children close to her breast—to protect them from the bitter chill.

All was silent in the house; a bullock cart passed along the street, its driver singing some sort of tune to induce the bullock to move on more quickly. The arrival of the bullock cart signified the time—five o'clock. And Sushila got up from her half realistic and sweet but illusive dream to the hard reality of her unhappy and barren life, her whole mind still merged in her dream which recalled those happy yet sad memories in a surprisingly tender tone, 'I find that I like my educated and modern daughter-in-law very much and cannot, therefore, afford to part with her.'

Love had won!

—*Victory of Faith and Other Stories* (1935)

Aunts and Cats!

Billu is our favourite kitten. The last time my brother Krishna and I went to our aunt's for our holidays we took him along with us to be a companion in case we felt lonely there. And, of course, there was a row about it.

Now, you must know, aunts are invariably divided into three classes, the young aunts, the old aunts and the middle-aged aunts. The young ones are the best among them because they are more friendly with you than the others. The old are a tolerable lot, sort of reserved persons who think it beneath their dignity to mingle with or talk to their young nephews and nieces; and if some error on the part of the latter occurs they just let it pass with a sort of dignified forgiveness. But the middle-aged aunts are the limit, those nearing forty-five or thereabouts. You can never please them, however hard you may try. They do not mix with the young folk like the young aunts, but neither are they reserved and aloof like the old ones. They think it their duty to lead the erring nephews or nieces to the right path. Nor can they help making themselves unpleasant by showing their displeasure whenever they come across any drawbacks or what seem to them as drawbacks of the younger folk. Aunts of this kind are most trying and harassing to the young generation. And well, our aunt was one of such type.

But to return to Billu. Our aunt Sulochana protested strongly against Billu sitting on the cushioned chair or sipping just a little, very little drop of milk from the milk vessel or helping himself to a piece of bread from the larder, which he was quite accustomed to do.

We, Krishna and I, tried our best to point out to aunt what a dear little thing Billu was. But our cries fell on deaf ears or if the good old saying suits the present situation, our words and remonstrances glided down over aunt 'like water down a duck's back.'

Aunt Sulochana, without the least prick of conscience, said that she would drown Billu—poor thing—in the extra well at the back of the house, that she would poke his eyes out or poison him. Good God! she said such horrible things about Billu that we almost felt like quarrelling with her tooth and nail.

Poor little Billu! Like all animals, he was quite ignorant of what human language meant and aunt Sulochana's threats about his very life meant nothing to him whatever, as if she had never uttered them at all. My aunt raged terribly about him from early dawn till late at night, but Billu went on occupying aunt's chair and snatching his share of bread and milk whenever he got an opportunity. It was the first time we had gone to aunt Sulochana's for spending our holidays; so though she spoke in the most unutterable terms about Billu she never dared to touch him or do him any personal harm.

Of course, Billu was a worthy kitten, though aunt Sulochana didn't seem to think so. We tried a hundred times to convince her of Billu's good points. We told her of the dreary, lonely nights before examination when we were forced to sit up long into the night in our study upstairs, to learn by heart the difficult lessons. We told her how, while the whole household slept—quite ignorant and indifferent of us there on the study upstairs, studying hard, hard until our brains seemed to crack—it was Billu who came to us and purred and comforted us, keeping us company and making it easy for us to drive the reluctant sleep from our tired eyes. We told her also about Billu chasing a grown-up cat, which used to make away with whatever eatables that were in sight, out of our house forever. As a last attempt to restore Billu into aunt's esteem we narrated to her—though with reluctance—of Billu's once catching a mouse which used to nibble all the clothes in our house and make disturbing noises at night. Indeed, we do not at all like to confess about our cat catching and eating a poor harmless mouse which just did what it could to carry on its livelihood. But you know how matters stood and it was all we could do to try to get Aunt Sulochana to have a better opinion of Billu. But even that wouldn't help to remove the frowns off her face whenever she saw Billu. There was ever the suspicious look in her eyes—which one casts upon a doubtful person—whenever Billu came in from somewhere and sauntered about the room.

In spite of our aunt's repeatedly coaxing us and often entreating us with almost tears in her eyes, to let her send Billu with a servant somewhere to the other side of the river and have it left there, we could not comply with her wishes. She was quite welcome to abuse him till her dear throat got hoarse but we could never, never let her hurt our dear Billu.

A fortnight had passed since our arrival at Aunt Sulochana's and, by that time, Aunt Sulochana was almost mad about Billu. To crown it all, he went and tore up two new sarees of hers and some other things. It all came about this way.

Aunt Sulochana burst upon us one day like a hurricane and rated Billu with all her voice and in all kinds of abuses that ever existed in our language. And finding them too few for her present frame of mind she invented some of her own.

'Your-y-your rotten, dust-eaten, burnt-faced crow of a cat has done— do you know wh—what it has done?' she exploded in wrathful accents. 'It—the wretched, scoundrel-faced thing that you call Billu has gone and torn two new—two NEW sarees that were bought only yesterday and an embroidered cushion cover finished only a week ago. And—and—,' her voice seemed to fail her, but she strove manfully—or womanfully— to retain the last bit of her fast shrinking self-control, and continued effervescently, 'and broken the couple of pretty vases that I had bought only a month ago.' Here she broke down completely. We thought she was going to weep—but no, with a mighty magnificent effort she gathered herself together to continue her speech.

At this moment Krishna interrupted.

'Aunt, dear Aunt,' he said going up to her and laying his hand upon her arm which she promptly shook off as she might have done a piece of rubbish. 'Do forgive Billu and us. In future we will see that he won't do any mischief. Indeed, we promise.'

'Your wretched Billu,' began Aunt Sulochana, 'ought to be at the bottom of the extra—'

'Aunt,' I exclaimed. 'Dear Aunt—please do not say—'

'Don't interrupt me, you undutiful girl,' she flashed up vehemently, 'how can I talk if you keep interrupting like this? Your wretched Billu ought to be, I say, at the bottom of the extra well. That is the right place for it.'

'Aunt, dear Aunt!' I protested feebly.

'It ought to be hung by the throat on the tamarind tree,' she went on ruthlessly, 'or else I will just drop a bit of poison in a cup of milk and let it drink—the poor dear!'

Krishna and I tried our best to stop our ears from hearing this foul talk about Billu. But stopping one's ears from hearing isn't as easy a job as holding one's breath to refrain from smelling something nauseating or shutting one's eyes to unpleasant sights; and we simply dared not shut our ears with our hands for fear of rousing Aunt Sulochana to greater fury—not that she was any less furious now. So there we sat hearing it and wishing ourselves at the end of the world or at the bottom of the sea—somewhere, anywhere if it was only somewhere far from Aunt's lecture!

Now if my aunt did write a real book of essays on a cat, there is not the least doubt that a vast public of cat-haters would welcome it with open arms. Even tolerators of cats would be converted to Aunt Sulochana's faith after reading a few lines of her book. But my Aunt cannot read or write. Well, well, Fate or Providence did a wise thing when it withheld education from Aunt Sulochana!

Billu was never seen until late at night and Aunt had gone to bed after a strenuous and most exhausting day. Then it was that Billu came to my room mewing softly.

Next day while my aunt and myself were strolling in the compound, my aunt suddenly stopped and turning to me said: 'Shashi, do not mind whatever I said about your kitten yesterday. You see,' she added a little kindly, 'I can't bear with cats.'

We remained there for a couple of days more and Billu having destroyed two more bed sheets, and dropped a cockroach into the curry utensil as well, we thought it best to leg it home before matters grew worse.

—*Victory of Faith and Other Stories* (1935)

Noor-un-Nisa Inayat Khan
(1914–1944)

In her book *Noor-Un-Nisa Inayat Khan (Madeleine)* (1971) Jean Overton Fuller tells us that Noor-Un-Nisa had always loved the Jataka Tales, the cycle of five hundred or so legends about the previous incarnations of the Buddha. 'In each one he is represented as some kind of animal which, by an act of sacrifice, furthered its evolution. Now the Baroness von Tuyll wrote to her suggesting a joint work. She fancied illustrating some of these stories. (Her professional name was H. Willebeck le Mair and she was well known as an illustrator of children's books). They existed in an English translation, but not in a form which a child could understand. Could not Noor adapt a few of the best to make a children's book? They picked out twenty, and each set out to work.'

Jean Overton Fuller continues, 'The story she loved most was one she called "The Fairy and the Hare." It seemed to her sublime, and there is no doubt that it affected her throughout her life.' The book *Twenty Jataka Tales Retold* was published by Harrap in 1939, and Fuller includes Noor's favourite story in her book.

Noor was the great-great grand-daughter of Tipu Sultan. Her own life was equally adventurous. She was born in Moscow, but the family had to flee because of the growing unrest which led to the Revolution. They lived in London, then in Paris, and Noor was educated in Paris, so she was fluent in French, and wrote articles and stories in both English and French. The family fled to England because of Hitler's advancing armies. Noor persuaded the British to take her on as a radio operator behind enemy lines with the code name 'Madeleine'. Although she escaped twice, the Germans finally caught up with her, and she was shot with three other British agents in September 1944. She was posthumously awarded Britain's highest civilian award for bravery, George Cross, and the French *Croix de Guerre avec étoile de vermeil*.

The Fairy and the Hare

A young hare lived once in a small forest between a mountain, a village and a river. My children, many hares run through the heather and the moss, but none so sweet as he.

Three friends he had: a jackal, a water-weasel and a monkey. After a long day's toil, searching for food, they came together at evening, all four, to talk and think. The handsome hare spoke to his three companions and taught them many things. And they listened to him, and learned to love all the creatures of the woods, and they were very happy.

'My friends,' said the hare one day. 'Let us not eat tomorrow, but the food we find in the day we will give to any poor creature we meet.'

This they all agreed to. And the next day, as every day, they started out at dawn in search of food.

The jackal found in a hut in the village a piece of meat and a jar of curdled milk with a rope tied to each handle. Three times he cried aloud: 'Whose is this meat? Whose is this curdled milk?' But the hut was empty, and hearing no answer, he put the piece of meat in is mouth, and the rope of the jar round his neck, and away he fled to the forest. And laying them at his side, he thought: 'What a good jackal I am! Tomorrow I shall eat what I have found if nobody comes this way.'

And what did the little water-weasel find on his rounds?

A fisherman had caught some sparkling golden fish, and after hiding them under the sand he returned to the river to catch more. But the water-weasel found the hiding-place, and after taking the fish out of the sand, he called three times: 'Whose are these golden fish?'

But the fisherman heard only the rippling of the river and none answered his call! So he took the fish into the forest to his little home, and thought. 'What a good water-weasel I am! The fish I shall not eat today, but perhaps another day.'

Meanwhile the monkey-friend had climbed the mountain, and finding some ripe mangoes, he carried them down into the woods and hid them in a tree, and he thought: 'What a good monkey I am!'

But the hare lay in the grass in the woods, and his beautiful eyes were moist with sadness. 'What can I offer if any poor creature should pass this way?' he thought. 'I cannot offer grass, and I have neither rice nor nuts to give.'

But suddenly he leaped with joy. 'If someone comes this way,' he thought, 'I shall give him myself to eat.'

Now, in the sweet little wood lived a fairy with butterfly wings and long hair of moonlight rays. Her name was Sakka. She knew everything that took place in the wood. She knew if a small ant had stolen from another ant. She knew the thoughts of all the little creatures, even of the poor little flowers, trampled over in the grass. And she knew that day that the three friends in the wood were not eating, and that any food they might find was to be given to any poor creature they might meet.

And so Sakka changed herself into an old beggar man bent over, walking with a stick.

She went first to the jackal and said: 'I have walked for days and weeks, and have had nothing to eat. I have no strength to search for food. Please give me something, O Jackal!'

'Take this piece of meat, and the jar of curdled milk,' said the jackal. 'I stole it from a hut in the village, but it is all I have to give.'

'I will see about it later,' said the beggar, and she went on through the shady trees.

Then Sakka met the water-weasel, and asked, 'What have you to give me, little one?'

'Take this fish, O beggar, and rest awhile beneath this tree,' answered the water-weasel.

'Another time,' the beggar replied, and passed on through the woods.

A little farther Sakka met the monkey, and said, 'Give me of your fruits, I pray. I am poor and starved and weary.'

'Take all these mangoes,' said the monkey. 'I plucked them for you.'

'Some other time,' the beggar replied, and did not stay.

Then Sakka met the hare and said, 'Sweet one of the mossy woods, tell me where can I find food? I am lost within the forest and far away from home.'

'I will give you myself to eat,' replied the hare. 'Gather some wood and make a fire; I will jump into the flames and you shall have the flesh of a little hare.'

Sakka caused magic flames to come from some logs of wood, and full of joy the hare jumped into the glowing fire. But the flames were cool as water, and did not burn his skin.

'Why is it,' he said to Sakka. 'I do not feel the flames? The sparks are as fresh as the dew of the dawn.'

Sakka then changed herself into her fairy form again, and spoke to him in a voice sweeter than any he had ever heard.

'Dear one,' she said, 'I am the fairy Sakka. This fire is not real, and it is only a test. The kindness of your heart, O blessed one, shall be known throughout the world for ages to come. So saying, Sakka struck the moon with her wand, and with the essence which gushed forth she drew the picture of the hare on the orb of the moon.

Next day the hare met the friends again, and all the creatures of the wood gathered round them. And the hare told them of all that had happened to him, and they rejoiced and all lived happily ever after.

—*Twenty Jataka Tales Retold* (1939)

Snehalata Sen
(n.d.)

We are told in the Publisher's Note at the beginning of her book that, 'As a short story writer, Mrs Snehalata Sen has long ranked high among Indian authors.' Snehalata Sen wrote in both English and Bengali but, as was the case with some of the other writers included in this anthology, the only biographical information available was from these Forewords or Prefaces.

Three of the stories that appear in *Nehal the Musician* (1923), including the title story, originally appeared in Bengali, in a book named *Yugalanjali* (1906). The others, including the story presented here, 'The Tale of the Buddhist Monk' were written in English.

The Publisher's Note continues, 'Mr Romesh Chandra Dutt, ICS, in the course of a review on the above book, wrote in the *Indian Ladies' Magazine* (Madras) in January 1907 as follows: 'Wild, weird stories in Bengali, melodious and powerful verses in English—such are the contents of this book written by the sisters, the talented daughters of the Hon'ble B.L. Gupta, now Judge of the High Court at Calcutta. Mrs Snehalata Sen, the elder sister, gives free scope to her imagination in composing stirring little tales in Bengali ... Mr Rabindranath Tagore, the gifted poet of Bengal, has prefaced the book with a letter to the young authoresses ...' Mrs Snehalata's tales always have something wild and supernatural about them.

Nehal the Musician appeared in translation in 1911, in *The Idler* a 'story magazine published in England. The artist Nandalal Bose designed the cover of the book.' The reference to the 'sisters' comes as a surprise, as no mention is made of the younger sister in the book, neither is she named in the review by Romesh Chandra Dutt.

Among other interesting features, 'The Tale of the Buddhist Monk' contains a ghost who speaks 'fluent correct English'. The tale is beautifully written, with an eye for detail. It documents an epiphany of sorts, experienced by a young prince who turns to religion.

The Tale of the Buddhist Monk

I had been commissioned by the Archaeological Society to undertake the excavations of some ruins and temples recently discovered in the heart of a dense jungle on a mountain in Ceylon. There was no house or bungalow there and I took up my abode in the ruins of an old Buddhist stone abbey, which with tent cloths and derries made a fairly comfortable dwelling place. Some hundreds of coolies had been engaged in the work of digging, and they too slept at night in another part of the ruins.

Years ago some one had evidently begun excavating but had left off, and parts of the jungle had been partially cleared, and slabs of stone, stone images, etc., lay here and there. The place was studded with shrines and stupas, caves and temples, all dedicated to Buddha, the great Teacher of humanity.

Wonderful architecture, beautiful sculpture and carvings met my eyes everywhere. Dark, gloomy, cool, subterranean caves, where no light penetrated, and lofty and stupendous structures rearing their temples to the blue sky were scattered all over the forest. Strange fantastic figures were sculptured on some, and the smaller shrines had beautiful carvings on them. Each day's work unearthed some stone image or figure of Buddha. In some of these, infinite labour had been given to every detail. While superintending the work I often wandered about, gazing at these specimens of a past art and musing on them. Neither Time nor the ruthless invader had succeeded in effacing the indestructible works of the ancient Hindus which tell of power, glory, strength and beauty. From Man's work I turned to Nature's, and the deep forest shutting out all sight of anything modern enclosed me in a strange and new world which seemed to belong to another sphere.

As the shadows of evening deepened around me one day, and the coolies ceased their work and retired, an unnatural weird gloom seemed to fall on the place. I stood leaning against the truck of a tree. Dark, erect and severe stood the shrines and temples. In the fading light they looked spectral and I fancied I could almost see the shadowy forms of Buddhist monks moving about. It was the consecrated ground of a great religion whose spirit was choked and entombed by a false superstition, like the caves and temples themselves. At last I rose to leave the gloomy place, and as I turned a tall form confronted me. It was of a handsome man in the garb of a Buddhist monk, in loose ochre-coloured voluminous robes, with a bowl in his hand. The features were fine and regular and not of the Mongolian type one usually connects with this costume.

Was it a ghost of the dead wandering about among its former haunts? I started and gazed in silence and wonder at the apparition when he broke the stillness around and spoke in fluent correct English, 'Does the Sahib wonder at the temples of the Master?'

'Who are you?' I asked. 'A poor Buddhist monk who dwells in yonder little ruin by the river,' said he, pointing to an edifice some distance away by which a little hill stream flowed downwards noisily. It was a little ruin of no particular shape.

Strings of beads and strange charms and pendants hung round his neck. As my eyes wandered over him they fell on a pair of rings on the hand which held the bowl. They were exactly alike except in size—one being smaller—and of peculiar design, with a great stone in the centre. A marvellous stone such as I have never seen before nor since! They seemed to be large brilliant diamonds with a bright spot of gold like a luminous spark in the centre of the stone. It glowed and flashed in the waning light like a point of fire! My eyes were rivetted on them, when the monk spoke again: 'The rings are strange. They are the relics from a temple and their story is stranger still, Sahib.' I took my eyes off the wonderous stones and said:

'May it please the Holy Sir to tell me the tale. The stones are marvellous, such as I have never seen nor heard of.' 'If the Sahib will come to my cell and rest awhile, I shall be pleased to do so.' I assented and we walked on silently, he leading the way, till we came to the little ruin by the river. The moon was just rising—a pale young moon in whose silver light the river shimmered along in a long line. It was a hot sultry night. The monk entered his abode and brought me a stone cup filled with cool clear water which I drank. There was a raised stone slab outside near the entrance and he requested me to sit on it while he did so beside me. Then, resting his hand on the begging-bowl, the strange stones flashing in the moonlight—he began his tale.

'I was a Prince, Sahib—the Prince of Ratanpur.' I looked at him and wondered no more at the noble princely bearing of the man. He continued:

'A cousin of mine now sits on the Gadi and rules the land. A few years ago I was the lord of those territories, but the mystery of Life was revealed to me, and I was called away from my worldly life of pleasure and vanity. I had been touring in Europe after five years of college training in England. I had just returned and intended to travel all over India before I went back to my State. I landed in Calcutta and from thence proceeded to Benares. I viewed the ancient city with a new interest contrasting it with the scenes I had just left. After going about in the city for two days I took a large green boat courteously lent me by a friend. The Raja of—lived a few miles up the river and I proceeded thither. As my boat glided along I stood and gazed on the varied scene of the riverside. It was a quaint sight.

The temples of Benares with its flights of steps, the hundreds of men and women, some bathing, some praying, some worshipping, all bathed in the rays of the morning sun and above them the towering temple, striking and unique. Here indeed I felt I was in the land of the Hindus—the land of Bharat with no touch of the West. The scene revealed even to the trivial observer the history of the past—for there among the numerous old temples in the sacred city of the Hindus a Moslem minaret lifted its brow to the blue sky. As my boat floated on slowly, it passed in front of the burning ghat, reminding me of Death in the midst of the Varied Life around—of Maya which is ever present to the Hindu. A dead body lay stretched on a litter, covered with a white shroud. Just then another boat glided in between ours and the riverside. An old man, a Buddhist priest, stood in it looking at me. He was tall, clean-shaven and thin. He had a number of brass fancy things, evidently for sale, and a little covered basket in his hand. The boat came alongside of mine and the old man held out some of his things saying in a courteous voice:

'Will the Maharaja be pleased to see these?'

'There were some quaint little figures, charms, amulets and pendants. 'I have bought many of these, Holy Sir, and care not for more,' I replied.

'Then will the Prince be pleased to see these stones and rings,' he said again, uncovering the little basket and takings out some rings set with various stones. I took them from him and as I looked at them a large brass ring set with a strange brilliant stone which looked like a diamond with a spark of yellow light in its centre attracted my sight. I had never before seen nor heard of such a stone. The ring was crude in its make.

'This is a strange ring with a wondrous stone in it,' said I, pointing to it. We had left the burning ghat behind, but the dead body with its rigid outlines from under its covering could be seen. The old priest turned his head in its direction and said in a dreamy tone:

'"The mystery of Life and Death is in that ring, Maharaja. It is a relic from a Buddhist temple. The Mahatma, whose pupil I was, gave it to me when his soul was departing from its earthly house."'

'If thou will part with it I would buy it,' said I.

'"I would not willingly do so, Prince," said he after a pause, but I have need of money. It is the great wish of my heart that I join the monks in the hermitage of Mansarovar in the Himalayas. If this ring could bring me the sum I need I may sell it.'

'And how much is that?' I asked. 'Two hundred rupees, Maharaja, neither more or less.'

'An irresistible desire came over me to possess this strange ring and I agreed to the price.

'As he handed it to me he said, "The ring is not of brass, Sir, but of Ashtadhatu[1] and the stone a marvellous one. It is not a ring only thou hast bought Maharaja, but *dreams*—dreams wonderful and strange and beautiful that will show thee glimpses of another world. There is one other only like it, and it lies hidden somewhere. Perhaps thy steps shall lead thee thither and to holier things, for the mystery of Life is in it. May the path be unfolded unto thee, the path that leads away from Maya. Farewell, Maharaja." He signed to the boatman who pushed away and soon his boat was lost among the crowds behind.

'I held the ring in my hands and turned it round examining it carefully. How the spot of gold flashed like a luminous spark. The word "Maya" was engraved inside in Sanskrit letters. It was a large ring of a man's size. I opened my cash box and put it by carefully. Our large luxurious boat glided along slowly. The glow of the setting sun on river and temples faded into the dusk and I went into my cabin for my evening meal. After my repast I sat out on the deck reclining lazily in a large armchair and smoking. We had left behind the crowded part of the river and the temples and houses. My boat had been anchored under the overhanging branches of a large tree for the night. Gradually an overpowering drowsiness came over me and the sound of distant music as of a hymn or a chant reached my ears and then a strange thing happened. The river bank faded from my view and I saw a band of women, tall and graceful, robed in the garments of the order of the yellow robe, with veils over their heads, walk forth slowly. In the centre was the black-robed figure of a maiden with head uncovered and long tresses streaming over her back. Her hands were bound. The procession stopped and a Buddhist priest led forth the women and stood facing them.

'But all was lost in a moment in the shadows of the night. Slowly, the moon rose flooding river and bank, and in its golden rays the face of a woman appeared before my eyes—a piteous face with a frightened look in the eyes. Her long flowing hair seemed to envelop her in a black shroud.

'Maharaja, it is late, and the dews of the night are falling.'

'I started. My old servant stood beside me. I rose and went to bed. Sleep came, bringing with it dreams, strange sights, fragments of scenes to which there was no end. I awoke late next morning and wondered.

'But why should I? I had bought these dreams. I bought them with two hundred rupees. I had paid for the Ring. A strange land was this of ours where dreams of an unknown past could be had for money—could be had with a ring. Fresh from England and Europe, it seemed exceedingly strange to me even though I was an Indian. Night after night these dreams came to me. Dreams of buddhist temples and caves, monasteries and shrines,

---

[1] A mixture of eight metals.

nuns and monks—in strange unknown countries. I often took out the ring and gazed at it. It had a mysterious fascination for me. Thus three weeks passed, and after going to Agra, Delhi and other places I returned to Calcutta. The maiden in black robes continued to haunt my dreams. Sometimes she appeared in beautiful robes performing the daily tasks of a temple, lighting the evening lamps, decorating the altar. Sometimes as a bride she stood before me radiant and beautiful but always the same face. One night I seemed to stand in a vast hall upheld by massive stone pillars sculptured in strange figures. On a raised dais sat an old woman in the yellow robe of the Order—stern, austere and silent. Lines of Buddhist nuns stood on each side and in the centre stood the black-robed maiden bound hand and foot with bent head. A young man—a Buddhist monk—entered the hall and, marvellous to relate, he had the face and figure of myself. He opened out a scroll of parchment and seemed to speak for some time. Slowly the stern looks of the old nun vanished and rising she came forward and unbound her who stood there. She turned her face for a moment to the young monk—and then all vanished.

'The dream was a very vivid one and I wondered more and more. One evening while looking over an album of old pictures at a friend's house, what was my surprise to see a picture of the hall I had beheld in my dreams. The resemblance was unmistakable and I resolved to go to that place. The writing under the picture said it was in a forest on a hill in Ceylon where excavations had been undertaken by the Ceylon Government. I turned to my friend and told him I meant to sail for Ceylon next week.

'Why, you passed it on your voyage and might easily have gone then,' he remarked.

'It was true but I did not reply. The next week I sailed in a large sailing boat for Ceylon. An irresistible desire, an uncontrollable impulse seemed to have taken hold of me.

'In due time I arrived there and proceeded at once to my destined place. 'And, Sahib, it was to *this* place I came.'

The monk ceased for a moment and I looked once more at the two strange rings on his hand and at his dark, earnest, dreamy eyes. Was his tale true? The rings were real without doubt. He went on again:

'I entered the vast hall of my dreams. The building was a Buddhist monastery of stone partly in ruins. I wandered about in its cloisters and little convent cells. I wandered at the gorgeous mosaic ceiling, the massive arches and carved walls and niches of the temple adjoining it. All was silent, dark and lone within. At eve I returned to my lodging in the house of a Singalese gentleman a few miles from there. But at night in my sleep it seemed that I rose and went out. Unknown though the place was, I found myself walking along and ere long reached the ruins.

'As I neared the abbey I stood still as if turned to stone, for a wondrous sight met my eyes. Shadowy forms moved about among the trees; bells rang out in peals; a procession came out bearing a dead body; and then all vanished into the darkness, and I awoke to find myself in bed. Was it a dream? I spent the next day in watching the coolies digging and in wandering about the ruins aimlessly. At eve I did not go home, for a strange fascination kept me, enchained, as it were, to the spot. As night closed around me, enshrouding the forest in a black darkness, a great restlessness overtook me and I roved about. Suddenly I found myself tracing my steps along a narrow path behind the abbey. I went on as if in a dream and entered a large enclosure in which was a number of tombs. Mechanically, as if directed by some invisible agent, I stopped at a tomb. The coolies had evidently been digging there, for a large oblong slab of stone, deep like a box, lay near some fresh earth, and the lid was open. A few bones—*human* bones—lay outlined in it and, marvellous to relate, another ring like the one I had bought in Benares lay in it. As I stopped and picked it up, a low chant reached my ears,

> I take my refuge in thy name and thee.
> I take my refuge in the Law of Good.
> I take my refuge in the order.
>
> Om.

'I gazed around with eager eyes, and there from the darkness above shone forth the face of the maiden in the black robes, the maiden of my dreams. A halo of light encircled her face pure and holy as an angel's. It seemed to speak of holy things, to call me away somewhere, Where? As I gazed, it faded slowly into the dense darkness and the low sweet chant died away into deep silence.

'When I awoke daylight had pierced the dense gloom of the forest and touched the trees and cupola-shaped stupas, and the heights of the temples and shrines with a golden light. It fell on the ring in my hand which flashed forth into a hundred sparks. I rose with it in my hand and retraced my steps to my lodging. As I walked a voice sighed with the wind, "I take my refuge in thy name and thee." A voice murmured among the trees, "I take my refuge in the Law of Good." It formed the music of the hill stream, "I take my refuge in the order. Om."

'A voice echoed from the caves and mountains, "Om". A face, sweet and pure, hovered round me. A voice whispered in my ear, "I take my refuge in thy name and thee."

'A great peace came over me. All longings and desires left me. The Path "where healing streams quench all thirst", "where bloom immortal flowers" lay disclosed to me—the path which leads away from Maya and the vanities of the world.

'Thus it was, Sahib, that I, the heir to an ancient line of Kings, have left my State and have entered the Path my Master trod. Om.'

His tale was ended and I perceived my two servants at a distance waiting respectfully. I beckoned to them. They came but they had forgotten my presence. With holy reverence they prostrated themselves at the feet of this Buddhist monk who murmured a blessing, laying his hand, on which the strange stones sparked, on their heads.

It was late, I rose and bade the Buddhist monk farewell.

—*Nehal the Musician* (1923)

Shovona Devi
(n.d.)

In her Prefatory Note to *The Orient Pearls* (1915), Shovona Devi writes: 'The idea of writing these tales occurred to me while reading a volume of short stories by my uncle, Sir Rabindranath Tagore, but as I have none of his inventive genius, I set about collecting folk-tales, and putting them into an English garb, and the tales contained in the following pages were told to me by various illiterate village folks, and a few by a blind man still in my service, with a retentive memory, and a great capacity for telling a story.'

The stories included here—The Princess with the Borrowed Life, The Hermit Cat, and The Hireling Husband, correlate with folk-tales from around the world, as far as certain themes are concerned: the prince turns into a pauper, a sly cat, and yet another prince woos a princess under the garb of a hireling.

The Princess with the Borrowed Life

Once upon a time there was a king who had an only son, but for some reason or other the latter had incurred his father's displeasure and, with his wife, had been banished from the kingdom.

The unfortunate couple took shelter in a forest, which was then nobody's property, and the Princess, wearied out with her long tramp, fell into a deep slumber, while her husband lay awake, keeping watch lest any harm should come to her; but, as ill-luck would have it, a deadly snake, which had its hole close by, crept out stealthily and bit the Princess.

The Prince, seeing her dead, set up a loud lamentation, which attracted to the spot a forest-hermit.

'Why dost thou weep, my son?' said the latter to the Prince, as he looked upon the Princess. 'Thy wife was never destined to live long.'

'Canst thou not, holy Father,' said the Prince, almost beside himself with grief, 'bring her to life again?'

'Yes,' replied the hermit, 'if thou wilt part with twenty out of the allotted years of thy life to thy wife.'

This the Prince speedily promised, and the hermit then asked him to join the palms of the dead Princess's hands together so as to form a cup; which done, he put into them a little water out of his gourd and then asked him to say to his wife—'Wake up, my wife! I part with twenty out of the allotted years of my life unto thee.'

No sooner was this said than she sat up with a start, as if nothing had happened to her beyond an evil dream, and that very moment the hermit disappeared into the forest like an apparition.

After this the royal couple did not consider it safe to dwell in the forest any longer, so they took to tramping once more, until after many adventures they found a home in a family of amateur dancers and singers.

The Princess was extremely fond of these arts and soon acquired remarkable proficiency as a dancer. Then, in order to judge by the test of public applause whether she had, in fact, attained such proficiency, she one day put on a disguise and slipped out with her friend, to give public exhibitions of her newly-acquired art.

The Prince, her husband, made a search for her, but, unable to discover her whereabouts, he reconciled himself to his fate at last, and took service with a nobleman, a high dignitary of the country.

Time passed on. The kingdom was astir with grand preparations for a festival, and the king had invited every nobleman in the kingdom to the palace to witness a performance by a famous dancer.

The Prince accompanied his master to the palace to witness the dance—and what a dance! The spectators were charmed no less with the dancing and singing than with the beauty of the performer, and applause greeted her at every turn, and gifts of great value poured in upon her. Among these gifts was a ring from the Prince, and, as she took it in her hand and looked at it, the dancer saw that it was her own ring with her name engraved on it, which she had exchanged for her husband's at her wedding; but she did not notice who among the crowd had given it to her.

After the dance was over, the spectators gathered round her, complementing her in Oriental hyperbole on her splendid performance, and showering gifts upon her; for their hearts were captivated by her dazzling beauty.

The king himself came round and lavished his praise upon her, and asked her what she wished him to do for her.

The lady handed him the ring and said: 'Your Highness! this ring belongs to me. Someone among the crowd presented it to me. He must be the thief. I beg Your Highness to find out who it is and punish him.'

As soon as the Prince heard the accusation made against him—for it was he who had given her the ring—he stepped forward, rubbed his eyes well, and discovered that the lady who had captivated the hearts of all the spectators, as well as his own, by her beauty, and who had won their applause by her exquisite dancing, was none other than his missing spouse, the Princess herself.

The Prince turned round and said to the King: 'I gave this ring to this lady. She is my wife; but she left me some time ago and has since taken to the life of a dancing girl. I did not recognize her at the time I gave her the ring. If she wants further proof, I say that she would have died of snake-bite, had I not revived her at the expense of a part of my life; and yet, for all that, she calls me a thief in public.'

The Princess, of course, knew nothing of all this, and took the Prince for an impostor. She burst out into sarcastic laughter at what she imagined was but an idle tale, and challenged him to prove it all to her.

The Prince then asked her to join her palms together in the shape of a cup, and, as soon as that was done, he put a little water into them and said: 'I have lent thee twenty of the best years of my life. I take them back.' No sooner was this said than the Princess staggered and dropped down dead on the spot!

The spectators were horrified at the sight, and would have beaten the Prince to death, then and there; but the King interfered, and, having heard the real truth from his lips, offered him his daughter in marriage, and the couple lived together long and happily.

—The Orient Pearls (1915)

The Hermit Cat

Once upon a time a tom cat, grown too old and infirm to catch his prey, stationed himself before the door of a temple, and fed on the crumbs of the offerings made to the idol by its votaries. Sometimes he used to sally out, holding up a rosary in one fore-paw, carrying a begging-bowl in the other, and limping along on his hind legs, in the hope of catching his prey by pious fraud instead of force, after the fashion of robber-mendicants.

On one of these sallies, the cat met with a mouse, and the latter, surprised to see a cat turned hermit, was bold enough to ask him whither he was bound.

'I have been abroad on a pilgrimage,' said the cat. 'I have just returned, and am now bound for my temple.'

The mouse, prostrating himself before the cat, at a sufficiently safe distance, for 'what is bred in the bone will come out in the flesh,' begged to be allowed to accompany him. Of course, the request was granted, the mouse following the hermit at a respectful distance.

The cat could not, even if he would, catch the mouse on open ground, lacking the energy to pursue his prey; but, once inside the temple, he could, said he to himself, pen him in and capture him with ease.

A little further on, a pigeon with a tuft of feathers on his head joined the party.

Arrived at the temple, the cat made his companions walk in, and himself stood at the door, telling the rosary as if he were engaged in prayer, so as to disarm the suspicions of his intended victims.

In the meantime the mouse, suspecting foul play, made a sufficiently long hole for himself in the floor of the temple, while the pigeon perched himself on the canopy over the idol, beyond the cat's reach.

After a time, hungry as he was, the cat lost patience, and cast about for an excuse before attacking his intended victims.

In a tone of haughtiness he demanded of the pigeon why he wore a tuft of feathers on his head.

'The tuft of feathers,' said the bird with much humility, 'is worn as a badge of caste.'

The cat next turned to the mouse and demanded, in a still more haughty tone, why he wore a beard and whiskers.

'My beard and whiskers, Thy Holiness,' replied the mouse, 'are as much symbols of my religion as thy rosary and begging-bowl are of thine.'

The cat, who now saw he had been found out, at once sprang upon the mouse, but, before his palsied paws could touch him, the little animal had slipped into the newly-made hole, while, as for the pigeon, it flew away to a place of safety.

Balked of his prey, the cat sulkily left the temple, and went and sat under a tree by a mouse-hole, with three paws up, sustaining his whole weight upon the fourth. The mice issued out of the hole, and, seeing the cat standing on one paw, enquired why he was practising austerities in front of their hole, of all places on earth. The cat winked at them and said: 'I am a cat turned hermit. I am standing on one paw out of consideration for Mother Earth, because, if I stood on all four, she would be burdened with a greater weight.'

The mice took him to be a very religious cat, and ceased to have any fear of him, and so, as they filed past, they prostrated themselves before him.

The wily cat used to snap up the last of the mice as they went past him, and, after they were gone out of sight, would devour him.

In this way his religious garb stood him in good stead, but, on the other hand, the mice kept missing some one or other of their numerous family every day. One missed her husband, another his wife, a third his sister, and so on, and there was much weeping and lamentation among the survivors, and their suspicions naturally fell upon the cat-hermit, the hereditary enemy of their tribe.

They accordingly determined to keep watch over the doings of the cat-hermit, and, as they filed out of the hole, the head of the party kept looking behind until the last mouse had left, and lo! as the latter came out, he was seized! The party then turned back, and the cat instantly let go his prey and resumed his former attitude. The mice filed back into the hole, and, acting on the principle of 'union is strength', caught hold of the cat's tail and dragged him, by sheer force of numbers, into the hole, and made a feast off him, which lasted for many and many a day.

—*The Orient Pearls* (1915)

The Hireling Husband

Once upon a time there was a proud and haughty monarch, and in his pride he neglected the gods and feared them not. He had married seven Queens, and each of them had borne him a son. 'What a joy to have such a family!' said he to himself, as he beheld his seven grown-up sons around him. 'I own extensive dominions, and would rather trust my sons to govern them for me than even the most trustworthy among my ministers.'

Filled with such thoughts, the King called his seven sons, and, intending to let them govern such of his possessions as their gratitude and affection for him should seem to deserve, said to them one by one: 'My dear son, who feeds thee and cares for thee?'

'Why, Father,' said the six oldest sons, 'who else should feed and care for us but thou? Has any of us been so ungrateful as to have denied that?'

'No,' replied the King; 'I was only thinking of making you governors of my provinces, and so, to know from your own lips which of you loved me best and were most grateful to me, so as to deserve my trust, I put the question to each of you. I am pleased with your answers and appoint you each a governor of one province.'

When the turn of the youngest Prince came to answer the question, he bluntly said: 'What a queer question to put? Father, who else can feed me but my own good destiny? "What's lotted can't be blotted."'

The King flew into a great fury and banished him then and there from his kingdom, saying: 'Oh, thou ungrateful wretch if thy good destiny feeds thee, look to it to feed thee in thy exile. Thou art henceforth no son of mine.'

Thus banished, the Prince bowed to his father and went away to seek his fortune elsewhere. He journeyed on and on, not knowing whither, until chance brought him to another kingdom. According to the laws of this country, every foreigner found therein had to be brought before the king, and only when he was found to be of good character was he ever allowed to stay. So no sooner had the Prince arrived there than he was seized and straightway taken before the King, who immediately took a fancy to him on account of his handsome appearance, and chose him to be companion to his son, a one-eyed Prince of equal age with him.

Thus did his good destiny befriend him in his darkest hour of trial.

As time went on, the father of the one-eyed Prince thought of getting his son married, but, as he was blind of one eye, none of the Princesses around cared to be his wife; at last necessity, which is said to be the mother of invention, suggested an ingenious way out of the difficulty.

'Why not get my son married by proxy?' said the King to himself. 'Why not let his companion, who is of the same age as he is and not a whit less handsome, play the bridegroom on his behalf, going through the marriage in his name, but letting him into the bridal chamber by stealth directly after the nuptials?'

And so, having thought out his plan, he proceeded to put it into action by sending out match-makers in every direction. It happened that another King, who had a grown-up Princess to marry, had, by a curious coincidence, similarly sent out a match-maker to look out for a bridegroom, and that he, having wandered far and wide without success, at last arrived at this kingdom quite exhausted and worn out. He soon discovered the son of the King to have but one eye, yet, having become too fatigued to go elsewhere to seek for a better bridegroom, he struck a bargain with the King then and there, promising to keep his tongue between his teeth as regarded his son's blindness.

Loaded with rewards, he returned to his master, told him how he had settled the marriage of the Princess with a remarkably handsome Prince, and thus received fresh rewards for his pains.

The wedding-day came, and the Prince's companion, dressed as a bridegroom, started in grand procession for the house of the bride in company with the King and his one-eyed son.

Arrived there, the sham Prince and his party were received in right royal style with every circumstance of pomp and grandeur. Everyone at the palace was captivated by the sweet manners and handsome appearance of the bridegroom, and the wedding passed off without a hitch. Immediately after the marriage, however, the bridegroom, according to his compact with his master, stole out of the bridal-chamber and rejoined his own party.

The Princess, missing him from her chamber, sent out her maid to look for him amongst the men of his party, and, sure enough, there she found him. After some persuasion she induced him to return with her to the Princess. On the way back, however, the Princess, who feared he might again leave her, had caused artificial tigers, bears, and lions to be set up. As soon as the Prince and the maid had crossed the road where these pretended beasts were concealed, they suddenly came in view, looking as fierce and threatening as if they had been alive.

The maid, pretending to be greatly alarmed, begged the Prince to hurry up as there were wild beasts behind them, and pointed to the sham tigers, bears, and lions with her finger; but the Prince, who knew not fear, offered to go back and kill them all with his sword. As that would have spoilt her plans, she entreated him to quicken his steps, saying she would fall down in a swoon if he tarried. The chivalrous Prince had to comply with her entreaties.

Thus was the wandering sheep brought back into the fold again, and, when the Princess saw her bridegroom, she took him to task for having run away from her, but soon she made it up with him and begged him to play a game of chance, before retiring, just to ascertain, she pleaded, how their married life would fare.

The Prince, to whom nothing came amiss, agreed to her request. While they were engaged in play, the Princess began to doze, and at last fell asleep, and the Prince, taking advantage of this, wrote in golden characters on the hem of her flowing robe his name and pedigree and the curious history of the marriage, and then decamped for good.

When the Princess awoke, it was daylight, and the bridegroom was not at her side. She consoled herself with thinking that he must have gone back to his friends among the men of his party, and, when night came on, he told her maid to go and fetch him as she had done the night before.

Now the one-eyed Prince, who had put on the dress of his proxy and was wearing a big turban which came down over the blind eye almost concealing it, met the maid and accompanied her to the Princess. On the way back they had to pass the same fierce-looking artificial beasts, and the maid entreated him to quicken his steps, as she pretended the animals were after them. No sooner had the one-eyed Prince looked behind and seen the beasts, than he began to quake all over through fright, and only kept himself from falling down in a swoon by catching hold of the maid, who screamed out and shook him off with much difficulty.

Arrived at the palace, the counterfeit bridegroom walked into the chamber, trembling with fear as if he had been suddenly seized with ague. The maid narrated to her mistress all that had happened on the way, wondering in her own mind whether he was really the bridegroom, for his behaviour had been so strange and unlike that of a Prince. However, the Princess had seen her bridegroom only for a short time, and so, to find out beyond all possibility of doubt, whether the gaudily-dressed young man before her was really her wedded husband, she asked him to play a game of chance with her. To her surprise he professed total ignorance of all games, and could not remember a single word of their talk on the wedding night. Suddenly the Princess noticed one of his eyes all but hidden by the turban, which she lifted up, when lo! she found him blind of one eye and had him instantly turned out of her chamber, neck and crop.

The one-eyed Prince ran back, weeping, to his father and told him of his woes. Finding that the fraud had been discovered, the King in great dismay beat a hasty retreat from the country.

In the meantime the Princess was at a loss what to do, not knowing who her husband was nor where he lived. In the end she could do nothing but keep her soul in patience in the hope of his some day returning to claim his bride.

In spring, when the earth is gay with flowers, and the birds fill the air with sound, the swinging carnival is held, and so it happened that the Princess put on her wedding garment and started swinging with her companions, when lo! the end of her robe swept the ground before her, and the golden letters recording the name and pedigree of her husband shone out in the sun. She quickly jumped down from the swing and learnt for the first time who her husband was and where he lived.

Overjoyed with the discovery, she ran straight to her father and thus said to him: 'O Father, the home of a married woman, be she a Princess or a commoner, should always be where her husband's home is. I am determined to go in search of my husband, so wilt thou be pleased to give me an army for my protection?'

The King tried to dissuade her from her purpose, pointing out the difficulty of the task, but she was not to be moved from her resolve. At last the King had no alternative but to give her an army consisting of his bravest and most trusted soldiers, and dressing herself in a man's clothes, the Princess set off on her travels.

The first thing she did was to go to the kingdom of her husband's father, and besiege it, challenging her father-in-law to give her battle; but the old King, not desiring bloodshed and fearing defeat, submitted to her, and was compelled to produce and give up his youngest Prince to her as a hostage. After that, she threw off her disguise as a Prince and declared herself to be the bride of his youngest son.

The King now realized the truth of what his youngest son had said to him, and, flinging himself upon his neck, said: 'My dear son, thou didst speak the truth. "What is lotted can't be blotted." Thy bride has won my kingdom for thee, and it is no longer mine to give away.'

From that time forward, the Prince and Princess lived happily together and ruled their people well and wisely.

—The Orient Pearls (1915)

Iqbalunnisa Hussain
(n.d.)

Who's Who of Women in India (1935) tells us that Begum
Iqbalunnisa was born and educated in Mysore, and that she was
the first Muslim lady graduate of Mysore. She started a school for
home industries as the Social Secretary of the Mysore State Women's
Conference, and 'has now proceeded to England for higher studies'.
The volume was published before Iqbalunnisa published her
novel Purdah and Polygamy in 1944. Teresa Hubel's article (see
Bibliography), 'The Missing Muslim Woman in Indo-Anglian
Literature: Iqbalunnisa Hussain's Purdah and Polygamy' connects
Iqbalunnissa with other Muslim women reformers such as Rokeya
Sakhawat Hossain, the writer, and Sakinatul Fatima Wazir Hasan,
an activist in the social reform movement of the 30s and 40s, who
in 1936 contributed to a collection of essays entitled Our Cause: A
Symposium by Indian Women. Certainly a sharpness of tone connects
all three. A quote from Hasan in the Hubel essay reads: 'Among
the upper and middle classes purdah is still the rule, and orthodoxy
which seems to have found its last resort among the Muslims of
India, is firmly entrenched. There is no other Muslim country in
the world where, in social matters like the purdah, marriage, and
status of women generally, so much dull-witted reaction prevails
as in India.'

Teresa Hubel writes, 'The issue of purdah was one of the principal
platforms of the pre-Independence Indian women's movement. ...
For those Hindu women who disagreed with the custom, it could
be combatted with a rhetoric that traced its origins to the Islamic
invasion of India and explained its subsequent adoption by the
Hindu elite classes as the effects of a corrupting influence. This
interpretation of purdah history in India, which, during the
Nationalist Movement, was used by Hindu revivalists to reconstruct
a Hindu history of women that was untainted by oppressive
structures from outside the Hindu fold, has been repeated so many

times by so many writers that it has entered the realm of common sense, though today in India there is a concentrated effort by feminist historians to uncover its racist overtones.'

Teresa Hubel continues, 'Unlike that of many Muslim women reformers, Hussain's analysis of the wrongs done to Muslim women is not embedded in a reinterpretation of Islamic scriptural teachings. ... Hussain's unwillingness to traffic in Islamic religious authority is tied up with her attempt to demonstrate that Muslim ideology regarding women, far from being divinely sanctioned, is, in fact, man-made. Again and again in the novel, through such techniques as narratorial comment, irony, and dialogue, Hussain suggests that the social system that confines women, physically and symbolically, is the product of male dominance.' For many Indian families, the strict seclusion of women was also a sign of prosperity. Finally, despite arguments against purdah advanced by prominent Muslim reformists, 'the custom continued to be so widely practised that when Hussain wrote her novel in the 1940s, she could depict every, single one of her middle-class Muslim female characters in a strict state of purdah and not stretch the bounds of the realist mode in which she was writing.'

Chapter II

Messages were sent to the relatives living in the city and telegrams to those out of it. Early morning trains brought swarms of them. Deaths, births, and marriages are events of great excitement and bring hundreds of womenfolk together. People who do not know a certain family can make a voluntary acquaintance on such occasions on the plea of human sympathy.

Zuhra fainted when she knew that her husband was dead. Her mother and sister who lived in the same city had come a few minutes before Umar passed away. They looked after her and her belongings. A death affords a good chance to the poor to get away with portable articles which can be hidden under the full-size veil. All big and small things were locked up in a lumber room. They were wholeheartedly her sympathizers. The neighbours had to send food to the house of calamity. The days of such consideration vary, but three days at least the bereaved family should be free from the worry of cooking. Luckily the three families, the tenants, agreed among themselves to feed the family a day each.

The dead body of Umar after washing and shrouding was kept in the common courtyard to enable hundreds of visitors to have their last look at him. All those who visited them that day had to be invited to the funeral dinners on the 7th, 10th, 20th and 40th days.

After the men finished their visits the doors were closed. The near and dear women relatives who did not observe purdah in front of him were asked to see the deceased. After all a man is a man even dead, and purdah before him is essential. The saddest ceremony in Zuhra's life had to take place before the dead body was taken for burial. Neither the mother had the heart to do it nor the married sister. No woman, with her husband living dared invite the calamity upon herself with open eyes. Umar's widowed sister came to Zuhra, an invalid who being aware of the dreadful ceremony began to sob, which made all the women shed sympathetic tears. There was a loud cry by the nearest relations. Umar's sister did not care for the general wailing; she had to do her duty. Holding up Zuhra's arm she made her stand. She could not do it. The great strain of nursing for years and the shock of his death had made her lifeless. Another old widow rushed to help her. In between them she had to walk to the dead body. When Zuhra was nearing the dead man she felt her sorrow uncontrollable.

'Don't make me a dark spot on the radiant world of womanhood! Kill me here and bury me here with him!'

An avalanche of indignant shouts burst on her from numerous ladies: 'You get what you deserve. You cannot go against God's will.'

'She will be a curse, a thing to be hated among women all her life,' said others. 'If you were lucky you would have died before him. He would have made you the queen of the day,' said a kinder woman.

Naturally such bitter remarks touched her sympathizers to the quick. They retaliated.

'This day is seen by hundreds. You are not alone in the sinking ship.'

'Think of other widows who are in a more miserable condition. Be brave, face the wrath of God with the same spirit as you do his favour.'

But even the well-wishers spoke from a distance.

The two unsympathetic supporters of Zuhra had to do their duty quickly. They pushed her forward between them. Her sobs were converted into loud weeping.

Don't for God's sake put my arms. They are aching. I don't want to live. For whom have I to live?' said Zuhra, frantically struggling. The hold on her arms was tightened.

'Oh kill me! My life will be worse than death. What interest have I in the world? Who will be my supporter? Oh God, the world is dark to me.'

Umar's sister who was holding the arm lost her temper. 'Whatever one gets is in return for what one does. You must have made his life unhappy, and must have disobeyed him, so you are bearing the consequences of his curse. Behave yourself in acknowledgment of your evil doings.'

A desperate condition of mind breeds imagination and recollection. 'I had no sleep, no rest, no peace of mind, and converted my nights into days, yet I deserve this. Is there justice in the world?' she said still weeping.

Such desperate expressions by the helpless daughter put courage in the heart of the mother. She came near to console Zuhra, and holding her to her breast said, 'Don't lose heart. You are judged now. Your son will be your helper and protector. You have to live and do a double duty for him.'

On the approach of her mother Zuhra's grief knew no bounds. She entreated her not to make her a widow, but the mother could not help her. The ceremony had to be performed. So they brought her to the dead man. She screamed when she saw him in the shroud and said, 'Oh heaven! what a condition he is in! I cannot bear to see him dead. Leave me. I shall kill myself and be buried with him.'

Umar's sister, who believed that Zuhra had been the cause of her brother's death, indignantly said, 'Don't pretend by saying that you want to kill yourself. You killed him all right,' and with force she made her squat near the corpse and commanded the mother to leave her in her charge.

'Bring a stone,' shouted Umar's sister. It was given. She broke the bangles from both the hands of the weeping Zuhra, then she pulled and threw the *Latcha* (black beads), the token of marriage, near the corpse, and removed the jewels and handed them over to a reliable widow relation. 'Bring a sheet,' she shouted. Zuhra's sister had brought a white dress (sari and blouse) for the occasion and sent it with someone. Zuhra was clothed and her coloured dress was taken and thrown near the dead body.

One of the experienced women said 'Cover her face; let it not be seen by *suhagans* (married women)'. 'Wash her face before you bring her inside the house,' cried another. 'Oh goodness, it ought to have been done before putting on the widow-clothes,' said someone else.

'One forgets what and how it is to be done because of the way she behaves. She is not ashamed of having caused the catastrophe; on the other hand she is howling and thinking of her own wretched self as if it is worth an atom. Shall I undress her, washing her face and then put on the clothes?' asked Umar's sister.

'No, no, to put on the widow-dress twice means making her a widow twice,' said one of the onlookers.

'Even if she is not made a widow twice, the curse will fall on someone else,' cried another.

It was decided that she should not be made a widow twice, nor to let the catastrophe fall on some innocent being, so she was taken back in the same way. She was not allowed to touch the corpse for fear of polluting it. They brought the reluctant creature away by force and laid her on her bed.

The thousands of men waiting outside for the women to make room were agitated. It was Friday, and the body had to be taken to the mosque before 1 o'clock. Umar had been lucky even in his death. His death on Friday meant an easy salvation which made others envy his fortune. The news that the men were coming in made the members of the opposite sex hide themselves in rooms. But they could not help peeping through the windows and doors, to see how the dead body was carried away. They were sure of their not being seen by the men. Even supposing they happened to see some women peeping no one could say who was who. The rooms were not enough to accommodate all. Some of the brave ladies sat down in the courtyard and shouted, 'Give us a sheet.'

It was searched for and given. Two old women beggars held the corners of the sheet. Thus it separated the women from the men in a corner of the open place. A second general wailing was started when the corpse was taken out. All women excepting the new widow came out to wash their faces and hands. The friends waited till the men returned from the burial ground and departed.

The relatives could not leave the place so soon. The near and dear ones coming from distant towns made up their minds to stay for forty days. They had to take part in various funeral ceremonies, and console the bereaved party.

The seventh day ceremony came on. 'Do everything very grandly to keep up his name and fame,' said Umar's sister.

'I have invited for dinner about five hundred people,' said Umar's brother.

'Were there only five hundred visitors that day?' asked the sister.

'There were more than a thousand,' was the reply.

'It looks mean and insulting if all of them are not invited for all the functions. In what way are the survivors going to show their regard for the man who left untold wealth?' said the sister.

'Ask his wife if she has no objection to what you say. I shall do it with pleasure,' said the brother, who knew that without Zuhra's signature no money could be drawn from the bank. Kabeer went to his mother who was in bed and said, 'Uncle wants to know if all the visitors have to be invited for all the functions or a part of them for each.'

Zuhra could not yet think of her position. 'Let them do anything they like. As for the expenses he has left enough.'

The reply satisfied all the organizers. The amount or each function was calculated.

'We have to make the dishes he liked the best,' said his sister. 'What about the clothes to be given to beggars?' said someone.

'They have to be clothed well or else the poor man will be seen naked in our dreams,' said the sister.

This ingenious idea gave birth to a new problem: whether ordinary clothes were to be given to many beggars or a costly set to one.

'Whatever you give you will see him in it,' said the sister.

'Then let it be a costly dress. Who will not be pleased to see him in a grand dress? He will look as if he was alive,' said the cousin widow. After some discussion it was decided that at the other functions ordinary clothes were to be given and on the fortieth day costly ones.

The fortieth day came. It had to be the grandest possible function. Many expensive dishes liked by Umar were prepared and the costly dress with gold embroidery was got made. It was arranged in a tray to keep ready for the night.

'No one will give such a grand dress to a beggar. No beggar will wear it. He will sell it and make money,' said the nephew of the deceased.

Kabeer was dissatisfied with all the extravagance, the daily expenses of maintaining five extra families and his mother's neutral policy.

'It was made for a Fakir,' said Kabeer. 'Let him have it. Why unnecessary discussion over a subject decided long ago?'

'The idea behind giving the clothes is just to part with them in the name of the dead man. It means the same even if it is given to a poor relation. Nazeer is getting married soon. It will suit him and will make a grand bridegroom's dress,' said the cousin.

The suggestion, as it was unselfish and useful, was unanimously supported. The prospective bridegroom was sent for and the dress was handed over to him after the *Fathaha* (prayer for the salvation of the soul).

The ladies who stayed for all these days did full justice to their sojourn. They helped, consoled and made them forget their sorrow. The motive of all of them was noble but the methods of carrying it out differed.

'What is the life of a woman after her husband? A woman lives for him and him alone. His death should mean the death of all her desire, comfort and happiness. Even the dogs are shown better consideration,' said one.

Once Kabeer was with his mother and heard someone saying, 'A widow has to be conscious of her sin in causing the death of her husband in thought, word and deed. She should avoid being present at happy events and not try to make others miserable.'

'My mother is different from other widows. I shall allow her to do anything she likes without caring for the ill talk,' said Kabeer.

Umar's sister, who was more tolerant to her nephew than to his mother, said 'You can allow her to do things after a long time, but now both of you should be very careful in what you do. So long as there is life in us we have to care for the opinion of others.'

The death of Umar had made Zuhra weak. Any mention of her husband or of her future wretched life made her shed tears for hours. Some of the guests were sincere and made a great fuss over her, attending to her needs in bed; some consoled her.

'God has chosen two extremes in writing your fate. One in giving you the best husband who sacrificed everything for you, and the other in making you the most unlucky in his loss. He has left money for you, but what is it? It does not give you happiness, respect and licence to take part in social activities.'

'He was very good to me. I was lucky in having him,' sobbed Zuhra.

'You didn't deserve the boon,' said one.

'If committing suicide was not a sin I would have done it long ago. The thought and the welfare of Kabeer prevent me. Oh, my son, who will take care of him? He will lose both father and mother,' cried Zuhra.

The over-crowded house, the seclusion, the constant taunts, the direct and indirect condemnation of widowhood and the frugal food—she being afraid of looking healthy—had made Zuhra pale and haggard. She could not sit or stand by herself. One day Kabeer took her to the courtyard for fresh air. She felt better while sitting there. Her sister-in-law rushed to the place and said, 'What will people say if they see you here? They will say that you were just wanting his death to be free. No widow will leave seclusion before four months and ten days. You are giving room to scandal. Even the servant will call you immoral.'

'Kabeer brought me here against my will. I am conscious of it,' said Zuhra.

'You should use your discretion. If you listen to children where is the difference between inexperienced boys and you? Unless you try to be careful in what you do and say I am afraid you will brig disgrace to the family,' said the sister-in-law rudely.

Days had passed since she had combed her air. She had a constant headache. She asked someone for oil, and a comb. When it was taken Umar's sister said, 'You are not making her a bride?'

The relations after performing the fortieth day funeral ceremony, and having exhausted all the cash in various banks, left one by one reluctantly. Thanks to the deceased the will was made and the property could not be sold before Kabeer reached his majority. This was well known to the male relatives.

Kabeer felt a great relief when the last family left. He did not ask anyone to stay behind and keep his mother company. He knew that he could do it better and make her forget her grief. The sense of responsibility had opened his eyes. Position in one's life works miraculously. He shunned his old friends and was the constant companion of his weeping mother.

'Don't make your life miserable in my company, Kabeer,' she said once.

'Your company gives me all that I need. You are to me both father and mother,' said he.

'You will be hopelessly disappointed in your expectations. No one will take his place. You lost in him everything in the world,' said she sympathetically.

Kabeer did not approve of her sentimentality. He felt that he was better able to look after himself. The sense of dependency had always been a cause of dissatisfaction to him. He was at liberty to spend and do what he liked, yet he did not exceed his privileges. His thoughts were turning towards the affairs of the estate. He had a sympathetic adviser in his mother.

'Both of us are equally afflicted. Let us feel the pang together. I would sacrifice my life to make you happy and comfortable,' he said with tears in his eyes.

'God bless you and give you long life, my supporter,' she said equally grieved.

Gradually he began to take an interest in outdoor affairs. All this time Umar's trusted servants and agents had managed the estate. He consulted his mother regarding the rent, interest and correspondence. He found her suggestions useful. This diverted her mind from the shock which seemed unbearable. They determined to keep aloof from their relatives. They felt that they were happier without their interference.

In a very short time he made the tenants, the staff and the people believe that he was sympathetic and lenient in his dealings. His generosity brought him more friends, and representatives of various associations for donations. His religious teaching had its effect. The Peers and the privileged demagogues whose high birth rules mankind were often invited. They were fed for days and given gifts to enable them to carry out their noble professions. No other method of propaganda to make a name for himself was needed. People began to talk of him as a rich and great man. His numerous visitors made it necessary to vacate the other part of Dilkusha which had been let during his father's time.

The wealth seemed to have an outlet, but what is money for if not to live happily and comfortably? was the thought of both the mother and the son.

Chapter IV

Human nature is not good everywhere. 'Birds of a feather flock together.' This is particularly true of business men and men with the mania of acquisition. When this instinct becomes a master sentiment it acts ruthlessly and knows no point of satiation.

When the capitalists and exploiters of the town came to know of the offer of a valuable house by a woman, all of them stuck together and offered a rock-bottom price. There was no time to wait for a better one. The building which had brought in nine hundred rupees a month was knocked down for fifty thousand. Zuhra's plans for the marriage were too grand to be carried out with that amount. She believed in being noticed.

'Kabeer, can you manage to raise a loan? We can easily economize in the future and repay it.' 'We shall have to sell or mortgage another property. There is no other alternative.'

'It will come to the notice of Doulath Khan. If he comes to know of our financial condition he will not respect you. I am told that he is spending double the amount yet he is not selling any property. He offered more money for the building, yet I refused his offer.'

'Then the only way is to buy things on credit. They charge more. ....'

'Let them take a few rupees more. We shall be able to pay soon after the marriage.'

'From where?'

'Out of the presents and the cash you get at the time of Jaiva.'

Kabeer in spite of his anxiety to say more could not do so freely in front of his mother. She spoke to him about it only when it was necessary. He wanted to say that she could not sell the presents, but it was too much for him.

'We have fifty thousand.'

'It is not enough for the jewels. I want to buy different kinds of sets. What about clothes and other expenses?'

'They won't be much.'

'The celebration will last fifteen days and the guests will be here eight days before it begins. We need at least twenty five thousand for feeding and clothing the near relatives.'

'Why all that? They know father is dead and we have spent a lot already.'

'Knowing our condition and expecting gifts are two different things. If we don't give them at least half of what they expect we will be making enemies.'

'Tell me what to do.'

'Send for one of your uncles. He knows what to do.'

398 • WOMEN'S VOICES

'Yes, swindle us. We know where we stand with our servants. Even if they steal it wouldn't come to hundreds.'

'If we do it ourselves there will be open hostility. If he were alive no one would have dared ask for the responsibility. Didn't you hear the sarcastic talk after the betrothal ceremony? Although I told them it was done in a hurry because of Jamila.'

'If father is dead you are alive. No one can blame you for it.'

'Have you ever heard of a purdah woman doing it? There are a thousand and one things to be bought, people to be consulted, houses to be hired, servants engaged, and what not?'

'If we ask one to be responsible the others will be annoyed. We have had enough experience of their work and their grumbling. Didn't they say if they had not rallied round Father would have been left unburied? Their anger will not do us much harm. We shall try to face their taunts boldly and patiently.'

'There must be a male member to look to things. You can't do them. What will people say? You can't put Mustafa in charge. It will make them furious. They will never be bossed about by him.'

'He will not order them to do things.'

'He dare not. Even if he commands servants it will put them off. They will set up their servants against him, and even us.'

'We shall ask Jamila's husband.'

'While his father is alive he will not accept.'

'Then let Mustafa do all that he can before they come. Then you can ask Jamila's father-in-law to act for father.'

It was decided. No relation was asked to come in advance. All those who had played important parts formerly waited anxiously for months. Nearing the months of the wedding they realized that they had to play a secondary part. The decision divided the relatives into two groups. Some of them were pleased and called Kabeer and Zuhra wise. They even prayed for his long life. 'The world will be better for the existence of such a clever young man,' said a very sincere relation. These came exactly on the date fixed for their arrival. This prompt action displeased the others who held meetings to discuss whether to go to the wedding or not. Women are keener than men on participating in marriages. The aunt said: 'Our presence at the marriage as mere spectators will not look so hideous as our non-cooperation. People will openly say that we did not attend because we were not made responsible.'

'To be at a distance and hear such talk will not be so humiliating as to be there on the spot. You will have to obey the orders of that insufferable Mustafa. I am sure he is acting the father. I shall murder him if he acts master to me,' said Umar's brother, who had been is charge of all the funeral ceremonies.

'You are prejudiced. He will neither be made responsible nor will he command you,' said his sister. The women supported the aunt, so they decided to start as soon as possible not to create any suspicion about their willingness. Intimation of their arrival was sent. Conveyances and escorts were sent to the station. Umar's brother suspiciously looked at the guides to discover Mustafa, but he was not there. He had many other important things to attend to. Jamila and her husband came with the first batch but her father-in-law arrived only with the malcontents. His excuse was that the house could not be left to itself for months, so he would try to engage a reliable watchman and join them.

The party reached home. Every one of them looked proud and serious as they had come with the policy of non-cooperation and non-violence. It gives a reasonable excuse to an unwilling partner.

'We want a separate room for ourselves. We are not quite well, that is why we came so late,' said Umar's sister.

'I see,' said Zuhra. 'The separate rooms have been kept ready.'

Unfortunately the rooms meant for them were occupied by distant relations who had come earlier So rooms in the other corner of the house were shown to them. The luggage was carried in and the party followed. Aunt and Uncle exchanged glances.

'This is the first humiliation, and many will follow,' said the uncle.

'The corner rooms will be much safer. We can give full vent to our feelings,' said the aunt.

All of them went to their rooms. Zuhra asked Jamila to seek out her father-in-law and tell him that the whole management had been done by her, but now that the men were there she wanted him to take the responsibility and to allow her to attend to other domestic duties.

Jamila told him confidentially. He said 'I shall think it over and send word to her.' He went to the sister and brother who were busy in talking over the insults and informed them about it.

'Something is better than nothing. The servants at least will have respect for us if you act prominently,' said the sister.

All of them grouped together and expressed their grievances to their hearts' content. When the meals were announced they intentionally went late.

'What a dirty place and plates! Do they take us for dogs?' said Umar's brother.

'You have to make the best of your position. Try to be patient and pass the days,' said the sister.

'This looks like a doll's marriage to me. The arrangements and the food at the funeral ceremonies were a hundred times better.'

'This is not the time to pass remarks. Even the walls have ears. As it is we are unwelcome guests. Our criticism will do us no good,' said the sister.

'We are insulted and treated like strangers. We ought not to have come to a place where we are not respected,' said he.

'Hush, someone is coming,' said the aunt.

'Rasam has been brought. Mother wants you all,' said Jamila to the ladies. The participation in the rasam would give them fresh ideas and cause for more gossip. All of them stood up quickly and departed.

Kabeer was made to sit on a stage in the middle of the famous courtyard which was brightly lit. It was packed with ladies, those who did not observe purdah in front of him, and children. Numberless trays with presents, eatables and flowers were set in front of him.

'Uncover the trays and show us the presents,' said the aunt.

One of the married woman obeyed her faithfully.

'What a cheap sort of ring, and shawl! This gives an idea of what they think of the bridegroom. If the bride's people had any respect for him they would have presented him lavishly,' said the aunt.

Kabeer's mother overheard the remarks from a distance.

'Those are a few of many. Other costly ones make up for them. We shouldn't judge the people on the basis of less expensive things,' said Zuhra.

'If it were my only son's marriage I would have picked a quarrel on that matter. I would have thrown them in their faces and asked them to replace them by suitable ones immediately,' said the aunt.

The girls, boys and the maidservant who had come from the bride's house looked horrified and stood like statues. They did not know whether to commence the ceremony or return with all their paraphernalia. Zuhra without caring for the suggestion asked them to start the ceremony. This annoyed the aunt, but there was nothing she could do. She pocketed the insult and gazed earnestly at the performance. Her associates also found many more grievances for discussion in their den.

The next morning Nikha was being performed. The bridegroom's party went to the uncle for permission to start.

'In the absence of the bridegroom's father your permission is to be obtained,' they said.

'You did not need any at the time of fixing the marriage and till to-day it was not necessary. Carry on with your work,' said the uncle.

'Does it mean you disapprove?'

'My approval or disapproval has nothing to do with it. The marriage is almost finished. One should know the time for such permission,' said the uncle.

There was confusion and agitation among the male members of the bride's party.

'What does it mean? Are they against the marriage?' said Doulath Khan.

Jamila's father-in-law overheard it and going to the over-anxious group said 'Carry on the Nikha with my permission.'

Many agreed and said, 'He is one of Umar's brothers. His permission is equally valuable.' The Nikha among men was over.

The bride was brought to the ladies for tying the Lacha. The poor thing was crying pathetically. Now was the time when she really felt the separation from her near and dear ones. She knew nothing of the people among whom she was going. She had not even seen them. She had been frightened to death from her childhood by stories of cruel mothers-in-law. How she would be criticized and faults found in everything she did. She had been given examples of heartless husbands who inflicted corporal punishment on their wives. She was asked to forget herself and be ready to face a hell in her future home. All these precepts began to crowd into her mind. The pathetic cry of the bride made almost all the ladies shed tears, thinking of their daughters who would one day have to face the same situation. Zuhra also shed tears thinking of her son who would not be so loving and obedient after that day.

'Go and ask Aunt who is an old suhagan to tie the Lacha,' said Zuhra to Jamila.

If a married woman who has lived long with her husband ties the Lacha the bride will have the same good fortune. So an old couple is particularly invited and the lady is requested to perform this act. As the demand for such a privileged woman is so great naturally she feels proud of her position.

Jamila went to her aunt. 'Ammajan wants you to tie the Lacha.'

'Is your mother dumb? From when did she lose her power of talking? Perhaps she thought it was beneath her dignity to come to me for it.'

'She is sitting at the other end of the hall. The place is overcrowded. She can't stir from her seclusion,' said Jamila.

'When you could manage to reach me, why couldn't she?'

'I pushed them and squeezed myself through and jumped over the children. One can't expect all that from Amma.'

'Just because there's no alternative she had to ask me. Ask her to do it herself, just as she did everything else,' was the curt reply.

'Don't be absurd and ask a widow to do it,' said the bride's grandmother who happened to be seated close by.

Jamila went back to the mother who gave her permission to do it herself. As Jamila was approached the bride the aunt's better sense prevailed. She got up and tied the Lacha without more ado. One of the ladies said, 'If she had done it without making a fuss, she wouldn't have brought ridicule on herself.'

'Don't talk through your nose without knowing the circumstances,' said one of the aunt's companions. The aunt finished her most sacred job and returned to her place. The widow sister of Umar, who had played a prominent part at the time of the funeral, said, 'Our talks and actions are watched and criticized. We must not show indifference or we shall leave the place with their enmity. It is better to preserve a nominal friendship.'

Experience is a good teacher, and bitter taunts are better. The aunt's friends in appreciation of her wisdom nodded their heads as a token of approval and jingled the heavy jewels in their ears and necks.

Jalva, when the bride is first shown to the bridegroom, now took place. Relations and friends from both sides had to give presents to the new couple. Kabeer's relatives who were annoyed, were discussing in a corner whether to give presents or not. The majority were against the proposal for more than one reason, but the opposing party though small carried the day. Some of them had brought with them superfluous articles from their homes and so felt an inner urge to deliver the goods. They stealthily handed them over to Zuhra with a request not to betray them. The rest followed suit.

The bride was brought home after the Jalva. A ceremony to make her coming an auspicious event took place, when her feet and hands were washed with milk. Similar observances were going on, to the utmost disgust of Kabeer, till he said that he was exhausted and needed rest.

The next morning the bride was sent for by her parents. Kabeer was left alone and had to wait for an invitation. The hours of separation were taxing. He was not allowed to go out of the house as on these days men literally observe purdah. He sat about impatiently or played with the children, keeping his eye on the front door not to miss the messenger bringing the invitation. The hours dragged on. He felt furious at the clock, which seemed cruelly antagonistic to his feelings. He thought of turning the hands of the clock to seven, but who would do the same in the bride's house? He went from one room to another, and to his surprise he found everyone asleep. He felt jealous, could not believe his eyes to see them so thoughtless; he went to his room and lay in bed till it struck seven. Each stroke put life back in his nerves. Each sound of a footstep thrilled him. But in vain. At eight o'clock, disappointed, he came to a decision not to go when the invitation arrived.

'It is past eight, and no sign of those people. Are they sending for you or not?' said the aunt, who came to him to put oil on the burning fire.

'I am not going there ever if they send for me,' said the enraged Kabeer.

'Don't pretend. You will jump up and forget your determination,' said Jamila who had entered the room.

'Have your dinner with us if you are feeling hungry,' said Zuhra who followed Jamila.

'I shall go to sleep right away. I don't want any food.'

This satisfied the opponents who felt sourly triumphant. Their spirit of revenge was making its way naturally.

'What inconsiderate people they are! Do they want to separate their daughter from him? The poor boy is pining from ten o'clock in the morning. One can imagine their treatment in future if it is such the very first day,' said the aunt very lovingly.

'Coming events cast their shadows before. You have to be ready for worse things. After all they are rich people. Pride and wealth go together. It suits them even if they do it,' said one of his cousins.

His mother's pride was touched to the quick. It was an open insult to her. The fear of hearing such a remark had made her spend thousands of rupees. She wanted people to say that both parties were equally rich. If they had said that her son was richer than his father-in-law she would have had nothing to complain of, as man being the superior animal everything that belongs to him ought to be so.

'If they are proud of their wealth we are prouder. A man after all is not the loser in such circumstances. If he is dissatisfied with one woman he can marry many. If they don't behave better I shall put down my foot and see that they come to their senses,' said Zuhra.

While the talk between the ladies was going on in his room Kabeer was becoming more and more exasperated. Patience has a limit. Once it is passed no one can control himself.

'Why this discussion on a subject that does not need any? I tell you I am not going there. If they send a car return it saying that I am not well,' said Kabeer.

'There will be many such hitches in life. If you begin to make a fuss over petty matters life will be impossible,' said Jamila, who by now had experience of a mother-in-law.

'That's your valuation of life,' said Kabeer.

'Don't be silly, Bhai. What will they think of you? After all what did they do to you? This is just the time for dinner. When there are guests dinner takes place at ten,' said she.

'What did they do to him? They treated him like a servant. They will send for him to feed him, as if he has no food in his house. You call him silly. You are a silly goose not to understand the situation,' said the aunt.

It was past nine. The car was announced. The young brothers and sisters of the bride came running into Kabeer's room, and seeing him in bed they began to pull his shawl and arms and made him sit up. A girl brought his sherwani (long coat) and turban from the hanger and forced him to put them on.

'Abba and guests are waiting for you. He asked us to bring you soon,' said they.

Kabeer forget all about his decision. He said to the little ones: 'All of you go to the car. I shan't be long.'

But one of the girls with more perseverance said, 'I am not going. You will sleep again.' She held his finger tight and pulled him out of the room. He did not resent it. The little girl had charmed him. The idea of asking his mother's permission went clear out of of his head. He followed the girl from the room.

The spectators exchanged sarcastic glances. The aunt was overjoyed. Revenge had laid the foundation and the construction of the edifice was in her power.

'To expect respect from sons especially after they are married is to build a house on sand. Soon after seeing his brothers-in-law he forgets all, even his own mother who is sacrificing her life and happiness and is working like a servant for him. If children only thought how difficult it is to bring them up they would have more respect for their parents' feelings. I can't get over the sight how he acted and treated all of us,' said the aunt very affectionately to Zuhra.

Zuhra was astounded at her son's behaviour and began to feel that her sister-in-law was her real friend. She controlled her emotion but in the absence of the aggressor wrath must find a satisfactory outlet.

'I shall serve him out if he does not mend his manners,' said the defeated mother.

'Unless you take this matter seriously and nip his impertinence in the bud he will treat you like a slave. It is up to you now to keep up your dignity. You have to deal with a person who has no blood relationship and respect for you. If he is indifferent to you one will be worse.'

'You have confidence in me. I won't allow anybody to have the upper hand with me. From the very first day I shall make her understand her position here.'

This was matter of no small elation to the aunt. She had put the poisonous seed in the cultivated ground. Circumstances would see to its proper watering. Zuhra's spirit towards her daughter-in-law was bitter; but would she not yield to the whims of her son?

'You have to be strict to both. There's every possibility of his losing his head. I can't imagine how he marched out of the room without looking at you when you were all the time supporting him.'

'Yes, I know.'

'I don't think the bride is chaste. I have my own reasons for saying so,' said Kabeer's cousin, who had been waiting all those years to give her daughter in marriage to him. His wedding was an irreparable shock to her.

Jamila had not heard the conspiracy going on among the ladies. She had left the room after Kabeer went to put her babies to bed. She entered the room when the last remark about the bride was passed. Her blood boiled with fury. From the first sight she had liked her sister-in-law.

'Don't start talking ill of the poor thing. She is an innocent child. Such suggestions will result in the destruction of both. You will make Bhai's life miserable. They are respectable and very orthodox people. One should think twice before condemning anyone.'

'I didn't mean anything ill. I just mentioned what struck me. Hereafter we will act like puppets,' said the cousin.

'It is better to be silent than to harm someone,' said Jamila.

Zuhra and the aunt looked at each other meaningly. The former detected a contemptuous look in the eyes of the latter which was rather disagreeable to her. She thought it was wise to support her daughter, or the mischief might take a hideous turn.

'The world will be better without presumption and hasty remarks. Sensible people avoid such expressions even if they are certain of it,' said Zuhra.

'Our own relations are our enemies. How would you feel if someone said such a thing about your daughter?' said Jamila to the cousin.

'They would be mad to say it. Nothing is said without cause,' said the cousin and left the room.

The matter was dropped. The mischief-monger was not very proficient. The design was erased before it could make its appearance. All of them had a quiet dinner and went to their rooms. The aunt thought that she had done her duty for the day. Her plan would have been more efficacious if the cousin had not unwittingly poked her nose into it.

They were together for some time. 'It is mere jealousy that made her talk so nastily. If she is angry with us she ought try to take revenge upon us and not on that poor creature,' said Jamila.

'Let us not think about it any more,' said Zuhra.

The next day the bridegroom and the bride came to spend the day. Everybody contrived to seem busy, except Jamila and the numerous children who came to welcome the pair. Jamila led the bride to her room while Kabeer paused to please the little ones. A servant came: 'Begum Sahib wants you.'

'Is anything the matter?'

'I don't know. She looks serious.'

'Why, what has happened?'

The servant went away.

He hesitated to go to his mother, but he had to. He went and greeted her very politely. Zuhra without blessing her son said, 'What happened to you last night? Had you gone off your head? You could see no one except your new friends.'

Kabeer stared at her and tried to recollect what he had done. 'What did I do?'

'What did you do? Are you still dreaming? Is it hypocrisy?'

'But what happened?'

'The very first day of your marriage you forgot your mother and your obedience to her.'

'All of you were waiting for the car to send me. The children worried me so much that I forgot to ask your permission.'

'That's what I say. You forget that your mother is alive. I wouldn't have prevented you from going. Isn't your interest my concern?'

'Ammajan, it was done unwittingly, and it shall never take place again.'

'Well, so long as I am alive you and your wife are expected to obey me implicitly. If you learn to obey, you will be able to rule. For whom am I labouring if not to make your life happy?'

Kabeer left her room and made to go out.

'Why are you so serious?' asked his aunt. 'A new bridegroom should be all happiness. When we are happy we don't know what we do.'

'Oh, nothing,' said Kabeer.

'Did you see your mother? She was rather upset last night. I tried my best to console her.'

'Thank you.'

'Zuhra is rather hasty in her actions. She should remember that a boy after losing his father is sad beyond words. Your sorrow will make that poor girl unhappy.'

'Please leave me. I have to go to the office. The business has been neglected for a long time.'

Kabeer knew his aunt's character well and couldn't be easily led astray. He entered the front building of Dilkusha. All the workers were having an easy time. No one would expect a bridegroom to go there.

'Something is wrong somewhere,' said one of the old clerks.

'The poor man seems used up,' said Mustafa.

Kabeer sat there checking and rechecking the accounts mechanically. A servant came and called him for lunch.

'I am not well. I don't want it.'

He sent servants for food and sat alone in his room.

'What made her so changed? She has never been so cold to me. Her attitude was quite different from what it has been all my life.'

The servant came back after an hour.

'Begum Sahiba is waiting for you and wants you to have some light food.'

He stood up. If he did not obey the second call there would be a break in the family. Her anger had a cause. She must have felt awkward when he went away without her permission. Four hours had passed since he was separated from his wife. He decided to go to his mother first and on the pretext of not feeling well go to his room.

He found her kinder and she smiled as he entered the room. She made him sit near her.

'Kabeer, I live for you and you alone. I wanted to kill myself after his death and save myself from lifelong misery. Only the thought of your loneliness made me surmount unbearable sufferings. What do I want from you but a little regard? You will have many wives but not your mother. How long will she live? Her days are nearing their end.'

'I am extremely sorry for what has happened. It has upset me. I shall have tea and no lunch.'

'Do as you please. Go and have a rest. I shall send for you.'

After bowing respectfully he left her and went to his room. He found Jamila and all the little ones there entertaining his bride who looked to him like the Sleeping Beauty. All of them were talking and laughing but she had closed her eyes and lips tight. Nothing made her smile or look about her. If there had been a competition to behave like a statue in the presence of mischievous spectators she would have won the first prize. She was not expected to open her eyes in her husband's house for five weeks and not to talk for about two months. The woman servant from her mother's house supplied all her needs. She closed the door when she fed her. She was not expected to eat more than a morsel. When Jamila found her brother in the room she sent all the little ones away and taking the bride's servant with her closed the door after her.

Chapter XI

Maghbool, Kabeer's third wife, was a beauty according to the feminine estimation. She was fat but well proportioned, and of medium height, the broad chest and comparatively slim waist making her figure very attractive. The broad, high forehead, with long nose, thin red lips with rosy cheeks, quite big almond-shaped eyes with dark, curved eyebrows, long lashes and the natural jet-black curls dressed round the forehead would have been a very good model for an artist.

She was an institution in herself. Her mastery over the Urdu language had made her crazy after papers, magazines, romance and poetry. She had a natural bent for music and had learnt many songs from the radio, pictures and even from beggars. Her rich voice had given them a feminine touch and sweetness. The whole family admired her singing and young girls and boys crowded the room to hear it. She made it a point to sing after the streets were quiet. Her father was fond of it and found solace in it after his day's hard work. Maghbool knowing of her father's liking used to try to learn something new and thrilling almost every day.

She was a good organizer and an economical manager of the house. From the day she took over the management she saved several hundreds a month. She kept accurate accounts. Her father often said that she was a son to him, his secretary and his right hand. She was active and hated to while away her time. Needlework, designing and painting were her hobbies. Everything she did was self-learnt, and she did it so exquisitely that an expert in that art would say that she had reached a fair level of perfection. There was nothing that she could not do and whatever she did she did beautifully.

Getting one's children married is the primary duty of parents, they are held responsible by God if they leave them unmarried. As a rule the unmarried man is the breaker of law, but a girl can under no circumstances be left a spinster. If unable to get a suitable husband of proper age for her, parents have to give up the search for a qualified man and hand her over to a blind or a lame man. This idea has put terror into the hearts of girls and their parents, and in view of the ill consequences of failure they often yield to the first offer. The idea of marrying and separating from her had always been painful to both her parents. Her father often said that she would not be separated by marriage or he would part with her only when he secured the best man in the world. But all offers that came to her were either from poor officials or rich widowers. He despised the former and hated the latter. A high official would consider it beneath his dignity to get himself married to the daughter of a Tahseeldar. Besides how could such a one come to know that here was such an invaluable hidden gem?

When she reached the age of twenty unmarried, her old lady relations began to look down upon her as a hideous being whom no man had condescended to recognize. Some of them found fault with her beauty and some said she could not get a husband because she came third in the family. She was a sinner and each breath of hers was equivalent to a curse. They would not be surprised if some terrible thing happened to one of the parents for their sin. They remarked sarcastically that she had wasted her age, energy and beauty which would have been advantageously used in wifehood and motherhood. Tired of taunts and the ceaseless remarks by the ladies at home her father resolved to get her married. As he could not get a man of his choice he determined to give her to a man who did not care to marry but valued money. Her savings with him had come to ten thousand rupees and he did not like to make use of it. He wanted to give her a big surprise in her marriage present. Poor man, if he had announced the gift he would have secured the best husband for her.

Maghbool's idea of life was quite different from that of other girls. Her vast study of romance and her passion for music had put before her an ideal married life. It meant to her a heaven on earth under the protection of a man who would be all love and would care for her desires, comfort and eve whims and fancies, a selfless man as depicted in love songs. The admiration and regard given her at home had developed a high sense of self-importance and self-respect in her. She believed that God by bestowing upon her unique gifts had reserved for her a superb life. He had meant her to be something in the world, and that part of her life was awaiting her after her marriage when she would be freer to make use of her talents.

When the talk of her marriage was going on at home she did not hide herself in a corner and leave her fate to the mercy of others. Unlike other girls she overheard every word about it. She condemned all those who supported Kabeer's proposal and could not understand how they could be blind to the consequences. She pitied those creatures who could not see beyond their nose, and had a strong confidence in her father's power of judgment. She thought that he would never be contaminated by the influence of the lunatic ladies at home. How could he, a sensible man, agree to make a prey of her to this three-headed dragon who had nothing to give her for all that he would take from her?

One day she managed to hide herself in a place from where she heard her father talk with her mother. To her surprise he was not an exception and was of the same mind as his better half. The shock had a paralyzing effect on her.

She stealthily went to her room and was lost in thought. Why had he not accepted the previous offer of Ahmed? Was it because he was not so well off? What more would she get by being the wife of a rich man except richer food and clothing? Would they give her entire happiness in life? Are they the only means of happiness? Are there not men and women living happily without those solaces? Could she not have tried to be happy with the frugal food and scanty garments given by that one master? Was it possible for her to please four masters, her rivals, her husband and her mother-in-law? Why had he demanded a heavy Mahar from Ahmed? Was it to keep up his name and prestige? Or was it to safeguard her interests? How many men pay it? Not even one percent. How many get it excused and then show their true colours? Will the registration of a house be a check on him? Will it make him a saint? Are not limited means to a certain extent a hindrance in the free play of one's instincts?

Maghbool's hopes in her father were shattered. She was miserable beyond words. She found herself among heartless people who were anxious only to get rid of their responsibility and to please society. She confined herself to her bed and gave up all her activities. When food was brought to her she made the servant eat it and take back the empty plates.

She thought she would express her dislike for the man and so escape the calamity. Whom to say it to and how? It meant a revolt against the established dogmas. She would be treated as a leper by everyone. No one would marry her if she was known as a rebel. She pictured herself married to lame and blind men. An awful fright entered her mind and she felt a palsy had smitten her. She thought that her refusal would be a sin against her God-sent parents. Would not that life be a worse torture than merely being one of many wives?

Should she let sleeping dogs life and yield? A girl of so pushful a nature could not be passive. A ray of light shone in her mind. She would go to her widowed aunt and beg of her to break the engagement. Many times she went to her aunt's room, but she could never bring herself to utter the fateful words. At length she gave up the idea as hopeless. She was so worried that she could not sing. Her father sent for her to sing, but she gave an excuse. He thought she felt shy to appear in front of him, and was sad at her coming separation from them. One day he became impatient to hear her sing and went to her room and compelled her.

'Don't desert us so room, Maghbool. We too have a claim on your gifts. Do oblige us now and then,' said he.

Maghbool took the harmonium and played a sad song which she had composed herself during her days of seclusion.

> Life is hard and harder for the ill-trained
> The world is dark and darker for the ill-omened.
>
> Social customs and dogmas are worshipped,
> Human feelings and interest are suppressed.
>
> The world moves with the rising tide
> And even the dear and the near ones ride.

Might is right and the mighty survive
The weak who yield and do not strive.

The sufferers are tormented and tortured
Even Death takes delight in their torture.

Death scorns and condemns his admirers
And humiliates himself and cringes before his haters.

O Death, do not anguish and distress the happy ones
To fulfil one's hopes is the noblest action.

The cheerful ones do not need you,
The sufferers invite and welcome you.

Their only resource is to escape with you,
Their wounds are healed only by you.

Do not turn your face from your aspirers,
Do not force yourself upon your haters.

Be just and respect yourself
And come to me, an adorer of yourself.

Faiz Mohammed was absorbed in listening to the sad tune and did not notice the words.

'You are playing something new to-day. It is so sad and pathetic that it brings tears even to the hardest soul. Do sing it again, you will make me wiser,' said he.

Maghbool opened her mouth to obey him and felt a big lump in her throat. She made an effort but it only brought tears to her big eyes. She looked at him lovingly and said,

'Abba, I can't. However I try to please you it is beyond me to sing.' She began to cry noiselessly and left the room. Her father was moved but was unaware of the cause of her unhappiness. At the same time he admired her sense of gratitude towards him. People would not write poems on the love of home, he thought, if it was not really dear to them. The girl was so sad because she had stayed at home so long.

A ladies' tailor was announced to make blouses for the bride. Her aunt went to Maghbool to take her for measurements.

'The tailor has been waiting a long time, come and be done with him,' said Aunt who was excited with the numerous activities going on at home in connection with the ensuring marriage.

'Measurement for what? Is it for my shroud? I shall give you a nice pattern for it,' said Maghbool.

'Girls should not talk like that. What will people say? Who does not get married? Girls are born to be separated from their parents one day or the other. You were lucky to be with them for twenty years. At the time of happy events you should not mention ill-omened names. Be thankful to God that your marriage is performed by your parents. Think of the orphans who cry their hearts out at their marriages because they are not lucky enough to have their parents to see their great day.'

Custom says that one must not embrace a widow, but Maghbool cried to her heart's content on her breast. She went mechanically to the tailor and after the measurements had been taken secluded herself in her den.

A girl friend came to see her one day and finding her extremely sad said,

'What's the matter with you, child? You are sad beyond words. New life should not be commenced with tears.'

'Tears are ahead of me for life, so I want to get used to them.'

'Marriage does mean sorrow.'

'Mine means more than that. It is a gallows waiting for a murderer.'

'But why? They say he is very rich.'

'They don't say other things about him. I mean his wives and children.'

'Oh goodness! Not wife but wives! Why did you not tell your mother secretly that you don't want him? She would have taken the blame herself and rejected him.'

'The idea has tortured me day and night, but how to say it? I found them all bent upon pushing me into the sea.'

'Shall I do you a little service?'

'If you dare do it you will make me grateful for life.'

The girl left the room with enthusiasm to do a good deed, but being snubbed by everybody returned dejectedly.

'Your mother asked me not to spoil you any more. I told her that I went to her to plead on your request.'

'Shall I tell you the exact words?'

'Do, please.'

'She asked me to tell you to shut your mouth and be contented with God's will. If you say anything more in that connection she will thrash you with a broom to serve you right. She added that she waited for twenty years to get a good man. You are unlucky and all her attempt failed. She can't wait even a day more as the other girls will pass the marriage age and will bring disgrace to the family.'

'Didn't I tell you the futility of it? All of them are bent upon killing me. No human power will change them.'

Maghbool, with no food, no peace of mind and no rest grew pale as pale could be, so much so that she fainted on the Takhat at the time of Jalva. In consequence Kabeer had to wait till very late in the night and so slept. When she came to her senses Faiz Mohamed took her to him and made a short speech asking him to make her life happy.

'I fell in love with you before seeing you. Now I adore you,' said Kabeer to Maghbool, and waited for an answer.

Maghbool had hated him right from the day she heard of his numerous wives. His words rang like a death-knell in her ears. His very touch seemed like a snake-bite. She would have abhorred to answer his questions and was thankful for the custom which forbids a bride to talk or look at the bridegroom at least for three months and his people for six. He could not be vexed by her silence and ill-treat her. The law was on her side.

'I sacrificed everybody else for you. I discarded them all before I came to you,' said he again. No answer. He was surprised. Nazni had begun to speak from the third day.

'The praise of your beauty and of your skill made me mad. I was dying to see you and to call you mine, but now I feel my love is one-sided,' said he again.

How could he pronounce such loving words? Perhaps he wanted to make up for divided regard and lost love. Could she use such endearing words to him when her mind was prejudiced?

'I gave you your Mahar in advance,' said he again. 'It is an enough proof of my love for you. I put no value on money where your happiness is concerned. You can buy lots of things out of the rent. You need not ask me or my mother for your petty needs. I gave nothing to the other two except what they got at the time of their weddings. Of course they do not count in our life now. One is only a servant and the other is a ghost. You are above them.'

It took her a long time to make up her mind to speak to him. Whenever she tried she found harsh and sarcastic words coming to her mouth. The ladies at home asked her what he said. She repeated his words. They were thrilled. Such a rich man to love her so dearly! Sometimes they asked her what she said. She told them that she had not opened her mouth yet. They were annoyed and said any other man would not have seen her face again.

'Are you still angry with me? What have I done to deserve such a severe punishment? Do you know what happened to me when you fainted? A little more strain would have killed me there. My whole body was shivering with fright. When your father brought you I was unconscious of his presence.'

'A beggar's anger does no harm to others. She is punished instead of punishing others. I was under a false impression that extreme sorrow drives away sleep, but you are lucky. A good sleep releases one from suffering and makes a man feel fresh,' said she in her first talk to him.

Kabeer at once knew where to put her. He could not deal with her in the same spirit. He must change his attitude.

'It was not sleep, I fainted. But being stronger than you I could stand it better. By the by, why did your father get the house registered in your name before he gave his consent?' said Kabeer. The matter of the house had been on his mind a great deal. He could not help but let it out.

'Did he do so? I have no idea. He must have done it on purpose.'

'Is it because he had no confidence in my love?'

'One can create confidence in others by one's selfless deeds. People without living together cannot have confidence in one another. Naturally he could not have it in you.'

'He ought to have known at least that if a man married a third time he usually becomes his wife's slave. He ought to have confidence in your unique powers, which will make any man give not only one house but all that he possesses. He did not have the magnanimity of heart.'

'He is not an ordinary man. You can't judge him so easily. Should he not have thought so much for me after the harm he did for me?'

'Yes, yes. He did you great harm by not trusting my sincerity. He tried to make trouble for both of us. My love for you is like a vast ocean, where all particles are washed away. Nothing can prevent the movement of its surging waves. In spite of his meanness I complied with his request,' said Kabeer and was proud of his ingenuity.

Maghbool felt like laughing but controlled herself. She wondered where to put him, with the lunatics or in the category of the highest type of rogues.

Kabeer had to please too many masters. When his sister wanted to go back home before her due date he stayed at home to effect a reconciliation with her. He had his dinner and even slept there. Then he wanted to bring Nazni home and had to follow the same procedure. Whenever such necessity arose he neither sent word to Maghbool nor told her of his plans beforehand. She did not ask him for the reason of his not coming and thought it was beneath her dignity to do so. But one day her patience reached its limit.

'Did the ghost or the servant influence you to stay away? Everyone was waiting for dinner for a long time. You at least ought to have sent word to me,' said she.

'My sister was disheartened with my cruel treatment of her. I was trying to clear her misunderstanding. It took a long time and it was time for dinner. They forced me to to have it with them. After that I felt too lazy to stir out of the house. Although my body was there my soul was with you and your picture was in my heart.'

'I see. Didn't you tell them that you had to come here?' she said sarcastically. She knew that he had married her without their knowledge.

'None of them knows of our marriage. They are very jealous people and would not have allowed me to marry you. I intend to tell them of it. I shall do it after my sister goes. Then I shall take you there and we shall never pass a day without seeing one another.'

'So I am only your mistress and do not deserve any recognition by your people.'

'You are my mistress,' said he, 'the queen of my heart and everything in the world to me. Usually love begins after the marriage but ours began before it. That shows our marriage was registered by God and heaven. If people recognize it or not what do we care? It is all God's work. I must be grateful to Mustafa who found you for me. He must have got an inspiration. Our marriage is sacred.'

'Are not all marriages sacred? Are they not based on selflessness and all kind of sacrifices for one another? It is said that a man and a woman have to be fated to live together, but some are destined to live with three or four.'

'Marriages performed by two loving persons are holy. Not others. The elders choose and do everything so the chief person concerned has nothing to do but yield.'

She often gave him a headache by her complicated questions. She always weighed her words before uttering them. She was a strong supporter of her parents and would get cross if he spoke lightly of them.

'Although our marriage is sacred you have no courage to announce it. One should be proud of having done a noble thing. You want to take me in by the back door.'

'I shall take you by the front door. When once my mother comes to know of it we will have no fear.'

'Will the ghost be there when I go? Of course the servant will be there to work for us. By the by did the servant get her baby?'

'Don't pronounce the names of those wretches. The very mention of them gets on my nerves. Life is short but full of miseries. Let us be happy without creating unnecessary unpleasant feelings. What do we gain by such talk?'

'Their names make me mad too but I thought you felt pleased with them. As you know, now and then you get into a mood to please them. Now I see you really don't like them. I read in a book that man has double teeth like an elephant. People have the audacity to write such rot and send it to be printed. What I don't like, you too despise, so where is the hidden tooth?'

'I discarded, rejected and despised them all when I married you. Even supposing I talk to them sometimes it is only to keep a smiling face on them. Otherwise they will curse us. A disappointed woman's curse had destroyed many a man. I don't care if they only do it to me but if they do it to you to destroy my happiness I will be helpless.'

'So one's love has a quality of change. Does it change with the winds?'

'Love is an ocean. It changes and yet it is the same. The tossing of the waves makes no difference as it is temporary. One should take the rise and fall of the waves as outside enjoyments. Love in the early stage of life is not constant and it is a mere child's play. There is no strong sentiment or attachment for one's object.'

'I see you speak very humorously. Your love for me is a product of old age. So there is no fear of its change. Don't they say that love comes only once in one's life?'

This was a hard question. The answers he had contemplated for days together were exhausted. There was no ready reply so he pretended to snore. Maghbool looked this side and that in the room to discover if there was a third person to overhear their talk, but how could there be?

—*Purdah and Polygamy* (1944)

Santha Rama Rau
(b. 1923)

Born in Madras in 1923, Santha Rama Rau is the daughter of Dhanvanthi Rama Rau (1893–1987) who can be credited for publicizing and making acceptable the idea of birth control in India. In the book *Santha Rama Rau* (Arnold-Heinemann, 1976), S.K. Desai says that Santha Rama Rau spent around ten years of her life in India, had her schooling in England and college education in the United States, after which she married Faubion Bowers in 1952, and settled in America. The marriage was dissolved in 1966.

Considered to be among the most gifted travel writers, her work includes a number of books of which four are travelogues: *East is Home, This is India, View to the Southeast* and *My Russian Journey.* Interestingly, even the two autobiographies she wrote, *Home to India* (1945) and *Gifts of Passage* are travelogues in terms of narrative style and content.

Apart from this, Santha Rama Rau also wrote a dramatization of E.M. Forster's *A Passage to India* (1960), and an excellent cookbook, *The Cooking of India.* Then, as a freelance writer since 1945, she wrote for magazines like *The New Yorker,* and also assisted Maharani Gayatri Devi in writing her memoirs, *A Princess Remembers* (1982).

An extract selected here, from *Gifts of Passage,* documents her visit to Dostoyevsky's apartment where she is asked by the current tenant about why she thinks of him as a great writer: 'I couldn't think of what to say, how to describe Dostoyevsky's calamitous power with words, his overwhelming sense of guilt and tragedy, the dark, dark world he lived in.' She finally replies, feebly, that she admires him because he wrote 'of such extraordinary things—such strange, unhappy people.' The tenant listens in growing bewilderment. '"Extraordinary?" she said. "Strange? But Dostoyevsky wrote of everyday, *ordinary* things and people."'

In the Author's Note to *Gifts of Passage* (1961), she writes, 'The stories which form the body of this volume have appeared in various magazines over a number of years. In rereading them with a view to book publication, I was interested to discover that, taken in sequence, they provide a sort of rough outline of my life story ... So it occurred to me that it would be amusing to weld together these very personal stories—each of which has a basis in a true happening—with autobiographical comment. The result is a curious kind of book, I suspect—a highly irregular self-explanatory essay which attempts to explain how the woman I am emerged from the child born thirty-odd years ago in Madras.'

Of her fiction, *Remember the House* (London: Victor Gollanez, 1945) can be described as a psychological novel that deals with an adolescent protagonist's coming of age. The development of consciousness is presented using dramatic situations.

Her second novel, *The Adventuress*, (New York: Harper and Row Publishers, 1970) has, at its core, the concept of 'survival' against all odds. It is set in the period after the World War, when traditional values are bypassed in the struggle for survival. Through the eyes of the narrator, Kay, Santha Rama Rau takes the reader through Japan, the Philippines, and Shanghai, bringing the reader face-to-face with characters who are Japanese, Filipinos, English, Americans, Chinese and Spanish. S.K. Desai describes the work as 'the story of a woman in search of security, both physical and psychological'.

Chapter IX

... The day we left Leningrad was moist and cold. Leningraders said that the summer was really over now. No more long mild evenings. Now autumn would spread, like the penetrating chill from the Neva, through the city. All afternoon I had been reading *The Insulted and Injured*, that early, inept, and curiously moving mixture of autobiography and fiction that Dostoyevsky had written nearly a century ago in St. Petersburg. When I came to passages like 'he pointed to the foggy vista of the street, lighted by street-lamps dimly twinkling in the damp mist, to the dirty houses, to the wet and shining flagstones, to the cross, sullen, drenched figures that passed by, to all this picture hemmed in by the dome of the Petersburg sky,' I had only to look out my hotel window to find an almost theatrical re-enactment of the scene. Although it wasn't actually raining, the Leningrad sky was soft with clouds and St. Isaac's golden dome was transformed by reflection to a sombre metallic gray.

After tea Faubion and I walked to Dostoyevsky's apartment. It was already deep twilight, the premature evening of misty weather. When we again stood outside the building we could feel the damp seeping up from the canal at the end of the next block. The first trickle of people coming back from work had begun and there were customers at both the cigarette stall and, surprisingly, at the cold-drink stand. Three women in dark winter-looking clothes with woollen scarves over their heads and holding shopping baskets stood talking on the corner. They looked at us with curiosity, two foreigners idling about indeterminately on the sidewalk, and then went back to their gossip and news.

Imitating Svetlana, we stopped the first person who passed us on the pavement, a middle-aged woman with an occupied air. Faubion asked her whether she knew which was the apartment of Dostoyevsky.

She looked at us unbelievingly. 'Which apartment?'

'Of Dostoyevsky. The writer.'

'You are a foreigner?'

'Yes. American.'

'I too am a foreigner. Czech. I know nothing of this.' She smiled and added 'Good evening' politely.

The entrance to the building was on the alleyway half blocked by the pile of lumber and building materials. 'There is an alley, dark and narrow, shut in by huge houses. ... The second house from the corner was under construction and was surrounded by scaffolding. The fence around the house came almost to the middle of the alley, and a footway had been laid round the fence.' The place must have looked very much like this when Dostoyevsky wrote that passage, I thought.

We walked through the arch way to a dank and messy courtyard. Firewood was stacked all across one side, partly covered with a length of tarpaulin. Next to it was a small shed or outhouse with a rotted door hanging unevenly from its hinges. Moisture had collected in shallow puddles between the flagstones. The children we had seen on our first visit were playing there, taking turns in climbing to the outhouse roof, jumping to the firewood, and then to the ground across a wide sheen of water. They stopped their game to stare at us, until we turned away uncertainly to examine the wooden board hung on a nail just inside the archway. It gave, in white painted letters, the names of the tenants and their apartment numbers, but that, of course, was no help to us.

We were trying to collect the courage to knock on the door of one of the apartments—any apartment—when the biggest of the children, the shaved-headed blond boy, came over to us.

'Foreigners?' he asked without smiling.

'Yes.'

'Poles?'

'No,' Faubion said, 'I'm—'

'Hungarian?'

'No, American.'

'Chewing gum?' the boy said hopefully.

'No chewing gum,' Faubion said, sorry to disappoint the child.

But the boy was already busy unbuttoning his coat and fishing in the pocket of his shorts with a chapped and dirty hand. He produced a small, rather tarnished gilt-and-enamel badge, made like a lapel pin, and held it out to us on the palm of his hand. On the badge, in Russian characters, was inscribed '1957 Youth Festival U.S.S.R.,' obviously a souvenir of the previous summer. 'Foreign money?' he asked.

'I'm sorry. But we will buy it for rubles if you want.'

'Rubles?' He turned down the corners of his mouth and put the badge away in his pocket. He looked resigned more than disappointed. While he was busy with the badge he said suddenly and casually, with his eyes averted, 'You are searching still for the same apartment?'

'Yes'.

'Second entrance, third floor, on your left.' He raced away to join his companions, leaving us wondering. Had he expected a tip? If so, he hadn't allowed us time to give him one. Had he been unwilling to talk the first time we saw him because of the intimidating presence of Svetlana and the official-looking car? Had it just been the general caution of people who live in a cautious world? Shyness? And then, this time, was he just being kind? Had he been pleased that we had offered to buy his badge, even in rubles? But why had he approached us anyway? We never came to a satisfactory explanation of his behaviour. It occurred to me much later that it is only in Russia that one searches so diligently for motives.

Inside the doorway marked '2' we found ourselves in a stone-floored hallway, colder than the evening outside. The stairs were uncarpeted stone too, with iron bars on each landing. On one landing a metal bathtub was propped against the wall with its four little claw feet sticking out toward the stairs. On the third floor two doors faced each other across the small hallway. Both were heavily padded and had strips of felt hammered along the edges to cover the cracks. We rang the bell of the door on the left.

All the way up Faubion had been composing sentences in his politest Russian. 'Please forgive us for disturbing you, but is this the apartment that was at one time occupied by Fyodor Mikhailovich Dostoyevsky, the writer?' but when the door was opened to us by a gray-haired woman in a dark dress with a sweater over it, he could only blurt out, 'Good evening—did Dostoyevsky live here?'

Understandably, she looked astonished. '*What* did you say?' she asked, and added as an afterthought, 'Good evening.'

The second time it came out sounding better, and she smiled. 'Ah, Dostoyevsky. You are foreigners?'

'Yes. Tourists. And we are so sorry to trouble you.'

'Ah, *tourists*. It is no trouble. Please come in. You are interested in Dostoyevsky?'

'We think him a great writer.'

'Come in, please come in. Yes, this used to be his apartment.'

She beckoned us through the outer and the inner door, equally padded, an arrangement like the light baffles of public buildings during wartime blackouts. I was suddenly aware of how drafty and freezing the Leningrad winter must be. She locked both doors behind us, and remarked pleasantly, 'You would like to see this apartment where he lived? It is nothing very special.'

A woman's voice from behind a closed door called out something to which our hostess replied, 'Come here, come here,' and, smiling at us, explained, 'My sister—my younger sister.'

The door on our left opened and a small round woman, dressed in black, emerged. She had a face like a bun, with bright, inquisitive raisin-coloured eyes, and dark hair drawn into a knot on the back of her neck. 'Foreigners,' her sister said, as though only that one word would explain our presence. The four of us stood uncomfortably close together, packed between the padded black bench on one side of the foyer and a tall white-painted cupboard on the other. There was an old-fashioned wooden coatrack in one corner, and simply no room for any other furniture.

The older woman said, 'I have often thought what kind of furniture Dostoyevsky had. This hall must have been empty—you can see that would be better. Really, there is only space for the waiting bench and the coatrack. Probably he had not much furniture to put here—he always had to sell things to pay doctors' bills, debts.' She smiled at us rather apologetically. 'I know all this because I have lived here so long—thirty years, even before I was married. When we first moved here there were still old people in the building who remembered Dostoyevsky. They are dead now, of course. But they used to tell us. Movers would come up the stairs. Another piece of furniture taken away. Another bill paid. He was very sick, you know. I was young when I heard these things, and it all seemed to me sad.' She shrugged her shoulders. 'Now ...'

Now worse things have happened to all of us? I wondered. Or, now I have other things to think about?

But Faubion said politely, 'Now he would have had free medical care?' She laughed as though we all shared a secret together. 'Yes. That is true.'

With a rush of housewifely indignation she said, 'You should have seen the place when we moved in! Dirt? Incredible! The people who had taken this apartment before us had done nothing to it. Of course, practically none of Dostoyevsky's things were here even when *they* came—even the books had been sold. Only this cupboard remained.' She pointed to the tall, cheap cupboard in the hall. 'It used to be in his bedroom. He kept his books in it. We had it painted white and moved here. There is so little space.'

The younger sister opened the door behind her. 'This was his room,' she said in a soft, deprecating voice. 'The coldest and darkest room in the building. This is where he lived.' *The Insulted and Injured* had opened with the hero looking for a place to live: 'All that day I had been walking about the town trying to find a lodging. My old one was very damp and I was beginning to cough rather ominously.' We followed the sisters into his room. Smallish, with two narrow windows set close together in the wall opposite the door, it too looked crowded although there was actually not much furniture. Two iron beds, one under each window, a cupboard, a round table covered with a plush tablecloth, a couple of straight chairs. I walked over to the windows, squeezing past the table, and stared out at Dostoyevsky's view. The dingy courtyard, the dark thin little figures of the children playing, the Leningrad evening closing in.

Behind me one of the sisters switched on the light and said, 'He worked here too, so I was told. He was in bed much of the time and had to do his writing here.'

I turned away from the window to face the Victorian look of the room in the lamplight, the pink-flowered wallpaper, the tablecloth edged with little round bobbles. 'Dostoyevsky's wallpaper was still here when we came to this apartment. It was a dark green, about this colour.' She indicated with her fingernail a fragment of leaf in the design of the present paper, a rather murky sage green. 'But it was so badly stained and torn that we had to change it.'

I could think of no questions to ask, could not even imagine the sick, tormented figure lying under that tidy white counterpane, writing away in the coldest, dampest room.

We crossed the tiny foyer to the door immediately opposite. This room was a bit bigger, with French windows opening on a narrow iron balcony that we had seen from the street. Here, too, there was a bed, but apparently the room was also used as a parlour—that is what it had been in Dostoyevsky's day—and there were three armchairs covered in white cotton and another round table. The wallpaper too was rather more formal, a plain, milky green the colour of celadon, with a decorative border of rather fanciful urns. 'The sun comes in here in the afternoons,' the gentle voice of the younger sister said, 'when we have some sun.' We all smiled with her. Leningrad weather, like London weather is always good for a mild crack.

While we were in this room the doorbell rang. The older sister hurried out to answer it, and we could hear fragments of a muttered conversation in the hall. Almost immediately our hostess returned with another woman of stocky build and slightly severe expression. She was still in her outdoor coat and scarf and was carrying a string bag filled with a bunch of onions, a large cabbage, a loaf of black bread and some packages wrapped in newspaper. She was introduced as 'my older sister. This is her room.'

In the awkward silence that followed I said, 'How nice that the family is all together.' When Faubion translated this, our hostess replied, without much interest, 'Yes. We all lived here together once, when we were young. Now we all live here together again. Three old women.'

'And in between?' my husband asked.

'In between, we married. And the war. All three husbands killed. Again we live together like girls.' She laughed to emphasize the absurdity of her description.

Back to the foyer and then into a thin sliver of a pantry next to the bedroom-parlour. Obviously part of the passageway had been partitioned off to make this pantry. The older sister was there unpacking her purchases. Eggs in a plastic bowl on the table, cookies on a blue china plate. There was a small electric hot plate on the table too, which transformed the narrow pantry into a makeshift kitchen. There was no proper kitchen and no bathroom. I supposed they must share those with other families somewhere in the building.

With a touch of eagerness the youngest sister led us through the pantry to curtained glass doors which opened into yet another bedroom, 'My daughter's room,' she said, almost whispering, and motioned us to follow her. She went directly to a baby's crib in the centre of the room, and when we all stood round it, staring at the small pink child asleep in his closely wrapped shawls, she said, after an admiring moment, 'My grandson.'

I looked around at the rest of the room. Two large wardrobes were placed side by side, jutting into the room to form a kind of screen for the double bed in the corner. A desk and a bookcase. Two or three chairs. And the baby in his crib. 'My daughter is a school-teacher. Her husband too. They are not yet back from work.' Rather timidly she asked, 'Perhaps you will stay and meet them?'

'Oh, no,' Faubion and I said together, suddenly aware of how long we had been there. He added, 'We have already disturbed you far too much.'

'But at least you will stay and have some tea with us?'

'No, really, we must go.' We stepped back into the pantry.

'But *something*,' the middle sister said, looking worried. She picked up the plate of cookies and handed them to us. We each took one and, since there wasn't room for more than one of us to sit at the pantry table, we all stood up nibbling cookies and smiling at each other with some constraint.

'Have we shown you what you came to see?' she asked.

'Yes, exactly,' I answered firmly, lying shamelessly, for nothing could have held less of Dostoyevsky's atmosphere than this neat, cramped life, the quiet, the three old widows, and the sleeping infant.

'I have been wanting to ask you something.' The first touch of diffidence came into her voice. 'What is it that you find in Dostoyevsky's writing?'

Before I could answer she went on hastily, 'I do not ask out of ignorance. I used to be a doctor, I am retired now. I get a pension of a thousand rubles a month.' (I assumed that this was intended as an indication of her accomplishment during her career). 'My husband, before he was killed, was an engineer. So you understand that we are not uncultured. I have read Dostoyevsky—with particular care, since we live in his apartment—but still I must ask, what do you see in him? Why is he great?'

I couldn't think what to say, how to describe Dostoyevsky's calamitous power with words, his overwhelming sense of guilt and tragedy, the dark, dark world he lived in. At last I said, rather feebly, 'He wrote of such extraordinary things—such strange, unhappy people—'

She listened to Faubion's translation with growing bewilderment. 'Extraordinary?' she said. 'Strange? But Dostoyevsky wrote of everyday, *ordinary* things and people. When I finish a Dostoyevsky novel I forget it before I put the book down. What is there to remember? Now *Tolstoy*— a truly great writer. Who can ever forget Anna Karenina?' Anna Karenina, the rich, the aristocratic, the eternally romantic woman.

'To *us*,' Faubion explained, 'Dostoyevsky's world is extraordinary. And powerful. And remembered forever.'

For the first time the oldest sister joined in the conversation. 'You are foreigners,' she said.

Faubion and I were silenced for a moment, hearing this familiar remark in an entirely new way.

At last the oldest sister continued, 'Is it permitted to ask what country you come from?'

Faubion said, 'I am American. My wife is Indian.'

'America and India,' she repeated wonderingly. 'And you have come such a long way just to see *this* apartment?'

—*Gifts of Passage* (1961)

G. Ishvani
(n.d.)

The Brocaded Sari, (1946), a novel by G. Ishvani (also spelt Isvani)
records the memories of life in a Koja Muslim community—the
protagonist's marriage, divorce, her stay in England for advanced
studies, and her eventual decision to settle in Florida with her six-
year-old son. The only information about the author is contained
in the brief Foreward which tells us the author decided to settle
in Florida because it reminded her of India.

Chapter XI

Raschid told me that we were going to make our home with his parents
for a few years. Indian families expected their sons and grandsons to live
with them, even after they were married; we were no exception. I had
met my husband's sisters, brothers, and mother before my marriage, and
according to our Muslim customs, had seen his father from a distance.
But I was completely unaware of the rest of the household. Nobody had
told me. Not even my beloved Lita had mentioned that Raschid's
grandmother, grandfather, three uncles, their wives, children, and half a
dozen cousins or so would be living with us too.

A small house in the garden, across the courtyard from the big house
where the family lived, was build for us. It consisted of a living room,
bedroom and dressing room. The furniture was a portion of my bridal
trousseau. This is a Koja custom. A few comfortable armchairs, a sofa, a
Persian rug on the floor furnished the living room; Raschid's books lining
the walls made the room attractive and gay. A circling veranda gave a
delightful view of the garden with its tall pipal trees, its clustering bushes
of red and white camellias.

With all this beauty I felt strange in my new home. In the midst of
my splendor, my beautiful jewels, my brocaded saris and embroidered

slippers (things I had adored and wanted all my life) I would rather a million times have returned home. While I was there my existence had seemed boring and stupid. But as each new day passed I began to realize how much I missed the warmth, gaiety, and love which lay beneath that seeming boredom. It had been fun stealing up to the terrace, pretending I was going to be a great dancer one day; walking with Yusuf in the garden watching the sun disappear down the far end of the blue sea. The long conversations with Lita; philosophizing idly over the eternity of time, the relationship of Eastern and Western cultures, the different religions in the world, the progress of science, and ultimately the everlasting question which ended all Indian conversations, 'When will India be finally free?'

But in my new surroundings no one seemed to be interested in any conversations except about what they were going to eat—how they were going to be dressed—when they were going to the mosque. It was impossible to practice, even dream about my dancing; they disapproved of it too strongly.

My one consolation was in having Amah. I could talk to her at least. She had looked after me since I was a child. But even she felt strange in her new home. In the kitchen, she said, the other servants refused to speak to her.

It was Grandmother-in-law who ruled this household. She had protruding black eyes, and wore her black hair pulled away from her forehead and tied into a stingy little knot at the nape of her neck. She was a devout Aga Khani and disliked me profoundly because I was a Shia, and the granddaughter of Bismail.

Grandmother-in-law was much younger than Grandfather-in-law. In deference to his age, she dressed in black. With still more deference, she garbed herself in the old-fashioned style. This meant a heavy silk robe hanging down to her ankles with a two-yard scarf flung over her head. As the house was packed with male relatives of all sizes and ages, she took great pains to conceal her bosom and head with the scarf. This required practice and skill, if one wanted to move around fast.

In the Koja molla (koja quarter) the women have a special walk, for which they are famous all over India. Their heads are bent with the elbows held stiffly on each side of the body and the hands held forward. Thus, head, shoulders, and bust are covered by the scarf. From the front they resemble belligerent pugilists; from the back, bulls enveloped by the toreador's cape. Grandmother was heavily built, short, but strong looking. When she entered a room all the loose ornaments and furniture rattled and shook; her backless Koja slippers clattered on the stone floor and could be heard a mile away. With swinging hands, flashing eyes, and head bent forward, she froze all the children and daughters-in-law into counting ten, before they dared reply.

Grandmother was thirty-two years old when she married Grandfather, who was seventy-two. This was his third matrimonial venture. The death of his second wife had dealt him a severe blow. After it he had changed completely. He showed no interest whatsoever in his life, or his surroundings. The family was perturbed. After a worried council it was decided to get him another wife. The results were excellent; he ate all his meals with appetite, smoked his hubble-bubble pipe and was at peace again with the world. Dressed in his white shirt buttoned up to his neck, with his white beard flowing down to the centre of his chest, a white cap jauntily perched on his silvery locks, he looked the picture of saintly contentment and dignity in his rocking chair. He resembled the late Rabindranath Tagore and could have been taken as his twin.

Strangely enough, the male members of Raschid's family seemed to follow the same marital pattern; their wives were always dying. Naturally, a new mother had to be found for the children. In our community, even if a man wanted to live without remarrying, it would have been impossible. His family would put so much pressure on him that eventually, in self-defense, he would be forced to take a new wife.

At the funeral of each successive dead wife, the women arrived in hordes to weep, mourn, and wail, with an alert eye kept open for their unmarried daughters over twenty. A girl over twenty was considered a very, very old maid in our community. She would have great difficulty in finding a husband, except, of course, a widower. These old ladies of twenty usually had some defects, physical or moral, and if their parents were not smart, they had the greatest trouble in getting them married.

Soon after the funeral of the departed wife, strenuous efforts were made by the parents of the would-be brides. In some way they would manage to approach the newly bereaved family in a friendly manner. Suddenly, apparently accidental meetings would take place in the mosque or, strangely enough, quite by chance, they would take it into their heads to take a stroll outside the house. Great affection and interest would be showered on the children after they had managed to worm their way in. Eyes would be raised to Heaven, tears would flow in stream, as they reviled, in broken, sobbing tones, a cruel destiny which left such beautiful, angelic children motherless, to be let to the helpless care of a man, one who was naturally incapable of taking the place of a mother and bringing them up properly. Presents would be produced, and the children would be kissed and patted tenderly on the head. Thus they hoped to make friends of them and to have them as allies. This, they hoped too would give them a wedge with the father. Naturally, he would be touched when he heard about it. Then all the virtues of their saintly daughter would be recited at great length: cooking capacities, saving capacities, sewing capacities and how she adored children, especially grown-up ones. All this would be exploited to the maximum. Beauty, on the contrary, would not be overstressed. These maneuvers were mostly successful. A few months later a new marriage would take place, and, perhaps several months or years later, another funeral.

Though we lived in a separate house our meals were taken in the large house with the family. The dining room was gloomy, as there were no windows. There were two long, narrow tables placed at the ends of the room. One table was reserved for the women, the other for the men.

Grandmother hovered over the men's table till they were seated and served. Then she signalled for us to enter. I followed the younger aunts-in-law into the dining room. They glanced modestly away from the men's table, pulled their saris lower, then with sedate, mincing steps took their places at the women's table.

The air was hushed and subdued. The servants pattered around noiselessly in their bare feet passing dishes from one table to another. Grandmother's eyes glinted like those of a general inspecting his troops, as she presided over our table. She made a special effort to be pleasant to me as a newcomer.

'You don't seem to have much of an appetite. You must eat, you know,' she said to me. Then with a grim smile, 'Don't forget that men don't like thin women.'

I nodded, then tried to smile as pleasantly as I could. But I noticed that her own plate remained untouched. Raschid's mother glanced at her pleadingly, from time to time, but to no avail. Grandmother sat as grimly as a stone without lifting a mouthful to her lips. Suddenly, for no apparent reason, she pulled back her chair and stomped out of the room. There was an embarrassed silence around the table, the glasses and plates echoed resoundingly as the door shut behind her. Being a newcomer I did not understand what it was all about.

I tried my best to appear at ease and smiled at my next-door neighbour, who was the third wife of Raschid's youngest uncle. She was young, modest, and wholesome but quite unhappy and plain looking. One could see from her manner and appearance that she was provincial. Her style in coiffure and her taste in saris all bespoke a small-town maiden. If I told all I knew about her, it would fill a book. I shall satisfy myself, however, by saying that she was extremely shy and that a great deal of coaxing had to be applied by the ladies around the table to make her eat. One day as she was leaving the table after her usual frugal repast, Grandfather, worried about her reported lack of appetite, decided to stop and speak to her.

His venerable age permitted him to take this liberty.

'Bless you, my child,' he said, thoughtfully stroking his beard, gazing down at her benignly from his august height.

She stood motionless for a second, too petrified to move. Finally, pulling her wits together, she did the correct thing when addressed by a male relative of one's husband. Lifting up her hands which were folded tightly across her chest, she pulled down her sari, completely covering her face.

Suddenly there was a gentle thud and her white handkerchief lay on the floor. Beside it were a couple of lamb chops. Shy of eating before people, she wrapped up anything she found when no one was looking, then slipped it into her bosom. I found out later that she was partial to lamb chops. In the southern village where she came from, nobody had heard of or seen such things.

After dinner I usually returned to my room where I would find Amah waiting for me. Raschid, like a good son, stayed to chat with his parents.

'Did you have a good dinner, Amah?' I asked. She shrugged her shoulders negatively; obviously, she had not enjoyed her dinner any more than I had mine. She then proceeded to move around the room patting a cushion, opening and shutting a blind, her silver ornaments tinkling musically.

Silver anklets and bracelets were Amah's one big vanity. Each Muslim New Year she received one of these as a gift; next year I was going to give her a pair of earrings, perhaps a nose ring. Her wrists and ankles were already covered. If more were added, she would have been unable to lift her hands or move her feet. Dressed in a spotless sari every day, she wore her grey hair drawn simply away from her lined, gentle face.

I picked up my embroidery; each time I put the needle into the material and took a stitch, my past seemed to appear before me, making my present life seem unsupportable.

'What's the matter, little one?' Amah took a piece of betel nut from the box beside her on the floor.

'Nothing,' I replied, bending over my needlework.

'Would you like me to tell you a story?'

'That would be nice, Amah,' I smiled. 'Tell me the one you used to tell me as a child. The one about the Lord Buddha.'

Amah told tales and fables delightfully. She raised or lowered her soft voice, and made her eyes shadow over in sadness or sparkle with joy, according to the mood of her story.

Putting another piece of betel nut in her mouth, Amah settled herself more comfortably on the floor. Then in a low, musical voice she commenced her story:

One day, Asita the wise old sage sat meditating as usual, beneath the pipal tree. Asita was a hundred years old. As his entire life had been devoted to pious works and prayers, his ears had long been closed to the sound of earthly joys. The people of India loved and revered him because they knew that his selfless devotion and worship had been rewarded by great spiritual insight.

This special day, however—Amah lifted her small hand and raised her silvery voice—while in the midst of his devotions, he was transfixed by what he overheard. He heard the gods rejoicing in Heaven. They were singing songs of joy and gladness to honour the birth of a baby. This baby, they said, was going to fulfill a great destiny. The universe had bestowed on him divine gifts, nobility of spirit, beauty, rank, wealth, as his just due. The people of the earth, below, who made their own sorrows and suffering, had not yet had the good fortune of such a clear spirit coming to mingle among them. His piercing intellect would see through the veil against which mankind struggled so hopelessly and ignorantly. Or if he deigned, he would become the greatest ruler of the mightiest kingdom in the world, and lead the greatest and noblest army of warriors into conquest.

This event had been heralded by the unloosing of a silver star shooting down from the sky. It had come to rest in the womb of Queen Maya, spouse of the blue-blooded King Voddoska, ruler of the mighty race of the Skyas.

The queen had awakened in trembling bliss. The night had been illuminated by a rosy glow. The flowers that opened their lovely petals only to the sunlight suddenly burst into full bloom and perfumed the night air with their fragrance. That same night, the ocean waves were lulled by a sweet, soothing breeze which swept up over the hills and mountains of India.

Asita's old bones rattled like a bag of pebbles after hearing this news. Picking up his wooden staff, he hobbled off in the direction of the king's palace. It was quite a distance for an old man of his venerable age, but that did not stop him. His thoughts were too full of the royal baby in the king's palace. After a little while, however, he became weary and stopped to rest by the roadside. Suddenly he was surrounded by a band of monkeys. Their shrill chatter accompanied by gesturing seemed to denote sympathy. Some hung their heads sadly, others screeched, beating their breasts, or two of them even staggered and fell down, imitating the feebleness of Asita. Finally, tired of this play-acting, they ambled off to the near-by stream to fetch him water. Trees were scaled, amidst a wild but friendly pandemonium, to bring him down fruits. When Asita got up to continue his journey, the monkeys showed no desire to leave him. They exhibited their friendliness by screaming encouraging cries from a respectable distance behind him. Others followed by swinging feverishly from tree to tree alongside the road. When Asita showed signs of wariness, they gathered together with cries of dismay to support him. Towards the end of the journey, the old man, unable to move, lay stretched out by the roadside. This again caused them to wail and beat their breasts. Finally after a long and noisy conference among themselves, the monkeys hoisted Asita on their shoulders and marched him triumphantly towards the palace gates.

When the king heard Asita was near, he ordered the courtiers, noblemen, merchants flocking the palace gates to make way for him.

Queen Maya wanted to lay down her first-born at the feet of the old man. In India the highest are humble before the wise.

But Asita stopped her. 'Not so, O Queen, not so,' he quavered in his thin old voice. 'The earth was carpeted by a million unknown flowers, the trees bent their great branches to makes an awning for his birth. The near-by hill produced a crystal-white stream for his bath. Not for nothing did all this happen, O Queen. Not for nothing,' he said reverently, kneeling before the infant. 'For thou art He, baby. Thou art Buddha. Come from your high birth to this lowly plane to help mankind.

Then Asita related to the king what the voices had told him concerning the prince's destiny. He would either renounce ambition to lead the life of a sage, or become the powerful ruler of the greatest kingdom in the world.

After listening carefully to Asita, the king called a council of his wise men. 'Sire,' the oldest amongst them spoke, 'we as the councilors of your state advise that the greatest precautions be taken till this dangerous period has passed. There is grave reason to believe that the first prophecy might come true.'

The king, rising from his golden throne, said, 'You have spoken well. The prince cannot forgo his royal heritage to wander forth into an unknown world.' He raised his august voice in scorn. 'To save mankind, indeed. To help the sufferings of the ignorant! My son will never wear the humble cape of the mendicant! Never! For other men, yes. But not for him. Ah—' he continued in a gentler tone, 'the second prophecy is more fitting. He will be a king of kings, nobler and greater than any of his mighty ancestors.'

Plans were made forthwith to build a new and marvellous palace for the young prince. It would consist of nothing except beauty for the eyes and joy for the heart. The rooms were to be studded with the richest jewels, the ceilings made of mosaic and designed in the most wonderfully artistic patterns, each depicting a new story of joy and harmony. In the ivory courtyards magical fountains would pour billowing cascades of opalescent water. The gardens would perfume the air with the rarest of fruits and flowers.

Surrounding the palace, miles and miles of smooth green lawns sloped gently towards the green hills in the distance. Beyond this were great forests filled with wild animals of all kinds. White deer roamed in graceful abandon and gaily coloured birds flew from one sweetly laden tree to another singing their eternal songs of love. Tall white-breasted swans filled the lakes; flocks of wild geese left their snowy homes in the Himalayan peaks to visit this enchanted spot.

To mention grief, sorrow, or death was forbidden in this paradise. The multitudes of attendants, singers, dancers, musicians, teachers were warned that if such words were ever uttered, the offender would be punished. He or she would immediately be removed. Even the dead flowers were plucked at dawn, the dying leaves hidden, so that the eyes of the prince would not rest on anything which foretold of sorrow.

The entrance to this unbelievable beauty was guarded by a huge iron gate. It required a hundred men to open. Within it was a second, then a third gate. Orders were that no one, not even the prince himself, could pass without the king's signet.

When the Prince Siddharta was eight years old, the most learned teacher that could be found was brought before him. At the first lesson a Sanscrit verse was inscribed which he was asked to copy. Bending his wonderfully handsome little face over his jewelled slate, the prince not only copied it but wrote it in every language in the world.

Falling on his knees, the teacher exclaimed in tones of bewildered awe, 'O Prince, I am not worthy of being a teacher.' But the prince soothed his instructor by kindly words and his radiant smile.

And so he grew up to manhood in grace, giving joy and happiness to all around him. The king, however, did not cease his vigilance. His spies reported in the minutest details everything concerning his son. They said that often when the prince was watching some wonderful performance, or hearing some marvellous tale, his eyes and thoughts were far away. He seemed to be listening to the sound of strange winds in the distance, which someday, his eyes seemed to say, would call him far away.

Efforts were redoubled so that the prince would never be alone, or have time to think of anything except beauty for the eyes and joy for the heart. The king sent his men in search of the greatest talent to be found in the world. Singers, dancers, athletes, poets, writers, scientists were brought to the palace.

One day, a special performer was scheduled to appear in the ivory courtyard. The prince with his entourage gathered to hear this recital. In a voice of unusual beauty, this great artist sang of new lands where at night the sun set low into the sea and where people with strange and unknown faces spoke different languages. Rewarding her with a handful of precious stones, the prince inquired, 'Tell me, beautiful one, are there such places? And such people?'

'Yes, my lord,' the great artist replied, 'I have seen them.'

The prince was heard to say to himself, 'I would give my kingdom to see such a world.'

This remark, as all others, was quickly carried to the king. 'It is well,' he told his councilors. 'It is time for the prince to visit the world and see his kingdom. Go, and give orders that all over the land the cities by swept, the houses repainted, and the people dressed in festive attire.' He commanded them then with raised voice, 'And tell them that the crippled, the sick, and the sorrowing must stay away from the roads. Only the gay, the young, and the beautiful must appear before him. The dangerous period has not yet passed. Nothing of sorrow or sadness must cross his eyes.'

So the prince accompanied by his gentlemen in waiting rode out through the huge iron gates. He was mounted on his beautiful white horse Tanaka, who was harnessed in gold with silver bridles laced across his arched white neck. Stepping over the flower-bedecked streets, he proudly carried his noble young master before the dazed wonderstruck eyes of his people. Men, women, children shouted with joy and admiration; to them it appeared like a celestial visitation, dazzling their eyes. Golden banners flew high over the houses, housewives wore fresh sandalwood caste marks between their eyebrows, and everywhere there was laughter and joy.

The prince stopped to smile and wave, then patted Tanaka's shining mane. 'You see, my friend, everyone is happy. All is well with the world.'

Suddenly from amongst the gaily thronged crowd there was heard a loud moan. An old man had crept up, and now lay exposed before the prince.

'Have mercy upon me, O Lord. End my sufferings,' he cried, before the people could stop him, or push him away.

Tanaka stamped his white hoofs impatiently on the ground and whinnied mournfully as his master dismounted.

'Tell me, Father, what ails thee?' the prince inquired in a gentle voice.

'For days I have lain without food or drink,' he replied, pointing feebly to his parched, cracked lips. 'All that awaits me now is death!'

After allaying the sick man's suffering, the prince demanded, 'How is it that men allow such pitiful beings to live amongst them without giving them help? And what is this thing he speaks about—Death—What is it?'

They shook their heads sorrowfully as they replied, 'Alas, so is life. O Prince, as all men are born so they must die.'

Returning to the palace, the prince mused over the old man, his misery, his fear of death. Now he realized the full meaning of all the different things he had seen and sensed as a child. He thought of the green fields where beneath the midday, flaming sun the peasant toiled for his bread. Of the lion prowling for his prey, how the lizard fed on the ant, and the snake on the lizard, till each killed and was destroyed in turn. A vast conspiracy of murder where the conqueror and the conquered, both, lived in mortal fear. A gigantic, rotating wheel which crushed each and all in turn. Riches, beauty, power, all went the same way. There must be something else—another answer to this bewilderingly, sorrowful maze.

The prince's preoccupation was quickly brought before the king. The wise men were called. 'Get him a wife, O King. There is nothing like the soft, clinging eyes of a woman to drive care away from the heart of a young man,' they advised him.

The news spread that the young, handsome Prince Siddharta, scion of the mighty Skyas, was to be wedded. From many distant lands lovely princesses arrived. They came garbed in rich brocades, adorned with precious jewels, and each one hoped to gain favour by her beauty and her wealth.

But Siddharta remained unmoved till the latest arrival stood before him. The Princess Yoddhasra looked like an ivory lotus arisen from a silver lake. Their eyes met, they stood motionless for a long time, gazing at each other.

Finally, as if in a dream, the prince spoke. 'I know thee, fair princess.'

'Yes, my lord,' she replies softly.

'I know thee,' he repeated, his luminous searching gaze turning to one of of radiant joy. 'The same slim, tall goddess form that I knew so well. The same pure and exquisite features, tender in their flawless perfection. Thy noble brow more lovely than a crescent moon. Long have I lived missing a part of myself, little knowing that it was hid in thee.' Kneeling, he unloosened his ruby necklace to clasp it around her slim, silken waist. 'Now we are rejoined.' His deep, musical voice ceased. His eyes clung to her in rapture.

So they were married amidst the inexpressible rejoicing of the populace. The ecstasy of these young mortals, each reflecting the other's perfection, even shaded the glory of the shining heavens. From the earth sprang crocuses, primroses, and other wild flowers; from the sky a silvery cloud hung suspended over their bridal chamber, as they lay in love.

So they lived in happiness. A year later a young prince, inheriting the grace and beauty of his parents, was born. The king, contented in his old age, dreamed of the day when Siddharta would be a king of kings, mightier than any of his ancestors. The second prophecy was well on its way.

But often in moments of greatest bliss, the princess noticed strange shadows darkening the face of the one she loved. An icy hand clutched at her heart as she begged, 'From whence springs this sadness, my lord?'

Then the prince would cast aside his secret visions and with words of tenderness and love hold her close to his heart.

One night the princess had a terrible dream. With tears streaming down her face, she flung herself into his arms.

'My lord,' she told him in a trembling voice, 'I dreamed a dream of terror. I saw a white bull for whom the people built a golden temple but he broke his golden fetters and escaped. Then my golden marriage robe turned into grey! The white jasmines in my hair withered! My jewelled anklets 'flew open! These are fearful omens, my lord. They mean that I will be taken from thee, or much worse and more terrible still—that thou wilt forsake me.' And she sank down before him.

Raising her, Siddharta spoke words of comfort. 'Be of good courage, beloved wife. Loving thee has made me love the people of the earth more than I ever dreamed I would do. Whatever comes, know that I will act only for the ultimate good that exists for us all. So with the brave spirit of thy warrior ancestors, smile and quit thy anguished little heart.'

When merciful sleep had closed her heavy eyelids, Siddharta got up and looked out of the pearl-encased window. The brightness of the stars slowly dimmed, the gentle breezes sweeping the horizon ceased, the leaves stilled their rustling. An untold sadness consumed him as he stood there gazing into the night.

'The times has come to choose between the two roads,' he said to himself. 'Which shall it be? The road of power? Shall my blood-stained, golden chariot trample over the earth to gain worldly victories? Or shall I tread the earth humbly till I am footsore and weary, searching for what my hearts tells me I must find?'

But from the darkness outside there was no answer. All was still. The universe itself seemed to be standing still, waiting with hushed expectancy.

His eyes filled with tears as he turned to watch his lovely young wife with his sleeping son cradled beside her. He strained to listen to the sound of their soft breathing, as though he were filling himself with this treasured sweetness for the last time. He knelt to kiss the silken coverlet on which she was lying, for he feared to wake her earlier than was necessary to the anguish that she would have to suffer on the morrow. Then he walked reverently around their marriage bed, knowing he would never lie there again. He bent over her. This time his strength nearly faltered.

He stretched out his golden arms, longing to enfold her once more. But he tore himself away, and turned his back on that jewel-studded room which held all that he loved.

As Siddharta stepped away from that chamber, the universe seemed to awake with a sigh. The stars shone brightly, the gentle breezes swept the horizon, the leaves continued their rustling. Then, as the dawn slowly overcame the darkness of the night, a supreme sadness filled him. Downstairs he aroused Rama, his trusted friend and servant, and told him to bring out Tanaka.

The old servant's tears flowed as he harnessed the beautiful animal, then led him out before the prince. Tanaka, his white hoofs raised, his neck arched, stood like some celestial steed, waiting for the command from his beloved master to unloosen his fleet wings and soar with him into the clouds.

Rama's tears continued to flow. 'Master,' he begged, 'do not leave us. Here is all that the heart desires. It has been foretold that the Prince Siddharta, if he so chose, would be a king of kings, ruler of the mightiest kingdom in the world. Do not leave us. Forget this other world,' he implored.

Siddharta embraced Rama and said: 'Be of good cheer, I shall still have a kingdom. But within it, no broken, tortured men will live in sorrow. Nor will vast cities be left bare and desolate after the tramp of conquering armies. Nor will the earth be soaked with the blood of innocent victims. In my kingdom'—he lifted his head—'The high and the low, the rich and the poor, the suffering and the deceased, all will tread the same path. But first, Rama, old friend, I must find that path. Who knows where it is— hidden within the depths of the darkest forest—concealed under the heaviest underbrush and covered with thorns. But find it I will.' So saying the beautiful Prince Siddharta mounted his white horse and rode out into the world.

Amah finished her story. Our unspoken thoughts were filled with the image of the golden Buddha leaving his beautiful young wife and child, to go out and help the suffering people of the earth. Our eyes glistened with unshed tears.

We heard footsteps mounting the stairs. Amah scuttled out of the room, her silver anklets and bracelets clinking, as Raschid came in through the door. He appeared to be nervous and upset tonight. He picked up a book, then just as impatiently threw it down again. Finally, he stood silently at the window, looking down into the garden.

'Father has been talking to me,' he said suddenly.

'Oh,' I murmured, bending over my needlework. It was difficult threading the filigree without spoiling the delicate form and then sewing it into the material.

'About Grandmother—look, put that stuff away,' he said, pointing to my needlework. 'I want to talk to you.'

Obediently, I put aside my embroidery and sat with folded hands.

'She won't eat.'

'I've noticed that. She never touches her plate. Why?'

'You mean to say that you don't know? Look—' he said, in an exasperated voice, 'she can't eat at the same table as you, she says, because you are not an Aga Khani. It's a small thing to you, but with her it's an obsession.'

I remained silent as he continued, 'Grandfather and Father are worried about her health. They told me that she fainted yesterday. She isn't strong. Her heart is weak.'

'I am sorry to hear all this,' I replied.

'Ishvani—you know that I wouldn't ask you anything I felt would be impossible for you to do. But this time, I am forced to ask you to enter the Aga Khani community.'

'Raschid, I would do anything for you in the world except this—'

'It's only a formality,' he broke in. 'You know to me it makes no difference what religion you belong to, be it Hindu, Muslim, or Christian. But Grandmother and our entire family feel quite differently about such things.'

'I know that it isn't important—to you, or to me—which religion one belongs to. But why wasn't I told before our marriage that they would be fanatic on this point?'

'I didn't know myself that they would be so insistent.'

'But, Raschid,' I said, 'you speak about them—what about us? Don't you think that we should have the moral courage to do what we think is right? After all, we represent young India. Our example will be watched and followed by others. Shouldn't we be able to think for ourselves now? Such ideas were all right a hundred years ago, but with our modern upbringing, it really makes no sense.'

He jumped up from his chair. 'You don't have to drag in India. This is a matter which is purely personal and affects nobody except ourselves.'

'But Raschid, what about my family? My grandfather spent his life fighting their bigotry and fanaticism. We suffered a great deal at their hands.'

'That is an old story which should be forgotten by now.'

'If I did, I would never be able to respect myself.'

He interrupted me impatiently. 'Let's end this conversation. I asked you nicely, once. But you replied with a lot of irrelevant arguments. Now I am going to command you and as a good Muslim wife, you should be only too happy to accede to my wishes. You must join the Aga Khani community.'

'But Raschid—'

He raised his hand. 'That's enough. Now it's time to go to bed. Good night.' He stalked towards the door and shut it noisily behind him.

—*The Brocaded Sari* (1946)

Brinda Maharani of Kapurthala
(n.d.)

In *Maharani: The Story of An Indian Princess*, Brinda, the Maharani of Kapurthala lets us in on what can undoubtedly be called a perspective reserved for a select handful. From the time of her betrothal to her experiences of married life, from difficulties with religion to family pride, culture and education, the book yields a number of interesting insights into the lives of those like her who 'lived between the traditional ancient world of India and the modern, frantic world of a Europe in the process of decay'.

The very first page startles: 'As a small Hindu princess I was not expected to evince any interest in my future life; it was only necessary for me to obey my parents and mind my manners.' Moving on, the Maharani's first meeting with her husband is depicted as a watershed moment. She writes about how the 'Tika Raja' was old and serious, while she simply stood in silence trying to understand why she had been given to this stranger. 'In that moment,' she writes, '[I] lost my childhood forever.'

The extract reproduced here epitomizes the Maharani's narrative. It goes from person to place to event to experience, encompassing everything from the Prince of Wales to grouse-shooting in Scotland, jazz players in America, gigolos in Paris, a meeting with the King and Queen in Buckingham Palace, and a rare admission of love: 'I had grown fond of my husband as the years passed and at last there was a good deal of understanding and quiet affection between us. But the Maharaja seemed determined to make trouble.

Possibly, since he disliked me, he could not bear for me to have the affection of his son. Seeing us happy together seemed to infuriate him.'

While details about her personal life are hard to come by except for what she writes herself, one can only agree with what Louis Bromfield, in his introduction to the book, says about the

Maharani—she 'makes no pretensions at being either an intellectual or a philosopher. Above everything, she is a human being.'

Chapter XII

Early in 1922 the Prince of Wales came to Kapurthala at the tail end of a long and strenuous tour; Kapurthala was the last state he visited.

We were charmed by the young heir to the English throne. Handsome and gay, he captivated the state by his lively interest in everything about him. By the time he reached Kapurthala he was exhausted from his weeks of official duties and speeches, but he remained cheerful and smiling throughout his visit.

The maharaja put on an elaborate spectacle for the prince with enormous banquets, entertainment, and fireworks. Since the maharaja's own wives were in purdah, it was up to me to act as hostess.

I was delighted. The prince and I had many friends in common and throughout the long ordeals of lunch and dinner we discussed, like ordinary people, the friends we knew. I was most impressed by the friendliness and democratic spirit of this young man who was later to become king. It seemed to me then that his ease of manner and warmth endeared him to everyone who met him, even on the first encounter.

At the state banquet, it was necessary that he rise to reply to the maharaja's toast of welcome. As the maharaja was saying his last words, the Prince of Wales reached for my hand under the table, smiled wryly, and whispered, 'This is always the worst part.'

As the Prince of Wales got up to speak, a sudden feeling like a premonition swept over me. Perhaps it was based on the fact that his genial manner seemed too democratic to be that of a king, but as I sat as the table and listened to his talk, I had the strong feeling that he would not rule England. I brushed the thought away as foolishness—how could he not be king? And yet, some accident, death, or illness—I could not visualize what would prevent it. I have thought of that moment many times since his abdication from the British throne—not for death but for love.

Some months after the visit of the Prince of Wales we left India with the maharaja and sailed for Europe. This time the three of us spent more time together than we ever had before. We were in London the spring of that year and the city was buzzing with excitement. The late King George and his bride-to-be, Elizabeth, were soon to be married and one April afternoon we were invited to a party at Buckingham Palace to view the wedding presents. There we met the late Duke of Kent who came over to us, introduced himself, and insisted on showing us all the presents. He was as excited as if it was his own wedding.

London was gayer that year than I had ever known it. For the first time it was more fun to be in England than in France. I was happy to see my old and beloved friend, Lord Hardinge, and we laughed together in remembrance of my career as an 'international incident'.

The Duke and Duchess of Sutherland entertained us and it was at their lovely home in Green Street that I once again had proof of how small the world is.

As I mingled with the guests while tea was being served I passed by a very beautiful woman who was pouring tea. There was something vaguely familiar about her. She was blonde and elegantly dressed, a typical English beauty.

'Who is she?' I asked Lord Hardinge. 'I have the feeling that I know her from somewhere.'

Lord Hardinge peered at the woman through his monocle. Then he told me her name. I had never heard it before.

But all afternoon her face nagged at me. It was not only her looks which were familiar; there was something about the way she moved, even about the way she poured the tea which I recognized.

The tea! Of course, *that* was it. I should have recognized her at once. For the elegant woman pouring tea was my little English friend, Sheila, with whom I had played 'tea' so many times in Dehra Dun.

I got up from my seat quickly and rushed over to where she was sitting. I introduced myself and we nearly fell into each other's arms. Sheila had grown into a charming woman, not without a sense of humour, for she picked up the teapot and swung it near my face.

'What you deserve now,' she laughed, 'is for me to take this pot of tea and dump it over *your* head!'

Sheila and I talked for hours about all that had happened to us in the many years since I had last seen her and we were both chagrined at the way we had behaved as children.

'I was a perfect little beast,' I confessed, 'to have plagued you the way I did.'

'It was exactly what I deserved,' retorted Sheila, 'I was an insufferable prig.'

Seeing Sheila had made the years dissolve and for a moment I could remember myself as a child. It is a shock to tear off the veil of age and realize the difference between what you thought life was going to be like and the way it turned out. There is more pain in the remembrance of innocence than there is in disillusionment.

In August of that year we went with the maharaja to Scotland to visit Lord Inchcape at Glenapp Castle, Ayrshire, for grouse-shooting. I had no idea what grouse were but I was game to join in the fun.

The morning of the hunt I arrived punctually in the downstairs hall. In India time means little, but I had learned in Europe that '*l exactitude c'est la politesse des rois.*' But unfortunately I had not yet learned about being correctly dressed for grouse-shooting. When Lord Inchcape saw me in what I thought an infinitely chic, bright red Paris suit, he said, 'My dear, you shall frighten the birds away.'

I suppose that my cheeks, too, would have frightened away the birds, for they took on the same colour as my dress.

Kind Lord Inchcape, however, asked me to follow the hunt on horseback. An enormous horse, as wide as it was long, was brought out of the stable, but the breadth of the horse was too much for me. After riding all day I ached all over and was all the more anxious to get back as I never enjoyed the spectacle of defenseless animals being killed.

The horse's tremendous breadth had another effect on me. Twisting about all day trying to find a more comfortable position had wrought havoc with my lingerie. On our return home as Lord Inchcape helped me to the ground, a tangle of pink silk slipped down my legs and twisted about my dangling feet. Even the staid Britishers standing about had to burst into gales of laughter. I am sure that a British princess would have been able to make a perfect riposte, but I admit that I never felt less a princess than when I bent down, picked it up, and stuffed it into my pocket as though it were a handkerchief.

Shortly after my debacle at Glenapp Castle we returned to Paris before going to India. Paris was at its height of gaiety and there were many changes since the last time we had visited France. Night clubs were swarming with people and for the first time my husband did not object to going about to the night spots.

We escaped one evening from a boring embassy reception with three Americans—reputed to be the three richest men in America (although that was always being said about Americans)—and wandered into an almost unknown little club called the Florence. It was completely deserted except for five Negro musicians who sat disconsolately at their music stand. The waiters stood about in boredom and we were the only guests in the place.

'Let's get out of this dead place,' suggested one of the American men.

We got up to leave but when the manager saw himself losing the only business of the night, he motioned to the musicians to start playing.

As if they were possessed by a strange magic, the five musicians suddenly sprang to life and played a hot jazz such as I have never heard since. We all sat down again quickly and stayed nearly until dawn listening to the wild excitement of these jazz players.

I could hardly wait to tell my friends. Before the next day had passed I had called almost everyone I knew in Paris and arranged to take them to Le Florence. A few days later we returned with a large party of people; within a week the Florence was crowded nightly with jazz fans. It soon became the most fashionable night club in Paris and remained so for twenty years. After that incident many of my friends teased me by saying they were going to rename the Florence *La Boîte à Brinda*.

Paris society was crowded with gigolos. I could feel nothing but pity for those handsome young men who pushed the old fat women around the dance floor; they more than earned their money. Most of their customers were women of sixty and seventy who covered their faces with rouge and their falling hair with wigs, frantically trying to appear to be in the bloom of youth.

When I was a young girl in Paris, a middle-aged French society woman was content to look her age. All that was changed now in the frenzy of excitement that was sweeping across the world in the twenties. Now there was only one way to look and that way was like a frisky young flapper with coal-scuttle hat, and hair cut straight across the forehead and bunched out at the ears. As I look back I am astonished that I was able to look at myself in the mirror without being horrified by the ugliness of my costumes.

The crazy desperation for gaiety from Paris to Rome, from London to the Riviera, brought out the ugliest aspects of human nature. There was a price for acceptance in this so-called society. Almost everyone was willing to pay it. You could buy a title and its papers then almost as easily as you can buy a tube of toothpaste today. The only difference was that the price was slightly higher.

Counterfeit letters of introduction to famous people, checks forged to pay for gambling debts, and fast motor cars, these were the standards of society of that time. Scandals were bursting like Roman candles all over Europe—only *some* of them were hushed up.

It was not only that people I had known all my life were so hard up for money that they allowed themselves to be mixed up in this sort of intrigue. It was more the story of the times. One could not help but be swept up by the wildness of the twenties.

In June of 1924 the Tika Raja and I, accompanied by the maharaja, were received by the King and Queen of England in Buckingham Palace. On such an occasion it was necessary that I wear formal Indian dress.

I was in a state over which one to wear. At first I chose the brightest and most gaily coloured of my saris but Eyres Monsell, who was then chief government whip, advised me that a more subdued sari would be in better taste. I finally chose a black silk chiffon, hand-embroidered with butterflies of gold and silver and coloured threads. On my head I wore a headband of diamonds and emeralds, matching emerald-and-diamond drop earrings, and twisted about my neck were three strands of gleaming pearls.

We were received by Their Majesties in a small anteroom. Queen Mary was dressed regally in pale blue and silver with magnificent diamonds. Across her corsage was the blue ribbon of the Garter. Queen Mary smiled cordially at me as I bowed low.

'You were a little uncertain of your English in Delhi some years ago,' she said kindly, 'but I am told you speak it now as well as you do French.'

I was flattered that the queen remembered me so well after all those years. The maharaja did not like the fact that I had been singled out, but King George was kind to me as well and was particularly insistent that I attend the horse show which was scheduled for the following week.

We were conducted by two guards to the ballroom where the maharaja and his son were placed on the dais behind the two thrones. I was given an ornately carved armchair a little to the right where I could see the proceedings clearly.

It was a remarkable occasion in many ways and I was impressed most of all by the efficiency of the English. It was far different from the more careless attitude of Indian royalty. In three hours, more than eight hundred debutantes were presented before the king and queen. The timing and the graciousness of the presentations could not have been better arranged.

Also present on that occasion were the Prince of Wales, the Duke and Duchess of York, the Duke of Connaught, and Prince and Princess Arthur.

When the royal family was ready to leave, a band hidden from sight burst into 'God Save the King' and the entire court rose to its feet as the king and queen and their family left at the head of a procession which included all the Indian princes who were present. I walked beside the famous Maharaja of Alwar, who towered above me like a brooding giant. As we passed slowly through the many state rooms lined on both sides with guests, I could overhear whispered remarks which speculated on who I was.

No one had any idea. I was the only Indian woman present and none of the guests realized that I understood English perfectly. It was difficult not to laugh as I walked down the aisle under the barrage of comments.

Some days later the king and queen invited us to lunch with Their

Majesties at the horse races at Ascot in the royal box. The road to Ascot was crowded with cars and in the confusion we lost our way. We arrived there three hours late, long after lunch was finished. We tried to be as unobtrusive as possible in the crowd, some distance from the royal box, but Lady Churchill spotted us and insisted that we join her until the race was over.

I was mortified by our inexcusable lateness and felt that our conduct deserved the worst possible punishment. But instead, when the king and queen learned that we had finally arrived, they sent for us and consoled us for having had the bad luck to lose our way. I was overwhelmed by their kindness and it was a great lesson to me to observe the graciousness of those monarchs.

Soon after this we returned to India. It was 1925. Winter in Kapurthala was usually an unhappy time for both my husband and myself. Somehow, there was always trouble of one kind or another.

In the last few years, the maharaja seemed to derive a perverse pleasure from interfering between the Tika Raja and me. This year he was worse than ever.

My marriage had never been a perfect one. But what marriage is? I had grown to accept the problems of our life together and it seemed to me that the Tika Raja had also become more content as the years passed by. He had always been in love with me; in the beginning, perhaps too much so. Not all the fault of our difficulties had been his. As a young girl I had not been ready for the burden of love and this had only accentuated his jealousy and insecurity. But, like many people, in some way he had been able to work out a more satisfactory relationship.

I had grown more fond of my husband as the years passed and at last there was a good deal of understanding and quiet affection between us. But the maharaja seemed determined to make trouble. Possibly, since he disliked me, he could not bear for me to have the affection of his son. Seeing us happy together seemed to infuriate him.

He began to hint to me that all was not well. He pretended to have great sympathy for me. It was almost as if he were consoling me on the failure of my marriage. At first I laughed it off since I could so easily see through his tactics but later it began to upset me.

There are none of us so secure that the constant tearing down of our defenses doesn't have some effect. Gradually, the maharaja's campaign began to work. His constant criticism of me to the Tika Raja also began to work. The result was that we both became irritable and many quarrels resulted. I began to get jittery and my nerves were at a breaking point from the strain.

Just when I was feeling my lowest the maharaja proposed that he and the Tika Raja go off to Europe together for the summer and that I remain in India. The separation, he said, would do our marriage good and he promised that when they returned, all would be well again. By that time I was so exhausted that I no longer cared what happened and I agreed to remain in Kapurthala while they made the trip together.

I took the children to Mussoorie for the hottest months of the year and then returned to our home. In the winter my father's health began to fail. He had never been well after the death of my mother and his exile from Jubbal had made him a broken man.

My late uncle, Rana Padam Chand, had left two sons. The elder son had died at the age of twenty-two so that Bhagat Chand, the younger, now ruled the state. He turned out to be a conscientious ruler and under his development the state's chief source of revenue, the timber forests, increased enormously in value. My father admired his brilliant nephew and also had a good deal of affection for him. But Bhagat Chand had been brought up to consider my father a villain. He had also been taught that my marriage had brought shame on the Jubbal family and believed that my father had purposely engineered it out of hostility for his relatives.

Still a proud man, my father was reproachful and demanding to his nephew while the raja remained aloof and unforgiving. My father wanted desperately to return to his own state of Jubbal but his nephew would not hear of it. Even when he was an old, sick man, the raja would not allow him to return.

On their last interview my father broke down and wept but it was to no avail.

'Very well,' cried my father. 'You refuse to honour your father's brother but the day will come when you will take my corpse to the burning ghat!'

This was in the nature of a curse for to carry a body to the funeral pyre is the most painful duty one can perform to the dead.

At the end of the winter, soon after the maharaja and my husband had returned to Kapurthala, we received the news that my father was dying. The maharaja was deeply saddened by the news for they had been lifelong friends. I could not believe it was so and was convinced that with proper care my father would live a long time. I began to prepare a small cottage near our home so that we could send for my father and nurse him back to health. In the meantime I sent my sister Madhvi and my brother Kaju to Simla to be with our father. At home we prepared for the invalid's arrival. ...

—*Maharani: The Story of an Indian Princess* (1953)

References

Primary Sources

Ali, Aruna Asaf *Travel Talk* (a collection of articles from 'Janata'), Delhi: Aundh Publishing, 1947.

Birdwood, Sir Geoge *et al. The Stree Bodhe and Social Progress in India* Bombay: The Stree Bodhe Office, 1908.

Chandra, Sudhir *Enslaved Daughters: Colonialism, Law and Woman's Rights* Delhi: Oxford University Press, 1998.

Chattopadhyay, Kamaladevi *et al. The Awakening of Indian Women* Madras: Everyman's Press, 1939.

Chattopadhyay, Kamaladevi *Japan: Its Weakness and Strength* Bombay: Padma Publications, 1943.

Chimnabai, Maharani of Baroda with S. M. Mitra *The Position of Women in Indian Life* London: Longman's Green, 1911.

Chitale, Venu *In Transit* Bombay: Hind Kitabs Ltd., 1950.

Choksi, Mithan and Evelyn Gedge *Women in Modern India (Fifteen Papers by Indian Women Writers)* Bombay: DB Taraporenula and Co., 1929,

Das, Harihar *Life and Letters of Toru Dutt* London: Oxford University Press, 1921.

Devi, Shonana *The Orient Pearls: Indian Folklore* London: Macmillan Co. Ltd., 1915.

Fuller, Jean Overton *Noor-un-nisa Inayat Khan* Rotterdam: East West Publishers with Barrie and Jenkins, London, 1971.

Futehally, Zeenuth *Zohra* Bombay: Hind Kitabs Ltd., 1951.

Grover, Verinder and Ranjana Arora (eds.) *Aruna Asaf Ali* New Delhi: Deep and Deep Publications, 1993.

———— *Sarojini Naidu* New Delhi: Deep and Deep Publications, 1993.

———— *Vijayalakshmi Pandit* New Delhi: Deep and Deep Publications, 1993.

———— *Sucheta Kripalani* New Delhi: Deep and Deep Publications, 1993.

Hossain, Rokeya Sakhawat *Sultana's Dream* Calcutta: S. K. Lahiri & Co., Originally published in *The Indian Ladies' Magazine* Madras, 1905. Originally written in English and translated by the author into Bengali.

Hussain, Iqbalunnisa *Purdah and Polygamy* Bangalore: Hosali Press, 1944.

Hutheesing, Krishna Nehru *With No Regrets* Bombay: Padma Publications, 1943.

Ishvani, G. *The Brocaded Sari* New York: John Day, 1946.

Jessawalla, Dosebai Cowasjee *The Story of My Life* Bombay: The Times Press, 1911.

Kosambi, Meera *Pandita Ramabai: Through Her Own Words* Delhi: Oxford University Press, 2000.

Lady Dorab Tata: A Book of Remembrance Bombay: J.B. Dubash, 1932.

Mote, S. V. *et al.* (eds.) *Vishrabdha Sharda* vol. I, Bombay, 1972.

Nehru, Jawaharlal *A Bunch of Old Letters* Bombay: Asia Publishing House, 1958.

Nehru, Shyam Kumari (ed.) *Our Cause: A Symposium by Indian Women* Allahabad: Kitabistan, 1938.

Nikambe, Shevantibai *Ratanbai: A Sketch of a Bombay High Caste Hindu Wife* London: Marshall Brothers, 1895.

Pandit, Vijayalakshmi *So I Became a Minister* Allahabad: Kitabistan, 1939.

———— *Prison Days* Calcutta: Signet Press, 1946.

Ramabai, C. T. *Victory of Faith* Ramnagar: T. Gopalkrishna Rao, 1935.

Rama Rau, Santha *Gifts of Passage* London: Victor Gollancz, 1961.

Reddy, Dr. S. Muthulakshmi *My Experiences as a Legislator* Madras, 1930.

Satthianadhan, Krupabai (ed. Chandani Lokugé) *Saguna* Delhi: Oxford University Press, 1999.

———— (ed. Chandani Lokugé) *Kamala: The Story of a Hindu Child-Wife* Delhi: Oxford University Press, 1998.

Sen, Ela *Gunpowder Women and Other Essays* Bombay: Thacker and Co., 1943.

———— *Darkening Days* Calcutta: Sushil Gupta, 1944.

Sen, Snehalata *Nehal the Musician* Madras: G. Ganesan Publishers, 1923.

Shah, A. B. (ed.) *The Letters and Correspondence of Pandita Ramabai* Bombay: Maharashtra State Board of Literature and Culture, 1977.

Sher-Gil, Amrita 'Evolution of My Art' in *Amrita Sher-Gil* Bombay: Marg Publications, (n.d.).

Sorabji, Cornelia *Love and Life behind the Purdah* London: Freemantle and Co., 1901.

———— *India Calling: The Memoirs of Cornelia Sorabji* London: Nisbet and Co., 1934.

———— *India Recalled* London: Nisbet and Co., 1936.

Sunity Devee, Maharani of Cooch Behar *Bengal Dacoits and Tigers* Calcutta: Thacker Spink and Co., 1916.

———— *The Autobiography of an Indian Princess* London: John Murray, 1921.

Tata, Herabai *A Short Sketch of Indian Women's Franchise Work* (n.d.).

Trivedi, A. K. (ed.) *The Baroda College Golden Jubilee Commemoration Volume* Bombay: The Times of India Press, 1933.

Turkhud, Nalini *The Jagirdar of Palna* Poona, 1936.

Vaswani, K. N. (ed.) *Sucheta: An Unfinished Autobiography* Ahmedabad: The Navjivan Trust, 1978.

Secondary Sources

Adhav, S. M. *Pandita Ramabai* Madras: The Christian Literature Society, 1979.

A. D. *The Indian Child's Mother* London: Church Missionary Society, 1922.

Alva, Violet *et al.* (compilers) *March of Events: Being the Case of the Indian National Congress 1942–45* Bombay: Bombay Provincial Congress Committee, 1945.

Baig, Tara Ali *Portraits of an Era* New Delhi: Roli Books, 1988.

Balfour, Margret and Ruth Young *The Work of Medical Women in India* London: Oxford University Press, 1929.

Begum, Atiya *Indian Music* 1913.

_____ *Music of India* 1925.

Brijbhushan, Jamila *Kamaladevi Chattopadhyay: Portrait of a Rebel* New Delhi: Abhinav Publications, 1976.

Brittain, Vera *The Women at Oxford* London: George G. Harrap, 1960.

Butler, Clementina *Pandita Ramabai Sarasvati* New York: Fleming H. Revell Co., 1922.

Chapman, Mrs E. F. *Sketches of Some Distinguished Women* London: W. H. Allen and Co. Ltd., 1891.

Chatterjee, Partha *The Nation and Its Fragments: Colonial and Post Colonial Histories* Delhi: Oxford University Press, 1997.

Chiplunkar, G. M. *The Scientific Basis of Woman's Education* Poona: Prof S. B. Hudlikar, 1930.

Cousins, James H. *The Renaissance in India* Madras: Ganesh and Co., 1918.

Cousins, Margaret E. *Indian Womanhood Today* Allahabad: Kitabistan, 1941.

Desai, S. K. *Santha Rama Rau* New Delhi: Arnold Heinemann, 1976.

Dinesh, Kamini *Between Spaces of Silence: Women Creative Writers* New Delhi: Sterling Publishers, 1994.

Diver, Maud *Royal India* London: Hodder and Stoughton, 1942.

Dongerkary, Kamala S. *On The Wings of Time* Bombay: Bhartiya Vidya Bhavan, 1968.

Engels, Dagmar *Beyond Purdah: Women in Bengal 1890–1930* Delhi: Oxford University Press, 1999.

Everett, Jana Matson *Women and Social Change in India* Delhi: Heritage Publications, 1978.

Forbes, Geraldine (ed.) *A Pattern of Life: The Memoirs of an Indian Woman* Columbia, 1977.

_____ *Women in Modern India* Cambridge: Cambridge University Press, Reprint of South Asian edition, 2000.

Forbes, Rosita *India of the Princes* London: The Right Book Club, 1939.

Fuller, Mrs Marcus B. *The Wrongs of Indian Womanhood* (with an introduction by Pandita Ramabai) Edinburgh and London: Olipant Anderson and Ferrier, 1899.

Grover, Verinder and Ranjana Arora (eds.) *Rajkumari Amrit Kaur* New Delhi: Deep and Deep Publications, 1993.

Ikramullah, Begum Shaista *From Purdah to Parliament* London: The Cresset Press, 1963.

Iyengar, K. R. Srinivas *Indian Writing in English* New Delhi: Sterling Publishers, 1984 edition.

Karve, Iravati *Hindu Society: An Interpretation* Poona: Deccan College, 1961.

Latif, Bilkees *Her India* Delhi: Arnold Heinemann, 1984.

Majumdar, P. C. *Keshub Chandra and His Times* Calcutta: The Brotherhood, 1917.

Mehta, Chandralekha, Nayantara Sahgal, Rita Sar *A 70th Birthday Tribute to Vijayalakshmi Pandit* New Delhi: Orient Longman, 1970.

Modak, Manorama R. *The World is My Family* Bombay: Thackers, 1970.

Mody, Rekha (ed.) *A Quest for Roots* Calcutta: Stree Shakti, 1999.

Murshid, Ghulam *Reluctant Debutante: Response of Bengali Women to Modernization 1849–1905* Rajshahi, Bangladesh: Sahitya Samsad, Rajshahi University, 1983.

Narasimhan, Shakuntala *Kamaladevi Chattopadhyay: The Romantic Rebel* New Delhi: Sterling Publishers Pvt Ltd., 1999.

Pal, R. B. *A Glimpse of Zenana Life* Calcutta, 1904.

Sarabai, M. (ed.) *The Mahatma and the Poetess* Mumbai: Bharatiya Vidya Bhavan, 1998.

Satthianadhan, Samuel *Sketches of Indian Christians* London and Madras: The Christian Literature Society, 1896.

Satthianadhan, Samuel and Kamala Satthianadhan *Stories of Indian Christian Life* Madras: Srinivasa Varadachari and Co., 1898.

Sengupta, Padmini *The Portrait of an Indian Woman* Calcutta: YMCA Publishing House, 1956.

Spencer, Dorothy *Indian Fiction in English: An Annotated Bibliograhy* Philadelphia: University of Pennsylvania Press, 1960.

Storrow, Rev. E. *Our Indian Sisters* London: The Religious Tract Society, (n.d.).

Tottenham, E. L. *Highnesses of Hindustan* London: Grayson and Grayson, 1934.

West, W. J. *Orwell: The War Broadcasts* London: Duckworth and BBC Publications, 1985.

Other Works of Women Writers Represented

Ali, Aruna Asaf *Private Face of a Public Person: A Study of Jawaharlal Nehru* New Delhi: Radiant Publishing, 1989.

———— *Fragments from the Past: Selected Writings and Speeches* New Delhi: Patriot, 1989.

———— *The Resurgence of Indian Women* New Delhi: Radiant Publishing, 1991.

Chattopadhyay, Kamaladevi *In War-Torn China* Bombay: Padma Publications, 1942.

———— *Uncle Sam's Empire* Bombay: Padma Publications, 1944.

———— *Towards a National Theatre* Aundh: Aundh Publication Trust, 1945.

———— *America: The Land of Superlatives* Bombay: Phoenix Publications, 1946.

———— *Inner Recesses, Outer Spaces* New Delhi: Navrang, 1986.

———— *Food and Milk*, Tract no. 1 of the All India Women's Conference, (n.d.).

Chitale, Venu (Weenoo) *Incognito* Poona, 1988.

Hossain, Rokeya Sakhawat *Motichur* part 1 & 2 (a collection of articles published between 1903–4 in various journals). Part 1, Calcutta: Gurudas Chattopadhyaya & Sons; Part 2, Calcutta: Mrs Rokeya Sakhawat Hossain.

———— *Avarodhbasini* ('The Secluded Ones'), Calcutta: Mohammadi Book Agency. Also appeared as a series of columns in the monthly *Mohammadi* (1928–30).

———— *Rokeya Racanavali* ('Collected works of Rokeya') ed. Abdul Quadir, Dhaka: Bangla Academy.

_____ (ed. Roushan Jahan, Afterword by Hanna Papanek) *Sultana's Dream and The Secluded Ones* New York: The Feminist Press, 1988.

Hutheesingh, Krishna Nehru *Shadows on the Wall* New York: John Day, 1948.

_____ *Dear to Behold: An Intimate Portrait of Jawaharlal Nehru* London: Macmillan, 1969.

Kripalani, Sucheta *Report of the Indusrial Finance Corporation Enquiry Committee* New Delhi, 1953.

Speeches and Writings of Sarojini Naidu Madras: A Natesan and Co., (n.d.).

Pandit, Vijayalakshmi *The Evolution of India* London: Oxford University Press, 1958.

_____ *The Scope of Happiness: A Personal Memoir* London: Weidenfeld Nicolson, 1979.

Rama Rau, Santha *Home to India* London: Victor Gollancz, 1945.

_____ *East of Home* London: Victor Gollancz, 1951.

_____ *Remember the House* London: Victor Gollancz, 1956.

_____ *My Russian Journey* London: Victor Gollancz, 1959.

_____ *View to the South East* London: Victor Gollancz, 1958.

_____ *The Adventurers* London: Michael Joseph, 1971.

Reddy, Dr S. Muthulakshmi *Autobiograhy* Madras, 1964.

_____ *Report on the Conference on Legal Status of Indian Women* Bombay: NCWI, 1943.

_____ (compiler) *Mrs Margaret Cousins and Her Work in India* Madras: Women's Indian Association, 1956.

Satthianadhan, Krupabai (ed. Chandani Lokugé) *Kamala: The Story of a Hindu Child-Wife* Delhi: Oxford University Press, 1998.

Sen, Ela *Testament of India* London: George Allen and Unwin Ltd., 1939.

_____ *Wives of Famous Men* Bombay: Thacker and Co., 1942.

_____ *Midnight on the Lakes* Bombay: Thacker and Co., 1943.

_____ *A Child is Born and Other Stories* Bombay: Thacker and Co., 1942.

_____ *Gandhi: A Biographical Study* Calcutta: Susil Gupta, 1945.

_____ *Indira Gandhi: A Biography* Calcutta: Rupa and Co., 1973.

Sorabji, Cornelia *Between the Twilights: Being Studies of Indian Women by One of Themselves* London: Harper and Brothers, 1908.

_____ *Therefore: An Impression of Sorabji Kharshedji Langrana and His Wife Franscina* London: Oxford University Press, 1924.

_____ *Susie Sorabji: Christian Parsee Educationist of Western India* London: Oxford University Press, 1934.

_____ *The Purdahnashin* Bombay: Thacker, Spink and Co., (n.d.).

_____ *Sun Babies* London: Blackie and Son Ltd., 1918.

_____ *Gold Mohur: Time to Remember* (A Play), London: Alexander Moring Ltd., 1930.

_____ *Indian Tales of the Great Ones* London: Blackie and Son Ltd., (n.d.).

Sunity Devee, Maharani of Cooch Behar *The Beautiful Mogul Princess*, 1918.

Tata, Herabai *The Sanctity of Womanhood* Bombay, 1917.